Sunset
P9-DVA-574

...1994 EDITION...

By the *Sunset* Editors

DARROW M. WATT

Colorful cattleya orchids (see page 18)

Sunset Publishing Corporation ■ Menlo Park, California

WILLIAM D. ADAMS

IT'S QUICK AND EASY *to grow these 'Champion' radishes. We tell you how on page 265.*

A Harvest of Ideas

Welcome to the first edition of our *Western Garden Annual,* a grand collection of ideas for gardeners throughout the West. This handsome new book gathers garden and outdoor living articles from all of *Sunset Magazine*'s 1993 regional issues into one convenient volume for easy reference and inspiration. Written specifically for home gardeners west of the Rockies, the articles provide a useful guide to seasonal tasks and current trends in Western gardening.

Each chapter begins with a Garden Guide, filled with garden news, ideas from around the West, and regional checklists of important tasks for the month.

Articles cover all facets of gardening, from plant selection guides and pruning techniques to landscaping reports that offer solutions to common problems. You'll learn about several community environmental action programs and discover ways to introduce children to the pleasures of gardening.

We're delighted to present this first *Western Garden Annual,* and we hope it provides many ideas for your enjoyment.

All material in this book originally appeared in the 1993 issues of *Sunset Magazine*.

Sunset Western Garden Annual was produced by *Sunset Books*.

Front Cover: *Outstanding perennials for seasonal color in Western gardens (see page 114). Cover design by Nina Bookbinder Design. Photography by K. Bryan Swezey.*

Back Cover: *Chinese witch hazel blooms brightly in a rain-soaked winter garden (see page 280). Photography by Bill Ross.*

Sunset Magazine
Editor: William R. Marken

Sunset Books
Editor: Elizabeth L. Hogan

First Printing March 1994

ISSN 1073-5089. ISBN 0-376-03855-1.

Printed in the U.S.A.

CONTENTS

Introduction 4
Enjoy this new *Western Garden Annual* for inspiration and easy reference throughout the year

January 6
The West's best climbing roses, orchids to grow indoors, new citrus varieties, dahlias from seed

February 24
Ornamental grasses, the West's top tomato, hanging baskets for quick color, bulbs to plant in winter

March 44
Southwest beans, the compost movement spreads, starting seeds from scratch, sharing the harvest

April...............72
Growing vegetables in small spaces, indoor-outdoor desert garden, ultimate rock garden, how to cut roses

May...............102
Top perennials for Western gardens, understanding "natural" fertilizers, extra-sweet corn varieties

June 124
Plants for drying, quick and easy garden projects, Colorado country gardens, a rabbit in your garden

July...............154
Landscaping a starter garden, converting to drip irrigation, pretty small gardens, creative containers

August 178
Natural gardens that attract wildlife, high-altitude gardening, imaginative birdbaths, crisphead lettuce

September 206
Fall planting in mild climates, 40 wonder plants for the Northwest, carrot varieties, colorful buckwheats

October 230
Olive trees, flowers and foliage for bouquets, tulips for the mild West, backyard composting essentials

November.......260
Rosemary, garden gloves, from seed to bread, plants for winter bloom, planting under oaks, artificial rock

December.......286
Western holiday wreaths, December-blooming camellias, cotoneasters, gift ideas

Indexes 314
Article Titles Index on page 314, General Subject Index on page 315

DARROW M. WATT

A New Guide for Western Gardeners

For some 65 years, gardeners all over the West—from the forests of Washington and Idaho to the Southwestern deserts—have learned to rely on Sunset for information and inspiration. Now, in response to our readers' requests, the writers and editors of *Sunset Magazine* and *Sunset Books* have created the *Western Garden Annual*, a new kind of guide intended especially for Western home gardeners. This 1994 edition of the annual provides a permanent reference to seasonal gardening information and articles published in *Sunset Magazine* during the past year.

Whether you're new to our pages or a long-time subscriber to *Sunset Magazine*, you'll appreciate our thorough, fresh approach to gardening subjects. You'll find a broad variety of topics as well as plenty of specific, useful information in each article. Only in

MICHAEL LANDIS

DON NORMARK

OUR READERS ENJOY THEIR GARDENS *throughout the year. From left: spring-blooming ceanothus covers the landscape with sapphire blossoms; a bountiful harvest of lettuce promises weeks of wonderful salads; the glow of autumn leaves invites outdoor activities; holiday decorations provide an opportunity to bring some of the winter garden indoors.*

Sunset are you likely to find information on such diverse themes as breakthrough citrus varieties, fall planting for spring color, "heirloom" beans from the Southwest, back-to-nature gardens, backyard and community composting programs, planting under oak trees, converting a sprinkler system to drip irrigation, and landscaping a desert garden.

In this volume you'll find feature articles from all of *Sunset*'s four regional editions: Northwest, Central, Southern California, and Southwest. This allows you not only to explore ideas for your own region, but also to see what's developing in nurseries and home gardens elsewhere in the West.

The *Western Garden Annual* is divided into 12 chapters, one for each month of the year. Starting off each chapter is the Garden Guide, offering timely news on garden-related topics and practical suggestions for the season in one or more regions of the West. Following the guide are four region-specific checklists, convenient listings of activities and tasks for the month.

The rest of each chapter is devoted to articles from that month's issue—plant selection guides, problem-solving landscaping articles, hands-on planting and pruning help, information on techniques and tools, and quick ideas for adding seasonal color to your garden. Many of the articles are applicable to all areas; some focus on a particular geographic region.

As you read this book, you'll notice references to climate zones. *Sunset* defines 24 such zones, ranging from the snowy-winter areas of the Northwest to the mild marine climate of Southern California. For detailed definitions of these climate zones and descriptions of plants that do well in the West, consult the *Sunset Western Garden Book.*

JANUARY

Garden guide 7
January checklists 10
Roses high and mighty 14
Orchids to grow indoors....18
Citrus breakthroughs 21
The dazzle of dahlias........23

Sunset's

GARDEN GUIDE

GOLDSMITH SEEDS

Bright pansies for winter gardens

NOW THAT THE HOLIDAY WHIRLWIND HAS PASSED AND CALMER January days are here, it's a good time to catch up on delayed gardening tasks, such as pruning, cleanup, and dormant spraying (wait for a dry day to prune and spray). In mild-winter areas, most nurseries have an abundance of 4-inch pots of winter annuals, like the colorful 'Universal' pansies shown above. This is also a particularly good time to shop for bare-root roses and fruit trees. In snowy climates, thumb through seed catalogs and plan your spring garden.

Saved from the scrap heap: two new sweet cherries

When Washington State University stopped fruit breeding at Prosser in 1985, it looked as if the program's promising new fruit varieties would never make it to market. Then the Central Washington Nursery Improvement Institute was formed to see that these and other promising fruit varieties would be released to the nursery trade. Two such cherries are now on the market.

'Glacier' is a large, dark cherry that ripens five days ahead of 'Bing' and tastes better. Best of all, it's self-fruitful, so you can get a harvest with a single tree.

'Olympus' looks and tastes similar, and ripens about 10 days later. Tree is smaller than 'Bing', but crops tend to be large. This one needs a pollinator; try a sour cherry like 'Montmorency'.

'Glacier' and 'Olympus' have done well in 10 years of testing in eastern Washington. Neither has been tried west of the Cascades.

More flowers for hummingbirds

After reading a *Sunset* article about hummingbirds, readers wrote to tell us about great hummingbird plants that didn't make our list. One of the most interesting is glory vine *(Eccremocarpus scaber)*, a tender climber that can scramble up a 10-foot trellis or fence in one season. You can order seed now, start it in early spring, and plant out in late spring.

By late summer or early fall, you'll get clusters of 1-inch trumpet flowers; colors include solid red, orange, and yellow. If a mild winter follows, the plant will regrow and flower the following spring, making plenty of nectar for hummingbirds.

In snowy winter regions, treat this as an annual. You can get seed of glory vine from Thompson & Morgan, Box 1308, Jackson, NJ 08527 (free catalog).

Best of the year: 1993 All-America Selections

Whether you shop by seed catalog or at your favorite nursery, watch for each year's top-rated vegetable and flower introductions. Four won All-America awards for 1993:

'Baby Bear' pumpkin has diminutive fruits about 5 inches in diameter and 1½ to 2½ pounds in weight. They're useful as small jack-o'-lanterns or in pies. The hull-less seeds are edible. Each plant yields 8 or 9 fruits on a 6- to 7-foot vine. Plants are easy to start from seed.

'Husky Gold' tomato bears shiny golden orange, 7- to 8-ounce fruits on small indeterminate plants. The first meaty fruits ripen about 70 days after transplanting and continue through the summer.

'Mont Blanc' nierembergia (pictured below) is an annual with pure white, star-shaped blooms. Plants spread to 15 inches and reach 3 to 5 inches tall. 'Mont Blanc' thrives in full sun and heat. It combines well with annuals or perennials at the front of borders or in rock gardens. It's slow to start from seed but easy to grow from transplants.

'Imagination' verbena is an annual with finely cut, lacy foliage and deep magenta flowers. This fast-growing plant for flower beds and hanging baskets reaches 2 feet tall with adequate fertilizer and water. It tolerates drought but won't grow as vigorously when water is short. 'Imagination' is easy to grow from transplants, more difficult from seed. Seeds of all four plants are available by mail from Park Seed Company, Cokesbury Rd., Greenwood, SC 29647; (800) 845-3369. Catalog is free.

ALL-AMERICA SELECTIONS

'MONT BLANC' NIEREMBERGIA *spreads low over path at front of border. Flowers start in late spring, last all summer.*

Great books for fruit-growing in western Oregon and Washington

West of the Cascades, damp winters and cool summers limit the kinds of fruit you can grow. To help out growers there, Oregon and Washington state universities have produced some excellent books that bear reading now, when you're deciding which fruit crops to plant or replace.

Growing Small Fruits for the Home Garden, by Charles A. Brun (WSU, Pullman, WA 1992; $5), tells how to grow blackberries, blueberries, currants, gooseberries, kiwis, raspberries, and strawberries. Advice about insects and diseases, culture, and recommended varieties is combined with drawings and color photographs.

Tree Fruit Varieties for Western Washington, by Robert A. Norton, J. King, and G. A. Moulton (WSU, Pullman, WA, 1992; $1.50), is the best book of the lot, covering apples, apricots, cherries, peaches, pears, and plums. It lists major varieties, and puts pollination information in easy-to-read charts.

Varieties were tested in Mount Vernon, Washington. Most also do well in western Oregon and British Columbia, but climate affects performance. To show prime planting areas, authors use climate-zone maps similar to ones in the *Sunset Western Garden Book.*

Growing Grapes in Your Home Garden (publication EC #1305) and *Grape Cultivars for Your Home Garden* (EC #1309), both by Dr. Bernadine Strik (OSU Extension Service, Corvallis, OR, 1989; $1.50 and 75 cents, respectively), offer complete coverage of homegrown fruits. Listing both European (mostly wine) grapes and American (mostly table) ones, the pamphlets discuss flavor, growing conditions, and pest problems.

Growing Grapes also has the best illustrations of grape pruning and training we've seen; the information is particularly useful this month.

You can order the first two booklets postpaid from Cooperative Extension Bulletins Office, Cooper Publications Building, WSU, Pullman, WA 99164. Order grape books from Agricultural Communications, Publications Orders, Administrative Services Building 422, OSU, Corvallis, OR 97331; add 25 cents for postage.

New tree roses have a weeping form

Tree roses are now available in new varieties. All have small leaves and flowers on long, supple canes that drape gracefully; they're grafted atop 36-inch stems.

They include several colors: 'Gourmet Popcorn' (white), 'Red Meidiland', 'Sea Foam' (white), 'Sweet Chariot' (mauve blend), 'The Fairy' (light pink), 'Weeping China Doll' (medium pink), and 'White Meidiland'.

Cascading roses look handsome in beds, but they are particularly showy in 30-inch-diameter urn-shaped pots (use fast-draining potting mix).

Look for bare-root plants at nurseries this month for about $25 each.

New house plant is a winner

Foliage plants that are easy to care for and tolerate low light don't come on the market very often. That's why the one shown at right is worth a look.

Homalomena (pronounced ho-*mal*-o-meena) 'Emerald Gem' is an attractive, dark green plant with glossy, heart-shaped leaves 4 to 5 inches across. It has a compact growth habit to about 14 to 18 inches tall when in a 6-inch pot. In larger (8- to 10-inch) containers, it develops slightly larger leaves and grows a bit taller.

Although 'Emerald Gem' tolerates low light, like any plant, it grows best in slightly brighter conditions (bright reflected light, such as near an east-facing window, is ideal). It's disease resistant and isn't bothered by insects.

'Emerald Gem' doesn't like to dry out, though. Water thoroughly (but don't let it sit in water), then water again when the top inch or so of the soil is dry. Fertilize regularly, following package directions.

If you can't find 'Emerald Gem' at a nursery or florist, either business can order it for you from these Southern California sources : Kallisto Greenhouses in Fontana (wholesale only), or Rancho Soledad Nursery in Rancho Santa Fe (wholesale and retail; call 619/756-3717).

DARROW M. WATT

WAXY, HEART-SHAPED LEAVES *of Homalomena 'Emerald Gem' practically glow when light strikes them.*

Crabapple tests in Colorado

For the last nine years, Dr. James E. Klett of Colorado State University has been evaluating crabapple *(Malus)* varieties for disease resistance and ornamental value.

In 1990 and 1991, severe outbreaks of fireblight, which blackens and kills foliage and branch tips, put trees through a rigorous test for resistance to this disease.

Of the more than 60 trees evaluated, 6 have shown superior resistance to fireblight and also have good looks. Nine commonly planted crabapples showed severe susceptibility to the disease.

The winners:

'Centurion'. Red buds open to rose; fruit is red. Reddish purple foliage ages to green.

'David'. Pink buds open to pure white. Fruit is red, foliage green.

'Indian Summer'. Rose-red flowers and large (about ⅝-inch) red fruit. Bronzy new foliage changes to green.

'Molten Lava'. Deep red buds open to white; fruit is red-orange. The tree developed a small amount of fireblight in 1991, but it still ranked very high for its ornamental value.

'Profusion'. Deep red buds open to deep pink; fruit is maroon. Purplish new foliage fades to bronze.

'Robinson'. Crimson buds open to pink; fruit is dark red. Reddish new foliage ages to bronze-green.

The losers:

These commonly planted crabapples include 'Dolgo', 'Mary Potter', 'Ormiston Roy', 'Red Barron', 'Red Jade', 'Royalty', ' Sentinel', 'Silver Moon', and 'Strawberry Parfait'.

Keep your cut flowers fresher longer

Using materials that you may already have in your house, you can make a cut flower preservative that keeps flowers looking fresh longer.

Mix 1 part lemon-lime soda (not diet) with 3 parts water. For each quart of the mixture, add ¼ teaspoon of household bleach. The sugar in the soda helps buds open and last longer, the acid improves water flow in the stems, and the bleach reduces the growth of bacteria and fungus.

Snowing? Get a broom

Get your broom ready if it appears that snow is going to fall west of the Cascades. In this part of the country, snow is usually wet and extra heavy. When it builds up on trees and shrubs, its weight can break or permanently damage branches.

Use the broom to knock or shake snow off branches before it builds up and causes problems.

The last word on drip irrigation

If you're planning or installing a drip system this year, Robert Kourik's new 118-page book, *Drip Irrigation for Every Landscape and All Climates,* is worth a read. It's the first comprehensive, yet inviting, book on the subject for home gardeners.

In Kourik's words, "This book is about how to put in a drip-irrigation system that's simple to install, efficient, and virtually invisible." The book is infused with good humor, abundant illustrations, and clear explanations of why and how things work. Kourik covers everything from basic drip components to when and how long to irrigate.

For a copy of the book, ask your bookstore to order from the publisher, Metamorphic Press, Box 1841, Santa Rosa, CA 95402. Or send the publisher a $16.93 check, payable to Drip Irrigation Book. ■

By Michael MacCaskey, Jim McCausland, Lynn Ocone, Lauren Bonar Swezey

WEST OF THE CASCADES, see items marked with a **W.**

EAST OF THE CASCADES, see items marked with an **E.**

January Checklist

HERE IS WHAT NEEDS DOING

☐ **BAIT FOR SLUGS. W:** A spell of mild, damp winter weather does two things: it makes pansies and primroses perk up and flower, and it brings out armadas of slugs. Bait for them with metaldehyde, or go out and handpick them. When you find pinhead-size white eggs in the soil, squash them: they've got baby slugs inside.

☐ **CARE FOR HOUSE PLANTS. W, E:** Feed only those bearing winter flowers or berries. Water all but only when the top inch of the soil dries out. Pinch off yellowing leaves. If plants have a layer of dust over them (which shelters plant-damaging insects), rinse it off with tepid water.

☐ **CHECK GERANIUMS. W, E:** Some foliage yellowing and dieback are normal during winter, but if they're extreme, give plants a brighter spot. Water only when the top ½ inch of soil dries out, and don't fertilize for another couple of months.

☐ **CHECK STORED BULBS, PRODUCE. W, E:** Check corms, tubers, and produce, sprinkling water on any that are shriveling, and throwing out ones that show signs of rot. Dahlias are the exception: cut out bad spots, dust with sulfur, and store away from the rest.

☐ **FERTILIZE ASPARAGUS. W, E:** Top-dress with rotted manure, or sprinkle with complete fertilizer.

☐ **ORDER SEED. W, E:** Mail-order seed catalogs are out now, offering a bigger selection of seed than you'll find in any supermarket. They also offer individual flower colors and hybrids you're unlikely to find on most racks.

☐ **PLANT BARE-ROOT. W:** This month, you can buy a remarkable array of bare-root plants, from vegetables (artichokes, asparagus, horseradish, and rhubarb) to berries, grapes, and fruit trees. Also look for bare-root ornamental trees and shrubs. All are less expensive than their counterparts in containers and tend to do better in the garden. Another advantage: these need minimal soil preparation before you plant them.

☐ **PRUNE FRUIT TREES. W:** Work on a day when temperatures are well above freezing. Cut out dead, diseased, closely parallel, or crossing branches, then prune for shape.

☐ **PRUNE ROSES. W:** Prune hybrid teas to a vase shape made from the strongest three to five canes, cutting top growth back by about a third.

☐ **SHOP FOR WINTER-FLOWERING SHRUBS. W:** You have a host of choices, some with remarkable fragrance, flower form, and color. Some good ones include *Camellia sasanqua*, *Cornus mas* (cornelian cherry), and witch hazel.

☐ **SOW PERENNIALS. W, E:** Put your coldframe or greenhouse to work by sowing seed of such hardy perennials as delphiniums, hellebores, veronicas, and violas. Set plants out as soon as they've developed two or three sets of true leaves, but not more than about a month before last frost.

☐ **SPRAY FOR PEACH-LEAF CURL. W, E:** Spray with fixed copper, Bordeaux mixture, or lime sulfur on a mild, dry day.

☐ **WEED . . . CAREFULLY. W:** The best way to beat weeds is to stay ahead of them. Start now by pulling up or hoeing the few dandelions and winter weeds that appear. Don't hoe over bulb beds: even if leaf tips aren't showing, they're likely just under the surface.—*J. M.*

IN HIGH ELEVATIONS and intermountain areas of California, and east of the Sierra, see items marked with an **H.**

IN LOW ELEVATIONS of Northern California, see items marked with an **L.**

☐ **APPLY DORMANT SPRAY. L:** To control fungus diseases and overwintering insects, spray fruit trees with a dormant spray such as bordeaux or lime sulfur. But hold off if temperatures are going to drop below freezing or if rain is expected.

☐ **CARE FOR GIFT PLANTS. L:** After they finish blooming, trim spent blossoms from hardier plants like azaleas, cinerarias, cyclamen, and cymbidiums, and move them to a protected spot outdoors. Keep tender plants such as amaryllis and kalanchoe indoors in a well-lighted spot. Water regularly. If plants dry out quickly, repot in fresh soil in the next larger container. Fertilize amaryllis, azaleas, and cymbidiums after bloom finishes. Fertilize others lightly every three to four weeks. **H:** Keep plants indoors until after the last hard freeze.

☐ **CARE FOR LIVING CHRISTMAS TREES. H, L:** If you haven't done so already, move living Christmas trees outdoors. Put them in a partly shaded spot to begin with, then move into full sun after a week or two. Rinse off the foliage and thoroughly soak the soil.

☐ **CONTROL SLUGS AND SNAILS. L:** Reduce their numbers by eliminating hiding places; clean out leaf litter and garden debris. Handpick, trap by allowing them to collect on the underside of a raised board, or use commercial bait.

☐ **ORDER SEEDS. H, L:** This is a good time to thumb through catalogs and order varieties you can't find on seed racks. Sow vegetable and flower seeds as soon as they arrive, so you can plant them out in February, March, and April.

☐ **PLANT ANNUALS. L:** For midwinter bloom, buy plants in 4-inch pots; smaller sizes will just sit until spring. Stuff plants into bigger decorative pots or set them out in flower beds. Try calendula, candytuft, cineraria, dianthus, English daisy, English and fairy primroses, Iceland poppy, pansy, snapdragons, stock, and viola.

☐ **PLANT BARE-ROOT. L:** This is the prime month to buy and plant dormant roses, shrubs, fruit and shade trees, and vines. Not only can you find the best selection of varieties in bare-root, but bare-root plants cost less and adapt more quickly. Plant them right after you bring them home. If you can't, heel them in: temporarily lay them on their sides in a shallow trench and cover with moist sawdust or soil.

☐ **PROTECT PLANTS FROM FROST. L:** Watch for dry, still, clear nights, and listen to the weather forecast. If frost is predicted, move tender container plants beneath overhangs or into the garage. Protect other frost-tender plants with burlap or a cloth covering. Do not let it touch the leaves; prop it on stakes and remove first thing in the morning.—*L. B. S.*

January Checklist

HERE IS WHAT NEEDS DOING

☐ **BUY AND PLANT BULBS. C:** January is one of the year's most important months for planting bulbs, corms, rhizomes, and tubers. Look in nurseries for tuberous begonia, calla, canna, crinum, dahlia, gladiolus, nerine, and tigridia.

☐ **CARE FOR BARE-ROOT PLANTS.** Keep roots moist before and after planting. If you can't put plants in the ground right away, heel in roots in moist soil or wood shavings until you set them out—no more than a week.

☐ **CONTROL SLUGS AND SNAILS. C:** Reduce their numbers by eliminating hiding places; clean out leaf litter and garden debris. Handpick, trap by allowing them to collect on the underside of a slightly raised board, or use commercial bait.

☐ **GROOM CAMELLIAS. C, L:** If camellia petal blight is a problem, keep the ground beneath camellia plants clean by removing fallen flowers and leaves promptly. Pick infected flowers from plants.

☐ **PLANT BARE-ROOT.** This is the planting month for dormant deciduous fruit and shade trees, artichokes, asparagus, cane berries, grapes, hardy perennials, roses, shrubs, strawberries, and wisteria vines. Plant as soon as you can.

☐ **PLANT BEDDING PLANTS. C, L:** It's not too late to plant these colorful cool-weather flowers: calendulas, cinerarias (very frost-tender), dianthus, English daisies, Iceland poppies, larkspur, pansies, primroses, snapdragons, stock, sweet alyssum, sweet peas, violas.

☐ **PLANT CAMELLIAS AND AZALEAS. C, L:** Nurseries are well stocked with blooming plants this month. Shop now to choose the flower colors and forms you want; plant right away in acid soil. Just after flowering is the time to transplant established camellias and azaleas.

☐ **PLANT VEGETABLES.** Set out seedlings of cabbage, chard, chives, endive, lettuce, onions, and parsley. In all but the desert, plant roots of perennial vegetables such as artichoke, horseradish, and rhubarb; plant asparagus in all zones.

☐ **PRUNE DORMANT PLANTS.** Make sure your shears and saws are sharp, then prune dormant fruit and shade trees, cane berries, grapes, roses, and vines. Wait to prune spring-flowering shrubs and vines until after blooms fade.

☐ **SPRAY DORMANT PLANTS. C, L:** Spray dormant roses and fruit trees to reduce numbers of overwintering pests, such as scale insects and peach leaf curl fungus. Rake up leaves and debris from around trees, then spray with horticultural oil, oil and lime sulfur, or oil and fixed copper.

☐ **START VEGETABLE SEEDS.** Coastal gardeners can still start seeds of broccoli, brussels sprouts, and cabbage for planting out next month. In all zones, experiment with early warm-season crops: start a few eggplant, peppers, and tomatoes to set out in warm, frost-protected areas in February or March.

☐ **WATER NATIVE PLANTS.** If winter rain is insufficient, or if persistent wind and bright sun desiccate plants, water fall-planted natives to help them get established. Now is when they seek out and store water in preparation for summer drought. Check soil moisture regularly; give new and established plants a slow, deep soak as needed.

☐ **WEED.** If you haven't done so already, mulch flower and vegetable beds to keep ahead of weeds encouraged by winter rains. Regular hoeing is also useful. Keep on top of areas seeded with wildflowers; as plants come up so will weeds. Hand-pull or carefully hoe to control them.—*L. O.*

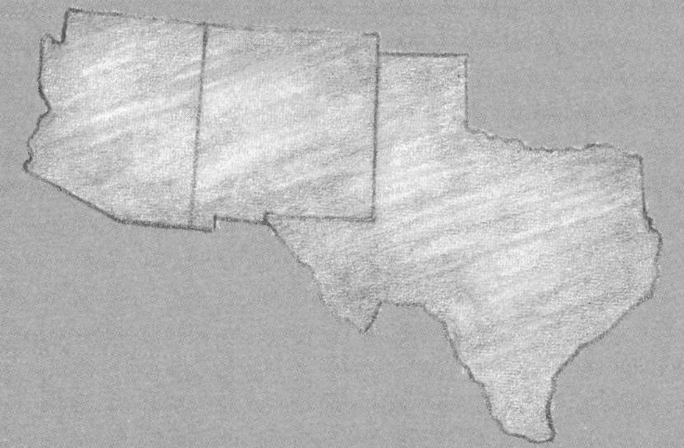

January Checklist

HERE IS WHAT NEEDS DOING

☐ **CONTROL APHIDS.** In mild-winter areas, these insects may attack a plant's young, succulent growth. Knock them off with daily blasts of water from the hose, or spray them with insecticidal soap.

☐ **FERTILIZE CITRUS TREES.** Citrus trees use nutrients most efficiently while they are flowering. Now, just before flowering, is the time to apply ammonium sulfate fertilizer to established trees. Wait another month before fertilizing young trees, and halve quantities.

Follow these guidelines for trees more than 4 years old: 2½ pounds for grapefuit, 3½ to 5 pounds for oranges and tangerines, and 5 to 6 pounds for large lemon trees. Water first; a day later, sprinkle fertilizer evenly over entire root area, then water to wash it into soil. Apply equal amounts in May.

☐ **MOVE LIVING CHRISTMAS TREES OUTDOORS.** To keep your living tree healthy, set it out of direct sun for several weeks, until it becomes acclimated. Then plant the tree in the ground (allowing plenty of room for its ultimate size), donate it to a local park or community, or keep it in a container for next year. If you keep the tree in a container, water it regularly. In low and intermediate deserts, place the tree where it will receive afternoon shade.

☐ **PLANT ANNUALS.** Most low-desert nurseries still have sixpacks and 4-inch pots of ageratum, calendula, cineraria, pansy, petunia, snapdragon, sweet alyssum, and verbena.

☐ **PLANT BARE-ROOT.** Berries, fruit trees, roses, and shade trees are available. Have the nursery wrap the roots to keep them from drying, then plant immediately after you get the plants home. In the high desert, wait another month or two before you buy and plant.

☐ **PLANT CHILLED BULBS.** If you live in a mild-winter area such as Houston, Galveston, Beaumont, Corpus Christi, or Phoenix, now is the time to plant the tulips, crocus, and hyacinths that you bought in November and stored in your refrigerator for a minimum of six weeks. Keep bulbs cool and shaded until you get them into the ground.

☐ **PROTECT CITRUS FRUITS.** Most citrus fruits are damaged if temperatures stay near 24° for 2 hours or more. If cold damages the fruits, pick and juice them within 24 hours. When temperatures below 28° are forecast, cover trees with a cloth before sunset and remove cloth in the morning.

☐ **TURN CUT CHRISTMAS TREES INTO MULCH.** If you have a compost shredder, grind cut Christmas trees to use as mulch (cut them into pieces first). If you don't have a shredder, check with your community: many cities now pick up and shred trees, then use the mulch in parks. Or you can make pea stakes: strip branches and trunk of needles, then cut them into pieces. As a last resort, dispose of trees—well before they become a fire hazard.

☐ **WATER PLANTS.** Between rainy periods, deep-water trees and shrubs every three weeks—oftener if temperature is above 70°.

☐ **WEED.** In low deserts—if you haven't done so already—mulch flower and vegetable beds to keep ahead of weeds encouraged by winter rains. Hoeing is also useful.—*M. M.*

Roses high and mighty

THESE 14 CLIMBERS DAZZLE GARDEN WALLS, FENCES, AND POSTS

If a single rose is enough to suggest romance, consider the impact of climbers. Their first shoots instinctively flirt with a picket fence or post. Gaining maturity, they'll overtake a trellis with a billowing bouquet of buds. The most lionhearted go for broke with an aerial flower show big enough to overwhelm a house wall.

Plant a bare-root climbing rose this month, and it'll start romancing your landscape this summer—and increasing its charms for years to come.

Climbers are the most vigorous forms of many kinds of roses, from polyanthas to hybrid teas. But their training and pruning requirements set them apart. "The quickest way to destroy a climber," says Southern California rosarian Clair Martin, "is to treat it like a bush rose."

Climbers won't clutch and twine with-

KATHLENE PERSOFF

LAVISH SPRING BLOOM *Climbing Lady Banks' rose envelops historic mill in Pasadena, California, with graceful drifts of dainty double flowers.*

out help; they need tying when canes are long enough to move into position. Though some rampant growers develop canes as long as 60 feet, others are compact and easily trained; choose one that's right for your situation. "It's for us to harness climbers," says Texas rosarian G. Michael Shoup, "not for them to harness us."

The chart below lists 14 of the best climbers for the West. Some will work in a small space, trained on a single post or a fan trellis, while the larger ones require large, sturdy structures.

Climbing sports (whose names start with the abbreviation Cl.) are naturally occurring mutations of bush varieties. They bloom off old wood and may take a few years to establish; the same is true of Lady Banks'. The other roses on the chart bloom on both

14 OF THE WEST'S BEST CLIMBING ROSES

Name	Color	Flower	Fragrance	Height/Habit	Comments
Altissimo	Blood red with yellow stamens	Single, up to 5 inches	None to slight	Stiff canes 7 to 10 feet	Continual light bloom if deadheaded. Showy hips in fall. Good all zones. Excellent disease resistance.
America	Coral pink	Full, 4 to 5 inches	Strong, spicy	Canes 10 to 12 feet	Recurrent bloom. Good on pillars. Slow starter. Good cut flower.
Cl. Cécile Brunner	Light pink	Dainty, 1½ inches, in large clusters	Moderate	Vigorous canes to 20 feet or more	Polyantha. Blooms on old wood; main flushes in spring and fall. Good all zones.
Dortmund	Cherry red with white eye	Single, 3 to 4 inches, in clusters	Slight	Flexible canes 10 to 12 feet	Heavy bloom in spring; continues if deadheaded. Hollylike foliage; showy hips. Good on pillar or wall. Excellent disease resistance; very hardy. Popular in the Northwest.
Dublin Bay	Dark crimson	4 to 5 inches	Slight	Canes 8 to 10 feet	Slow to start climbing; early flowering. Recurrent bloom. Excellent disease resistance. Popular in the Northwest.
Golden Showers	Clear yellow, fades in hot sun	Semidouble, 4 inches, in clusters	Moderate, sweet	Upright, stiff canes to 14 feet	Flowers open fast; bloom is recurrent. Stems almost thornless. Good on pillar or wall. Does best in cool-summer climates.
Handel	Ruffled white with pink edging	Semidouble to double, 3 to 5 inches	Slight	Stiff canes 12 to 14 feet	Two main flushes of bloom; pink edges fade in hot sun. Excellent disease resistance. Popular in the Northwest.
Cl. Iceberg	White	Double, 3 to 4 inches, in clusters	None to slight	Flexible canes to 12 feet	Slow to start; vigorous once established. Continual bloom. Good on pillar or wall. Hard to find, but supplies increasing.
Joseph's Coat	Changing hues of red, pink, orange, yellow	Double, 3 to 4 inches, in clusters	Light, tangy	Stiff canes 8 to 12 feet	Intermittent bloom with two main flushes. Somewhat cold-tender; not recommended for the desert.
Lady Banks'	Yellow 'Lutea' or white 'Alba Plena'	Double, 1 inch, in clusters	'Alba Plena' has light violet scent; 'Lutea' has none	Massive; canes to 25 feet or more	Species rose. Profuse bloom on old wood in early season only. Evergreen, thornless. Prune only to shape. Hardy to 15°. Excellent disease resistance.
Madame Alfred Carrière	White with pink blush at center	Double, 3 to 4 inches, cupped	Strong, sweet	Stiff canes 15 to 20 feet	Noisette. Strong bloom in spring, then light. Easiest to train flat and fanned. Few thorns. Outstanding in Texas and Southern California. Hardy to 15°.
New Dawn	Light pink	Double, 3 to 4 inches	Moderate, sweet, fruity	Vigorous canes to 15 feet or more	Profuse bloom in spring, then light. Best on wall or fence. Very thorny. Hardy.
Royal Sunset	Orange changing to apricot	Semidouble to double, 3½ to 5 inches	Moderate	Upright, stiff canes to 10 feet	Recurrent bloom. Thick, glossy, deep green leaves. Heat bleaches flowers. Excellent disease resistance.
Sombreuil	White	3 to 4 inches, flat, old-fashioned	Potent, rich	Canes 10 to 12 feet	Tea rose. Recurrent bloom. Good on pillar or fanned. Outstanding in Texas and Southern California. Hardy to 15°.

PHOTOS COURTESY OF WEEKS ROSES, JACKSON & PERKINS, HUNTINGTON BOTANICAL GARDEN, ANTIQUE ROSE EMPORIUM, INGRAHAM'S COTTAGE GARDEN, EDMUNDS' ROSES

new and old wood; they will start flowering the first year they're planted.

PROVIDING SUPPORT

Choose a structure that's large and sturdy enough to support the plant at maturity. Use pressure-treated wood for posts, and set the posts in concrete.

If you build or buy a structure like an archway or pergola, construction must be solid and the base long enough to set 2 feet into the ground. Some prebuilt units are not hefty enough for climbing roses.

You can place a trellis in front of a masonry wall and train the rose on it, or secure plant attachments directly in the wall. Nurseryman Ray Sodomka of Santa Barbara, California, suggests threading plant ties through eye screws attached to the wall with expansion bolts. Or train canes on a grid of 14- or 16-gauge wire threaded through the eye screws. Either way, the eye screws should extend a couple of inches beyond the wall to provide air circulation.

One of the best structures for a climbing rose is a chain-link fence: it's strong, and its links provide air circulation and spaces for tying branches.

PLANTING AND TRAINING

For best results, plant roses in full sun and well-drained, fertile soil. Place them about 15 inches from their support structure, and avoid planting next to trees or shrubs that will compete for water.

All climbers bloom best when canes are trained horizontally. This causes growth buds to emerge and grow upward, producing an abundance of flowering branches. Untrained, upright-growing canes produce fewer flowers.

Roses that do best on pillars have flexible canes to about 10 feet. These climbers need little space, yet give a dramatic display, especially if you twist the canes around the post.

Although small, stiff-caned bushes like 'Altissimo' can be trained to a post, they bloom better when canes are fanned or horizontal.

In mild climates, where canes grow rapidly, you may need to start training the first year the rose is in the ground. In colder regions, growth may stay in bounds without training until the second year.

To attach canes to the support, use a stretchy, strong material like plastic nursery tape or strips of old nylon stockings; avoid wire or cord that can cut into branches.

PRUNING AND CARE

For the first two or three years, just remove faded flowers to promote repeat flowering. Once some wood has matured and strong climbing canes are established, prune to stimulate growth of new canes and flowering laterals. Each winter (at the same time you prune bush roses), shorten flowering laterals to 3 to 6 inches long, or to two to four buds. Remove weak or dead wood at the base.

Keep as many productive shoots as possible. If you can't redirect a wayward stem by tying it, cut it back to a bud headed the right way.

Climbers' other needs—water, fertilizer, and pest and disease control—are similar to those of bush roses.

'JOSEPH'S COAT' *accents railing with a kaleidoscope of 3- to 4-inch blooms.*

RUSS A. WIDSTRAND

CHARLES MANN

'NEW DAWN' *softens pergola and frames garden retreat.*

FRAGRANT WHITE CLIMBERS *'Sombreuil' and 'Madame Alfred Carrière' (behind) twine over walkway. Design: James Yoch, Diane Johnson.*

SOURCES

You'll find a good supply of plants in nurseries this month. Collectively, these mail-order sources offer all the roses in our chart except 'Cl. Iceberg' (available in some nurseries).

The Antique Rose Emporium, Route 5, Box 143, Brenham, TX 77833; (800) 441-0002. Catalog $5.

Edmunds' Roses, 6235 S.W. Kahle Rd., Wilsonville, OR 97070; (503) 682-1476. Free catalog.

Jackson & Perkins, Box 1028, Medford, OR 97501; (800) 292-4769. Free catalog.

Pickering Nurseries, Inc., 670 Kingston Rd., Pickering, Ontario, Canada L1V 1A6; (416) 839-2111. Catalog $3.■

By Lynn Ocone

DARROW M. WATT

COLORFUL GROUPING *of cattleya orchids shows range of flower colors, from subtle green with a red lip to vivid purple. In front are miniature cattleyas.*

Elegant and easy . . . orchids to grow indoors

They're corsage orchids, lady's slippers, and moth orchids

SOMETIMES BIZARRE, but more often elegant and exotic, orchids are the royalty of the flower kingdom. More than 25,000 species have been named so far.

These beauties, while much admired and cherished, have a reputation for being finicky and difficult to grow. But many are simple to raise indoors, once you learn their basic needs.

Three types of orchids are easy and reliable to grow: *Cattleya, Paphiopedilum,* and *Phalaenopsis.*

All can be grown on a windowsill and will rebloom indoors without artificial light (except cattleya, which requires artificial light in winter in the Northwest and in foggy coastal areas). Long-lasting flowers come in a variety of shapes, sizes, and colors.

THE CORSAGE ORCHID

Familiar to many from prom nights, cattleya is the flamboyant, colorful orchid used in corsages. This large-flowered type normally grows 1½ to 2 feet tall; miniature cattleyas are 6 to 12 inches tall with smaller flowers.

The thick, leathery leaves are attached to pseudobulbs (enlarged stems), which send up stems topped with one to five or more flowers. Flowers last two to six weeks and may be scented. Under ideal conditions, some varieties of cattleya may rebloom in summer.

Of the three types, cattleya offers the widest color range; varieties with lavender, purple, or white flowers, or white flowers with colored lips, are the best known. Yellow and green flowers are also popular. New colors include port, apricot, and copper.

FOR THE UNUSUAL, GROW LADY'S SLIPPERS

To some, paphiopedilum (lady's slipper) is beautiful; to others, it's bizarre. Flowers may be mahogany, green, brown, pink, white, or yellow with warts, hairs, and bold stripes or subtle color blends.

Like cattleya, this orchid sends up one bloom stem from each cluster of leaves. It's crowned with a single pouch-lipped flower that lasts up to three months.

Paphiopedilums with solid green leaves require cool temperatures (50° to 60° at night); ones with mottled leaves are warm growers (60° to 65° at night). The latter fare better under average household conditions.

ORCHIDS THAT LOOK LIKE MOTHS

Graceful, elegant flowers of phalaenopsis (moth orchid) seem to flutter along arching stems. Flower stalks arise from flat leathery leaves; flowers open from the bottom. Flower sprays last two to three months.

Commonest colors are white and pink, but candy-stripe, rose-pink, purple, and spotted yellow are becoming more available. Phalaenopsis blooms from the same leaf cluster year after year.

After bloom, cut off the flower stalk just above the node that produced the lowest flower; it may send out a new flower spike. Since flowering saps the plant's strength, it's best to cut the stalk back to the base after two or three cycles or if the plant is unhealthy, so it can put energy back into leaf growth.

CARING FOR ORCHIDS

To be successful with orchids, it's important to mimic their native conditions.

Temperature. All three

grow well if temperatures stay 60° to 65° at night and 70° to 75° during the day.

Light. Proper lighting is critical for getting plants to rebloom. Cattleya needs the most light. Set plants in a south window filtered by a sheer curtain (or set them back a few feet). Leaves should be yellowish. If they're leggy and dark green, give them more light.

Paphiopedilums and phalaenopsis need less light; both types prefer African violet conditions (an east or lightly shaded west window).

Humidity. Ideal is 50 to 60 percent. To keep it high, cluster pots with other house plants and set them on trays filled with gravel and water (pot bottoms must sit above the water level).

Misting helps, if your water doesn't have a high salt content. But don't mist after noon; water on the leaves overnight causes disease. Provide air circulation.

Fertilizer. To rebloom, plants need fertilizing regularly. Bark, the standard growing medium, uses nitrogen as it breaks down. Apply a high-nitrogen fertilizer (like 30-10-10) at quarter strength every time you water (never fertilize a dry plant). Use low nitrogen (6-30-30) every fourth feeding. Paphiopedilum is the most sensitive to overfeeding; flush with plain water once a month and cut back fertilizing in winter.

Water. Cattleya likes to dry out between waterings; paphiopedilum and phalaenopsis like to stay evenly moist but not wet.

To test moisture several inches down, stick a sharpened pencil into the bark; if it comes out dry, the plant needs water. Also, if the pot feels light, it's time to water.

As the bark breaks down, air spaces compress and the bark stays wet longer. Don't overwater or roots will rot.

Potting medium. All three types require a well-drained potting medium with plenty of air spaces.

REPOT PERIODICALLY

Repot orchids periodically (every two to three years for cattleyas, every one to two years for paphiopedilum and phalaenopsis) to replace growing medium that has decomposed and lost its air space, and to move plants into larger containers, if needed.

Repot after flowering before new roots are more than ½ inch long (they're often seen at the base of new growth). Use ¼- to ½-inch-diameter fir bark. You can add perlite for water retention and aeration. Soak the bark overnight before using.

Water the orchid thoroughly. Then lay the pot on its side and gently tug out the plant (use a knife to loosen roots from the pot). Wash off any old bark that clings to the roots, and cut off any dark or rotted roots.

Position cattleya in the new container so old growth is nearest to the pot rim and new growth is at the center. The base of the plant should sit ½ inch below the pot rim. Stake large cattleyas.

Arrange paphiopedilum or phalaenopsis in the pot's center so bottom leaves sit on top of the bark, ½ inch below the rim. Set plants in a shady location for four to six weeks. Don't water for the first two weeks, then water sparingly for the first few months.

ARCHING FLOWER SPIKES *are crowned with delicate spotted or striped phalaenopsis flowers.*

PAPHIOPEDILUMS *with all-green leaves (left) tolerate cool temperatures; ones with mottled leaves prefer warmer conditions.*

DARROW M. WATT

WHERE TO GET PLANTS BY MAIL

Ready-to-bloom plants cost from $17 to $35 for cattleya, $17 to $18 for paphiopedilum, and $15 to $30 for phalaenopsis. Catalogs are free unless otherwise noted.

Beall Orchid Co., 3400 Academy Dr. S.E., Auburn, WA 98002; (206) 735-1148.

The Rod McLellan Co., 1450 El Camino Real, South San Francisco, CA 94080; (800) 237-4089. Brochure $2.

Stewart Orchids, Box 550, Carpinteria, CA 93014; (800) 621-2450, or 831-9765 inside California. ■

By Lauren Bonar Swezey

'Melogold'
grapefruit-pummelo
hybrid
'Rio Red'
grapefruit
'Moro'
blood orange
'Variegated Pink'
lemon
'Lane Late'
navel orange
'Page'
mandarin
'Wekiwa'
tangelolo

Citrus Breakthroughs

Here are new varieties to try

By Lauren Bonar Swezey, Linda Lau Anusasananan

'Oroblanco' grapefruit-pummelo hybrid

NORMAN A. PLATE

LEMONS WITH PINK FLESH, ORANGES WITH RUBY red flesh and a mouth-tingling flavor that hints of raspberries, and tangelolos that look like miniature grapefruits: these are some of the new (and not so new, but lesser-known) citrus—trees and fruits—now coming from growers in the citrus belts of California, Arizona, and Texas. All together, the chart on the next page lists 13 kinds.

Choose a variety suitable to your region

If you live in a mild area of inland Southern or central California, or the lower deserts of California or Arizona, you can grow most kinds of citrus. Along the coast and in the San Francisco Bay Area, citrus may not get enough heat to ripen. Periodic freezes in northern and inland areas can damage trees.

While most blood oranges are marginal in coastal Northern California, 'Moro' colors well and produces a good tart-sweet flavor there. And grapefruit-pummelo hybrids are adapted to cool coastal temperatures; they'll sweeten up much better than grapefruit. Unlike other pink grapefruit, 'Rio Red' colors well on the coast, although it's fairly tart.

Gardeners in Northern California's inland valleys can grow a variety of citrus, but in these areas be sure to protect trees from freezes.

Planting and care

To give your tree the best growing conditions, take advantage of microclimates in the garden. In cool, coastal areas, plant trees where they get reflected heat from paving, the south side of the house, or a masonry wall.

Provide good drainage. Water trees regularly; they don't tolerate drought. Fertilize with a complete acid food that also contains iron, manganese, and zinc.

Prune only to shape trees. In the desert, let the branches grow to the ground to protect the trunk from sunburn.

Mandarins tend to bear a heavy crop one year and a light one the next. During a heavy year, pick off a third to a half of the fruits when they're marble-size so trees will produce more the next.

When to harvest citrus

Warm temperatures speed ripening. The same variety of citrus will ripen two to three months earlier in the desert

SANDRA WILLIAMS

FRESHLY PICKED *'Oroblanco' is a breakfast treat for Claire and David Guggenheim.*

than in coastal areas and about a month earlier than in southern inland areas.

When you grow citrus at home, you can pick fruits at peak flavor. Near the estimated first-harvest date, pluck off a fruit and taste it. If it's not to your liking, wait to pick. It's best to store fruits on the tree unless a hard freeze is predicted. Then you should pick fruit and store in a cold area.

Different kinds of citrus hold on the tree for different lengths of time. But climate plays a big role. Fruit holds on the tree longest on the coast and shortest in the desert (high temperatures eventually deteriorate fruit).

'Melogold' and 'Oroblanco' eventually drop fruit. Grapefruits hang on for months near the coast and slowly grow sweeter. Lemons also hang on a long time.

Pick mandarins at peak flavor; don't leave them on the tree until their skins get puffy or most kinds will lose flavor. Oranges can hang on the tree for several months, although some may drop off. Harvest before the flesh gets dry. Blood oranges don't hold on as long. Harvest tangelolo when fully sweetened.

Where to buy trees

Pacific Tree Farms, 4301 Lynwood Dr., Chula Vista, CA 91910; (619) 422-2400. Sells all citrus listed, except 'Spring' navel orange. Due to quarantines, trees can be shipped only to Southern California counties. Catalog $2.

Wholesale sources

These California nurseries outside quarantine areas sell wholesale only.

B & Z Nursery, Porterville. Sells grapefruit hybrids, 'Rio Red', 'Lane Late', and blood oranges.

Four Winds Growers, Fremont. Sells 'Oroblanco', 'Rio Red', and blood oranges.

Menlo Growers, Gilroy. Sells 'Oroblanco', 'Encore', blood oranges, and 'Variegated Pink' lemon in Northern California only.

Willits & Newcomb, Arvin. Sells grapefruit-pummelo hybrids, 'Rio Red', 'Pixie', 'Lane Late', 'Spring', and blood oranges.

Young's Nursery, Thermal. Sells 'Oroblanco', 'Rio Red', 'Encore', 'Lane Late', 'Moro', and 'Tarocco'. Also retail. ■

Type of citrus	Looks? Taste?	Needs in the garden? When ripe?
GRAPEFRUIT AND GRAPEFRUIT HYBRIDS		
'Melogold' grapefruit-pummelo hybrid	Large, 6- to 7-inch yellow fruit with medium-thick rind. Sweet with minimal tartness, no bitterness.	Needs less heat to ripen than grapefruit. Slightly more cold-sensitive than 'Oroblanco'. Starts mid-December; holds to March.
'Oroblanco' grapefruit-pummelo hybrid	Large, yellow 5- to 6-inch fruit with thick rind; few seeds. Sweet-tart; often more flavorful than 'Melogold'.	Needs less heat to sweeten than grapefruit; good in all areas. Early November; holds in some areas until March.
'Rio Red' grapefruit	Yellow 5- to 6-inch fruit with pink blush, red flesh; no seeds. Mild, sweet with tang.	Needs heat to sweeten fully; flesh colors on coast. Starts January; holds to May or longer.
MANDARINS		
'Encore' mandarin	Small (2 to 3 inches), light orange fruit; seedy; peels easily. Sweet-tart; complex flavors.	Isolate from other mandarins to minimize seeds. March to May; holds to July or later.
'Page' mandarin	Small, 2- to 3-inch fruit with deep orange flesh and skin; has few seeds, thin skin. Very sweet and juicy.	Better (but seedier) fruit with pollinator, such as 'Valencia' orange. December to February; holds until March or mid-May.
'Pixie' mandarin	Small, 2- to 3-inch yellowish orange fruit; no seeds. Bumpy rind, irregular fruit. Very sweet and flavorful; low acid.	Late-maturing mandarin for coastal and inland areas, not deserts. March to April; holds until June or July.
LEMON		
'Variegated Pink' lemon (also called 'Pink Lemonade')	Small, 3-inch-long lemons with green stripes and light pink flesh. Typical tart, highly acid lemon flavor.	Natural dwarf tree to 8 feet; 'Sungold' is similar, with yellow flesh. November to February; holds until April or later.
ORANGES		
'Lane Late' navel **'Spring'** navel	Medium, 3- to 4-inch orange fruit; no seeds. Flavor similar to other navels. 'Spring' is dark orange and sweet.	Peelable oranges when other navels are out of season; may not grow on coast (try 'Trovita'). December to March; holds to June or August.
'Moro' blood orange	Medium, 3- to 4-inch fruit with deep burgundy flesh, reddish orange rind. Sweet-tart, with raspberry undertones, juicy.	Colors and flavors better than other types in coastal Northern California. December to February; holds until March or April.
'Sanguinelli' blood orange	Small to medium, 3½- to 4-inch oblong fruit; flesh orange with red streaks. Sweet-tart flavor; juicy.	Not suitable for coastal Northern California. December to March; holds until April or May.
'Tarocco' blood orange	Medium to large, 4½-inch fruit; internal red color unreliable. Sweetest, most flavorful blood orange.	Adapted to inland valleys of California and the desert. Starts December; holds to April or May.
TANGELOLO		
'Wekiwa' tangelolo (lavender gem, pink tangelo)	Looks like mini-grapefruit (3 to 4 inches wide) with pinkish flesh. Sweet, mild grapefruit taste; very juicy.	Cross between grapefruit and tangelo. Not widely available. November to January; holds until February or later.

RENEE LYNN

SINGLE-FLOWERED *14- to 18-inch-tall 'Coltness' dahlias bloom in a rainbow of colors.*

The dazzle of dahlias . . . from a pack of seeds

FOR A FRACTION OF the cost of tubers or nursery sixpacks, you can grow dozens of dahlia plants from seed to brighten your summer landscape. You'll be surprised at how easy they are to grow: start them indoors in flats or cells, and you'll have vigorous seedlings in just eight weeks.

Sunset head gardener Rick LaFrentz tried seed-starting dahlias recently for the display gardens at our Menlo Park, California, headquarters. He grew dwarf varieties (12 to 14 inches tall), including single-flowered 'Coltness' and double 'Redskin', which has dark reddish foliage.

For the back of a planting bed, try taller kinds, such as cactus types and 'Showpiece', which can get up to 5 feet. They're just as easy to grow and also bloom the first year.

In mild climates, you can sow seeds in January and have transplants by March; in cold-winter climates, wait until February or March to sow seeds.

HOW TO PLANT SEEDS

The papery, ⅓-inch-long seeds are easy to handle. Fill a sixpack or other seed-starting tray with a peat-type potting soil, moisten it well, and plant one or two seeds per cell. Cover with about 1/16 inch of soil and water lightly.

Place the trays in a warm spot (65° to 70°) until the seeds germinate, in 5 to 20 days. When the seeds sprout, move the trays to a bright window (no direct sun) or place them under grow lights; you can also start them in a greenhouse. Keep the soil moist but not soggy. If you plant two seeds per cell and both germinate, snip off the weaker plant.

When the seedlings have at least two sets of true leaves, they're ready to plant in the garden. Move the trays outdoors to a shady area for several days, then slowly expose them to more light over the next week.

Once the dahlias are acclimated to full sun, plant them 10 to 12 inches apart in a sunny location. Mix plenty of organic matter into the soil first. Water regularly.

To keep dahlias blooming continuously, remove faded flowers before seeds form, pinching or cutting stems off at the base (don't just remove the flower head). If spider mites become a problem when the weather warms, spray with insecticidal soap.

PETER CHRISTIANSEN

PLANT SEEDS *in sixpacks or flats of premoistened soil. Eight weeks later, when seedlings have about two or three sets of true leaves, dahlias are ready to plant.*

WHERE TO GET SEEDS

Most nurseries carry dahlia seeds, but you'll have a wider selection if you buy them by mail. The following sources offer free catalogs; a packet of seeds costs $1.25 to $4.95 (plus shipping), depending on variety.

W. Atlee Burpee & Co., 300 Park Ave., Warminster, PA 18991; (800) 888-1447. Sells 'Redskin', 'Rigoletto' (double flowers on foot-tall plants), and two tall types.

Territorial Seed Company, Box 157, Cottage Grove, OR 97424; (503) 942-9547. Sells 'Coltness' and 'Redskin'.

Thompson & Morgan, Box 1308, Jackson, NJ 08527; (800) 274-7333. Sells 13 varieties. ■

By Lauren Bonar Swezey

FEBRUARY

Garden guide 25
February checklists..............30
The graceful grasses.............34
The top tomato?..................38
A tiered effect for roses.........40
Pruning a hybrid tea rose......41
Hang up some quick color 42
Bulbs to plant in winter 43

Sunset's
GARDEN GUIDE

RUSS A. WIDSTRAND

Star of the late-winter garden

FEBRUARY BRINGS UNCERTAIN WEATHER TO LOW ELEVATION WESTERN GARDENS. Will it be mild and wet, or frosty and dry? You'll need to keep a watchful eye on the forecasts so you can care for your plants accordingly. If long spells of dry weather settle in, plants in the garden may need water. On nippy nights, you might have to protect tender plants. February is also bloom time for clivia; this colorful shade plant, shown above, thrives in low elevations of California and Arizona (Sunset climate zones 13–17, 19–24).

NORMAN A. PLATE

BRIGHT LEAVES *of gold locust (Robinia pseudoacacia 'Frisia') add a sunny touch to a Palo Alto, California, garden. Design: Jonathan Plant & Associates, Inc., Lafayette.*

A locust with golden leaves

If you're looking for an unusual deciduous tree that will provide shade in summer but allow the sun to shine through in winter, consider gold locust (*Robinia pseudoacacia* 'Frisia'), shown in the photo at right.

Unlike the more familiar 'Sunburst' honey locust (*Gleditsia triacanthos*), whose yellow foliage turns green as it matures, the gold locust has yellow foliage throughout the season. It makes a handsome contrast to any green plant and to purple-foliaged ones like Japanese maple (*Acer palmatum* 'Ornatum') or smoke tree (*Cotinus coggygria* 'Royal Purple').

Gold locust is a moderately fast-growing tree (about 2 feet a year) that, in time, will reach 30 to 50 feet. It withstands drought once established and tolerates heat, cold, and poor soil.

Trees may be difficult to find, but you can order by mail from Greer Gardens, 1280 Goodpasture Island Rd., Eugene, OR 97401; (800) 548-0111 (catalog $3). An 18- to 30-inch-tall gold locust costs about $30 plus shipping.

'HEATWAVE' TOMATOES *are deep red and juicy; plants are bred for hot climates.*

The latest word on newspaper mulch

Is newspaper safe to use as a mulch in the garden? Maybe not, says U. S. Department of Agriculture soil scientist Jim Edwards. Although black ink used for newspaper printing usually doesn't contain heavy metals, colored inks often do, and these metals can leach into the soil.

Edwards found barium in red inks, copper in blue and green inks, and cobalt, lead, and manganese in paper with metallic coatings.

Colored inks used in newspaper advertising inserts can contain metals that should not be allowed to leach into soil. To be on the safe side, don't make mulch from any sections of the newspaper that have colored ink.

A new tomato for hot inland areas

All tomato plants thrive in warm weather, but when temperatures soar above 90° most won't set fruit. 'Heatwave' is a new tomato with a gene that allows it to set fruit when daytime temperatures range from 90° to 96° and nighttime temperatures are from 70° to 75°.

High temperatures also affect the viability of pollen. 'Heatwave' produces much more pollen than standard tomato varieties, so there's a much greater chance that pollination will occur.

'Heatwave' is a bush-type, 30- to 36-inch-tall, determinate tomato (all the fruit develops at about the same time) that is also disease-resistant. The tomatoes are about 3 inches in diameter and weigh 6 to 7 ounces.

Started from seed, tomatoes need six to eight weeks to reach transplant size, so order seed as soon as possible. From planting, harvest will take about 68 days.

Order seed from W. Atlee Burpee & Co., 300 Park Ave., Warminster, PA 18991; (800) 888-1447.

Keep hummingbird feeders clean

Watching these fascinating creatures feed is a captivating experience. For the health of the birds, the Wild Bird Center in San Carlos, California, recommends regular cleaning to keep feeders bacteria- and algae-free.

To clean your feeder, prepare a solution of 2 cups water, 1 teaspoon mild dishwashing liquid, and 2 tablespoons laundry bleach. Scrub the container and base with a bottle brush or other stiff brush. If you can't reach the black algae inside, add a few tablespoons of sand to the solution and shake the feeder vigorously. Rinse thoroughly and dry before refilling.

A good recipe for nectar is 1 part granulated sugar (do not substitute honey) with 4 parts water. Boil water for 2 minutes, cool to room temperature, measure, then add sugar.

Lettuce seed that's easy to handle

Lettuce seeds are tiny and hard to handle, which can cause frustration at planting time. Because it's difficult to pick up just one seed, you often end up with crowded seedlings that need thinning, and seed is wasted.

Now seed catalogs are offering pelleted lettuce seed, originally developed for commercial seeders. Each seed is covered with diatomaceous earth—an inert, nontoxic material. The coating increases the seed's dimension, which allows you to set it where you want it.

The coating doesn't affect plant growth in the long run. However, in tests at *Sunset,* germination was a few days slower than for the same variety of nonpelleted seed. But the pelleted type caught up,

RUSS A. WIDSTRAND

TEMPTING TO TOUCH, *drumstick flowers on strong, wiry stems are long-lasting in the garden and excellent air-dried for bouquets.*

and all seedlings were the same size at transplant time.

You can buy pelleted seed from these two sources: Harris Seeds, 60 Saginaw Dr., Box 22960, Rochester, NY 14692; (716) 442-0410 (catalog free; sells nine varieties). Ornamental Edibles, 3622 Weedin Court, San Jose, CA 95132; (408) 946-7333 (catalog $2; sells five varieties).

Unusual everlasting flowers to plant now

As you order seeds this month for your spring and summer garden, consider unusual everlastings that are attractive in the ground and that extend the beauty of the season when dried in bouquets or wreaths. Here are six to try. All of them can be air dried; in the garden, all prefer sunny locations.

Drumstick flower (*Craspedia globosa*). Golden globes of tiny flowers (pictured above) grow atop 2-foot wiry stems. This full-sun perennial requires little water once established. Plants are sometimes available in well-stocked nurseries; a 1-gallon plant costs about $7.

Paper daisy (sold as *Helichrysum cassianum* or *Lawrencellia rosea*). Annual, to 24 inches tall, produces sprays of small papery rose-colored flowers.

Winged everlasting (*Ammobium alatum*). Inch-wide white flowers with yellow centers grow in clusters on annual plants about 2 feet tall.

Helipterum (also known as *Acroclinium*). Petite strawflowers in shades of pink and white have yellow or black centers. Yellow center turns brown when dried.

Safflower (*Carthamus tinctorius*). Orange 1½-inch thistlelike flowers on plants to 36 inches tall. It's sensitive to transplanting, so start seeds in peat pots or sow directly in the garden.

Xeranthemum annuum. Wiry-stemmed annual has pink, white, and purple single and semidouble flowers.

Several mail-order catalogs carry a good selection of seeds for everlastings. Among them, Thompson & Morgan offers all of these varieties. For a free catalog, write to Box 1308, Jackson, NJ 08527.

If your bearded irises don't bloom . . .

It may be that they don't get enough fertilizer. According to Jeanne Plank, curator of the iris garden at Descanso Gardens in La Cañada, CA, "Irises should be fed at least as often as roses, three or four times each year, depending on variety." Just don't overdo the nitrogen—too much inhibits blooms.

Fertilize plants in very early spring with a complete, low-nitrogen product. Feed again about six weeks after the plants flower. Plank lists other reasons irises may not bloom.

• ***Not enough sun***. Plants need full sun along the coast or 6 hours of sun inland, with afternoon shade.

• ***Depleted soil.*** Although irises can tolerate many kinds of soil, they prefer it rich and well drained. Before you plant iris divisions, amend the soil with compost.

•***Overcrowded clumps.*** Divide every three or four years, about six weeks after flowering in coastal areas; in hottest regions, wait until fall.

•***Recently planted divisions.*** Divided and planted at just the right time, irises have a good, but not certain, chance of blooming the first year.

•***Divisions too small.*** Each division should have a healthy section of rhizome several inches long, with a good fan of leaves, and roots growing from the bottom.

The last of the pony packs

Pony packs with six 1½- by 2-inch cells are becoming a thing of the past, according to retail nurseries. Most annuals are now sold in jumbo or color packs that have six 2- by 2½-inch cells each.

If you can find pony packs, they are still the best buy at about $1.25 (21 cents per plant), compared to jumbo packs at about $2.75 (46 cents per plant).

You'll also find the most popular annuals like marigolds and pansies sold in mud flats, cell-less 2-inch-deep flats that hold 64 plants each.

A mud flat of annuals costs about $18.95, or 30 cents per plant. Soon you'll see half- and quarter-flats.

Pony packs cost less, but they dry out more quickly and offer less space for root development than color packs and mud flats.

If you are shopping for flats, check to see that plants are growing at an even height and are not tall and spindly. Plants should not be so small that they slip out of the soil easily.

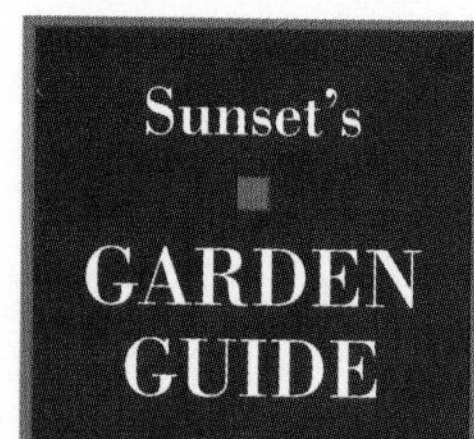

STEVEN R. LORTON

GLOWING *in the chill gray of February, bright bloom of Bergenia crassifolia tops waxy cluster of leaves in an old stone urn. Clipped English ivy twines behind.*

The expert's dahlia stakes

Look at the blue ribbons on Mii Tai's wall in Spokane and you know that she grows picture-perfect dahlias. But when it comes to making the stakes for her dahlias, credit goes to her husband, Sumio. During the dark winter months, he heads for the basement to make (and maintain) the stakes that hold the dahlia heads high.

He paints the sturdy steel rebar stakes (which he buys precut in 5-foot lengths) with a moss green rustproof paint. To apply the paint, he uses a 6-inch square of medium-pile wool carpet (cut from remnant strips he buys at a carpet supply store). Wearing rubber gloves, he folds a paint-soaked carpet square around the rebar and runs it up and down until the rebar is thoroughly covered. One square is enough to paint about 50 stakes.

He stands the painted rods diagonally along the wall (which is protected with layers of newspaper) to dry.

Every few years, he gives old rods a fresh coat of paint while he's painting new ones.

How to use strong fertilizer

Whenever we recommend a complete fertilizer for your plants, we mean one that contains a balance of nitrogen (N), phosphorus (P), and potassium (K). Fertilizer labels show, in numbers like 10-10-10 or 12-12-12, the percentage of each nutrient the fertilizer contains.

The higher the number, the greater the amount of a particular nutrient. That means 20-20-20 is a strong fertilizer. How to use such strong fertilizer? Many good gardeners broadcast the high-powered stuff this month over garden beds and under shrubs and trees. Rains are usually plentiful in February, and plants are just coming out of dormancy. Rain quickly dissolves the fertilizer, which soaks into the ground, and the plants awaken to a hearty (but well-diluted) breakfast. Then they race into action.

Use amounts specified on the label (*never* exceed manufacturer's directions for coverage per square foot).

SAM KWONG

HALF BLUE, HALF GREEN, *uniformly thick with short, stiff needles, two-spruce arch forms grand entry into garden.*

You enter through a spruce archway

When it comes to dramatic entries into a garden, the bicolor spruce arch that Gordon Page designed for the Walla Walla garden pictured at bottom left may take the cake. The arch combines two spruces—a green form of Colorado spruce (*Picea pungens*) and a Colorado blue spruce (*P. p.* 'Glauca'). The saplings were planted 8 feet apart, one on each side of the walkway.

Page sheared the young trees each spring to keep their branches dense. When they grew tall enough, he cut out the top growth tips, pulled the tops together at a height of about 12 feet, and grafted them. Then he began to shear the spruces into the rounded arch shape.

The arch is now four decades old, but it has looked about the way it does now for the last 30 years.

In early June, the arch gets a serious annual shearing with electric clippers. In late summer, errant shoots are snipped off. During last summer's drought, the owner soaked each plant around the trunk about twice a month "just to be on the safe side." Other than that, the trees have flourished with no irrigation or feeding.

Except for Sitka spruce (*P. sitchensis*), spruces don't do well in mild-winter climates. There, a similar arch could be developed from such conifers as *Chamaecyparis lawsoniana, Cupressus forbesii, C. glabra, Juniperus* (columnar), *Sequoia sempervirens, Taxus, Thuja, Tsuga canadensis, and T. heterophylla.*

Simple and elegant flowers for winter

A favorite February bloomer, *Bergenia crassifolia* heralds spring simply and elegantly in Barbara Thomas's Seattle garden. In an old English limestone urn (shown in the photo above), it sends up a brilliant rose flower cluster or two (which often stay on well into March) above a rosette of waxy oval green leaves.

MICHAEL MacCASKEY

PURPLE SAGE *bears clusters of purple flowers above gray-green foliage in late spring. It thrives in hot, dry gardens with little water once established.*

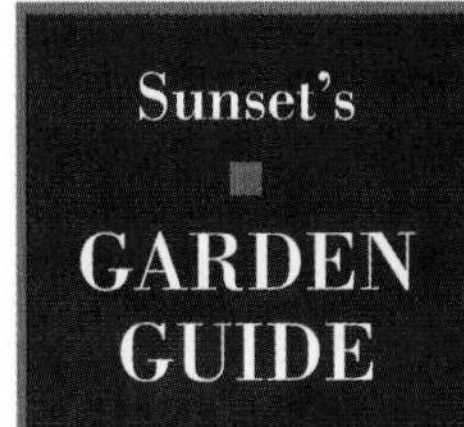

The plant has been happy in the pot for three years—like a treasured and very undemanding garden pet. The owner waters it when she thinks about it, pours a bit of liquid plant food in the urn when she happens to be making the rounds for other plants, and picks off yellow leaves whenever they appear.

After blooms fade in midspring, Thomas buys a six-pack of *Lobelia erinus* 'Crystal Palace' and spaces the plugs evenly around the edge of the urn. Through summer, the lobelia rings the bergenia with brilliant deep blue flowers.

A host of new bergenias have recently been introduced from Europe through British Columbia. (Many come from Bressingham Gardens in England, others from Germany.) Flowers range from white through pink to deep red; leaves are sometimes larger than those of the species and have a bronzy cast, especially in cold weather.

You can find these new bergenias at well-stocked nurseries throughout the west except for the southwest deserts. Plant them anywhere in coastal gardens, in shade inland.

A new purple sage for Arizona and California gardens

Purple sage (*Salvia dorrii*) is one of the sages to most recently make the transition from the wild into our gardens. It grows wild over a wide swath of the desert, from southeastern California to southern Nevada and northeastern Arizona, usually at elevations between 2,500 and 5,000 feet. Purple sage is common in washes and usually grows in association with creosote bush and one-seeded juniper. Just recently the cultivated plants became available to gardeners.

Purple sage (pictured above), which is also known as gray ball salvia, develops into a low, rounded 3-foot-tall shrub after about three seasons; once established, it grows fast (mostly during the cool season). Small gray leaves are about ½ inch long. Papery purple flowers cover branch tips mostly in May and June, though scattered flowering is common virtually all year.

Plant this sage in sunny, hot, dry, and low-care sections of your garden. Although established plants need only a bare minimum of irrigation water, new transplants will need water approximately twice a month during their first summer. Plant in well-drained soil so the rootball is an inch or so above soil level—not in a low basin that collects water. Pinch off faded flowers to keep blooms coming; cut back plants in early fall to control their size.

Plant annuals before they bloom

There was a time when the only annual flowers a gardener could buy at the nursery were tiny seedlings in flats. Cut and lifted out with a knife and spatula, such seedlings were delicate and rarely in flower. We didn't know it at the time, but these nonflowering plants established more quickly, and produced stronger plants in the long run, than plants that you buy in bloom.

Now, most bedding plants are sold in bloom. And once a plant begins to flower, most of its energy is diverted to the development and maintenance of the flowers and seeds that normally follow. Root and leaf growth are put on hold.

If you can't find nonblooming bedding plants at nurseries, choose the youngest ones you can find; before planting, pick off flowers or buds to help divert the plant's energy into root growth. You can also ask your nursery to special-order plants that are a week or two younger.

New guide to water-conserving gardens

If you want to grow a maximum number of flowers on a minimum amount of water, a new book—*The Low-Water Flower Gardener*, by Scott Millard and Eric A. Johnson (Ironwood Press, Tucson, 1993; $14.95)—tells you how.

Directed primarily to Southwestern gardeners, the 144-page book includes an encyclopedia of 270 colorful, unthirsty grasses, ground covers, perennials, and small shrubs. Each description includes the plant's native range and cultural guidelines. Several of the newest plants for the Southwest—such as *Calylophus hartwegii*, *Gaura lindheimeri*, and 20 ornamental grasses—are included, as are more common plants such as bougainvillea and daylily. More than 125 color photographs and 40 illustrations accompany the text.

The Low-Water Flower Gardener is available at many bookstores or from the publisher, 2968 W. Ina Rd., Room 285, Tucson, AZ 85741; include $3 for shipping and handling. Or order from the distributor, Johnson Books, at (800) 258-5830. ■

By Steven R. Lorton, Lynn Ocone, Michael MacCaskey, Lauren Bonar Swezey.

WEST OF THE CASCADES, see items marked with a **W.**

EAST OF THE CASCADES, see items marked with an **E.**

February Checklist

HERE IS WHAT NEEDS DOING

☐ **BAIT FOR SLUGS AND SNAILS. W, E:** Put bait around new transplants, plants that send up new shoots early in the year, or winter bloomers like hellebores. Remember that bait is toxic to pets; don't let them out unattended in areas where bait is scattered.

☐ **BUY FLOWERING PRIMROSES. W, E:** Nurseries, florists, even supermarkets abound with primroses this month. Pop ones with bright red or white flowers into decorative pots or baskets for Valentine's Day giving. All colors—including yellows, blues, and purples—make cheerful containers indoors. Or plant primroses in sweeps to perk up winter-brown beds (east of the mountains, put them in pots in a protected spot).

☐ **CARE FOR HYDRANGEAS. W:** Prune plants lightly to shape them. Feed plants with a complete granular plant food. In February's cool, moist weather, hydrangeas can take a strong food—15-15-15 (scatter it according to manufacturer's specifications).

☐ **EXAMINE STORED BULBS AND PRODUCE. W, E:** Check fruits, vegetables, and bulbs in storage for signs of rot. Remove spoiled ones and throw them out; one bad apple can spoil the barrel.

☐ **FERTILIZE HOUSE PLANTS. W, E:** House plants that are showing new growth, blooms, or fruits should be fed now. Give them a half-strength solution of fertilizer monthly until April, when days grow longer, the sun shines brighter, and plants start to grow faster.

☐ **FORCE FLOWERING TREES AND SHRUBS. W, E:** Flowering apricot and plum, forsythia, and ornamental quince are among the plants that can be cut for switches and taken indoors for early flowering. Place these branches in a vase in warm water; display them in a bright place. Pussy willows (and almost any willow) can also be forced. Most of them will root and can be planted out in the garden.

☐ **PLANT BARE-ROOT. W:** Many trees, shrubs, vines, and cane berries, as well as asparagus and strawberries, are available now bare-root. Plant them as soon as you get them home; if you can't, pack their roots in moist compost, wood shavings, or soil until you're ready to plant. Water thoroughly.

☐ **PRESPROUT PEAS. W:** Soak peas overnight in warm water, then put them between several layers of wet paper towel on a cookie sheet. Set them aside in a warm place. Once they have sprouted, plant them outdoors where you want them.

☐ **PRUNE ROSES. W, E:** West of the mountains, cut hybrid teas back by about a third. On the east side of the Cascades, you can cut them back further. Cut out injured or dead canes. Cut out parallel or crossing branches. Prune to shape plants.—*S. R. L.*

IN HIGH ELEVATIONS and intermountain areas of California, and east of the Sierra, see items marked with an **H.**

IN LOW ELEVATIONS of Northern California, see items marked with an **L.**

☐ **CHOOSE FLOWERING PLANTS. L:** Nurseries should have a good selection of early spring–blooming shrubs and vines, such as azalea, camellia, Carolina jessamine, and daphne.

☐ **CONTROL SLUGS AND SNAILS. L:** As nighttime temperatures rise above 40°, slugs and snails are more active and can quickly consume favorites such as daffodil, pansy, and primrose. One of the best ways to control them is to search for them (flashlight in hand) at night; handpick and destroy. Or use beer traps. Commercial baits can be toxic to pets; use them only where pets can't get to them.

☐ **CUT BACK FUCHSIAS. L:** To produce lush new growth, cut woody stems back to main branches, then remove interior twiggy growth. Prune fuchsias growing in containers back to the pot rims.

☐ **FERTILIZE PLANTS. L:** Fall-planted annuals and perennials benefit from feeding now. Also feed established trees and shrubs—if they lack vigor or their leaves look pale—as new growth begins. Wait to feed azaleas, camellias, and rhododendrons until after bloom; use an acid fertilizer. Later this month, feed lawns.

☐ **PLANT FOR SPRING BLOOM. L:** Choices include calendula, candytuft, cineraria, dianthus, English daisy, English and fairy primroses, forget-me-not, Iceland poppy, pansy, *Primula obconica*, snapdragon, stock, sweet William, and viola.

☐ **PLANT VEGETABLES. L:** Set out artichokes and asparagus, and seedlings of broccoli, cabbage, cauliflower, celery (only in *Sunset Western Garden Book* zones 15, 16, and 17), green onions, kohlrabi, and lettuce. From seed, start beets, carrots, chard, lettuce, peas, spinach; they grow easily and seeds are less expensive than transplants. Sow eggplant, pepper, and tomato indoors. **H:** To get a jump on the season, at the end of the month start seeds of broccoli, cabbage, and cauliflower indoors or in a greenhouse. When seedlings are ready to plant (in six to eight weeks), set out and drape with floating row covers.

☐ **PRUNE TREES AND SHRUBS. L:** If you haven't pruned deciduous fruit and ornamental trees, grapes, roses, and wisteria, do so by midmonth. Wait to prune spring-flowering plants such as rhododendrons until after bloom. **H:** Wait to prune until toward the end of the dormant season, but before growth starts.

☐ **REPOT CYMBIDIUMS. L, H:** If your cymbidium orchids are bulging out of their containers, it's time to repot them. Do this between mid-February and early July. Repotting too late in the season will prevent bloom and may make cymbidiums that live outdoors in milder climates more susceptible to cold.

☐ **WATER. L:** If rains are light or there are long periods between them, deep-water plants when soil is dry (check soil moisture first with a soil probe).

☐ **WEED. L:** Soon after weeds germinate, hand-pull, hoe, or spray with non-toxic SharpShooter weed killer (made from fatty acids) or more toxic glyphosate. Spray on a calm, dry day; do not let spray drift onto desirable plants.—*L. B. S.*

☐ **BUY AZALEAS AND CAMELLIAS. C:** Nurseries carry many blooming azaleas and camellias now; you can select the exact flower color and form you want.

☐ **CUT BACK FUCHSIAS. C:** Prune fuchsias to main branches, then remove all twiggy interior growth.

☐ **FERTILIZE PLANTS. C, L:** Two to three weeks before deciduous fruit trees bloom, feed them with a complete fruit-tree fertilizer. Feed spring-blooming flowers with complete fertilizer now. **L:** Treat mature trees and shrubs when spring growth starts. Fertilize citrus with a complete citrus food. Follow label directions.

☐ **ORDER SEEDS.** Buy seeds of warm-season flowers and vegetables to plant indoors now for the spring and summer garden. Mail-order catalogs offer the greatest choice of plants, and growing plants from seed is cheaper than buying seedlings.

☐ **PLANT ANNUALS. C:** Near the coast, there's still time to squeeze in a planting of cool-season annuals and have time for them to perform before summer heat knocks them out. Try calendulas, Iceland poppies, lobelia, pansies, primroses, stocks, and sweet alyssum.

☐ **PLANT BARE-ROOT.** In many areas, nurseries still have fruit and shade trees, cane berries, grapes, hardy perennials, perennial vegetables such as artichokes and asparagus, roses, shrubs, and strawberries. Plant as soon as you get them home; water well.

☐ **PLANT BULBS. C:** Buy and plant caladium, calla lily, canna, crocosmia, dahlia, gloxinia, rhodohypoxis, tigridia, and tuberous begonias. **H:** Finish planting gladiolus by Valentine's Day.

☐ **PLANT VEGETABLES OUTDOORS. C, H:** Where temperatures stay cool into spring, plant seedlings of broccoli, chives, lettuce, and onions. If soil isn't soggy, sow seeds of cool-season plants, including beets, broccoli, carrots, chard, chives, kohlrabi, onions (bulb or green types), and radishes. **L:** After midmonth, plant warm-season vegetables such as tomatoes.

☐ **PREPARE SOIL. C, L:** Before planting, add compost to vegetable and flower beds, especially in sandy or clay soil. Work in 20 to 30 percent compost by volume; add a complete high-nitrogen fertilizer according to label.

☐ **PRUNE DECIDUOUS PLANTS.** Before spring growth appears, prune dormant plants such as roses, most fruit trees, berries, grapes, and vines.

☐ **PRUNE HYDRANGEAS.** Remove old, brittle hydrangea canes clear to the ground; shorten others halfway, cutting just above a bud. Leave canes with large, flat flower buds at tip.

☐ **WEED.** Stay on top of winter weeds. Remove them by hand or with a hoe while they are small, before they go to seed.—*L. O.*

February Checklist

HERE IS WHAT NEEDS DOING

☐ **CARE FOR ROSES.** In intermediate and high deserts, finish pruning. After mid-February in low and intermediate deserts and South Texas, spread a complete fertilizer around each established rose. Water first, let drain, apply fertilizer, and water again. Don't fertilize if below-freezing nights are expected.

☐ **CLEAN AND REPAIR DRIP SYSTEMS.** Flush out sediment from filters and check screens for algae growth; clean with a toothbrush, if necessary. Turn on the water and check to make sure that all emitters are dripping water; clean or replace clogged ones. If you can't remove a clogged emitter, simply install a new one next to it.

☐ **FERTILIZE BULBS.** For the best spring bloom in the low desert, feed bearded irises in late February with a low-nitrogen fertilizer. Sprinkle it into trenches alongside the plants, then water well. Feed daffodils and tulips with a water-soluble or liquid fertilizer, also low in nitrogen.

☐ **FERTILIZE OVERSEEDED RYE LAWNS.** For the last time this season, feed winter rye lawns. Use 2½ pounds of ammonium sulfate per 1,000 square feet. Broadcast over dry grass (or use a fertilizer spreader); water thoroughly.

☐ **PLANT GROUND COVERS.** In the low and intermediate deserts and in South Texas, plant these ground covers this month: Baja evening primrose (*Oenothera stubbei*), Hall's honeysuckle, prostrate myoporum, periwinkle (*Vinca minor*), star jasmine, and perennial verbena. In the low and intermediate deserts only, you can also plant trailing indigo bush (*Dalea greggii*).

☐ **PLANT PERENNIAL WILDFLOWERS.** In the low and intermediate deserts, shop for sixpack or container plants of African daisy, coreopsis, evening primrose, paperflower (*Psilostrophe cooperi*), and penstemon. Planted this month, they'll bloom in spring. Mulch so that grassy weeds don't take over.

☐ **PREPARE SOIL.** To prepare for spring planting, work generous amounts of compost into alkaline desert soils; use 2 pounds of ammonium phosphate per 100 square feet, and 3 pounds of soil sulfur per 100 square feet. Instead of sulfur, acidic soils of East Texas often need 5 to 10 pounds of dolomitic limestone.

☐ **SET OUT VEGETABLES.** For May harvest, plant winter vegetables such as lettuce, radishes, and spinach. But leave room for March planting of corn, peppers, and tomatoes.—*M. M.*

SPIKY YET SOFT *blue oat grass sets off Pacific Coast iris in front entry garden. Design: Kiillkkaa Group.*

NORMAN A. PLATE

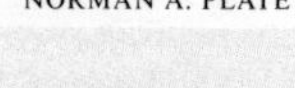

RENEE LYNN

NONINVASIVE *yellow pampas grass (Cortaderia selloana 'Gold Band') bears white plumes that punctuate purple-leafed fountain grass, other grasses, and shrubby gray Artemisia 'Powis Castle'. Design: Michael D. Barclay and Mary Wildavsky.*

GIVING AIRY LOOK *to informal, water-thrifty garden, fluffy plumes of Oriental fountain grass bloom from early summer into fall. Design: Randy Baldwin.*

CLAIRE CURRAN

The graceful grasses

They're easy to grow and useful in your garden . . . as edging, accents, ground covers, focal points

THE CURRENT RAGE in Western gardens, ornamental grasses are here to stay, according to landscape designers and nursery people. Their beauty and versatility have long been recognized in Europe, and more recently on the East Coast. But given their adaptability, these perennials are in their element in the West.

Thanks to the increased diversity and availability of grasses in nurseries, it's easy to capitalize on their attributes. Here we feature ornamental grasses and sedges selected for low to moderate water needs and noninvasiveness. Our chart, which lists the grasses by foliage height, will help you use them to fill almost any design niche or environment in your garden.

You'll find low-growing grasses to serve as edging and

ground covers (bulbous oat grass, sedges, fescue), towering grasses with strong silhouettes for accents and focal points (eulalia grass, yellow pampas grass), and midsize grasses to mass together or mix with flowering perennials in beds and borders (giant blue wild rye, blue oat grass, fountain grass).

Because of their fine linear structure—ranging from upright to arching—grasses catch light and wind as few other perennials can. They glisten in early-morning and late-afternoon sun, and introduce movement and sound to otherwise rigid plantings.

When selecting grasses, evaluate them as you would other perennials. Consider their ornamental qualities (color, variegation, flowers), growth habits (pendulous, mounding, vertical), growth and bloom seasons, light requirements, and water needs.

Since many are deciduous, plan so adjacent plants compensate with flowers or foliage when grasses go dormant.

INVASIVENESS—A CAUTION

Some ornamental grasses, such as *Cortaderia jubata* pampas grass and *Pennisetum setaceum* fountain grass, have become tenacious weeds that threaten native plant habitats and invade urban open space. The grasses listed in our chart are not considered invasive in the West. However, many are new here, and their potential as weeds is not yet fully understood.

Some grasses, such as *Miscanthus sinensis,* do not spread in summer-dry gardens but may self-sow with overhead irrigation. To help keep grasses in bounds, use drip irrigation, and water

Guide to the grasses . . . what they need, how to use them

	GRASS	LIGHT	WATER	FOLIAGE	BLOOMS	LANDSCAPE USES
UNDER 2 FEET	**Bulbous oat grass** *Arrhenatherum elatius bulbosum* 'Variegatum'	Part shade	Moderate	White striped	Summer	Plant with perennials in borders or in groups as accent. Dormant in summer. Short-lived in hot inland areas. Cut back after bloom.
UNDER 2 FEET	**Quaking grass** *Briza media*	Sun, part shade	Moderate	Green	Spring	Use in shrub and perennial borders or as accent. Good cut flower. Evergreen.
UNDER 2 FEET	**Feather reed grass** *Calamagrostis acutiflora* 'Stricta'	Sun	Low to moderate	Green	Late spring to fall	Good accent plant with strong vertical form. Good cut flower, but bloom varies. Deciduous; semievergreen in mild areas.
UNDER 2 FEET	**Fox red curly sedge (Curly-top sedge)** *Carex buchananii*	Sun, part shade	Low to moderate	Rusty brown	Not showy	Use as accent, in groups, or combined with blue- and gray-foliage plants. Upright with curled leaf tips. Short-lived. Evergreen. May self-sow.
UNDER 2 FEET	**Variegated Japanese sedge** *Carex oshimensis aurea-variegata*	Shade, part shade	Moderate	Bright yellow striped	Not showy	Bright yellow accent in borders; good in groups or spilling over rocks or walls. Evergreen. May self-sow.
UNDER 2 FEET	**Orange-colored sedge** *Carex testacea*	Sun, part shade	Low to moderate	Orange-brown	Not showy	Let spill over rocks and walls or use as accent. May be short-lived. Evergreen. May self-sow.
UNDER 2 FEET	**Blue fescue** *Festuca amethystina* and *F. cinerea*	Sun, part shade	Drought tolerant	Green, blue, gray	Spring	Use as ground cover, in groups, or as accent or edging. Divide every 3 years. Selections vary in color. *F. a.* 'Superba' is best bloomer. Evergreen.
2 TO 4 FEET	**Giant blue wild rye** *Elymus condensatus* 'Canyon Prince'	Sun, part shade	Drought tolerant	Blue	Summer to fall	Use in masses, as accent, or in shrub and perennial borders. In heavy soil, use instead of blue oat grass. Evergreen.
2 TO 4 FEET	**Blue oat grass** *Helictotrichon sempervirens*	Sun, part shade	Low	Blue-gray	Late summer to fall	Stiff form makes good accent. When given frequent summer water in hot areas, may rot in heavy soils. Evergreen.
2 TO 4 FEET	**Evergreen maiden grass** *Miscanthus transmorrisonensis*	Sun, part shade	Low to moderate	Green	All year	Use as specimen or at back of border. Good cut flower. May be hard to find. Evergreen.
2 TO 4 FEET	**Deer grass** *Muhlenbergia rigens*	Sun, part shade	Drought tolerant	Gray-green	Summer to fall	Use in mass plantings or as accent; striking with night lighting. Evergreen.
2 TO 4 FEET	**Red switch grass** *Panicum virgatum* 'Haense Herms'	Sun	Low	Blue-green with red tips	Summer to fall	Use as specimen or in groups as accent. Upright, airy. Orange-red fall color. Prefers light soils. Deciduous.
2 TO 4 FEET	**Oriental fountain grass** *Pennisetum orientale*	Sun	Low to moderate	Gray-green	Spring to fall	Use in drifts, as specimen, or with perennials; backlighting plays up pink flowers. Good for erosion control. Dormant in winter.
2 TO 4 FEET	**Purple-leafed fountain grass** *Pennisetum setaceum* 'Rubrum'	Sun	Drought tolerant	Purple	Summer to fall	Use as accent; striking with blue and gray plants. Heat tolerant. Evergreen to deciduous. Cold-hardiness varies greatly. A noninvasive variety.
2 TO 4 FEET	**Giant feather grass** *Stipa gigantea*	Sun	Drought tolerant to low	Gray-green	Summer	Use as specimen or in groups. Six-foot bloom spike makes good cut flower. Evergreen.
OVER 4 FEET	**Yellow pampas grass** *Cortaderia selloana* 'Gold Band' or 'Sun Stripe'	Sun	Drought tolerant	Yellow striped	Late summer to fall	Use as accent with shrubs or in background plantings. A noninvasive type of pampas grass. Evergreen.
OVER 4 FEET	**Eulalia grass** *Miscanthus sinensis*	Sun, part shade	Moderate	Green, some with white or yellow	Late summer to fall	Varieties differ greatly in size and color. Use as specimen, in groups, or at back of border. Good cut flower. Deciduous. May self-sow.

only the plants' root zones.

If your neighborhood borders a native plant community, don't plant grasses that may self-sow, and consider using only those native to your area. For a list of native grasses to plant, check with a local botanical garden or native plant nursery.

PLANTING AND CARE

Fall and spring are the best times to plant grasses. Nurseries most often sell them in 1-gallon containers.

Minimal soil preparation is enough for most grasses, but some, like blue oat grass and fox red curly sedge, require excellent drainage.

Plant the grass so the soil level is the same as it was in the container, and water well. Mulch to conserve water and suppress weeds. Where gophers and rabbits are pests, protect plants with wire baskets and fencing.

Most ornamental grasses thrive in fertile soil, although too much nitrogen may force rapid, weak growth and delay flowering. Use a complete, controlled-release fertilizer according to label directions.

In all but the hottest inland climates, most grasses featured here require water no more than once a week. Some are drought tolerant and thrive with little or no summer water; most of these still tolerate regular summer watering. Even drought-resistant species need frequent watering until they are established.

Carex and *Miscanthus* get by with weekly water, but are larger and more vigorous if watered more frequently.

All grasses are best watered by drip irrigation. Because it directs water to roots, this method conserves water and reduces weeds (including grass seedlings). Overhead water may damage grass flowers, and massive foliage may prevent the spray from reaching roots.

Though grasses are low-maintenance plants, deciduous types look neater with a yearly trim. In addition, dried grasses or plants allowed to build up a thatch of dead foliage can be a fire hazard.

Use a power weed or hedge trimmer or heavy shears to cut grasses back to a couple of inches above the crown. As a general rule, cut winter-dormant grasses when new growth shows at the base, usually in late winter or early spring. You can also cut actively growing grasses to force new foliage.

Every three years or so, divide overgrown clumps or clumps with outward growth and bare centers. For most types, the best time to divide is early spring.

DARROW M. WATT

TALL-GROWING *eulalia grass accents curving pathway edged with wispy variegated Japanese sedge (foreground) and perennials. Design: Lawrence Fleury.*

Grasses have a way of standing up for themselves

RUSS A. WIDSTRAND

PERENNIAL BORDER *features blue oat grass and variegated society garlic flanked by coral bells (behind) and erigeron (foreground). Design: Jana Ruzicka.*

MAIL-ORDER SOURCES

Nurseries commonly carry many of these grasses. Two California sources offer a wide selection by mail:

Greenlee Nursery, 301 E. Franklin Ave., Pomona, CA 91766; catalog with growing information, $5. Plants are shipped September through May.

Ya-Ka-Ama Native Plant Nursery, 6215 Eastside Rd., Forestville, CA 95436; send $1.50 for a price list. ■

By Emely Lincowski, Lynn Ocone

BEST OF THE WEST

The top tomato?

" 'Early Girl' has everything I want in a tomato. It's very flavorful, juicy, thin-skinned, and so versatile in the kitchen. And I get a huge harvest that starts early."—Elaine Schlegel

WESTERNERS give a high five to tomatoes as the all-time favorite vegetable. And there's no squabbling about the favorite variety: From Salem, Oregon, to Flagstaff, Arizona, everyone loves 'Early Girl'. Out of 45 varieties mentioned by *Sunset* readers, 'Early Girl' earned 28 times more votes than most of the other varieties, and 2½ times the votes of its nearest rival, 'Sweet 100'.

What's so great about this tomato? Respondents described its flavor with glowing words. "It's loaded with fresh, sweet flavor," writes Kathy Sansone of Salem, Oregon. "I love its rich tomato taste," writes Barbara Todd of North Shore, California. Lise Wilkinson of Irvine, California, finds 'Early Girl' so tasty that she eats it like an apple.

A tomato that produces early

A big part of the attraction of 'Early Girl' is its earliness (Elaine Schlegel of Carmel Valley, California, pictured at right, enjoys fresh, ripe tomatoes long before her friends who plant other varieties). Time from setting out transplants to first crop is about 52 days—give or take a few days—compared to as long as 80 days for beefsteak types. 'Early Girl' also is an indeterminate variety, so it keeps producing all season long.

Its earliness is a real advantage in cold climates. "We've been unsuccessful with other varieties that are supposed to be suitable for high altitudes," write Barbara and John Fisher, who garden at 7,000 feet in Flagstaff, Arizona; they find that 'Early Girl' is one of the few tomatoes that matures for them.

Tips for a successful crop

Most nurseries sell seedlings of 'Early Girl', or you can start it from seed.

At the nursery, buy young, stocky seedlings. Plant them after last frost in a spot that gets full sun. In mountain climates, you may have to protect plants from sudden late frosts with a plastic tepee or other device.

Space seedlings 3 to 4 feet apart in soil amended with plenty of organic matter, such as compost or peat moss. Before planting, mix in a low-nitrogen fertilizer or a fertilizer formulated especially for tomatoes. In cooler climates, use a mulch of black plastic to warm the soil.

Deep planting is best for tomatoes. Set them in up to the top two sets of leaves (remove lower leaves first); roots will sprout along the stem. Water regularly for the first few weeks until roots are established, then cut back on frequency and water more deeply.

As plants grow, they'll need support. The easiest way is to build a wire cage. Cut an 80-inch length of 6-inch-mesh concrete-reinforcing wire (available in 5- and 7-foot widths), and bend it into a cylinder. ■

By Lauren Bonar Swezey

NORMAN A. PLATE

The look is "controlled wildness"

How to prune and tie roses for a tiered effect

NOTCHED STAKE *and tie hold cane down so it arches across the ground. New growth will hide the stake.*

K. BRYAN SWEZEY

YOUNG CANE *of 'Madame Alfred Carrière' is tied to older cane.*

CASCADE OF COLOR *was created by securing lower canes of dark pink 'Zéphirine Drouhin', white 'Mrs. Herbert Stevens', and light pink 'Madame Ernst Calvat' to stakes. Arbor at rear holds pinkish white 'Madame Alfred Carrière' and a pink moss rose.*

An artist in the garden, British-born designer Michael Bates of Santa Rosa, California, trains his 200-plus roses the English way—pruning, tying, and working with their natural growth habit—to achieve a look of controlled wildness.

Using roses as a framework for the landscape, Bates intermingles colors and creates a tiered effect with layers of old-fashioned and modern varieties. He started the 8-year-old plantings during the dormant season, selecting roses that would give him the appropriate look.

Over pergolas and trellises, he trains climbing and noisette roses to cascade, producing a shower of color each spring. Below the climbers grow large Bourbon, hybrid musk, and hybrid perpetual shrub roses, with arching branches that encroach on the lawn and intertwine with adjacent bushes. Some shorter roses support taller ones to produce graduated bloom.

STAKING AND TYING TO DIRECT GROWTH

"Plants often have a will of their own," says Bates. "There are general rules and guidelines, but you need to be flexible and improvise."

For climbers and large shrub roses, Bates allows new canes to grow upright the first year. In subsequent dormant seasons, he ties some of them to other canes in loose arches for a garland effect.

The second year, the canes produce lateral growth. In the next dormant season, Bates cuts these shoots back to about 4 inches, much as grapevines are pruned. After the fourth year or so, he prunes out woody canes completely.

To give depth to the plantings, Bates also trains canes to grow on different planes, so flowers form in layers. One way to accomplish this is to pull down two upright canes, lift up a third one from below, and then tie them together loosely. You can also tuck some canes into position without tying them, especially thorny ones.

Another way to get a layered effect is to prune roses growing in the foreground more severely to keep them low. Plants behind can grow up and arch over them.

Bates also uses stakes and ties to train canes to grow in a certain direction or to arch just above the ground. Trained horizontally, the canes produce flowers along their entire length instead of just at the tip.

Bates offers words of advice to anyone trying his techniques: "Some roses have vicious spines, so I always wear a T-shirt topped by two heavy shirts. You'll still get stuck once in a while, but I view it as part of the experience." ■

By Lauren Bonar Swezey

Pruning a Hybrid Tea Rose

The magnificent plant family, the *Rosaceae*, gives us many shapes and forms of rose-producing plants, but the one class that has remained most popular with home gardeners over many decades has been the hybrid teas.

That huge group of ever-busy flower producers needs an annual pruning just to keep the flower production abundant and handsome. Here we show the basic steps in this simple process.

The best time to prune roses is shortly before new growth begins. Throughout most of the low-elevation west, that means mid- to late January. In the coastal northwest, rose pruning season begins in late February. In the high-elevation west (snowy winters), the season usually comes in late March.

Remove dead wood. You'll see: it's dark brown, gray, or black, and shriveled-looking. Just getting rid of this is a big help.

Cut to outward facing buds. When you leave a little bud of new growth, it should point away from the center of the plant (see step 3). An exception: if the plant is especially low and sprawling, cut to inside-facing buds. Make each final cut about ¼ inch above the bud and angled so water will drain off the cut.

Hold shears with blade down. There's a reason for holding the shears in the position shown in drawing 3 (blade lowest and hook side up): the blade makes a clean cut and, if the hook is going to bruise any wood, it will be wood that's being cut off.

As a nice extra, paint cuts. To protect the freshly pruned branches from borers and dehydration, daub and coat each cut larger than ¼ inch diameter. Use a drop of the white glue that comes in a plastic bottle with dispenser top.

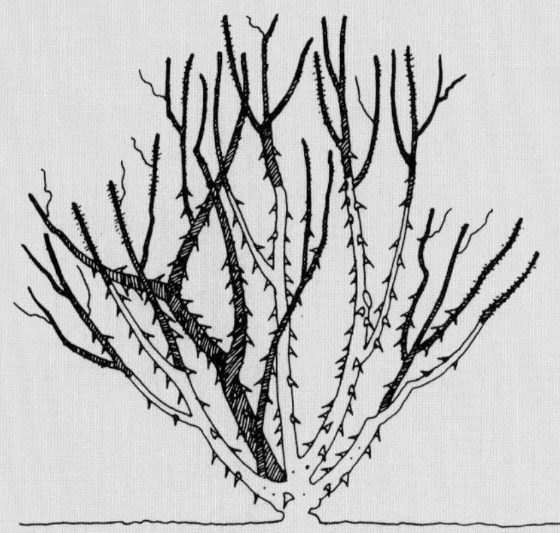

1 EXAMINE THE PLANT *to determine what should be cut out and what should stay. Remove canes that are old and woody, that grew crosswise or are misplaced, and that seem weak.*

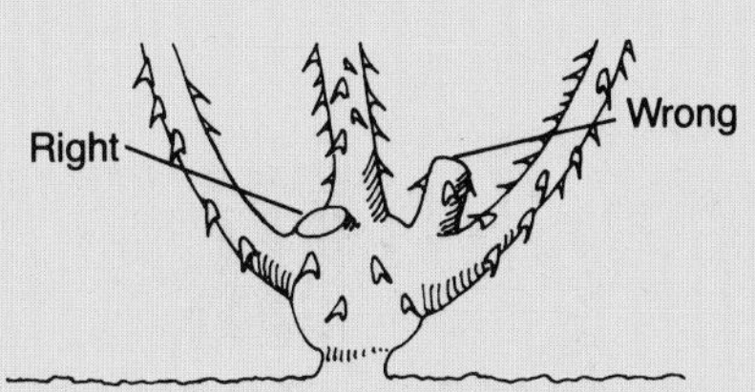

2 WHEN REMOVING A CANE, *make the cut as close to its base as possible. Don't leave stubs.*

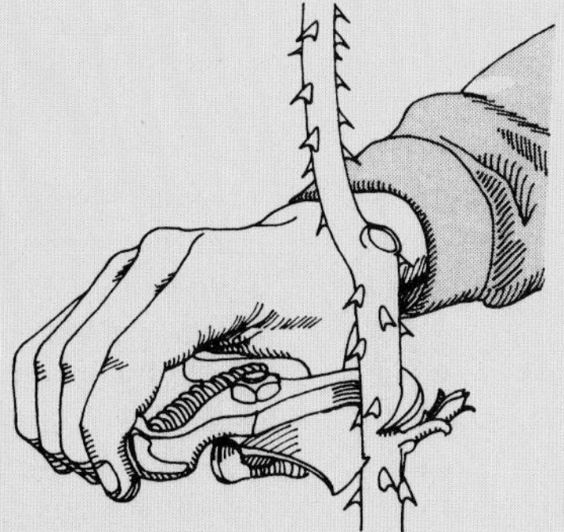

3 FINALLY, CUT BACK EACH YOUNG VIGOROUS CANE *by about one-third. Make all final cuts just above buds that face out from center of plant, like this.*

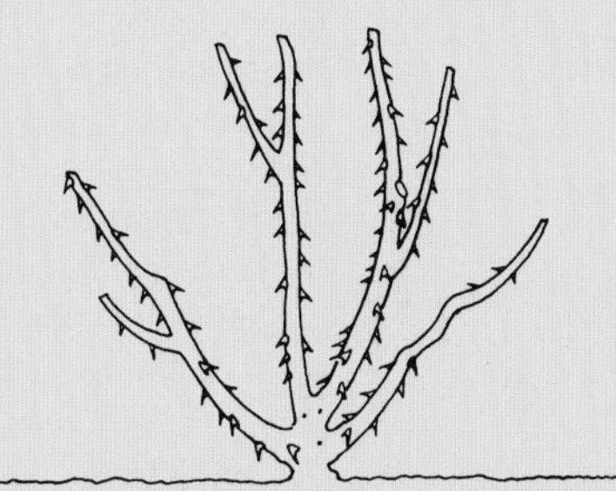

4 HERE IS A FINISHED HYBRID TEA ROSE PLANT, *with only its most vigorous young canes remaining. Typically, from 4 to 6 such canes remain after pruning.*

ILLUSTRATIONS: VERNON KOSKI

RENEE LYNN

HANGING POTS *display blooming Brachycome 'Blue Splendor', light blue trailing lobelia, and multicolored portulaca—all started from seed.*

Hang up some quick color

Start annuals with transplants or seeds? Either. At Sunset, we've done it both ways

FLOWERS AND foliage dangling close to eye level practically shout for attention. Just one hanging pot of colorful trailing annuals can immediately brighten a drab corner, soften a hard wall, or block an unwelcome view.

Showy flowers make the annuals pictured here great for containers. They're relatively inexpensive, and they're fast and easy to grow. You can grow them from transplants or seeds; we've used both methods in *Sunset*'s garden, and share the pros and cons here. Either way, the plants live just a year or less, but they bloom generously through their short lives.

Annuals that grow fast and bloom furiously need regular watering and fertilizing, especially where they're growing in containers. Hanging baskets require even more water since they're exposed on all sides to sun and air.

GROWING FROM TRANSPLANTS

Most nurseries offer an assortment of transplants that are well suited to hanging baskets. In mild-winter, hot-summer climates, you'll find the last of the cool-season plants in nurseries this month; nemesia, sweet alyssum, and sweet William are among them. If you want quick color before summer heats up, choose cool-season plants with flower buds that are just opening. Overgrown plants in full flower are often potbound or stressed.

As the weather warms and the threat of frost passes, you can plant your spring and summer baskets with warm-season plants like impatiens, nasturtiums, petunias, and portulaca. Choose young, healthy plants not yet in bloom. Plants that establish and develop in hanging baskets give the longest season of flowers.

GROWING FROM SEEDS

If you're starting summer baskets from seeds, now is the time to order and plant them. Good mail-order catalogs offer a greater assortment than nurseries do, including seeds of new, unusual, or uncommon annuals.

There's more work to starting plants from seed, but it's less costly, and the results are more personal and distinctive since you can fine-tune plant selection to match your taste and garden situation.

Plant seeds directly in the baskets, or start them in flats, trays, or peat pots and later transplant the seedlings into the baskets.

Direct seeding works best with large-seeded plants like nasturtiums. Sow seeds of only one kind of plant per container, in containers filled with premoistened potting mix; cover seeds according to package directions. Shade the containers, and keep soil moist until seeds germinate and begin to grow. Once seedlings are growing well, move pots to provide plants with adequate light.

When seedlings are a couple of inches tall, thin them to 4 to 6 inches apart. Wait to hang the pots until plants are well established.

The two-step approach takes more time, soil, and containers, but it works with both large and small seeds. There's another advantage, too: it's generally easier to maneuver and maintain flats or peat pots (especially if you're starting seeds indoors) than the larger hanging baskets. Follow the seed-starting directions given earlier. If you start the seeds indoors, gradually acclimatize the seedlings to the outdoor environment before moving them to full sun.

For more variety, you can make a living bouquet by mixing several types of plants from seedlings in a single basket. For a rounded, mounding look, place tallest plants in the center, ringed by slightly shorter ones, and plant low, trailing plants near the container's edge.

CARE FOR HANGING BASKETS

Densely planted baskets may require daily watering in summer. Frequent watering flushes nutrients from the soil quickly, so frequent fertilizing also is necessary.

Feed hanging baskets every two weeks from spring through summer with a complete liquid fertilizer at half strength. Exact timing and amounts depend on the type of fertilizer used; follow label directions.

Water plants by drip irrigation or by hand. When watering by hand, apply a gentle, dispersed stream. Lightweight, porous clay pots can be lowered into buckets of water up to the rim; leave them in the buckets until the soil is thoroughly wet.

To encourage more flowers, regularly pick spent blooms. ■

By Lynn Ocone

NORMAN A. PLATE

INTENSE, SWEET FRAGRANCE *is the main reason to grow tuberose (left). Glads, dahlias, and lilies make a colorful display in late spring (right).*

Bulbs to plant in winter

In mild climates, plant some of summer's most colorful bloomers in February and March

BULB PLANTING IS most often associated with fall, when nurseries stock dozens of varieties of daffodils and tulips. But there's another important season to plant bulbs.

In the West's mild-winter climates, bulbs, corms, and tubers of some of the showiest and most colorful warm-season flowers can be planted now through March. (In cold or wet climates, wait a month or two before planting bulbs outdoors.)

Begonias and dahlias are well known for their brilliant colors and long bloom season. Callas, gladiolus, lilies, and tigridia produce a showy display in pots or garden beds in late spring or summer. Along with Asiatic lilies, acidanthera and tuberose add intense fragrance to the garden, or to the house when brought in as cut flowers. Crocosmia, an old-fashioned favorite, spreads freely. And liatris's flower plumes offer something a little unusual for a perennial or flower border.

To get a jump on the season, start begonias and tuberose indoors and plant after last frost.

FLOWERS THAT CASCADE OR GROW 6 FEET TALL

Many of these 10 plants come in a range of colors and sizes. Climate zones listed are from the *Sunset Western Garden Book*. Unless noted, plants grow in all zones.

In cold or wet areas, lift, dry, and store begonia, calla, dahlia, gladiolus, tigridia, and tuberose before winter.

Acidanthera (*Gladiolus callianthus*). Fragrant white flowers marked with brown or maroon appear in spring or summer on 2- to 3-foot-tall stems. Full sun; moist soil.

Tuberous begonia. Upright plants 1 to 1½ feet tall have flowers up to 5 inches wide; hanging plants have 3-inch flowers. Both come in dozens of colors and bloom summer to fall. Filtered shade or an eastern exposure; moist soil.

Calla (*Zantedeschia*). Showy part is a flower bract that looks like an upturned bell. Dwarf pinks, yellows, and oranges grow to 1½ feet tall; common white calla grows to 3 feet. Full sun (partial shade inland). Moist soil; common calla grows in many soils. Blooms spring or summer. Zones 5, 6, 8, 9, 14–24.

Crocosmia (montbretia). Small orange, red, or yellow flowers on 2½- to 4-foot branched stems. Full sun (part shade inland); drought tolerant. Blooms summer. Best in zones 5–24 (in colder zones, plant in sheltered area and mulch).

Dahlia. Dozens of colors and forms. Plants range in height from 15 inches to over 6 feet with flowers up to a foot wide. Full sun (light shade inland); moist soil. Blooms summer to fall.

Gladiolus. Garden glads send up flower stalks 4 to 6 feet tall, miniature glads to 3 feet, baby glads to 1½ feet. All have flaring flowers in many colors. For a succession of bloom, plant every 15 days. Plant year-round in frost-free areas. Full sun; moist soil. Blooms spring or summer.

Liatris. Plumes of purple or white flowers, 2 to 3 feet tall or more, top tufts of narrow, grassy leaves. Grow in full sun; any soil. Tolerates drought. Blooms summer. Zones 1–10, 14–24.

Lily (*Lilium*). Many shapes and colors. Heights range from 1 to 6 feet or more. Asiatic are some of the most popular, with flowers to 7 inches wide. Grow in full or filtered sun, moist soil; shade roots. Blooms mainly in summer.

Tigridia. Vividly colored triangular flowers, 3 to 6 inches wide on 1½- to 2½-foot stalks, bloom in July and August. Provide full sun (afternoon shade inland) and moist soil.

Tuberose (*Polianthes tuberosa*). Fragrant, white flared flowers on 3-foot stems; grassy foliage. Needs heat to bloom. Sun or part shade; moist soil. Can be permanent garden plant in Zone 24; elsewhere dig in winter or plant in containers and protect. Blooms summer to fall.■

By Lauren Bonar Swezey

MARCH

Garden guide 45
March checklists 52
Southwest beans 56
Tapestry of herbs 59
Spreading compost movement......60
Start seeds from scratch? 62
Sharing the harvest.....................64
The real geraniums.....................66
When leaves turn yellow 67
Wildflowers in Golden Gate Park..68
The right hoe for the job.............69
Garden of the future...................70
Inviting beneficial insects 71

Sunset's GARDEN GUIDE

NORMAN A. PLATE

Spring in Northern California

HERALDING THE BEGINNING OF SPRING, MAGNIFICENT BLOOMING SAUCER *magnolia fills this Menlo Park, California, garden with lovely pink petals. This seasonal display is a good indication that mild weather is here to stay (in colder climates, blooming—and mild weather—comes later), and it's a good time to take action on those spring planting projects you were daydreaming about during those drenching winter rains. If you live where frost or snow still threatens, you can start flower and vegetable seedlings indoors.*

Petunias with a sweet fragrance

Some old-fashioned petunias are fragrant, but, in breeding new varieties, hybridizers have often sacrificed fragrance for large blooms and dramatic colors. Two sweet-scented kinds you can still grow from seed are climbing petunias (shown at right) and The Pearl.

Climbing petunias grow 4 feet tall when trained up a trellis or netting. If left to sprawl, they mound to about 18 inches. The blooms range in color from lavender to white and have a light, sweet fragrance. Since these aren't hybrids, you can save the seed for planting out next year and you'll get the same flowers.

Pearls are recent hybrids of old-fashioned multifloras that have maintained their sweet fragrance. Flowers come in white, light pink, deep rose, salmon, royal blue, and lavender; plants grow 12 to 14 inches tall.

Order seeds of climbing petunia from *Seeds Blüm*, Idaho City Stage, Boise, ID 83706 (catalog $3). Order The Pearl from *Shepherd's Garden Seeds*, 6116 Highway 9, Felton, CA 95018; (408) 335-6910 (catalog $1).

NORMAN A. PLATE

SOFTLY FRAGRANT *old-fashioned climbing petunia plants bloom in a mixture of pastel pink, lavender, and white.*

Conditions that lead to root rot

Root rot, caused by soil fungus, is a common problem. The fungus is present in most soils, and when conditions are right (if the soil is too damp, for instance) it can attack plant tissue. Earliest symptoms are yellowing leaves and branch dieback.

Here are some of the conditions, reported to the University of California Cooperative Extension Service, that lead to root rot. We offer some practical solutions to help prevent root rot from occurring around trees.

Problem: An old irrigation system was replaced with a new system regulated by an automatic controller. Sprinkler heads are positioned close to a tree trunk. The soil stays wet, or water puddles, around the crown (the base of the trunk).

Solution: Make sure your controller isn't scheduled to water too often. Check soil moisture with a probe or a trowel. The soil shouldn't stay soaking wet; allow it to dry out somewhat between waterings. If puddles form, cut back on watering, improve drainage by aerating the soil, or slope soil away from the trunk. Do not allow sprinklers to hit tree trunks. Changing to a ½- or ¾-inch spray pattern can help.

Problem: Either lawn or plants were installed around a tree, so the trunk gets wet during irrigations.

Solution: Remove plants placed near the trunk, and keep new plants and lawns several feet away from it. If possible, do not plant within the drip line of native oaks. When planting grass around a new tree, leave a ring of open soil around the trunk about 3 feet in diameter and expand it as the tree grows. The open soil can be covered with mulch.

Problem: The grade was raised and the crown was buried. Raised flower beds were built under the tree. This keeps the trunk too moist, which makes it vulnerable to entrance by soil fungus. Raising the grade also can suffocate roots.

Solution: If you've raised the grade or plan to raise it, call in an arborist to advise you on techniques to keep the soil away from the trunk (such as building a retaining wall circling the trunk and at least several feet away).

Why aren't my strawberries sweet?

This is one of the commonest questions you hear from gardeners who grow strawberries. What's the answer? Most likely it's a cultural problem.

To develop their sweetest fruit, strawberry plants need at least 6 hours of direct sun at midday. If grown in partial shade, or if they get only morning or late-afternoon sun, strawberries will be on the tart side. Also, keep beds free of weeds, so the weeds don't shade and compete with the strawberry plants. And give plants plenty of room to grow—about a square foot of space per plant.

Applying too much fertilizer or water can reduce sweetness, too. Excess nitrogen causes overly lush growth instead of good berry production. Feed once when growth begins and again after the first crop. Overwatering dilutes flavor. Keep the soil moist but not wet.

A watermelon that captures the moon and stars

For a taste of history, this season try growing Moon and Stars, an heirloom watermelon that's thought to have originated in the Volga region of Russia and was later preserved by the Amish.

Moon and Stars isn't actually a melon variety; at least 20 slightly different kinds of melon are called the same thing. However, they do have similar characteristics, with a few variations.

The melons all have dark green rinds covered with yellow spots that are said to represent the moon and stars. The leaves also are splashed with yellow.

The large, 25-pound melons have pinkish red or yellow flesh. Some are oblong with black seeds; others are round with white seeds. All are sweet and succulent, and grow well even in marginal (cool) watermelon climates.

Plant seeds as soon as the

soil warms (in cooler climates, start seeds indoors four to six weeks earlier); plant through black plastic, and cover with fabric row covers in cool climates. Keep the soil moist. Each plant should produce two melons.

Seeds are available by mail from two sources. *Seeds Blüm* (Idaho City Stage, Boise, ID 83706; catalog $3); sells round 'Moon and Stars #2' and 'Yellow-fleshed Moon and Stars'. *Shepherd's Garden Seeds* (see address in petunia item on page 46) sells a round one.

DARROW M. WATT

BRIGHT SPOTS *that fleck the rind give Moon and Stars its name; leaves are also speckled. Inside, this 25-pound watermelon has sweet, red flesh.*

Sunset's
GARDEN GUIDE

Plant these shrubs for fragrance

Mild climate gardeners are familiar with gardenias and lavender, both of which add wonderful fragrance to the garden. And, of course, everyone loves the heady fragrance of roses. But if you're looking for something a little different, here are five more suggestions to add to your spring planting list.

Butterfly bush (*Buddleia davidii*) is a large deciduous or semievergreen shrub that grows to 10 feet tall (but a few kinds are lower growing). The fragrant, lilaclike purple, pink, or white flowers appear throughout summer and are attractive to butterflies. Flowers are good for cutting.

Jasmine (*Jasminum*) includes many kinds of vines and shrubs, some very fragrant. Spanish jasmine is a semievergreen vine with white flowers that appear all summer. Italian jasmine is shrubby with yellow flowers in mid- to late summer. Shiny-leafed *J. polyanthum* is an evergreen vine with white-and-rose flowers in late spring.

Mexican orange (*Choisya ternata*) is a 6- to 8-foot evergreen shrub with glossy yellow-green leaves. It can be kept as a 3-foot-tall hedge. White flowers appear in spring and intermittently through summer (bees like them). Plant in full sun in cool-summer areas, part (not dense) shade elsewhere. Prune regularly to encourage new growth. It prefers well-drained acid soil.

Sweet olive (*Osmanthus fragrans*) is a versatile evergreen shrub with glossy green leaves. It grows to 10 feet or more and can be trained as a small tree, hedge, screen, or espalier, or grown in a container. The flowers, which appear in spring and early summer (occasionally at other times), are powerfully fragrant but inconspicuous. Plant in part shade inland, in shade or sun in coastal areas.

Winter daphne (*D. odora*) is a 4-foot-tall evergreen shrub with variegated leaves. Extremely fragrant pink and white flowers appear in late winter. Plant in very fast draining sandy soil or containers. Plants should get only partial sun. Water sparingly in summer. Shape by cutting at bloom time.

This is the year of the uncommon citrus

California Rare Fruit Growers (CRFG) is a non-profit club dedicated to research, education, and preservation of subtropical and tropical fruits.

Each year, the group centers its activities on a fruit-of-the-year. This year is dedicated to new and unusual citrus (such as blood oranges, 'Oroblanco' grapefruit-pummelo hybrid, and kumquats) not readily available in markets. Other annual activities include seed, scion, and plant exchanges; garden tours; plant sales; and classes on propagation, pruning, and grafting. Monthly chapter meetings and activities are open to the public. To join, write to CRFG at the Fullerton Arboretum, California State University Fullerton, CA 92634 (annual dues, which include six issues of *Fruit Gardener* magazine, are $16). The group has 15 chapters throughout the state—six of them in Northern California.

CLAIRE CURRAN

GREEN GROWTH *at base of maiden grass indicates time to cut back old growth.*

Cutting back ornamental grasses

Dried grasses that gave beautiful fall color can become a fire hazard in summer. And if they're not cut back, new green growth mingling with bleached old growth gives gardens an unkempt look.

In late winter or spring when new growth begins at the base of these grasses, cut back old growth just above the new growth as shown at left—a couple of inches above the plant crown. Use a mechanical weed trimmer with a blade (wear protective ear and eye gear); string trimmers do not work with most grasses. If you have just a few clumps of grass to cut, use sharp pruning shears. Some grasses have sharp edges that can cut hands; wear gloves.

LYNN OCONE

'GEM' CALLAS *bear rosy lavender flowers spring to summer. Eight rhizomes were planted in this 12-inch-diameter container.*

Growing callas in containers

Callas *(Zantedeschia)* are especially handsome when massed in containers; they bloom for six to eight weeks from spring to early summer in the mild-winter nondesert climates. Flower colors range from yellow to rosy lavender (like the ones in the photo at right) and from cream to orange. Look for rhizomes in nurseries this month, and plant now.

Space rhizomes 2 to 4 inches apart in premoistened, fast-draining soil and cover with an inch of soil. Water sparingly until leaves appear. When the plants are established, water regularly to keep the soil moist, not wet.

Reduce watering after plants bloom; once leaves start to die back, withhold water entirely.

Begin watering again next January, or when plants start to show new growth. As new leaf shoots develop, feed with a balanced fertilizer according to package directions.

Rhizomes of callas cost $2 to $5 each, depending on their size and the variety you choose. Small, $1\frac{3}{4}$-inch rhizomes are sufficient for pot culture.

NORMAN A. PLATT

GRUBS *of green fruit beetles grow 2 inches long; they thrive in warm compost piles.*

From grub to green fruit beetle

When you turn your compost pile this month, you might find the creamy white, dark-headed grub of the green fruit beetle (pictured below left) nestled in the decomposing debris. The grubs, which feed on decaying matter, are harmless.

But they develop into fruit-eating adults. Grubs pupate in late spring and early summer, and, by July, they emerge from the soil as iridescent green beetles about $1\frac{1}{4}$ inches long and $\frac{5}{8}$ inch wide. The beetles, sometimes called figeaters, feed on ripe fruits such as figs, grapes, peaches, plums, and tomatoes. They penetrate the fruit with a small horn located just above their mouths; damaged fruit becomes inedible.

To help manage the beetles, screen your compost now and destroy the grubs. Keep ripe fruit picked and the ground clear of dropped fruit. If trees are small, protect the fruit with fine netting.

You can trap adults by suspending a 1-gallon plastic container from a branch. For bait, put an inch of a 1-to-1 mixture of water and grape or peach juice into the container. Insert hardware cloth, or a plastic funnel with at least a $\frac{3}{4}$-inch opening in the tip, in the container opening.

Beetles attracted by the bait will enter the container and be unable to escape.

Mahonias for hedges, ground covers, accents

Mahonia is a Western native evergreen shrub that easily adapts to a range of garden situations. There are many kinds. The leaves, which range in color from glossy green to blue-gray, are divided into leaflets that often have spiny edges. Lemon yellow, spring-blooming flowers develop in summer into berries that attract birds.

The plants are easy to grow and are disease resistant; most resist oak root fungus. All are drought tolerant once established.

A small looper caterpillar is the one pest known to disfigure leaves; when caterpillars first appear, apply *Bacillus thuringiensis.*

Here are five excellent mahonias to consider for your garden:

M. aquifolium (Oregon grape). Erect shrub grows to 6 feet or more and spreads to about 4 feet. Flowers in 3-inch sprays form edible berries. Variety 'Compacta' averages about 2 feet tall and spreads freely. Grows well in sun or shade.

***M.* 'Golden Abundance'**. A heavy-blooming, 5- to 8-foot shrub that spreads to 6 feet. Bears glossy green leaves and blue fruits. Takes full sun on coast, partial shade inland. Good screen or hedge.

M. nevinii (Nevin mahonia). Usually in the 3- to 10-foot range, but may reach 15 feet. Leaves are gray. Flowers bloom in 1- to 2-inch clusters followed by decorative red berries. Takes sun to light shade. Good screen, hedge, or barrier.

M. repens (creeping mahonia). Low-growing ground cover to 3 feet tall. Spreads to 3 feet by underground stems. Dull blue-green leaves turn bronze in winter. Tolerates coastal sun, needs shade inland. Useful under oaks or on banks for erosion control.

***M.* 'Skylark'.** Roundish shrub to 5 feet or more with shiny dark green leaves, brilliant red when new and purple tinted in winter. Good screen, hedge, or accent.

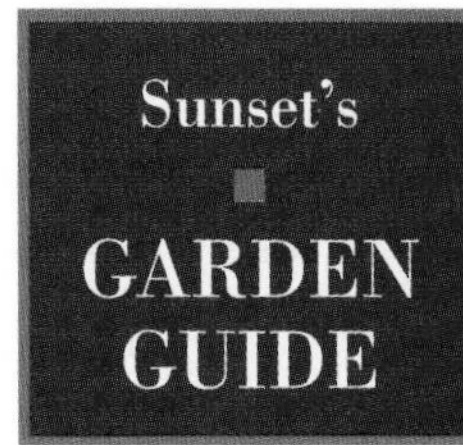

Welcome spring with winter hazel?

An early sign of spring in the Northwest, winter hazel (*Corylopsis*) is much appreciated but not as well known as it should be. Its haze of soft yellow, fragrant flowers comes on about the same time as daffodils, covering this shrub from bottom to top.

The one pictured at right is a *Corylopsis sinensis,* near its maximum height of 15 feet. This multitrunked beauty is native to western China and grows well west of the Cascades and in northern California's coastal and coastal valley country.

If you like the looks of this plant but want something smaller, try buttercup winter hazel (*C. pauciflora*) or spike winter hazel (*C. spicata*). Both can grow to 10 feet, but they're so slow-growing and so easily pruned that you can keep them to half that height.

The smaller winter hazels are fairly easy to find at nurseries. If you have room for the kind pictured here, order it from Forestfarm, 990 Tetherow Rd., Williams, OR 97544; (503) 846-7269. The catalog costs $3.

JIM McCAUSLAND

DAFFODIL YELLOW *winter hazel flowers perfume the air in this Seattle neighborhood. Blooms come on in March, well ahead of leaves, and hang in thick clusters.*

Succession-plant broccoli . . . all at once

If you start open-pollinated broccoli from seed, it matures over a fairly long season so you're not stuck with a big crop to freeze or eat all at once. But compared with hybrid broccoli (which does mature all at once), the open-pollinated kind doesn't have much size or vigor.

Pondering this inequity, a major breeder decided to simply package together three broccoli hybrids with different harvest seasons. You plant them in the same place at the same time and get all the advantages of hybrid broccoli, but with a harvest season that spans three to four weeks.

This new mix—called Super Blend—comes both in seed packages and as transplants. As an extra interest, the three hybrids in the blend are commercial varieties not normally available to home gardeners.

Plant early this month for harvest in late spring and early summer.

Blue flowers for sunny, dry places

Though plenty of plants are said to be blue, few really are. So when a new blue shows up, it's news. This year's addition to the true blues is *Oxypetalum caeruleum* 'Blue Cheer', whose 1-inch star-shaped flowers in circular clusters start out powder blue and age to lavender. They come atop a tender perennial that grows to about 2 feet with an open, spreading, sometimes slightly vining habit.

Treat this plant as you would a seed-grown pelargonium; start it this month or next and plant it out in May. Give it a fast start, with regular light feedings and good soil, and you'll be able to back off on watering later in summer

You can buy 'Blue Cheer' from W. Atlee Burpee & Co., 300 Park Ave., Warminster, PA 18974. The company's catalog is free.

Give plastic pots another life

To help you recycle, an increasing number of nurseries throughout the West are serving as drop sites for plastic nursery pots and plastic nursery flats. The nurseries reuse what they can and send the rest off to a plastics recycling station. Most sites are open daily, though busiest (as you'd expect) on weekends. Call your nursery for more information.

Gender-biased asparagus

A few years ago, we reported the first all-male asparagus, which was bred to produce more and larger spears because it didn't have to put energy into seed production. 'Jersey Giant' seeds seem regularly to produce about six male plants for every female.

Now a new variety called 'Jersey Knight' has been developed. Only about 1 in 20 'Jersey Knight' plants is female. The plant, new on the market in the spring of 1993, is sold mostly in bare-root form at nurseries. You can also mail-order seed from Park Seed Co., Cokesbury Rd., Greenwood, SC 29647. The catalog is free.

Planted now, it will give you a crop next spring. To give the plant a strong root system, don't cut this year's spears.

Lawn-feeding holidays in the Northwest

If you can never remember when to fertilize your lawn, learn one of the great rules of thumb of Northwest gardening: fertilize on Easter, Memorial Day, the Fourth of July, Labor Day, and Halloween. Each time, apply ½ pound actual nitrogen per 1,000 square feet of turf. If there's a summer water shortage where you live, skip the July feeding, or cut it in half.

The best lawn fertilizers for the Northwest, by the way, come in a nitrogen-phosphorus-potassium (N-P-K) ratio of 3-1-2. The N-P-K listing on the bag, for example, might be 12-4-8. That's the approximate ratio at which western Oregon and Washington's cool-season grasses are believed to use the three primary nutrients.

Ideas from a desert courtyard

"I favor as much color as I can get, but always in keeping with the Sonoran Desert environment," landscape designer Phil Hebets says of the garden pictured at right, which he designed.

Several elements make the small garden perfectly suited to this region.

Suitable plants. Throughout the garden, unthirsty shrubs add splashes of color in spring and summer. Bold red bougainvillea drapes a wall. *Ruellia peninsularis* and red-flowered *Salvia greggii* border the pathway. Adding shade around the garden's perimeter are trees such as desert ironwood *(Olneya tesota)*, in center of photo at right, and Texas ebony *(Pithecellobium flexicaule)*, the bushy tree to the right. Both are native to the Sonoran Desert.

Contrasting shapes. The garden uses lots of stones in contrasting shapes, from irregular-shaped boulders to bold, geometric walls. Round pots are displayed on walls of different heights.

PAM SINGLETON

BOUGAINVILLEA *brightens courtyard of desert house. Plants such as salvia soften hard edges. Design: Phil Hebets, Sonoran Desert Designs.*

Details. Sculpture, such as a glass-inlaid stone by local artist Otto Rigen and a smooth black stone by Juan Hamilton, blend well in to the desert theme. As with a potent spice, just a few such details make a big impact.

Water. A small reflecting pool and waterfall, designed and built by Steve Oliver, is tucked into one corner. It's refreshing to look at, and tumbling water is refreshing to listen to.

MICHAEL MacCASKEY

GREENISH WHITE FLOWERS *cluster on plains yucca's short stalk in spring.*

The short-stalk yucca

If you haven't yet encountered the yucca pictured at left, look for it at a nursery. Plains yucca *(Y. glauca)* looks much like other yuccas—in a nursery container. But unlike the others, which sprint skyward once you plant them, plains yucca rarely grows much taller than 3 feet. Overall, it's a much more manageable plant.

This yucca is native to the vast region from South Dakota to Texas. It's also known as small soapweed, since its crushed roots produce a respectable lather.

In home gardens, it works well as an accent plant and is handsome even in containers. It's the best yucca for small spaces.

Pale green leaves are 1 to 2½ feet long and 1 to 2 inches wide; they're pointed at the tips, but not daggerlike. Greenish white flowers bloom on a short, asparaguslike stalk over an eight-week period beginning in midspring. Individual flowers last 10 days or so.

After bloom is finished, cut the stalk as low as you can reach. Plants are not demanding: provide full sun and well-drained soil and they'll thrive.

Plains yucca is widely available, but you might have to ask your nursery to order it. A 1-gallon plant costs about $5, a 5-gallon one about $16.

What to do about giant palm borer?

The damage these tenacious borers can cause is awesome. As one desert resident out for a stroll looked up into her neighbor's palm, its top half suddenly snapped off and fell to the ground. On a golf course, three palms also broke in half when lightly ruffled by wind.

So, if you're a palm tree owner, you'd be wise to learn about the creature that does the damage in its two forms: adult beetle and larva.

Adult beetles are about 2 inches long and ½ inch in diameter. They are most active in late summer, but you're unlikely to see them even then. What you are likely to notice are the ¾-inch-diameter exit holes they leave in tree trunks after they pupate inside them.

Upon emergence, adult beetles fly to the crowns of nearby palms to lay eggs. The larvae hatch, then burrow inside the trunk, working their way up and down the top third of it. Their extensive tunnels disastrously weaken some palms so that their trunks snap.

Giant palm borers have long coexisted with *Washingtonia filifera* in California. As with many tree pests, these beetles seem to select primarily stressed, weakened trees. Transplanted palms that are planted too deeply or that are severely pruned are most vulnerable.

If you own a palm, check the upper third of the trunk for large holes. If you find any or have questions, notify Terry Mikel, at Maricopa County Cooperative Extension, 4341 E. Broadway Rd., Phoenix, AZ 85040; (602)

MICHAEL THOMPSON

LIGHTWEIGHT *concrete planter is made for bonsai, but it makes a good platform for herbs and flowers as well.*

255-4456. And if you're shopping for a palm, keep in mind that the insect originates in California; plants imported from there are most likely to be harboring the pest. There is no chemical control. If you have a palm that is heavily infested, you might need to have it removed.

And about those lawn weeds

A new preemergent herbicide that's now on the market can help you get broad-leafed lawn weeds under control. The substance, called isoxaben (and sold as Gallery), works by killing weed seeds as they germinate and start to put down roots.

You apply it this month, before most weed seeds germinate, because it has no effect on them after they begin to become mature. (It also has no effect on most growing landscape plants.)

You can buy this in a granular formulation to apply with a spreader, or as a component of dry fertilizers.

Garden color in the Northwest in March

Like the year's first vine-ripened tomato, the first color of spring is much appreciated in western Oregon and Washington. Here are some star March performers (trees, shrubs, perennials, annuals) there.

Trees include cornelian cherry (*Cornus mas*), Sargent's magnolia (*Magnolia sargentiana robusta*), saucer magnolia (*M. soulangiana*), star magnolia (*M. stellata*), autumnalis flowering cherry (*Prunus subhirtella* 'Autumnalis'), 'Shirotae' flowering cherry (*P. serrulata* 'Shirotae', usually sold as *P. s.* 'Mt. Fuji'), Yoshino flowering cherry (*P. yedoensis*), and flowering plum (*P. blireiana*).

Shrubs include camellia (*C. japonica* and *C. sasanqua*), flowering quince (*Chaenomeles*), the winter hazels (*Corylopsis*), *Forsythia intermedia, Osmanthus burkwoodii*, lily of the valley shrub (*Pieris japonica*), and red-flowering currant (*Ribes sanguineum*).

Perennials include wood anemone (*A. nemorosa*), bergenia (*B. cordifolia*), Corsican hellebore (*Helleborus lividus corsicus*), forget-me-not (*Myosotis sylvatica*), and primroses (especially the little ground cover 'Wanda'). Beyond these are the bulbs you can't plant until next spring, flowering vines like *Clematis armandii* that you can plant now, and annuals like pansies that you buy as bedding plants.

Because these are flowering, they'll be available only in containers or balled-and-burlapped. Plant immediately.

Bonsai planters that look cut from nature

Traditional bonsai containers are simple and shallow—designed as well-finished foils for ancient (or ancient-looking) plants. But some newer planters, made of a mix of concrete and a lightweight substance, look as if they were cut from nature with the plants they contain (see photo above). As much platforms as containers, these planters come with soil pockets of different depths, and they look as good with succulents, alpines, and small herbs as with bonsai. Moss or ground covers planted along their rims act as vegetative dams that hold water back while it soaks in.

The containers are sold in different sizes and in earth tones ranging from sandy brown to charcoal black—with or without plants. Prices of unplanted containers range from $10 to $80. If you have trouble finding them at your nursery, get a mail-order catalog. ($2) from Oregon Outcroppings, Box 178, Trail, OR 97541; (503) 878-3318.

Desert hero: Mexican bird of paradise

Mexican bird of paradise (*Caesalpinia mexicana*), an evergreen shrub, grows quickly to 12 feet or more. Leaves are about an inch long and half as wide.

Its showiest month is October, when plants are covered with flowers at a time most other desert plants are pretty worn out. Flowers are in clusters about 6 inches long and 4 inches wide; they're followed by 2½-inch pods, each one full of seeds. They rarely germinate or become weedy.

Mexican bird of paradise grows easily in hot sun and survives frosts. It's a good choice for a tall screen.

A 5-gallon plant costs about $15.

Wanna buy a historic tree, buddy?

Sounds like a scam, but it's not. A division of American Forests (formerly the American Forestry Association) is selling offspring of historically significant trees from all over the United States. You could have in your garden a ponderosa pine whose parent is the Forty-niner tree, a 200-footer that served as a landmark for forty-niners crossing the Sierra Nevada. There are also significant oaks, presidential trees, and many others. To get a free catalog, write or call Famous & Historic Trees, 8555 Plummer Rd., Jacksonville, FL 32219; (800) 677-0727. Trees cost $35 to $50 each, plus $7 for shipping. Proceeds benefit American Forests and the historic sites. ■

By Michael MacCaskey, Jim McCausland, Lynn Ocone, Lauren Bonar Swezey

Northwest

GARDEN GUIDE

WEST OF THE CASCADES,
see items marked with a **W.**

EAST OF THE CASCADES,
see items marked with an **E.**

March Checklist

HERE IS WHAT NEEDS DOING

☐ **BAIT FOR SLUGS, SNAILS. W:** If you don't have pets that might get into it, put bait out around areas where you've just sown seed or planted seedlings. Otherwise go on handpicking raids at night or after a rain.

☐ **DIVIDE PERENNIALS. W:** Dig, divide, and replant summer and fall bloomers such as asters, chrysanthemums, and coral bells, but leave the spring bloomers alone until fall. Even then, divide them only if you want to increase your stock or if growth is so congested that flower production is suffering. To cut clumps apart, use a spade or sharp knife, as shown below.

☐ **FERTILIZE EVERGREENS. W, E:** Feed both broad- and needle-leafed kinds with high-nitrogen fertilizer.

☐ **FERTILIZE LAWNS. W, E:** To support the grass growth that starts this month, give lawns their first feeding of the season. Apply ½ pound actual nitrogen per 1,000 square feet of lawn in a mix whose nitrogen-phosphorus-potassium ratio is 3-1-2.

☐ **FERTILIZE SHRUBS. W, E:** Fertilize established roses with high-nitrogen fertilizer, and feed early-flowering shrubs as soon as they've finished blooming.

☐ **FERTILIZE SMALL FRUITS. W, E:** Feed blackberries, blueberries, and raspberries, or apply a top dressing of manure before new growth starts.

☐ **HOE SPRING WEEDS. W, E:** Eliminate spring weeds while they're still small, and chickweed before it takes over. You can control broad-leafed lawn weeds with an application of pre-emergent herbicide (see "And about those lown weeds. . ." on page 51).

☐ **INSTALL IRRIGATION SYSTEM. W, E:** After you prepare annual and vegetable beds for planting, install drip or ooze irrigation lines to carry you through the summer. It's easier to put them in now, when soil is loose and root-free, than in summer, when roots and hardened soil make the job tougher.

☐ **MAKE COMPOST. W, E:** Use spring weeds and early grass cuttings as the basis for your next compost pile. Be sure to mix in some seasoned compost to get it all started. Turn it regularly, keep it moist, and you'll have compost by summer. Give long-term compost—rose prunings, thistles, and branches—a shrub pile. Eventually they, too, will break down.

☐ **PLANT BARE-ROOT. W, E:** Bare-root season ends this month as nurseries pot up unsold bare-root fruit and ornamental trees, shrubs, cane fruits, and vegetables. Prices go up as soon as bare-root plants go into pots. Also, some plants (plums, apricots) flower late this month, so buy and plant them early, before top growth appears.

☐ **PLANT NEW LAWNS. W, E:** If you live in an area that gets enough water to carry a lawn through the summer, amend the top 6 to 12 inches of soil (deeper is better),and lay sod or rake in a blend of bent, bluegrass, fescue, and rye. West of the Cascades, bluegrass should be a minor part of the mix; on the east side, it can be the major part. Keep moist. You'll be mowing by April.

☐ **PLANT SUMMER BULBS. W:** Late in the month, set out ornamental bulbs and bulblike plants, including calla, dahlia, gladiolus, tigridia. Also plant root crops like potatoes.

☐ **PREPARE PLANTING BEDS. W, E:** Now's the time to use all that compost you prepared last fall. Dig it into vegetable and flower beds that you'll plant next month, then water and let the soil settle before planting. Reserve a little compost to get your new pile started, and use coarse, uncomposted leftovers as mulch on shrub beds.

☐ **PRUNE CLEMATIS. W:** You can prune summer bloomers now, but wait until after flowering to prune spring bloomers such as *C. armandii.*

☐ **REPAIR OLD LAWNS. W, E:** Rake out moss and thatch in dead or damaged parts of your lawn, rough up the soil, and scatter seed that matches the kind of grass you already have (otherwise the overseeded section will have a different color, texture, and growth rate). Cover with a mulch of peat and don't let it dry out. Avoid using herbicide (alone or in fertilizer) on the repaired section until it matures.

☐ **RESTART FUCHSIAS, GERANIUMS. W:** Bring overwintered begonias, fuchsias, and geraniums into a warm, well-lighted room or a greenhouse. Water and fertilize lightly to get them ready for planting out in May.

☐ **RETROFIT SPRINKLER SYSTEMS. W:** If you live in an area where summer watering was controlled last year, now is the time to think about ways to save for this year. Consider retrofitting existing lawn sprinklers with low-flow heads. They apply water more slowly, reducing runoff and allowing water to soak in gradually and deeply. Also, check sprinklers at the end of every watering cycle. If there's runoff, set your timer for shorter cycles.

☐ **SOW COOL-SEASON VEGETABLES. W:** Beet, carrot, lettuce, pea, radish, and spinach can all be sown this month, as can most cabbage family members. A cloche helps warm the soil and gives seedlings an early start. To sow in neat rows, stretch a string between two stakes and plant beneath it, as shown below.

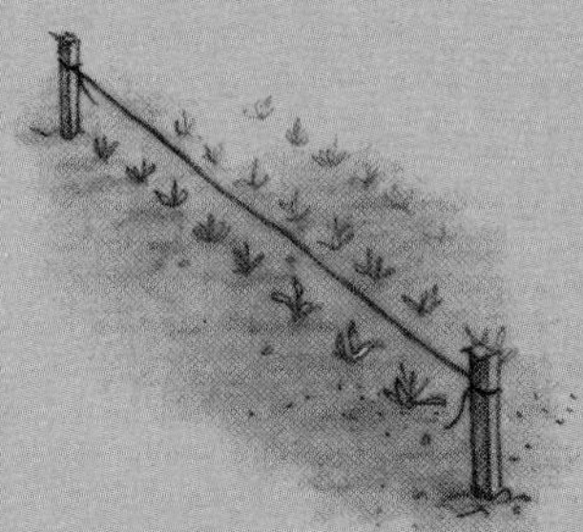

☐ **SOW FROST-TOLERANT PERENNIALS, ANNUALS. W:** You can sow arabis, calendulas, columbine, coral bells, delphiniums, pansies, sweet alyssum, sweet peas, and veronica directly in the ground.—*J. M.* ■

Central

GARDEN GUIDE

IN HIGH ELEVATIONS and intermountain areas of California, and east of the Sierra, see items marked with an **H.**

IN LOW ELEVATIONS of Northern California, see items marked with an **L.**

March Checklist

HERE IS WHAT NEEDS DOING

☐ **AMEND SOIL. H, L:** Before planting in very sandy or heavy clay soils, add organic matter such as compost or ground bark to help improve soil texture and water retention. If you use ground bark or another wood product, make sure it has been nitrogen stabilized (read the label or ask the supplier). If it hasn't been, add a high-nitrogen fertilizer so plant growth will not be retarded. Use 2½ to 5 pounds of 20-10-10 or 16-9-12 per 500 square feet.

☐ **CHECK FOR OAK MOTH LARVAE. L:** Many small worms descending on silky threads and large quantities of dry, light green droppings beneath an oak tree signal a serious infestation. Trees can be completely stripped of foliage. If the tree is small enough to treat yourself, spray with *Bacillus thuringiensis* (which has low toxicity to mammals); repeat every 7 to 10 days for several weeks. Otherwise, call in a tree service.

☐ **COMPOST. H, L:** Save grass clippings, prunings, and other garden refuse for the compost pile. To help branches break down faster, chop them into smaller pieces, add a layer of garden soil every foot or two, and throw in a few handfuls of a complete fertilizer. Turn the pile frequently and keep it damp.

☐ **CONTROL PESTS. L:** Succulent spring growth and tender seedlings attract many kinds of raiders this month. Take action early. Wash off aphids with a jet from a hose, or spray with insecticidal soap. Handpick, bait, or trap earwigs, slugs, and snails. To repel birds, cats, and squirrels, cover newly planted beds with netting, floating row covers, or temporary wire screens.

☐ **DIVIDE PERENNIALS. L:** Summer- and fall-blooming perennials such as agapanthus, chrysanthemums, daylilies, Michaelmas daisies *(Aster),* and yarrow can be divided now, while they are still semidormant. Do this if clumps are crowded or if last year's bloom was sparse. Lift clumps with a spading fork and make a clean cut with a spade. Use the young outer portions of the clumps, discarding the older, coarser center growth. **H:** In colder areas, wait to divide perennials until they are just starting to sprout.

☐ **FERTILIZE. L:** Feed roses when spring growth starts. Give annual flowers, berries, citrus, fuchsias, and vegetables high-nitrogen fertilizer. Apply acid fertilizer to azaleas, camellias, and rhododendrons when bloom stops. Give container plants, especially citrus, an extra boost with a foliar feeding of a liquid fertilizer containing iron and other micronutrients.

☐ **PLANT PERENNIALS. L:** Shop for drought-tolerant perennials such as artemisia, coreopsis, gaillardia, *Gaura lindheimeri*, penstemon, salvia, Santa Barbara daisy, and wallflower. Many perennials are available in sixpacks, 4-inch pots, and 1-gallon cans. To plant from a sixpack, push with your thumbs from the bottom and lift plant out. Be sure to loosen roots by gently pulling apart the bottom part of the rootball (see illustrations at right).

☐ **SHOP FOR NURSERY PLANTS. H, L:** Look for plants with healthy foliage. If plants have green leaves, they should be a deep color, not pale or chlorotic. Avoid plants with brown leaf edges and dead or damaged branches. To avoid purchasing rootbound plants, choose ones that are in scale with the size of the pot and make sure no roots are growing out the bottom. The biggest plant is not always the healthiest one.

☐ **SOW SEEDS IN STRAIGHT ROWS. H, L:** Shown at left are two ways to plant in straight rows. Lay a board on the soil surface; furrow or plant along its edge. Or stretch a string between two stakes; plant beneath it.

☐ **START VEGETABLES. L:** Make successive sowings right in the ground of these spring vegetables: beets, carrots, lettuce, peas, radishes, Swiss chard, turnips. Set out broccoli, cabbage, and cauliflower seedlings. Plant potato tubers. Also, plant young herbs, including chives, parsley, rosemary, and thyme. If last frost has passed, you can also start planting the first warm-season crops when they appear in nurseries. Most need warm (at least 60°) soil. Plant through black plastic and use floating row covers. **H:** Start seeds of warm-weather crops such as eggplant, peppers, and tomatoes indoors now so they will be ready to move outside when danger of frost has passed.

☐ **TEND LAWNS. L:** Cool-season grasses—bent, bluegrass, fescue, rye—begin a spring growth spurt now. Feed with a high-nitrogen fertilizer. If drought isn't a factor, you can plant new lawns now from seed or sod. In low elevations, consider less thirsty turf-type tall fescues. Keep lawns small (600 square feet is large enough for most family activities) and in shapes that are easy to water.—*L. B. S.* ■

March Checklist

HERE IS WHAT NEEDS DOING

☐ **BUILD COMPOST.** Put prunings, leaves, grass clippings, and kitchen waste on compost pile. Chop or shred branches into small pieces, add a layer of garden soil every foot or two, and add some high-nitrogen fertilizer. Turn and mix pile frequently; keep moist.

☐ **DIVIDE PERENNIALS.** If summer- and fall-blooming perennials (agapanthus, asters, bellflowers, callas, daisies, daylilies, rudbeckia, yarrow) are weak and crowded and last year's blooms were sparse, it's time to divide. Dig each clump so the rootball comes up intact. Wash or gently shake off excess soil so you can cut divisions with a sharp knife. Each division should have some leaves and plenty of roots. Plant immediately.

☐ **FEED LAWNS. C, L:** Warm-season lawns require nitrogen fertilizer to grow well. But don't overdo it; 1 pound of actual nitrogen per 1,000 square feet is plenty.

☐ **FERTILIZE PLANTS. C, L:** Most bedding plants, citrus, ground covers, shrubs, trees, tropicals, and vines benefit if fed this month. Use a complete fertilizer according to package directions. If plants were damaged by frost, hold off until new growth shows.

☐ **LANDSCAPE. C, L:** Cool, moist weather now through next month is ideal for planting. Set out hardy trees, shrubs, and ground covers now; wait for soil to warm before planting cold-tender tropicals. To save water, choose unthirsty plants like the mahonia described in the item on page 48. **H:** In Las Vegas and Lancaster, plant apricots, cane berries, grapes, peaches, pecans, plums, and pomegranates.

☐ **MULCH PLANTS.** To conserve moisture and smother weeds, mulch ground covers, perennials, shrubs, and trees with a 3-inch layer of bark chips, compost, or weed-free straw. Keep mulch away from the base of plants. In windy areas, work it into top of soil so it doesn't blow away.

☐ **MANAGE SNAILS.** Control them now to reduce their numbers for the rest of the year. If you find small holes in foliage and slime trails in flower beds or vegetable gardens or on young plants, hunt for snails at night. Hand-pick, trap by allowing them to collect on the underside of a slightly elevated board, or use commercial snail bait.

☐ **PLANT ANNUALS.** Nurseries have an abundance of flowers in sixpacks and 4-inch pots. To plant, remove rootball carefully and gently loosen roots at bottom, as shown at right; transplant immediately into moistened and prepared soil. **C, L:** As weather warms, replace fading winter-spring annuals with summer flowers. Plant ageratum, marigolds, petunias, and scarlet sage. **H:** Late this month, set out marigolds, petunias, and zinnias.

☐ **PLANT BULBS, CORMS, TUBERS. C:** This is the time to plant summer "bulbs" such as caladium, calla, canna, dahlia, gladiolus, gloxinia, nerine, tigridia, and tuberose, and tuberous begonias. See item on page 48 for instructions on planting callas in containers.

☐ **PRUNE. C, L:** After flowers fade, prune to shape ornamental flowering fruit trees, and shrubs such as cherry, crabapple, peach, plum, and quince. On frost-tender plants such as bougainvillea, calliandra, citrus, and Natal plum, remove damaged wood and shape plants as new growth appears. Prune most evergreen shrubs, such as boxwood, before spring growth surges. **H:** Finish dormant pruning. After bloom, prune spring-flowering plants such as forsythia, lilac, and spiraea.

☐ **START FLOWERS FROM SEED. C, L:** Sow seeds of the following annuals in flats, or directly in the garden where you want them to grow: aster, bachelor's button, marigold, nasturtium, and zinnia. To sow seeds in a straight line, lay a board on the soil surface and furrow or plant along its edge, or stretch a string between two stakes and plant beneath it (see drawings below left). Plant seeds shallowly and firm the soil over them with your hands.

☐ **TEND HERBS.** To rejuvenate established perennial herbs such as mint and sage, cut back old or dead growth, then feed with a complete fertilizer and water them. Also set out young plants of chives, mint, parsley, rosemary, sage, and thyme.

☐ **THIN FRUIT. L:** Apricot and peach trees usually produce too much fruit. Remove extras when they're the size of large peas or marbles. On each 12 inches of stem, leave only the two largest fruits.

☐ **THIN TREES. L, H:** To minimize damage from spring winds, thin vulnerable trees like acacia, African sumac, carob, and pepper. Stake trees only in windiest areas.—*L. O.* ■

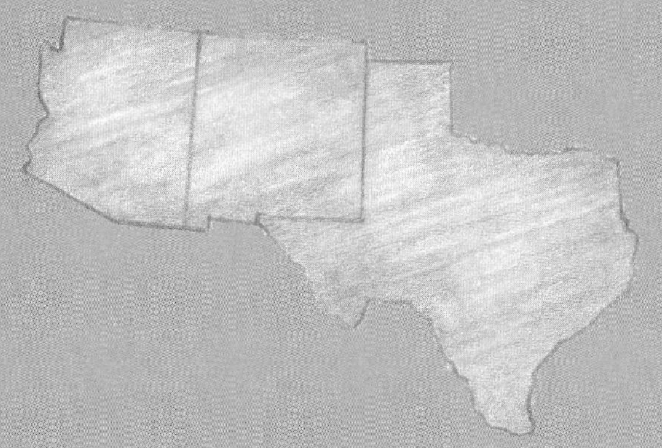

March Checklist

HERE IS WHAT NEEDS DOING

☐ **BUY SUMMER BULBS.** In low and intermediate deserts and mid- to southern Texas, shop for bulbs—caladium, canna, and crinum—this month, but wait another month until soil warms to 65° to 70° before planting. Throughout mid- and low elevations, plant dahlia, gladiolus, and iris.

☐ **CARE FOR HERBS.** In low and intermediate deserts and throughout most of southern Texas, cut back perennial herbs like mint and sage, then fertilize and water deeply to stimulate new growth. Also set out new plants of mint, rosemary, sage, and thyme in loose, well-drained soil or in large containers.

☐ **CLEAN AND REPAIR DRIP SYSTEM.** Throughout the Southwest, this month is your last chance to do these chores before reliable irrigation is essential. Check filters for algae growth and clean them with a brush and bleach if necessary. Check emitters while operating to be sure they're not clogged or watering excessively. Warm vinegar will dissolve alkaline deposits if they are not too thick.

☐ **DISCOURAGE WHITEFLIES.** Many kinds of these annoying insect pests rapidly increase their numbers beginning this month. Avoid using chemical sprays such as diazinon that harm beneficial predators and parasites more than whiteflies. Commercial soap sprays or homemade versions (up to ¼ cup liquid dish soap per gallon of water) will restrain the pests, but don't overdo it: soaps can burn leaves. Be sure to spray leaf undersides thoroughly.

☐ **DIVIDE PERENNIALS.** At high elevations, and in Dallas and north, it's not too late to dig and divide clumping perennials such as bearded irises, chrysanthemums, and daylilies. With rootball aboveground, separate by hand or use a shovel to slice through clump.

☐ **ENLARGE WATERING AREA.** As a plant grows, roots spread more widely and the demand for water increases. If you water by drip, add emitters or replace old ones with new ones with a greater capacity. Also, move emitters out from the crown to the drip line to accommodate spreading roots.

☐ **MULCH PLANTS.** Once soil has warmed (late March in most of the Southwest), spread 3 to 4 inches of bark chips, compost, or other composted organic material over root area of flowers, roses, shrubs, and trees, and in containers. The layer helps prevent weeds and insulates roots from temperature extremes. Wait another month before mulching heat-loving plants.

☐ **PLANT ANNUALS.** Many choices are available in sixpacks, and 4-inch and sometimes 6-inch pots. In low and intermediate deserts and southern Texas, you can plant warm-season flowers such as blackfoot daisy (*Melampodium*), celosia, gomphrena, lisianthus, Madagascar periwinkle, marigold, portulaca, and salvia. In high-elevation deserts and in northern Texas, there is still time to plant cool-season flowers such as pansy, primrose, and snapdragon. If plants are somewhat rootbound, gently loosen their roots before planting. Protect new plants from rodents with netting or screen.

☐ **PLANT CITRUS.** In Arizona's low and intermediate deserts and in Texas's Gulf Coast and Rio Grande Valley, you can plant citrus this month. In Arizona, try Algerian tangerine, Arizona Sweet orange, 'Kinnow' mandarin, or 'Marsh' grapefruit. Gulf Coast gardeners should plant hardy kumquats, 'Improved Meyer' lemon, and Satsuma mandarins. Rio Grande Valley gardeners can plant grapefruits, lemons, mandarins, sweet oranges, and tangelos. In Texas where frost is sometimes severe, plant nongrafted varieties that come back true to type from roots.

☐ **PLANT GROUND COVERS.** In low and intermediate deserts, plant aptenia, calylophus, dwarf rosemary, white lantana, Mexican evening primrose, verbena, or vinca. In high elevations, consider Baja evening primrose (*Oenothera stubbei*), cotoneaster, dwarf rosemary, trailing indigo bush, ivy, Mexican evening primrose, prostrate juniper, sedum, and snow-in-summer (*Cerastium*). In Texas, use Indian mock strawberry, ivy, liriope, or sedum; also consider natives such as horseherb (*Calyptocarpus vialis*) or silver king artemisia (*A. ludoviciana*).

☐ **PLANT PERENNIALS.** In lower elevations, set out aster, autumn sage (*Salvia greggii*), chrysanthemum, coreopsis, feverfew, gerbera, helianthus, hollyhock, penstemon, Shasta daisy, and statice.

☐ **PLANT VINES.** These vines are hardy throughout the Southwest: Boston ivy, Carolina jessamine (mid- and low elevations), Japanese honeysuckle, Lady Banks' rose, mandevilla 'Alice du Pont' (low elevations only), silver lace vine, trumpet creeper (*Campsis radicans*), Virginia creeper, and wisteria. Plant now in low and intermediate deserts and in southern Texas; wait another month to plant elsewhere. Wait until warm weather to plant these tender vines: bougainvillea, pink trumpet vine, and queen's wreath.

☐ **PRUNE FROST-DAMAGED PLANTS.** Once new growth appears on frost-damaged plants, it is safe to prune away damaged wood. Use hand pruners or loppers to cut off dead wood and reestablish the plants' natural shapes. Wait longer before pruning bougainvillea. Unlike most plants, its new growth starts at the base and moves up the stem.

☐ **START VEGETABLES.** In the low desert and southern Texas, sow seeds of asparagus beans, bush beans, cucumbers, lima beans, melons, summer squash, and sweet corn. Also set out plants of peppers and seedlings of tomatoes, but provide protection from frosty nights as necessary; in mid- and north Texas, wait another two to four weeks. In the high-elevation desert, you can still plant cool-season vegetables, such as broccoli, cabbage, and lettuce.

Start sweet potato shoots now to plant next month. Set a potato in a loaf pan and half-cover with fresh water. Shoots will form along the waterline.—*M. M.* ■

Southwest beans

GROW THEM FOR THEIR GOOD LOOKS AND GOOD TASTE

Heirloom beans native to the American Southwest and Mexico are finding their way into home gardens, markets, and restaurants around the West. These are bean varieties that date back hundreds or even thousands of years, with such descriptive names as 'Anasazi', once grown by cliff dwellers of ancient New Mexico; 'Montezuma Red Twiner', said to be discovered in 3,000-year-old Mayan tombs; and 'Aztec Dwarf

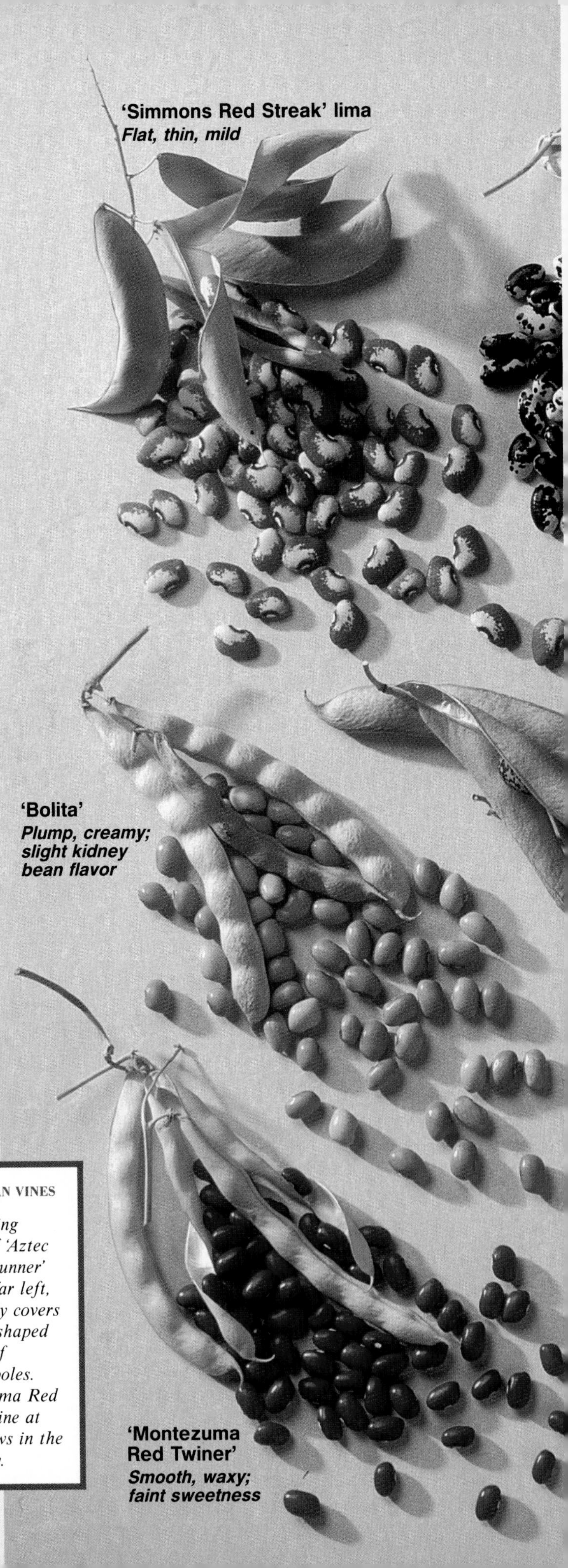

NORMAN A. PLATE

TRADITIONAL SUPPORT FOR BEAN VINES

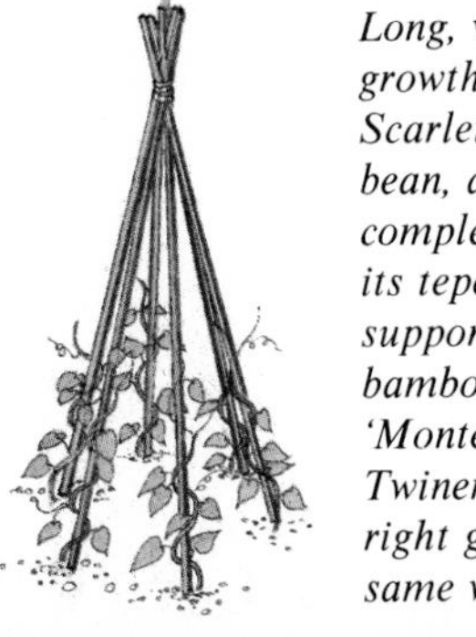

Long, vining growth of 'Aztec Scarlet Runner' bean, at far left, completely covers its tepee-shaped support of bamboo poles. 'Montezuma Red Twiner' vine at right grows in the same way.

'Simmons Red Streak' lima
Flat, thin, mild

'Bolita'
Plump, creamy; slight kidney bean flavor

'Montezuma Red Twiner'
Smooth, waxy; faint sweetness

'New Mexico Appaloosa'
Smooth, creamy, mild
'Anasazi'
Creamy, smooth; cooks quickly
'Hopi Red' lima
Mealy, mild; peppery skin; cooks up plump
'Aztec Dwarf White'
Plump; mashed potato texture
'Mitla Black'
Small, firm, dense, creamy, mild
'Aztec Scarlet Runner'
Meaty, firm; chestnut-like flavor
'Blue Speckled' tepary
Small, firm, dry, mild

NORMAN A. PLATE

BRIGHT *'Aztec Scarlet Runner' and 'Mitla Black' beans are at the shelling stage—seeds are soft but fully expanded.*

White', possibly cultivated by the Aztecs.

Long touted in health food circles for their nutritional value, dried beans like these Southwest natives are also gaining status in the gourmet world—for their high protein, high mineral, low fat, and high fiber content, and their attractiveness and versatility.

Now gardeners and cooks can grow and harvest their own Southwestern heirlooms to use in Southwestern recipes. If you don't have space or time to grow your own beans, you can order most by mail.

CHOOSE A BEAN FOR FLAVOR, TEXTURE, OR SIMPLY ITS GOOD LOOKS

The beans shown on pages 56 and 57 have varied flavors, textures, and appearances. Check the pictures and descriptions to choose varieties that appeal to you.

Size is a consideration. 'Aztec Scarlet Runner' and limas grow much taller than the rest (8 to 15 feet tall). For best production, train them on a trellis or tepee at least 6 feet tall (see page 56).

The other bean vines are short climbers (usually about 3 feet tall). Grow on short trellises, or allow to sprawl on the ground.

'Aztec Dwarf White' (also called potato bean) and tepary beans are drought tolerant. If overwatered, they produce foliage rather than beans. Scarlet runners don't do well in the low desert. The limas are unsuitable for cool, foggy, coastal climates or cold-winter areas; they need a long, fairly warm growing season (about a hundred days).

PLANT IN WARM SOIL

When soil has warmed to above 60°, plant seeds 6 inches apart and an inch deep, except tepary seeds: plant these 4 inches apart and ½ inch deep. Rows should be about 4 feet apart. If growing beans on poles, plant six seeds per pole; thin to three plants when they are a couple of inches high.

Keep soil moist during germination and plant growth (drought-tolerant beans noted previously can dry some between waterings). If plants are moisture-stressed while beans form, pods may not fill properly.

You can harvest scarlet runner beans and 'Mitla Black' as green beans, and any of them as shelling beans (when seeds have swelled but are still soft), or wait until they're dry and hard.

The best way to dry beans is to leave them on the vine until pods are crackling dry and seeds don't dent with a fingernail. If you expect rain or frost before the beans are dry, harvest them and lay them out on a tarp in a covered area, then put them out in the sun to finish drying.

SHELLING THE BEANS

There are several ways to harvest dried beans. Valerie Phipps of Phipps Ranch in Pescadero, California, gave us some tips. She has harvested heirloom beans for years. She says, "By the time you've done all the work, the beans are like a treasure."

One way to harvest beans is to pop their shells open, as with fresh peas. It's work, but Phipps says time flies if you're watching a movie on the tube. To speed things up, she suggests placing the pods in a burlap bag or pillowcase and stomping on them.

At the ranch, the pods are piled on a tarp and beaten with a flail—a long supple pole of willow wood. Or, you can just use a long board.

If harvesting pods from the vine seems like too much work, Phipps offers another option. Pull plants up by their roots, dry the vines thoroughly on a tarp in the sun, then bang them back and forth in a new trash can until the beans fall from their shells.

After you've beaten or stomped on the pods, you're left with a pile of beans covered with chaff. Place all on a tarp. Remove as much large plant material as possible. Then throw the chaff and beans up in the air; let the wind carry the chaff away—or blow it away with a fan.

STORING THE BEANS

Store dried beans in an airtight container. If moisture forms inside the container within the first 24 hours, beans aren't completely dry. Lay them out to dry further.

To kill weevils or eggs that can come in on beans, place beans in a freezer overnight.

MAIL-ORDER BEANS TO GROW OR COOK WITH

The first three catalogs offer seeds for planting; the last three, beans for cooking. Not all beans listed in this article are sold in every catalog.

Native Seeds/SEARCH, 2509 N. Campbell Ave., Box 325, Tucson, AZ 85719; (602) 327-9123 (for information or a catalog only). The catalog is $1.

Plants of the Southwest, Agua Fria, Rte. 6, Box 11A, Santa Fe, NM 87501; (505) 471-2212. The catalog is $4.

Seeds of Change, 1364 Rufina Circle, Suite 5, Santa Fe, NM 87501; (505) 438-8080. The catalog costs $3 (refundable with order).

The Bean Bag, 818 Jefferson St., Oakland, CA 94607; (800) 845-2326. 'Anasazi', 'New Mexico Appaloosa', 'Hopi White' lima, scarlet runner, and brown and white tepary.

Gallina Canyon Ranch, 144 Camino Escondido, Santa Fe, NM 87501; (505) 982-4149. 'New Mexico Appaloosa', scarlet runner.

Phipps Ranch, Box 349, 2700 Pescadero Rd., Pescadero, CA 94060; (415) 879-0787. 'Anasazi', 'New Mexico Appaloosa', 'Bolita', scarlet runner, 'White Aztec' (pueblo), brown and white tepary. ■

By Lauren Bonar Swezey, Linda Lau Anusasananan

JEFF HALSTEAD

TAPESTRY OF GREEN AND GRAY: *basking in sun, assorted thymes surround a blue-flowered Lithodora in front-yard border.*

Tapestry of herbs for a Northwest border

And it thrives during Seattle's dry summers

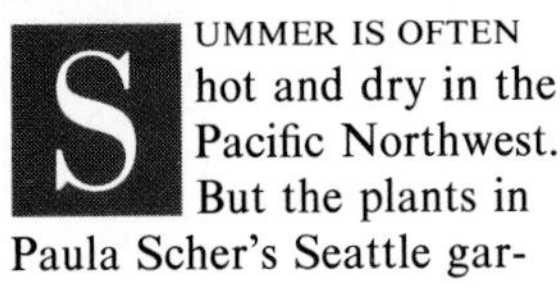

SUMMER IS OFTEN hot and dry in the Pacific Northwest. But the plants in Paula Scher's Seattle garden—on an unshaded south-west-facing slope—won't be drooping. Herbs and other drought lovers fill a colorful border, offering a good lesson in water-wise gardening. (In recent years, the need for saving water in the garden has become a serious concern, even here in the often-rainy Pacific Northwest. Our population continues to grow, but our water supply doesn't.)

IN FULL JULY BLOOM, *common Thymus vulgaris is a mass of pale purple.*

Herbs are her core plantings. She grows many thymes: lemon thyme (*Thymus citriodorus*), creeping thyme (*T. praecox arcticus*), woolly thyme (*T. pseudolanuginosus*), common thyme (*T. vulgaris*), and silver thyme (*T. v.* 'Argenteus'). Add to those lavender (*Lavandula angustifolia*), marjoram and oregano (*Origanum majorana* and *O. vulgare*), dwarf rosemary (*Rosmarinus officinalis* 'Prostratus'), and tarragon (*Artemisia dracunculus*). She also grows several kinds of sages (*Salvia*) with foliage that runs from silvery gray to chartreuse to purple-red.

Drought beaters that aren't herbs are also woven into the tapestry: epimedium (most often grown as a woodland plant), *Lithodora diffusa* (often sold as *Lithospermum*), and heaths (kinds of *Erica carnea*). Here and there clumps of annuals pop up. Snapdragons and zinnias are favorites.

Plants were set out from 4-inch pots and gallon cans three or four years ago.

WATER? ONLY OCCASIONALLY

On rare occasions during driest summers, Scher turns the sprinkler on these beds, as much to wash off accumulated dust as to water plants. She sprinkles for a half-hour early in the morning, once a month at most. If a plant gets leggy, she shears it back with hedge clippers.

In mid-February, she broadcasts a complete dry fertilizer (16-16-16) around the beds for robust bloom. ■

By Steven R. Lorton

K. BRYAN SWEZEY

EXPERT COMPOSTER *Cindy Havstad demonstrates the art of making compost at a free workshop in Livermore, California. It's one of many workshops in the nation based on a model developed in Seattle.*

The West's spreading compost movement

Town by town, people are learning how to keep their clippings to themselves

On a cool Saturday morning in June, Cindy Havstad begins to talk about composting. A woman with a passion for her topic, she addresses her audience, a handful of homeowners and their children from Livermore, California, with surprising energy considering the early hour. After ticking off the benefits and ease of composting, she shows the attentive group how to get started.

Havstad has her listeners in the palm of her hand, and she knows why: they are enticed to her demonstration by a desire to do their part to solve our nation's garbage crisis—ready to compost, rather than dump, their yard waste.

Out of such motivations movements are made and sustained, and the West has an impressive new social movement under way. With landfill sites filling up fast, people are banding together to reduce their solid waste. Curbside recycling for cans, bottles, and newspapers is now common in many areas. Some cities and counties have voluntary programs designed to cut solid waste by specific amounts by specific years. And a few have gone even further, mandating the cutting of solid waste dumping by as much as half by 1995.

Of course, that means dumping far less yard waste. The Environmental Protection Agency estimates that grass clippings, leaves, and prunings account for 19 percent of household trash, and as much as 50 percent in summer and fall. While some communities have started huge municipal composting sites with curbside pickup, such efforts can get expensive. So, using a program launched in Seattle four years ago as a model, several cities are persuading thousands of residents to make their own compost.

THEY'RE MASTER COMPOSTERS: THEY SPREAD THE WORD

Seattle had promoted composting for more than a decade when, in 1989, it took the big leap—setting a goal of composting three-quarters of all yard waste by 1998. How would that be possible? To help find out, the city hired Seattle Tilth Association—a nonprofit organization that specializes in urban organic gardening and home ecology—to experiment with ways to promote backyard composting.

The success of Seattle Tilth's program has led dozens of other communities—including Vancouver, British Columbia; Portland; Burbank, Glendale, Ventura, and the counties of Sacramento and Alameda, California—to pattern programs after it. Alameda County's program, which includes the Livermore demonstration project, so closely mirrors Seattle's that cities nationwide are now going there, too, for information about what works.

There's nothing magic about Seattle Tilth's approach—it just takes hard work, volunteerism, and city funds. The city distributes at no charge home composting brochures, other educational materials, and a compost bin (plus an hour-long training session) to any Seattle resident who asks. It also maintains five demonstration sites: all display commercial and homemade bins and offer self-guided tours to explain composting methods. Perhaps most important, the city has mimicked the USDA Cooperative Extension Service's highly successful Master Gardener program by training hundreds of Master Composters to spread the word.

MICHAEL THOMPSON

DEMONSTRATION CENTER *in southwest Portland teaches home composting.*

In Alameda County, Master Composters receive 50 hours of classroom, field, and hands-on training in composting biology, bin construction, and troubleshooting. They also get tips on teaching methods. In exchange, Master Composters commit at least 50 hours to educating the public about composting—setting up displays at fairs and festivals, teaching in classrooms, staffing compost hotlines, and leading workshops similar to the one at Livermore.

Multiply passion and effort by the hundreds of Master Composters in the West, and it's clear something big is cooking: hundreds of workshops a year, thousands of backyard composting bins (24,000 distributed in Seattle alone, so far), enormous quantities of waste intercepted between the yard and landfill.

In Seattle, consultants have estimated that 2,900 tons of yard waste are being diverted from dump sites each year—59 percent of the goal. "We've persuaded people to change their behavior toward yard and food waste," says Madelon Bolling, public information specialist with Seattle Tilth. "Don't throw it in the garbage; learn how to compost it."

PARTIALLY COMPOSTED *straw and other organic matter are used as a mulch in a vegetable and flower bed.*

START YOUR OWN PROGRAM OR BECOME A MASTER COMPOSTER

Seattle Tilth Association helps communities start composting programs. The group's $5 information packet describes a model program and includes designs for three home composting bins, a resource guide to composting products and equipment, and a tour guide for a home composting demonstration site. For an additional cost, the group offers a *Master Composter Resource Manual,* a home composting brochure, and several slide shows. For more information, write or call Seattle Tilth at 4649 Sunnyside Avenue N., Seattle 98103; (206) 633-0451.

To find out if your area has a program, or to learn how to become a Master Composter, call your local waste department or sanitation service. ■

By Lauren Bonar Swezey

NORMAN A. PLATE

TWO SPINACH SEEDS *go into premoistened potting mix in each 1½-inch-wide cell of plastic foam flat.*

Start seeds from scratch?

We offer four good reasons . . . and some reliable step-by-step instructions

FOR MOST GARDENERS, the bottom line is economics: for the cost of a sixpack of lettuce, for instance, you can buy a packet of 600 seeds.

Then there's selection. Seed catalogs give you a choice of dozens of tomatoes, in various colors and shapes, where a nursery might carry four or five types.

And for those who garden in cold or wet climates, getting a head start on the growing season is key. If you start seeds of squash indoors, you can get a month's jump over direct sowing in the ground.

Add the satisfaction of watching plants sprout and grow, and you've got four good reasons to overcome any hesitation about trying your hand at seed sowing.

Just how tricky is it? With some plants, like sweet peas, it couldn't be simpler: just push the seeds into your garden soil, keep moist, and two weeks later, you'll see the first shoots. Some others take more coddling. For instance, eggplants, peppers, and tomatoes should be started indoors in containers to give them the heat and light they need, but the numerous types available as seed make the extra effort worthwhile.

TAKING THE MYSTERY OUT OF SEED STARTING

Sowing in containers gives you better control of growing conditions and keeps seedlings out of harm's way. But some seeds are best sown directly in the ground (see list on opposite page).

In either case, you should start with fresh, high-quality seeds (look for the date on the packet) and follow these guidelines for successful germination:

Timing. If you're planning to transplant from containers, start peppers eight to ten weeks ahead, eggplants and tomatoes six to eight weeks, cole crops (such as broccoli) and leafy greens about four weeks, melons and squash two to four weeks. Flower seeds are variable, but give them at least four weeks.

Growing medium. For direct sowing, dig plenty of compost or soil conditioner into the soil.

For containers, you can buy seed-starting mixes, but it's easy to make your own. One of the best mixes is ⅓ peat moss, ⅓ vermiculite, and ⅓ perlite. But you can also use equal parts of peat moss and vermiculite, or packaged potting soil.

Moisture and fertilizer. Moisten the soil thoroughly before planting. Afterward, water with a fine spray that won't wash away small seeds. Keep the soil evenly moist but not soggy, so seeds don't rot or dry out.

To retain soil moisture in containers, cover them with wet newspaper, damp burlap, or aluminum foil until the first seeds germinate. Use clear plastic for seeds that need light to germinate; make sure air can get in or fungus may grow.

Start fertilizing container seedlings when they have two sets of true leaves. Every fourth watering, use a liquid fertilizer diluted to half strength, or use a fertilizer sold for starting seeds.

Before direct sowing, mix a complete fertilizer into the soil according to package directions.

Temperature. Most garden seeds germinate when soil temperature is between 75° and 95°. But cool-season vegetables, such as cabbage and

CELLS WITH SLOPING SIDES *direct roots downward (left), helping seedlings establish faster in the ground than ones grown in cylindrical cells, which tend to have circling roots (right).*

TO HELP PEAT POTS *retain moisture, place 1½ inches of soil in the bottom of a flat and set pots in it.*

spinach, tolerate temperatures as low as 45°. Keep in mind that seeds take longer to germinate at cool temperatures. And depending on the type of plant, germination times vary from a few days to two weeks or more.

To speed germination of eggplants, melons, squashes, and tomatoes in containers, use a soil-heating cable or heat mat, or set seed trays on a water heater.

After germination, container-grown seedlings grow best when kept between 60° and 70°, with nighttime temperatures about 10° cooler. Cool-season vegetables develop well even at 50°.

Air. All seeds need air to grow. Except as noted below for seeds that need light to germinate, plant shallowly (two to three times as deep as the seed diameter). Set containers where air circulation is good.

Light. Most vegetable seeds germinate equally well in light or dark; onions and chives prefer dark. Some flower seeds (columbine, gaillardia, impatiens, lobelia, Oriental poppy, petunia, primrose, snapdragon, sweet alyssum) need light to germinate, so don't cover with soil. Others (calendula, delphinium, nasturtium, pansy, other poppies, sweet pea, verbena) prefer dark; cover these with well-firmed soil.

Once seeds germinate, all plants need light to grow. Move containers into light just after sprouts stick their heads through the soil. If you move them too late, seedlings become leggy and weak.

If you're not using a greenhouse, move plants to a sunny south window or use fluorescent lights, set 6 to 8 inches above plants, for 12 to 14 hours a day. If the weather is mild, you can move seedlings outdoors into morning sun. Spindly growth is a good indicator that plants aren't getting enough light.

When seedlings are ready to transplant outside, you need to harden them off so they can withstand full sun. Don't fertilize the week before. Set seedlings outdoors in filtered light for several hours; protect from wind. Over the next week or 10 days, increase exposure until they get full sun.

CHOOSING A CONTAINER

Convenience, cost, and reusability will determine which container is best for your situation. If you can't be around to water daily or don't plan to transplant young seedlings into another container before planting them out, use containers with 2- to 4-inch-wide openings.

Plastic flats with no dividers are an old favorite. They're readily available, and free when you buy seedlings at nurseries. (Foil baking pans are an inexpensive alternative.) Just fill them with planting mix and sow rows of seeds. Make sure they have drainage.

The drawback is that roots get tangled and can be difficult to separate at transplant time, which can shock the seedlings. Gently separate roots when plants have one set of leaves, or wait until they have several sets, snip out unwanted seedlings, cut soil into blocks with a knife, and then wait a week before transplanting them.

Plastic sixpacks, like the ones you buy seedlings in at the nursery, are inexpensive (about 10 cents apiece) and reusable. Many home gardeners find them easy to use. Exposure to sun eventually degrades plastic.

Peat pots or peat strips are inexpensive (6 to 16 cents for each 4-inch pot), but not reusable. They dry out easily and roots may not penetrate them readily; see a helpful technique above left. You can plant them pot and all or tear away the pot.

Plastic foam flats with tapered individual cells are our favorites. They come in six different cell sizes ($5.50 to $9.50). One of the advantages is that roots are directed downward instead of circling around the rootball (shown opposite, bottom). Plants pop out easily with a knife.

Sources. Nurseries carry most of the common types. Seed catalogs usually carry their own designs. All those mentioned here are available from *Peaceful Valley Farm Supply*, Box 2209, Grass Valley, CA 95945; (916) 272-4769. ■

By Lauren Bonar Swezey

Good bets for beginners

Growers we consulted consider the following seeds easy to start.

To start in containers or direct-sow:

Bachelor's button, basil, calendula, chives, cole crops (broccoli, cabbage, cauliflower), cosmos, cucumber, leafy greens, lettuce, marigold, melons, penstemon, pumpkin, sage, salvia, scabiosa, squash, sweet alyssum, yarrow, zinnia.

These do best when direct-sown:

Beans, corn, nasturtium, nigella, pea, radish, sunflower, sweet pea, most wildflowers.

COLLECTION OF SEED-STARTING TRAYS AND POTS *shows the wide array of products available at nurseries and through mail-order gardening catalogs.*

Sharing the harvest

How some Northern California gardeners pool their resources and talents to feed the hungry

By Lauren Bonar Swezey

VOLUNTEERS OF EVERY AGE *help Marge Cerletti (in blue hat)*

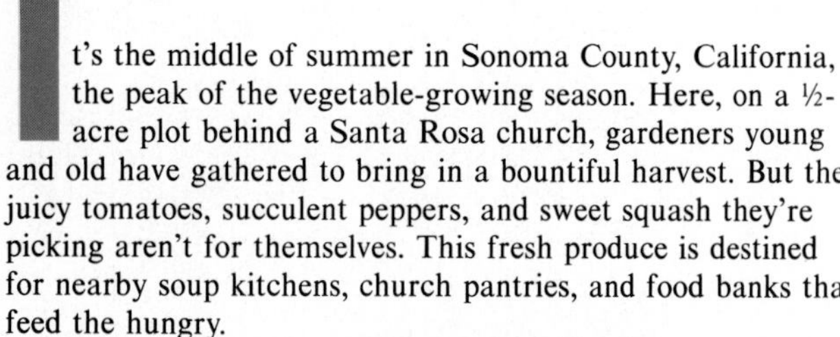

It's the middle of summer in Sonoma County, California, the peak of the vegetable-growing season. Here, on a ½-acre plot behind a Santa Rosa church, gardeners young and old have gathered to bring in a bountiful harvest. But the juicy tomatoes, succulent peppers, and sweet squash they're picking aren't for themselves. This fresh produce is destined for nearby soup kitchens, church pantries, and food banks that feed the hungry.

The volunteers who tend this particular garden are a diverse group of civic-minded people who donate time and resources to feed their less fortunate neighbors. Together, they form Growing Food for the Hungry, which has grown and distributed to the needy more than 20,000 pounds of fresh vegetables since its inception just five years ago.

The birth of a notion

Marge Cerletti, one of GFFTH's founders, recalls the origin of the project. "We started this vegetable garden because we wanted to offer a nutritious, fresh alternative to Twinkies, candy bars, and canned food," she says. Cerletti's concern about the increasing hunger problem in Sonoma County was shared by Muchtar Salzman, formerly of the UC Cooperative Extension in Santa Rosa. Salzman, it turns out, had dreamed of starting a large garden as a solution to the problem. Once the seed of that idea was planted, it didn't take long for Cerletti to locate a patch of earth behind a local church for their garden.

It also wasn't very difficult to find the volunteers to work the land, thanks to the UC Master Gardeners and the Organic Garden and Nutrition Club of Sonoma County. Since then, dozens of other individuals have offered their services, including children from 4-H and Scout troops and teenagers from local high schools. "It's turned out to be a project for all ages—a true community effort," says Janet Sanchez, one of GFFTH's coordinators.

Volunteers needn't be experienced gardeners. Plenty of jobs—such as shoveling compost, monitoring irrigation, and harvesting—don't require gardening skills. "Volunteers have a great opportunity to learn," says Cerletti. "Not only do we give them organic gardening classes, but the volunteers learn a lot working side by side with Master Gardeners and knowledgeable members of our organic gardening club."

Though many volunteers are now involved, much of GFFTH's success is due to the dedication of Cerletti. "Marge, an 81-year-old live wire, is the heart of the program," says Sharon Malm Read of Catholic Charities, one of the groups

K. BRYAN SWEZEY

harvest vegetables in Santa Rosa garden.

BOXES OF PRODUCE *are picked up by organizations such as Catholic Charities and distributed to soup kitchens. Other groups take food to low-income families.*

that benefit from GFFTH's harvest. "Without Marge's devotion to the project, it just wouldn't run as smoothly."

A diverse crop, from spring through fall

After the vegetables begin producing, the real work starts: distribution. "We harvest two to three days a week," says Sanchez. "It takes a tremendous amount of organization and a strong network of dependable contacts to pick up the food on time; otherwise it rots."

Over the years, GFFTH has learned a great deal about which vegetables are most useful to soup kitchens and food banks. In most cases, lettuce is too fragile to handle. Swiss chard is better than spinach because the harvest lasts longer. And many facilities don't use eggplant. Green beans and carrots are appreciated by the kitchens, but the beans are very time-consuming to harvest and the carrots require scrubbing to get the mud off, although the GFFTH volunteers grow them both anyway.

The crops grown in the greatest quantities are broccoli, cabbage, cauliflower, corn, garlic, leeks, onions, sweet and hot peppers, potatoes, summer and winter squash, and tomatoes. Planting dates are staggered so that the harvest doesn't come all at once.

Finding the resources

Groups such as GFFTH are totally dependent on donations from the community. Many people who don't have time to help in the garden pledge a monthly donation that helps pay the water bill and purchase miscellaneous supplies. Local companies have also gotten into the act by donating irrigation equipment and time on rented tractors and tillers. In addition, GFFTH has raised money through raffles, potluck dinners, and plant sales.

Even the seeds and seedlings are donated, thanks to the hard work of Joe Spicer, who is the Northern California representative for America the Beautiful Fund's Operation Green Plant. He locates outdated (but still viable) seeds and leftover seedlings from local suppliers and nurseries, and distributes them to groups such as GFFTH and to low-income families who grow food for themselves.

How to get involved

To learn how to start your own garden modeled after GFFTH, or to volunteer, write or call Marge Cerletti at Growing Food for the Hungry, Box 3626, Santa Rosa, CA 95402; (707) 539-6598.

America the Beautiful Fund will supply both information and seeds to help you start your own charitable garden. Ask the group if there's an existing garden in your community where you can participate. Send a self addressed, stamped envelope to ABF, Operation Green Plant, 219 Shoreham Building, Washington, DC 20005. To those starting their own charitable gardens, ABF will supply 50 packets of vegetable, herb, and flower seeds for $4.95 (to cover postage and handling) or as many as 750 packets or bulk seeds for large gardens (write for shipping costs).

If you have extra fruits or vegetables in your garden, The Salvation Army can direct you to the nearest food bank or soup kitchen that can take your harvest. If you live in the Sacramento Valley, an organization called the Senior Gleaners will harvest your excess fruit and vegetables for you, or you can take produce to 3185 Longview Drive, Sacramento; call (916) 971-1530 before delivering. ■

RUSS A. WIDSTRAND

PURPLE CARPET *of Geranium incanum lines garden path. In mild climates, foliage is evergreen.*

The real geraniums: versatile and hardy

GERANIUMS HAVE AN identity problem. The bright bloomers you probably think of as geraniums are really, botanically, pelargoniums. True geraniums go by the common name of cranesbills. It doesn't help that they're named for one of their least prominent features: small beak-shaped fruit that develops into seed heads.

Overcoming lack of recognition, cranesbills have finally made their way into the mainstream nursery trade. And no wonder: these versatile perennials have a relaxed look well suited to perennial beds and borders. Depending on species, they form low carpets, mounds, or clumps, offering a range of choices for edgings, borders, and ground covers.

The five-petaled flowers, about an inch wide, form soft drifts of color—in shades of pink, blue, violet, or white—that integrate easily with other garden bloomers. Most types reach peak bloom in spring or early summer, and some bloom sporadically into fall. In mild coastal areas, some are evergreen and bloom on and off throughout the year.

Most species of these hardy perennials withstand temperatures to at least 10°. They're relatively care-free but bloom best when spent flowers are cut off.

Although the cultural needs vary from species to species, most cranesbills need sun to light shade (especially in hot inland areas), average soil, and moderate water. A few, including *G. incanum* (pictured at left) and *G. dalmaticum,* tolerate drought. Mulch plants in the desert.

Most nurseries that specialize in perennials carry at least a handful of species, including some of the following strong performers:

G. cantabrigiense 'Biokovo'. Lacy foliage reaches 1 foot tall, 18 inches wide. Pale pink flowers.

G. cinereum 'Ballerina'. Clumps 4 to 6 inches high. Gray-green leaves. Lilac pink flowers to 1½ inches with purple veins, dark centers. Long bloom season. Place in front of borders or in rock gardens. Evergreen on coast.

G. dalmaticum. Shiny lobed leaves form 4-inch-tall mat. Dainty light pink flowers. Needs light shade in hot climates. Good in containers.

G. endressii 'Wargrave Pink'. Compact, mounding plant 6 to 12 inches high, spreading twice as wide. Deeply lobed light green leaves. Salmon pink flowers with darker veins. Self-sows.

G. incanum. Ground cover with wispy foliage mounding to 1 foot high, 5 feet wide. Rosy violet flowers bloom year-round in mildest climates. Self-sows.

G. 'Johnson's Blue'. Spreading plant about 18 inches tall. Clear blue flowers have long bloom season.

G. macrorrhizum (pictured at left). Fragrant foliage, 8 to 10 inches tall, turns reddish in fall. Magenta flowers; 'Album' is white. Vigorous grower, can be invasive.

G. sanguineum. Trailing foliage spreads about 2 feet, grows 1½ feet tall. Magenta flowers. *G. s.* 'Album' flowers are white, 'Striatum' flowers (pictured at far left) are light pink with dark veins. Use in front of borders. ■

By Lynn Ocone

SILKY FLOWERS *of G. sanguineum 'Striatum' grow to 1½ inches across.*

CHAD SLATTERY

CLUSTERED BLOOMS *of G. macrorrhizum rise above aromatic foliage.*

JACK K. CLARK/COMSTOCK

FIRST SIGN *of iron chlorosis on gardenia leaves is yellowing between green veins. Eventually, whole leaves may yellow.*

When leaves turn a sickly yellow . . .

Suspect iron chlorosis. Here are causes and cures

SICKLY YELLOW leaves like the ones in the photograph above are often the first signs that a plant in your garden may be suffering from the nutritional disorder called iron chlorosis.

Plants need iron to make chlorophyll, the green color in plant cells necessary for photosynthesis. But in the West, many plants don't get enough iron because their roots are unable to obtain it from the soil. Roots may be damaged by a lack of oxygen in overwatered or poorly drained soils—typical after a rainy spring—or by extreme soil temperatures. High concentrations of limestone (calcium carbonate) make the soil more alkaline, which makes the iron less soluble.

In severest untreated cases, the leaves can even turn almost white, and the plant can decline and eventually die.

Iron chlorosis is easy to confuse with other nutrient deficiencies. If a plant is iron-deficient, its newest leaves are yellower than old ones. If it's nitrogen-deficient, the old leaves are yellow and the new ones green.

Just about any plant can become chlorotic, but a few—including citrus and gardenia—are more susceptible than others.

CURING IRON CHLOROSIS

Here are some remedies. You may need to try more than one—improve your soil and apply iron chelates, for example—to cure your plant.

Improve the soil. Dig about four breathing tubes—holes about 2 to 3 feet deep and a foot wide—evenly spaced around each tree's drip line; fill them with compost. If necessary to improve soil drainage, regrade the soil surface or install an underground drainage system. Or move plants to raised beds with good soil.

Acidify the soil. Reducing soil pH below neutral to slightly acidic is the single best way to remedy iron chlorosis (it also improves air and water movement through soil). You can apply powdered soil sulfur, but that may require a lot of sulfur and a year or more to produce results. More soluble forms of sulfur with iron and manganese (such as Disper-Sul Plus Fe Mg) are available in some nurseries. To lower pH from 8.5 to 8 before planting, and to increase iron availability to roots, work 5 pounds of this type of product per 100 square feet into the top 4 to 6 inches of soil (but no more than 6 pounds per 1,000 square feet over turf). Water heavily, let soil drain, and then plant.

Apply iron sulfate. This is the cheapest and most widely available iron fertilizer; it's fine as a foliar spray but becomes insoluble on contact with alkaline soil (pH greater than 7.0). It stains concrete, stucco, or anything that contains lime. To increase its effectiveness, blend it with organic matter—2 pounds of iron sulfate to 2 pounds of peat moss or any good compost—and concentrate the mix in soil near plant roots. It costs $5 for a 5-pound bag.

Make acid spots. Instead of amending a large area to lower pH, apply soil sulfur in just a few places around a plant. Around a mature citrus tree, for instance, make four holes each about a foot wide and deep. Into each hole, place a mixture of 5 pounds soil sulfur, 1 pound ammonium sulfate, and 1 pound iron sulfate. Refill holes with soil.

Apply iron chelates. These organic compounds keep iron soluble and available to roots. Scatter dry granules within the plant's drip line, then water thoroughly so the chelate soaks into soil around roots. Leaves should start to green up in two to three weeks. Or spray liquids on the leaves. Follow package directions.

Some iron chelates hold onto iron more tightly than others. The four commonest ones listed below range from those that hold iron the least (top) to those that hold it tightest (bottom). Generally, the latter are the ones that work best in alkaline soils.

Citric acid. Best as foliar spray (it oxidizes rapidly in soil). If you apply too much, it can burn leaves. Inexpensive, and widely available.

EDTA (ethylenediamine tetraacetic acid). Effective only at a soil pH of 6.8 or less, a rarity in the low-rainfall West. Deactivated upon contact with clay or calcium carbonate in soil.

DTPA (diethylenetriamine pentaacetic acid), sold as Sequestrene 330 and Sprint 330, is useful where soil pH is 7.2 or less and soils are not high in clay. But in any soil it is useful on lawn grasses. Cost is about $30 for 5 pounds of 6 percent chelated iron.

EDDHA (ethylenediamine di-o-hydroxy-phenyl acetic acid), which is sold as Sequestrene 138 and Sprint 138, is a powder you mix with water. It's effective in soils of pH 7 to 8.7 or higher, and is the most reliable chelate for Western soils (it does not fix to clay); it's not recommended for turf.

Cost is about $100 for 5 pounds of 6 percent chelated iron (to treat a mature citrus in heavy soil, use ½ to 1 pound). ■

By Michael MacCaskey

CHARLES WEST

GOLDEN CALIFORNIA POPPIES *mix with Pacific Coast irises in sunny meadow.*

Wildflower time in Golden Gate Park

Bright blooms offer planting ideas you can use at home

JUST A FEW HUNDRED yards from San Francisco's busy streets is a garden that's every bit as dazzling in spring as the wildflower meadows planted by nature on California hillsides. The Menzies Garden of California Native Plants, in Strybing Arboretum, displays plants that grow naturally along California's central coast.

The 3½-acre garden features the best ones from four plant communities: bunchgrass meadow, chaparral meadow, redwood grove, and mixed woodland are represented in a carefully orchestrated symphony of colors. Most of the plants are tough and drought tolerant.

Starting this month and going through May, the garden is at its most colorful; it's a good time to visit for ideas on plant combinations to try at home, or just to relish the brilliant blooms.

Walking through the garden is like taking a stroll through scaled-down California terrain. Paths meander through the cool redwood grove to the sun-filled bunchgrass meadow with its dry, rocky outcrops.

In midspring, wildflowers such as California poppies, Pacific Coast irises in shades of blue, white, and purple, and golden yellow meadowfoam spread a dazzling carpet against a backdrop of brilliant blue ceanothus and other spring-flowering chaparral shrubs. The ceanothus, which include 'Julia Phelps' (dark indigo blue flowers) and 'Ray Hartman' (medium blue flowers), make handsome hedges or screens. Manzanitas, cloaked with blooms in soft shades of pink and white, are also used as backdrops to complement the bright wildflowers.

Later in spring, bright pink and red clarkias, several types of lupines and shimmering white Matilija poppies bloom among soft green mounds of native grasses, offering a more subdued but still appealing effect. During late summer and through fall, buckwheats and California fuchsias form a very textured, softer look.

Strybing Arboretum (open 8 to 4:30 weekdays, 10 to 5 weekends) is in Golden Gate Park; the arboretum entrance is near Ninth Avenue and Lincoln Way. ■

By Emely Lincowski

MEADOWFOAM *(Limnanthes douglasii), native to Northern California, spreads carpet of yellow and white flowers.*

NORMAN A. PLATE

3 Waring hoe. The deceptively simple hooked blade of this hoe can loosen the top 4 inches of soil and pull out weedy subsurface grass runners without breaking them off. The long-handled version shown here (it's also available as a hand tool) lets you spot-weed without bending over.

4 Trake. This is made for gardeners who get sidetracked (read: most of us). Take it into a perennial bed for cultivation and light weeding in close quarters, then switch over to the trowel end to pop out thick-rooted dandelions, divide daisies, or transplant overcrowded perennials. The elongated handle gives the trake excellent leverage.

5 Multi-hoe. Though this looks like a medieval combat relic, its functions are simple. Use it rounded side down to scoop out planting rows or to chop out weeds. Flip it over, and use its straight blade to chop out roots that encroach on vegetable and flower beds. It can also edge grass on a small scale.

6 Dutch hoe. This hoe cuts out young weeds as you push it along under the soil surface, its blade parallel with the ground (people over 5 feet 6 inches might find this difficult). It can be flipped over and used to smooth beds after cultivation. It's sold in several versions.

The right hoe for the right job

EACH OF THE HOES and cultivators pictured here does at least one job better than its all-purpose counterparts and is well worth the cost if you have a garden chore that calls for what it does best. If not, it just becomes stock for your next garage sale.

Good hoes are rarely sharpened when you buy them, so you'll likely have to do the job yourself. To put an edge on a flat hoe, use a flat-sided, single-cut medium file. To sharpen a hooked blade, use a half-round file.

SIX SPECIALTY HOES

1 Collinear hoe. Equipped with a thin, sharp, straight blade, the collinear hoe is for frequent light cultivation around seed beds and vegetables. It's not good for heavy hoeing. It's available with a short or long handle.

2 Hand mattock-ax. This tool works best where competition from invading roots is serious. Just hoe until you encounter roots, then chop hard if they're perpendicular to the blade. If they're parallel, flip the hoe over and cut with the opposite blade.

WHERE TO FIND THEM

Look for these tools at well-stocked nurseries and garden centers, or in mail-order tool catalogs. Here's where to find the most uncommon of them.

The collinear hoe is sold by Smith & Hawken, 25 Corte Madera, Mill Valley, CA 94941; (415) 383-2000. For the hand mattock-ax, write or call Brookstone Company, 5 Vose Farm Rd., Peterborough, NH 03458; (800) 846-3000. The Waring hoe is sold by The Gardener's Eye, Box 100963, Denver, CO 80250; (800) 624-4192. ■

By Jim McCausland

CHAD SLATTERY

ON SOUTH SIDE *of Microclimate House, plants chosen for sunny exposure include blue-flowered Salvia clevelandii. Yellow-leafed trees are 'Sunburst' honey locust.*

Garden of the future in Riverside

It's a demonstration garden devoted to conserving water and other resources

POINTING THE WAY for Western gardens of the future, Landscapes Southern California Style shows how to make the most of our arid climate. This demonstration garden in Riverside is a study in thrifty use of water and other resources—with serendipitous savings in time and effort spent on maintenance.

The 1-acre garden, created by the Western Municipal Water District and University of California Cooperative Extension, is devoted to education. In 1992, some 13,000 visitors attended open-air lectures, studied the materials at the educational stations, or simply enjoyed the plantings.

The garden, located at 450 Alessandro Boulevard, is open 10 to 4 daily except holidays. For group tours, call (909) 780-4177. This year, the annual sale of water-efficient plants is April 17.

FEATURES OF THE GARDEN

Structural elements approximate those around a typical house: pathways, a covered patio, a wood deck. A small building called the Microclimate House illustrates how to deal with the different sun and shade patterns on each side of your house.

Bisecting the garden is a dry stream bed. Two lawn areas—one Bermuda grass, the other tall fescue—demonstrate water-sensible choices in turf. In addition, you'll see more than 150 water-thrifty plants combined in a home garden setting.

The 50 educational stations address planning, installation, and maintenance. Planning tips include ways to analyze your site: its soil and exposure, as well as your personal or family needs. You learn how to select low-water-use plants for particular microclimates and to group together those of similar water needs so irrigation is simpler and more efficient.

Installation information includes ways to improve the soil and the proper planting techniques for shrubs and trees. Panels explain when to use drip and when to use sprinklers, with sample systems on display.

To make maintenance as carefree as possible, there is information about getting the garden established through its first season and how to handle problems that arise.

TAKE-HOME IDEA: *yellow-flowered Sedum rubrotinctum grows in combination with Cistus purpureus.*

WHAT'S THE PAYOFF?

If this garden were given over to a sweeping expanse of evergreen lawn accented with thirsty flower and shrub beds, it would need about 54 inches of water a year to remain healthy and attractive. But last year this water-thrifty landscape used only 27 inches of water.

As plants become deeper rooted, water needs will decrease further. Meanwhile, 3½ years after planting, the richly varied landscape has filled in, and it promises to be at its most colorful this spring. ■

By Michael MacCaskey

PETER CHRISTIANSEN

BORDER FOR BENEFICIAL INSECTS *includes California poppy, pink corn cockle, and blue bachelor's button.*

Plants that invite beneficial insects into your garden

CHOOSE THE RIGHT plants, and you can encourage beneficial insects—those good bugs that feast on such garden pests as aphids and whiteflies—to stop and stay awhile in your garden.

What are the right plants? They're ones that offer beneficial insects the food and shelter they need for survival. Beneficial insects' preferred food source is other insects, but to complete their life cycles they also require pollen and nectar, which they dine on when the pest insect population is low.

The plants listed at right offer a haven for beneficial insects. Plant them in flower borders or use them to edge vegetable plots.

Insectary plants generally come from the carrot, daisy, and pinks families and bear small, shallow flowers. Luckily for gardeners, these include many favorite border flowers such as cosmos, sweet alyssum, and yarrow.

The key to attracting beneficials is a diverse planting. Mix many different plants; the broader the spectrum of food and shelter you provide, the greater the variety of insects your border will attract. Plan to have something in flower all year, so the insects are not forced to find pollen and nectar sources outside your garden. To offer a continuous food source, select plants such as feverfew and common fennel for a long bloom season, and plants such as buckwheat and corn cockle for late-fall bloom.

While the benefits of planting to attract beneficials have not been widely evaluated, one recent study conducted by University of California researcher Bill Chaney proved that planting rows of white sweet alyssum between rows of lettuce actually increased the number of beneficial insects that visited the plantings. It also suppressed aphids on lettuce crops 50 feet away.

As you experiment with plants to attract beneficials, remember that the goal is not complete elimination of pests, but keeping their numbers down so that damage to plants is at a tolerable level. ■

By Emely Lincowski

15 plants for beneficial insects

Annuals

Baby blue eyes (*Nemophila menziesii*). Blue flowers on 6- to 10-inch plants; blooms March to May. *Attracts:* parasitic wasps, pirate bugs.

Bishop's weed (*Ammi majus*). Similar to Queen Anne's lace; blooms April to October. *Attracts:* parasitic wasps, pirate bugs, syrphid flies.

Coriander (*Coriandrum sativum*). Small white flowers on fine-textured plant; blooms May and June. *Attracts:* hover flies, parasitic wasps, pirate bugs.

Corn cockle (*Agrostemma*). Tall, wispy plants with pink cuplike flowers; blooms November through April where winters are mild, May to August elsewhere. *Attracts:* lady beetles, parasitic wasps.

Cosmos (*C. bipinnatus*). White works best; 1- to 4-foot ferny foliage; blooms April to November. *Attracts:* insidious flower bugs, lacewings, lady beetles.

Sweet alyssum (*Lobularia maritima*). White to purple flowers on 6- to 8-inch plants; blooms all year in mild-winter areas. *Attracts:* hover flies, lacewings, parasitic wasps, pirate bugs.

Tidytips (*Layia platyglossa*). Yellow and white flowers on 5- to 16-inch plants; blooms March to August. *Attracts:* parasitic wasps, pirate bugs.

Perennials

Buckwheat (*Eriogonum*). White, yellow, pink, and rose flowers on 1- to 4-foot plants; blooms May to October or later. *Attracts:* hover flies, pirate bugs.

Common fennel (*Foeniculum vulgare*). Soft, ferny foliage; yellow, flat flower clusters; blooms April to November. *Attracts:* hover flies, lacewings, lady beetles, paper wasps, soldier bugs.

Coreopsis. Yellow, orange, and maroon flowers on plants 1 to 3 feet tall; blooms May to September. *Attracts:* hover flies, lacewings, lady beetles, parasitic wasps.

Crown pink (*Lychnis coronaria*). Soft gray foliage on 2-foot plants; magenta, pink, and white flowers; blooms April to August. *Attracts:* hover flies, parasitic wasps.

Feverfew (*Chrysanthemum parthenium*). White daisy flowers on 1- to 3-foot plants; blooms from April to September or later. *Attracts:* hover flies.

Rue (*Ruta graveolens*). Beautiful blue-gray foliage, yellow flowers; blooms in early summer. *Attracts:* mud wasps, parasitic wasps, potter wasps.

Tansy (*Tanacetum vulgare*). Yellow flowers on plants 2 to 3 feet tall with ferny foliage; blooms June and July. *Attracts:* lacewings, lady beetles, parasitic wasps, pirate bugs.

Yarrow (*Achillea*). Pink, yellow, red, lavender, and white flowers; blooms April to September. *Attracts:* lady beetles, parasitic wasps.

APRIL

Garden guide 73

April checklists.................. 80

Small vegetable gardens 84

Impatiens: garden show-off ... 91

Saguaros on the sofa 93

A superlative rock garden 96

Daisy standouts from seed..... 98

Keep your roses blooming 99

Sunroses in spring gardens .. 100

New ardor for Arbor Day 101

Sunset's

GARDEN GUIDE

K. BRYAN SWEZEY

River of yarrow in Healdsburg

APRIL SHOWERS ALTERNATE WITH SPARKLING CLEAR BLUE SKIES THIS month, creating a refreshing backdrop for the vibrant array of spring-flowering bulbs, perennials, and roses blooming in gardens now. Bright yellow yarrow (Achillea taygetea) is the centerpiece of the border pictured above and described on page 76. As tempting as it may be to sit back and enjoy the spring show, allow plenty of time for gardening, too; you'll find planting opportunities and chores that need attention so your summer garden will also glow with bloom.

Sunset's

GARDEN GUIDE

PANAMERICAN SEED

CREAMY WHITE FLOWERS *cover 'French Vanilla', a new hybrid marigold.*

More hardy fuchsias

Until recently, if you wanted a hardy fuchsia on the perimeters of fuchsia country, you had only one choice—*F. magellanica.* This tiny-flowered plant grows 3 to 5 feet in a season. In hard winters, it dies to the ground. After a mild winter, it leafs out from last year's growth.

Now a number of hardy fuchsias with similar characteristics are appearing in many nurseries. Some have tiny flowers, others have blossoms like the big hybrids that fill hanging baskets. Most grow 3 to 4 feet in a year, then die back with the first hard frost. They're excellent in mixed borders and are hardy in all low elevations except deserts.

Specialty nurseries sell hardy fuchsias this month through summer. If you buy and plant now, they'll give a full season of bloom this year and put down a good network of roots long before cool weather returns.

JAN SILVER

BLOSSOMS *of 'President' fuchsia dangle in dappled light beneath a tree.*

Give these plants light shade and rich, well-drained soil. During the bloom season, feed them lightly once a month with a complete dry fertilizer, or twice a month with liquid. In the Northwest, after the first hard frost, you should cover the root zone with a 6-inch mound of mulch.

Names of plants with big blossoms to look for include *Fuchsia* 'Cardinal' (scarlet flowers), 'President' (pictured below), and 'Chillerton Beauty' (light pink sepals, rose petals).

'French Vanilla': a new white marigold

A vigorous creamy white marigold now adds diversity to the traditional yellow-to-gold-flowered marigold clan. This beauty (pictured above) is the result of many years of hybridizing.

The first white-flowered plants, which were introduced in 1976, had a few problems. They lacked vigor, and flowers tended to have a green center.

The new hybrid, 'French Vanilla', is bushier and more vigorous than previous white marigolds and has fuller, larger flowers. Plants grow about 24 inches tall, with flowers up to 3 inches across.

The flowers stay a uniform creamy white, are odorless, and are good for cutting. White marigolds' petals tend to sunburn in hot, inland areas (this variety less so than the older whites), so plant them where they get afternoon shade or grow them in late summer. West of the Cascades, they do fine in full sun.

Order seeds from W. Atlee Burpee & Co., 300 Park Ave., Warminster, PA 18991; (800) 888-1447. The catalog is free.

Giving hot soil a chance to cool

In the spring, Eric Nelson and Toni Haun dug a new perennial bed 2 feet deep, sifted rocks out of the soil, backfilled and added yards of nutritious rotted steer manure. Then they got worried: if they planted the bed too quickly, the manure might burn plant roots. It's a common mistake, and worth remembering before you plant expensive shrubs and perennials in hot, overly rich soil, then watch them slowly burn to a crisp.

Nelson and Haun played it safe; after amending the bed in the spring, they planted pumpkins in it to test its heat. When the plants shot out, covered the bed with big beautiful green leaves, then produced large, handsome fruits, Nelson and Haun knew the bed was safe.

So when October—optimum planting time—arrived, they put in the expensive plants with confidence.

New lightweight sod is fast and easy to install

If you've ever installed a conventional sod lawn, you know how much work it can be. Each 5-square-foot roll weighs at least 25 pounds, which makes installing even a small, 600-square-foot lawn an exhausting process.

Now a new type of lightweight sod is available—8 square feet weigh about 18 pounds. The sod is grown in lightweight humus on top of plastic.

When the sod is harvested, growers lift it off the plastic with roots intact (conventional sod-harvesting cuts off more than 90 percent of roots).

This means that light sod is much less prone to transplant shock. Roots grow into the soil and establish much faster (within 7 to 10 days) after planting.

What kinds of grasses can you get this way? Two kinds: "dwarf fescue," a shorter growing form of tall fescue, suited to all of Southern California; and St. Augustine, good in all low elevations of Southern California and Arizona.

Both the fescue and St. Augustine are grown as light sod. Prices range from 35 to 50 cents per square foot, about the same as for conventional sod. One wholesale source is Pacific Sod; call (800) 942-5296 to find out where to purchase it retail.

CLAIRE CURRAN

ABUNDANT FLOWER CLUSTERS *crown 4-foot Geranium maderense in spring.*

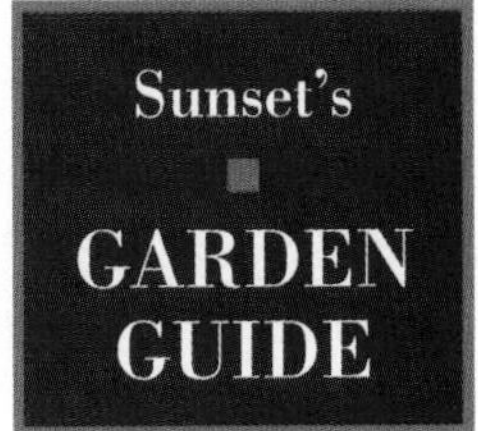

The giant among geraniums

A purple haze of quarter-size flowers covers *Geranium maderense* (pictured above in a garden designed by Lynn Woodbury) in spring. It's a true geranium—not a pelargonium, the common pot plant that's usually called geranium. Since temperatures around 22° damage or kill *G. maderense*, gardeners in mild-winter regions are among the privileged few who can grow it outdoors.

When in flower, this largest of all geranium species reaches up to 5 feet tall. The rosette of 15- to 18-inch-wide, deeply cut leaves grows to about 3 feet tall and equally wide. The plant is classified as a biennial (which flowers and dies within two years). But some plants actually take up to three years to produce the magnificent bloom, and then self-sow as they gradually die.

Inland, *G. maderense* is best suited for dappled shade, such as under tall-growing trees; in this somewhat protected situation, plants require infrequent watering in summer, and leaves are shielded from scorching summer sun. On the coast, the geranium can take full sun.

G. maderense may be difficult to find, but it's worth the search. Check geranium shows this month and next, and nurseries that specialize in perennials and Mediterranean plants.

New encyclopedia of ornamental grasses

With a passion for ornamental grasses and a zeal to share his expertise, Southern California horticulturist John Greenlee gives us a new comprehensive reference on these versatile plants. *The Encyclopedia of Ornamental Grasses* (Rodale Press, Emmaus, PA, 1992; $29.95) tells how to grow and landscape with more than 250 grasses.

Accompanying each plant description is a color photograph of the grass, along with information on its landscape uses, USDA hardiness zones, tips on culture and propagation, and pests and other problems.

The introductory section covers such basics as how grasses grow and how to select, buy, and plant them. The closing section covers designing with ornamental grasses. Plans show grasses in cutting gardens, a prairie garden, mixed borders, and foundation plantings. Grasses appropriate for both sun and shade are listed.

New uses for sabadilla

This insecticidal dust, derived from finely ground seeds of the sabadilla lily *(Schoenocaulon officinalis)*, is not new. Aztecs and Incas used it, and it was one of the most popular insecticides in the United States until it was abandoned for DDT after World War II. But it's been reintroduced within the last few years, and availability is increasing. Now it has been approved for use on a broader range of plants.

Sabadilla is a good choice for vegetable crops because its toxic properties dissipate quickly in sunlight. It is deadly to such troublesome insects as flea beetle, grasshoppers, green stink bug, harlequin bug, and striped cucumber beetle (but it is also toxic to honeybees, lady beetles, and spiders).

The material is registered for sale and use in all western states except Alaska, Arizona, California, Hawaii, and Utah. In most of those not-registered states, the processes by which new insecticides become registered are moving forward.

Sabadilla isn't equally effective against all insect pests, and it won't kill all of your target pests. But it will diminish the number of troublemakers. Apply it while there's moisture on the leaves, so the dust sticks to both leaf tops and bottoms. Wear a mask.

Sabadilla is available by mail from Necessary Organics, 1 Nature's Way, New Castle, VA 24127; (800) 447-5354 (catalog free). In Nevada, it's also available in some retail garden centers. A 1-pound can costs $9.95, a 5-pound bag $35.

RUSS A. WIDSTRAND

SPRING BOUQUET—*including roses and sweet William—grows in glazed ceramic pot. Design: Roger's Gardens.*

Water wisdom for container gardening

One of the joys of spring gardening is the chance to mix blooming plants in pots for a splash of bright color on a deck or patio. But container plants require more frequent watering than plants in the ground. They have a limited amount of soil to draw on for water, and their aboveground roots are more exposed to the drying effects of sun and wind. Consider these pointers to conserve moisture and reduce irrigation frequency:

Use containers made from less-porous materials. Plastic, metal, concrete, and glazed ceramic containers (such as the one pictured above) are less porous than terra-cotta, pressed peat, or sphagnum moss–lined wire baskets.

Don't give a plant more sun than it needs. If it thrives in part shade or sun, give it shade; it won't dry out as quickly.

Double up pots. To keep a pot from drying out too fast, put it inside a larger one and fill the space between them with moistened peat moss or sand.

Cluster pots. They'll shade and cool each other.

Mulch. To prevent the soil surface from drying out and repelling water, cover it with a layer of pebbles or bark.

Don't water unnecessarily. Use a moisture meter or soil sampler to check soil moisture content before watering.

Repot rootbound plants. They dry out quickly. Trim the roots and put plants into containers that are one size larger.

Rust fungus weakens lawns

NORMAN A. PLATE

POWDERY ORANGE *pustules indicate grass blade is infected by a rust disease.*

If your bluegrass or rye grass lawn has an orange tint to it, look closely at a leaf blade. A reddish orange powder on older leaf blades is a sign that your grass is infected with rust fungus (to test, rub a white cloth over the leaf blades; if the cloth picks up an orange color, it's rust).

Bluegrass and rye grass are most susceptible, but other lawn grasses are sometimes affected. Rust is a common disease of many plants, but it's host specific; for example, lawn rust won't infect other plants such as roses.

Rust thrives in warm, moist conditions. In order for spores to germinate and infect the grass, the leaf surfaces must be wet for 4 hours. To control it, water in the morning so grass blades dry out during the day. Apply a high-nitrogen fertilizer to get the grass growing vigorously. If necessary, apply a fungicide containing chlorthalonil; mancozeb is less effective but will help. If necessary, reseed bare spots.

Two low-growing summer perennials

If you're looking for low-growing perennials for the front of a border, *Coreopsis verticillata* 'Moonbeam' and *Scabiosa* 'Butterfly Blue' are easy, long-blooming choices.

'Moonbeam' was named Plant of the Year by the Perennial Plant Association in 1992. It has fine-textured, threadlike foliage. Creamy yellow, daisylike flowers, 1 to 2 inches across, appear in profusion throughout the summer. The plant grows 18 to 24 inches tall.

'Butterfly Blue' is a compact (about 12 inches tall), trouble-free plant that produces dozens of lavender blue flowers 2½ to 3 inches across all summer long. As its name implies, the flowers are attractive to butterflies.

Both plants are available from Park Seed Co., Cokesbury Rd., Greenwood, SC 29647; (800) 845-3369 (catalog free).

Spring garden is deer and drought resistant

Drought and deer can take their toll on gardens. But with the right plants, you can have a showy display of plants that deer don't particularly like—and on modest amounts of water.

Cathryn Rose's garden in Healdsburg (pictured on page 73) contains a winning mix of yellows, greens, and purples. She combines yellow yarrow (front), lime green *Euphorbia myrsinites* (behind), purple-leafed 'Crimson Pygmy' Japanese barberry (front, right), and purple-flowered *Erysimum linifolium* 'Bowles Mauve' (behind the barberry).

All of the plants need only periodic deep irrigations. The bed is watered by a drip system and mulched heavily with well-rotted poultry manure. To keep plants looking well manicured, Rose cuts back flowers of yarrow and euphorbia after they fade.

Have a ball with a new zucchini

A new hybrid zucchini—'Roly Poly'—is aptly named: it's round. Like other zukes, it's a prolific producer and can be eaten raw like an apple, shredded to make bread or casseroles, sliced and sautéed, or hollowed out and stuffed.

The flesh has a creamy texture and nutty flavor. Order

KARL SPREITZ

LIKE A GARDEN MIRROR, *pond reflects shapes, textures, and colors around it. Clouds of white flowering cherry close to far shore are doubled in still water.*

toneaster buxifolius in fruit, or a cut arrangement of naked vine maple twigs and sprigs of longleaf mahonia.

The pot looks spiffy in all seasons. After bloom is finished, plants can be transplanted into the garden—or given to friends. Blooming plants are given plenty of liquid plant food, so soil stays full of nutrients. If the soil loses a loose fluffy texture, it's time to replace it with fresh mix.

Cotoneaster and other good inland plants

Will any cotoneaster grow as a ground cover in the cold winters, hot, dry summers, and alkaline soil east of the Cascades in the Northwest? Yes. Two do just fine: *C. dammeri* and *C. horizontalis.*

This and other questions about gardening in eastern Oregon and Washington plus western Idaho are answered in a 70-page booklet, *Landscape Plants for the Inland Northwest,* published by the Washington State University Cooperative Extension.

The booklet is chock-full of useful and straightforward advice for inland gardeners. It lists ground covers, rock plants, shrubs, small trees, and vines by height: 1½ to 4 feet, 4 to 15 feet, 15 to 30 feet, and trees over 30 feet. Information on each plant includes the common and botanical names, description, potential height and width, and what exposure to give it.

For a copy of the booklet, request EB1579 and send a $3 check or money order to Bulletin Office, Cooperative Extension, Cooper Publications Building, WSU, Pullman, WA 99164.

seeds now from W. Atlee Burpee & Co. (address on page 74) for May or June planting. From seed to table takes 50 days.

A mirror in the garden

In spring, the pond in the photograph above adds a new dimension to gardens of Royal Roads Military College near Victoria, B.C. White and pink blossoms of shrubs and trees planted near its edges reflect in still waters, doubling their power in the landscape. If you're lucky enough to have a pond in your garden, here are some simple lessons that can increase your pleasure from it. For powerful reflections, think tall and think bright.

Mix heights and shapes for interesting reflections. The images in the pond above include a cone-shaped tall dark conifer, sky, and the black lines of deciduous trunks and branches. This diversity of plants gives the reflection shape and texture.

Choose plants with bright-colored flowers. Flowering cherries at pond's edge are brilliant spots of white that double in number when reflected in the still water. If the cherries were planted farther back on the lawn, they'd be white splotches on a green carpet.

Light-colored blossoms reflect the best: examples include *Cornus mas,* forsythia, *Magnolia stellata,* spiraea, and weigela.

Royal Roads Military College is in Colwood, about 7 miles west of Victoria. Gardens are open from 10 to 4 daily. This month, the gardens will be an impressionist's blur of infant leaf and early blossom.

A concentrated spring display

One great pot, filled to bursting with blooms and set in just the right spot, can often have more impact than clusters of pots.

The single cast-stone pot pictured below shows off just a few plants for spring bloom. Red and white English daisies *(Bellis perennis* 'Goliath') surrounding yellow tulips add a bright splash of color to the otherwise all-green garden. These replaced winter-flowering blue pansies. Next will come white lobelia and magenta geraniums for summer, then mums for autumn.

For winter, the gardener might put in a 1-gallon *Co-*

KEVIN MILLER

CAST-STONE POT *is brimful of spring color: yellow tulips, white and red English daisies.*

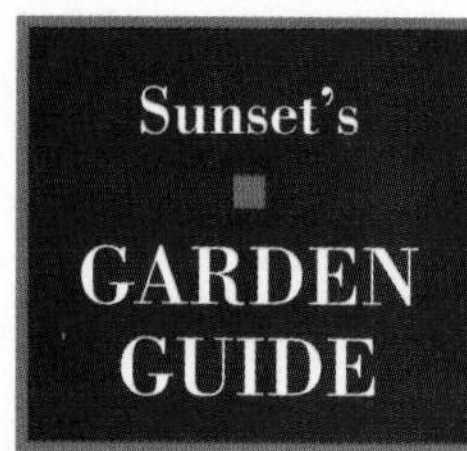

Golden crownbeard—a summer wildflower to sow now

The picture below shows this little-known plant at its best. In the wild, golden crownbeard *(Verbesina encelioides)* grows throughout most of the West—from Montana to Arizona, New Mexico, and Texas; it blooms for about two weeks in late summer.

This hardy bloomer has much to recommend it. It needs virtually no water beyond a little rain, it's a profuse bloomer, it provides cover and food for birds, and it's useful for reclaiming weedy areas. Sow seed this month.

Golden crownbeard grows in proportion to the water it gets. During years of average rainfall, it gets 1 to 2 feet tall; with abundant rain, it'll reach 4 feet tall. Flowers are about 2 inches in diameter, with golden yellow centers and petals. Since it's not a neat or refined plant, use it to cover outlying areas, or to the rear of cultivated areas.

Two seed packets are enough to cover 100 square feet or so. Scratch the seeds into the soil and wait for rain to start them; or use sprinklers. They should sprout in about a week. Flowers start as early as June in some areas but don't appear till late summer in Santa Fe. After plants and flowers die, they turn a pleasing tan. Collect seeds then for next year, or let nature take its course.

Seeds are available for $1.75 per packet from Plants of the Southwest, Agua Fria, Route 6, Box 11A, Santa Fe, NM 87501; (505) 471-2212. The color catalog costs $3.50; an availability listing is free.

CHARLES MANN

GOLDEN CROWNBEARD, *an interior West wildflower. Sow it now.*

Plants that rabbits may find resistible

"They're cute," admits Tucson Master Gardener Dawn Dixon, "but allowing rabbits to use your garden as a smorgasbord is wasteful of your time and money." In her garden, Dixon noticed that rabbits seem to avoid plants with aromatic foliage or milky sap. That observation led to others, and soon she had compiled a list of rabbit-resistant plants. Here are some of her favorites; all are attractive garden plants that, in Dixon's garden, have thrived despite the presence of rabbits. (But keep in mind that when there's nothing else to eat, rabbits will nibble on just about any plant.)

Dalea greggii (trailing indigo bush). Ground cover to 3 feet wide, 1½ feet tall.

Eremophila (emu bush). Several species of Australian natives that are well adapted to desert (see item, page 79).

Euphorbia rigida. Evergreen perennial or low shrub; showy. About 2 feet high and 3 feet wide. Good in containers or borders.

Feijoa sellowiana (pineapple guava). Evergreen shrub or small tree, to 20 feet tall, has edible fruit.

Gazania. Low ground covers (some trailing-spreading, others clumping) produce large, daisy flowers.

Iris (bearded kinds). Usually evergreen; mostly showy flowers.

Rosemary. Evergreen shrub or ground cover, grows to 2 to 6 feet tall, depending upon variety. Light blue flowers.

Salvia clevelandii (Cleveland sage). Evergreen shrub to 3 feet high, 5 feet wide. Gray-green leaves are strongly scented; blue flowers are abundant in late spring.

Sophora secundiflora (Texas mountain laurel). Evergreen shrub or small tree to 25 feet tall. Grape-scented violet blue flowers come late winter through spring.

CRANDALL & CRANDALL

'HUSKY GOLD' TOMATO, *a 1993 All-America winner, bears flavorful 5- to 7-ounce fruits on compact plants. The tomatoes ripen to bright golden yellow or orange-yellow.*

Two new tomatoes: one is gold, one loves heat

'Husky Gold,' one of a new series of tomato plants developed specifically for home gardeners, is a dwarf indeterminate (vinelike) type—it grows only about 4½ feet tall.

The 5- to 7-ounce fruits taste sweet and mild, and as the name suggests, they're bright golden. Stems and leaves are dark green. Plants are resistant to verticillium and fusarium wilt. They begin fruiting about 70 days after transplanting and continue until frost. Grow 'Husky Gold' in the ground or in raised beds, patio planters, or large pots.

Another new tomato, 'Heatwave,' is discussed on page 26 (February), where it is suggested to start that variety from seed.

In April, both kinds would best be set out as transplants. Differences between the two are many: 'Husky Gold' ripens gold, 'Heatwave' red; the first grows as a vine, the other as a bush. The two ripen in almost exactly the same number of days.

Look for transplants of either tomato at garden centers. Transplants of both tomatoes (and other vegetable and flowering plants) are also available by mail from W. Atlee Burpee & Co, (800) 888-1447; a minimum purchase of 48 plants (6 per variety) for $25 is required.

An Aussie comes to the Southwest

Emu bush *(Eremophila glabra)*, pictured at right, is one of more than 150 plants in a genus found in Australia (only a handful are grown in the West). What makes the newly introduced Australian shrub so special? Perhaps it's the brilliant red flowers that contrast strikingly with silver-gray leaves. Or the plant's toughness: it thrives in the extreme heat and dry, alkaline soil of the low and intermediate deserts. Plants survive temperatures in the mid-20s.

Emu bush is a highly variable species. The form most common in nurseries grows about 4 feet tall and wide with silver oval leaves—about 1½ inches long—that feel stiff and leathery to touch. Flowers, attractive to hummingbirds, are also about 1½ inches long.

Plant emu bush in full sun and fast-draining soil. Set slightly high in the planting hole to further aid soil drainage. Water every two weeks during dry weather. Once plants are established (next spring), the time between irrigations can stretch to a month or more. Most often, plants are damaged by too much, not too little, water.

As the plant matures, prune lightly to help maintain dense growth. Look for blooming plants in nurseries this month. A 1-gallon pot costs about $2, a 5-gallon one about $7.

With ground covers, be a barber, not a butcher

Most ground covers need periodic trimming to keep them from looking ragged. To keep the chore simple, do it regularly. For quick tidying up, you can shear or mow. Either method works well with ground covers such as ivy, lippia, star jasmine, trailing indigo bush, and verbena.

A rotary mower is particularly useful for low-growing bloomers like verbena, whose seed heads hang on after flowers die. To shear blooms without ripping the foliage, set the mower at 2 to 3 inches. Within a few weeks, new blooms will appear.

Use hand shears to trim mounding ground covers such as trailing indigo bush. New growth will soon hide evidence of your pruning. Also use shears to avoid a butchered look on slow-growing plants like star jasmine and periwinkle; selectively trim each runaway stem.

Don't prune ground covers such as juniper and rosemary after their branches become tough and woody—these plants recover slowly and unattractively. Sheared woody branches will no longer send out much new growth. To maintain shape and size on this type of ground cover, frequently pinch newest growth at shoot tips; start when plants are young.

Do's and don'ts of composting

This month, weather warms and days lengthen. Grass starts growing fast, weeds sprout, and it takes plenty of trimming to keep plants in bounds. This abundance of organic waste makes spring a good season to start or rebuild a compost pile.

Alternate layers of high-carbon organic material (such as straw, tree prunings, and old leaves) with layers of high-nitrogen material (kitchen waste, green grass clippings, succulent weeds, and manure).

Some materials are unsuitable for composting. Avoid plants with disease or insects that could survive the composting process and spread in the garden. Don't compost weeds with seed heads, or warm-season lawn grasses like Bermuda or St. Augustine that reproduce by runners. Keep out plants recently treated with pesticides or herbicides. Avoid meat scraps or oils from the kitchen; they may attract animal pests. Exclude waste from dogs, cats, and birds that may contain organisms that are harmful to humans.

Suitable materials that are slow to compost, such as banana peels, magnolia leaves, and woody brush, should be shredded or chopped before going into the pile. The smaller the pieces, the quicker the decomposition; reduce material to ¾-inch pieces or smaller. ■

By Steven R. Lorton, Michael MacCaskey, Lynn Ocone, Lauren Bonar Swezey

MICHAEL MacCASKEY

FIRE ENGINE RED FLOWERS *contrast strikingly with silvery leaves on emu bush. This new arrival from Australia blooms in waves, peaking spring and fall.*

Northwest

GARDEN GUIDE

WEST OF THE CASCADES, see items marked with a **W.**

EAST OF THE CASCADES, see items marked with an **E.**

April Checklist

HERE IS WHAT NEEDS DOING

☐ **ADD TO COMPOST. W, E:** Prunings, spent flowers, and lawn clippings, all go on the pile. Accelerate decomposition by mixing in old compost, high-nitrogen fertilizer, or commercial compost starter. If the pile seems dry, soak it well. You may want to cover it. A sheet of black plastic works well.

☐ **AMEND SOIL. W, E:** As soon as soil is dry enough to work, dig in generous amounts of organic matter (up to 4 inches for the top foot of soil). Rake the amended soil, let it settle for a week, then plant early crops or bedding flowers.

☐ **BATTLE SLUGS. W, E:** Slugs and snails chew off seedlings as they emerge. Handpick at night, or bait thoroughly now to get as many as possible, as early as possible. Keep pets out of areas where you've put down bait.

☐ **BUY BEDDING PLANTS. W:** The year's best selection of bedding plants is available now. Shop early, but shop with a list. Choices include celosia, geraniums, impatiens, lobelia, marigolds, and sweet alyssum. If weather is still chilly in your area, hold off planting tender summer annuals for a few more weeks. **E:** Look for frost-tolerant bedding plants such as dusty miller and lobelia.

Wherever you live, try to have a planting plan in hand before you mosey into a nursery; otherwise, the fever will seize you and you'll buy what looks pretty (which is just about everything), and head home with a hodgepodge of plants. Water transplants often.

☐ **CHECK DAHLIA TUBERS. W:** If you don't let dahlias overwinter in the ground, you can take them out of storage and plant them now. **E:** Wait until May. Check stored bulbs for signs of rot or drying. If you find rot, cut out bad spots and dust tubers with sulfur. If tubers are dry, sprinkle them lightly with water, but continue to store them in a cool, dry place.

☐ **CONTROL TENT CATERPILLARS. W:** Break up their tents with a strong jet of water from your hose, then spray with *Bacillus thuringiensis* (BT), sold in nurseries and garden centers. Or cut off entire branches—tents intact—and burn them, or close them up in plastic bags that you've sprayed inside with household insecticide.

☐ **DEADHEAD FLOWERS. W, E:** If you remove blooms as they fade, spring-flowering plants will look better, perform better, and sometimes flower longer. Plants that don't have to put their energy into seed production will channel their energy into blossom and foliage growth. Look at what you're pulling off. You don't want to grasp a flower that has a bee working in it. You'll get stung.

☐ **DIVIDE PERENNIALS. W, E:** There is still time to divide most summer-flowering perennials. Daylilies, hostas, phlox, and Shasta daisies are good candidates. Dig now, divide with a spade or sharp knife, and replant. A clump the size of a dinner plate will divide nicely into quarters. Do the same for early-flowering perennials as soon as blooms fade.

☐ **FEED AND WATER ASPARAGUS AND RHUBARB. W, E:** Demand for water and fertilizer increases as new growth emerges. Mulch with finished compost or well-rotted manure, or sprinkle high-nitrogen fertilizer over the soil and mulch the ground around the base of the plant with straw or black plastic.

☐ **FEED CONIFERS. W, E:** Conifers zoom into action early in the spring. Now is the time to scratch the soil under the plant and scatter a high-nitrogen fertilizer (always follow manufacturer's instructions). Plants that are yellowish but not a golden form will green up almost immediately. Golden forms will shine brighter. Water plants well if seasonal rains are scant.

☐ **FEED SPRING-FLOWERING SHRUBS. W, E:** As soon as blooms fade on shrubs such as azaleas and camellias, apply high-nitrogen fertilizer. This encourages strong, new growth and gets the plant in shape for later in the year when it sets next year's flower buds.

☐ **HOE WEEDS. W, E:** Get them now while they're young and root systems are easily destroyed. If you wait a month, plants will be established and you'll have to pull, and, even then, many will come right back.

☐ **MOVE OVERWINTERED PLANTS OUTDOORS. W:** Put cymbidiums outdoors early in the month. Around midmonth, move begonias, fuchsias, and geraniums outdoors; these plants will take a chill but not a frost. **E:** Save this job for May.

☐ **MOW LAWNS. W, E:** Lawns get ratty-looking in winter. When the surge of spring growth starts, mow frequently; don't remove more than a third of the length of the grass blades. Edge lawns, too. If you're considering hiring a lawn service, line up help soon. About the time dandelions bloom, their phones start ringing off the hook.

☐ **PLANT BARE-ROOT. E:** This is the month to plant everything from cane berries to ornamental trees during the brief bare-root planting season. The ground is thawed and workable, but spring has not yet broken. Be certain to keep roots moist between nursery and planting hole. If they dry out, even for a short time, you may lose the plants.

☐ **PLANT SMALL FRUITS. W, E:** Blueberries, blackberries, raspberries, and strawberries can all be planted now.

☐ **PLANT SUMMER BULBS, CORMS, TUBERS. W:** In coastal nurseries choices this month include acidanthera, calla, crocosmia, dahlia, gladiolus, montbretia, ranunculus, tigridia. Dig planting holes, set stakes, put in bulbs and cover with soil. Some gardeners drop a pinch of 12-12-12 fertilizer (or one with a lower N-P-K) in a couple of inches of loose soil in the bottom of the planting hole and stir it up well. Or you can mix a trowelful of finished compost into the bottom of the hole.

☐ **PLANT VEGETABLES. W, E:** Cabbage, carrots, lettuce, parsnips, peas, potatoes, radishes, spinach, Swiss chard—all cool-season crops should go in now.

☐ **RENEW PATHWAYS. W, E:** Use bark, conifer needles, gravel, straw, or wood chips to keep established paths from getting muddy. Sawdust gets soggy.
—*S. R. L.* ■

Central

GARDEN GUIDE

IN HIGH ELEVATIONS and intermountain areas of California, and east of the Sierra, see items marked with an **H.**

IN LOW ELEVATIONS of Northern California, see items marked with an **L.**

☐ **APPLY ANT CONTROL. H, L:** Ants feed off honeydew secreted by aphids, scale, and other pests. They also protect the pests from natural predators. To keep ants off trees and shrubs such as camellias, citrus, and roses, wrap the trunks with a 1- to 2-inch-wide strip of masking tape and coat with a sticky barrier like Tanglefoot. Keep the barriers free of dirt and check them periodically for breaks; reapply when necessary.

☐ **APPLY DORMANT SPRAY. H:** If you found aphids, mites, or scale insects last year on fruit trees, after pruning this year apply a dormant spray—a mixture of oil and lime sulfur or oil and copper. Follow label directions; if rains wash it off, repeat the application. Be careful not to stain walks and walls.

☐ **CARE FOR POTATOES. L:** If you have the time or inclination, pinch off flower buds before they open so more energy goes into tuber production. Also keep plants evenly watered, especially while tubers are beginning to set (this happens shortly after plants flower, if not pinched off); potatoes do not do well in soggy soil.

☐ **CONTROL MILDEW ON GRAPES. L:** Powdery mildew infects leaves, shoots, stems, and berries with a white fungus. Apply sulfur dust when shoots are 6, 12, and 18 inches long and then every two weeks (except when temperatures are above 95°).

☐ **CORRECT CHLOROSIS. L:** If plants such as camellias, citrus, grapes, and gardenias are chlorotic (yellow mottling between leaf veins), spray leaves with a foliar fertilizer containing iron and zinc. For longer-term results, apply chelated iron or an acid-forming fertilizer containing chelated iron.

☐ **MULCH THE SOIL. H, L:** To save water, smother weeds, and keep soil cooler, spread 1 to 3 inches (depending on the size of the plant) of bark chips, compost, wood shavings or other organic material under shrubs and trees, around flowers and vegetables, and in pots. To prevent crown rot, keep mulch away from stems and trunks.

☐ **PLANT BARE-ROOT PERENNIALS. L:** Perennials purchased by mail sometimes come bare root. Before planting, carefully untangle roots. Spread them over a cone of soil in the center of a good-size planting hole as shown below. Refill hole, burying roots to just below the crown (where new foliage emerges).

☐ **PLANT VEGETABLES AND HERBS. L:** Sow seeds of beans, corn, cucumbers, squash, most root crops (beets, carrots, radishes, turnips), greens (chard, lettuce, mustard, spinach). Leave space for another planting—two to three weeks later—of bush beans and root crops. Set out seedlings of eggplant, peppers, and tomatoes. This month, nurseries will have sixpacks of many herbs, including basil, mint, oregano, and parsley.

☐ **PRUNE. H:** Finish pruning deciduous fruit and ornamental trees before new growth emerges. Also prune flowering vines, grapes, and roses. Wait until after bloom to prune forsythia, spiraea, and other spring-flowering shrubs or, as flower buds begin to swell, cut branches and let them bloom in indoor arrangements. **L:** After new growth appears, prune freeze-damaged wood on tender plants, such as bougainvillea and citrus. Also, prune to shape spring-flowering shrubs (after bloom) and overgrown hedges. Prune camellias and rhododendrons right after bloom finishes.

☐ **ROTATE VEGETABLE BEDS. H, L:** If you have room in your garden, rotate planting sites to avoid a buildup of diseases and insects that can survive in the soil or on plant residue. Don't plant the same or closely related plants in the same locations they grew in the last two to three years.

☐ **SET OUT BARE-ROOT PLANTS. H:** Now available in nurseries are many kinds of deciduous plants, including cane berries, deciduous fruit and nut trees, flowering shrubs, flowering vines, grapes, rhubarb, roses, and strawberries. Bare-root planting is the best and least expensive way to start these plants. Select plants with well-developed root systems. Don't let roots dry out before planting.

☐ **SOW HARDY VEGETABLES. H:** As soon as soil can be worked, sow seeds of beets, carrot, endive, kohlrabi, lettuce, onions, parsley, parsnips, peas, potatoes, radishes, spinach, Swiss chard, and turnips. Set out transplants of broccoli, brussels sprouts, cabbage, cauliflower, and onions. Plant seed potatoes. Use floating row covers to warm soil and get plants off to a fast start.

☐ **THIN VEGETABLE SEEDLINGS. H, L:** Use scissors to snip out seedlings of basil, carrots, green onions, lettuce, and other vegetables that were sown too thickly (see drawing below); cut out at soil level.

☐ **WATCH FOR INSECTS. H, L:** Be on the lookout for aphids; hose them off with a strong blast of water or spray them with insecticidal soap. If pest problems arise that you aren't familiar with, county extension agents and Master Gardeners in your area can help identify them and suggest solutions.

☐ **WATER. H, L:** As the weather warms, increase watering frequency. Deep-water established plants often enough to prevent wilt and promote deep rooting, but not more than necessary (check soil moisture around roots with a soil auger or by digging down with a trowel).—*L. B. S.* ■

April Checklist

HERE IS WHAT NEEDS DOING

☐ **AMEND SOIL.** Before planting your summer flowers, herbs, and vegetables, add organic matter to the soil. Spread compost 2 to 3 inches deep over planting area, then sprinkle a regular or controlled-release fertilizer at label rates. Deeply cultivate the mixture into the soil.

☐ **BUILD A COMPOST PILE.** Put prunings, leaves, some types of grass clippings and kitchen waste on the compost pile (see item on page 79). For fastest breakdown, chop or shred branches; add a layer of garden soil and a handful of fertilizer every foot or two. Turn and mix pile frequently, and keep it as moist as a damp sponge.

☐ **BUY AND PLANT BULBS. C, L:** Cannas and dahlias are available now, and both grow fast and provide a long season of bloom. Tuberoses are also available for planting this month. In low-desert areas, buy gladiolus corms, but store them at 40° until planting time in August. **H:** For continuous summer bloom, plant gladiolus at two- to three-week intervals.

☐ **CARE FOR GRAPES. L, H:** Once new shoots are 5 to 8 inches long, control mildew with sulfur dust or lime sulfur spray. Repeat applications if needed. Water deeply while plants are growing actively.

☐ **CHECK PLANTS FOR IRON DEFICIENCY. C, L:** If bottlebrush, camellias, citrus, eucalyptus, gardenias, geranium (*Pelargonium*), hibiscus, pyracantha, and roses have yellowing leaves with green veins, feed them with fertilizer containing chelated iron.

☐ **CHOOSE ANNUALS CAREFULLY.** To conserve water, use annuals sparingly and cluster them for impact. Choose less-thirsty kinds such as celosia, cosmos, portulaca, sanvitalia, and sweet alyssum. Pick healthy plants that are not rootbound; plants in cell-packs will generally adjust without as much stress as overgrown plants in 4-inch containers.

☐ **DIG OR HOE WEEDS.** Dig out deep-rooted weeds such as dandelion with a hand weeder (water first to loosen soil). Slip weeder into soil and pry against taproot to make sure you get its entire length. Use a sharp hoe to scrape out other kinds of weeds when they're small by cutting just below the soil surface.

☐ **DIVIDE CYMBIDIUMS. C:** If pots are packed and have a few leafless and brown bulbs visible, this is the time to refresh plants. Knock the root mass out of the pot and separate as many clumps as you can by hand, or use pruning shears. Keep at least three healthy bulbs, with foliage, in each division. To discourage rot, dust cuts with sulfur.

☐ **FEED WARM-SEASON LAWNS.** A healthy lawn is more water efficient; apply no more than 10 pounds of a 10 percent nitrogen fertilizer, or 50 pounds of compost, per 1,000 square feet. Feed again in four to six weeks.

☐ **FERTILIZE PLANTS.** Most plants benefit from a feeding of all-purpose fertilizer (such as 10-10-10). Apply with a light touch; overfeeding now will result in softer, more water-hungry growth. Conversely, plants struggling for nutrients also use water less efficiently.

☐ **GROOM GARDEN.** Remove weeds, leaves, and other debris from your garden. To prevent the spread of petal blight, rake up fallen camellia blossoms. On daffodils and other bulbs, wait to cut off leaves until they have turned completely brown. Remove flowers as they fade.

☐ **MANAGE PESTS.** Wash aphids from citrus and roses with water or a soap spray. Trap slugs and snails under raised boards, hand-pick, or use bait, especially around young plants.

☐ **PLANT ANNUALS. C, L, H:** This is the month to start summer flowers such as ageratum, coleus, dahlias, dianthus, impatiens, lobelia, marigolds (for a new one, see item on page 74), nicotiana, petunias, and zinnias. To save water, minimize the size of planting beds, and mulch them. **H:** There's still time to plant pansies, snapdragons, stock, sweet alyssum, and violas.

☐ **PLANT ORNAMENTAL GRASSES.** Many nurseries have a good assortment of ornamental grasses available in 1- and 5-gallon containers. Choose noninvasive grasses that are right for your climate. For a list of native grasses and sources, check with a local botanic garden or plant society. Plant so that the soil level of the container plant is even with the soil level in the garden. Water immediately after planting, and keep the root zone moist while plants become established. To conserve moisture, spread mulch at the base of plants. (The item on page 75 reviews an excellent new reference book on grasses.)

☐ **PLANT SUMMER VEGETABLES. C, L:** If you live within sight of the ocean, you can continue planting cool-season crops like broccoli, cabbage, cauliflower, leaf lettuce, and spinach. Inland, shift attention to warm-season crops—beans, corn, cucumbers, eggplant, melons, okra, peppers, pumpkins, squash, tomatoes. **H:** Delay planting two to four weeks; until midmonth, there is still danger of frost.

☐ **SPRING-CLEAN INDOOR PLANTS.** Take house plants outdoors into the shade for a tune-up. Hose off dust with a fine spray and, if necessary, control pests with insecticidal soap. To leach out salts, drench the soil with water, let it drain, then drench it again.

☐ **THIN VEGETABLE SEEDLINGS.** In small, intensely planted beds, use scissors to snip out seedlings of basil, beets, turnips, and other vegetables that are usually sown too thickly. Cut out at ground level.

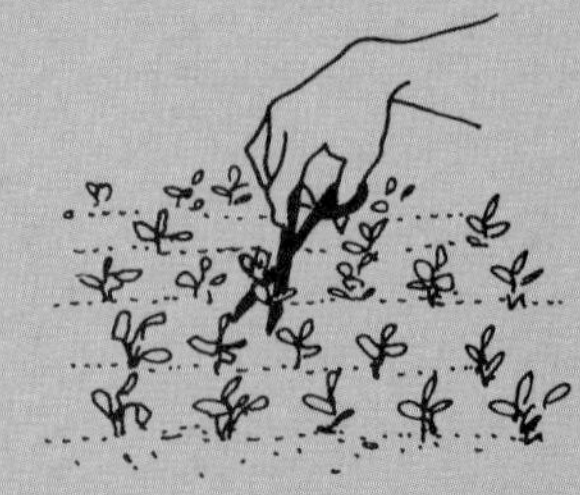

☐ **WATER WISELY.** Irrigate newly planted perennials, shrubs, and trees regularly to establish; as plants grow, water deeply and less often. Adjust automatic sprinklers to meet water needs.
—L. O. ■

Southwest

GARDEN GUIDE

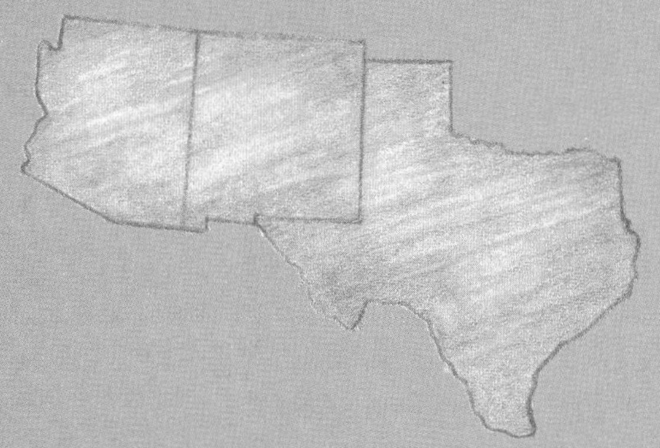

April Checklist

HERE IS WHAT NEEDS DOING

☐ **CURE IRON CHLOROSIS.** Waterlogged, alkaline soil makes iron unavailable to the roots of many plants. Iron is essential to make chlorophyll; without it, leaves turn sickly yellow. Susceptible plants include arborvitae, bottlebrush, boxwood, citrus, cotoneaster, crape myrtle, eucalyptus, and pyracantha. Cure by improving soil aeration and drainage. Be sure you are not overwatering. Also, acidify soil by adding peat moss or products containing sulfur, and use chelated iron.

☐ **DIG OR HOE WEEDS.** Use a hand weeder to dig out deep-rooted weeds such as dandelions; water first to loosen soil. Slip the weeder into soil and pry against taproot to make sure you get the entire root. Use a sharp hoe to remove all kinds of weeds when they're small; cut just below the soil surface. After weeding, apply a 3-inch-thick mulch to prevent weed regrowth.

☐ **FERTILIZE LAWNS.** Encourage strong summer growth of Bermuda grass by fertilizing with high-nitrogen fertilizer. Two weeks after green-up, apply 3 to 4 pounds of a fertilizer with 20 percent nitrogen (such as 20-0-0) per 1,000 square feet. Repeat every six weeks throughout the growing season. In the high desert, fertilize cool-season grasses (blue, fescue, rye) the same way.

☐ **FERTILIZE PLANTS.** Apply a complete fertilizer (such as 10-10-10) to annuals, bulbs, container plants, perennials, roses, shrubs, and trees. Use about 1 pound per 100 square feet of garden space. Soil should be moist before application (water it the day before fertilizing). Water again afterward.

☐ **FINISH POST-FREEZE PRUNING.** New growth is now plentiful on most trees and shrubs, making damaged areas easy to identify. As you prune, keep the plant's most natural shape in mind and cut to accentuate that shape. If heavy pruning is necessary, cut back on watering.

☐ **PLANT ANNUALS.** This month, you can plant ageratum, calliopsis (*Coreopsis tinctoria*), celosia, cosmos, four o'clock, globe amaranth, gloriosa daisy (*Rudbeckia*), kochia, lisianthus (*Eustoma grandiflorum*), marigold, Mexican sunflower (*Tithonia*), portulaca, strawflower, vinca rosea (*Catharanthus roseus*), and zinnia. Before planting, mix organic amendments such as compost into soil; add water-holding polymers to planting mix in containers.

☐ **PLANT CITRUS.** In low and intermediate deserts (Phoenix and Tucson, primarily), and in the Rio Grande Valley, this is the best month to plant citrus. Choose 5- to 7-gallon-size plants; they're likely to establish and produce faster than larger sizes. Plant in full sun, and make planting holes at least twice as wide as the rootball but no deeper. To protect the trunk from sun, wrap it with newspaper at planting time. In average soil, water two or three times a week at first, tapering off to once every five to seven days during the summer; water less often in heavy clay soils, more often in sandy soils. To aid water penetration, maintain a soil berm over the outer edge of the rootball.

☐ **PLANT LAWNS.** In Casa Grande, Phoenix, Tucson, Wickenburg, and Yuma, plant hybrid Bermuda grass as soon as minimum nighttime temperature is above 70°. If you live in Albuquerque, Bisbee, Globe, Las Cruces, or Nogales, plant a cold-hardy grass such as buffalo grass or blue grama. Tall fescue is an option for intermediate-elevation Tucson and Wickenburg, but fall is a better time to plant it.

☐ **PLANT PERENNIALS.** Sow seed of chrysanthemum, columbine, coreopsis, gaillardia, gerbera, hollyhock, and Shasta daisy. Plant small plants of gazania and geranium. From either seeds or transplants, try Michaelmas daisy (hybrids of *Aster novi-belgii* and *A. novae-angliae*) or salvia.

☐ **PLANT SUMMER BULBS.** After last frost, plant bulbs, roots, or tubers of caladium, canna, crinum, dahlia, daylily, gladiolus, iris, montbretia; buy and plant container-grown agapanthus, society garlic (*Tulbaghia*), and zephyranthes.

☐ **PLANT VEGETABLES.** In low-desert areas such as Phoenix and Yuma, and in the Rio Grande Valley, sow bean and cucumber seeds by mid-April; also plant eggplant, okra, peanuts, squash, and sweet potatoes. Gardeners in intermediate elevations can plant seeds of cucumber, melons, okra, pumpkins, soybeans, squash, and watermelons. Also plant seedlings of eggplant, pepper, sweet potato, and tomatoes, and tubers of Jerusalem artichoke. If you live in the high desert, wait until mid-May to begin these plantings.

☐ **PRUNE TREES.** In Arizona, spring winds are typically 15 to 45 mph but can be stronger. Check tree stakes and ties to confirm they are strong and not gouging the trunk. Lightly thin African sumac, Brazilian and California peppers, eucalyptus, Mexican palo verde, and South American mesquites so that wind can pass through more easily. The same advice is good in New Mexico and West Texas, even though winds have already started there.

☐ **STOP CURLY TOP VIRUS.** This disease, which spreads by a ⅛-inch-long greenish yellow beet leafhopper, affects cucumber, melon, and tomato plants. Symptoms—curled, stunted leaves and deformed fruit—usually appear this month as weather warms. The leafhoppers avoid shade, so you can protect plants by covering them now with shadecloth or a row cover. Remove infected plants as soon as symptoms appear, and plant in another location next year.

☐ **THIN VEGETABLE SEEDLINGS.** Use scissors to snip out seedlings of basil, carrots, green onions, and other vegetables that are impossible not to sow too thickly; cut them off at ground level.

☐ **WATCH FOR OLIVE DIEBACK.** If new shoots and upper stems of your olive trees wilt and die back this month or next, the cause is most likely verticillium wilt fungus. More acidic soil slows its progress: use ammonium sulfate fertilizer, soluble sulfur, and organic mulches. Prune out dead branches.—*M. M.* ■

No space, no time? Yes, you can grow vegetables

WE OFFER PROOF, INSPIRATION, AND GROWING IDEAS ON THESE SEVEN PAGES

Traditional vegetable gardens—large, rectangular plots with rows of crops and footpaths between rows—are fine for large backyards and gardeners who have the time to tend them. But where gardening space (and time) is limited, can you grow vegetables at all? The answer is a resounding yes, as the photographs on these pages show.

Every square foot counts in these small gardens. "All you need is good soil and

SANDRA WILLIAMS

Boxes 4 by 8 feet yield abundant harvest for first-year gardeners

Jayne and Tom Olson of San Diego treat each 12-inch-deep bottomless box as a separate garden, customizing drip irrigation and soil amendments for two to four rows of crops in each. The wood frames create small, defined spaces, manageable for both children and adults. Each box takes a few hours to turn and replant. Portable trellises attach to each box.

LAURIE DICKSON

In a 20- by 25-foot space, an all-in-boxes deck garden

Reclaiming an unused part of the garden between the garage and the house, landscape architect Karen Langhart of Durango, Colorado, created a space for vegetables that would be productive, attractive, and fun for the family. Raised beds in the center, built by husband Rick, are each 4 feet long by 4 to 5 feet wide. Long, 2-foot-wide beds border the fence. Lattice trellises hold up vining plants and make for easy picking. Plants are on a drip system.

Raised beds make maximum use of small space . . . and your efforts

water and fertilizer, and anything will grow—even in a 4- by 8-foot box." says gardener Tom Olson, who is pictured on page 85.

Any space will do as long as it gets at least 6 hours of sun each day and is near a water source. Planting near the house is best since the garden is more likely to grab your attention and invite you out to enjoy it and maintain it. And the convenience of harvesting from an easy-access garden will encourage you to use the crops regularly for family meals.

Once installed, small gardens don't take a lot of time to maintain. Even at peak growing season, David Lansing spends just an hour a week caring for his 52-square-foot established vegetable garden (pictured on page 90). "With my busy schedule and family commitments, that's the way it has to be," he says. "I used to enjoy spending more time in the garden, but now I have to get in and out as fast as possible."

PLANNING AND DESIGNING A SMALL GARDEN

A successful vegetable garden is usually the product of careful design and planning, and an up-front investment of time and resources.

Most of these gardens feature raised beds, which neatly organize small spaces. The change in level from the ground to planting beds makes these small gardens appear larger. And beds that curve or meander—like the one pictured above right—give a further illusion of space; also, their less structured look makes them at home in the landscape.

Raised beds have other advantages: Their contained area makes it easy to improve the soil, especially if it requires lots of amendments. Filled with light, rich soil, they drain well. They warm up quickly, and they're easy to plant, tend, and harvest.

If you don't have room for raised beds, you can still grow vegetables in nooks and crannies—in narrow side yards,

RUSS A. WIDSTRAND

A 200-square-foot vegetable bed edges the courtyard

Elevated planting area, curved edging of broken concrete, plants in drifts, and contrasting adobe pavers give depth and dimension to this productive vegetable garden. The perennial border at its base adds visual interest as well as flavor and fragrance. Design: Howard Folkman The Gardenmaker for the Pasadena (California) Showcase House of Design.

A hundred square feet of raised beds and walls transform Los Angeles side yard into a productive garden

Edible-landscape designer Janie Malloy tends herbs while seated atop a 3- by 3-foot raised bed. Trellises mounted to painted brick wall add vertical growing space for vining vegetables like 'Roman' and scarlet runner beans. For a year-round harvest, Malloy mixes annuals with perennials.

along garage walls, and on patio overhangs.

Whichever design you choose, start with a plan on graph paper. Figure how big beds can be in the space you've got, how much wood or trellising you'll need, and what kind of irrigation system you want. If you plan to install drip irrigation, an irrigation supply specialist can help you figure the components you'll need. Thoroughly prepare the soil, adding fertilizer and amendments such as compost as needed.

GARDENING TECHNIQUES FOR HIGH YIELDS

Besides designing your garden well, there are other ways to maximize harvest from a small space. Choose productive plants that suit your tastes and don't grow too large; the list on page 89 can help you decide what to grow. Plant only what you can use, Interplant fast-maturing crops like lettuce and spinach with slower-growing crops like broccoli and cauliflower. The lettuce and spin-

30 square feet, 15 minutes a day . . . she grew vegetables for two

Beans, eggplant, squash, tomatoes, and more

Rectangular bed, edged with four rough-cut redwood 2-by-12s, is perfect size for time-pressed gardener Susan Hobson Dormitzer, who tells her story below. Bed was planted in May (left) and still going strong in October (right). Corner braces double as trellis posts: trellis at right holds beans; cucumbers and melons were already harvested.

ach will be ready to harvest before they are crowded out by the slower-growing plants.

Plant quick-maturing plants like radishes, beans, and carrots in succession so you can harvest several crops in one season. Plant intensively in blocks or wide rows.

Plant at the correct season. Fertilize and water consistently so plants grow vigorously. Keep vegetables picked—daily during peak season—so more will grow. Don't waste space on diseased or overmature plants.

WHAT CAN YOU GROW IN 30 SQUARE FEET?

We decided to find out. Bud Stuckey, who tends the *Sunset* test garden in Menlo Park, California, designed the raised bed and trellis system pictured above to make use of every inch of space—including trellises for pole beans, cucumbers, and melons. First-time gardener Susan Hobson Dormitzer planted and tended the garden for a season.

"My grandfather spent hours tending his big garden," she explains, "so I always thought having a vegetable garden was a Herculean adventure. But I found that it doesn't have to be an all-consuming hobby."

Since Dormitzer works five days a week, she couldn't give the garden a lot of time. She spent 1 to 1½ hours planting it, then about an hour every other weekend throughout the growing season for maintenance. During the week, she needed only 10 to 15 minutes a day to water and harvest vegetables—a job she could do in office clothes.

Dormitzer attributes much of her success to the fertile soil. Before she planted, Stuckey amended it with compost, chicken manure, and redwood soil conditioner. Later, plants were fertilized weekly with fish emulsion.

She chose vegetable varieties that are known for their flavor and productivity: one plant each of 'Ambrosia' melon, Japanese eggplant, 'Sunburst' squash, and yellow cherry tomato; two each of

NORMAN A. PLATE

'Jalapeño' chili pepper, 'Lemon' cucumbers, and yellow bell peppers; and a row of 'Blue Lake' pole beans. She filled in with green and purple basil, lettuce, and thyme and, for color, ageratum and marigolds.

The experience wasn't without failures. The squash tried to take over the garden, so Dormitzer pruned off leaves to keep them from shading other plants. "It was *too* prolific. I would rather have more melons, peppers,

(Continued on page 90)

Which vegetables to grow in small spaces? Here's advice

We asked avid gardeners, including extension specialists and vegetable growers, what they would grow if they had limited space. Here is their advice. Numbers after named varieties correspond with seed suppliers listed at bottom right.

Beans

"My standard is 'Blue Lake' [2, 3]. Yellow 'Romano' [3] has stupendous flavor if not overcooked, but is less productive." *—Rosalind Creasy, author of Cooking from the Garden*

"In the long run, pole beans are more productive than bush beans. Scarlet runner beans, with attractive red flowers, are best in cooler areas."*—Wendy Krupnick, Shepherd's Garden Seeds*

Beets

"Baby beets such as 'Kleine Bol' ('Little Ball') [2, 3] are good at any stage."*—W. K.*

"Mix seeds of different-colored beets, then sow them in small blocks. Harvest young leaves for salads, the beets when they're about 1 inch in diameter."*—R. C.*

Broccoli

"Sprouting types such as 'Mercedes' [3] are practical for small gardens because they allow harvest of small quantities over a long season."*—W. K.*

Carrots

"Mix 1 radish seed to 4 carrot seeds ('Chantenay' or 'Nantes') and plant in one row. The radishes will be up and gone by the time the carrots start growing." *—Shepherd Ogden, The Cook's Garden seed company*

Corn

"I recommend 'Early Sunglow' [2, 3]. It produces two or three ears on a 4½-foot stalk. For baby corn, pick as soon as they show silk. They're wonderful steamed, stir-fried, or pickled."*—W. K.*

Cucumber

" 'Salad Bush' [2, 3] makes full-size slicing cucumbers on a vine that spreads to 2 feet. Train it inside a small wire cage." *—Nona Koivula, All-America Selections*

"Cucumbers like to grow vertically. 'Lemon' cucumber [1, 3] is always good; another favorite is 'Kidma' [3]."*—W. K.*

Eggplant

"One of my favorites is 'Osterei' [1]. It makes white egg-size fruits."*—S. O.*

"Eggplants take a long time to mature; start with good-size transplants. 'Agora' [3] is prolific."*—W. K.*

Greens

"Mixed baby greens are the best crop for a small garden. You harvest quickly, and over a long season. I mix seeds of bok choy, chard, baby spinach, lettuces, and mizuna, then sow seeds over a 2-foot-square area. Harvest with scissors."*—R. C.*

"Lettuce is great because it will grow for such a long time. 'Reine des Glaces' [1] is a full-flavored Batavian. Of the romaines, I recommend 'Rouge d'Hiver' [1, 3]."*—R. C.*

"The best spinach is 'Melody' [2]. It's dependable and flavorful. I scatter seeds in blocks, not rows, and use thinnings in salads."*—R. C.*

Peas

"Edible-pod kinds are most space-efficient. I like 'Super SugarMel' [2, 3]."*—W. K.*

Peppers

"My favorite is 'Corno di Toro' [1, 3]. Plants are productive; peppers are huge and sweet."*—Elizabeth Berry, Galina Canyon Ranch Produce*

" 'Poblano' chilies [3] are best. They have an intense flavor."*—R. C.*

Potatoes

"The trick with potatoes is to grow a small amount and leave them in the ground until you're ready to use them."*—R. C.*

Pumpkin

"They're hardly small plants, but two are suited to small gardens: 'Jack Be Little' [1, 2], which bears 3- to 4-ounce pumpkins, and new 'Baby Bear' [1, 2, 3], which bears 1½- to 2-pound fruits. Train vines up a trellis."*—N. K.*

Radish

"I plant 'Easter Egg II' [1, 2, 3]. Each one is a differently colored surprise when you pull them up."*—R. C.*

Squash

"Most aren't too practical where space is limited, but vining 'Zucchetta Rampicante' [3] is good for small spaces because it can ramble up a trellis."*—W. K.*

"Plant only one hill of squash, but more than one variety. Harvest them all as babies."*—S. O.*

Tomatoes

"In limited spaces, plant compact, bush-type 'Chello' [3]. It produces yellow cherry tomatoes."*—W. K.*

"Try growing 'Sweet 100' [1, 2, 3] in an 18-inch pot at the base of a drainpipe, then tie stems to the pipe as it grows."*—S. O.*

Sources

1. *The Cook's Garden*, Box 535, Londonderry, VT 05148. 2. *Park Seed Co.*, Cokesbury Rd., Greenwood, SC 29647; 3. *Shepherd's Garden Seeds*, 6116 Highway 9, Felton, CA 95018.

By Michael MacCaskey

Patio arbor supports rambunctious vines

Fuzzy gourds, used in Chinese cooking, grow through and over the patio arbor in Tina and Al Lee's Westminster, California, garden.

CHAD SLATTERY

DAVID LANSING

RUSS A. WIDSTRAND

Trellis adds 6½ feet of vertical growing space

To take advantage of vertical space in a 3-foot-wide bed along the back edge of her Orange, California, garden, Nellie Brogle trains beans up trellises made of 1¼-inch redwood (left). Expansion bolts attach trellises to block wall; they extend a couple of inches from the wall to provide air circulation.

Lattice supports pumpkin vine, hides compost

Vining pumpkin on decorative lattice conceals a compost bin against garage wall. Lattice bin is lined with chicken wire; it opens from the side. Design: David Lansing, Newport Beach, California.

Where else to find space for vegetables? Along a wall or overhead

and cucumbers. They're good investments in space."

Powdery mildew was a problem, especially toward season's end. But the small garden yielded enough produce to feed her and her husband, with extras for friends.

FINDING SPACE FOR VEGETABLES

If your growing space is so limited that you can't accommodate even a raised bed, you may be able to find space for a few crops along a wall or patio. Stroll through your garden and seek out wasted spaces. Do you have a narrow strip between the garage and the house, a planting bed bordering a pathway, or space for an arbor over a walkway? Consider extending a low garden wall with trellises, which create valuable vertical growing space for vining and sprawling plants like beans, cucumbers, and tomatoes.

By attaching trellises to an existing block wall along the back border of her property (pictured above), veteran gardener Nellie Brogle grows enough beans and cucumbers in her 10-foot-long, 3-foot-wide garden to keep her family and neighbors well supplied, and she still has plenty left for canning (98 quarts of cucumbers one season). "A small space will produce tremendously, if you take care of it," says Brogle.

The trellis above right supports a pumpkin vine and hides a small compost pile in an otherwise wasted space next to the house. "Nothing is more fun than making compost," says Lansing, "and the plants respond immediately when you use it."

SPEAKING OF COMPOST . . .

It's not always easy to find space for it in a small garden. But a compost pile puts garden waste to work—creating a ready supply of beneficial amendment and mulch. To serve your garden well, it can be as small as 3 feet high and 3 feet wide. ■

By Lauren Bonar Swezey, Lynn Ocone

BILL REITZEL

CLOSE-UP *shows flowers that continually make impatiens the top seller.*

Impatiens: the easy garden show-off

For 25 years a garden mainstay, it's now number one bedding plant

DOES ANYONE NEED an introduction to the flower producer shown here? It's *Impatiens wallerana,* now the top-selling bedding plant in America. It does everything well and asks little. This month, in recognition of its 25th year of popularity (before that, it was relatively obscure), we tell of nine kindnesses that these shade-loving plants and the gardeners who tend them have come to expect from each other spring through fall.

Selection. Today you can choose from numerous strains and series, shades of every color except yellow and true blue, single and double flowers from the size of a dime to that of a silver dollar, and plants 8 to 20 inches high. Buy them by the color and size you want rather than by name; different growers often give different names to plants that are essentially the same.

Landscape use. Single-flowered kinds make the biggest splash in beds and borders. Double-flowered kinds aren't as showy en masse; plant them in pots. Both kinds combine well with begonias, ferns, fuchsias, and hydrangeas.

How much midsummer shade? Give them a minimum of 2 hours on the coast, 6 in inland valleys, 8 to 10 in the mountains and deserts.

Spacing. Plant dwarf varieties about 6 inches apart, big guys 12 inches apart. Adjoining plants of different varieties and heights always manage to develop into an unbroken, softly contoured leaf-and-flower surface.

Pests. Aphids and mites have been recorded; use diazinon. Snails use impatiens as daytime dormitories and can feed on seedlings.

Fertilizing. Feed often enough to keep plants vigorous, plump, and sassy; use a complete fertilizer. Plot intervals according to how long vigor continues after each application. In frost-free climates where impatiens will grow year-round, reduce or eliminate feeding in winter.

Watering. If a tree supplies the needed shade, its roots may steal moisture; water extra there. In containers or in the ground, timely watering recovers drooping impatiens.

Seed heads. Petals fall to reveal seed pods shaped like little footballs. When ripe, they'll burst in your hand with a muscular twitching motion you don't expect from the plant kingdom. Self-scattered seeds of single-flowered varieties sprout and grow if soil is wet enough.

Cutting back. It's a tonic. Any time during the growing season, you can cut back impatiens as close as 6 inches from the ground. New growth emerges in a few days; flowers cover it in two weeks. ■

By Joseph F. Williamson

IMPATIENS *bloom during summer and fall in Golden Gate Park, San Francisco.*

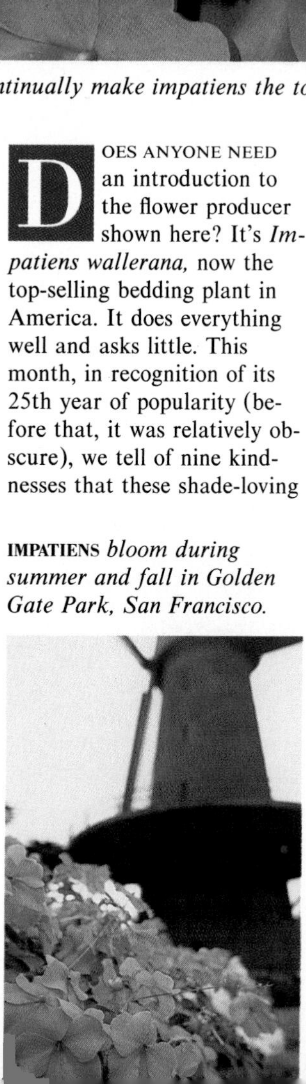

DISPLAYING VERSATILITY, *impatiens fill hanging basket, pots, and beds.*

LINDA YOUNKER

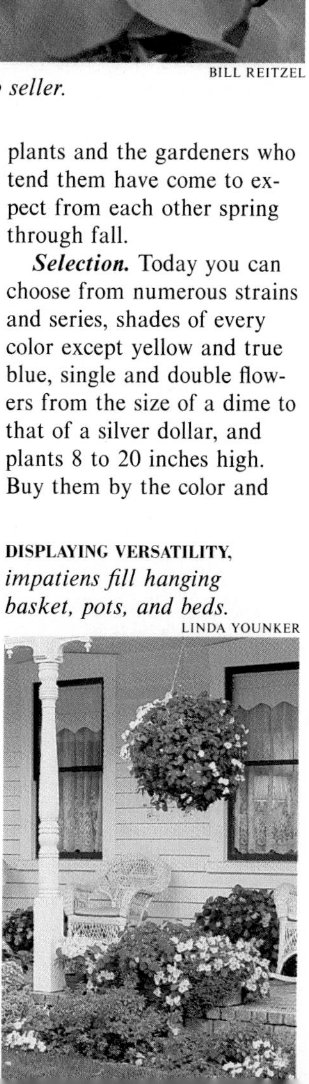

Saguaros on the sofa

Beautiful things happen when indoors and outdoors work together

By Lynn Ocone

LIKE AN OUTPOST IN THE WILDERNESS, THE RANCHO MIRAGE, California, garden of interior designer Steve Chase gives respite from the sun, yet is open to the untamed desert at its edge. In an intriguing interplay, manmade spaces mesh with the natural desert.

Areas immediately surrounding the house are formal extensions of the interior. These outdoor rooms, a pergola off the library, and manicured garden beds filled with bold, textural plants are designed for viewing from both indoors and out. Pebble and rock paths, flanked by cholla and saguaro cactus and palo verde trees, lead from these manicured areas to the wild-looking landscape beyond, where sunlight plays over more casual plantings.

"I want the garden to look wild, but to cooperate with the formal geometric architecture of the house," Chase says. Order and formality characterize

PETER CHRISTIANSEN

CRAGGY PEAK *and stately saguaros (far left) create a majestic backdrop for outdoor room, off the living room. Beds (above left) break expanse of aggregate patio; rock paths (above right) lead from patio to wildlike plantings.*

STACKED SANDSTONE *makes handsome outdoor table (left). In flamboyant gazebo (right), cast-cement furniture capped with broken tile contrasts with serene landscape beyond.*

"I want the garden to look wild, but to cooperate with the house design."

LIKE SURFACING BUBBLES, *barrel cactus, interspersed with ocotillo in this formal courtyard planting (left), shape views from inside the house and out. Magenta verbena illuminates spring garden (below).*

PETER CHRISTIANSEN

the outdoor rooms: furnishings of cast cement are bold and blocky, planting beds contained by poured aggregate paving are geometric, and barrel cactus are planted in lines. But Chase preserved the desert aesthetic in the 10-year-old garden with his choice of colors, textures, and materials that harmonize with the desert's sand, stone, and vegetation.

Though gardening in this wild slice of desert poses unique challenges—not the least of which is seriously armed plants—it offers its own rewards. Among them are the unsurpassed views of the majestic Santa Rosa Mountains towering beyond, bats sipping nectar from saguaro blossoms at dusk, and parched land that explodes into spring green following winter rain. Chase feels his garden's strength is visual, and his greatest pleasure is the tremendous serenity that it brings.

"There's a fine line between *looking* wild and being wild," he says. "People think my garden is low maintenance because it looks natural. But the look requires constant maintenance. The cactus have minds of their own. They outgrow their bounds. They lean when I intend them to grow straight. I have to move plants, rescale, and trim."

Chase says it's not a garden to play in, but evidence of his wit and artistry suggests it's a garden he enjoys playing with. Bold color and fanciful mosaic-tiled furniture electrify the dining gazebo. But even this assertive design is tempered by the natural landscape beyond, which partial glass-block walls both keep at bay and integrate visually.

The garden is a stage for Chase's outdoor art collection; sculptures, stone and metal artifacts, and natural objects like the stacked flagstone table (pictured above) are displayed and enjoyed. ■

DOUGLAS BOND

LESSONS FOR ROCK GARDENERS FROM THE ULTIMATE ROCK GARDEN

• **Keep the proportion of rock to plants high.**

Look closely here and on the facing page: the most eye-catching visual element in this garden is stone, which is used flat or crushed for paths, in large slabs for stairs and seating, and also to line the stream and pond.

• **Salt steep slopes with plenty of large, flat-topped rocks.**

Use them to climb, sit, or stand on (as below) while you work in the garden. This trick can make the most formidable-looking rockeries easy to plant and maintain.

A rock garden to end all rock gardens

On Vashon Island, it recalls the natural art of the Washington Cascades

HIGH ART? YES, landscape designer T. M. Holtschlag decided, the alpine plants and rocks of the Washington Cascades are high art, and well worth mimicking in the lowlands. Holtschlag designed this rock garden on Vashon Island, Washington, for his parents, Peggy and Ralph Holtschlag, and the result is a superlative blend of plants and stone (125 tons at last count) that calls to mind the mountains above.

Before the garden went in, the Holtschlags looked out onto a steep, dry, salal-covered bank. Now the view takes in running water, stone,

DOUGLAS BOND

and a profusion of alpine plants that push up out of fissures, mold into rock hollows, and flow like lava over beds of scree (shalelike gravel).

Apart from its obvious scale and expense—not everyone wants the *ultimate* rock garden—this landscape has lessons that translate into any rock garden, of any size.

Most kinds of alpines look best in spring and summer. Look for them in nurseries now, and plant anytime between now and fall. Water new plants well. ■

By Jim McCausland

JIM McCAUSLAND

• Choose plants to fit the rockwork, not the reverse.

Saxifrages, sedums, and other rock garden plants pack the cracks and fill pockets in the stone. Taller shrubs (like the tree heath pushing up above the candytuft at left) and perennials fit among larger rocks and in vertical cracks. Spreading plants like evergreen candytuft, heather, prostrate juniper, and lithodora grow in scree here, where they spread as they might in alpine meadows.

• Leave dirt to dirt gardeners.

One reason for this garden's success is that, while it shows plenty of rock, plants, water, and sky, almost no soil is visible. Even the flat areas are covered with scree (see the path beyond the girl at left).

• Be fanatic about weed control at first, and you'll have little to worry about later.

To further discourage weeds from coming up in paths, Holtschlag put a layer of landscaping fabric under the scree.

NORMAN A. PLATE

'GOLDEN ROSETTE' COREOPSIS *is an annual daisy with 1½-inch flowers and ferny foliage.*

Daisy standouts—from seed

Sow these 10 now for summer color

THE DAISY FAMILY of flowers is made up of dozens of species that vary widely in plant form and flower color. Started this month from seed, daisies deliver a lot of summer color without draining your budget or drinking much water.

The 10 daisies described here were among the top performers selected from 36 drought-tolerant varieties in testing by UC Cooperative Extension in Santa Cruz County. Plants were evaluated on form, length of bloom time, ease of care, and resistance to disease and insects.

Coreopsis (*C. stillmanii* 'Golden Rosette'). Mounding plant to 1 foot; yellow 1½-inch flowers; ferny deep green foliage.

Creeping zinnia (*Sanvitalia procumbens* 'Mandarin Orange'). Compact ground cover 4 to 6 inches tall, spreading to 1 foot or more; orange-yellow ½-inch flowers with deep brown centers.

Dahlberg daisy (*Dyssodia tenuiloba*). Plants form neat mounds to 1 foot tall and 2 feet across; bright yellow 1-inch flowers; ferny foliage.

Feverfew (*Chrysanthemum parthenium*). Ferny foliage to 2 feet, covered with white ¾-inch flowers; self-sowing.

Fleabane (*Erigeron* 'Blue Beauty'). Foliage grows in a neat rosette to 8 inches; purple 1½-inch flowers with yellow centers.

Gloriosa daisy (*Rudbeckia hirta* 'Green Eyes' or 'Irish Eyes'). Upright plant to 2½ feet; golden yellow 4- to 5-inch flowers with olive green centers.

Mexican sunflower (*Tithonia rotundifolia* 'Goldfinger'). Upright, dense plant to 3 to 4 feet; red-orange 3-inch flowers; velvety blue-green foliage.

Monarch of the Veldt (*Venidium fastuosum* 'Zulu Prince'). Mounding plant to 2 feet; creamy white 4-inch flowers with black centers; gray-green foliage.

Palm Springs daisy (*Cladanthus arabicus*). Compact mounding plant to 1½ feet; golden 1½- to 2-inch flowers; feathery gray-green foliage.

Purple coneflower (*Echinacea purpurea*). Upright plant to 4 to 5 feet; 3½- to 4½-inch blooms ('Bravado' has lavender pink petals; 'White Swan' has fragrant greenish white flowers).

Seed sources. Nurseries may sell seeds for some of the varieties listed here. Seeds of six of the named varieties are available by mail from Thompson & Morgan, (800) 274-7333. Another source is Park Seed Co., (800) 845-3369.

How to sow daisies. Plan to sow seeds directly in the ground. The daisies listed prefer well-drained soil and full sun (feverfew, gloriosa daisy, and purple coneflower tolerate light shade, especially in hot inland areas).

Before sowing, prepare the soil by loosening the top 6 to 8 inches and mix in a complete granular fertilizer (10-10-10). Add compost or other organic matter if the soil is heavy clay, gravelly, or sandy. Rake soil smooth, then scatter seeds. (Follow directions on the seed packet for sowing depth and spacing.) Cover seeds lightly with soil. For best germination, water and keep soil moist. When seedlings have two or three pairs of leaves, thin plants to desired spacing. Water young plants regularly until they are established. ■

By Emely Lincowski

PALM SPRINGS DAISY *has fragrant 1½- to 2-inch flowers, feathery foliage.*

MONARCH OF THE VELDT *'Zulu Prince' has striking 4-inch flowers, deeply lobed leaves. Plants reach 2 feet.*

DOTTED LINES *show where to cut a rose at different times during the growing season.*

LUCY I. SARGEANT

Keep your roses blooming . . . by cutting them properly

APRIL MARKS THE beginning of the payoff season for year-long rose care as the queen of flowers unfurls her first colorful blooms of the year. While some gardeners are content to enjoy the shapely blooms in the garden, others pursue long-stemmed beauties to use in bouquets.

If you are among the second group, these guidelines for cutting hybrid teas, offered by Keith Zary, hybridizer and director of rose research at Jackson & Perkins, should help you get long-stemmed cut flowers without compromising the plant's continued growth, shapeliness, and productivity.

Each time you cut a stem, you remove leaves that manufacture nutrients for the plant. Newly planted rose bushes, and those that are weak or small, need all their leaves for plant growth. Zary's guidelines are for established, healthy plants that can spare some leaves.

Depending on your climate, your roses may get two to five bloom cycles (the longer your growing season, the more cycles you can expect). When you cut flowers during the first bloom cycles, in spring and early summer, Zary recommends leaving at least two five-leaflet leaves (as shown in the drawing at left) on the branch you cut the flower from. Cutting above the leaf node will force one or two new canes to grow from that node.

RUSS A. WIDSTRAND

AT PEAK SEASON, *cut under the hook to get extra-long-stemmed roses.*

By mid- to late summer, when plants have plenty of food-manufacturing foliage, it's possible to cut extra-long stems like the one indicated. Make the cut "under the hook" (where the offshoot of new growth joins the older cane below a previous cut) and just above an outward-facing node. You can leave just one five-leaflet leaf on the remaining stem.

Continue cutting extra-long-stemmed roses up to the second to last bloom cycle in your region (late October or early November in mildest-winter regions). Thereafter, cut shorter stems, leaving two five-leaflet leaves.

Toward the end of the growing season, as days shorten and light is limited, plants need to manufacture as much food as possible to store in stems and roots for use early the next spring before leaves are present.

CARE DURING THE GROWING SEASON

Roses are hungry and fairly thirsty plants. For vigorous growth and abundant blooms, they need water at all times during the growing season; water deeply to moisten the entire root system. To help save water, improve soil, and minimize weeds, spread a 2- to 3-inch layer of mulch on the soil at the base of your plants.

Your first fertilizer application in late winter or spring should coincide with the onset of new growth. For subsequent feedings, apply a complete fertilizer when a bloom period has come to an end and the next cycle is just beginning.

Check plants for pests and diseases during the growing season. For recommended controls, ask your nursery. ■

By Lynn Ocone

BRIGHT YELLOW *sunroses are difficult to resist.*

RED SUNROSES *brighten entry garden of blue bellflowers and pinks.*

DARROW M. WATT

Showy sunroses add zest to spring gardens

See, choose, plant, and enjoy them, all this month

CASCADING brilliantly over walls, rocks, or anywhere you want color, sunroses (*Helianthemum*) add to a garden what a strong spice adds to a meal: zest and pungency. They put on a big show in spring and continue to bloom, though less splashily, over several months. And when the colors depart, the 6- to 8-inch plants (spreading to 3 feet) display neat green or gray foliage year-round.

Sunroses are growing in popularity in the West because they need water only two or three times a month in summer. They're flowering at nurseries now in 1-gallon pots (priced at $4 to $8). Choose your colors—varieties include orange 'Prima Donna', yellow 'Wisley Primrose', pink 'Rose', and white 'St. Mary's'—and set out plants now, too.

Pick a sunny spot with good drainage; plants won't do well with lots of water. If you are combining them with shrubs or other flowers, just make sure those don't need much water either, or you'll have healthy sunroses but parched neighbors. For a ground cover, space plants 2 to 3 feet apart.

Then watch the sunrose: within days, clusters of 1-inch blossoms will cover the low mounds. Though each lasts only a day, flowers should open through June (later in the Northwest), with scattered bloom all summer. To encourage repeat flowering in fall and keep plants tidy, shear after spring bloom. ■

By Emely Lincowski

SUNROSES COME *in many colors—such as 'Wine' (left) and striped 'Raspberry Ripple' (right)—besides pink and yellow.*

EMELY LINCOWSKI

DARROW M. WATT

ARBOR DAY *poster art conveys nuances of timber politics, an unusual subject for a second-grade artist.*

HIGH SCHOOL *students advise younger ones on how to get their trees from pot to ground.*

COMMUNITY ACTION

New ardor for Arbor Day

Second graders in Livermore, California, try their hands at suburban foresting

AT A TIME WHEN native stands of trees are shrinking because of logging and urban encroachment, the simple act of planting a seedling has taken on new meaning. So, too, it seems, has the observance of Arbor Day.

For the past two years, Livermore, California, has combined a planting celebration with an Arbor Day program designed to instill respect for trees in the people who will be around the longest to enjoy them: children in elementary schools.

AT AGE 6 OR 7, THEY EACH ADOPT A TREE

Livermore's celebration, organized by a local beautification committee, made trees a part of Livermore's second-grade curriculum—and each second grader's life. Last year, the Davey Tree Surgery Co. and Livermore Rotary Club donated a total of 1,400 seedlings of Chinese elm, crape myrtle, and redwood. Each child became the parent of a single tree, planting it near his or her home and taking responsibility for its care.

Of course, the kids weren't the only ones involved: they could not adopt until an adult signed a "contract" with the school promising to help take good care of the tree. Meanwhile, high school students in horticulture classes and members of a local garden club were recruited to teach the youngsters how to handle, plant, and take care of their seedlings.

Finally, classroom teachers incorporated a one-week curriculum on trees, based on one prepared by the Alameda County Resource Conservation District. It covered trees and their relationships to animals, other plants, and the environment. Teachers added poems, songs, and art projects about trees and had children create posters expressing what they had learned.

SOWING THE SEEDS OF A TRADITION

What did Livermore gain from the program? Besides 1,400 new trees and an Arbor Day tree-planting tradition, the city might have sown the seeds of a generation in love with trees. Said Michelle Ridolfi, a former Livermore High School student who helped some second-grade tree planters, "They seemed really happy to be responsible for giving a tree life." ■

By Emely Lincowski

MAY

Garden guide........................103
May checklists 110
Perennials come back 114
"Natural" fertilizers...........121
What sweet corn's best?.......122

Sunset's GARDEN GUIDE

K. BRYAN SWEZEY

It's bean-planting time

BRIGHT BLUE SKIES AND WARM TEMPERATURES ARE SURE SIGNS THAT it's peak planting time for warm-season vegetables like 'Blue Lake' beans, shown here growing on an A-frame trellis (described on page 104). It's also transition time for flowers: as cool-season annuals fade, interplant with flowers that thrive in summer conditions. If a hot spell hits while plants are becoming established, keep them well watered and shade them temporarily with cloth or a board. As weather warms, the rest of the garden will also need watering.

NORMAN A. PLATE

DOUBLE-FLOWERED *'Teddy Bear' sunflower forms clusters of 6-inch-wide yellow blooms on 2-foot-tall plants.*

Sunflowers step out from the back border

Traditional sunflowers are fine if you have space for 10-foot giants. But for smaller gardens or border fronts, you can choose from several dwarf varieties.

Music Box is a mix of dwarf sunflowers (to 28 inches tall) with 4- to 5-inch-wide single flowers in colors from yellow cream to mahogany red. 'Sunspot' has 8- to 10-inch-wide flowers that look similar to the old-fashioned giants, but on plants only 18 to 24 inches tall.

'Teddy Bear', shown at right, produces very full 6-inch-wide pom-pom blooms. The plant grows only 2 feet tall. New 'Orange Sun' has double apricot-orange blooms on 3½-foot plants.

Sunflowers are easy to grow. Sow seeds in place, and water regularly. Flowers appear in late summer and fall.

You can order seeds of these kinds from Thompson & Morgan, Box 1308, Jackson, NJ 08527; (908) 363-2225. The catalog is free.

K. BRYAN SWEZEY

COLORFUL SUCCULENTS *tumble from 8-inch-wide pots. In front is round-leafed Cotyledon orbiculata with Senecio mandraliscae cascading below. Cotyledon undulata grows in rear pot.*

Pots of succulents thrive with little water

Succulents make handsome arrangements in containers. And most types require only minimal water and care.

The ones shown below grow in landscape designer Chole Morgan's coastal mountainside garden in California. Since the garden can reach 90° to 100° in summer, the pots are kept in an area that gets morning sun and afternoon shade.

The succulents are watered about once a week in summer. Too much water rots them; too little and leaves will shrivel.

Look for succulents at specialty nurseries. Or you can order by mail from K & L Cactus & Succulent Nursery, 9500 Brook Ranch Rd., Ione, CA 95640, (209) 274-0360 (catalog $2; refundable with first order); or Cactus Unlimited, 21030 Gardena Dr., Cupertino, CA 95014, (408) 257-1047 (catalog $2.50).

A-frame trellis supports 'Blue Lake' beans

To produce a bumper crop, pole beans like 'Blue Lake' need strong, upright support. One attractive trellis, pictured on page 103, supports beans at Crow Canyon Institute in San Ramon, California.

We've adapted this 15-foot-long trellis to one 6 feet long—the best size for most home gardens. Four 7-foot 1-by-1s (each pair forming an A-frame) make up the trellis's end supports; for stability, the 1-by-1s were sunk 6 inches into the ground.

Between the A-frames, three 1-by-1s function as horizontal stretchers, one across the top, one along each bottom side. The bottom crosspieces, each attached about 8 inches up from the ground and overlapping the vertical supports by about 1½ inches, were secured with 1¼-inch nails. The top crosspiece rests in Xs formed near the top of the supports and also overhangs each one by 1½ inches; twine secures the crosspiece.

To allow the vines to climb, twine was strung between the top and bottom pieces; it wraps around 1-inch nails pounded every 6 to 8 inches halfway into both sides of the top crosspiece and into the outsides of the bottom two crosspieces. Start and end the row of nails about 2 inches from each end of the crosspieces.

To steady the trellis, a 7½-foot-long piece of rope was tied around each end of the top crosspiece to a 1-by-2 stake pounded into the soil about 1½ feet out from each end of the trellis. Nails near the top of each stake keep the twine from slipping off.

What causes flower drop from citrus trees?

Just because your citrus tree's blossoms drop like rain in spring doesn't mean there's something drastically wrong with the tree.

Citrus trees produce an overabundance of flowers and couldn't possibly sustain all of them if they were to develop into fruit (less than 1 percent of a tree's flowers ever mature into fruit). During the bloom stage, trees naturally shed most of what they can't support.

But they still retain more flowers than they can support later. So trees have a second shed, called June drop (in June or July), when tiny fruits drop off the tree. This allows the remaining fruit to mature to full size. Once fruits reach about an inch in diameter, they usually stay on the tree.

If your tree sheds all of its fruit, the problem could be cultural or weather-related.

The tree could be too young (1 to 2 years old)

to support fruit. A sudden heat spell (up to 110°) when soil is dry can also cause fruit drop. And trees that are regularly underwatered or deficient in nutrients may drop much or all of their fruit (especially if they grow in containers).

ANDY AND SALLY WASOWSKI

MASSES OF WHITE FLOWERS *like little stars cover desert plumbago in spring. Use this shrub-vine as a ground cover in shady areas.*

Desert plumbago: handsome, but tough

In the wild, desert plumbago *(P. scandens)* grows in Pinal and Pima counties, particularly in the canyons of the Santa Rita Mountains at elevations between 2,500 and 4,000 feet. Now, this Arizona native is available to southwest gardeners. Masses of white flowers, good shade and sun tolerance, and all-around hardiness make it a choice plant for southwest gardens.

Desert plumbago grows to 3 feet high and then sprawls, eventually making a 6-foot-diameter clump. Oblong leaves are about 4 inches long. Masses of white, ½-inch-diameter flowers (see photo above) come in late spring. A few flowers come through summer, followed by another burst in fall. Though the plant grows well in shade, it will produce fewer flowers. Seed pods are sticky enough to cling to clothes and pets.

Plants freeze to the soil at about 22° but renew themselves quickly in spring. If a hard freeze doesn't kill them back, their leaves turn an attractive purple during cold weather. Pruning is necessary only to keep the plants in bounds.

Though desert plumbago is very drought tolerant in shady areas, it needs regular irrigation in full sun. Plants are now available in some southwest nurseries in 1- and 5-gallon cans ($7 and $14, respectively).

CRUSTY CLAY POTS *like the one shown at left look like new when coated with linseed oil (as the one at right was).*

NORMAN A. PLATE

Linseed oil makes clay pots look like new

If your clay pots are crusted with white (from accumulated salts and mineral deposits) and caked with dirt and grime, the following technique, developed by Bud Stuckey for *Sunset*'s test garden, will give them new life. Linseed oil is the magic potion; you rub it into the pots' exteriors.

A stiff brush and a little elbow grease help, especially if the crusts are thick. Remove as much of the crusts as you can with water and the brush. Then allow the pots to dry for several hours. (If a pot just has a thin white film, you don't need to brush it off before applying the oil.)

Use a cloth to wipe the linseed oil over the outside of the pots. Don't skimp on oil. Let the pots sit for an hour or so. If the oil soaks in and the pots have dry patches, apply a second coat.

A mosquito repellent you can grow?

Perhaps. Citrosa is its name, and its parentage is unique. This plant, recently introduced in California, was literally created from two unrelated plants—rose-scented geranium *(Pelargonium graveolens)* and citronella grass *(Cymbopogon nardus)*—by a high-tech process called protoplast fusion.

According to the plant's creators, combining the two plants—both naturally rich in fragrant oils—resulted in this one that's extraordinarily rich in citronella oil, a traditional mosquito repellent.

Does citrosa ward off mosquitoes? Some gardeners say yes; others aren't so sure. The citrus fragrance is most pronounced when the plant is brushed, but the creators say that the leaves constantly release tiny amounts of citronella that are detectable by mosquitoes but not by people.

Whether it works or not, citrosa is an attractive plant; it looks like a robust rose-scented geranium with lobed, slightly fuzzy leaves. Plants can grow to 5 feet tall in a season. Plant citrosa in a container with room for vigorous growth—at least 10 inches in diameter—or plant in the ground. Give it afternoon shade. Roots aren't fussy about soil, as long as it drains well.

If you'd like to give citrosa a try, it's available in retail nurseries. For sources and growing advice, call Bailey's Nursery in Lodi, California, at (800) 888-6149. A 4-inch pot costs about $9. One mature plant per 100 square feet is recommended for mosquito repellent.

Sunset's
GARDEN GUIDE

The long and short of wisteria blooms

Though wisteria is often spoken of as though it were one plant, it's really several, all in flower in April and May. Vigorous and almost impervious to cold, wisterias deserve their popularity; just be sure you know which one you're getting before you buy.

The commonest is the violet blue Chinese wisteria *(W. sinensis)*. It's popular for all-at-once bloom that occurs before leaves unfurl. It also comes in a white version *(W. s.* 'Alba'). Both kinds are sold as single or multitrunked vines or as small, single-trunked trees. All three forms result from simple training: anyone can take a young Chinese wisteria, stake it, and prune it into a tree.

The bloom of Japanese wisteria *(W. floribunda)* isn't as much a tour de force as that of its Chinese cousin because leaves and flowers open together, and flowers bloom sequentially (instead of all at once) from base to tip of the cluster. But clusters are half again as long as those of Chinese wisteria and come in blue, white, lavender, pink, or purple, often marked with yellow and white. They're also more fragrant than Chinese wisteria flowers.

One Japanese wisteria *(W. floribunda* 'Longissima') has especially long flower clusters. It's pictured at right.

Both kinds of wisteria are common in nurseries. Buy grafted varieties (look for obvious swelling at the base of the plant or ask your nursery). These flower earlier than seedling-grown kinds.

Wisterias do well in an impressively wide range of climates, performing beautifully from the balmiest sections of the Southern California coast to the coldest parts of high-elevation snowy-winter regions (extreme winter cold may cause some damage to flower buds).

DON NORMARK

THE LONGER FLOWER CLUSTERS *of 'Longissima' Japanese wisteria set it apart. These are 1½ to 3 feet long.*

NORMAN A. PLATE

SEASIDE PLANTING *of pink and yellow seaside daisy, gray Eriophyllum staechadifolium, and 'Yankee Point' ceanothus in Carmel, California, withstands salt, sand, and wind.*

Plants that thrive in salt, sand, and wind

For plants to grow well near the beach, they've got to be tough. Beach soil is very sandy, so it retains little moisture. Wind blows almost constantly near the sea. And the salt spray and salty soil are enough to shrivel nearly any plant.

Some tough plants can take these inhospitable conditions, according to Denise Henry of the Forest and Beach Department of Carmel, California. These 12 plants can take a direct hit of sea spray and look great: bush morning glory, ceanothus, *Echium, Eriophyllum staechadifolium, Erysimum linifolium* 'Bowles Mauve', French lavender *(Lavandula dentata), Lavatera assurgentiflora*, myoporum (it can be damaged in a hard frost, but it grows back from the roots), Pacific Coast iris, rosemary, seaside daisy, and statice *(Limonium perezii)*.

Rockrose *(Cistus)* can't take salt spray. Protect it with a taller plant.

Plant your own flowering prairie

Call it black-eyed Susan, coneflower, gloriosa daisy, or just plain rudbeckia—it's all the same plant, *R. hirta*. Though it's native to the East, it grows well in the West.

To achieve the look of a flowering prairie in your own garden, sow the gloriosa daisy strain of *R. hirta* in regular garden soil that gets full sun. (It won't take soggy soil.) The seeds you plant this month will come up quickly, and a few will likely flower this fall. Most, however, will bloom next summer and fall. Some will flower for more than one year, and all will self-sow.

Single-flowered gloriosa daisy blooms are 5 to 7 inches across, while the doubles are about a third smaller. Colors are yellow, russet, orange, and mahogany with dark centers. Plants grow 3 to 4 feet tall. If you want shorter plants, try 'Marmalade' (tops out at 2 feet) or 'Goldilocks' (to 10 inches tall).

Leave faded flowers on the plant to ripen seed for the birds and to start future generations of daisies

DAVID STUBBS

OLD-FASHIONED HOLLYHOCKS *stand out against a log wall, where they'll bloom July through frost.*

Queen of the mallows

Some plants seem place-specific: while they can grow almost everywhere, they're unparalleled in certain regions. For hollyhocks *(Alcea rosea)*, prime growing area runs from the Sierra-Cascades east to the Rockies.

Old-fashioned single hollyhocks like the ones pictured at right are at their best stretching skyward against a wall or fence, but breeders seem to have it in for tall plants in general. They know our gardens have less space but forget that we have just as much height as ever.

Newer hollyhocks are selected for double flowers, exotic colors, and shorter stature (and no stakes).

Try one of the classic tall single varieties (sometimes sold as 'Single Mixed') for 5-foot spires of pink, rose, white, and carmine. Sown this month, this biennial will give you a few flowers this year, the main crop in 15 months. Another good single is *A. r.* 'Nigra', whose bloom is almost black (a hollyhock color popular early this century).

Or plant Chater's Double (a perennial also sold as Fordhook Giants) for double flowers in several colors, including yellow and apricot.

Plant either in full sun and well-draining, rich soil.

One mail-order source of hollyhocks, including singles and Chater's Double, is Thompson & Morgan, Box 1308, Jackson, NJ 08527; the catalog is free.

Bellwethers for mildew: roses and yuccas?

If you travel through the vineyard country of the West, you'll occasionally see roses or yuccas planted at the ends of grape rows.

The French (and more recently, California vintners) have grown roses in their vineyards for generations, partly because they're beautiful, partly because they get powdery mildew more easily than grapes. When mildew showed up on roses, the French would spray the grapes.

Yuccas are grown for exactly the same reason: they're bellwethers.

Some years ago a Prosser, Washington, vintner brought this custom to eastern Washington by planting roses in his vineyard (others have since planted the yuccas as well). After he wrote the roses off on his taxes, the IRS investigated, and the grower successfully used the mildew-indicator argument to keep his deduction.

We wanted to know, deductions aside, how effective roses really are for this. Not very. "Anybody who relies on roses to tell him when to spray grapes just isn't very wise," says WSU extension agent Jack Watson. "For starters, the mildew that attacks Northwest grapes isn't the same kind that roses get. It's more realistic to just plant the roses because they're pretty."

Another good garden blue

Veronica hybrids are among the best fillers for perennial borders. They're almost impervious to insects and disease, and they're long-blooming. For that reason, the Perennial Plant Association made one of them, 'Sunny Border Blue', its plant of the year for 1993.

First hybridized about 40 years ago, the plant was thought to be lost soon after. But in the late 1970s it was rediscovered and reintroduced. *Veronica* 'Sunny Border Blue' is perfectly hardy and should grow well anywhere in the West, although it seems to be offered by retail nurseries mostly in the Pacific Northwest.

As the name implies, 'Sunny Border Blue' does best in full sun. Give it a spot with well-draining garden loam and regular water, and it will grow to almost 2 feet, with violet-blue flowers coming from spring through much of summer. Deadheading should prolong bloom.

A new source book for wildflowers

If you've ever thought of including more native plants in your garden, you should pick up a copy of the *National Wildflower Research Center's Wildflower Handbook* (Voyageur Press, Inc., Stillwater, MN, 1992; $15.95 postpaid).

Opening chapters cover the whys and hows of native gardening, seed collecting, seed buying, and propagating native seed, and the prose ends with a discussion about gardening to attract wildlife. Most of the book is given over to state-by-state listings of native seed and plant sources.

You'd most logically use this book to track down plants that grow wild in your own state, but you might also want to find sources of natives you grew up with in another state: For former Californians, there's Monterey cypress from Big Sur, for example, or toyon (the "holly" that gave its name to Hollywood).

There's also a list of native plant societies, government and conservation organizations that are involved with plants, and even landscape architects and designers who specialize in native plants.

You can order this book directly from the National Wildflower Research Center, 2600 FM 973 North, Austin, TX 78725.

Sunset's GARDEN GUIDE

New source for 'Cl. Iceberg' rose

Indeed, 'Iceberg' rose—that well known and much celebrated white-flowered floribunda—is one of the great roses of modern times. Its climbing form, shown at right, is just as beautiful as the bush form but often difficult to find for sale. A few retail nurseries have offered it in limited quantities, but, until recently, it has been even more difficult to get by mail.

Now, one mail-order source offers plants in 3-inch-wide by 6-inch-deep containers for $9.95 each, plus shipping ($1.25 per plant to California, $1.75 to Nevada). For a descriptive catalog, send $5 to Heirloom Old Garden Roses, 24062 N.E. Riverside Dr., St. Paul, OR 97137; (503) 538-1576. Order and plant now, before summer's heat sets in. Plants are slow to start climbing but vigorous once established. They're outstanding in large pots, as shown in the photograph above, or trained over an arbor.

RUSS A. WIDSTRAND

FLOWER-LADEN *canes of 'Cl. Iceberg' rose are trained to trellis. Design: Sandy Kennedy, Woodland Hills, California.*

CHAD SLATTERY

PINK FLOWERS *of Digitalis mertonensis bloom on 3-foot spikes in this San Clemente garden. Design: Rogers' Gardens.*

An elegant foxglove for your garden

The colorful perennial pictured at bottom left is *Digitalis mertonensis*, often called strawberry foxglove. This foxglove is a hybrid of common foxglove *(D. purpurea)* and *D. grandiflora.* Bell-shaped flowers, 2 inches long, are an unusual coppery pink; they bloom on 2- to 3-foot spikes starting in spring. Evergreen 6- to 8-inch leaves form an attractive rosette at the plant's base.

Plant it from seed or transplants now for bloom next spring. It prefers partial shade and moist, rich, fast-draining soil. Cut back main spikes after flowering, and smaller flowering shoots will bloom into summer. Dig and divide crowded clumps after they flower in spring or fall. Plants may self-sow; they come true from seed.

Strawberry foxglove looks best planted in groups of at least five. The color sometimes fights with other pinks, but it combines well with white or pastel blue flowers such as baby blue eyes. The flowers attract hummingbirds.

Look for strawberry foxglove in nurseries that offer good selections of perennials or order seeds from Thompson & Morgan (address in the first item on page 104).

How to avoid getting skunked

Skunks can be serious pests in home gardens; they often migrate to residential neighborhoods from nearby open land and adapt quite well to populated areas. While they're most notorious for their odorous encounters—often with household pets—skunks have other bad habits that take their toll on gardens. They dig holes in irrigated areas to search for grubs, and they may scatter compost piles or garbage as they look for food scraps.

Getting rid of skunks can be a smelly and costly proposition. Professional removal costs $45 to $150 per skunk. "The best way to get rid of a skunk is not to attract one to your property in the first place," says Vincent Lazaneo, horticulture adviser for UC Cooperative Extension in San Diego County.

Skunks are omnivores; they feed on everything from pet food to mice, fruit, and eggs. In the wild, skunks live in burrows, brush piles, hollow logs, and rock piles, but on your property, they could also live quite happily in or under buildings or decks or under piles of firewood, lumber, or debris.

To discourage them, Lazaneo suggests minimizing their food and shelter. Feed pets indoors. If you must feed them outdoors, don't leave the food out overnight. Harvest fruit and vegetables as soon as they ripen, and keep dropped fruit picked up. In lawns, control grubs that skunks feed on; use beneficial nematodes or consider chemicals such as diazinon. Store garbage in cans with tight lids, and don't add food scraps to an unenclosed compost pile.

To minimize their shelter, seal off holes in your foundation or in outbuildings and openings under decks. Contain or stack landscape materials so skunks can't burrow into the piles.

If skunks live in your garden and you need help trapping them, call your county agricultural office or a professional pest control operation. The type of assistance offered by the county varies from location to location.

Mexican honeysuckle

As a magnet for hummingbirds, with a long bloom season and an undemanding temperament, Mexican honeysuckle *(Justicia spicigera)* deserves a place in many southwest gardens where summers are very hot, and winter temperatures seldom drop below 15°.

As you see in the photograph at right, tubular orange flowers grow in clusters, mostly at the ends of the stems. Basic blooming season comes in spring, with somewhat of a repeat in late summer after monsoons. With supplemental water (one watering every 1 or 2 weeks through midsummer) flowers can form nearly year-round.

If left untrimmed, Mexican honeysuckle grows 2 to 3 feet tall in sun, 3 to 4 feet tall in partial shade. Cut it back to a few inches above the soil if frozen (28°); it will regrow in spring.

Plant in well-drained soil. Fertilize lightly in spring; use a complete fertilizer according to label directions. Pinch growing tips in spring to encourage bushy growth.

Mexican honeysuckle is widely available. Gallon-size plants cost about $5.

DON NORMARK

HERE'S THE MEXICAN HONEYSUCKLE *(also called firecracker plant) showing its mostly-in-spring flowers in the Phoenix garden of Steve and Cincy Leshin. Design: Carol Shuler.*

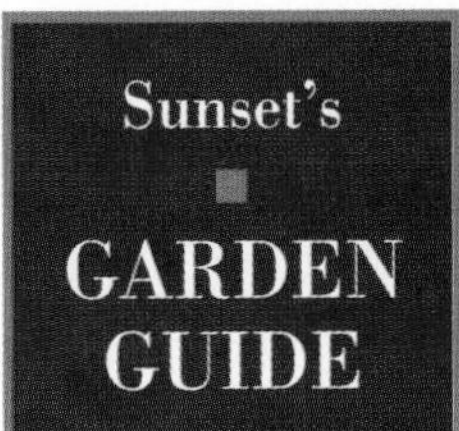

Javelinas are sloppy eaters. They bite a chunk of a cactus pad and strain it through their teeth, leaving long fibers hanging from the pad. These animals will also completely uproot plants that have fleshy roots.

Pack rats sit on top of a pad and nibble on an edge. They eat a couple of inches a night and come back to the same location several nights in a row.

Giant cactus beetles usually climb to the highest part of a cactus and gnaw on the top edge. They ultimately create scallop-shaped wounds in the pads.

Sunscreen for plants

To survive hot weather just ahead in the desert, many new transplants will need some shade. If you can't provide them with shadecloth or other protective devices, you can spray them with a sun-reflective coating. This liquid dries quickly, leaving a thin, white film on the plant's foliage.

This product, called Snow, is intended to keep fruit and vegetable crops from drying out, but it also eases plants through transplanting. Calling it "a sunscreen for plants," Scottsdale landscape architect Marcus Bollinger sprays it over newly planted cactus, as well as transplanted citrus, palo verde trees, and sago palms.

Mix about 1 pound Snow to 5 gallons of water (exact proportions depend upon the degree of protection desired) and apply from a sprayer. If you notice some sunburning after spraying, spray again.

You can buy Snow from Phoenix-based Artistic Arborist, Inc.; call (602) 263-8889. Cost is $19.50 for 50 pounds.

Stalking the cactus nibblers

Damage to cactus in desert gardens, like that shown in the picture below, usually happens in the dead of night when some animal decides to dine in your garden. Before you can decide what to do about it, you need to figure out who the culprit is. A jackrabbit? A javelina (wild boar)? A pack rat? A cactus beetle? Here's how to make educated guesses.

A jackrabbit was likely the cause of the fresh, green, scraped-looking area in the picture. It uses its teeth like tiny chisels, leaving characteristic marks.

MICHAEL MacCASKEY

LIGHT GREEN SCAR *indicates nibbling by a jackrabbit.*

Which beans to plant? Pole or bush?

Gardeners usually choose pole beans for flavor, crop size, and length of bearing season. Most kinds keep growing all summer, flowering as they lengthen and producing bean pods until frost shuts them down in autumn. Pole beans will keep bearing as long as you keep picking; they stop flowering when you stop picking.

In short-season areas, bush beans' shorter season (the main crop comes earlier) and all-at-once harvest give them an advantage. You might get two pickings over two weeks from a bush bean plant.

Both kinds of beans thrive in loose, sun-warmed soil but sulk if you try to grow them where soil is shaded or cold. Sow either kind in full sun as soon as all danger of frost is past. ■

By Michael MacCaskey, Jim McCausland, Lynn Ocone, Lauren Bonar Swezey

Northwest

GARDEN GUIDE

WEST OF THE CASCADES, see items marked with a **W.**

EAST OF THE CASCADES, see items marked with an **E.**

May Checklist

HERE IS WHAT NEEDS DOING

☐ **BUILD COMPOST. W, E:** Spring weeding and grass-cutting give you plenty of garden waste. Throw it into the compost pile, preferably in layers, so that you'll have compost to dig into the summer garden as earliest crops come out. Turn it often with a spading or hay fork, and keep it moist.

☐ **CONTROL SLUGS. W, E:** Slugs and snails can mow down newly germinated seedlings before you even know they're up. Bait around seedbeds (if you don't have pets that might lick it up); otherwise, handpick snails and slugs on evenings or damp days. An effective antislug weapon is a mixture of 1 part ammonia to 5 parts water. Spray slugs with it and they die.

☐ **CONTROL WEEDS. W, E:** Spot-spray, hoe, or handpick weeds while they're tiny. Do the job on a sunny morning: the sun will quickly dry out displaced and exposed weed roots before they can take hold again.

☐ **DIVIDE PERENNIALS. W, E:** If you act right away, you can divide most perennials that bloom in late summer and fall and still get bloom this year.

☐ **FERTILIZE FLOWERING SHRUBS. W, E:** Scatter high-nitrogen fertilizer among bloomed-out spring-flowering shrubs to support the summer's leaf, branch, and bud growth. Deadheading (picking off spent blooms before they go to seed) also directs more energy into plant growth.

☐ **FERTILIZE INDOOR PLANTS. W, E:** Warmer weather and long days put house plant growth into high gear. Feed that growth with monthly doses of fertilizer.

☐ **FERTILIZE LAWNS. W, E:** Sometime around midmonth, apply high-nitrogen fertilizer to turf at the rate of ½ to 1 pound actual nitrogen per 1,000 square feet. Use the lower number if your lawn looks green and healthy and doesn't get much use, and the higher number if the opposite conditions apply.

☐ **FERTILIZE LONG-FLOWERING PLANTS. W, E:** Annuals, begonias, fuchsias, geraniums, and container plants—anything with a long and taxing season of bloom—should be fertilized now and at monthly intervals throughout summer.

☐ **GROOM BULBS. W, E:** Deadhead spring-flowering bulbs, fertilize, and continue to water until leaves die down in summer. Now—between flowering and dormancy—is when bulbs multiply, replacing (tulips and crocus) or rebuilding (daffodils) their bulbs for next spring's show. Cut leaves off now, and you damage or destroy the bulbs themselves.

☐ **MOVE HOUSE PLANTS OUTSIDE. W, E:** You can induce a quick recovery in house plants that have grown lean and lanky over winter by moving them outside. Put them in a warm spot that's protected from midday sun and pinch them back. They'll look great by the time you bring them back inside next fall.

☐ **MOW LAWNS. W, E:** Abundant warmth, light, and moisture give lawn growth an extra push this month. Mow every four or five days, or often enough that you never remove more than a third of the grass's length at once.

☐ **PLANT ANNUALS. W, E:** You can plant almost anything this month, since danger of frost has passed. Sow bachelor's button, calendula, clarkia, cosmos, impatiens, marigold, nasturtium, nicotiana, pansy, salvia, and sunflower. Direct-sow any of these in well-prepared soil that's relatively weed-free; otherwise start seeds in flats so you won't get stuck trying to separate flower seedlings from weed seedlings.

☐ **PLANT FUCHSIAS, GERANIUMS. W, E:** Plant any of these in the garden now west of the Cascades, but wait until month's end if you live on the east side. Geraniums need full sun, while fuchsias favor dappled shade.

☐ **PLANT HERBS, VEGETABLES. W, E:** This is the one month of the year when you can plant everything and when you must plant all your warm-season crops (beans, corn, cucumbers, eggplants, melons, peppers, and tomatoes) to guarantee a crop by the end of the year.

☐ **PLANT PERENNIALS. W, E:** Nursery tables are full of perennials this time of year. You can buy and plant bleeding heart, bluebell, columbine, daylily, geum, hosta, Oriental poppy, penstemon, Siberian iris, yarrow, and more. To cool off the hot colors of Oriental poppies and daylilies, plant whites and blues (feverfew and bluebells, for example).

☐ **PLANT SUMMER BULBS. W, E:** It's the last good month to plant summer-flowering bulbs like acidanthera, begonias, dahlias, and gladiolus. Put stakes into the hole at planting time so you won't risk spearing the bulbs later, when they grow tall enough to need staking.

☐ **PROTECT COLE CROPS. W, E:** Use floating row covers to keep flies and butterflies away from your plants; that in turn will keep them from laying the eggs that turn into root maggots (from the flies) and cabbageworms (from the butterflies).

☐ **PRUNE LILACS. W, E:** Start the process by removing blooming branches, pruning out those that are crossing, poking out too far, closely parallel, or just growing at wrong angles. Take flowers inside for the fragrance and color.

☐ **PRUNE RHODODENDRONS. W, E:** Immediately after they flower, shape rhododendrons by pinching out new buds or simply go ahead with the year's major pruning. Do it early so you won't remove next year's flower buds, which form later in summer. Don't be shy: most rhododendrons (dwarf kinds are the exception) take to pruning like cloth to scissors—you can remove a third to half of the plant with no problems, and cut badly overgrown plants back by even more.

☐ **SPRAY APHIDS. W, E:** Blast aphids off new growth with a strong jet of water, then follow up with a spray of insecticidal soap if some are still present.

☐ **SPRAY TENT CATERPILLARS. W, E:** Blow webs apart with the strongest jet of water your nozzle can make, then spray with *Bacillus thuringiensis.* Repeat if necessary.—*J. M.* ■

IN HIGH ELEVATIONS and intermountain areas of California, and east of the Sierra, see items marked with an **H.**

IN LOW ELEVATIONS of Northern California, see items marked with an **L.**

May Checklist

HERE IS WHAT NEEDS DOING

☐ **CHECK DRIP SYSTEMS. H, L:** Before the weather turns hot, check your drip-irrigation system to make sure it's operating properly. Clean filters, check emitters and sprays to see that they're working (replace ones that aren't), inspect lines for leaks, and (if necessary) adjust the timer for warmer weather. After making any repairs, open end caps and flush lines before running the system.

☐ **COMBAT PESTS. L:** Spray aphids with insecticidal soap, or—if water is not restricted—knock them off with a strong stream of water from the hose. Trap, handpick, or bait for snails, slugs, and earwigs. Set out traps for gophers and moles, or protect beds by burying wire mesh before planting.

☐ **CONTROL TIP MOTH. L:** Brown, dead tips on cypress, junipers, or thuja are signs of cypress tip moth infestation. To confirm an infestation, shake the foliage vigorously this month. If you see large numbers of silvery tan moths flying around, they're cypress tip moths. The larvae do the damage when they tunnel into the leaf scales. Spray once with acephate or diazinon.

☐ **CONTROL WEEDS. H, L:** Pull or hoe whenever possible. If you must spray stubborn weeds with an herbicide, protect nearby plants from spray damage by holding a piece of cardboard against stems or trunks. Angle the board toward the weed to block the spray.

☐ **FERTILIZE. H, L:** Feed many plants, from summer-blooming perennials to roses. If you are trying to conserve water, fertilize only if plants look pale and spindly; this way, you don't force too much moisture-loving new growth. For continued flowering or fruiting, feed flowering annuals and vegetables regularly with a complete fertilizer.

☐ **HARDEN OFF TRANSPLANTS. H:** Move warm-season flower and vegetable seedlings to a coldframe, or expose them gradually over a week to 10 days to longer periods of sunlight, so eventually they can take full sun. Also cut back on fertilizer to further prepare seedlings for transplanting.

☐ **MULCH THE SOIL. H, L:** A 3-inch layer of mulch around trees and shrubs helps retain soil moisture, suppresses weeds, and keeps the soil cooler. To cover 100 square feet to a depth of 3 inches, you need about 1 cubic yard (27 cubic feet) of mulch. For smaller plants, apply an inch or two, which takes about 9 cubic feet or 17 cubic feet, respectively.

☐ **PINCH. H, L:** To encourage branching on shrubs and newly planted flowers such as azaleas, fuchsias, geraniums, marigolds, rhododendrons, verbena, and zinnias, pinch back the growing tips. Use small pruning shears or your fingers.

☐ **PLANT FOR PERMANENCE. H, L:** Now is a good time to plant almost any perennial, shrub, or tree. **H:** If necessary, wait to plant until the soil is workable and, in coldest areas, danger of frost is past.

☐ **PREVENT RUNOFF. H, L:** To channel irrigation water to roots, build basins of soil around plants—especially those on slopes and hillsides. If using drip irrigation on a slope, set the emitter or emitters on the upper side of the plant.

☐ **PROTECT COOL-SEASON CROPS. H:** To keep vegetables such as broccoli, cauliflower, lettuce, and spinach from bolting (going to seed) when the weather turns warm, cover them with shadecloth.

☐ **PRUNE. H:** Tip-prune evergreens to encourage compact growth. Remove dead branches from euonymus, junipers, Oregon grape, pyracantha, and yews. Prune spring-flowering shrubs such as lilac, mock orange, and spiraea after bloom ends. On lilacs, remove spent flower clusters just above points where leaf buds are forming.

☐ **REMOVE SUCKERS. H, L:** Leafy, fast-growing shoots arising from rootstocks (base of plants) of roses, fruit trees, and some ornamental trees compete for water and nutrients. They also ruin plant form. Cut back flush to the trunk or ground. On trees, also snap off any unwanted sprouts that emerge from along the main trunk.

☐ **THIN FRUIT. L:** On apples, Asian pears, nectarines, and peaches, gently twist off enough immature fruit to allow 4 to 6 inches between remaining fruit—which can then grow larger.

☐ **START COMPOSTING.** You can add these items to the compost pile: annual weeds, coffee grounds, egg shells, evergreen needles, fruit and peels, grass clippings, garden waste, leaves, prunings, sawdust, small wood chips, and tea leaves. Do not add kitchen scraps that contain butter, bone, cheese, chicken parts, fish, lard, mayonnaise, meat, milk, oils, peanut butter, pet manure, salad dressing, or sour cream.

☐ **WATER. H, L:** Water trees and shrubs deeply with drip, soaker hoses, or a deep-root irrigator. To avoid overwatering, check soil moisture with a trowel or soil probe. Water small to medium shrubs when the top 3 to 6 inches of soil is dry, large shrubs and trees when the top 6 to 12 inches is dry. Unthirsty plants such as cotoneaster and rockrose can go longer between watering than thirstier plants like azalea, hydrangea, and rhododendron.—*L. B. S.* ■

☐ **COOL OFF CONTAINER PLANTS.** As days get hotter, place containers where they'll get afternoon shade. Plants in pots need irrigation more often than plants in the ground. To wet the entire root zone and reduce salt buildup, drench until water runs out bottom. Apply pebble mulch to soil. Check plants for slugs and snails. To rewet a dry rootball, set pot in a large pan of water; also water the soil surface. When the soil is thoroughly wet, lift out pot and drain.

☐ **FERTILIZE SUBTROPICALS. C:** The first flush of new growth on bananas, bougainvillea, citrus, gardenia, hibiscus, lantana, and Natal plum tells you that this is the right time to give plants a dose of high-nitrogen food. Feed regularly through the active growing season.

☐ **HARDEN OFF SEEDLINGS.** A week or two before planting out seedlings that you've started in a greenhouse or other sheltered place, stop fertilizing them and stretch periods between waterings. Gradually increase time exposed to outdoor light; protect from afternoon sun.

☐ **MAKE COMPOST.** Pile prunings, leaves, grass clippings, and kitchen waste (except for oils or meat scraps), wetting each layer. For fast breakdown, chop or shred twigs and branches into small pieces, and add soil to pile as it builds. Keep pile moist, and turn and mix it often.

☐ **MANAGE PESTS.** Spray or dust plants that have pest caterpillars (such as cabbage worm, geranium budworm, and oak moth) with *Bacillus thuringiensis.* Spray aphids, mites, and whiteflies with insecticidal soap or horticultural oil. Green lacewings can also help control them. Trap, handpick, or bait for snails and slugs.

☐ **PINCH FOR BUSHIER GROWTH.** Some annuals, such as petunias and phlox, and many perennials and small shrubs need light tip-pruning now. Pay particular attention to azaleas, fuchsias, geraniums, and marguerites. Remove dead flowers.

☐ **PLANT BULBS. C:** Acidanthera, caladium, calla, canna, dahlia, gladiolus, gloxinia, tigridia, tuberous begonia, and tuberose are still available, but selection is dwindling. Plant now for summer bloom.

☐ **PLANT FRUIT TREES. C:** For best production, fruit and nut trees need regular water. But once established, the following can tolerate drought in water-lean years: fig, jujube, loquats, macadamias, persimmons, sapote, and strawberry and pineapple guavas. **C, L:** Subtropical fruits with higher water needs to plant this month include avocados, bananas, cherimoyas, citrus, and mangoes. To prevent sunburn, wrap trunks of thin-barked trees like avocados and citrus with tree wrap or paint with whitewash or white latex paint.

☐ **PLANT PERENNIALS.** The selection in nurseries this month is better than at any other time of year. See the article on page 114 for ones to try. Before shopping, decide where your plants will go in the garden; plant as soon as possible.

☐ **PLANT SUMMER COLOR. C, L:** As soon as possible, set out seedlings of annual coreopsis, celosia, cosmos, creeping zinnia, four o'clock, gaillardia, globe amaranth, kochia, Madagascar periwinkle, marigold, portulaca, salvia, sunflower, tithonia, zinnia. **H:** From nursery packs or seeds, try ageratum, annual coreopsis, aster, begonia, celosia, cosmos, creeping zinnia, four o'clock, gaillardia, globe amaranth, gloriosa daisy, marigold, mignonette, nasturtium, periwinkle, phlox, portulaca, scarlet flax, strawflower, sunflower, sweet sultan, tithonia, zinnia.

☐ **PLANT VEGETABLES. C, H:** Sow seeds of beans, corn, cucumbers, melons, okra, and pumpkins. Set out plants of cucumbers, eggplant, melons, peppers, squash, sweet basil, and tomatoes. **L:** Plant Jerusalem artichokes, okra, peppers, and sweet potatoes.

☐ **SUPPRESS WEEDS.** Spread a 3- to 6-inch layer of mulch around trees, shrubs, perennials, and annuals. Leave a clear area around the base of trunks and stems to prevent diseases. Around newly planted trees, maintain mulch for at least three years. Mulch also conserves moisture.

☐ **TEND ROSES.** Roses should be in full bloom this month. Continue feeding and watering. Drip irrigation and a 3- to 6-inch layer of mulch around plants reduce water needs. For best flowering, remove faded blooms promptly, cutting stems just above a leaf with five or more leaflets.

☐ **TEND TOMATOES AND PEPPERS.** To help prevent blossom-end rot, mulch to maintain uniform soil moisture and don't overfertilize with nitrogen. **L:** To prevent sunburn on peppers and tomatoes, cover plants with shadecloth or screening.

☐ **WATER.** Young plants may need watering daily to keep from drying out. Irrigate just-planted container-grown trees and shrubs slowly to soak original rootball and reduce runoff. Water established plants deeply to encourage deep root growth. If using drip irrigation on a slope, set emitter or emitters on the upper side of the plant.

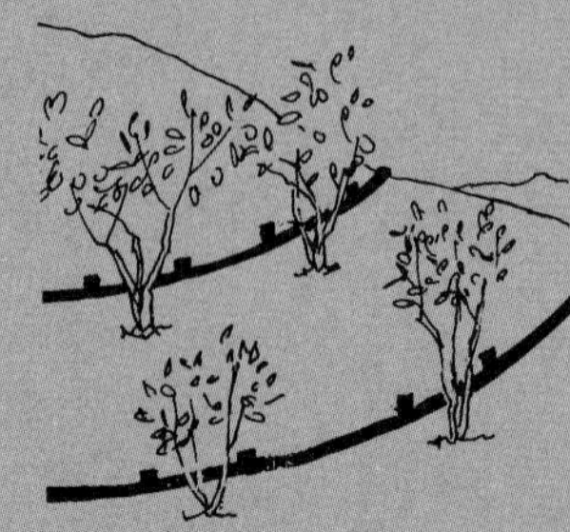

Use a soil probe to test for moisture content. Water only when necessary. Adjust or override automatic sprinklers to meet water needs.—*L. O.* ■

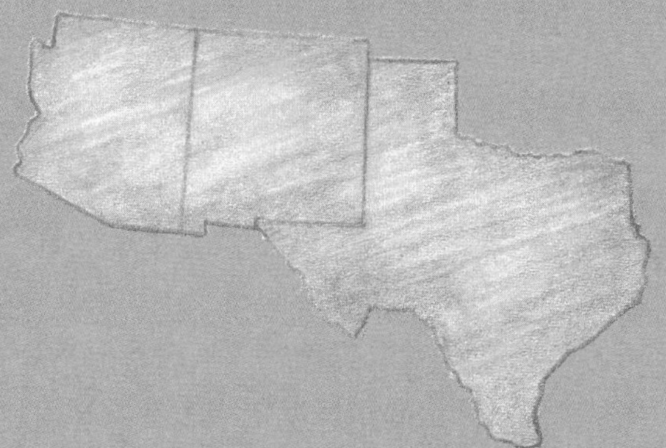

May Checklist

HERE IS WHAT NEEDS DOING

☐ **CARE FOR TOMATOES.** Large, indeterminate tomato vines need support or they'll flop and sprawl. Encircle the plants with wire cages, or tie the main stems to stakes. To minimize blossom-end rot, maintain uniform soil moisture; mulch and drip irrigation both help. In hottest desert areas, prevent sunburn by covering or partially shielding plants with row covers.

☐ **CHECK LAWNS FOR IRON DEFICIENCY.** If you fed your lawn with a high-nitrogen fertilizer at the recommended rate (5 pounds of 20-0-0 per 1,000 square feet) and it still isn't green, it may lack iron. Apply iron sulfate (also known as copperas) at the label's recommended rate. Apply it carefully: it stains paving and clothes on contact. You should see results—a green color—within a week.

☐ **FERTILIZE VEGETABLES.** Before planting, fertilize soil with 1 to 2 pounds of 16-20-0 per 100 square feet. Once vegetables are growing, give them a 1-tablespoon boost, placed 6 inches from stem, at the following times. *Beans:* after first picking and every three to four weeks thereafter. *Corn:* when it's knee-high and again when tassels form. *Cucumbers and melons:* just before the vines begin spreading. *Eggplant:* when blossoms or first small fruits are visible. *Peppers and summer squash:* at blossom time. *Tomatoes:* when small green fruits appear.

☐ **HINDER PESTS.** Aphids and whiteflies are abundant this month. Later, as weather warms, they'll naturally diminish. In the meantime, reduce their numbers by washing plants with a stream of water, or use insecticidal soap.

☐ **INCREASE WATERING.** This month usually brings the year's first 100° days. Pay particular attention to all new plants, and to plants producing new growth. Check plants for signs of wilting afternoon and morning. Almost everything, including cactus and succulents, needs extra water this month.

☐ **MAKE COMPOST.** Pile prunings, leaves, grass clippings, and kitchen waste (no oils or meat scraps), wetting each layer. For fast breakdown, chop or shred twigs and branches into small pieces before adding them to the pile, and add soil as the pile builds. Keep the pile moist, and turn and mix it often.

☐ **MULCH PLANTS.** To enrich soil, keep roots cool, prevent weed growth, and conserve soil water, spread an organic mulch—bark chips, compost, or dried grass clippings—over the plant's root zone. Make the layer 3 to 4 inches thick under large shrubs and trees, about 2 inches under smaller shrubs, and 1 inch around bedding plants and in containers. (Always leave a space clear of mulch around tree and shrub trunks.) In windy or wet areas, use a heavier material such as decomposed granite.

☐ **NURTURE ROSES.** They begin the month at their peak of bloom, but end the month stressed by high temperatures. In the Phoenix area, provide plants with afternoon shade. If leaf color is pale, deep-water, then give each bush a fertilizer formulated for roses (follow rates recommended on label); water again to carry fertilizer into soil. By midmonth, mulch each bush with a 3- to 4-inch layer of compost or bark.

☐ **PLANT FLOWERS FOR SUN.** Choices include ageratum, celosia, coreopsis, cosmos, firebush (*Hamelia patens*), four o'clock, gaillardia, globe amaranth, gloriosa daisy, kochia, lantana, lisianthus, nicotiana, portulaca, salvia, strawflower, tithonia, vinca rosea (*Catharanthus roseus*), and zinnia.

☐ **PLANT SHADE-LOVING FLOWERS.** Choices include begonia, caladium, chocolate plant (*Pseuderanthemum alatum*), coleus, gerbera, impatiens, lobelia, oxalis, pentas (*P. lanceolata*), and spider plant.

☐ **PLANT VEGETABLES.** In most of the Southwest, now is the time to plant heat-loving crops such as eggplant, okra, peanuts, peppers, soybeans, summer squash, and sweet potatoes. In the mountains (Santa Fe and Taos), early May is the last chance to set out broccoli, cabbage, and cauliflower plants. Plant seeds of beets, carrots, lettuce, onions (sets), and turnips. Wait for warmer soils at month's end to plant heat-loving beans, peppers, and tomatoes.

☐ **PROTECT CROPS FROM BIRDS.** Spread netting to protect ripening fruits from hungry and thirsty birds. Net is available at garden centers in sizes large enough to cover the crown of a tree.

☐ **PROVIDE FOR CITRUS.** If leaves are not dark green, trees need fertilizer. At the drip line of each established tree, spread 1 cup of ammonium sulfate per inch of trunk diameter. Water deeply. As temperatures rise, water trees more frequently. Mature trees need a 2- to 3-hour sprinkler soaking every two to three weeks (oftener in sandy soil, less often in clay soil). Soak soil around young and dwarf trees for 1 to 2 hours every 5 to 10 days.

☐ **REDUCE WEEDS.** Remove weeds by hand, hoe, or mower. Prevent their return with a thick mulch. Don't spray systemic weed killers such as glyphosate around established plants—spray drift is damaging. Spot-treat the weeds instead.

☐ **START LAWNS.** Throughout most of the Southwest, the best-adapted lawn grass is Bermuda. Plant it anytime night temperatures average above 70°. Improved varieties of buffalo grass (such as 'Prairie' and '609') are low-maintenance options for all but the hottest regions.

☐ **THIN GRAPES.** Once berries are the size of match heads, prune clusters. Leave no more than two clusters on each shoot—a maximum of 40 to 80 clusters per mature vine, many fewer on 3- and 4-year-old vines.

☐ **TRANSPLANT CACTUS.** Now, before daytime temperatures peak, is the best time of year to move these plants. Plant only nursery-grown plants; collecting them from their natural habitat is illegal.

☐ **WATCH FOR GRAPE LEAF SKELETONIZER.** If plants are only lightly infested, pick off and dispose of damaged leaves. If caterpillars are too numerous for that, spray undersides of leaves (evening is best) with *Bacillus thuringiensis.* Follow label directions.—*M. M.* ■

Perennials come back—stronger than ever

THEY'RE OVERFLOWING NURSERIES NOW. HERE'S A GUIDE TO TODAY'S TOP 47

Perennials have been around the West as long as gardeners have been gardening here. And for more than 60 years, *Sunset* has been introducing these great-for-the-long-haul plants to home gardeners (see the cover below). But now perennials are coming on stronger than ever, and nurseries are offering more selections. Choices are almost endless in colors, textures, shapes, and sizes, making perennials suitable for lavish flower beds, mixed borders, and small pockets around the garden.

MATILIJA POPPIES *(Romneya coulteri)* *on 1931 cover.*

From this wonderfully diverse group, how do you choose the best ones

K. BRYAN SWEZEY

COLORFUL BORDER
Front to rear are pink penstemon, lavender scabiosa, light and dark blue delphiniums, and yellow yarrow (Achillea). Design: Chole Morgan, Santa Barbara, California.

CLAIRE CURRAN

SUPER SALVIAS—*blue S. chamaedryoides, white and pink S. greggii, and spiky purple S. leucantha—brighten garden.*

All-time top choices Of the four dozen plants we describe on these pages, the perennial favorites are salvias, pictured above, and campanula, true geranium, and lavender.

for your garden? We asked perennial growers, specialty nurseries, and serious gardeners around the West to list overall favorites, as well as ones with great flowers, striking foliage, or unthirsty good looks, and for shady areas, low borders, or accents.

Choose plants from the categories that address your garden's needs; the listings (alphabetical by botanical name) that follow give information on each plant. Zones are from the *Sunset Western Garden Book.* Boxes list the best in each category.

47 great plant groups for your garden

Yarrow (*Achillea*)
Sun, foliage

Generously blooming carefree plants 4 inches to 5 feet tall. Aromatic leaves are finely divided, gray to green; flowers grow in flattish clusters. Many excellent choices. Hybrids of *A. millefolium* and *A. taygetea* (Galaxy series, Summer Pastels, Debutante) bear flowers that range from creamy pastels to vivid colors on 2-foot stems; ferny gray-green foliage. 'Moonshine' bears yellow flowers, silvery leaves. All zones.

How to grow. Give full sun, cut back after flowering, divide crowded clumps. Tolerates drought once established but looks best with water.

Lady's mantle
(*Alchemilla*) ***Shade***

Mounding clumps of nearly circular 4- to 6-inch, gray-green leaves with scalloped edges. Stems of airy lime green flowers appear in late spring. Grows 12 to 18 inches high and 2 feet across. Zones 1–9, 14–24.

How to grow. Plant in sun in mild-summer areas, partial shade inland. Needs well-drained, moist soil.

Japanese anemone
(*A. hybrida*) ***Shade***

Graceful, spreading plants with dark green maple-like leaves. Pink or white flowers on branching 2- to 4-foot stems in late summer, early fall. All zones.

How to grow. Sun or partial shade on coast, shade inland; moderate water.

Thrift, sea pink (*Armeria*)
Low beds, borders

Tufted mounds of grassy blue-green leaves 4 to 24 inches tall. Globular flowers on 6- to 8-inch stems in shades of pink, red, or white. Blooms almost all year near coast, spring elsewhere. *A. maritima* has fine foliage. *A. alliacea* has wider blades and larger flowers. *A. m.* 'Alba' has white flowers. All zones.

How to grow. Plant in full sun in soil with good drainage. Water moderately in dry areas, sparingly in moist climates.

Artemisia
Sun, foliage, accent

Woody and herbaceous plants with feathery, aromatic silvery white or gray-green foliage. Many good choices, from 6 inches to 5 feet or more. Shrubby, dome-shaped *A.* 'Powis Castle', to 2½ feet tall, spreads at least 4 feet. Prostrate *A. stellerana* 'Silver Brocade' has woolly white leaves. Zones vary by type.

How to grow. Full sun, well-drained soil. Moderate to little water.

Aster ***Flowers***

Daisy-flowered perennials; most bloom summer to fall, but a few in spring. *A. frikartii,* 3 feet tall, has fuzzy, gray-green leaves. *A. f.* 'Mönch' and *A. f.* 'Wonder of Stafa' are both lavender blue. Michaelmas daisies, 3 to 4 feet (dwarf hybrids 1 to 2½ feet) have white, pink, rose, red, blue, violet, or purple flowers. All zones.

How to grow. Plant in full sun and well-drained soil. Average water.

False spiraea
(*Astilbe*) ***Shade***

Light, airy, plume-like flower clusters May through July. Dark green foliage. In bloom, plants grow 1 to 4 feet tall. Many kinds: 'Avalanche', white flowers; 'Betsy Cuperus', pale pink; 'Fanal', garnet red, bronzy foliage. Best in zones 2–7, 14–17; short-lived in zones 8, 9, 18–24.

How to grow. Plant in partial shade inland, sun or partial shade near coast. Needs rich, moist soil.

Bergenia ***Shade***

Large glossy leaves form bold clumps that can be massed as a ground cover. Rose, lilac, purple, or white flower clusters form on erect stems. *B. cordifolia* blooms in spring, *B. crassifolia* in winter. Zones 1–9, 12–24.

How to grow. Plant in partial shade (sun near coast). Takes neglect but responds to regular watering.

Swan River daisy
(*Brachycome multifida*)
Low beds, borders

Mounding ground cover, 6 to 8 inches tall and 1½ feet wide, with finely divided leaves. Purplish blue, 1-inch-wide flowers spring through summer. Zones 14–24.

How to grow. Best in sun. Needs good drainage and moderate water.

Brunnera macrophylla
Shade

Small-scale, clumping ground cover to 1½ feet tall. Dark green 3- to 4-inch-wide heart-shaped leaves. Airy clusters of blue flowers in spring. All zones.

How to grow. Plant in part shade in warm areas; takes sun near coast. Prefers moist soil but tolerates some dryness. Self-sows.

K. BRYAN SWEZEY

FOUNTAIN OF WHITE *Dierama pulcherrimum spreads over Senecio leucostachys (left) and Centranthus ruber.*

9 favorites for accents

Artemisia 'Powis Castle', fairy wand (*Dierama pulcherrimum*), lion's tail (*Leonotis leonurus*), Russian sage (*Perovskia*), Jerusalem sage (*Phlomis fruticosa*), Matilija poppy (*Romneya coulteri*), salvia (*S.* 'Costa Rica Blue', *S. leucantha, S. uliginosa*)

DARROW M. WATT

GOLDEN COREOPSIS *(foreground) mingles with gaillardia, catmint (Nepeta), penstemon, and delphinium.*

17 perennials for showy flowers

Aster, chrysanthemum, coreopsis, delphinium, *Diascia*, Santa Barbara daisy (*Erigeron*), *Erysimum linifolium*, gaillardia, gaura, *Geranium*, daylily (*Hemerocallis*), lavender, catmint (*Nepeta*), evening primrose (*Oenothera*), penstemon, phlox, verbena

Bellflower (*Campanula*)
Shade; low beds, borders

Many kinds, from 3 inches to 6 feet. All zones. *C. poscharskyana* grows 1 foot tall, spreads, and bears blue flowers in spring. *C. persicifolia* bears 2-foot flower spikes in summer. *C. portenschlagiana* grows 4 to 7 inches high, bears violet-blue flowers in summer.

How to grow. In warm areas, plant in partial shade; in cool areas, give full sun. Moist, well-drained soil.

Chrysanthemum
Flowers

This large group includes many garden perennials. Try painted daisy (*C. coccineum*), Shasta daisy (*C. maximum*), or marguerite (*C. frutescens*), a short-lived perennial to 3 feet tall with white, pink, or yellow daisy flowers. Zones vary by species.

How to grow. Plant in full sun and well-drained soil. Needs moderate water.

Coreopsis ***Flowers***

Most bear yellow flowers over a long season. *C. auriculata* 'Nana' grows 6 inches tall, 2 feet wide. *C. grandiflora* 'Sunburst' and 'Sunray' reach 2 feet. *C. verticillata* 'Moonbeam' is 1½ to 2 feet. All zones.

How to grow. Hardy plants need little except full sun and well-drained soil.

Delphinium
(*D. elatum*) ***Flowers***

Tall flower stems are dramatic. Excellent cut flowers. Pacific Coast Hybrids grow to 8 feet. Choices include 'Summer Skies' (light blue)

CHAD SLATTERY

'MIDNIGHT' PENSTEMON *and 'Moonshine' yarrow (Achillea) contrast in sunny border.*

11 favorites for sun, unthirsty good looks

Yarrow, artemisia, Santa Barbara daisy (*Erigeron*), euphorbia, gaillardia, gaura, lavender, evening primrose (*Oenothera*), Matilija poppy (*Romneya coulteri*), salvia, verbena

and 'Galahad' (white). Medium-height strains include the Blue Fountains, Blue Springs, and Magic Fountains. Best as annual in hot-summer areas. Zones 1–10, 14–24.

How to grow. Plant in full sun and porous soil. Plant slightly high; bait snails.

Pink (*Dianthus*)
Low beds, borders

Mostly grassy-leafed, evergreen clumps. 'Tiny Rubies' (3 inches tall) bears ruby flowers in early summer. Maiden pink (*D. deltoides*), to about 1 foot tall, blooms in summer. Fragrant cottage pink (*D. plumarius*), 10 to 18 inches tall, with rose, pink, and white flowers, blooms summer to fall. All zones.

How to grow. Plant in full sun in light, fast-draining, slightly alkaline soil.

Twinspur (*Diascia*)
Flowers

Low, spreading plants with small leaves. Spikes of pink flowers from spring to fall. *D. fetcaniensis* (salmon flowers) grows 18 inches tall; *D. rigescens* (rich pink flowers), 18 inches; *D.* 'Ruby Field' (deep pink), 10 inches; *D. vigilis* (light pink), 18 inches. Zones 5–9, 14–24.

How to grow. Full sun or part shade, well-drained soil. Moderate water.

Bleeding heart (*Dicentra*)
Shade

Graceful fernlike foliage with long stems of heart-shaped flowers that rise above it. Dies back in winter. *D.* 'Luxuriant' (reddish pink flowers through summer), 12 to 18 inches tall; *D.* 'Snowdrift' (white flowers, spring), 16 inches; *D. spectabilis* (rose pink flowers, late spring), to 3 feet. Not reliable as perennial in Southern California and Southwest deserts. Zones 1–9, 14–24.

How to grow. Prefers filtered or part shade and moist, well-drained soil.

Fairy wand
(*Dierama pulcherrimum*)
Accent

Graceful, clumping plant with grasslike leaves and slender 4- to 7-foot flower stems. Flowers, in late spring and summer, are pendulous, bell-shaped, from near white to bright purple. Zones 4–24.

How to grow. Plant in sun or light shade and well-drained soil; water regularly.

Santa Barbara daisy
(*Erigeron karvinskianus*)
Flowers, sun

Trailing plant to 20 inches tall spreads 3 feet or more. White to pinkish daisy flowers appear spring to fall. Zones 8, 9, 12–24.

How to grow. Plant in full sun. Takes drought and poor soil. Can be invasive; to keep it in bounds, cut it back periodically.

Erysimum linifolium 'Bowles Mauve' ***Flowers***

Rounded, shrubby perennial 1 to 2 feet tall with narrow gray-green leaves. Spikes of purple flowers over a long period, most heavily in spring. Zones 14–24.

How to grow. Plant in full sun and well-drained soil. Best with regular water but can take some drought.

Euphorbia ***Sun***

Rugged plants, many with showy flowerlike bracts. Diverse in form and size. Milky sap (poisonous in some species) causes skin irritation. *E. characias wulfenii* is rounded plant with narrow, blue-green leaves and yellow to chartreuse bracts in late winter, early spring. Zones vary by species.

How to grow. Full sun, well-drained soil, little water.

Blanket flower
(*Gaillardia grandiflora*)
Flowers, sun

Red and yellow daisy flowers atop 2- to 4-foot plants over a long season. Several strains and varieties; 'Goblin' is compact (to 1 foot), with deep red flowers bordered in bright yellow. All zones.

How to grow. Give full sun, well-drained soil, low to moderate water.

Gaura (*G. lindheimeri*)
Flowers, sun

Erect plant with branching flower spikes 2 to 4 feet tall. Pink buds open to white through summer. All zones.

How to grow. Give full sun. To keep blooms coming, cut back seed-bearing spikes.

True geranium
Flowers; low beds, borders

Upright, trailing, or mounding plants about 1 to 2 feet tall with five-petaled flowers mostly in spring or early summer. *G. dalmaticum* (hardy to at least 10°) has light pink flowers; *G. incanum* (zones 14–24), rosy violet flowers; *G. sanguineum* (all zones), magenta flowers.

How to grow. Most need sun (light shade in hot inland areas), average soil, moderate water (*G. dalmaticum* and *G. incanum* tolerate drought).

Hellebore
(*Helleborus*) ***Shade***

Evergreen plants with large, leathery, sharply toothed leaves. Flowers (2 to 4 inches wide) look like single roses, bloom in winter

NORMAN A. PLATE

VARIEGATED *Houttuynia cordata 'Variegata' has striking pink, yellow, and red on green foliage.*

11 perennials for striking foliage

Yarrow (*Achillea taygetea*), artemisia (*A.* 'Powis Castle', *A. stellerana* 'Silver Brocade', *A. schmidtiana* 'Silver Mound'), plantain lily (*Hosta*), *Houttuynia cordata* 'Variegata', dead nettle (*Lamium maculatum*), sedum (*S. spurium* 'Dragon's Blood', *S. s.* 'Tricolor', *S.* 'Vera Jameson'), lamb's ears (*Stachys byzantina*)

or spring. *H. orientalis,* to 1½ feet, bears greenish, purplish, or rose flowers. *H. argutifolius,* to 3 feet, bears chartreuse flowers. Zones vary.

How to grow. Prefers shade or part shade. Plant in soil well amended with organic matter. Moderate water.

Daylily hybrids
(*Hemerocallis*) ***Flowers***

Tough, deciduous and evergreen clumping plants, 1 to 6 feet tall with arching, sword-shaped leaves. Lilylike blossoms open on branched stems. Repeat-blooming varieties give two or three bloom cycles. All zones.

How to grow. Give sun (afternoon shade in hottest areas). Takes most soils. Water while in bloom.

Coral bells (*Heuchera*)
Shade; low beds, borders

Compact plants form clumps of roundish leaves with scalloped edges. Bell-shaped flowers April to August on stems 15 to 30 inches tall. *H.* Bressingham hybrids bear white, pink, or crimson flowers; *H. maxima,* white; *H.* 'Palace Purple', purple foliage; *H. sanguinea,* red or coral pink. Zones vary.

How to grow. Full sun near coast, light shade inland. Best with ample water (*H. maxima* needs less).

Plantain lily (*Hosta*)
Foliage

Handsome green or variegated foliage. Blooms in summer. Plants range from 6 inches to 5 feet tall. Choose by leaf shape and color (green, white, yellow, cream). Zones 1–10, 12–21.

How to grow. Takes heavy to light shade. Needs moist soil during growing season. Bait for snails, slugs.

Houttuynia cordata 'Variegata' ***Foliage***

Ground cover to 1½ feet tall. Heart-shaped leaves are cream, pink, yellow, and red. Deciduous in winter. Spreads by underground rhizomes. Zones 4–9, 14–24.

How to grow. Plant in sun near coast, morning sun or light shade inland. Can be invasive in damp or wet soils.

Evergreen candytuft
(*Iberis sempervirens*)
Low beds, borders

Reliable plants 8 to 12 inches tall. Narrow, dark green leaves. White flower clusters in winter and early spring. 'Snowflake' (4 to 8 inches tall) is showiest; 'Little Gem', 4 to 6 inches tall; 'Purity', 6 to 12 inches tall and spreading. All zones.

How to grow. Plant in sun or partial shade. Shear lightly after bloom to stimulate bushy new growth. Average water in well-drained soil.

Dead nettle
(*Lamium maculatum*)
Shade, foliage

Ground cover (1 to 1½ feet) with heart-shaped leaves. Blooms in spring or early summer. Deciduous in cold winters. Silver-leaf types: 'Beacon Silver', rosy pink flowers; 'Pink Pewter', pale pink; 'White Nancy', white. 'Aureum' has gold leaves, pink flowers. All zones.

How to grow. Light shade, moist but well-drained soil.

Lavender (*Lavandula*)
Flowers; sun; low beds, borders (smaller types)

Rugged evergreen plants 8 inches to 3 feet. Tiny fragrant flowers, usually lavender to purple, cluster along tips of slender stems. Aromatic leaves usually grayish. Excellent choices include compact *L. angustifolia* 'Hidcote' (to 1½ feet) and *L. a.* 'Munstead' (to 1½ feet). Larger types include *L. angustifolia* (3 to 4 feet) and *L. intermedia* 'Provence' (to 3 feet). Zones 4–24, depending on species.

How to grow. Sun, well-drained soil, moderate to little water. Cut back after bloom.

Lion's tail
(*Leonotis leonurus*) ***Accent***

Branching, shrubby, 4- to 8-foot plant with toothed leaves; velvety, bright orange flowers in tiered whorls bloom around upright stems summer through fall. Zones 8–24.

How to grow. Needs sun, excellent drainage, little water. Cut back in winter.

Catmint (*Nepeta faassenii*)
Flowers; low beds, borders

Soft, fragrant, gray-green leaves on mounding plant 1 to 2 feet tall. Lavender flowers bloom in early summer. 'Six Hills Giant' and 'Snowflake' are especially showy. All zones.

How to grow. Plant in full sun; give regular water. Shear off faded flowers to stimulate repeat bloom.

Evening primrose
(*Oenothera*) ***Flowers, sun***

Carefree plants with abundant broad-petaled flowers in warm season; some open during the day, others at night. *O. berlandieri* (rose pink) blooms during the day; *O. b.* 'Siskiyou' (lighter pink) is more compact. Both can be invasive. Yellow blooms of *O. missourensis* open in the evening. All zones.

How to grow. Give sun, fairly well-drained soil. Moderate to little water.

Penstemon ***Flowers***

Diverse group of more than 250 species, all with tubular flowers. Some are mat-forming alpines, others grow 2 to 4 feet tall. Showy hybrids include 'Firebird' (red), 'Huntington Pink', 'Midnight' (purple). In desert, try *P. parryi*, pink flowers; *P. eatonii,* red. Zones vary.

How to grow. Plant in full sun (light shade inland) in soil with good drainage. Give modest water; hybrids take regular water.

Russian sage
(*Perovskia*) ***Accent***

Woody, multistemmed plant to 3 feet tall. Finely cut or toothed gray-green leaves. Lavender blue flowers in many branched spike-like clusters. All zones.

How to grow. Likes warmth, full sun. Tolerates some drought.

Jerusalem sage
(*Phlomis fruticosa*) ***Accent***

Coarse, semishrubby plant to 4 feet or more. Gray-green leaves, yellow flower clusters along upper stem in early summer; bloom repeats with regular water. All zones.

How to grow. Give full sun. Tolerates poor soil, drought. Cut back for repeat bloom.

Phlox *Flowers*

Many kinds; all have showy flowers. Favorite perennials include summer phlox (*P. paniculata*), with dome-shaped white, pink, lavender, and red flowers on 3- to 5-foot stems (zones 1–14 and 18–21), and moss pink (*P. subulata*), a ground cover that makes sheets of bloom in white and shades of pink, rose, and lavender in late spring or early summer. (zones 1–17).

How to grow. Summer phlox needs regular water and full sun. Moss pink is moderately drought tolerant.

LITTLE PINK DAISIES *cover mounding brachycome.*

16 choices for low beds or borders

Thrift (*Armeria*), Swan River daisy (*Brachycome multifida*), bellflower (*Campanula poscharskyana*), pink (*Dianthus deltoides, D. plumarias, D.* 'Tiny Rubies'), geranium (*G. dalmaticum, G. sanguineum*), coral bells (*Heuchera*), evergreen candytuft (*Iberis*), lavender (*Lavandula angustifolia* 'Hidcote', *L. a.* 'Munstead'), catmint (*Nepeta*), germander (*Teucrium chamaedrys*), mother-of-thyme (*Thymus*), speedwell (*Veronica*)

Matilija poppy
(*Romneya coulteri*)
Sun, accent

Big, crepe-papery white flowers on 8-foot stems in summer. Gray-green leaves. Can be invasive. All zones.

How to grow. Needs sun. Cut back in late fall. Can withhold summer water.

Salvia
Sun, accent (tallest ones)

Diverse, undemanding plants with flowers from white to pink, blue, and scarlet. Foliage often coarse, aromatic. Dozens to choose from. *S. chamaedryoides* (true blue flowers, gray-green leaves) grows 2½ feet tall, 5 feet across; *S. clevelandii* (lavender blue flowers, gray-green leaves), to 4 feet; *S. greggii* (red, purple, pink, or violet), to 4 feet; *S. leucantha* (velvety purple or deep rose spikes), to 4 feet; and *S. uliginosa* (sky blue), to 6 feet. Zones vary with species.

How to grow. Most need sun and well-drained soil. Moderate to little water.

Sedum *Foliage*

Succulents with fleshy leaves and stems and star-shaped flowers in clusters. Size, form vary by type, usually not exceeding 2 feet tall. Dramatic *S.* 'Autumn Joy' (to 2½ feet) has gray-green leaves and 3- to 6-inch pink flower heads that age to deep bronze. Zones vary by type.

How to grow. Sun or some shade, average to low water.

Lamb's ears
(*Stachys byzantina*) ***Foliage***

Gray-white leaves are soft, thick, woolly. Leaves of 'Primrose Heron' are yellow in spring, gray by summer. 'Silver Carpet' spreads rapidly; no flowers. All zones.

How to grow. Plant in any well-drained soil, sun or light shade. Moderate water.

Germander (*Teucrium*)
Low beds, borders

Evergreen perennials that are sun, drought, and heat tolerant. *T. chamaedrys,* to about 1 foot tall, twice as wide. 'Prostratum' (pink blooms), 4 to 6 inches high, to 3 feet wide. Flowers attract bees. All zones.

How to grow. Needs well-drained soil. To force side branching, cut plants back in early spring and late summer.

RUSS A. WIDSTRAND

JAPANESE ANEMONES *bear white blooms, like part shade.*

10 favorites for shade

Lady's mantle (*Alchemilla*), Japanese anemone, false spiraea (*Astilbe*), bergenia, *Brunnera macrophylla,* bellflower (*Campanula*), bleeding heart (*Dicentra*), hellebore, coral bells (*Heuchera*), dead nettle (*Lamium*)

Mother-of-thyme
(*Thymus praecox arcticus*)
Low beds, borders

Dense mats 2 to 6 inches high of roundish, dark green, aromatic leaves. Purple-white flowers, summer. 'Albus' has white flowers; 'Coccineus', crimson flowers; 'Reiter's', rose red flowers. All zones.

How to grow. Needs sun. Best in light, well-drained, dryish soil.

Verbena
Flowers, sun

Mostly low, spreading, drought- and heat-tolerant ground covers. *V. bonariensis* has 6- to 7-foot-tall flower stalks with fragrant lilac purple flowers. *V. peruviana* (pink, lavender, red, and white flowers, spring and summer) is 8 inches tall; *V. pulchella gracilior* (rose violet to pink or white, spring), 8 to 12 inches tall. Zones vary.

How to grow. Needs sun, heat. All dislike wet foliage.

Speedwell (*Veronica*)
Low beds, borders

Small flowers in spring to summer on 4-inch to 2½-foot plants. Varieties include 'Barcarole' (rose pink blooms), 10-inch plants; 'Crater Lake Blue' (bright blue), 10-inch plants; 'Icicle' (white), 15-inch plants; and 'Sunny Border Blue' (violet-blue), 1- to 2-foot plants. All zones.

How to grow. Full sun or light shade; regular water. ■

By Michael MacCaskey, Lynn Ocone, Lauren Bonar Swezey

What about "natural" fertilizers?

You need to understand the terms . . . and how plants take up nutrients

DOUGLAS BOND

GARDENER SPRINKLES *blood meal, a high-nitrogen natural fertilizer, into pot of flowering annuals.*

IN RECENT YEARS, several companies have introduced lines of "natural" fertilizers. What are they, how do they work, and are they worth the cost? First you need to be sure you know what you're buying.

WHAT'S IN A NAME?

Products labeled fertilizer must show how much of the three primary plant nutrients—nitrogen (N), phosphorus (P), potassium (K)—they contain. If a bag isn't labeled fertilizer—if it's called a growth enhancer, for example—it isn't fertilizer.

The word *natural* is more vague. Most chemical companies use it to mean fertilizers extracted from living things or from the earth with minimal processing. Synthesized ingredients—like ammonium nitrate and urea formaldehyde—are usually (not always) excluded.

To most laypeople, *organic* means unsullied by chemicals, or straight from nature; to a chemist, the word simply means carbon-based. Thus some synthesized nitrogen fertilizers are technically organic.

FROM BAG TO PLANT

To a plant, nutrients are nutrients. Whether a nitrogen ion originated in horse manure or in a chemical factory, it has the same chemical structure and is used in the same way by plants.

Most natural fertilizers contain modest amounts of mostly slow-release nitrogen, so they're unlikely to burn plants to which they're applied, and they continue working for a long time. To compensate for relatively low nutrient value, apply more to get the same results you'd see from synthesized fertilizer.

In addition, over time natural fertilizer can improve soil texture by adding organic matter, which helps soil hold water, air, and nutrients. The worse your soil is, the more important it is to increase organic content.

Mined nutrients like rock phosphate and limestone don't contribute much organic matter to the soil. Only those derived from recently living things (manure and cottonseed meal, for example) build soil's organic content.

A WORD ABOUT NITROGEN

The most heavily used plant nutrient, nitrogen, comes in both water-soluble (fast-release) and water-insoluble (slow-release) forms.

Water-soluble nitrogen gives plants a quick dose of nutrients as it washes down around the root system. It dissolves slowly, so it isn't likely to be carried into the water supply by runoff. Synthesized water-soluble nitrogen sometimes used in otherwise-natural fertilizers includes ammonium nitrate, ammonium sulfate, and urea.

Water-insoluble nitrogen must be slowly broken down by microorganisms for plants to use it. Synthesized forms used in natural fertilizers include IBDU, sulfur-coated urea, and urea formaldehyde (methylene ureas nitrogen).

A QUESTION OF PRICE

Nitrogen in natural fertilizers costs 2 to 25 times as much as nitrogen in synthetics. For that reason, natural fertilizers are often sold in small boxes. Bagged lawn fertilizers tend to be the least expensive of the naturals (they're fine for plants, too).

Natural fertilizers sell for more because they cost extra to make. Many also contain biodegradable ingredients designed to increase microbial activity in soil; such activity is said to decrease disease and improve growing conditions.

SOURCES

Most garden centers and nurseries sell packaged natural fertilizers. If you'd like to buy individual bulk ingredients and mix your own, write or call Down to Earth, 532 Olive St., Eugene, OR 97401; (503) 342-6820.

NATURAL MINED NUTRIENTS

Dolomitic lime raises the pH of acid soils, making more nutrients available to roots. It also supplies calcium and magnesium.

Langbeinite ore contains magnesium, potassium, and sulfur. Of the three, only potassium, at 20 percent, is a major nutrient. Langbeinite ore is used in blends, but rarely alone.

Limestone raises soil pH and supplies calcium.

Rock phosphate contains calcium and lots of phosphorus—20 to 30 percent—of which only about 2 percent is readily available to plants.

NATURAL ANIMAL- OR PLANT-DERIVED NUTRIENTS

Alfalfa meal has about 5 percent water-insoluble nitrogen, 2 percent phosphorus, 1 percent potassium.

Bat guano contains 10 percent nitrogen, most of it water soluble. It also has 3 percent phosphorus, 1 percent potassium.

Blood meal is dried blood from slaughterhouses. At about 12 percent nitrogen (mostly water-insoluble), it's quite strong for a natural fertilizer. Store it away from cats and dogs, which eat it. In Oregon State University trials, this was the most effective natural fertilizer.

Bone meal contains 3 to 5 percent water-insoluble nitrogen, 12 percent phosphorus.

Cottonseed meal has 6 percent water-insoluble nitrogen, 2 percent phosphorus, 1 percent potassium.

Dried poultry waste (chicken manure) contains about 5 percent nitrogen (3 parts water-insoluble to 1 part water-soluble), 3 percent phosphorus, and 2 percent potassium.

Feather meal has 12 percent nitrogen, most of it water insoluble.

Kelp meal provides about 3 percent potassium, abundant trace elements.

Soybean meal has 6 percent water-insoluble nitrogen, 2 percent phosphorus, 1 percent potassium. ■

By Jim McCausland

DARROW M. WATT

SWEET CORN *comes in two colors and a mix. The newer extra-sweet varieties are available in each of these. Shown here—freshly harvested and at peak eating quality—are yellow sugary enhanced 'Breeder's Choice', white supersweet 'How Sweet It Is', and bicolor supersweet 'Top Notch'.*

Sweet? Sweeter? Sweetest? What's best?

We taste-tested and checked out some extra-sweet corn varieties

CORN IS SWEETER than ever, and gardeners are raving about the newer varieties. Not only do they taste sweeter, but the sweetness lasts much longer after harvest than it did in the old-fashioned corn our parents and grandparents grew.

What makes the corn so sweet? It's in the genes. One type, called "sugary enhanced" has a gene (labeled "se" in catalogs) that modifies the normal gene for sweetness, making kernels much more tender and sweeter (although sweetness varies among varieties). The conversion from sugar to starch is somewhat slower after harvest than in older varieties, so the corn stays sweeter for many days after picking.

The supersweet varieties (shrunken-gene types, labeled

LATE-SUMMER HARVEST *towers over gardener, yields dozens of succulent ears.*

"sh_2") are even sweeter than sugary enhanced varieties, and they'll stay sweet up to two weeks if they are stored in a refrigerator.

May is an ideal time to plant sweet corns. (If you live in the lower deserts, plant earlier in spring or in late summer.)

SWEET OR SUPERSWEET, WHICH IS BETTER?

All this sweetness has initiated a debate among gardeners. One side claims the sugary enhanced varieties have a perfect balance between sweetness and old-fashioned corn flavor—and that supersweets are too sweet and don't taste like corn. On the opposite side are gardeners who prefer the supersweets.

At *Sunset*'s Menlo Park, California, headquarters, we decided to join the debate, so we planted sugary enhanced and supersweet corn in our test garden. A jury of "experts" rated the harvest (see box at right).

Since many breeders are focusing on these sweeter corns, gardeners can now choose from dozens of varieties. One catalog mentioned at right lists 25 types of sugary enhanced and 13 types of supersweet, with names like 'Kiss and Tell' (se) and 'Sweet Desire' (sh_2).

How do you select from all these choices? The best way is to grow several kinds and evaluate their taste. (Planting tips follow.) Earliness may be important, depending on your climate. Some take less than 60 days to mature; others, more than 90.

Other things to look for in catalog descriptions are tolerance of cool soil, disease resistance, and plant sturdiness, especially if you live in a windy climate.

BEFORE PLANTING SUPERSWEETS, WAIT UNTIL THE SOIL WARMS

Differences in growing requirements for sugary enhanced and supersweet varieties are well documented. These differences may help you decide which kind to plant.

Most sugary enhanced types germinate much more readily than the supersweets. Because of the shriveled seed, supersweets generally need warmer soil (65° to 75°) and less moisture to sprout.

One trick is to plant the supersweets shallower, from ¾ to 1 inch deep rather than the typical 1 to 1½ inches. Also, plant in moist, not wet, soil. Both kinds need full sun.

To avoid tough, tasteless corn, isolate the supersweets by at least 60 feet from all other corn types (including other supersweets), so they won't cross-pollinate. Or, time planting so that maturity dates are at least 10 days apart. (If a 69-day variety is planted next to a 77-day type—an 8-day maturity difference—you need to plant the 77-day corn at least 2 days after the 69-day corn.) Sugary enhanced types don't need to be isolated from themselves or other corn, but you should isolate white and bicolor from yellow or they all will be bicolor.

GIVE ALL CORN PLENTY OF FERTILIZER AND MOISTURE

All varieties are heavy feeders. At planting time, till in a high-phosphorus fertilizer (for instance, 10-15-15 or 8-10-8). Then side-dress with the same fertilizer when the corn is 6 inches high and again when it begins to tassel. Place the fertilizer 6 to 8 inches from the stalks and mix it into the top 1 to 2 inches of soil (keep it away from tender corn shoots).

To ensure pollination, plant in blocks of at least four rows and do not overcrowd. Plant seeds 3 to 4 inches apart in rows 30 to 36 inches apart; thin to 10 to 12 inches apart. If you're tight on space, plant two rows a foot apart, with the double rows 3 feet apart. If your soil is heavy clay, either use a soil conditioner or plant in raised beds.

Water corn regularly and deeply to encourage deep rooting. Also, be sure to supply plenty of moisture when the ears are forming; if the soil dries out during pollination, ears may not fill completely. Rain at this stage may also cause unfilled ears.

DARROW M. WATT

SUNSET JURORS *sink their teeth into steaming corn fresh from the test garden, then jot down their remarks.*

SUNSET TASTE PANEL PUTS EXTRA-SWEET CORN TO THE TEST

ON AN AUGUST AFTERNOON we gathered our jury of "experts" for a sweet corn taste panel.

The group included a food writer, a garden writer, and our head gardener (a corn aficionado raised in the Midwest). Other members were a second corn aficionado from the Midwest and the director of *Sunset*'s test garden.

The jury tasted eight varieties of corn just harvested from the test garden. Three were sugary enhanced varieties ('Breeder's Choice', 'Double Treat', and 'Seneca Dawn'). The other five varieties were supersweets ('Honey 'N Pearl', 'How Sweet It Is', 'Top Notch', 'Phenomenal', and 'Silver Extra Sweet').

After cooking the corn until hot, the hungry jurors dug in. The hands-down winners were the sugary enhanced varieties, with 'Double Treat' and 'Breeder's Choice' the favorites. Four out of five tasters liked their "good corn flavor," which was "sweet but not too sweet," and their "tender and crunchy" texture.

One juror dissented, preferring the "very sweet and crunchy" 'How Sweet It Is'.

WHERE TO FIND SEEDS

For the best selection of corn varieties, order by mail. Catalogs are free.

Johnny's Selected Seeds, 310 Foss Hill Road, Albion, ME 04910; phone (207) 437-9294.

Harris Seeds, 60 Saginaw Dr., Box 22960, Rochester, NY 14692; (716) 442-0410.

Park Seed Co., Cokesbury Road, Greenwood, SC 29647; (800) 845-3369.

Stokes Seeds Inc., Box 548, Buffalo, NY 14240; (416) 688-4300.

W. Atlee Burpee & Co., 300 Park Ave., Warminster, PA 18991; (800) 888-1447. ■

By Lauren Bonar Swezey

JUNE

Garden guide....................125

June checklists..................132

The easy everlastings..........136

Quick garden projects 140

Colorado country gardens ...144

A rabbit in your garden?.....150

Quick and easy compost......152

Summer pruning...............153

Sunset's GARDEN GUIDE

RUSS A. WIDSTRAND

Magnificent marguerites

GARDENS THROUGHOUT THE WEST PRACTICALLY BURST WITH COLOR AND FRESH growth this month. In the low elevations of California, Oregon, and Washington it's peak bloom time for perennials, and early-summer vegetables are ready to harvest. If you act soon, you can still plant summer vegetables and flowering plants like the marguerite pictured above. Everywhere this is the month when spring's tentativeness gives way to summer's abundance—and to its heat. You need to begin supplying water, mulch, and shade as needed.

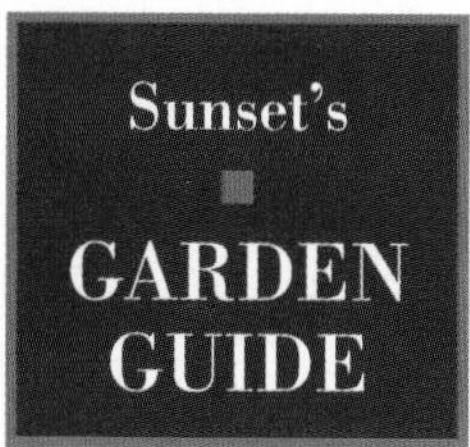

RUSS A. WIDSTRAND

GRAY-GREEN LEAVES *of salvias and centaurea contrast with deep purple leaves of cordyline (left) and New Zealand flax (right).*

Marguerites, the nonstop bloomers

When it comes to abundant blooms over a very long season (spring through fall), *Chrysanthemum anethifolium* (pictured on page 125) and *C. frutescens,* both commonly called marguerites, are tough to beat. These short-lived perennials practically bloom themselves to death; sometimes they last only a year. They are excellent for containers and for quick effects in mixed borders or as accents. The two species look similar, but only *C. frutescens* is commonly available in nurseries.

Marguerites grow in *Sunset* climate zones 14 through 24 but seem to do best in frost-free coastal areas with hot summer days. Inland, they may freeze. Since they grow extremely fast, start with small, nonwoody plants in 1-gallon containers. Plant now in full sun and well-drained soil; by fall, marguerites should grow to 4 feet high and 4 to 5 feet wide.

For maximum bloom, cut off flowers at planting time and prune lightly after each bloom cycle. Feed monthly with a complete liquid fertilizer. Water regularly.

WILLIAM D. ADAMS

TO TEST CORN *for ripeness, nick a plump kernel with your thumbnail and look for cloudy milk.*

When is corn ripe enough to pick?

That's not always easy to tell. But picking corn as soon as it's ripe is important for best flavor.

To confirm peak ripeness, try the technique pictured at left. About four days after the silk (threadlike strands at the top of the ear) turns brown, feel the corn. If the ear feels full, gently pull down the husks. If the kernels look plump and moist, push your fingernail into one of them to check the milk. Cloudy milk indicates that the ear is perfectly ripe. Thick, white milk indicates it's overripe. But if the milk is clear or nearly so, the ear is unripe; fold the husks back over it and hold them in place with rubber bands so the ear can ripen longer.

Check corn daily, since it ripens surprisingly fast in the heat of early summer and optimum ripeness doesn't last long.

A medley of Mediterranean plants

Plants from areas with Mediterranean climates combine handsomely in the simple pots pictured above. Garden designers David Mason and Robert Tainsh created the container garden for last year's Pasadena Showcase House of Design.

To give the plantings a soft, informal look, the designers used plants of varied forms and textures. Bold, reddish, strap-leafed cordyline (left) and New Zealand flax (right) contrast with the soft, airy textures of purple-flowered salvias and the gray foliage and thistlelike pink flowers of upright *Centaurea gymnocarpa* (center). *Scaevola aemula* 'Blue Wonder', with fan-shaped flowers, adds volume and lushness while softening the edges of the container at center.

To look their best, the containers require monthly fertilizing during the growing season and consistent water; they're irrigated by an automatic low-volume minispray system with spaghetti tubing fed up through the drainage hole in each container. Placing the pots on a gravel surface lets them drain freely. Gardeners keep spent blooms picked.

Since most of the plants naturally grow large, they must be repotted yearly or transplanted into the garden and replaced with young plants.

Why gladiolus flowers fail to open

It's early summer and you've been patiently waiting for your gladiolus flowers to unfurl, but for some reason they don't. Look closely at one of them; if you notice that the petal margins are brown or dry, the flowers are deformed, and the foliage has silvery streaks, the culprit that's robbing your plant of glorious blooms is probably gladiolus thrips. These insects feed on buds of glads as well as of iris and other garden flowers.

To confirm the presence of thrips, pull open the glad blossoms. Thrips are tiny (1/16-inch-long) brown or black elongated insects that scurry across the petals.

Control is difficult because the insects hide in the blossoms. In warm climates, they live in the soil during winter; in cold climates, they live on the corms. Your best bet is to dig the corms after tops have died down and dust them with diazinon before replanting or storing. Replant in a new location. You can also treat young growth in spring with acephate.

Star clusters: ideal for hot summers

Not many plants flower right through summer in all parts of the Southwest. But star clusters (*Pentas lanceolata*), pictured at right, does. This perennial, often grown as an annual, bears flowers in shades of red, pink, lilac, or white in dense, 4-inch, ball-like clusters. Slightly hairy leaves are about 4 inches long. The plant grows 1 to 4 feet tall, depending on variety.

Named varieties include 'Lavender Delight' (1 foot tall), 'Pearl White' (2 feet), 'Pink Profusion' (3 feet), 'Ruby Glow' (to 4 feet), and dark pink 'Starburst' (to 2 feet).

You're going to use your garden shears if you grow star clusters: to cut back dead flowers in summer and to cut back dead stems after the winter's frost have finished.

Although star clusters is hardy to only 28° (it's native to tropical eastern Africa), it often grows back from roots.

Star clusters does well in sun but prefers partial or afternoon shade in the hottest and driest areas, such as Phoenix. Give it fertile and well-drained soil. It tolerates drought but is at its best with regular irrigation—frequency depends on your climate and the garden's exposure.

Look for star clusters at nurseries in 1-gallon containers (about $5). Or write to Logee's Greenhouses, 141 North St., Danielson, CT 06239 (catalog $3).

RUSS A. WIDSTRAND

TIGHT CLUSTERS *of tiny pink flowers bloom above glossy, deep green leaves on star clusters spring to fall.*

It's palm pruning time, but don't overdo it

If your date or Washingtonia palm is getting overgrown, this month is the best time of year to prune.

Remove all dead fronds, leaving the green ones. Some people advise removing some green fronds as well, so you won't have to redo the job as soon. But if you leave only a few green fronds on the tree, the palm will have a reduced energy-producing capacity, making it more susceptible to pests. Periodic overpruning also deforms the shape of the trunk: over time, heavily pruned palms develop a bottlelike shape.

Pruning should be done from a lift-bucket raised to frond height, since tree climber's spikes damage the trunk and create opportunities for insects to enter the tree. To prune Washingtonia palms, use a linoleum knife or small pruning saw to remove dead fronds with a clean cut. Use the same tools for a date palm, even though you can't cut as close to the trunk.

Eight outstanding perennials for mountain climates

Choosing perennials for high-elevation areas such as Fort Collins, Colorado, or Salt Lake City can be a bit of a

Sunset's

GARDEN GUIDE

gamble, since extreme temperatures are tough on plants. But in test plots at Colorado State University in Fort Collins, the following eight perennials have proven outstanding at high elevations; all survived at least five years of testing.

***Anemone vitifolia* 'Robustissima'** has pale pink flowers about 2 inches across from July into September. It grows 3 to 3½ feet tall.

Blue oat grass (*Helictotrichon sempervirens*) is an ornamental grass about 12 inches tall. Flower heads appear in early summer.

Desert four o'clock (*Mirabilis multiflora*) is drought tolerant and suitable for native gardens. Leaves are heart-shaped; flowers are magenta or rose pink.

Goldenrod (*Solidago virgaurea* 'Peter Pan') has bright green leaves and dense plumelike heads of yellow flowers topping leafy stems from July into early September.

***Heliopsis helianthoides scabra* 'Incomparabilis'** has yellow-orange flowers on 30- to 36-inch stems from July to September.

Mother-of-thyme (*Thymus praecox* 'Coccineus') is a mat-forming evergreen plant with aromatic leaves. Magenta flowers appear from June to September.

Penstemon pinifolius has shrubby, needlelike foliage to 6 inches tall (15 to 18 inches when in bloom). Scarlet flowers appear continually from June into early September.

Sea lavender (*Limonium latifolium*) has a rosette of leathery evergreen leaves; cloudlike blue-violet flowers appear continually from June into October.

Sunset's

GARDEN GUIDE

RUSS A. WIDSTRAND

SMALL-LEAFED *English ivy gets wrapped around galvanized wires attached to wall by anchor bolts; eventually, plants will form leafy diamond patterns.*

Green graphics of ivy dress up a blank wall

English ivy (*Hedera helix*) traces decorative leafy diamonds on the blank wall pictured at right. Training ivy in this way is especially useful in small gardens where planting space is limited.

To create this design, Kevin Campbell inserted bolts 34 inches apart across the top and bottom of the wall (the bolts extend ¼ inch from the wall surface so the wire can wrap around them). He attached galvanized wire at a 45° angle to the top and bottom of the wall. Then, at each point where the wires intersect near the ground, he planted ivy from 6-inch containers. As shoots grow, they are wrapped around the wires to form the leafy grid.

Small-leafed forms of English ivy suitable for wall covering include 'California', 'Emory', 'Glacier', 'Hahn's Self Branching', and 'Needlepoint'. The ivy will cover a 6-foot wall in two to three years.

Six months of petunias

The opulent bed of petunias pictured below belongs to Elmer Tiegs of Nampa, Idaho. Although summers here are often hot and dry, Tiegs manages to get seven months of flowers from his plants (he sets them out in mid-April and enjoys them until the first hard freeze hits in mid-November).

PETUNIAS—*'Sugar Daddy' and 'Snow Cloud'—bask in dry heat and bright sunshine of an Idaho summer.*

STEVE BLY

To keep petunias thriving for so long, Tiegs grows them in beds that he enriches in early spring with ample amounts of well-rotted manure. When he sets out seedlings from sixpacks in the amended soil, he pinches back each plant. He spaces plants 12 inches apart in rows 12 inches apart. Between the rows, he hoes in an irrigation ditch 3 inches deep and 3 inches wide.

Once a week, Tiegs floods the ditch with water flowing slowly from a garden hose. If the weather is particularly hot and dry, or plants are dusty, he may sprinkle overhead. Otherwise the plants flourish on their own. He occasionally snips off errant shoots, but once plants are bedded out, he doesn't pinch back, deadhead, or fertilize all summer.

In all of the West except the low desert, you can have such a show in a month if you set out plants now.

In fall when plants flop, brown, and go dry, they're easy to pull out and add to the compost pile.

A shopping center palm collection

Some 60 kinds of palms from around the world now thrive in the Crystal Court area of Costa Mesa's South Coast Plaza. Many are rare and unusual, and all are labeled. The older specimens, some dating back to the 1940s, were transplanted from Beverly Hills in 1986.

With guidance from the International Palm Society of Southern California, Crystal Court management adds uncommon types yearly. Some of the more unusual ones to look for are a 40- to 50-year-old clump of slender lady palms (*Rhapis humilis*), a 40-foot Cuban royal palm (*Roystonea regia*), and a Hawaiian loulu palm (*Pritchardia hillebrandii*).

For help finding the many palms, pick up a self-guided tour map (free) at the Crystal Court management office (open week days) or by mail; call (714) 435-2160 to request one.

To get to Crystal Court from I-405, take Bristol Street north about ¼ mile to Sunflower Avenue. Turn west on Sunflower and go about ¼ mile to Bear Street.

The statuesque nicotiana

Highly prized as a bedding and container plant for summer gardens, *Nicotiana alata* bears flowers of white, lime, pink, or dark red that fill the evening air with a sweet, powerful fragrance. Now its taller cousin—*N. sylvestris*—is growing in popularity and availability.

This excellent bedding plant for sun or partial shade grows up to 5 feet tall and is topped with long, tubular white flowers (also pungently sweet). Its large, coarse green leaves look handsome against the glossy leaves of a hedge like photinia, privet, or pittosporum, the waxy needles of yew, or the thick foliage of Canadian hemlock, Leyland cypress, or boxwood.

Plant *N. sylvestris* in quick-draining, rich soil. It will not tolerate drought; if soil goes dry, give it a good soaking at its base after the sun is down. Fertilize the plant as you do other summer bloomers.

DON NORMARK

FRAGRANT WHITE *trumpets of Nicotiana sylvestris play to dainty yellow marigolds and dusty miller below.*

The chard with pizzazz

Few plants are as colorful as rhubarb chard: it flaunts its jewel red stems with such chutzpah that it almost says, "So who needs flowers?"

Do you eat it or look at it? Take your choice. In the photograph at left, its stems enliven a perennial border.

Rhubarb chard is easy to grow. Plant it any time from early spring to early summer in rich, well-drained soil and full sun.

Sow seed now. When the first set of true leaves appears, thin plants to a foot apart, and by August you'll have a plant that looks like the one pictured. For a speedier display, set out seedlings.

Chard is quite cold tolerant; it will stand through a mild winter. Leaves and stalks are edible, and the stems are attractive in flower arrangements.

RUBY STEMS *of rhubarb chard are nearly iridescent.*

Rethinking rhody relocation

Northwest gardeners are accustomed to being able to move rhododendrons anytime—except just before and during bloom. Drought has changed all that.

Rhododendrons can be transplanted successfully—even during a hot, dry summer—but they need to be in constantly moist soil so that their network of fine, close-to-the-surface feeder roots can get the water they need. In many recent summers, we didn't have water to spare for this kind of irrigation.

If you're thinking about moving a rhododendron, wait until late October or early November to do it. By then, the plants are going dormant, temperatures are lower, days are shorter, and water should be more abundant.

When you move it, slice into the ground around the drip line of the plant with a shovel. Then slice under the shallow root system and pry the plant up. Move it to a new planting hole slightly larger than the rootball and enriched with lots of organic matter. Water the plant in well, then let nature take over. Don't fertilize until next summer.

Zing went the thing in your salad

"What's that nice nutty taste in the salad?" The chef you've questioned smiles smugly: "Arugula. Perhaps you know it as roquette or rugola."

This old herb is enjoying the spotlight again as cooks continue their relentless search for little-known ingredients. And arugula is easy to grow. Though a bit weedy, this freely self-sowing annual grows to a height of about 3 feet. The leaves taste best when they're 1 to 4 inches long and ruffled, like small mustard leaves. You can harvest them until the plant blooms and the leaves become hot tasting.

To ensure a succession of leaves, sow seeds at one-month intervals. Allow plants to set seeds. Collect some to sow next year and to give to friends; allow other seeds to scatter in the planting beds. You will have plenty of arugula next year. Simply thin out the plants you don't want.

Arugula seed is available through Abundant Life Seed Foundation, Box 772/1029 Lawrence St., Port Townsend, WA 98368. This nonprofit foundation is dedicated to the collection, preservation, and distribution of seeds worldwide. Donation for the catalog is $2. A foundation membership (which includes three newsletters and the catalog) costs $20.

Sunset's

GARDEN GUIDE

RENEE LYNN

TALL, GLOWING HEADS *of 'Illumination' amaranth brighten Elizabeth Gamble garden in Palo Alto, California, from midsummer to frost.*

Glowing amaranths for summer gardens

Brightly colored foliage makes amaranth (*Amaranthus*) a standout in sunny borders. Plants are easy to grow from seed and look good from midsummer to frost. Young, tender leaves also are edible and can be used in place of spinach in summer.

'Illumination' (shown at right) develops a glowing head of bright crimson and yellow foliage on 3- to 4-foot stalks. Lower foliage is purplish green. 'Early Splendor' and 'Flaming Fountain' also have foliage in brilliant autumn hues.

A. tricolor (Joseph's coat) has leaves blotched with green, red, and yellow on 1½- to 2-foot stalks.

For best germination, plant seeds when soil has warmed to about 70° (early summer) in an area that gets full sun. Use the tall kinds as accents or in the back of a border. Water plants regularly and fertilize lightly.

Seeds are available from Ornamental Edibles, 3622 Weedin Court, San Jose, CA 95132 (catalog $2).

SILVERY SPOTS *indicate that mites have been hard at work sucking sap from this avocado leaf's cells.*

JAMES McMURTRY

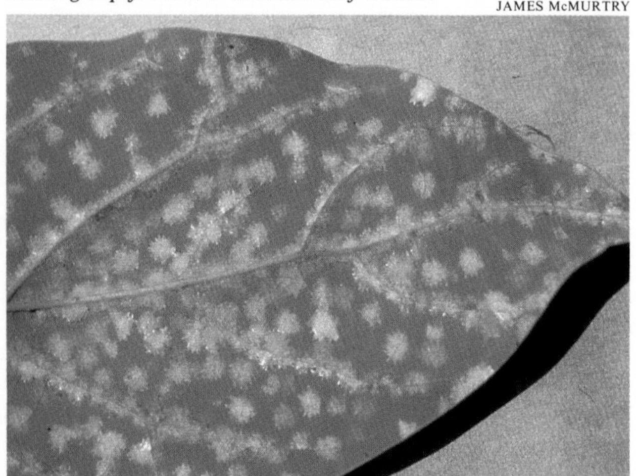

Mite plagues avocados in San Diego County

An avocado mite *(Oligonychus perseae)* that feeds on the tree's leaves has recently established itself in San Diego County. The tiny mites collect under a protective webbing on the undersides of leaves, where they feed along the midrib and veins. Their sucking creates patches of dead tissue that appear tan on the upper sides of leaves and silvery underneath. Serious infestations can defoliate trees, sometimes causing fruit to sunburn and drop. The mites seem to prefer Guatemalan varieties such as 'Gwen', 'Hass', and 'Reed'.

Biological controls offer the best hope for managing the pest. Although some naturally occurring beneficial insects found feeding on the avocado mites are having some impact and are increasing in numbers, they haven't kept the pests in check. A predatory mite from Florida (*Typhlodromus helveolus*) does show promise; it can burrow under the webbing to feed on the eggs, young, and adults, and it reproduces quickly. Insectaries are producing the beneficial mite, but for now supplies are limited and available primarily to commercial growers.

Until beneficial mites are readily available, there is little you can do to suppress the avocado mite. UC Cooperative Extension recommends spraying affected trees with wettable sulfur; consult a professional pesticide applicator.

Why pick beans early?

In the low and intermediate deserts, now is harvesttime for snap beans. If you pick the beans at the right stage of maturity, you'll get the best flavor as well as more abundant production.

For tender, flavorful beans, harvest when pods are ¼ to ½ inch in diameter. If you wait until they're larger and bulging with seeds, the beans will be stringy and tough. Picking early also helps ensure a long harvest season.

Trailing wine-cups: new native perennial

Wine-cups (*Callirhoë involucrata*) is cold-hardy and heat tolerant. Its native range extends from Texas and New Mexico to as far north as Montana. Plants grow 6 inches to 1½ feet high and 2 or more feet wide; plants grow larger with summer water.

This native perennial is aptly named: 2½-inch-diameter brilliant crimson flowers are shaped much like wine glasses. Plants are becoming more available this season; you might notice them in gardens or in the wild this month, when they bloom most heavily (flowering season lasts until August, depending upon climate and weather).

The nearly round leaves are divided into five to seven narrow segments. Flowers close at night and don't reopen after pollination; to prolong bloom, remove pollinated flowers.

Trailing wine-cups is an ideal plant for rock gardens or in low borders. It also grows well in containers and hanging baskets.

It prefers well-drained, gravelly soils. You can start it from seeds in fall or from carrotlike tubers now. Seeds take a month or so to germinate and need at least another year to begin flowering. Space tubers 8 to 12 inches apart. If watered frequently, wine-cups will bloom all summer. In extreme heat, plants die back to the ground but will grow again in fall.

Seeds are available (100 for $1.75) from Plants of the Southwest (address given at far right). Or order tubers ($3.50 each) from Wildseed Farms, Box 308, Eagle Lake, TX 77434; (800) 848-0078 (catalog free). Plants (about $4 for a 2½-inch pot) are available from A High Country Garden (address given at far right).

Grow your own insecticide?

Neem may be one of the most remarkable plants on the planet. Powerful insecticides are distilled from its leaves and seeds. But for various reasons, including the tree's reluctance to grow just anywhere, this plant has been slow to reach nurseries. Now, limited quantities are becoming available.

As a general guide to where neem can be grown out doors, try it wherever summers are hot (and the hotter it gets, the better) and winters don't go much below 30°.

Neem is the common name for *Azadirachta indica*. Not only does it protect crops from many pests, but it has some antibacterial and antiviral properties, too. The tree has been well known throughout the Old World since ancient times.

Some gardeners make a mulch from its leaves; others make an insecticidal spray by soaking leaves or seeds overnight in water.

Neem grows well in poor, infertile soils. In India, it's known as an evergreen tree to 50 feet.

One nursery has a limited supply of neem trees available by mail. A 10-inch-tall seedling costs $36 from Pacific Tree Farms, 4301 Lynnwood Dr., Chula Vista, CA 91910; (619) 422-2400 (catalog $2).

A new book, *Neem: A Tree for Solving Global Problems* (National Academy Press, Washington, DC, 1992), provides additional information on neem trees. It's available from Agribookstore, 1611 N. Kent St., Arlington, VA 22209; (703) 525-1744. Cost of $24 includes handling and air-mail shipping.

The easiest penstemon?

Nature has given us many kinds of penstemons and man has hybridized some more. What all the kinds have in common are bright-colored, two-lipped flowers that hummingbirds like, and a need for fast soil drainage.

Pineleaf penstemon (*P. pinifolius*) is perhaps the easiest to grow of all penstemons. From late spring into August, it sends out 1½- inch-long scarlet-orange flowers that glow like bursts of fire, beckoning the hummingbirds. Evergreen, needlelike leaves turn purple in freezing weather.

In the wild, this diminutive perennial (12 to 18 inches tall and about 2 feet wide) grows in the southwestern corner of New Mexico east of the Chiricahua Mountains. It also adapts well to gardens in Taos and Phoenix. The plant tolerates heat, cold (to –30°), and mild summers.

A more compact version grows about 8 inches high; its flowers are slightly more orange, and they bloom over a slightly shorter season. Yellow-flowered 'Mersea Yellow' is about the same size.

Plant pineleaf penstemon in borders, along pathways, and in rock gardens: it's adaptable enough to grow well with many different kinds of plants. In the photograph below, it makes a handsome edging to a river of gray stone.

Plants are available in some nurseries ($6 for a 1-gallon can). You can also start plants from seeds; they're available from Plants of the Southwest, Route 6, Box 11A, Santa Fe, NM 87501; (505) 438-8888 (catalog $2). Or order 2½-inch plants (about $4 each) from A High Country Garden, 2902 Rufina St., Santa Fe, NM 87501; (800) 925-9387 (catalog free). ■

By Steven R. Lorton, Michael MacCaskey, Lynn Ocone, Lauren Bonar Swezey

CHARLES MANN

BLAZING FLOWERS *cover pineleaf penstemon beginning this month and into August.*

Northwest

GARDEN GUIDE

WEST OF THE CASCADES, see items marked with a **W.**

EAST OF THE CASCADES, see items marked with an **E.**

June Checklist

HERE IS WHAT NEEDS DOING

☐ **BAIT FOR SLUGS. W, E:** The battle goes on. These guys can do more damage than ever this month, nibbling off newly emerging shoots of bedding plants and vegetables. Bait around rocks, in dark, moist areas along house foundations, and through ground covers such as dwarf periwinkle and ivy. Be careful to keep pets (especially dogs) away from bait.

☐ **BUY PERENNIALS. W, E:** Nurseries will sell blooming plants this month, mostly in 1-gallon cans. Display them in decorative pots or baskets by entries, on a patio table, or even in cool sunrooms. After flowers fade, plant them in borders or spot them around the garden.

☐ **CARE FOR BEDDING PLANTS. W, E:** As blooms fade, snip them off. Pinch back plants that you want to bush out. Water when soil is dry. Fertilize plants in the ground and in pots regularly—monthly at full strength or twice a month at half strength. Plant growth surges right now; a liberal application of 12-12-12 is like rocket fuel.

☐ **CLIP HEDGES. W, E:** To ensure that rain and sunlight reach all the foliage, shape the hedge so that the base is wider than the top. If you are a twice-a-season hedge trimmer, clip early this month, then again in late summer or early autumn. If you are a once-a-year clipper, do the job late this month or in early July. The new growth that follows either style of trim will be shorter and neater through fall and winter.

☐ **CULTIVATE SOIL. W, E:** Water runs off crusty soil. Work the top ½ to 1 inch of soil into the consistency of dry granola or coffee grounds. This is something you can do as you weed. When you irrigate, watch the water soak down right around the roots.

☐ **CUT ROSES. W, E:** Look carefully at the leaves before you cut a flower. The leaves closest to the rose have three leaflets each. The leaves farther down have five leaflets. Cut the stem just above a group of five leaflets. New growth will begin just below your cut. If you cut above a group of three leaflets, you'll get a stub and no new growth.

☐ **DEADHEAD RHODODENDRONS. W, E:** To keep the plant looking tidy and to channel its energy into growth and next year's buds rather than into seed production, remove blossoms as they fade; be careful not to break off new growth buds. Examine what you're pulling off before you grasp it so you don't squeeze a flower that has a bee working in it.

☐ **DIVIDE PERENNIALS. W, E:** After perennials bloom, cut back flowering stalks, then dig, divide, and replant them. Water plants well from now through the end of summer.

☐ **FEED PERENNIALS. W, E:** As soon as flowers fade, apply a complete fertilizer.

☐ **GROOM SPRING BULBS. W, E:** Keep watering bulb plantings until leaves begin to brown. Then snip off old flower heads. Remove brown, withered foliage only when it pulls away with a gentle tug (removing foliage before it has totally died back weakens the bulb, and next year's flower will be spindly, if one comes up at all).

☐ **MANAGE COMPOST. W, E:** Turn the pile. If it seems dry, soak it well. You may want to cover it—a sheet of black plastic works well. Prunings, spent flowers, and lawn clippings all go on. Accelerate decomposition by mixing in old compost, high-nitrogen fertilizer, or commercial compost starter.

☐ **MIX IN AMENDMENTS. W, E:** If you are establishing new beds, getting ready to replant rows in the vegetable garden, or digging a planting hole, mix in plenty of organic matter—such as compost or well-rotted manure—to enrich the soil. Be cautious with manure. If it's too fresh (hot), it will burn what you've planted. Builder's sand loosens up soil.

☐ **MOW FREQUENTLY. W, E:** Lawns grow fast in the long days of a Northwest June. Cut often enough that at each mowing you are removing only a third of the length of the grass blades.

☐ **PLANT DAHLIAS. W, E:** There's still time to get dahlias into the ground, but get moving. As you plant tubers, put stakes in place. If you wait until plants are up and need staking, you'll likely puncture the tuber with the stake.

☐ **PLANT TREES AND SHRUBS. W, E:** Dig a generous planting hole (twice as wide as the rootball) and enrich soil with organic matter. Remove the plant from the can. If big roots are wound around the rootball, knead the rootball gently to loosen the tangle. Or score the rootball with a knife to stimulate the development of new feeder roots. Put plants into the ground and fill in with enriched soil. Press soil firmly in place and water well. Don't fertilize newly set-out shrubs and trees. Wait a year or at least until early next spring.

☐ **PUT OUT FUCHSIAS. W, E:** Plant them in pots of rich, quick-draining soil and water well. Pinch back growth to encourage bushier plants; as blossoms fade, snap them off to keep seed pods from forming. Apply a complete liquid fertilizer. If you use it at half strength, you can feed fuchsias weekly. If you use it at full strength, feed them every other week.

☐ **SET OUT VEGETABLES. W, E:** Plants in flats and 4-inch pots are still abundant in nurseries. Buy and plant immediately. If seedlings have knotted roots, use a knife to shave off some of the bottom of the rootball and score the sides to stimulate growth. Put plants in rich loose soil. Water well. Don't let plants dry out.

☐ **STAKE TOMATOES. W, E:** While plants are young, get them going in the right direction. Put stakes, a trellis, or growing frame in place and loosely tie young plants up (fabric strips, 2 inches wide and a foot long, make great ties). Prune off suckers and other unwanted shoots now and throughout the growing season.

—S. R. L. ■

Central

GARDEN GUIDE

IN HIGH ELEVATIONS and intermountain areas of California, and east of the Sierra, see items marked with an **H.**

IN LOW ELEVATIONS of Northern California, see items marked with an **L.**

June Checklist

HERE IS WHAT NEEDS DOING

☐ **ATTACH SHUTOFF VALVES. H, L:** To conserve water, attach shutoff valves or hose-end sprayers that shut off the hose.

☐ **CARE FOR ROSES. L:** To encourage growth and new flushes of bloom on repeat bloomers, remove faded flowers and feed plants with a complete fertilizer and iron chelate (if necessary); water afterward. For deep watering with a hose, build basins around the plant. If using drip, place two emitters, on opposite sides. Mulch to conserve soil moisture and keep roots cooler.

☐ **CHECK SPRINKLERS. H, L:** Inspect your system to see if it's working properly and there are no broken, malfunctioning, or misaligned heads. Turn the system on and inspect each head; replace broken ones. If a head is bubbling or squirting irregularly, it may be clogged. Check slits for dirt or small pebbles. To readjust a misaligned head, turn it until it's spraying in the right direction.

☐ **FEED HOUSE PLANTS. H, L:** Although there's plenty to do outdoors, don't neglect house plants; this is their best growing season. Fertilize once a month or every time you water (dilute to quarter strength). To prevent sunburn, move them away from hot south- or west-facing windows, or cover windows with translucent curtains.

☐ **HARVEST VEGETABLES. L:** If you planted an early crop of beans, short-season corn, cucumbers, or squash, harvest should be starting. Pick in the early morning when temperatures are cool and vegetables are at their peak maturity—firm, fully colored, and full flavored, but not too large. Harvest lemon cucumbers before they yellow; harvest beans before seeds swell. Zucchini and pattypan squash also can be harvested as baby squash when just a few inches long. For tips on corn harvesting, see item on page 126.

☐ **PICK HERBS. H, L:** For the best flavor, harvest individual leaves or sprigs before flower buds open. If plants are blooming, use flowers to decorate foods.

☐ **PLANT UNTHIRSTY SHRUBS. L:** For color with minimal water, try *Anisodontea hypomandarum*, blue hibiscus, Cape plumbago, ceanothus, euphorbia, feathery cassia, lavender, phlomis, rockrose, and Russian sage. Score each rootball to loosen roots. Dig a planting hole no deeper than the rootball but about twice as wide. Half-fill the hole with soil, tamp with the shovel handle, and soak well. Fill the hole with soil and tamp with your foot; soak the soil thoroughly.

☐ **PLANT VEGETABLES. H, L:** No matter which zone you live in, June is prime vegetable planting time. Sow seeds of beans and corn. Set out transplants of cucumbers, eggplant, melons, okra, peppers, pumpkins, squash, and tomatoes.

☐ **PROTECT FRUIT CROPS. L:** To keep birds from raiding fruits such as sweet cherries, cover trees with plastic bird netting or row cover fabric (available at nurseries). To keep it from blowing off, fasten it around the trunk or to branches with wire or twine.

☐ **PRUNE HEDGES. H, L:** Since shrubs grow faster at the top, hedges are usually heavier on top; the tops shade the base and make them sparser. To counteract top-heavy growth, clip the hedge slightly wider at the base and slanting in at the top as shown below.

☐ **REMOVE FIRE HAZARDS. H, L:** In fire-prone areas, clean up brush and debris to reduce the fuel volume. When grasses turn brown, mow them to about 4 inches. Clean off any plant debris that may have accumulated on the roof. Prune out dead and diseased wood from trees and shrubs. Prune tree limbs at least 20 feet off the ground. Cut branches back at least 15 to 20 feet from the house.

☐ **SET OUT SUMMER COLOR. H, L:** For instant color, look for blooming plants in 4-inch pots or 1-gallon cans. Good choices include coreopsis, gaillardia, globe amaranth, Madagascar periwinkle (*Catharanthus roseus*), penstemon, perennial statice, portulaca, salvia, sanvitalia, sunflower, verbena, and zinnia. Good foliage plants for fillers include low-growing artemisias, dusty miller, and golden or purple sage.

☐ **SNIP OFF SPENT FLOWERS. H, L:** To encourage continued bloom on annuals, perennials, and flowering shrubs, remove faded flowers before they start to form seeds. Make sure you remove the entire flower head, including the ovary, where seeds form (such as the bulbous part of the dahlia flower), and not just the petals.

☐ **STAKE TALL, FLOPPY FLOWERS. H, L:** To hold up sprawlers like bachelor's buttons, carnations, and yarrow, insert four stakes at least 2 feet tall (depending on height of flowers) into the soil around the plant; wrap the outside with two layers of twine, as shown below.

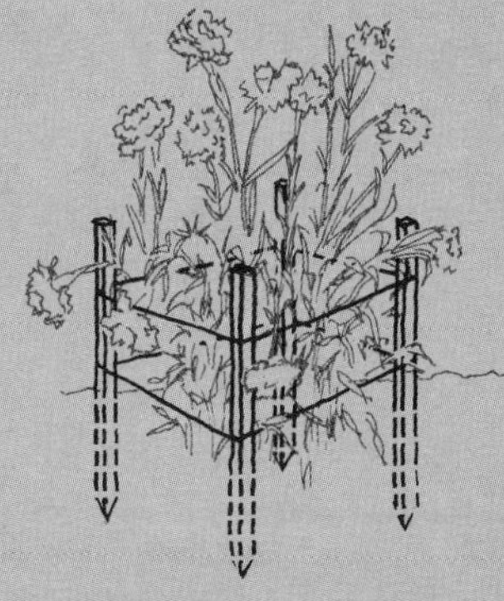

☐ **THINK TWICE BEFORE YOU FERTILIZE. H, L:** Too much fertilizer is as damaging as too little. It also encourages overly lush, weak growth. Check the plant first to see if it needs feeding. Healthy, full-size foliage means the plant's fine. Pale leaves (starting with older ones), indicate nitrogen deficiency. Chlorosis (yellowing between veins) usually indicates iron deficiency (see below).

☐ **TREAT CHLOROSIS. H, L:** A common ailment in alkaline soils is iron chlorosis (yellow leaves with green veins), which is caused by an iron deficiency. For fastest response, apply chelated iron to soil.—*L. B. S.* ■

☐ **CARE FOR CORAL TREES. C:** If your coral tree (*Erythrina*) grows in a lawn or is otherwise overwatered, it's probably growing fast and needs pruning now. Shorten long shoots by a third to a half and remove any branches that cross. If possible, reduce the amount of water your tree receives. It will grow more slowly, need less pruning, and flower just as well or better.

☐ **CARE FOR ROSES.** Feed roses after each bloom cycle and water regularly. If aphids or spider mites are a problem, wash plants frequently with soapy water, then rinse with clear water.

☐ **CONTROL CHEWING WORMS.** Spray or dust plants that have pest caterpillars (such as cabbage worm, corn earworm, and geranium budworm) with *Bacillus thuringiensis* (BT). Apply sparingly, starting when caterpillars are small.

☐ **PLANT FOR COLOR. C, H:** Some choices that aren't water guzzlers include amaranthus, coreopsis, dusty miller, evolvulus, gaillardia, gazania, gloriosa daisy, Madagascar periwinkle (*Catharanthus roseus*), nierembergia, portulaca, scarlet sage, semperflorens begonia, verbena, and yarrow. Colorful plants that need more water, especially inland, include aster, coleus, impatiens, lobelia, melampodium, petunia, salpiglossis, and zinnia. Before planting, work in compost and a complete fertilizer.

☐ **PLANT SUBTROPICALS. C:** Exotics you can plant now include banana, floss silk tree (*Chorisia*), figs, gold medallion tree (*Cassia leptophylla*), orchid tree palm, and snowflake tree (*Trevesia*). Subtropical shrubs to plant now include gardenia, hibiscus, philodendron, and bird of paradise (*Strelitzia*).

☐ **PLANT VEGETABLES. C:** Set out seedlings of cucumbers, eggplant, peppers, squash, and tomatoes. Sow seeds of beans, beets, carrots, corn, cucumbers, pumpkins, and summer squash where you want them to grow. In cool coastal areas, you can still plant lettuce seeds and seedlings. **H:** Sow seeds of corn, cucumbers, muskmelon, okra, squash, and watermelon.

☐ **PRUNE HEDGES.** To counteract top-heavy growth, prune hedges so they are slightly wider at the base and slanting in at top, as shown below. Use hedge shears on fine- to medium-leafed shrubs. Use pruning shears on large-leafed shrubs, cutting branch by branch.

☐ **PRUNE PALMS CAUTIOUSLY. C, L:** Midsummer is the time to prune, but don't overdo it. Use a sharp knife to cut into the trunk at the base of a dead frond and lightly pull to remove it. Don't cut palm fronds that are still green.

☐ **REJUVENATE IRIS.** Lift, wash, and separate 3- to 4-year-old clumps of bearded iris. Throw away punky old rhizomes and let cut ends of healthy ones heal overnight before replanting. To compensate for root loss, shorten leaves by cutting them with scissors. To replant, set the rhizome top just below soil; point the leafy end in the direction you want growth.

☐ **SPREAD MULCH.** To suppress weeds, enrich soil, and conserve water, spread a 2- to 3-inch layer of organic mulch around vegetables, trees, shrubs, and flowers; keep mulch away from stems and trunks of plants. Use compost, ground bark, weed-free straw, or dried grass clippings.

☐ **STAKE TOMATOES.** For easy picking and to prevent fruit rot, support tomatoes off the ground with a cage or stakes. It's best to stake when you plant. As plants grow, tie them up with plastic ties or strips of old nylons.

☐ **STOP WATERING NATIVE PLANTS.** Many, such as ceanothus, flannel bush, and oaks, are especially disease-prone in summer's warm, wet soils. If plants are not yet established, let water drip slowly over the rootball several inches away from leaves and trunk. Also, water at night or during cool weather, not in the heat of the day, when soil is hottest.

☐ **SUPPORT FLOWERS.** Tall flowers like delphiniums need stakes close to the mature plant's height. Tie bloom spike to stake as it grows. Use ties that won't cut stem or stalk. Corral sprawlers like bachelor's buttons in a support fence as shown below; to make one, wrap twine around stakes placed in a square around the plant.

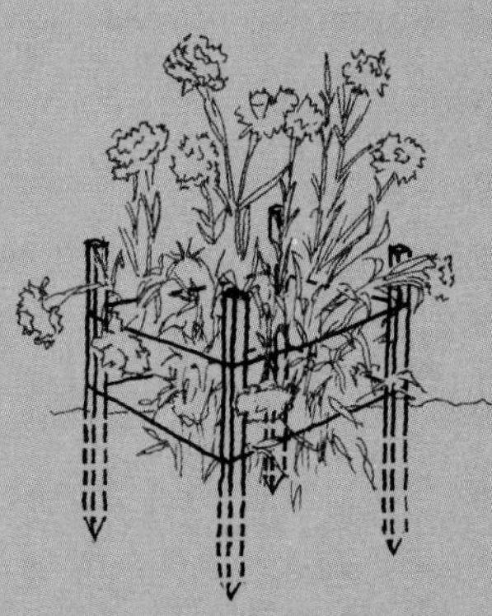

☐ **TEND CITRUS. C, L:** Feed with high-nitrogen fertilizer; water thoroughly. To protect newly planted trees from sunburn, wrap trunks with burlap, cloth, or commercial tree wrap or paint with white latex tree paint. Apply a sticky ant barrier such as Tanglefoot. To lessen June fruit drop, water mature trees deeply every two weeks through this month; water young trees weekly.

☐ **TURN COMPOST.** For quicker decomposition, move the bottom of the pile to the top, and the sides to the middle. Add water and perhaps nitrogen fertilizer, then cover to retain moisture.

☐ **WATER WISELY.** Use an efficient irrigation system that doesn't mist, fog, or create runoff; drip irrigation, moisture sensors, soil soakers, and automatic shutoff valves for sprinklers and hoses are all good ways to save water. Don't give plants more water than they need; let their appearance be your guide. Pull moisture-stealing weeds from beds.—*L. O.* ■

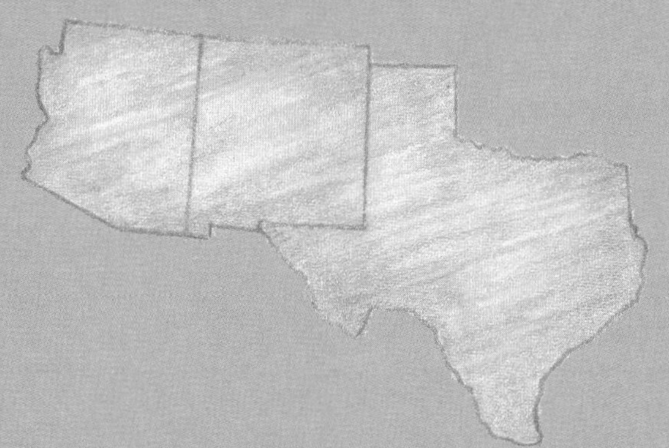

June Checklist

HERE IS WHAT NEEDS DOING

☐ **CHECK TREE TIES.** Reattach trees to stakes—and replace stakes if necessary—to protect young trees from winds.

☐ **DIMINISH SPIDER MITES.** They thrive in heat and on dusty plants. Mottled leaves and fine webs indicate their presence: watch for them on undersides of leaves on campanula, delphinium, hollyhock, and salvia. Wash plants frequently with a strong spray from the hose. Use an insecticidal soap if necessary.

☐ **HARVEST VEGETABLES.** In low and intermediate deserts, early vegetable plantings are ready to harvest when you see these signs: corn, at milk stage (see related item on page 126); eggplant, when skin is glossy; cantaloupe, when stem slips off with light pressure; watermelon, when tendrils nearest fruit turn brown. Pick in the early morning, when it's cool.

☐ **INSPECT SQUASH VINES FOR BORER.** Check plants daily this month for the tiny eggs of this insect. If you see them, rub them off. After hatching, larvae bore into the vine, damaging it.

☐ **MINIMIZE SPOTTED SPURGE.** It is one of the most annoying summer weeds. Pull or hoe it out before it forms seeds. Throw away pulled plants; if you leave them on the soil's surface, they'll still scatter seeds. Use mulches to minimize weeds. If weeds are severe, use a preemergence herbicide.

☐ **MOW LAWNS.** Mow lawns once or twice a week. Set the mower to cut common Bermuda 1 to 1½ inches high, hybrid Bermuda 1 inch high, St. Augustine up to 1½ inches high, and zoysia 1 to 1½ inches high. In the high desert, cut bluegrass 1½ to 2 inches high.

☐ **MULCH TREES AND SHRUBS.** To help reduce weeds and minimize evaporation, apply a layer of organic material or gravel 2 to 4 inches thick (deeper for bigger plants) under shrubs, trees, and vines, and on flower and vegetable beds. Keep mulch several inches from trunks, and don't use organic matter around drought-tolerant plants.

☐ **PLANT (OR TRANSPLANT) PALMS.** This is the best month to plant palms. Set them in holes at least twice as wide as the rootball and of equal depth. Use excavated soil as backfill, and water well. Use heavy twine to tie fronds up and cover bud. You can cut twine once new growth occurs or wait for twine to break naturally.

☐ **PLANT SUMMER COLOR.** In the hottest areas it is nearly too late, so act fast. Choices include cockscomb, firebush, globe amaranth, Madagascar periwinkle, portulaca, purslane, salvia, starflower, and zinnia. In cooler areas, choices include ageratum, aster, calliopsis, cockscomb, cosmos, gaillardia, globe amaranth, kochia, Madagascar periwinkle, phlox, portulaca, purslane, sanvitalia, sunflower, tithonia, zinnia. To protect young plants from the hottest sun, shade their west sides.

☐ **PLANT SWEET POTATOES.** They thrive with the heat that comes this month. Check at your nursery for young plants or order from a catalog.

☐ **PLANT VEGETABLES.** It's not too late to sow seeds of heat-loving vegetables: amaranth, black-eyed pea, melons, okra, peanuts, and yard-long beans. In the high desert, there's still time to plant beans, corn, cucumber, eggplant, and squash.

☐ **POLLINATE SQUASH.** Pick male flowers from atop their thin stalks and remove petals. Locate female flowers by their swollen stalks and daub each with a male flower.

☐ **PREVENT BLOSSOM-END ROT ON TOMATOES.** It is caused by stress, usually induced by fluctuating soil moisture and high soil and air temperatures or calcium deficiency. Prevent it with heavy mulching; also provide afternoon shade and water plants by drip. Scatter a tablespoon of gypsum at plant roots weekly to ensure available calcium for the enlarging fruit.

☐ **PROTECT WATER PLANTS.** Aphids and midges are abundant on pond plants such as arum, taro, and water lily this month. If you have fish, avoid using insecticide; instead, dust plants with diatomaceous earth.

☐ **SHIELD RIPENING GRAPES.** Birds and other animals are watching your ripening grapes as closely as you are, and they're likely to get there first. Cover bunches with a brown lunch bag, stapling the open end snugly against the stem.

☐ **SOW TOMATOES.** It's time to sow seeds for the fall crop. Try heat-tolerant 'Heatwave' or 'Solar Set'. Also recommended are 'Champion', 'Early Girl', and 'Surefire'. Set out plants in late July.

☐ **SUSTAIN ROSES.** Rebuild watering basins around plants so that water soaks in deeply, then mulch to conserve soil moisture and to keep roots cooler. Remove faded flowers and fertilize with a product designed for roses. If leaves are pale instead of dark green, use a fertilizer that contains iron chelate.

☐ **TEND CITRUS.** Feed young trees with nitrogen fertilizer. Feed mature trees only if you didn't do so last month. Water thoroughly. To protect newly planted trees from sunburn, wrap trunks with burlap, cloth, or commercial tree wrap, or paint the trunk with white latex paint.

☐ **WATCH FOR CURLY TOP.** Infected plants wilt, are stunted, and grow poorly. Greenish yellow, ⅛-inch-long beet leafhoppers spread the virus, which affects cucumber, melon, and tomato plants. The leafhoppers avoid shade, so you can protect plants by covering them now with shadecloth or a row cover. Remove infected plants as soon as symptoms appear—they're safe to add to compost.

☐ **WATER ATTENTIVELY.** Most plants—but especially new plants—benefit from deep watering this month. Flood or drip irrigation makes this easier. Before and after watering, check soil moisture by digging down with a trowel. Water in the morning to recharge the soil's reservoir before the day heats up. If you use a drip system, water slowly and deeply once a month to leach salts from the root zone.—*M. M.* ■

The easy, enchanting everlastings

GROW THESE FLOWERS TO DRY . . . FOR BOUQUETS

The enchanting beauty of fresh flowers needn't fade with the seasons. Dozens of cool- and warm-weather bloomers lend themselves to drying and can be preserved for years in arrangements and wreaths.

Strawflowers and statice—often referred to as everlastings—are well known to many gardeners. Botanically, everlastings are a group of plants in the sunflower family that have papery bracts

GLENN CHRISTIANSEN

DARROW M. WATT

FLOWERS FOR DRYING
At peak bloom, yarrow and statice (left) are ready to pick for drying. Dried flowers await arranging at Sonoma Flower Company (right); they include, from left to right, pink pokers, roses (above), bright yellow goldenrod, Mexican sage, pink strawflower, yellow and pink roses, and blue and dark pink larkspur.

(petal-like structures). But the broader definition includes any flower (and seed pod) that retains form and color after it dries.

Many flowers suitable for drying are common annuals, perennials, and shrubs, delphinium, feverfew, hydrangea, lavender, larkspur, liatris, roses, salvias, and yarrow. But a wide variety of materials beyond these common plants can be dried. They range from delicate-looking fillers like cloud grass (*Agrostis nebulosa*) and statice (*Limonium latifolium*) to dramatic artichokes and poppy pods. Many wildflowers, grasses, and pods also dry well. The chart on the facing page lists 30 plants that are suitable for drying.

You can are dry most of them by hanging them upside down; a few of them are dried upright.

GLENN CHRISTIANSEN

DRAMATIC ARRANGEMENT *is made from bunches of dried flowers. Starting at the back are hare's tail grass, larkspur, drumstick allium, white immortelle, pink pokers, strawflower, lavender, roses, globe amaranth, and salvia.*

GETTING STARTED

If you're new to gardening or just want to grow a small patch of flowers, you can buy nursery transplants instead of sowing seeds; many better nurseries now carry good selections of perennials in containers; you can also buy small plants through the mail. Fewer annuals for drying (cockscomb, gomphrena) are sold as seedlings.

If you want to try some special varieties, you need to start from seed. Sow love-in-a-mist, safflower, and grasses directly in the ground. Others can be started in flats or small pots filled with a mixture of equal parts of peat moss, perlite, and vermiculite. Add a controlled-release fertilizer. Most seeds germinate readily in household temperatures (60° to 75° during the day, 50° to 60° at night).

For all seeds, keep the soil moist. Once seeds have germinated, move containers to a sunny window. Thin seedlings so they have plenty of room to develop.

Before planting outdoors, harden off seedlings by placing containers outdoors in a sheltered area. Slowly expose them to sun over the next week or so until they can take full sun.

Prepare the soil as you would for any flower garden. Cultivate, add organic matter, and mix in a fertilizer. If you don't want to strip your flower garden bare at harvest time, set out extra plants (space permitting) so some flowers can stay on the plants.

To produce healthy flowers with optimum color, fertilize and water regularly. If you use sprinklers, water in the morning so the flowers aren't wet overnight.

HARVEST FLOWERS AT THE OPTIMUM STAGE

Depending on the kinds of flowers you grow, harvest can last for months. Flowers must be harvested at the proper stage (see chart) to retain good color and form after drying. With some flowers, you may need to experiment.

When multiple flowers develop on a single stalk, you can either harvest individual flowers with short stems (you can extend the stems with wire) or cut the entire stalk when flowers are at various stages of development.

To harvest, pick flowers after the dew has dried but before temperatures rise. If you want to strip off large leaves, do it before drying.

To air-dry flowers, make small bunches (15 to 20 or so) of a single kind and tie them together with a rubber band (don't use string; the bunches will fall apart when the stems shrink). Then you can hang them upside down on a coat hanger or drying rack; leave plenty of space between bunches for air circulation.

Allium, statice, yarrow, and tall grasses like pampas grass can be dried upright in an empty vase. For baby's breath and hydrangea, fill the vase with 2 inches of water.

Place materials in a dark, dry area with good air circulation and temperatures between 70° and 110°—an attic, warm basement, or water heater or furnace room, for example. Keep them out of light and high humidity.

Allow about three days (and at least 24 hours) for most flowers to dry well. If stems are still soft after several days, temperatures may be too cool, and rotting or loss of quality may occur.

Most flowers are dry when stems snap. The exception: dense flowers such as cockscomb. Break one in half to check. Seed pods, grains, and roses need a couple of extra weeks to dry.

After drying the materials, you can leave them hanging in bunches away from sunlight or store them in boxes in a warm, dry area. Wrap them in newspaper and layer them. Don't overcrowd the boxes or flower heads may be crushed.

DESIGN TIPS

Just before arranging flowers, recondition them by spraying lightly with water to make them more pliable and less prone to breakage.

To protect the flowers and prevent shattering, finished arrangements can be sprayed with a dry-flower sealer (available at craft stores).

Some flower stems are weak and must be wired if used in arrangements.

WHERE TO BUY SEEDS OR PLANTS

The following catalogs are free from the growers unless otherwise noted.

Goodwin Creek Gardens, Box 83, Williams, OR 97544; (503) 846-7357. Sells seeds and plants. Catalog $1.

Nichols Garden Nursery, 1190 N. Pacific Highway, Albany, OR, 97321; (503) 928-9280.

Park Seed Co., Cokesbury Rd., Greenwood, SC 29647; (800) 845-3369.

Territorial Seed Company, Box 157, Cottage Grove, OR 97424; (503) 942-9547.

Thompson & Morgan, Box 1308, Jackson, NJ 08527; (800) 274-7333.

By Lauren Bonar Swezey

30 choice plants to grow for drying

MICHAEL THOMPSON

STAR EVERLASTING *pod* SEA HOLLY *bloom*

Flower	Color	How does it grow?	When to harvest
Acroclinium, Swan River everlasting (*Helipterum*)	Shades of pink, rose, or white	Annual, 1 to 2 ft.	Just before flowers are fully open
Artichoke (*Cynara*)	Purple	Perennial, 4 to 8 ft.	When buds just open
Baby's breath (*Gypsophila*)	White, pink	Annual or perennial, to 4 ft.	Just when fully open
Chinese lantern (*Physalis alkekengi*)	Bright orange red	Perennial, 2 ft.	When lanterns color up
Cloud grass (*Agrostis nebulosa*)	Tannish	Annual, about 1 ft.	When heads form but before seeds mature
Cockscomb (*Celosia*)	Jewel tone colors	Annual, 8 in. to 3½ ft.	When heads reach full color
Cupid's dart (*Catananche caerulea*)	Lavender blue	Perennial, 2 ft.	In the morning when fully open
Drumstick (*Craspedia globosa*)	Golden	Perennial, 2 ft.	When fully colored
Feverfew (*Chrysanthemum parthenium*)	Yellow or white	Perennial, 1 to 3 ft.	When flowers have just opened
German statice (*Goniolimon tartaricum*)	Silvery white	Perennial, 1½ ft.	When fully open
Globe amaranth (*Gomphrena globosa*)	Pink, purple, red, white	Annual, 9 in. to 2 ft.	When color is intense
Globe thistle (*Echinops*)	Steel blue	Perennial, 3 to 5 ft.	Just before flowers open
Goldenrod (*Solidago*)	Golden yellow	Perennial, 1 to 5 ft.	At peak color
Hare's tail grass (*Lagurus ovatus*)	Tan	Annual, 1½ ft.	When heads are fully open but before seeds mature
Immortelle (*Xeranthemum annuum*)	Mixed colors	Annual, 2½ ft.	When fully open and at peak color
Lamb's ears (*Stachys byzantina*)	Pink with gray leaves	Perennial, 1 to 1½ ft.	Just before full bloom, lay leaves on screens
Larkspur (*Consolida ambigua*)	Blue, pink, purple, white	Annual, 1 to 5 ft.	When flowers are open ⅔ up stem
Love-in-a-mist (*Nigella damascena*)	Pale brown	Annual, 1 to 2½ ft.	When pods are mature
Money plant (*Lunaria annua*)	Silvery white	Biennial, 3 ft.	When pods begin to dry but before seeds turn yellow
Onion family (*Allium*)	Pink, purple, yellow, white	Perennial, bulbs, 1 to 5 ft.	When fully open
Pink pokers (*Psylliostachys suworowii*)	Lavender pink	Annual, to 1½ ft.	When all flowers are fully open
Poppy (*Papaver*)	Light brown	Perennial, to 4 ft.	When pod is well formed
Quaking grass (*Briza maxima, B. minima*)	Brownish green	Annual, 1 to 2 ft.	When heads form but before seeds mature
Safflower (*Carthamus tinctorius*)	Yellow-orange	Annual, 1 to 3 ft.	In bud or just at peak color
Sea holly (*Eryngium*)	Light to dark metallic blue	Perennial, 1½ to 4 ft.	When flowers turn blue
Starflower (*Scabiosa stellata*)	Greenish to bronze	Annual, to 1½ ft.	As soon as petals drop
Statice (*Limonium*)	Many colors, many forms	Annual, perennial, 3 ft.	When fully open
Strawflower (*Helichrysum*)	Many vibrant colors	Annual, 1 to 3 ft.	Before yellow centers are visible or in bud; wire stems
Winged everlasting (*Ammobium alatum*)	White, yellow	Annual, 1½ to 3 ft.	When buds start to open, before yellow centers show
Yarrow (*Achillea*)	Yellow, white, or pastels	Perennial, to 5 ft.	At peak size and color

30 minutes or less

These six summer projects for the garden are quick and easy

CHEERFULLY PAINTED *pots brighten a garden or house. Design: Françoise Kirkman.*

IT'S FINALLY THE weekend, and you're ready to tackle a garden project. But you don't have time to devote the entire weekend to it. Take heart: not all garden projects are time-consuming. The six projects shown on this and the following pages are quick and easy, and all add a little pizzazz to the garden.

How about an easy-to-install plant shelf that places flowers right at your kitchen window? Or a simple, low-cost flagstone table that adds an elegant touch to a corner of the garden? Or a sturdy pot stand on wheels that's utilitarian *and* attractive?

Once you have the materials in hand, each of these simple projects can be put together in 30 minutes or less (two of the projects also require drying time). And none of them require special skills, although a little imagination helps when painting pots.

Shopping for the materials is the most time-consuming part of each project, but shopping lists can help you plan exactly what you need. All of the materials are readily available at nurseries and building supply stores (look in the yellow pages under Building Materials). Flagstone (for the table) is also sold at some businesses that sell landscape materials.

1 Paint redwood or clay pots
(30 minutes, plus drying time)

What you'll need

Clay or redwood pots Saucers
Water-base nontoxic waterproofing
Roofing compound Latex paint
Paintbrush Paint roller Sponges

NORMAN A. PLATE

With colorful paints, you can transform any mundane-looking clay or redwood pot into a bright, even abstract piece of art that's suitable for displaying indoors or out. Because each pot is waterproofed first, it's both functional and long-lasting.

The designs shown here were created with a sponge, paintbrush, and paint roller. If you choose a wood pot, sand it first. Otherwise, the steps are the same for both wood and clay.

First, coat the pot thoroughly inside and out with waterproofing; let dry 24 hours. Next, coat the inside of the pot with roofing compound, stopping within 2 inches of the pot rim. Then comes the fun. Follow the designs pictured above or create your own.

The three pots above with solid backgrounds (yellow and purple) were painted on the outsides with a roller. After the base coat on the yellow pots had dried, designs were painted on with brushes; masking tape helped define the zigzag lines on the large yellow pot at far left. Saucers were waterproofed, then painted along the rims.

The small, spatter-painted pot in front was first sponge-painted with red, light green, and dark green and then brush-spattered with yellow.

The Southwestern cactus pot in the center was painted with triangular pieces of sponge (apply paint to one side of the sponge piece with a brush and press painted side onto pot as shown in the photograph at bottom left). The long wooden planter box was covered with a solid coat of blue paint, allowed to dry, then painted with 1-inch squares of sponge to make the purple checkerboard design. A small brush was used to dab on orange dots.

Circular pieces of sponge made the yellow dots on the pot at right rear in the photo; lines of purple and turquoise were painted around them.

All of the pots were allowed to dry thoroughly before filling.

2 Display chimney pipe plant stands (10 minutes)

What you'll need

Round terra-cotta chimney pipes (various sizes)

Potted plants

Empty pots or wood blocks

The attractive containers shown at right are not actually containers, but pipes sold for lining chimneys. They're inexpensive (about $11 to $28, depending on size) and available at masonry supply stores. Unlike typical containers, they add height to potted plants and bring flower colors and plant textures into closer view.

The pipes come in two heights: 24 inches with a 12- or 14-inch inside diameter, and 30 inches with an 8-inch inside diameter. If you cluster three pots as shown, use two taller ones behind with a short one in the foreground.

Since the pipes are hollow, fill the interior with stacked pieces of wood or empty pots so the potted plants can be set at the right level. Mix seasonal pots of color with foliage plants that have interesting textures and shapes.

3 Put together a flagstone table (5 minutes)

What you'll need

24-inch-tall oval terra-cotta chimney flue liners: 2

A piece of flagstone about 21 inches wide by 32 inches long

Although this flagstone and chimney-flue table is extremely simple and inexpensive to make (about $10 for each flue liner at a masonry supply store and $6 for the flagstone), it is attractive and elegant, and durable enough for use in the garden or on a patio.

The flues are just the right height for a coffee table or end table. The buff-colored Arizona flagstone was handpicked from a building supply store that sells flagstone and other outdoor paving. To install, just set the legs 6 to 8 inches apart and center the flagstone on top.

FLAGSTONE TABLE *was designed by Richard William Wogisch, San Francisco.*

CHIMNEY PIPE *containers add height to plants. Design: Richard William Wogisch.*

PETER CHRISTIANSEN

4 Make a plant shelf
(15 minutes)

What you'll need

Rough-sawn 2-by-8 cut to window length plus 6 inches

Rough-sawn 1-by-12 (optional) cut to length of 2-by-8

8-by-10 shelf brackets: 2 or 3, depending on width of window

#8 flathead woodscrews: 6 per bracket

A screwdriver or drill with #8 screw bit

Plants in 1-gallon cans

PLANT SHELF *lifts potted flowers into full view from indoors. Design: Ken Smith, Newbury Park, California.*

This project allows you to create a living bouquet outside a window where its color and fragrance can be enjoyed from indoors.

Because the plant shelf is designed to hold 1-gallon containers, you can have an instant continuous show of seasonal color. When one season's flowers fade, you can purchase the next season's show and just set it on the shelf. To save money, you can also plant sixpacks of color in 8-inch clay or plastic pots and use them when they come into bloom.

The plant shelf is suitable for stationary, double-hung, or sliding windows; it's not suitable for casement windows that open outward. Before buying materials, measure the width of the window; add about 3 inches to each end so the board will extend a bit beyond the window. For a 4- to 6-foot-wide window, buy three angle supports; smaller windows need only two.

Position the angle supports with their tops 12 inches below the bottom of the window. (This allows the flower pots to sit about 2 inches below the window, plus 8 inches for the height of the 1-gallon cans and 2 inches for the thickness of the wood.) Level the supports before screwing them in.

Lay the 2-by-8 on top and screw it to the angle supports. If you plan to use utilitarian containers and the plant shelf is highly visible from outdoors, you can hide the pots and the side of the shelf with a 1-by-12 fascia nailed to the shelf horizontally.

NORMAN A. PLATE

TWO-TIERED POT *brings an entire herb garden to any deck or patio. Design: Lauren Bonar Swezey.*

5 Plant an herb pot
(15 to 20 minutes)

What you'll need

Bowl-shaped clay pots: one about 16 inches in diameter and one about 24 inches in diameter

Herbs: about 13, in 2- or 4-inch pots (number varies, depending on size of containers)

Potting soil: 2 cubic feet (deeper pots may need more soil)

Soil polymers

This herb pot provides an almost limitless variety of fresh cuttings to use in your favorite recipes. It also makes an attractive display on a sunny patio or deck.

To find a suitable style of pot, look at a nursery or store that specializes in pots. Choose bowl-shaped containers with wide openings and narrow bottoms; these come in several sizes. The top pot should be small enough so there's plenty of room to plant around the edges of the bottom one once they're stacked.

To plant, fill the bottom container with soil and mix in soil polymers according to package directions; level the soil. Center the small pot on top of the large pot; fill with soil and polymers.

Plant cascading and low, bushy herbs, like lemon basil, oregano, parsley, and thyme, in the lower pot. Save extra-tall ones, such as large-leaf and purple basil, for the top pot; fill in with shorter herbs, like chives and spicy globe basil. Water regularly; feed every week or two with fish emulsion.

6 Construct a plant stand
(about 30 minutes)

What you'll need

1-by-3 clear pine: 10 feet for 14½-inch-diameter stand

1¼-inch (3d) galvanized nails: 30 Compass

Coaster wheels with screws: 4 Epoxy Wood stain

Water-base waterproofing

This sturdy pot stand makes large containers easy to move. When the plant—such as the cymbidium orchid pictured below—goes out of bloom, the pot can be rolled out of view. The stand is also attractive enough to use indoors. If you don't need wheels, you can substitute 2- to 4-inch-high legs of wood.

Directions are for a 14½-inch-diameter stand to hold a 13-inch saucer. But the stand can be made to fit any size saucer by adjusting the wood length and the number of slats or the slats' spacing.

Make a paper pattern 14½ inches square (or 1½ inches larger than the diameter of the saucer). Cut eight pieces of wood 14½ inches long. Lay five of the pieces vertically on the paper, leaving a ½-inch gap between pieces.

Position and glue the three remaining pieces horizontally across them, gluing the middle one first; space them 2 inches apart (see drawing below). Secure all slats with nails as shown in the drawing (keep nails away from cutting line and the area where the wheels will be installed).

With a compass, draw a 14½-inch-diameter circle and saw along the line; sand the rough edges. Screw the wheels onto the cross-supports through the second and fourth slats (predrill holes). Stain and allow to dry 24 hours. Apply the waterproofing and let dry. ■

By Lauren Bonar Swezey

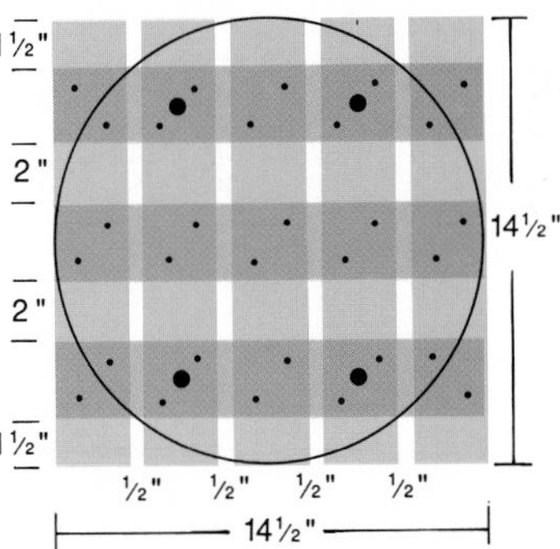

PLANT STAND *holds heavy pots. Drawing shows dimensions. Design: Françoise Kirkman.*

Colorado Country Gardens

By Lynn Ocone

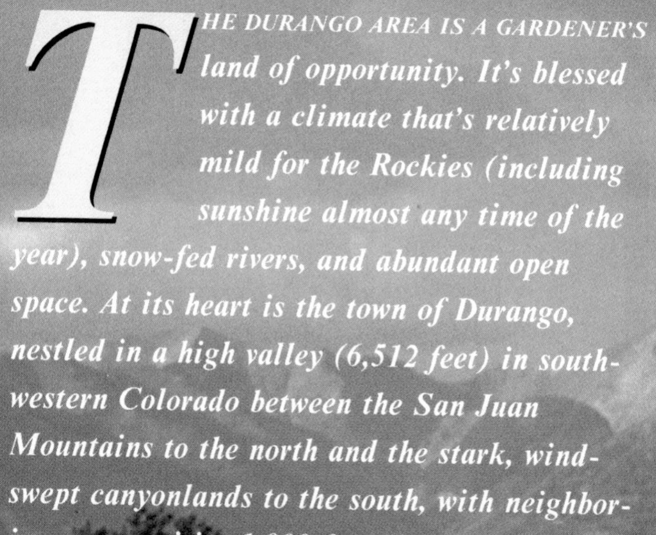

THE DURANGO AREA IS A GARDENER'S land of opportunity. It's blessed with a climate that's relatively mild for the Rockies (including sunshine almost any time of the year), snow-fed rivers, and abundant open space. At its heart is the town of Durango, nestled in a high valley (6,512 feet) in southwestern Colorado between the San Juan Mountains to the north and the stark, windswept canyonlands to the south, with neighboring communities 1,000 feet higher.

"We're surrounded by so much natural beauty, all we can do is embellish it," says one gardener. But gardening here—as elsewhere in Sunset climate zone 1—has its challenges: unpredictable weather and just a three- to four-month growing season. The time between planting and harvest is compressed, as is the season of flowers. What blooms in quiet succession elsewhere unfurls here in frantic profusion.

Pictured on these pages are gardens shaped by the land and climate, and by the artistry of the people who tend them. Study the photographs for plant combinations you can try.

SUNFLOWERS *bask in summer sun at Blue Lake Ranch in Hesperus. They were started from seed sowed by raincoat-clad gardeners in "a moment of free-spirited planting madness" during a spring shower.*

LAURIE E. DICKSON

Blue Lake Ranch: 5 acres of blooms

GARDENERS AT THIS bed and breakfast inn in Hesperus (11 miles west of Durango) harvest golden and orange calendulas, which grow together in rows (pictured below), along with the bachelor's buttons to dry for edible garnishes to sell (right). But it's the gardens that we hope draw people to us," says owner David Alford. The Alfords grow everything from sunflowers—pictured on the previous pages—to irises (more than 4,000 plants). They save and sell seeds of some of their favorites—old-fashioned hollyhocks, petunias, Shirley poppies, and dianthus. For information on lodging and garden products, write to Blue Lake Ranch, 16919 Highway 140, Hesperus, CO 81326.

Perennial meadow at the back door

MARY J. VANDEWIELE, NOW IN HER 80'S, CAN'T SAY exactly when she planted the pink painted daisies, golden Iceland poppies, and towering bearded irises that form her meadow. She's been gardening this spot for more than 50 years, and the perennials now ebb and flow naturally through the seasons, encouraged by summer watering, occasional fertilizing, shearing back in fall, and leaving clippings in place as a winter mulch. The Iceland poppies reseed themselves, and the painted daisies come back each year. The irises get divided every few years. "Perennials are always there—you just have to let them do their thing," she advises.

LAURIE E. DICKSON

LAURIE E. DICKSON

Colorful annuals at Clear Water Farm

"Gardening is my favorite thing to do, and it's a way to stay home and make money," says Suzy McCleary of the 2 acres of flowers and vegetables that blanket her Hesperus farm. She spends long summer days tending plants for the wreaths, soaps, and seasonings she sells by mail and in the local stores. She grows mostly annuals. Scarlet cosmos, pink snapdragons, and orange zinnias brighten the entry border, picture at left; petunias and nasturtiums (along with geraniums) tumble from pots (above). Yellow statice edges the cabbage row (right). "I can cut annuals several times in one season. They give me more flowers than perennials that bloom only once each summer," she says. McCleary starts most plants—more than 2,000—indoors in March to plant out in late May or early June, depending on the weather. For a free Clear Water Farm catalog, write to 21055 Highway 140, Hesperus, CO 81326. ■

DON NORMARK

HANDSOMELY WEATHERED *and overgrown with roses, hutch is home to Margo Kramer's garden companion, Max, a family member for eight years.*

What about a rabbit in your garden?

Domestic rabbits make cuddly garden pets—and there's a bonus

CUDDLY *mixed Holland lop weighs 4½ pounds.*

DOUG WILSON

PERHAPS IT'S A BEATRIX Potter revival, or maybe another grass roots back-to-the-earth movement, this time focusing on hare husbandry. Whatever the impetus, a growing number of Westerners are keeping a rabbit or two in their gardens.

Stan Andreasen, of Seattle, explains his affection for his long-eared garden pet this way: "I love everything about a domesticated rabbit in my garden. The hutch is garden art, Nibbles is a happy resident—sort of the spiritual keeper of the garden—and he's a loving, cuddly little manure factory."

If you'd like a domestic bunny in your garden, you'll find rabbits for sale in pet shops and through rabbit breeders. The selection is wide—from the diminutive Netherland dwarf to the floppy-eared, lovable lops to the Flemish giant, which can reach 25 pounds.

MAKING A HOME FOR A PET RABBIT

The simple shed-roofed hutch illustrated on the facing page is a good basic design. Modify it to suit the location, the number of rabbits you wish to house, and the amount of space you want to give your rabbit (also consider how much out-of-cage exercise it will get). Most pet rabbit owners agree the very minimum is 1 square foot of floor space per pound of body weight. Err on the side of generosity. A 10-pound rabbit needs a hutch that measures about 3 by 4 feet and is at least 14 inches tall.

A shed roof with overhanging eaves handles rain and shades the hutch, which should be enclosed on the better part of three sides to block the wind. Since rabbits gnaw on wood, use untreated 2-by-4s to frame the interior housing area; sheath the housing with 1-by-6s or with plywood.

For the floor and open areas, use ½-inch hardware cloth (normally available in 3-foot widths). The idea is to use cloth big enough to let droppings fall through but small enough that the rabbit's feet won't slip through. One area of the floor should be solid so the bunny can sit and stretch out in comfort. A pair of 1-by-6s across the floor (covering the depth of the cage at one end) works well.

Build the hutch to stand 3 feet aboveground (with legs made of pressure-treated 4-by-4s). This allows air circulation under the cage and room for droppings to fall well away from the pet. At this height, dogs are more likely to ignore the rabbit, and you'll find it easy to see your pet, feed and water it, and clean the cage.

FLEMISH GIANT *can reach 25 pounds.*

Build in a door that allows you to lean completely into the cage to reach the far corners, and affix a strong, animal-proof latch.

Inside the hutch, place a wooden hiding box: a box 12 inches wide and high by 18 inches deep is a good size for most rabbits. It should be solid on all sides except for a foot-square opening at one end for the rabbit to get in and out of. Straw, hay, or excelsior pushed loosely into the box provides insulation and softens hard surfaces.

BUNNY FOOD

The staple of any pet rabbit's diet is the commercial food (usually called rabbit pellets) available at feed stores. Rabbits tend to get obese, especially in captivity, so don't overfeed.

Add to the basic diet a daily treat—an apple or a carrot. You may want to get a mineral lick (also available at feed stores).

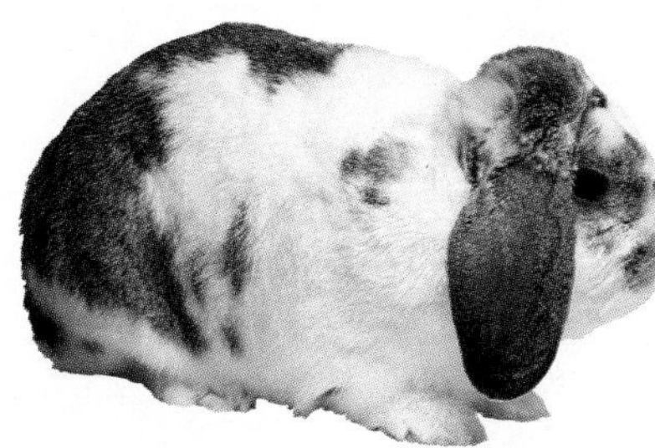

DOCILE MINI LOP *is an adorable 6-pound pet.*

A constant supply of clean, fresh water is essential. Plastic bottles with feeding tubes that hang on the side of the cage are one good answer. Unbreakable dishes filled with water also work. Be vigilant; water evaporates quickly, and it could be fatal to deprive the animal of water.

THE DIVIDEND FROM YOUR INVESTMENT IN FOOD

In addition to being cuddly, docile pets, rabbits are prodigious fertilizer producers. Two rabbits will build up a hefty pile—ample to give a thorough November manuring over planting beds and vegetable plot on a standard 60- by 120-foot city lot. The gentle manure breaks down during winter while plants are dormant; seasonal rains soak the nutrients into the ground. For plants, it's like downing a protein drink. You can broadcast 8 to 10 pounds of rabbit droppings per 100 square feet in late fall. Sandy soils will benefit most from the larger amount; for a finer-textured soil, use the smaller amount.

Gardeners often add the droppings to their compost piles. You may want to put a shovelful or two in a 15-gallon plastic bucket, fill it with water, let it stand for a week until it becomes the color of strong tea, then irrigate plants with the elixir.

Of course, you should prevent children from handling rabbit droppings or playing in fertilized beds.

PROBLEM RABBITS AND RABBIT PROBLEMS

Loose hare. To let your pet out for a regular romp, you need an enclosed space. A fence must go to the ground, and, even then, a rabbit can dig underneath and hop away. Watch your rabbit's habits. If it keeps returning to the same corner, check for signs of digging (though it may just be returning to a comfortable siesta spot). Don't let a rabbit loose where you've used slug bait or weed killers.

Gnawing problems. Rabbits nibble permanent plants in the garden. It usually isn't very damaging. They love to munch lawn.

But newly set out or emerging plants (annuals, perennials, and vegetable seedlings) are prime targets. As one rabbit owner sums up. "Seedlings and rabbits are incompatible."

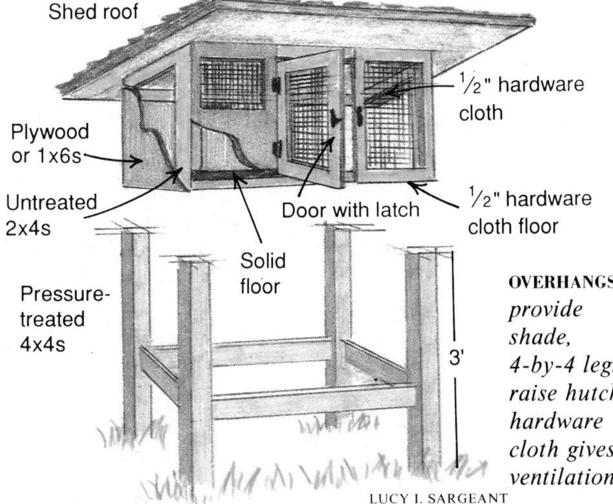

OVERHANGS *provide shade, 4-by-4 legs raise hutch, hardware cloth gives ventilation.*

LUCY I. SARGEANT

THICK, PETTABLE *fur covers 8-pound rex.*

To protect seedlings, keep your rabbit in an enclosed pen, put protective fences around areas you want the rabbit to stay out of, or fashion a portable playpen of sorts from 1-by-1 garden stakes and a roll of chicken wire.

Heat and cold. Heat stroke is one of the primary rabbit killers. Rabbits can't stand direct sunlight in their cages. *Be certain your rabbit has constant access to shade.* Bunnies are happiest in 55° to 65° temperatures. (At 85° they head underground in nature—rabbits are not good pets for hot climates.) In hot weather, they must be in a shady place, preferably cool and breezy.

One California rabbit owner wraps a frozen plastic water bottle in a towel and places it in her rabbit's cage in hot weather to cool her pet. Another drapes wet towels over the cage.

Rabbits do well in most cold weather if they have a hiding box to snuggle up in. If you live in a normally mild-winter climate and the temperature suddenly plunges well below freezing, bring the rabbit indoors, or into a garage at least.

Myxomatosis. Well-kept rabbits are relatively disease-free, but in California (especially around coastal hills and Sierra foothills) and in coastal Oregon, domesticated rabbits can contract myxomatosis, which is nearly always fatal. The virus that causes the disease is carried by native pygmy cottontail rabbits and can be transmitted by mosquito. Philip Tillman, campus veterinarian for UC Davis, advises anyone living within 3 miles of a semiwild area with a population of native pygmy cottontails to forgo keeping a rabbit as an outdoor pet. ■

By Steven R. Lorton

TINY, PERKY *Netherland dwarf weighs 2 pounds.*

BUILD A COMPOST PILE *by layering greens (grass and weeds) with browns (straw, dead leaves).*

MICHAEL THOMPSON

USE A GARDEN FORK *to turn and aerate working compost, and to dig fresh compost into garden beds.*

Quick and easy compost

Using this method, you'll have finished compost in about a month

THE BAD NEWS IS your garden's endless capacity to produce organic waste, from weeds and cut grass to played-out vegetables and flowers. But the good news is your compost pile's power to recycle it.

Lake Oswego gardener Kathy Elshire uses the system pictured here. It works in all seasons, producing coarse, black, finished compost in about a month. For finer-textured compost (to make a seedbed, for example), Elshire keeps the pile working for an extra couple of weeks.

THE RECIPE

Elshire builds a 5-foot-wide pile on rough soil, alternating 6-inch layers of brown matter (old leaves, potting soil, straw, wood chips, or sawdust) with green matter (weeds, grass, soft shrub clippings, or alfalfa pellets).

Once a week, she mixes and aerates the pile by moving it a few feet with a pitchfork. In warm, dry weather, she hoses it down at the same time, since the pile needs to be kept as moist as a squeezed-out sponge.

THE SCIENCE

The pile's 50-50 green-brown mixture is important, since it helps maintain the optimal carbon-nitrogen ratio. If there's too much of one or the other, the composting process slows down.

DIRECT-SOWN SEEDS *start fast in pure compost.*

But, as Elshire says, "Any time you make a mistake, you can always fix it. The compost pile is more forgiving than your best friend." When her garden doesn't supply enough brown matter, for example, she just adds straw (not hay, which contains weed seeds). When she's short on green matter, she adds alfalfa pellets; a little goes a long way. She buys the straw and alfalfa pellets at a feed store.

UNCOMPOSTABLES

To keep the pile clean, fast-working, and free of rodents, she doesn't try to compost diseased leaves, thorny plants (like rose and blackberry prunings), food, or gone-to-seed weeds. Vegetable scraps go into a worm bin; everything else goes to a commercial composting station. ■

By Jim McCausland

Summer pruning for more apples and pears

It's easy to do, once you know how

MOST GARDENERS associate pruning apple and pear trees with the winter dormant season, when it's important to work on a tree's shape. But summer pruning has many benefits, too, including a significant boost to fruit production.

According to Mark Sammons of UC Santa Cruz's Agroecology Program, summer pruning is actually a very simple technique that's been used for years on espaliers and other intensively trained trees typical of some densely planted orchards. For home gardeners with one or several apple or pear trees, the method is easy to master and quick to perform.

WHAT ARE THE BENEFITS?

The biggest benefit of summer pruning is a greater quantity of fruit relative to the size of the tree. Pruned trees channel more nutrients into fruit production, rather than excessive foliage. The fruit also grows larger, and blushed or red types develop better color.

Enhanced disease resistance is another benefit. Pruning opens up the tree and improves air circulation, which helps prevent diseases.

The technique also has a dwarfing effect. The 'Mutsu' on a dwarfing rootstock (MM106) shown here has been kept at 8 feet, rather than growing the typical 18 to 25 feet. This can be a big plus for gardeners with little space. It also means fruit is easier to harvest.

WHICH TREES CAN BE PRUNED? WHEN?

Any healthy apple or pear tree older than three years (it should have developed its main structure) that's growing on a dwarfing rootstock can benefit from summer pruning. It's not suitable for standard-size trees, which are too vigorous. In hot inland areas, the technique should be modified to remove less foliage, or the fruit will sunburn.

The best time to prune is when new growth is about pencil-thick; the stem tip should be succulent and the base starting to turn woody. In Southern California, this is normally about the beginning of June. In the Santa Clara Valley, south of San Francisco, it's usually about the third week of June. In cool, northern coastal areas, trees may not be ready for pruning until early August.

Pruning is confined to shoots on the lateral branches; branches that form the main structure of the tree are left unpruned. Also, leave the two shoots closest to the ends of the branches unpruned until the tree has reached the size you want.

When conditions are right, all of the dormant buds in the remaining leaf axils (where a leaf joins the stem) of the pruned shoots will form fruit in the following year. ■

By Lauren Bonar Swezey

SIMPLE STEPS FOR BOOSTING APPLE OR PEAR PRODUCTION

LATERAL SHOOT *in hand is ready to be pruned; stem is about pencil thickness and wood is half-ripe.*

STARTING AT BASE *of shoot, count up two or three leaves above basal whorl of leaves; prune just above the leaf.*

WITH LATERAL SHOOTS *pruned back, branch is narrower and allows more light into center of tree.*

NORMAN A. PLATE

TO BEGIN PRUNING, SELECT a branch and find the third shoot from the end (start at the top if your tree is already the size you want it).

Prune the stem back to just outside the third leaf. If the stem is somewhat thinner than a pencil (under ½ inch), prune just above the second leaf. Prune weak and thin lateral shoots above the first leaf. Work down the branch, pruning the remaining laterals, then work your way around the tree, pruning the other branches the same way.

In areas with long growing seasons where trees are irrigated, buds may grow into new shoots after pruning. If this happens, repeat the pruning operation a second time during or right after harvest (don't do this second pruning in colder climates if new shoots appear).

ONE YEAR LATER, *the pruned lateral shoot produces a fruiting spur with an apple, instead of just foliage.*

JULY

Garden guide....................155
July checklists 160
First house, first garden 164
Switching to drip...............167
Pretty small gardens 170
Creative containers............176

Sunset's GARDEN GUIDE

NORMAN A. PLATE

A fuchsia-blossom wall

ALL OVER THE WEST, GARDENS ARE AT PEAK BLOOM NOW. NEAR THE COAST, FEW plants speak of summer's colorful bounty better than fuchsias, shown above espaliered on a trellis in Carmel, California. Although they're special plants for mild-winter, mild-summer areas, fuchsia plants can produce their pretty flowers through the summer in any climate except the low and intermediate deserts, where it's just too hot and dry for them. Whether you grow fuchsias or something else, there's still time to set out plants that will bloom into fall.

Sunset's

GARDEN GUIDE

NORMAN A. PLATE

SPIKES OF PURPLE *flowers appear all summer on low-growing, dark green Prunella vulgaris.*

Ground cover blooms through summer

Prunella vulgaris (sold as *P. incisa*), a member of the mint family, is an attractive 4- to 8-inch-tall, mat-forming ground cover that is closely related to the well-known ground cover ajuga. Prunella's coarse, dark green, deeply cut leaves handsomely set off short spikes of small, purple blossoms all summer.

Prunella grows well in full sun or part shade, and in most soils; it needs regular watering through the dry season. It tolerates cold down to at least –10°. Plant it in a border where it can be allowed to spread to about 3 feet (it can overgrow less vigorous plants), as shown above.

If your nursery doesn't carry plants, it can order (wholesale only) from Suncrest Nurseries, Watsonville, California. Or you can order it by mail from ForestFarm, 990 Tetherow Rd., Williams, OR 97544; (503) 846-6963 (call between 9 and 3). A tube-size plant costs about $3.

Water meters track usage indoors or out

Here in the arid West, it seems that good reasons abound for conserving water in homes and gardens. The always-dry summers and the increasing pressures from an expanding population on limited water supplies are two basic reasons for avoiding waste.

The best way to tell just how much water you're using is with a meter. Two battery-operated flow meters that attach directly to a water source—such as a hose bibb, irrigation system, or indoor water faucet or shower head—are now available.

WaterTracker ($65 with one adapter) snaps onto either a ½- or ¾-inch fitting, with an adapter for each. It gives current readings from 0.1 gallon to 999.9 gallons and cumulative readings (in full gallons) to 9,999. You can buy meters to read in either gallons or liters; they will last for at least five years.

WaterMate ($50 to $60) fits a specific pipe fitting (½ or ¾ inch). This unit has a clock and calendar, and measures water usage from 0.1 gallon to 999,999.9 gallons. It also displays in liters, cubic feet, or water billing units (748 gallons).

Both meters can be ordered from the manufacturers. For WaterTracker, call Muir Products, Inc., at (800) 354-5161; for WaterMate, call WaterMate Technology Corporation at (800) 769-2837.

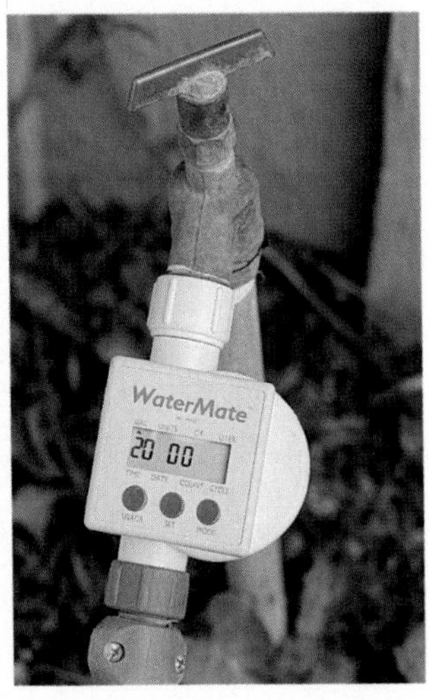

FLOW METER *attached to hose bibb or other water source measures water use.*

Tree basins for summer

Though most well-established trees do well without much extra summer water, any tree you planted during the past year needs regular water just to survive.

To make such irrigation really count, build a watering basin 3 feet across (inside diameter) and 6 inches high. Cover it with organic mulch that doesn't touch the tree trunk. (Use straw or coarse leftovers from the compost pile; ground bark floats, so it's not as easy to keep well dispersed.)

If your area gets a lot of winter rain and your soil drains poorly, break the wall of the basin in late fall to let water escape during the winter. Otherwise standing water won't allow roots under the basin to breathe.

New book for water-conserving gardeners

If you're looking for desert-adapted plants that don't need much water, here's a book that can help. *Low-Water-Use Plants for California and the Southwest,* by Scottsdale landscape architect Carol Shuler (Fisher Books, Tucson, 1993; 144 pages; $14.95), opens with a thorough discussion of low-water-use gardening; it's followed by a 95-page encyclopedia, complete with color portraits of most of the described plants and a creative plant selection matrix.

The 16-page chapter on horticulture reflects the most current thinking about planting, and the section about irrigation systems and scheduling will be useful to many gardeners. There's little information about pests; perhaps that is because the right plant, placed in the right spot and cared for properly—the theme of the book—is not particularly pest prone.

Low-Water-Use Plants for California and the Southwest is available at most bookstores or directly from the publisher at Box 38040, Tucson 85740; (800) 255-1514.

Tough new white dogwoods

Across the United States, both major native dogwoods—Western (*Cornus nuttallii*) and Eastern (*C. florida*)—have taken a beating from disease in recent decades. Anthracnose has been the main problem. To beat it, Elwin Orton of Rutgers University, in New Jersey, developed disease-resistant hybrids as replacements.

Crossing Eastern dogwood with kousa dogwood (*C. kousa*), he produced six white-flowered hybrids. Two of them—*C.* 'Aurora' and *C.* 'Ruth Ellen'—won gold medals from the Pennsylvania Horticultural Society this year and are available at retail nurseries now. We use trademark names here. You might also find these under their official hybrid monikers: 'Rutban' ('Aurora') and 'Rutlan' ('Ruth Ellen')—names only a university could love.

'Aurora' produces wide flower bracts whose parts overlap. The tree itself is slightly taller than wide and rather rounded. 'Ruth Ellen' has leaner bracts whose adjacent edges don't touch one another. This tree is more oval, and wider than tall. Both trees bloom profusely in May.

Both these trees are sterile; they won't produce fruit.

Look for balled-in-burlap plants this month. Choose the bloom you like best.

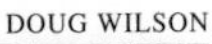
DOUG WILSON

OOZE-STYLE SOAKER HOSE *puts water right over roots of these vegetables.*

MICHAEL THOMPSON

BRICK PATIO *started out as a water-guzzling rear lawn. New fence adds privacy; pots of annuals brighten it.*

Soaker hoses save water

For irrigating rows of homogeneous plants, from roses to carrots or tomatoes, it's difficult to beat ooze-type soaker hoses. (Don't confuse these with perforated hoses that shoot water out in streams.)

They're easier to install and maintain than drip irrigation and more efficient than overhead sprinklers, and they share an important benefit with drip tubing: water from them never touches plant leaves. For roses, that means less black spot, botrytis, and leaf spot, while for vegetables it means less blight.

In addition, water oozes out of these too slowly to run off or evaporate; most soaks deep into the root zone.

Hoses with different flow rates are available. Canvas soakers put out the highest volume, but water flow falls off severely from end to end. We don't recommend these. Next come rubberized hoses (one is made partly from recycled tires). As you'd expect, the ⅝-inch diameter puts out more water than the ½-inch.

Lay soakers on the soil surface. You can also bury the rubberized kind (but not the fabric one, which would rot).

Shade gardening revisited

"Casually, quietly, I would observe her weeding, perhaps a bed of marigolds. Four hours or so was her usual stint. There she would be, kneeling before marigolds under an August sun, sequestered beneath a great limpet of a straw hat, saved from the sins of telephone and daytime TV, a marigold woman pure and simple."

So goes George Schenk's

description of a neighbor in *The Complete Shade Gardener* (Houghton Mifflin Co., Boston, 1991; $17.95), one of the classic books about growing things in abundant shade. Newly updated and revised, it's better than ever.

As nurseryman, designer, and maker of gardens, Schenk has had decades to perfect his craft in gardens from Seattle to New Zealand. In *The Complete Shade Gardener,* he walks you through the design process, explains how to prepare all kinds of soils for planting, and discourses on pruning and much more.

Nothing is idealized. Explaining how he chose a particular plant to stand against a wall, he writes: "Reader, my considered answer is: I don't know. I never know. . . . My Finance Committee plumped for a vine. . . . My Corps of Engineers likewise endorsed a vine. . . . My Don't Fool Around Lobby . . . rallied in behalf of a vine. . . . But my Art Commission argued against a vine and, with its single vote, won. (It always does.)"

Expect insight, humor, and as strong a shade-plant encyclopedia as you can find anywhere, and this book won't disappoint you. It's available in bookstores.

Trading in the lawn

Faced with a rear lawn that seemed more work than it was worth, Jo Leech decided she'd rather have a patio and planting beds. Her husband, Arnie, started by replacing the grass with bricks set in sand. (If you do this, strip out the sod first, or the patio surface will become uneven as the sand settles into the dead grass.)

Then she added color to the area with a border of annual baby's breath, blue salvia, cornflower, cosmos, geum, impatiens, lobelia, marigolds, nemesia, and stock.

To cool the garden down, she let plants wall it off. English ivy covers the chain-link fence, English laurel screens the alley, and a large rhododendron grows against the garage. A shady woodland of vine maples borders the patio, while a lath screen (pictured on page 157) completes the courtyard.

If summer watering restrictions during the past several years have tempted you to remove your water-guzzling lawn, now is a good time to take action. Grass is growing more slowly and is easier to remove.

CLAIRE CURRAN

DECORATIVE TASSELS *of summer-blooming Origanum hybridum conceal the perennial's low-growing, scented foliage.*

Selecting a peach variety for Southern California

Several low-chill peach varieties, like the genetic dwarf 'Southern Rose' pictured below, ripen this month. It's a good time to get out and taste ripened fruits of different varieties to determine which you like best. Some Southern California nurseries, like Pacific Tree Farms in Chula Vista, offer fruit for tasting. Also check farmers' markets for vendors who sell locally grown peaches.

If you find a peach you like, in mild summer areas you can still plant container-grown trees this month—the sooner, the better. Consider only varieties that have a low chill requirement (the amount of cold weather required for the tree to grow and fruit normally). Good varieties for Southern California should require no more than 200 to 300 hours of chilling, depending on where you live. Among the excellent choices for standard trees are 'Early Amber', 'Eva's Pride', 'Flordaprince', 'Gulf Queen', 'May Pride', and 'Santa Barbara'. 'Southern Rose' is a low-chill dwarf tree with good-tasting fruit; it grows to 5 feet.

For a selection of container-grown peach trees, check full-service nurseries. One mail-order and retail source offering several varieties is Pacific Tree Farms, 4301 Lynwood Dr., Chula Vista, CA 91910; (619) 422-2400. Catalog costs $2.

RUSS A. WIDSTRAND

'SOUTHERN ROSE' *dwarf peach bears ripened fruit in July.*

A safe way to remove algae from ponds

Algae can ruin the beauty of a pond and completely block the view of koi or goldfish swimming around. The slimy green growth is also dangerous for fish, because it can use up available oxygen.

Until recently, algae, which multiply quickly with a combination of sun, warm water, and nutrients in the pond, have been difficult to control without chemicals that can be harmful to fish. Now, two nontoxic, organic liquid products (sold as Bio-Restoration 1 and 2) can be used in tandem to rid your pond of these unwelcome plants.

The first formulation, when applied to the water, disrupts photosynthesis and locks up phosphates. The treated water temporarily turns lilac, and the algae drop to the bottom of the pond. (Even if no algae are present, this formulation can be used alone to prevent their formation.)

The second formulation—a combination of enzymes and microorganisms—biodegrades the algae and other organic wastes, clearing the water in the process.

Neither of these formulations harms fish or pond plants such as water lilies and *Iris pseudacorus*.

Bio-Restoration is available from Enviro-Reps International, 2646 Palma Dr., Suite 455, Ventura, CA 93003; call (805) 650-9187. Cost is about $25 for a gallon of either product (enough to treat 15,000 to 20,000 gallons of water).

Showy oregano for long summer bloom

Summer-blooming *Origanum hybridum* (pictured above) is best used in the front of a border, a hanging basket, or a rock garden. It needs sun, good drainage, and little water once established.

This perennial spreads to about 1½ feet. Flower clusters with overlapping rose purple bracts embellish the plant from summer to fall. The tassel-like clusters, dangling from slender, 18- to 24-inch stems, are attractive in arrangements. When crushed or rubbed, the slightly felty dull green leaves have a strong, pleasant scent (it's related to mint and oregano).

In winter, when the plant is semidormant, the foliage dies partially back. By early spring, new growth appears, signaling the best time to cut back the old flower stems.

Summer-blooming *O. hybridum* is sold in 4-inch pots for about $2 and in 1-gallon containers for about $5.

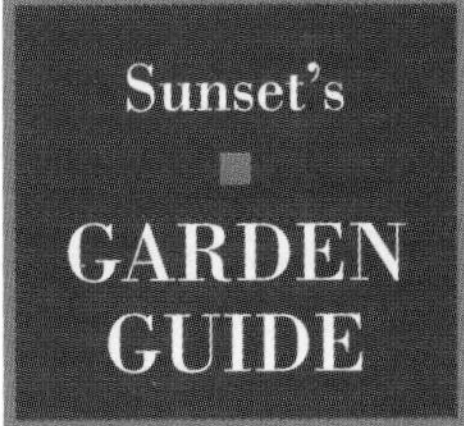

New reference book for gardeners in the dry West

Gardeners serious about growing plants that are naturally adapted to their own part of the arid West will find a comprehensive new reference, *Landscape Plants for Western Regions,* by Bob Perry (Land Design Publishing, Claremont, Calif., 1992; $59), especially useful.

The book is an investment in a well-designed landscape. Opening chapters provide a strong foundation for choosing plants based on environmental impact, climate, and their natural origins and habitats. Charts give the estimated water needs of about 650 plants for eight climate and habitat regions of California and portions of Arizona and Nevada.

Perry recommends plant combinations for good looks and cultural compatibility. The combinations include trees, shrubs and vines, ground covers, perennials, and accent plants.

Design checklists give the size, flowering season, and wildlife value of each plant. The same plants are shown in color photographs and described in greater detail in an encyclopedia.

For a copy of the book, check bookstores or order directly from the publisher, 409 Harvard Ave., Claremont, CA 91711; (909) 621-2179.

A grasshopper strategy

Last year, grasshoppers inundated El Paso, and in Fort Worth they even ate the vinyl off window screens. Is there an effective and environmentally sensible control for these voracious pests? Yes. This month, use a chemically treated bait; next spring, use the biological control *Nosema locustae.*

De-Bug is wheat bran bait treated with a small amount (2 percent by weight) of the insecticide carbaryl. Although other formulations of carbaryl can be dangerous to groundwater and beneficial insects, this one—according to USDA tests—is not. De-Bug does not leach into groundwater and is not toxic to honey bees. Only insects such as grasshoppers that feed on the bait are affected.

Apply De-Bug with a dry spreader (drop or whirly type) at a rate equal to 1½ to 3 pounds per acre; it can reduce grasshopper numbers by 75 percent within two days.

Next spring, when grasshoppers are immature (about ½ inch long), use *Nosema locustae,* the most effective (and safest) grasshopper control. Also mixed into a wheat bran bait, the protozoa, a natural parasite of grasshoppers, works more slowly than most insecticides, but it affects grasshoppers only.

De-Bug and *Nosema locustae* baits are available in nurseries or by mail from Bozeman Bio-Tech, Box 3146, Bozeman, MT 59772; (800) 289-6656. Cost of both is less than $10 to treat 1 acre.

RUSS A. WIDSTRAND

BOUNTIFUL HARVEST *of tiny pink lingaro berries begins midmonth and continues into August.*

Lingaro . . . fruits for you and for birds

The picture above shows a plant that promises to be a welcome addition to many desert gardens. Lingaro (*Elaeagnus philippinensis*) is native to the mountains of Luzon in the Philippines; it thrives in heat, is drought tolerant, and takes cold to 18°.

Fruits of lingaro are pale red to pink, and they taste juicy and tart. They hold well on the bush for weeks if birds don't reach them first. You can make a brightly colored jam with them; small seeds inside are soft and edible. Evergreen leaves are about 3 inches long, mottled green on top and silvery underneath. The plant develops into an arching shrub about 9 or 10 feet tall; with pruning, you can train it into a small tree.

You can plant lingaro anytime in almost any soil. Like legumes, lingaro is able to extract nitrogen from the soil, so fertilizer needs are minimal. Water regularly to establish.

Bare-root 1- to 2-foot plants ($36) are available from Pacific Tree Farms, 4301 Lynwood Dr., Chula Vista, CA 91910; (619) 422-2400.

Two colorful heat lovers

Among the few fast-growing annuals you can grow for summer color are portulaca and its cousin purslane. Plant them now for color soon.

Many gardeners first encounter purslane (*Portulaca oleracea*) as a persistent weed. But hybrids—with names such as 'Candy Cane', 'Fuchsia', and 'Hot Pink' are now available. The stems and leaves of these showy hybrids are larger than those of the weedy kind, and their flowers reach 2 inches across. They're colorful additions to hanging baskets and garden beds.

Portulaca (*P. grandiflora*), also called rose moss, has flowers 1½ inches across in yellow, orange, magenta, and rose. The Sundial Series bear flowers of scarlet, pink, fuchsia, yellow, cream, orange, and white. Space seedlings 6 to 8 inches apart to make a bed of shimmering colors. Or scatter seeds in the ground for bloom in about six weeks. Mix the seeds with about three-fourths sand and sprinkle from a salt shaker for even distribution. Cover very lightly and keep moist.

Both portulaca and purslane have fleshy stems and leaves that enable them to withstand fairly dry soil once established. Planted this month, both continue blooming until frost. ■

By Michael MacCaskey, Jim McCausland, Lynn Ocone, Lauren Bonar Swezey

Northwest GARDEN GUIDE

WEST OF THE CASCADES, see items marked with a **W.**

EAST OF THE CASCADES, see items marked with an **E.**

July Checklist

HERE IS WHAT NEEDS DOING

☐ **DIG SPRING-FLOWERING BULBS. W, E:** After tops have dried, you can dig bulbs and replant them. If you want to store them for later replanting, brush the dirt off, cut off dead tops, and dry them in a warm, shady spot with good air circulation. Store in slatted boxes in a dry, dark place.

☐ **FERTILIZE CHRYSANTHEMUMS. W, E:** Do it every three weeks until buds show color, then feed weekly.

☐ **FERTILIZE YOUR LAWN. W, E:** Around July 4, give your lawn ½ to 1 pound actual nitrogen per 1,000 square feet. Water in well.

☐ **MULCH AZALEAS, CAMELLIAS, AND RHODODENDRONS. W, E:** A 3- to 4-inch layer of organic mulch helps maintain soil moisture, which in turn helps keep these shrubs healthy as they set buds for next spring's flowers.

☐ **ORDER FALL-PLANTED BULBS. W, E:** If you plan to make an especially large order, or you want hard-to-get bulb varieties, you can order now.

☐ **PLANT DAHLIAS, MUMS. W, E:** For fall bloom, you can fill holes in the garden now with dahlias and chrysanthemums. The dahlias sold as bedding plants are mostly the shorter varieties.

☐ **PLANT LATE-SEASON ANNUALS. W:** Nurseries still have annual seedlings in stock. Planted now, many will flower into fall if you keep them well fed and watered. (Avoid rootbound seedlings.)

☐ **PLANT VEGETABLES. W:** There's still time to sow seeds of beets, broccoli, bush beans, carrots, chard, Chinese cabbage, kohlrabi, lettuce, disease-resistant peas, radishes, scallions, spinach, and turnips.

☐ **PRUNE AZALEAS, RHODODENDRONS. W, E:** Cut back oversize, leggy, or misshapen plants as early in the month as possible. Generally speaking, the most rampant growers take pruning best.

☐ **RENEW FLOWERING GROUND COVERS. W, E:** After bloom, shear ground covers, fertilize, and water.

☐ **RENEW SHASTA DAISIES. W:** Cut bloomed-out Shasta daisies to within 3 or 4 inches of the ground, then feed and water to encourage fall bloom.

☐ **TEND COMPOST. W, E:** Keep the pile working by turning it often to aerate it and watering it to keep the moisture content up.

☐ **TEND FUCHSIAS. W, E:** Many fuchsias bloom less during the hottest part of summer. Pinch out grapelike berries (and nip out growing tips for a bushier plant), then fertilize and water well for another round of bloom next month.

☐ **TEND RASPBERRIES. W, E:** After the June harvest is finished, remove canes that have produced fruit (they'll be brown and withering). Leave new green canes. On everbearing raspberries, remove only the half of each cane that bore fruit; the lower half will bear next summer.

☐ **TEND ROSES. W, E:** Keep bushes fed and watered. When you pick hybrid tea flowers, cut them off just above a five-leaflet side shoot.—*J. M.*

IN HIGH ELEVATIONS and intermountain areas of California, and east of the Sierra, see items marked with an **H.**

IN LOW ELEVATIONS of Northern California, see items marked with an **L.**

☐ **CONTROL BUDWORMS. H, L:** If your geraniums, nicotiana, penstemons, and petunias appear healthy but produce no flowers, budworms are probably eating the buds before they can open. Look for small holes in buds and black droppings on leaves. Spray every 7 to 10 days with *Bacillus thuringiensis* (BT), a nontoxic biological control.

☐ **CONTROL TOMATO HORNWORMS. H, L:** Look for chewed leaves and black droppings, then hunt through foliage and handpick and destroy the worms. If they're still small, spray them with BT.

☐ **DIVIDE BEARDED IRIS. H, L:** Dig old clumps with a spading fork, then cut the rhizomes apart with a sharp knife; be sure to include a leaf with each division. Replant the younger, vigorous sections of rhizome.

☐ **FERTILIZE CYMBIDIUMS. L:** To encourage flower formation for next winter's bloom, feed cymbidiums with liquid fertilizer diluted to ¼ strength every time you water.

☐ **MULCH. H, L:** To conserve moisture, cool plant roots, and discourage weeds, cover the soil around plants with a 2- to 3-inch layer of organic mulch.

☐ **PLANT SUMMER FLOWERS. L:** Nurseries still have a wide variety of summer flowers that will bloom into fall. Choices include ageratum, celosia, dahlias, marigolds, petunias, portulaca, salvia, sweet alyssum, and zinnia.

☐ **PLANT VEGETABLES. H:** For harvest in fall (except in highest altitudes), plant beets, broccoli, cabbage, carrots, cauliflower, green onions, leaf lettuce, peas, spinach, and turnips. Below 5,000 feet, plant winter squash among spinach; it will cover when you harvest the spinach. **L:** You can still plant corn and summer squash.

☐ **POLLINATE MELONS AND SQUASH. H, L:** If you live in a hot, inland area and you're not getting good production, high temperatures may be inhibiting fruit set. Use an artist's brush to gather pollen from freshly opened male flowers and transfer it to female flowers (the base of the female flowers is slightly enlarged). Dust pollen onto the stigma in the center of the flower. (You can also pull off male flowers: gently remove petals and shake flower directly over the female flowers.)

☐ **PRUNE CANE BERRIES. H, L:** After harvest, remove old raspberry canes as they begin to die; cut off blackberry and boysenberry canes that have fruited and tie new canes onto the trellis. In coldest climates, wait until August.

☐ **START PERENNIALS. L:** To get ready for fall planting, take cuttings of dianthus, geraniums, scabiosa, Shasta daisies, verbena, and other herbaceous perennials, dip stems in rooting hormone, and plant them in a mix of 2 parts perlite and 1 part peat moss. Sow seeds of campanula, columbine, coreopsis, delphinium, forget-me-not, foxglove, purple coneflower, and rudbeckia in the same mix.

☐ **WATER CAREFULLY. H, L:** Before watering, check soil moisture by digging down with a trowel or using a soil probe; water only when necessary. Use drip irrigation or soaker hoses when possible. If hand-watering, construct soil basins and furrows to direct water to plant roots. —*L.B.S.*

ADJUST MOWING HEIGHT. If your lawn is tall fescue or a similar cool-season grass, use a rotary mower set 1½ to 2 inches high. For Bermuda lawns, reel mowers work best; cut to an inch or shorter.

CARE FOR ROSES. Feed after each bloom cycle, and water (deeply) only when needed. Cut flowers just above a leaf node with five or more leaflets. Check for aphids and spider mites. If you find any, wash plants with a strong jet of water from the hose, or use an insecticidal soap.

DIVIDE IRIS. C: Lift old, overgrown clumps of bearded iris, and divide rhizomes with a sharp knife. Discard woody centers and replant large, healthy rhizomes 1 to 2 feet apart, just barely covering them with soil.

HARVEST VEGETABLES AND FLOWERS. For a longer harvest and to keep plants attractive, pick heat-loving vegetables such as beans, cucumbers, eggplant, peppers, and squash at their prime; harvest often to keep them coming. To encourage more flowers, cut off developing seed heads of cosmos, dahlias, marigolds, rudbeckias, and zinnias.

MOVE HOUSE PLANTS OUTDOORS. C: Give them a summer vacation and cleaning. Many grow faster and look healthier if they spend all or part of the summer outdoors. Just don't expose them to strong winds or to much more light than normal. Occasionally spray leaves with water to wash off dust.

MULCH. To suppress weeds, cool the soil, and reduce evaporation, spread a 2- to 3-inch layer of compost, ground bark, weed-free straw, or dried grass clippings around vegetables, fruit trees, shrubs, roses, and perennials. Keep soil clear around stems and tree trunks.

PLANT QUICK COLOR. C, H: Set out soon-to-bloom annuals in full sun; choices include globe amaranth, marigolds, portulaca, salvia, verbena, vinca rosea, and zinnias.

PLANT VEGETABLES. C: If you water diligently, you can still plant some vegetables for an extra and late harvest. Plant seeds of beans, carrots, corn, cucumbers, and summer squash. Set out seedlings of cucumbers, eggplant, melons, peppers, pumpkins, squash, and tomatoes.

TEND CYMBIDIUMS. Next year's flower spikes are developing now. To ensure proper development, water weekly and feed this month and next with high-nitrogen fertilizer. Apply it according to label instructions.

THIN TREES. L: Prune to open up top-heavy trees such as acacia, Brazilian pepper, and mesquite; thin branches and suckers so wind can pass through. If necessary, stake or guy young trees to support them in wind.

TIP-PRUNE. C, H: Force more branching and encourage bushier plants by pinching out the tips of chrysanthemums, fuchsias, and recently planted marguerites.—*L. O.*

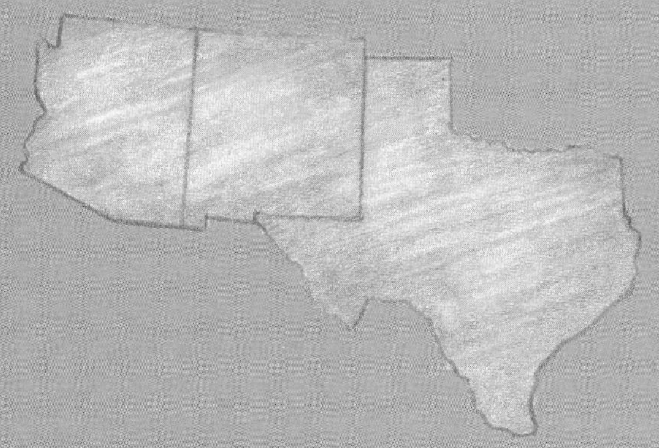

☐ **FEED ROSES.** If the leaves of your roses look pale and growth is slow, apply a complete fertilizer, preferably one that also contains chelated iron. Water thoroughly before and after applying fertilizer, then cover soil with 2 to 3 inches of organic mulch.

☐ **PLANT FLOWERS.** In the high desert, plant right away so that plants have time to mature before frost. Everywhere, choose plants that love heat, such as cockscomb, cosmos, globe amaranth, gloriosa daisy, marigolds, portulaca, purslane, vinca (*Catharanthus roseus*), and zinnia. Also try perennial shrubs such as firebush (*Hamelia patens*), Cape plumbago (*P. auriculata*), or *P. scandens* 'Summer Snow'.

☐ **PLANT PUMPKINS FOR HALLOWEEN.** Many varieties take 120 days to mature (July 3 plus 120 days equals Halloween). Choose such varieties as 'Big Max' and 'Big Moon'. Sow six to eight seeds about an inch deep in well-amended soil in a sunny area with enough room for vines to ramble (about 8 to 12 feet diameter); when plants are 4 to 6 inches high, thin to the best two plants. Water regularly, taking care not to wet foliage.

☐ **PLANT VEGETABLES.** In the Rio Grande Valley, Phoenix, and Yuma, plant pumpkins in early July, muskmelons after mid-July, and winter squash any time this month. In Austin, El Paso, Las Cruces, San Antonio, and Tucson, plant muskmelons in early July. In Albuquerque, Flagstaff, Prescott, and Santa Fe, plant beans, corn, and summer squash. In Bisbee, Douglas, Globe, and Willcox, plant beets, broccoli, short-season cauliflower, cabbage, carrots, chard, leaf lettuce, and turnips for fall crops.

☐ **POLLINATE MELONS, PUMPKINS, AND SQUASHES.** If you don't see many bees, and you notice that the first immature fruits shrivel and drop, you may need to help pollinate these plants. Use an artist's brush to gather yellow pollen from male flowers and transfer it to female flowers (the ones with swollen bases that will develop into fruit). Dust the pollen onto the stigma in the center of the flower.

☐ **PREVENT SOUTHWESTERN PINE TIP MOTH.** In Las Cruces, late June to early July is usually the time to take action to control the second generation of pine tip moth to occur this year. To find out the best method for your trees, check with your local nursery or cooperative extension agent.

☐ **SOLARIZE SOIL.** To clean soil of weeds and other garden pests, now, during the hottest temperatures of the year, is the time to put the sun to work in your garden. Cultivate, clean, and water the soil to be treated. Cover with clear plastic sheets; mound soil over edges to hold plastic in place. Leave plastic in place for two to three weeks, then roll plastic back, dig soil, and re-cover for another two weeks.

☐ **SOW TOMATO SEEDS.** In the low desert, sow seeds near midmonth—they'll germinate quickly, and seedlings will grow fast. You should get fruits from September until frost.

☐ **THIN TREES.** Before summer rainstorms and winds arrive, lightly thin top-heavy trees such as olives; cut out branches.
—*M. M.*

First house, first garden

FROM BARE DIRT
TO BLOOMS,
THE HARRISONS
CREATED A
STARTER GARDEN

Gardeners, like painters, often start their creations with nothing more than a blank slate and a vision. Then come the work, a little trial and error, perhaps a few setbacks, before vision becomes reality. That's what Vicky and Steve Harrison found out when they bought their spanking new first house in Rancho Santa Margarita, California. The Harrisons' blank slate was the backyard—bare dirt from wall to wall. Their vision of what it could eventually become

CHAD SLATTERY

TWO-PURPOSE DECK
With lid on sandbox (left) deck is ready for lounging or parties; with lid off, it's a play space (right). Blooming plants include purple lavender, golden gazanias and broom, white lantana (foreground) and Salvia greggii (rear), and bright purple Geranium sanguineum.

CHAD SLATTERY

TWO-LEVEL BEDS *keep edibles like beets, chard, fennel, lettuce, peppers, and strawberries growing just outside the kitchen window. Bark chips cover paths between.*

was simple: "A pleasant place to relax, entertain, and grow herbs and vegetables—also a place for our daughter to play."

But the yard was small—barely 30 by 60 feet—and the soil was heavy clay. "After we bought the house, we didn't have much money left over for costly landscaping," says Vicky Harrison.

Undaunted, the Harrisons (both first-time gardeners) set about creating the garden pictured here. At its heart is a three-level deck with built-in planters for colorful perennials and shrubs. A few steps down on one side are raised beds for herbs and vegetables.

How did this busy working couple find time to design and install a garden from scratch by themselves? By using the carefully laid out four-step plan given here. The Harrisons worked weekends on the project for 16 months and spent about $7,000.

STEP 1: DRAW A PLAN

The Harrisons pooled their ideas to design the deck. To choose plants suitable for their climate, Vicky pored over garden books. She visited nurseries regularly to see what certain plants looked like in bloom and dormant. Then she made a plant list and drew up a plan.

Cost: none.

Time: about 30 hours spread over about six months to research plants; about 6 hours to draw the plan.

STEP 2: GRADE THE SOIL, BUILD DECK FOOTINGS

The Harrisons graded the soil, then dug holes for concrete deck footings. "We had to do it with shovels," Steve explains, "because we made the mistake of landscaping the front yard first. Hauling heavy equipment over it would have ruined it."

Cost: none.

Time: about 2 hours to grade the soil, 20 hours to dig the holes.

STEP 3: BUILD DECK AND PLANTERS, INSTALL IRRIGATION

After building concrete footings for the deck, Steve put down PVC pipe for drip tubing. "I nailed the first board the day after Thanksgiving, then dabbled on deck construction—sometimes in rain—for four months."

The deck was built of redwood 2-by-6s and stained to match the house trim. Besides the planters, it has built-in benches, a barbecue storage cupboard, and a 2-foot-deep sandbox that can be concealed beneath a removable 4-foot-square section of deck.

The vegetable garden is made up of three triangular raised beds (also built of redwood 2-by-6s) with 2-foot paths between them. "We wanted easy access to all parts of these beds without getting into the dirt," says Steve. Each bed has two levels, one 10 inches tall and one 15 inches tall. The beds range from 8 to 12 feet long.

Soil in the bottom of the planters was amended with sand before the Harrisons brought in topsoil (about 27 cubic yards) by wheelbarrow.

Cost: $5,700 for deck and raised beds, including concrete, drip-irrigation supplies, lumber, stain, mulch, soil amendments, topsoil, and 2 cubic yards of sand.

Time: about 16 days total.

STEP 4: CHOOSE PLANTS, SET THEM OUT, AND SPREAD MULCH

At the nursery, Vicky picked out most of the plants from her wish list, choosing substitutions—when necessary—with the help of a nurseryman. "I wanted plants that were evergreen, drought tolerant, free of thorns, and good-looking, as well as ones that could stand up to frost and Santa Ana winds," she says. Her choices include citrus trees, as well as blood-red trumpet vine, Japanese honeysuckle, lantana, lavender, rockrose, and salvia.

"We planted as a team," Steve says. "Vicky put the plants in the ground, and I followed her, installing drip tubing and putting down black plastic, then redwood mulch to prevent weeds. We finished just after guests arrived one Sunday afternoon."

Cost: $1,300 for 100 plants (mostly gallon size).

Time: about 5 hours to buy plants, 12 hours to plant. ■

By Kathleen Norris Brenzel

Raised beds keep vegetables just outside the kitchen door

LASER-DRILLED SOAKER TUBING *winds through closely spaced annuals and perennials, delivering water all along its length.*

Switching to drip

Converting an existing sprinkler system is easier than starting from scratch. It also saves time, money, and water

BY NOW, JUST ABOUT everyone knows that drip (or low-flow) irrigation is an efficient way to water plants. Because a drip system applies water slowly—in gallons per hour (gph) instead of gallons per minute (gpm) like conventional sprinklers—it eliminates wasteful runoff. By applying water directly to plants' roots, it also avoids overspray, evaporative loss, and uneven coverage that results when growing plants block sprinkler spray patterns.

But if you already have sprinklers, switching to drip can seem an intimidating proposition. However, you can simplify installation and minimize expense by retrofitting your existing sprinkler system. Because the distribution lines from the main water source are already in place, you don't have to start from scratch. And there's little or no digging involved.

Over the past couple of years, irrigation manufacturers have introduced many new

K. BRYAN SWEZEY

TO INSTALL *new heads, unscrew old sprinkler and screw on low-flow replacement, such as a multioutlet head.*

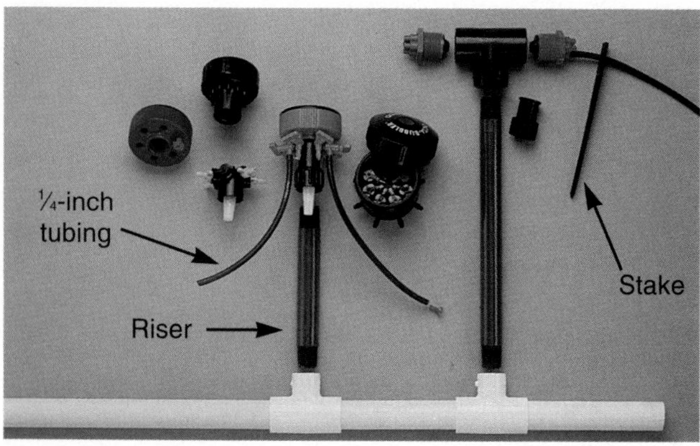

NORMAN A. PLATE

SYSTEM 1: *Multioutlet bubbler heads on risers deliver water through ¼-inch tubing staked in place. Units range from 4 to 12 outlets per head. For most flexibility, look for heads with adjustable flow (changeable inserts or adjustable valves).*

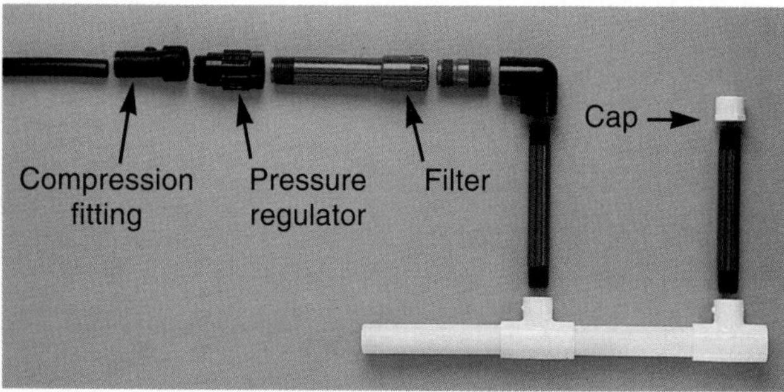

SYSTEM 2: *Simple retrofit uses one riser; others are capped (as at right). Remove sprinkler, screw on threaded elbow, nipple, filter, pressure regulator, and compression fitting; attach ½-inch tubing and emitters.*

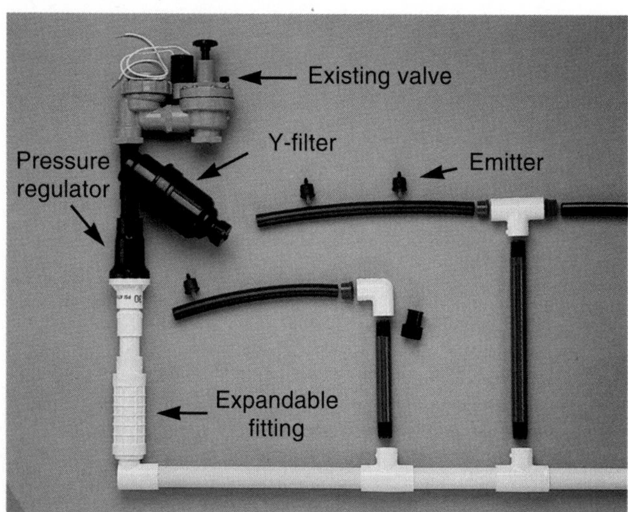

SYSTEM 3: *For larger gardens, start installation at valve. Cut and remove PVC pipe from valve to water line; screw on Y-filter, pressure regulator, and threaded/slip coupling. For easier connection, use expandable coupling such as a Slip-Fix (bottom left) and slip street elbow to tie into water line; if expanding arm won't reach adapter, add a piece of PVC with a coupling. Remove sprinklers on risers, screw on threaded-slip elbows or Ts, glue in compression fittings for ½-inch tubing, install tubing and emitters.*

products that make installation easy for just about anyone. We show four ways to retrofit sprinklers. Which system you choose depends upon the layout of your garden, how plants are arranged, and the number of sprinklers you plan to change over.

Generally, it's best to change over the entire line on one valve, rather than mix sprinklers and drip along it. Because of different water output from sprinklers and drip fittings, it's difficult to adjust watering times on a mixed system. But, in some cases, you may have no choice.

WHICH SYSTEM IS FOR YOU?

The four systems shown here all use existing underground polyvinyl chloride (PVC) pipe that distributes water through the line from a valve. If your system has galvanized pipe, it's better to start from scratch since pieces of flaking metal can clog the drip emitters.

The photograph for system 1 shows the variety of multioutlet heads available to screw onto sprinkler risers and distribute water to plants through ¼-inch or laser-drilled soaker tubing. The other three retrofits use traditional drip components.

System 1 is especially useful with mixed plantings of trees, shrubs, and ground covers that aren't grouped according to water usage, gardens where plants are clustered around risers, and small gardens with just a few sprinklers.

If you have extensive plantings and relatively few sprinklers, this system may not work. Each head has a limited number of outlets (from 4 to 12), and you need enough to water each plant individually. If this poses a problem in only a couple of areas, you can add risers.

The heads—called bubblers because they have a higher flow rate than drip—are designed to screw directly onto risers and work under varying pressure, generally from 10 to 100 psi. They come in flow rates from about 2 to 20 gph, depending on pressure.

All of the heads contain small filters or screens and are flow-regulated, so you don't need to install a separate filter and pressure regulator. However, if you irrigate with well water, it's advisable to install a drip filter at the valve.

System 2 is best used in a simple, linear planting bed, such as a parking strip or flower bed, and in beds with widely spaced plants. It makes use of one central sprinkler on the line, with the rest capped off as shown.

A filter and pressure regulator (20 to 30 psi) are installed directly on a riser, and ½-inch polyethylene tubing weaves around plants to deliver water; one or more emitters (depending on the size of the plant) are punched into the tubing to supply water to each plant's root zone.

The tubing can run 150 feet in any direction (use T-fittings to go in different directions) and can deliver up to about 240 gph. For beds that are fully planted with ground covers or flowers, it's best to use soaker or emitter line instead of ½-inch poly.

System 3 is for larger gardens that require more distribution lines and emitters. It's also useful if sprinklers on one line are separated by paving, or if the line serves a large number of plants. To save money, a filter and a pressure regulator are installed at the valve (as shown), rather than on multiple risers. Any number of risers on the line can be retrofitted with polyethylene tubing. The rest are capped off.

System 4 converts pop-up sprinklers to drip; this solution is currently available only for Rain Bird pop-up sprinklers 4 inches tall and up. The system is useful for borders with pop-up heads or gardens where the lawn has been replaced with shrubs and

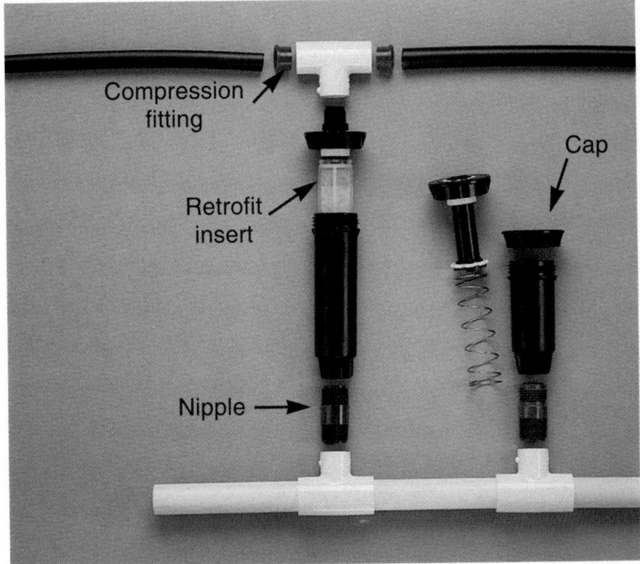

NORMAN A. PLATE

SYSTEM 4: Pop-up sprinklers made by Rain Bird are adaptable to drip. Unscrew cap and remove innards (right); replace with retrofit (left) that includes a filter and pressure regulator. Screw a threaded/slip/slip T onto cap, glue in compression fittings, and install ½-inch tubing.

ground covers. It can also work as a mixed system if a lawn has been reduced in size and the area has been replanted with flowers and small- to medium-size shrubs.

To retrofit one or several sprinklers, you replace the pop-up innards with a cap and an insert that includes a filter and pressure regulator. You cap off the other sprinklers. Poly tubing or soaker tubing delivers water to plants.

DESIGNING THE SYSTEM

To make your shopping trip as efficient as possible, plan a system on paper first. It also may help you decide whether you want a system that uses ½-inch tubing or the multioutlet heads with ¼-inch tubing.

Draw your garden bed on graph paper and then mark locations of plants. If you choose the multioutlet heads, how much ¼-inch tubing will it take to deliver water to each plant? If plants are too widely spaced and some of them are a good distance from the sprinkler, the garden may end up looking like a plate of spaghetti with tubing running long distances in all directions (generally a maintenance nightmare). If this is the case, system 2 or 3 with ½-inch tubing may be a better choice.

On the other hand, if the landscape configuration is fairly simple, with plants clustered around sprinklers, it may not be worth the trouble to install drip components. A system using multioutlet heads might do the trick with less work.

IF YOU HAVE TO MIX SPRINKLERS WITH DRIP

In some gardens, it may not be practical to convert an entire line to a low-flow system. The answer may be a mixed system, even though it makes watering trickier.

For instance, if you have a small garden with only one line that waters both the lawn and a small border, you can retrofit a few sprinklers with multioutlet heads to water the border plants while keeping your lawn sprinklers.

Another situation that may call for mixed watering is a reduction in lawn size. If you're planting shrubs and other plants where the lawn used to be, the sprinklers can be retrofitted to water the plants (a good application for system 4).

With a mixed system, you must plan drip output that will water the plants in the same time it takes to soak the grass—usually 15 to 20 minutes two or three times a week. Because of the frequent watering, most drought-tolerant plants won't be suitable.

To water deep-rooted trees and shrubs, you will need a high flow rate (up to 20 gph), such as with system 1. Since water streams out of the ¼-inch tubing at higher flow rates, install a high-flow diffuser on the end of each piece of tubing.

WHERE TO FIND COMPONENTS

For selection and service, the best place to shop is at an irrigation supply store (look under Irrigation or Sprinklers in the yellow pages). If you can't find what you're looking for locally, you can order by mail from The Urban Farmer Store, 2833 Vicente St., San Francisco 94116; (415) 661-2204. Catalog $1. ■

By Lauren Bonar Swezey

Installing extra risers

To install more risers on an existing line, you need to cut into the PVC pipe. You can then install the riser with an expandable coupling to bridge the gap. Or you can use standard fittings with the following method.

Start by cutting out a 12-inch section of the PVC sprinkler line. Using pipe glue, install an elbow on each cut end.

Make a U-shaped insert by installing four short pieces of PVC (3 to 4 inches long, depending on fittings and pipe used) on either end of two additional elbows. Add a slip/slip/½-inch threaded T between the elbows.

After you've adjusted fittings so the insert fits into the elbows on the cut pipe ends, apply glue to each end of fittings; you may need to recut one piece of pipe for proper fit. Install a ½-inch threaded nipple and elbow to the T; screw on the riser. Glue the whole unit in place; after glue dries, flush line, cap off to test for leaks, then bury.

K. BRYAN SWEZEY

Pretty small gardens

By Lynn Ocone

Visual trickery lies at the very heart of these successful Southern California gardens. Their creators employ all means to leap the visual bounds of garden walls and to instill interest and intrigue without clutter. Though each of the five landscapes on these six pages has its own style and personality, all incorporate basic techniques and design principles to defy their boundaries.

To create an illusion of space, the designers used plants to blur walls and fences, making the plots seem

Secluded streetside cottage garden

Plants in the ground, on the walls, and overhead blur the boundaries of the Laguna Beach garden pictured at left, designed by Lew Whitney of Roger's Gardens. That's a staghorn fern growing at far left; a trumpet vine edges the house eaves. Simple weathered brick paths set off colorful pockets filled with such plants as foxgloves, campanulas, violas, white roses, and gray dusty miller. Visual eddies created with accents such as a sundial, an inviting wooden chair, and containers like the one pictured below—it holds a fancy-leafed geranium—bestow a warm romantic character.

RUSS A. WIDSTRAND

larger. In the cottage garden shown above, curving brick paths disappear near the garden's edges, hinting that more lies beyond. Other techniques that make gardens seem larger: changing levels, creating depth through layering plants and structures, borrowing scenery from neighbors' gardens, and using cool colors and fine textures to help backgrounds recede.

Simplicity in design helps the elements work together to make the gardens feel spacious; each designer started with a plan that reflects a single garden style. Repeating plants and colors helps simplify. In the photograph on page 172, gray-green plants throughout the garden unify paving and plantings.

Details make the difference when space is limited. Everything shows in a little garden, and each plant, structure, and ornament must contribute to the overall design. Without enough detail, the garden is bland; with too many details, it's cluttered and confining.

Focal points and accents, such as a single showy or sculptural plant, or water features and statuary, attract attention and keep the viewer from taking in the whole garden at once.

RUSS A. WIDSTRAND

Open-air dining in a backyard hideaway

WILLIAM B. DEWEY

With a flair for the practical and aesthetic, landscape contractor Rob Lane designed his Santa Barbara backyard for privacy and an expansive view from the bedroom doors that open onto it. He softened the potentially stark and towering privacy wall (inset) with a potato vine. The contrast between brick and flagstone paving provides variety in color and texture, while pockets of gray-green plantings throughout the garden, including the side yard leading to it (above), visually tie pavers together. Unified by their color scheme, the plants—which range from ground-hugging woolly thyme to spiky fox red curly sedge (*Carex buchananii*)—are eye-catching accents in varied textures and forms.

Pretty small gardens

Restful and rustic backyard sanctuary

Every inch counts in this intimate garden in Fullerton. The patio, partly shaded by a Chinese elm, is made of puzzle-like pieces of broken concrete. Around it, billowing and vining greenery unifies and softens hard edges of concrete, walls, and doorways. Landscape architect Jana Ruzicka countered the boundary walls by layering plants. She planted vines on the neighbor's wall and, in one bed, trained ivy up three 7-foot-tall cones of wire mesh (inset); the variegated Algerian ivy on the cones contrasts with the green Boston ivy on the wall, giving the bed an illusion of depth.

Opposite the ivy-covered wall, perennials—including coreopsis, *Geranium incanum,* Jupiter's beard, lavender, and snow-in-summer—grow in a bed between the broken-concrete patio and the garage. Instead of mixing individual plants, Ruzicka massed plants of the same kind, which gives the small space a more unified look.

Pretty small gardens

Small wonder within a zero lot line

Plants and paving contribute equally to this Irvine landscape, designed by Steve Mudge and Hudson Elliott. Flagstone rich with color and pattern brings interest to the foreground, while cobblestones blend paving and planting bed; plants within the bed echo colors in the flagstone.

To make the back wall appear smaller and farther away, the designers gently mounded the garden in front of it. They created an uncluttered look that gives the sense of openness by using only a few varieties of plants—mounding blue fescue accented with dollops of green aeonium and purple echeveria (above) and kangaroo paws (inset)—by choosing plants that are in proportion to the bed, and by planting in groups. The main accent—a tile fountain—and secondary accents like kangaroo paws and boulders, focus attention within the garden rather than on boundaries.

Country charm in a city side yard

Sandy Kennedy of Kennedy Landscape Design in Woodland Hills combined pathway, plantings, and a sitting area to transform a once-wasted strip between a garage and property line into the flower-filled retreat in Venice pictured below.

The chair and arbor at the garden's far end draw your attention through the garden, away from the imposing side boundaries. Poured concrete pavers meander through a pea gravel path leading to the sitting area. This curve interrupts the path's straight line, inviting a visual pause midway to the arbor and making the space seem longer. Plants—white-flowered lamium, lilac purple *Verbena bonariensis,* and deep purple statice—are arranged with the tallest against the garden walls and smaller ones spilling toward the pathway. The size gradation provides a sense of depth, while the soft textures of the centermost plants further obscure the linear path. Lattice-topped fencing gives privacy and masks the views of nearby neighbors, yet its open pattern eliminates any sense of confinement by letting light shine through. ■

RUSS A. WIDSTRAND

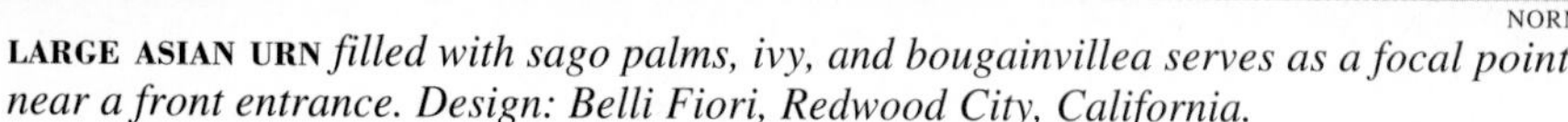

NORMAN A. PLATE

LARGE ASIAN URN *filled with sago palms, ivy, and bougainvillea serves as a focal point near a front entrance. Design: Belli Fiori, Redwood City, California.*

PETER CHRISTIANSEN

ENGLISH VICTORIAN *water filter, 16 inches tall by 8 inches in diameter, makes a handsome pot for kalanchoe.*

ANTIQUE SOUP TUREEN, *11 inches tall by 18 inches in diameter, holds foliage plants such as coleus and colorful annuals such as impatiens. Design: Belli Fiori.*

Creative containers

Tureens, crocks, and pipes can make handsome homes for plants

GARDENING IN containers is taking on a new sophistication that goes beyond conventional clay pots stuffed with marigolds. Now, innovative gardeners and designers are creating floral and foliage displays that direct as much attention to the containers as to the plants that go into them.

Although plenty of attractive containers are manufactured and sold specifically for use with plants, many other containers also work well. These two pages show a variety of unusual choices in different sizes, shapes, and materials that can be used to display plants.

But this is just a sample of striking kinds you might discover if you hunt around.

GREAT CONTAINERS COME FROM MANY SOURCES

Designer Jean Manocchio of Belli Fiori in Redwood City, California, has used a variety of materials with great success. "I have an aversion to plastic, but I've tried just about everything else, including bronze, glass, naturally hollowed out rocks, a claw-foot bathtub, and even a birdhouse."

She hunts for containers everywhere—nurseries ("I always look in the dark, dusty corners for the unique pot that was pushed aside"), specialty pottery stores, antiques shops, and garage sales. "My greatest recent discoveries came

CORRUGATED STEEL CULVERT PIPES *are inset in deck so bottomless containers drain to soil below. Pipe is 12 inches in diameter and was cut with a torch to make 8-, 14-, and 18-inch-tall containers (one is hidden behind the others). Design: Richard William Wogisch.*

PETER CHRISTIANSEN

SALT-GLAZED CROCKS, *once used to hold food, now display annuals and perennials on a deck. Crocks range from 9 to 17 inches tall, from 8½ to 14 inches in diameter.*

NORMAN A. PLATE

TERRA-COTTA *bowl's clean lines complement spa. Bowl holds alstroemeria, asters.*

from San Francisco's Chinatown: two beautiful pots that had been filled with kim chee (Korean pickled cabbage). The merchant sold both to me for $6."

San Francisco landscape architect Richard William Wogisch often makes containers from building materials, such as terra-cotta chimney pipes or flue liners, or culvert pipes like the ones shown at left.

HOW TO CHOOSE THE RIGHT CONTAINER

According to Manocchio, the pots should enhance the plants that go in them. In the garden, a container full of plants becomes a focal point. And if it will be viewed from inside the house, Manocchio likes to coordinate it with the interior design.

For instance, if the interior is Asian, she might use an Asian pot (see the facing page) planted with timber bamboo or a Japanese maple. For a Southwestern room, she might choose a Mexican clay urn or carved stone container.

Wogisch often uses containers to solve architectural problems. If the front entrance to a house has no planting areas, he'll add large containers that match the architecture, and fill them with plants. When designing the deck shown above left, he needed a transition where the stairs ended, so he added containers that complement the house's modern architecture.

Other tips from these designers: Don't use too many small containers—they're a maintenance nightmare. For a focal point, use one large container with a single dramatic plant. For bright, fussy plants, use plain pots. An ornate pot should contain a simple planting—a broad-leafed foliage plant, for example. If a container is made of low-fired clay, paint the inside with roofing compound or line it with heavy plastic (punch holes in the bottom). ■

By Lauren Bonar Swezey

AUGUST

Garden guide....................179
August checklists 184
An oasis for wildlife............188
High-altitude gardening.......191
Plain or fancy birdbaths......193
Like a slice of the woods 196
Cool backyard oasis............199
Crisphead lettuces..............200
Gunnera: Dinosaur food? 202
It's a cloister garden 203
Is it nematodes?..................204
A backyard jungle 205

Sunset's GARDEN GUIDE

RUSS A. WIDSTRAND

It's harvesttime

AUGUST'S WARM, BRIGHT DAYS ARE MORE LIKELY TO DRIVE GARDENERS UNDER the nearest shade tree than into the garden for a hard day of digging and planting. That's all right; you can enjoy lounging in the garden now and save the heavy tasks for cooler weather. Maintenance is your main priority; pots and beds need regular watering. Also, check vegetable gardens daily for ripe produce; that way, you can be sure to pick vegetables and fruits, such as the luscious red 'Supersteak' tomatoes above, at their peak.

Sunset's

GARDEN GUIDE

NORMAN A. PLATE

NARROW RAISED BED *between driveway and fence overflows with bloom. Ivy geraniums climb the grapestake fence, with purple statice and lobelia below.*

Slice of color along a driveway in Carmel

With proper soil preparation and the right combination of plants, even the narrowest planting bed can produce a dramatic impact.

This driveway planting in Kim and Bruce Marcus's oceanside garden grows in a narrow raised bed just 8 inches high and 6 to 7 inches wide. The lush display of pink and white ivy geraniums, purple statice (*Limonium perezii*), and blue and purple lobelia blooms from spring until fall.

Before planting, the sandy soil was amended with redwood conditioner and water-absorbing soil polymers. For watering, a drip system was installed along the length of the bed after planting.

Ivy geraniums trained up the fence give height to the display. The only maintenance required is deadheading the flowers and fertilizing.

PETER CHRISTIANSEN

LARGE CLAY FEET *raise container off ground for better air circulation. Decorative lion's feet are also available.*

Feet of clay raise pots off ground

Outdoors, terra-cotta pot feet dress up ordinary containers. They're also practical. Depending on their size and style, they raise pots 1¾ to 3½ inches off the ground, improving air circulation beneath and preventing staining on decks and patios.

The pot feet come in a variety of designs; two types are pictured below left. The lion's feet come in large and small sizes, and the traditional step design feet come in large, small, and wide (for trough planters). Feet shaped like lion faces, frogs, and hedgehogs are also available.

Use large feet and bulkier designs (such as frogs) beneath large pots. Since dimensions vary according to design and manufacturer, it's a good idea to try them out on different styles and sizes of pots to see which combination looks best. The small feet are suitable for pots about 6 to 8 inches in diameter. Use three feet for pots and four feet for troughs. Prices for three run about $4.50 to $19.50.

Two mail-order sources are Gardeners Eden, Box 7307, San Francisco, CA 94120, (800) 822-9600, and Kinsman Company, Inc., River Rd., Point Pleasant, PA 18950, (800) 733-5613.

Perennials for bloom late summer and fall

It's easy to create a riot of color with perennials in spring and summer. But what can mild-climate gardeners plant in August to carry the show into fall?

Here are five choices with showy late-summer bloom. Nurseries should have a good selection of them in bud or bloom. Most perennials in bloom are sold in 1-gallon cans. To save money, you can plant from smaller-size containers, but they won't give the full impact until next year.

Aster puts on a dramatic show of daisylike blue, lavender, pink, purple, red, or white flowers, generally in summer and fall. Most garden varieties range from 2 to 4 feet.

Chrysanthemum types that bloom into fall include white Shasta daisies ('Esther Read' blooms longest) and florists' chrysanthemums in a wide range of colors.

Japanese anemone (*A. hybrida*) is a graceful, spreading plant with dark green maple-like leaves and pink or white flowers on 2- to 4-foot stems. Flowers appear from late summer to fall.

Sedum telephium 'Autumn Joy' and ***S. spectabile*** are succulents that produce dramatic flower heads starting in late summer. 'Autumn Joy' changes from light pink to salmon to rosy rust. 'Brilliant' has deep rose red flowers; 'Meteor' has bright pink blooms.

New guides to gardens in Northern California

Gardens in Northern California are incredibly diverse, with design influences that vary from Mediterranean to Japanese. Two books show and describe gardens to visit that represent this great range of styles.

Visiting Eden: The Public Gardens of Northern California, by Melba Levick and Joan Chatfield-Taylor (Chronicle Books, San Francisco, 1993; $18.95), features 21 gardens from Mendocino to Santa Cruz and east to Amador County. Each garden in this paperback book is beautifully illustrated with glossy color photographs by Levick.

The text gives a short history of each garden and describes the layout and some of the plants. Details include address, hours of operation, and brief directions to the garden.

Glorious Gardens to Visit in Northern California, by Priscilla Dunhill and Sue Freedman (Clarkson Potter Publishers, New York, 1993; $16), highlights 65 gardens—

large and small, public and private—in five regions.

The 197-page paperback book has just a few black-and-white photographs but plenty of information on each garden's history and design. Some of the gardens are open by appointment only

CHARLES MANN

MAHOGANY EYES *surrounded by golden petals make flowers of black-eyed Susan stand out in this Southwest garden. This perennial blooms in summer and fall.*

Help for successful food preservation

If you're drowning in tomatoes and can't pick cucumbers fast enough, perhaps it's time to consider the tried-and-true art of food preservation. Gardeners attempting drying, canning, or freezing garden produce for the first time have help—and experienced food preservers have new recipes and information on the latest techniques.

In Los Angeles, University of California Cooperative Extension's Common Ground Garden Program offers classes, an informative free newsletter, and expert phone advice to food preservers.

In August, most of the questions Susan Giordano, coordinator of the food preservation programs, receives relate to tomatoes: "What do I do with so many of them?" Giordano is full of helpful tips and assures gardeners not to panic. "If you can't process them all at once, wash and dry them, then freeze them individually on a cookie sheet," she advises. "Once they're frozen, store them up to three months in a plastic bag. Use them to make sauces, ketchup, or other products."

For additional tomato tips, class information, or answers to food preservation questions, call Common Ground at (213) 744-4348.

Glorious black-eyed Susan

When it blooms in summer, black-eyed Susan is a show-stopper. Yellow-to-mahogany flowers reach 4 to 7 inches across; when plants are massed, as in the photograph above, they produce a sea of dazzling color that is especially appealing against banks of greenery or stone walls. August is the month these classic daisies usually bloom in the high desert; it's also a good month for high-desert gardeners to set out plants for next year's bloom.

This hardy American perennial, also called gloriosa daisy (*Rudbeckia hirta*), grows 3 to 4 feet tall and produces rough, hairy stems and leaves. Established plants are winter hardy throughout the Southwest, and roots tolerate all soils except boggy ones. If you remove faded flowers promptly, bloom will continue into fall.

Nurseries sell most gloriosa daisies in spring because that's when plants look best. But if you buy young plants and set them out in your garden this month, they'll be stronger and bloom better next year than any you could buy then. That's because they'll have time to put down roots before winter, coming into next spring as fully established young plants. Water and mulch new plants just as you would if planting in spring. You'll find plants in 2¼- and 4-inch pots ($1.50 to $3) or in 1-gallon containers ($4 to $6).

California native plants at two nurseries

If you're looking for native plants in Northern California, two nurseries are worth a visit. Both offer a wide selection of plants, and they're located in scenic areas of California.

Mostly Natives Nursery, just north of Tomales Bay about an hour's drive north of San Francisco, specializes in coastal natives and drought-tolerant plants. The small nursery is packed with 600 varieties of 200 species, including bunchgrasses, perennials, shrubs, and trees.

To get there from the Bay Area, take U.S. Highway 101 north to Petaluma, then take the Washington Street exit and drive west 16 miles to Tomales (follow signs). The nursery is at 27235 State Highway 1. Hours are 9 to 4 Tuesdays through Saturdays, 11 to 4 Sundays; call (707) 878-2009. (Catalog of native plants costs $3.)

Ya-Ka-Ama Native Plant Nursery, north of Forestville, near the Russian River about 15 minutes northwest of Santa Rosa, grows and researches plants indigenous to California, as well as plants adapted to the area.

To get there from Santa Rosa, take U.S. 101 north 4 miles; take River Road west 5½ miles to Trenton-Healdsburg Road, then go north 1 mile to Eastside Road and turn left; the nursery is about 50 yards down on the right. Hours are 9 to 5 weekdays, 10 to 4 weekends; phone (707) 887-1586.

ORANGE-FLOWERED *Zauschneria arizonica blooms in the pot at Mostly Natives.*

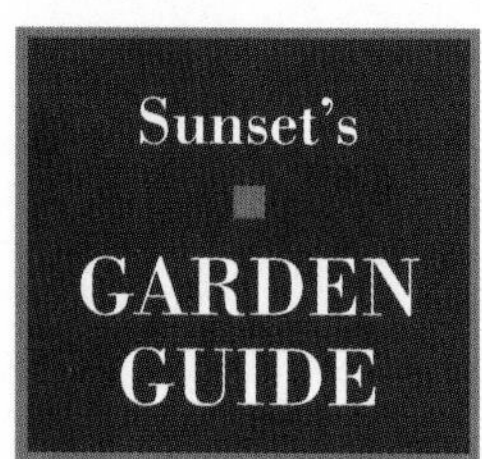

Shear now or forget it

West of the Cascades in Oregon and Washington, the most-used broad-leafed plants for hedges are probably English laurel, *Photinia fraseri, P. glabra,* Portugal laurel, and Zabel laurel. Part of their management is to shear them at the best seasons.

In these climates, August is your last chance of the season to clip broad-leafed hedges. By trimming now, you'll give them a chance to send out new leaves before the growing season ends. New leaves will soon cover the pruning cuts, and the hedge will retain a full, lush look through fall and winter, and then resume active growth next spring.

If you clip a broad-leafed hedge much past August, it has no time to regenerate. You'll be looking at a thatch of leafless twigs and cut ends through the winter.

Use hand clippers and snip gingerly, almost one branch at a time (if you use electric shears, you'll cut the big glossy leaves in pieces, giving the hedge a mutilated look).

Keep moisture in clay pots

Reports from England tell us that even Windsor Castle has replaced clay pots with difficult-to-break, water-retentive, heavy terra-cotta–colored plastic. Although Her Majesty the Queen may be able to give up her mossy old clay pots, many Western gardeners may not want to, even if clay pots do dry out fast in summer; after all, terra-cotta pots are attractive.

To keep terra-cotta from drying out and pulling water away from plant roots, regularly moisten the clay. Completely submerge pots in big tubs of water for several hours, or overnight if they begin to look dry. Hardware and discount stores sell large plastic utility tubs (often called grub tubs) that work well. Plastic garbage cans also do the trick.

Lift clay pots from the bath, then continue to irrigate plants regularly. Replace cracked pots. They're hopeless moisture losers.

A white-flowered yarrow

Frothy clusters of sparkling white blooms that cover *Achillea ptarmica* 'The Pearl' give it the look of a cumulus cloud hovering 2 feet above the ground. This rambunctious grower has an appealingly old-fashioned, wild look; small double flowers (a bit like the blossoms of double feverfew) stand in upright clusters above dark green, solid leaves (not lacy like those of other yarrows).

It blooms prolifically from late June well into September. Plants set out this month will pep up a summer-weary garden and be ready to take off next spring.

Like other yarrows, it is not finicky about soil, and it grows happily anywhere in the West. Give it a sunny location where it has room to sprawl. Water newly set-out plants regularly—especially if the weather is extremely dry.

In a few years, the center of established plants will get woody and may not produce well. Dig them out in fall, chop off the young side growth for replanting, and throw the hard old centers on the compost.

Look for plants at nurseries in 4-inch pots.

Northwest native makes a fine shade tree there

Western larch (*Larix occidentalis*), a much-loved Northwest native, is well known for its vivid yellow autumn color. But whoever thought of this stiff-needled conifer as a shade tree for a patio or deck?

In the wild, this larch can grow to 150 feet or more in as many years. But in gardens, it is surprisingly well mannered; it grows fast, straight, and tall to a height of 30 to 50 feet, then slows down. You can shear it to keep it narrow. Several planted in a line or clustered close to a deck will stretch up, casting shadows as their spring green needles filter the sun. If plants get too tall, you can top them.

When fall arrives, expect a great show of golden yellow foliage. Then the needles drop—they're easy to sweep up (and they make excellent mulch). Through winter, the naked tree branches allow low sunlight to warm the deck.

If water is plentiful, you can plant it from a nursery container in August (otherwise, wait until fall); nurseries sell it in 1-, 5-, and 15-gallon containers.

Plant labels for woodland gardens

Smooth river rocks serve as plant labels in Elizabeth Lair's Eugene garden. Resting unobtrusively on the ground beneath the plants, they look almost as though put there by nature.

Lair chooses each stone carefully, making sure it has a flat side to write a plant's name on, as well as a pleasing shape and color. Before marking on the stones, she cleans them thoroughly with detergent and a scrub brush. (If you write over dirt, the ink disappears when moisture dissolves the soil beneath the ink.)

After letting the stones dry, she applies the names of the plants with an indelible felt-tip marker (if you're skilled

HANDSOME HEDGE *of Zabel laurel (Prunus laurocerasus 'Zabeliana') gets summer clipping.*

DON NORMARK

RUSS A. WIDSTRAND

GOLDEN YELLOW *gloriosa daisies and blue mealy-cup sage bloom into fall.*

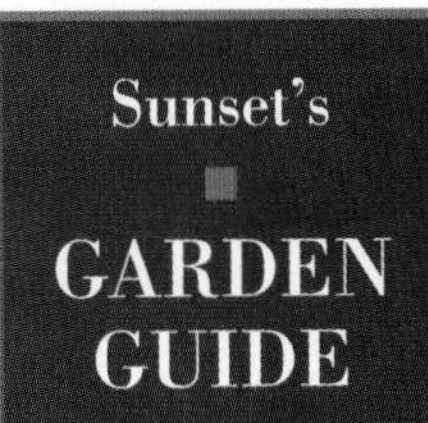

with a brush, you might choose to paint the names on).

Once dry, the stone labels go in place next to the plants.

Summer sizzlers take the heat

By late summer, many annuals (and perennials treated as annuals) have passed their bloom peak and are starting to look faded and tired. But some flowering plants, including gloriosa daisies and blue mealy-cup sage (*Salvia farinacea*) pictured above, are hot-weather workhorses that continue blooming into fall. The daisies are short-lived perennials, and the sage is a perennial in mild-winter climates; both are usually treated as annuals. When planted in early spring, they bloom from early summer into October.

Listed below are other excellent heat-tolerant annuals (and perennials treated as annuals) for summer into autumn bloom:

Bedding begonia (*B. semperflorens*), blanket flower (*Gaillardia pulchella*), cosmos, creeping zinnia (*Sanvitalia procumbens*), four o'clock (*Mirabilis jalapa*), globe amaranth (*Gomphrena*), love-lies-bleeding (*Amaranthus caudatus*), Madagascar periwinkle (*Catharanthus roseus*), marigolds, Mexican sunflower (*Tithonia rotundifolia*), morning glory (*Ipomoea tricolor*), and spider flower (*Cleome spinosa*).

Check them out in gardens and nurseries now. You can plant some now, to fill holes left in the garden by spent annuals. For a full season of bloom, wait until spring to plant.

Octopus agave: born again

In the low elevations of California and Arizona, several winters of plentiful rain prompt octopus agave *(A. vilmoriana)* to flower prolifically in the spring. But then it dies. If you have an octopus agave that's slowly withering, you can take steps now to propagate it.

First, check the flower stalk. Beginning this month and through fall, many hundreds of tiny plantlets develop along its length. When these plantlets reach about 4 inches across, pick them off the stalk. Notice the little bumps at their bases? These will grow into roots if you set the plantlets base down in moist soil. Water plantlets generously at first. They'll grow fast. You can cut back on water to limit their size.

Mother plants take as long as a year to completely shrivel and die. You can dig them up for compost anytime after you've harvested as many plantlets as you (and your neighbors) can use. Do it while plants are still somewhat moist; once they dry completely, they are more difficult to uproot.

Mosquito (and tick) protection update

Balmy summer evenings often bring out mosquitoes that can turn a backyard barbecue into a swatting match. There is no sure-fire way to prevent mosquito bites, short of completely covering yourself. But insect repellents can do a good job of keeping mosquitoes at bay.

Most effective are repellents that contain DEET. Now, new formulations with reduced concentrations of DEET are designed to release the chemical slowly to prolong its effectiveness. One example is Ultrathon Insect Repellent. It's available in a cream with 33 percent DEET that provides 12 hours of protection, or as a spray with 24 percent DEET that protects for 8 hours.

Manufacturers do not recommend the use of traditional DEET products on children 2 years old or younger (it can cause allergic reactions or other problems). For ages under 5, the American Academy of Pediatrics recommends repellent products containing 10 percent DEET or less. An example is Skedaddle! Insect Protection For Children, a lotion that contains 6.5 percent DEET and provides 2 hours of protection. The AAP also advises dressing children in long pants and lightweight, long-sleeved shirts of muted colors (bright colors seem to attract mosquitoes).

Small-leafed succulents for small containers

Just a single ornamental pot planted with succulents adds visual surprise to patios, decks, or in-ground plantings.

Here are five small-leafed trailing succulents for small containers:

Delosperma nubigenum has bright green leaves that turn red in fall, but green up again in spring. Showy, golden yellow 1-inch flowers bloom in spring.

Sedum album (often sold as *S. brevifolium*) grows 2 to 6 inches tall. Its ¼- to ½-inch green leaves are sometimes tinted red. Small, starlike flowers are white or pinkish.

S. repens (often sold as *S. anglicum*) has yellow-green leaves to ⅛ inch long. It's a compact grower to 2½ inches, with solid carpet of yellow flowers in spring.

S. spathulifolium has small blue-green leaves tinged with reddish purple; they form rosettes on trailing stems.

S. spurium has 1-inch dark green or bronzy-tinted leaves; pink flowers bloom in summer on 4- to 5-inch stems. ('Dragon's Blood' has rosy flowers and bronze leaves that turn red in winter.) ■

By Steve Lorton, Michael MacCaskey, Lynn Ocone, Lauren Bonar Swezey

WEST OF THE CASCADES, see items marked with a **W.**

EAST OF THE CASCADES, see items marked with an **E.**

August Checklist

HERE IS WHAT NEEDS DOING

☐ **BAIT FOR SLUGS. W, E:** In hot weather, slugs head for cool places. Put bait around rocks; in dark, moist areas along house foundations, garden walls, and fences; and under ground covers such as ivy and *Vinca minor*. Be careful to keep pets (especially dogs) away from bait.

☐ **COMPOST GARDEN WASTE. W, E:** Add spent flowers, inedible vegetable parts, weeds without ripe seeds, and prunings to the compost pile. Turn the pile and moisten it to the texture of a damp sponge. Small, chopped-up bits decompose quicker than big pieces. If you don't have a compost shredder, spread nonwoody waste on the lawn and run over it with a power mower.

☐ **CONSERVE WATER. W, E:** Water gingerly, even if supplies are ample. Northwest gardeners need to think in terms of water conservation—our population is growing, our water supply isn't. Use soaker hoses or drip irrigation, or build basins around trees and shrubs and run the hose slowly to get water right to plant roots.

☐ **DEADHEAD FLOWERS. W, E:** As blooms fade, remove them. Clipping off spent flowers helps extend the bloom period of most plants and keeps them from channeling their energy into seed production. Many gardeners like to get up early each morning and, with a mug of coffee in one hand and pruners in the other (and often in their bathrobes), wander through the garden, admiring and snipping.

☐ **DIG, DIVIDE, AND REPLANT EARLY PERENNIALS. W, E:** Bearded iris and Oriental poppies can be divided now. Use a spade or shovel to cut small clumps in half, large clumps in quarters.

☐ **FERTILIZE PLANTS. W, E:** Long-blooming perennials and container plants can still benefit from regular feeding. Apply full-strength, high-nitrogen fertilizer monthly, or half-strength fertilizer twice each month through October.

☐ **HARVEST HERBS. W, E:** They'll retain more flavor if you harvest them in the morning just after the dew has dried. If you're not using them right away and the weather is dry and warm, dry the cut herbs on a screen in the shade.

☐ **PROPAGATE SHRUBS. W, E:** Camellia, daphne, elaeagnus, euonymus, hebe, holly, hydrangea, magnolia, nandina, rhododendron, and viburnum can all be propagated by tip cuttings. Strip leaves off the lower end of the cuttings, dip them in rooting hormone, and put them in pots filled with rooting mix (equal parts potting soil and sand work well). Water cuttings. Place them in a bright spot out of direct sun. Mist daily, or cover with a plastic bag to keep moist. When frost hits, move the cuttings into a protected area.

☐ **PRUNE CANE BERRIES. W, E:** On June-bearing plants, remove all canes that bore fruit this summer—they won't bear again. On everbearing plants, cut off the half of each cane that's already produced fruit.

☐ **WEED. W, E:** Before weeds set seed and scatter it around your garden, pull them (you'll be reducing next year's chores). Put pulled plants on the compost pile.—*S. L.*

IN HIGH ELEVATIONS and intermountain areas of California, and east of the Sierra, see items marked with an **H.**

IN LOW ELEVATIONS of Northern California, see items marked with an **L.**

☐ **CARE FOR ANNUALS. H, L:** To keep warm-season annuals blooming through the end of summer and into fall, water and fertilize them regularly, and remove spent flowers before they go to seed.

☐ **CHECK FOR NUTRIENT DEFICIENCIES. H, L:** Inspect leaves for signs of nutrient deficiencies. Pale yellow leaves indicate that plants need nitrogen; if leaves are yellow and veins are green, apply chelated iron.

☐ **DEEP-WATER LARGE TREES AND SHRUBS. H, L:** If they depend for their water on rain rather than on irrigation, they may need a deep soaking now. Apply water with a soaker hose, deep-root irrigator, or hose running slowly in a basin until the soil is well soaked at least to the plant's drip line. Check moisture penetration by digging down with a trowel.

☐ **HARVEST FLOWERS FOR DRYING. H, L:** For dried arrangements, harvest plants that keep well, such as celosia, English lavender, globe amaranth, roses, statice, strawflowers, and yarrow. Cut with as long a stem as possible, strip off leaves, tie in small bunches, and hang upside down in an area that is dark, dry, and well ventilated.

☐ **LIGHTLY SHAPE SHRUBS AND VINES. H, L:** After summer growth, some plants may need a minor trimming to shape. Snip out wayward shoots, but don't do any major pruning. Avoid shearing shrubs into gumdrops, which destroys their natural shapes.

☐ **PICK UP FALLEN FRUIT. H, L:** Collect decaying fruit that could be harboring insects and diseases. If they look suspect, toss them in the garbage; don't compost them.

☐ **PLANT OR SOW ANNUALS. L:** Start seeds of fall- and winter-blooming annuals, such as calendula, Iceland poppy, pansy, primrose, stock, and viola. If you're having a summer party and need instant color, nurseries still should have many warm-season flowers in 4-inch pots.

☐ **PREPARE BEDS FOR FALL PLANTING. H, L:** Cultivate the soil at least 12 inches deep (if possible) and then work in a 2- to 3-inch layer of organic matter and fertilizer or compost. Rake planting beds smooth.

☐ **START VEGETABLES. H:** Where frosts aren't expected until late October, sow seeds of beets, carrots, spinach, and radishes; they should be ready by fall. **L:** Start seeds of broccoli, Brussels sprouts, cabbage, and cauliflower; they need six to eight weeks to reach transplant size. Sow seeds of carrots, chard, lettuce, peas, and radishes directly in the ground.

☐ **WATER AND FERTILIZE ROSES. H, L:** To get good fall bloom from your rose bushes, make sure they get plenty of water during August's hot days; also give them a shot of rose fertilizer. Snip off any old blooms that remain.—*L. B. S.*

August Checklist

HERE IS WHAT NEEDS DOING

BUY AND PLANT BEARDED IRIS. Iris rhizomes begin to arrive in nurseries this month. Plant them 1 to 2 feet apart in an area that gets at least a half-day of sun. In cool coastal areas, rhizome tops should show just above the soil surface. In hot areas, bury tops slightly to prevent sunburn. Water immediately after planting.

FEED CYMBIDIUMS. Next year's flower spikes are developing now. Continue weekly watering, but shift this month from a high-nitrogen fertilizer to one that is high in phosphorus. Use the dose recommended on the label.

GROOM FLOWERS. To encourage more blooms from annuals and perennials, keep fading flowers picked off.

HARVEST VEGETABLES. C, H: Once vegetables begin to mature, keep harvesting or production will slow down. Harvest eggplants, peppers, and tomatoes regularly. Pick prolific and fast-growing cucumber, squash, and zucchini daily.

MULCH. The mulch you applied in spring might be nearly decomposed by now. Check depth, and if less than 1 inch, reapply compost, shredded bark, or composted bark to a depth of 3 inches. Keep mulch away from bases of tree trunks and plant stems.

PLANT FALL-BLOOMING BULBS. Starting midmonth, you can buy and plant autumn-blooming bulbs such as *Colchicum*, fall-blooming crocus, or spider lily (*Lycoris radiata*). If you plant soon, you may have flowers next month; if you plant later, leaves will appear in winter or spring, with flowers the next fall. Plant among unthirsty California or Mediterranean natives.

PLANT FALL VEGETABLES. C: If you live near the coast (*Sunset* climate zones 20 through 24), plant the following from seeds (S) or transplants (T): cabbage (T), cauliflower (T), celery (S, T), kohlrabi (T), and peas (S). Inland, in zones 18 and 19, plant beets (S), broccoli (T), Brussels sprouts (T), cabbage (T), carrots (S), cauliflower (T),chard (S, T), kohlrabi (T), lettuce (S, T), peas (S), potatoes (eyes), and radishes (S). **L:** Sow seeds for corn and snap beans by mid-August, cucumbers by early September. In late August, indoors or in a protected area, start seeds of cool-season crops like broccoli, cabbage, cauliflower, and leaf lettuce; transplant in September or October. **H:** Sow seeds of carrots, spinach, and turnips; set out plants of cabbage, chard, kale, and lettuce; plant potato eyes.

TEND ROSES. Cut flowers for bouquets, or remove spent blooms. Feed with complete fertilizer after each bloom cycle, mulch heavily, and water deeply and regularly. Prune lightly, removing dead, weak, or crossing canes.—*L. O.*

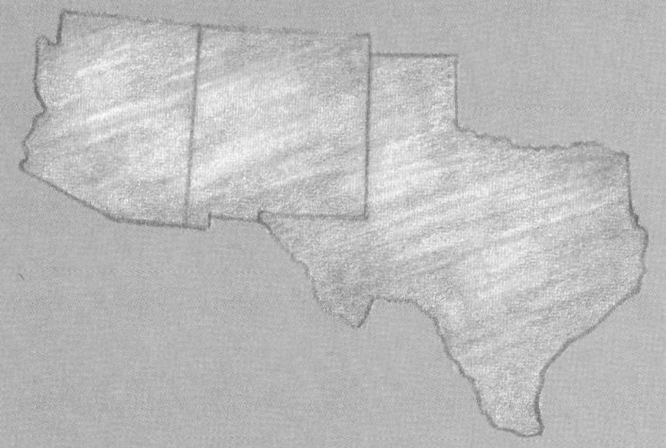

August Checklist

HERE IS WHAT NEEDS DOING

☐ **CARE FOR LAWNS.** Warm-season grasses such as Bermuda are growing fast this month. Water them regularly and deeply. Mow common Bermuda weekly at least to about 1½ inches high; cut hybrids lower, to ¾ inch or less. Cut St. Augustine and zoysia to 1½ to 2 inches. Cut cool-season grasses such as buffalo grass, Kentucky bluegrass, and tall fescue higher, to 2 to 3 inches.

☐ **CONTROL SOUTHWESTERN CORN BORERS.** Young larvae feed on the surface of the corn leaf, producing translucent, skeletonized areas. They can also destroy the plant's growing tip. When damage first appears, spray with *Bacillus thuringiensis.* Spray thoroughly where leaves attach to stalk—that's where these larvae hide. Repeat according to label directions.

☐ **FEED AND WATER ROSES.** For a burst of flowers in fall in mild-winter areas, acidify soil early this month by sprinkling Disper-Sul, a soluble form of sulfur (usually ½ cup per bush; follow label directions), over the root zone. At the same time, apply a controlled-release fertilizer, such as 7-10-5, and an iron chelate. Then water thoroughly.

☐ **FERTILIZE SHRUBS.** To help shrubs recover from summer heat stress, apply a dilute application of a controlled-release fertilizer such as 18-5-10.

☐ **PLANT OR SOW VEGETABLES.** In mild-winter areas such as Phoenix, Tucson, Dallas, and San Antonio, plant early in the month for a late crop of warm-season vegetables like cucumbers, snap beans, summer squash, sweet corn, and tomatoes. By late August, set out transplants of beets, broccoli, cabbage, carrots, cauliflower, chard, and spinach. Apply a 2-inch layer of organic mulch, and shade transplants and seedlings from hot afternoon sun using pieces of cardboard or shadecloth.

☐ **PREVENT FRUIT SPLIT.** Drought followed by sudden heavy watering (from monsoon rains, for instance) can cause fruits such as citrus, pomegranates, melons, and tomatoes to split. Abundant moisture causes the fruits to swell, but outer skin is unable to stretch. Keep soil around plants evenly moist—don't allow it to fluctuate from moist to dry.

☐ **PRUNE PEPPERS AND TOMATOES.** If the long, hot season has ravaged your plants and you live in a mild-winter area, you can encourage a fall crop by pruning. Cut spring-planted tomatoes back by a quarter to a third of their height in mid- to late August. Prune pepper plants lightly. Protect newly exposed stems from sun with shadecloth until new leaves come out; fertilize and water. —*M. M.*

An oasis for wildlife—and people

SOUTHERN CALIFORNIA GARDEN HAS A PLANTED-BY-NATURE LOOK

Rooted in native soil on a hot slope in Bel Air, dry-climate plants seem to swell and surge as they reach to the sun, yet at the same time ramble downhill. This "simulated natural hill-side," as designer Sandy Kennedy of Kennedy Landscape Design Associates in Woodland Hills refers to it, reflects the owners' vision of an informal garden that's inviting to wildlife and mimics nature.

Owners Stephanie Lynn and David Mills collaborated with Kennedy to choose unthirsty plants adapted to the Mediterranean climate—plants that are also resistant to

RUSS A. WIDSTRAND

WILD GARDEN
Water gently cascades down hot, lush slope planted with rosemary, purple-spiked pride of Madeira, fortnight lily, and Mexican bush sage (left); rushlike horsetail fills container. Hammock (right) invites lazing on warm days; evergreen orchid rockrose blooms in foreground.

RUSS A. WIDSTRAND

SEED-FILLED FEEDER *lures finch from nearby cover (including pink New Zealand tea tree at bottom left) to top of garden.*

insect pests and disease. "My garden is truly an example of survival of the fittest," says Lynn. "I don't waste time and resources trying to make things grow that don't want to." Lynn uses organic fertilizers and least-toxic pesticides.

Among the stalwart plants thriving on the hot, south-facing slope are large accents (lion's tail, Matilija poppy, pride of Madeira), flowering shrubs (Mexican bush sage, rockrose, trailing lantana), and low-growing fillers (Cape weed, lavender, nasturtium, prostrate rosemary, society garlic). Two ground covers especially valued for erosion control are yellow-flowering *Acacia redolens* (a favorite of hummingbirds) and coyote brush (*Baccharis pilularis* 'Twin Peaks'). Deer, which graze the slope, usually ignore all of these plants.

"The hillside is chaotic by intent," Lynn explains. "While most gardeners are itching to clip and prune, I simply trim plants to allow them to grow independent of each other. And I intentionally leave the plant litter for insects and other animals to live in." Lizards dart about, and birds such as sparrows, thrashers, and towhees are heard and seen rustling in the accumulated duff.

Lynn says it's the diversity of plants that attracts creatures. Herbs, shrubs, perennials, and fruit trees intermingle, providing food, shelter, and nesting sites. Despite losing fruit and occasional plants, Lynn encourages even ground squirrels, rabbits, and deer—considered pests by many. (When all creatures are welcome to share the harvest, Kennedy advises that young trees be given protection from gophers, moles, and ground squirrels that could kill them. Plant trees in 3-foot-deep hardware cloth baskets and ring them with 6-foot-tall chicken-wire cages, supported by poles positioned 3 feet from the tree trunks.)

The hillside pond (pictured on page 188) is both attractive and an important source of water for the creatures. Bird feeders and birdbaths dot the landscape, strategically placed near garden seats so Lynn and Mills can enjoy the beauty and activity.

REFINEMENT NEAR THE HOUSE

While the hillside is devoted to informality, the garden entrance and swimming pool area are more refined; roses and cutting perennials dominate. Although these smaller close-in plantings require more maintenance and water than the hillside does, Lynn is uncompromising in her nontoxic approach to gardening. She handpicks snails and spot-sprays insecticidal soap to help control aphids. In the absence of toxic pesticides, there seem to be healthy populations of naturally occurring aphid-eating insects such as lacewings, ladybird beetles, syrphid flies, predatory midges, and parasitic wasps. The area is fenced to keep deer out.

Thorough soil preparation and choice of disease-resistant varieties help ensure successful rose growing. When planting, Kennedy digs each hole 2½ times as wide and twice as deep as the plant's rootball. She backfills the planting hole with a mixture of ½ to ⅔ decomposed organic matter (like redwood compost), ⅓ to ½ garden soil, and 1 cup bonemeal (for each 5-gallon container plant). Some varieties thriving without chemicals are pink 'Bewitched', apricot 'Brandy', 'Double Delight', and 'King's Ransom'. ■

By Lynn Ocone

POOLSIDE PLANTING *combines hybrid tea roses such as yellow 'King's Ransom' (foreground) with floribundas such as white 'Iceberg' (background) and perennials for cutting.*

R. VALENTINE ATKINSON

YOUNG MOUNTAIN ASH TREES *border a bench-ringed plot of grass in demonstration garden.*

Lessons for lofty landscapes

Lake Tahoe garden demonstrates ways to go easy on the land

MOUNTAIN DWELLERS are drawn to high-altitude settings by verdant forests, crisp air, and clear water. But home building and insensitive landscaping can have a detrimental effect on the fragile alpine environment. A recently planted demonstration garden in South Lake Tahoe, California, shows how to minimize such impact.

In the decades of development following the 1960 Winter Olympics at Squaw Valley, the Tahoe Basin has suffered increased erosion, bringing greater runoff to the lake. The runoff contains chemical fertilizers with nutrients that foster the growth of algae, which threaten to turn Tahoe's jewel-clear waters cloudy.

The Lake Tahoe Demonstration Garden was created by several public agencies to show homeowners how they can control erosion, irrigate less, and minimize or avoid use of fertilizers. Its precepts are applied in four different situations, with different exposures and shade patterns. These range from a relatively high-maintenance garden of adapted and ornamental plants (as well as natives) to a simple cabin's undisturbed forest understory that requires thoughtful initial siting, then needs no attention.

The garden shows mulches—from straw to pine needles to slope netting—that lessen watering needs and hold nutrients in place. In place of sod lawns, which make heavy demands for water and feeding, the garden proposes deeper-rooted low-maintenance grasses that form natural-looking pockets of mountain meadow.

EASY-GROWING NATIVES

This project makes widespread use of native plants, which, once established, require little watering and no fertilizing. It employs at least 150 of the 1,000 or so species native to the area. We list a few here.

Trees. Besides the conifers you'd expect, look for Western water birch (*Betula occidentalis*), attractive in loose groups along a stream; mountain alder (*Alnus tenuifolia*), useful for stabilizing soil in moist areas; quaking aspen (*Populus tremuloides*), which shimmers gold in fall; mountain maple (*Acer glabrum*), a small multi-trunked tree that thrives in well-drained soil; and mountain ash (*Sorbus aucuparia*), with ferny foliage and colorful summer berries.

Shrubs. Rabbitbrush and serviceberry, sage and spiraea all have their places, but you'll also see dwarf Arctic willow (*Salix purpurea* 'Nana'), which can form a hedge or windbreak in wet soil; creek dogwood (*Cornus californicus*), for erosion control in moist areas; and greenleaf manzanita (*Arctostaphylos patula*), a good barrier planting or evergreen ground cover on rocky slopes.

Flowers. Columbine, creeping phlox, lupine, penstemon, and yarrow might be predicted. Others here include blue-flowered Lewis flax, for dry, exposed slopes; sulfur flower (*Eriogonum umbellatum*), spreading low clusters of yellow-orange flowers in sunny rock gardens; monkey flower (*Mimulus guttatus*), for glowing color in damp spots; and evening primrose (*Oenothera hookeri*), for an afternoon lift of bright yellow bloom.

Grasses. Of those in sample plots arrayed here, sheep fescue and hard fescue need the least fertilizer. Tall fescue mixes well with red fescues such as 'Ensilva'.

Most of the plants you'll see in the demonstration garden are available from nearby suppliers. The garden's interpretive center has information on appropriate species.

From U.S. Highway 50 in South Lake Tahoe, drive east on Al Tahoe Boulevard. Turn right on College Drive and follow signs to Lake Tahoe Community College. From the parking lot, a sandy path leads through pines to the demonstration garden. ■

By Marcia Williamson

KATHLEEN N. BRENZEL

Robin romps *in cool, clear water that fills glazed-bottom birdbath. Fired clay rim is textured—easy for birds to grip. Saucer slips out of pedestal for easy cleaning.*

Flagstone birdbath *nestles in cactus patch. It's two layers thick; triangle was cut out in top layer with masonry blade. The two pieces were mortared together. Clear polyurethane and silicone caulk seal the cracks.*

NORMAN A. PLATE

Basic or fanciful baths for birds

They entice feathered friends to your garden for a splashing-good time, but they're for people to look at, too. You can buy or build one this weekend

By Peter O. Whiteley

IF YOU WANT TO ATTRACT A CROWD OF FRIENDS THIS SUMMER, just say, "Come on over for a drink and a swim." It's a sure bet they'll come flocking. The same goes for birds, who never turn down an invitation to sip and frolic in cool water—especially on a warm summer day.

All birds need water for drinking and bathing. They'll happily frolic in a streambed or a puddle, but a birdbath in the right spot in your garden—kept filled and clean—is the ultimate watering hole for all kinds of feathered visitors. On these four pages, we show a collection of birdbaths that you can buy or build yourself. Some are basic bowls. Others, like the sleek triangular flagstone bath or the whimsical miniature swimming pool carved in wood, are as much for people to look at as for birds to splash in; you can display them as sculpture among garden plants.

Once the birds discover this reliable water source, they'll bring your garden alive with color, sound, and activity. You'll discover the quiet pleasure of watching finches, jays, robins, sparrows, and other songbirds swoop into the bath for a splashing-good time. If you add a bird feeder nearby, there's sure to be an even bigger crowd. (You might even see birds washing berries in the water.)

While a bath can cool off the birds and enhance your garden in summer, it's beneficial to birds in winter, too; bathing then actually helps insulate birds by keeping their feathers free of dirt and leaving space between them for pockets of trapped air.

Miniature swimming pool was carved in redwood plank made of two 16-inch-long pieces of 4-by-10. The pool was coated with copper and blue acrylic paint, then sealed with polyurethane.

Sunken bath, *enhanced with the sound of water from a dripper, attracts Steller's jay. The bath took less than 2 hours to assemble from a kit; sod was removed, then the hole was leveled and lined with a 3- by 5-foot piece of synthetic rubber ($35 for liner, $40 for dripper). Rocks, which anchor the liner's edges, are from a building supply yard.*

Birdbath basics

Whether you buy or build a birdbath, here are a few rules of thumb to help you choose and locate it.

Keep it shallow but roomy. Most birds bathe by wading into shallow water that's no deeper than their legs are long, so 2 to 3 inches is deep enough. The bath's sides should slope gradually, so birds can wade in to a depth that's comfortable for them. If the bath has vertical sides, some birds find it difficult to judge the depth; add a flat rock in the bath's center.

To allow room for more than one bather, choose a bath that's at least 24 to 36 inches in diameter.

Consider materials. Birdbaths can be made from many materials—concrete, glazed ceramic, metal, plastic, and terra-cotta, to name five. The photographs on these pages show a sampling of ones available. Plastic and metal withstand many types of weather, but surfaces can be too slippery for birds. Some plastic can get brittle with age and crack; metal should be stainless steel or other material that resists rust. The surface texture should be rough enough to offer traction; you can add gravel to slick-bottomed ones, but that makes cleaning a little more difficult. Lightweight birdbaths need firm pedestals to keep from tipping.

Keep it clean. Mosquitoes and algae love standing water, but stagnant water isn't healthy for birds. Change the water daily during summer, every three to four days in cooler months when the bath is used less. Use a strong jet of water from the hose to clean the bowl; if the bottom is dirty, scrub it.

Keep it safe. If you're going to attract birds to your garden, you'll need to make sure they're protected from predators. Put the birdbath next to shrubs or trees that provide cover and escape routes. But make sure the plants aren't so close to the bath that they create hiding places for cats and other marauders. Putting a bath on a pedestal base isn't enough—there still should be some open space around it. Avoid clustering pots too close to a birdbath's pedestal; cats can climb them to get to a bath (they'll sip the water, too).

Certain kinds of birds prefer ground-level bathing, but that leaves them even more vulnerable to predators. Place ground-level baths where they have 10 to 20 feet of open space around them (but no more, or you'll leave damp birds exposed to hawks, owls, and other birds of prey).

For greater viewing pleasure, place the bath where you can see it from the patio or house. To keep the water cooler and encourage day-long use, try to choose a location that receives morning sun but some shade at midday.

Copper bath *on rusted steel base has domed fountain with recirculating pump. Design: Tom Torrens; $750.*

PETER CHRISTIANSEN

Glazed terra-cotta saucer *has pedestal made of slender metal rods that stick into the soil; $39.95.*

NORMAN A. PLATE

Hanging birdbath *with ornate outer rim can dangle from tree or house eaves; $39.95.*

Baths you can buy—to hang, to mount on walls, to nestle among plants

Deck-rail bath *is three-quarter circle of glazed terra-cotta mounted on post; $29.*

Birdbath extras

To keep birdbaths especially inviting to birds year-round, you can add the following devices to them.

Running water. The sight and sound of moving water are appealing to birds and can increase the number of birds visiting the bath. Some baths come with built-in fountains. Or you can create a miniature fountain by adding a submersible pump with a spray head. In a more natural-looking, ground-level pond, the same style pump can also recirculate water in a streambed or waterfall. Pumps should be plugged into receptacles with a Ground Fault Circuit Interrupter (GFCI).

Drippers hook onto outdoor faucets and let you add as little as a few drops a minute to keep a bath full and clean (many have their own pressure reducers and needle valve controls). Freestanding misters put out a fine spray that will attract hummingbirds, which enjoy hovering for midair baths.

Heaters. If you live in a climate where water in the shallow baths can easily freeze solid, consider adding a small heating element that will keep it thawed and available to birds during cold spells.

Wall-mounted birdbath, *called Deck Oasis, has plastic saucer secured in steel ring; $42.95.*

Sources for birdbaths and extras

The birdbaths picture on these pages are available from the following sources.

Synthetic rubber pond liner: Avian Aquatics, Inc., 6 Point Circle, Lewes, DE 19958; (800) 788-6478.

Terra-cotta bath on steel pedestal (also birdbath heaters, drippers): Duncraft, Penacook, NH 03303; (603) 224-0200.

Three-quarters railing birdbath: Gardeners Eden, Box 7307, San Francisco, CA 94120; (800) 822-9600.

Wall-mounted birdbath: Iron Design, 26309 146th St., Zimmerman, MN 55398; (612) 856-4700.

Fiberglass boulder: Second Nature Inc., Box 217, Alamo, CA 94507; (510) 943-6333.

Copper birdbath with fountain, hanging birdbath: The Nature Company, 750 Hearst Ave., Berkeley, CA 94710; (800) 227-1114. ■

Fiberglass boulder, *molded from real rock, has water basin in its top. It weighs about 60 pounds; $425.*

Like a slice of the wild North woods

NATIVE PLANTS AND WILDLIFE SHARE THIS SHADED GARDEN NEAR SEATTLE

In late afternoon on a summer day, sunlight pokes through conifer branches and dances over a pool edged with moss and ferns. Squirrels forage on the mossy carpet, and birds seek berries among the shrubs. This tranquil retreat could be a patch of native Northwest forest, but it isn't. It's a backyard garden at Issaquah, east of Seattle, where tough plants that nature has put in this climate grow happily in cultivated beds and borders.

What makes the garden remarkable is its origin—as a bulldozed lot; only three badly scarred cedar trees survived the construction of the

DON NORMARK

COOL AND MOIST *Gurgling under an old cedar tree, a natural-looking stream meanders past drought-tolerant ferns, mosses, and native creepers; all make this garden an oasis for people and wildlife, even during rainless summers.*

house. For the owner, the goals were simple: develop a canopy of native trees and an understory of native shrubs, establish native ground covers, and create a handsome water feature to attract wildlife and give a cooling effect throughout the dry months of summer.

To supplement the cedars, Douglas fir and dogwood seedlings were spaced throughout the garden, far enough apart so they wouldn't touch one another or produce complete shade even when mature. Vine maples give the garden delicate vertical lines in winter and wands of lacy summer foliage. Deciduous wild currant provides vibrant deep pink spring flowers, summer greenery, and fall leaf color; one of the plants is particularly useful outside a bedroom window, where it provides a view and a privacy screen. Redtwig dogwoods are handsome green bouquets throughout the garden in summer, then drop their leaves to show off big white berries and sparkling red stems in the winter. And evergreen and deciduous huckleberry give handsome foliage and fruit that is tasty to both the resident birds and the owner. For spectacle, brilliant red berry clusters explode in June on four elderberries spread out under cedar trees (birds eat the berries, but humans can't). Ground covers, planted in plugs around the garden, include bunchberry, kinnikinnick, and the difficult-to-find twinflower; all provide food and cover for birds.

The plants in this garden came from native nurseries, arboretum and plant society sales, friends' gardens, and even areas red-taped and primed for development.

POOLS, STREAM, AND PLANTS FOR WILDLIFE

A stream filled with river rock meanders through the middle of the garden with a little pond at each end; it attracts dozens of birds at a time. Native granite lines the water, and plants like salal and native rushes grow along the stream, often popping out of a mulch of pea gravel. (Be careful with rushes; these statuesque plants self-sow like fury. But you can enjoy them if you clip off the flowers before seeds ripen.) A pump recycles water from the lower pond back to the upper one.

Besides birds, other wildlife forages in the garden: squirrels, raccoons, butterflies. Frogs are at home in the ponds and croak through the summer nights.

Maintenance is easy—just removing debris and fallen leaves from the stream, pond, and paths. To build the soil and provide a natural, water-retaining mulch, the owner allows leaf litter to remain on the ground around plants. No other amendments are used. ■

By Steven R. Lorton

DON NORMARK

BOARDWALK LEADS PAST NATIVE FERNS, *conifers, and rock-edged streambed (above). Poking out into pool (below), licorice fern (Polypodium glycyrrhiza) grows on a mossy downed limb.*

NATIVE PLANTS IN THIS GARDEN

Trees, shrubs

Dogwood (*Cornus nuttallii, C. stolonifera*)
Douglas fir (*Pseudotsuga menziesii*)
Elderberry (*Sambucus callicarpa*)
Huckleberry (*Vaccinium ovatum, V. parvifolium*)
Salal (*Gaultheria shallon*)
Vine maple (*Acer circinatum*)
Wild currant (*Ribes sanguineum*)

Ground covers

Bunchberry (*Cornus canadensis*)
Kinnikinnick (*Arctostaphylos uva-ursi*)
Licorice fern (*Polypodium glycyrrhiza*)
Sword fern (*Polystichum munitum*)
Twinflower (*Linnaea borealis*)

PETER CHRISTIANSEN

BACKYARD FOREST *of birches, greenery, and lily pond is cool in summer.*

Mountain retreat or coastal dell?

No, it's a cool backyard oasis . . . in hot-summer Denair, outside Modesto

A GROVE OF WHITE-barked birch trees protects and shades Sonja and Jack Sperry's house, so that on hot summer days their house and garden can feel as much as 20° cooler than the neighbors'. Although the verdant garden has the look of mountain country, it's in California's hot-summer, low-elevation Central Valley where daytime temperatures usually hover in the 90s.

FREE-FORM DECK-BENCH *wanders through the trees.*

To create the forest, the Sperrys began with an exposed, flat site that had areas of heavy clay soil. They created level changes with low berms of sandy loam, and excavated a long pond, which they contoured with sand and sealed with a vinyl liner.

Then they planted seven European white birches (*Betula pendula*) and a few cutleaf weeping birches (*B. p. 'Dalecarlica'*), and began building the garden. They developed one area at a time, adding berms and an irrigation system for each zone. They used drip, mister, or impulse sprinklers depending on plant size, and the slope and exposure.

Now, 15 years after planting, the birch forest has grown; it surrounds the house and is thicker—several hundred offspring have come up from those original trees.

As in a true forest, this one has a rich green carpet of undergrowth beneath the birches' protective mantle. Ornamental strawberries, baby's tears, nandina, and dwarf agapanthus fill much of the garden in summer months. Palms, ferns, daylilies, succulents, and small Japanese maples appear in different areas as well. To make the garden seem as natural as possible, the Sperrys added tree stumps and rocks, now overgrown by the ground covers.

A free-form deck projects into the forest from the rear of the house; the deck skirts some trees and lets a few rise through it. Only 16 inches above ground level, it is at the right height to serve as a broad bench.

Birch trees can be water hogs, but in this garden they combine with underplantings to shade and cool the soil. In summer, each zone in the garden usually gets a 15-minute irrigation every morning. Periodic spraying protects against aphids. ■

By Peter O. Whiteley

The crinkly, colorful crispheads

DARROW M. WATT

FALL-PLANTED *'Reine des Glaces' develops a full head in 60 to 65 days.*

CRINKLY, CRISP, AND often colorful, Batavian lettuce combines the best characteristics of looseleaf and iceberg types.

Handsome textured leaves give young Batavian (a type of crisphead) lettuce the look of a looseleaf type. But as a Batavian matures, it forms a small head similar to that of an iceberg lettuce, with crunchy ribs. Yet a Batavian is much more flavorful and less watery than iceberg, and its deep green (sometimes burgundy-tinged) leaves are full of vitamins.

You won't find Batavian lettuce in the grocery store because it doesn't ship and store well. If you want to enjoy its crunchy-sweet flavor, you'll have to grow it from seed.

In the mild climates of lowland California and Arizona, now is the time to order and start the seeds, setting out seedlings in fall. In climates with colder winters, you can order seed now, start it in October, and plant the seedlings after spring's last frost.

CHOOSE APPLE GREEN OR BURGUNDY RED

Batavian lettuce is as ornamental as it is tasty. It even looks handsome mixed with flowers in a flower bed. Try an apple green variety such as 'Centennial', 'Reine des Glaces' (shown), or 'Victoria', or a burgundy-tinged type such as 'Rosy', 'Rouge Grenobloise', or 'Sierra' (all shown below). All of these varieties do well when planted in fall and spring.

'Anuenue', 'Centennial', 'Nevada', 'Sierra', 'Verano', and 'Victoria' are noted for their heat tolerance and bolt resistance. They also can be grown successfully in summer near the coast, but they probably won't stand up to high temperatures in inland areas.

START SEEDS IN FLATS OR CELL-PACKS

Fill containers with potting soil or a mixture of potting soil and perlite. Place seeds on top of premoistened soil (about four seeds per inch in flats, one or two seeds per cell-pack), press in, and cover with about ¼ inch of soil.

Place containers in bright light but not in direct sun. Keep the soil constantly moist but not soggy. Soon after seeds germinate, thin them to about an inch apart. Fertilize lightly with a seed-starting fertilizer.

When seedlings are about 2 inches tall, slowly introduce them to stronger light to harden them off, then plant them 8 inches apart in the garden. If the weather is warm, you may want to protect the tender seedlings with shadecloth or pieces of wood. Fertilize weekly with fish emulsion or other fertilizer (follow label directions).

Check regularly for aphids, slugs, and snails. Control aphids with a spray of insecticidal soap. Pick off slugs and snails at night or ring plants with finely ground diatomaceous earth.

You can harvest outer leaves as plants grow or wait for heads to develop.

WHERE TO BUY LETTUCE SEED

You probably won't find Batavian lettuces at a nursery. The following sources sell seeds of several varieties, but one catalog may not carry all of the ones mentioned here.

The Cook's Garden, Box 535, Londonderry, VT 05148; (802) 824-3400. Catalog $1. Listed as spring lettuce.

Johnny's Selected Seeds, 310 Foss Hill Rd., Albion, ME 04910; (207) 437-4301. Catalog free. Sold as summer crisp lettuce.

Ornamental Edibles, 3622 Weedin Court, San Jose, CA 95132. Catalog $2.

Shepherd's Garden Seeds, 6116 Highway 9, Felton, CA 95018; (408) 335-5311. Catalog $1. ■

By Lauren Bonar Swezey

LETTUCE VARIETIES TO START FROM SEED

FRENCH IMPORT *'Sierra' is blushed with bronze.*

BURGUNDY *leaves wrap apple green head of 'Rosy'.*

SERRATED *leaves of 'Reine des Glaces' form dense head.*

CROSS SECTION *of 'Rouge Grenobloise' shows how a small green head forms inside burgundy-tinged outer leaves.*

CRINKLY *'Rouge Grenobloise' looks especially ornamental.*

MICHAEL THOMPSON

BIG, CRINKLY, GRASS GREEN *leaves of Gunnera tinctoria (also sold as G. chilensis) grow in dense upright clumps.*

Dinosaur food? Not exactly

But this big-leafed perennial has a steamy jungle look. You can plant it this month

I LOVE GUNNERA. IT looks like dinosaur food," says Tim Hohn, curator of Seattle's Washington Park Arboretum, about the lush, huge-leafed native of South America you see in the photograph above.

It's a humorous notion, but accurate. The leaves are so large you can easily imagine a giant reptile munching them. It's an exotic, almost prehistoric-looking plant. "You either love it or you hate it. Either way, you can't miss it," says landscape architect Ron Rule, of Vancouver, British Columbia. He uses gunnera as an anchor in the middle of a mixed border.

Only five years ago, gunnera was rarely seen in the Northwest. It was most commonly visible in photographs of English estate gardens—usually at the edge of a pond. But now a growing number of daring gardeners are growing this water lover, sometimes away from water and even in small city gardens. Nurseries are responding to the trend with an increased supply of the large plants.

Late summer is a good time to plant gunnera. By getting plants in the ground before temperatures drop, they'll have plenty of time to get established before cold weather comes.

CHOOSE FROM TWO GIANTS

Gunneras come in a variety of shapes and sizes; of about 40 identified species in the genus, only five are used in cultivation. Of those, only two big-leafed ones (*Gunnera manicata* and *G. tinctoria,* also known as *G. chilensis*) are well known. These two are the powerful, statuesque plants that the genus is known for. *G. manicata* has a somewhat open form; its leaves can measure 9 feet across. A leaf of *G. tinctoria* rarely gets broader than 5 feet, but leaves grow up in denser clusters. The leaves are covered with fleshy prickles that make them rough to the touch, but they're not painfully thorny. They're brittle, and easily torn by wind.

Flowers that look like large, greenish yellow corncobs appear atop thick stalks in summer. Both plants can grow 6 to 8 feet tall.

PLANTING AND CARE

Give these plants partial or light shade and rich soil that is kept constantly moist. In Victoria's Beacon Hill Park, a large clump of *G. tinctoria* grows well away from any visible water supply, but in a low spot in the ground, sheltered from strong sunlight by the shade of tall trees. The trees are far enough away that their roots don't steal water from the soil around the gunnera.

Gunneras don't need bog conditions, but they won't take drought. If the soil dries out, the leaves droop, but will come back after watering. Overhead watering (if our water supply allows) coupled with a deep watering at the roots, will help keep plants perky through a hot dry spell.

If water is a problem, grow gunnera in soil that stays moist—such as at a pond's edge, where the plant will become a startling accent, mirrored in water; keep the plant's crown well drained. Or try one in a large pot.

Gunnera will survive all but the toughest cold snaps in zones 4 and 5 of the *Sunset Western Garden Book.* Young, newly set out plants will be killed if their first winter is a hard one.

Well-established plants die down in winter but come up again in late spring. Before winter sets in, cut the plant back almost to soil level. To protect it from frost, mound a 6-inch layer of mulch over the crown. In April, gently pull the mulch away (take care not to damage emerging leaves). Scatter high-nitrogen fertilizer around the base of the plant to encourage robust growth.

SMALLER GUNNERAS . . .

Three other gunneras merit attention—all ground covers with small leaves that form thick mats in moist, peaty soil. In late summer, *G. prorepens* sends up spikes of brilliant red fruits above 3-inch-diameter rosettes of bronzy green leaves. *G. magellanica* is less spectacular in bloom, but leaves are 5 inches wide. *G. monoica* has tiny leaves that form a dense carpet.

. . . WHERE TO FIND THEM

Ground cover gunneras are difficult to find. One source (which also sells *G. manicata*) is Heronswood Nursery, 7530 288th St. N.E., Kingston, WA 98346; catalog $3. ■

By Steven R. Lorton

MICHAEL THOMPSON

'AUTUMN JOY' SEDUM *adds bright spot in cloister's center.*

It's a cloister garden

And the arbor around this colorful pocket in Portland supports vines

LIKE A PAINTING, THIS Portland garden is an eye-catching pocket of color within a neat frame. "It's a cloistered garden," says landscape architect Laurence Ferar. The "frame" is a large, sturdy arbor that provides shadowy walkways where you feel a sense of enclosure. The arbor also draws visual lines around the garden and says, "This is it. Look in here."

Just inside the arbor, broad-leafed evergreens such as *Daphne odora* and sarcococca provide rich fragrance in the cold months and thrive in summer's dappled shade. Farther out in the garden, perennials and roses provide spring and summer bloom; a katsura tree (*Cercidiphyllum japonicum*) stretches up in the center to give the garden more summer shade and to provide foliage color in autumn, a sculptural form in winter, and flower buds in spring.

The 65-foot-long arbor fits neatly between house and garage.

But it does more than frame the garden and visually connect the two buildings: the arbor also supports plants. Vines—grape for fruit and shade; wisteria for twisting trunks, lacy leaves, and spring blossoms; and clematis for bursts of color from spring through summer—climb up the posts and are beginning to crawl over the trellis roof.

The arbor is built of cedar; 6-by-6 vertical posts, spaced 8 feet apart, support 2-by-8 horizontal beams topped with 2-by-4 rafters and a 2-by-2 roof grid. The posts are supported by steel braces set in concrete. Brick pavers, set in a grid design to match the grid overhead, cover the walkway and patio under the arbor.

Lawn fills in between the property line and the arbor. ■

By Steven R. Lorton

GRAPE *(foreground) and wisteria (behind) climb arbor's posts and will eventually shelter walkway.*

When plants die mysteriously. . .suspect nematodes

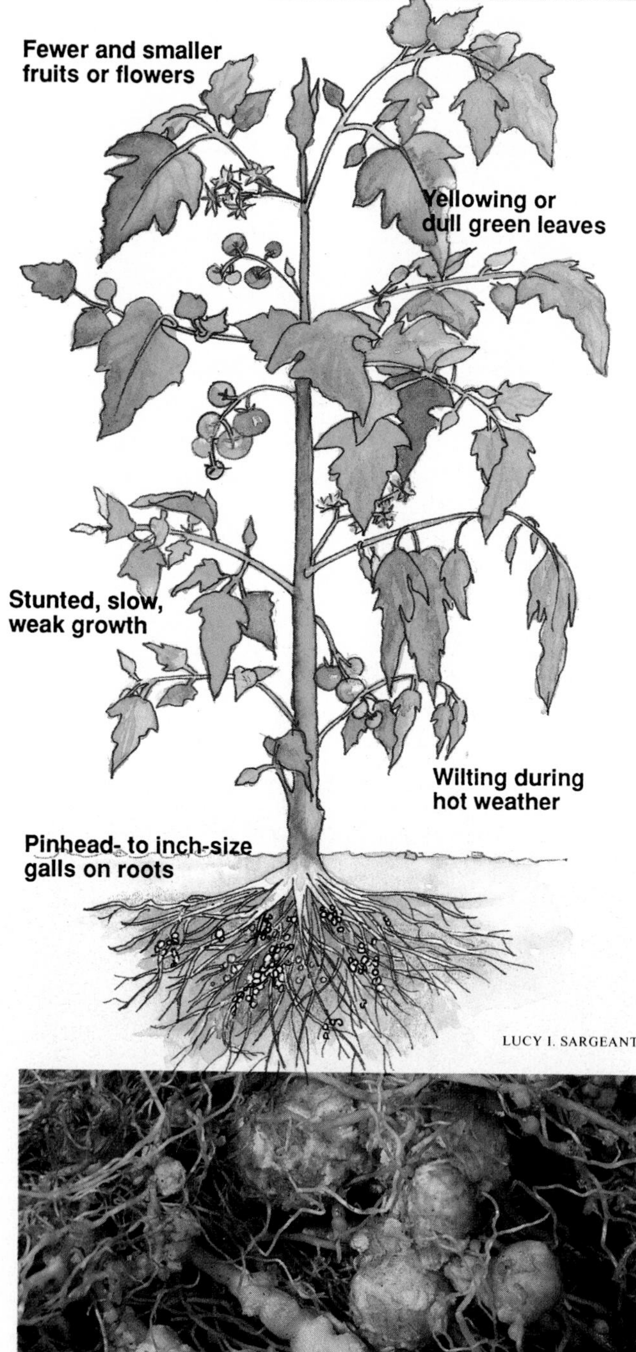

LUCY I. SARGEANT

JACK K. CLARK

SWOLLEN SECTIONS *of roots, called galls, are caused by root knot nematode (Meloidogyne incognita). Unlike beneficial nitrogen-fixing nodules, these pinhead- to walnut-size galls don't snap easily off root.*

AMONG THE MANY creatures inhabiting garden soils are nematodes. Various types of these tiny, translucent roundworms live in all Western gardens. If you're lucky, nematodes in yours can remain a mystery. But if your fruits and vegetables languished or died despite your best efforts, parasitic species of nematodes may be flourishing in your soil. Now is the time when plants may show symptoms of nematode damage. You can take certain steps to control the pests.

Root knot nematodes, found throughout the West, are the commonest plant-damaging type. Sandy or sandy loam soils, especially in areas with long warm seasons, are most susceptible to them.

Likely targets of parasitic nematodes include most stone fruits, citrus, grapes, and strawberries. Other victims are beans, cole crops, cucumbers, eggplant, lettuce, melon, peas, peppers, spinach, squash, and tomatoes, and root crops such as beets, carrots, white and sweet potatoes, and radishes. (Root knot nematodes damage the roots of asparagus, corn, garlic, olives, and onions, but to a lesser degree.)

HOW TO KNOW AND WHAT TO DO

If your plants have any of the symptoms shown in the drawing above, along with root galls that don't easily detach, you may have a nematode problem. To be sure, check with your university extension service or farm advisor for names of laboratories that can identify the nematodes in your soil samples.

Here is what you can do if root knot nematodes are found.

Amend soil. Before planting, mix in plenty of organic matter; after planting, apply a 4- to 6-inch layer of organic mulch. Plants in organic-rich soil are better able to tolerate nematode damage, most likely because soil holds moisture better and has more nutrients.

Try organic fertilizers. Organic kinds such as blood meal, cottonseed meal, and fish emulsion also stimulate beneficial organisms, to the detriment of harmful nematodes.

Plant only resistant plants. Tomatoes with the code letter N in their names, as in 'Better Boy VFN', are resistant to most root knot nematodes. For fruit trees, use Nemaguard or Nemared rootstocks on almond, nectarine, and peach; 'Royal Blenheim' on apricot.

Plant in early spring or late fall. Cool-season crops like carrots, cole crops, lettuce, peas, and spinach are more damaged by nematodes in warm soil. Plant when soils are cool.

Solarize planting beds. If you live inland (coastal climates are too cool), you can cover empty planting beds with thin, clear plastic for four to six weeks during July and August. Solarization heats up the top 8 to 12 inches of soil enough to kill most parasitic nematodes. Cultivate and moisten soil first.

Summer fallowing is also effective. Cultivate frequently, maintain soil moisture so nematode eggs hatch, and keep area weed-free to starve nematodes out.

Avoid chemicals. More toxic nematode controls such as Vapam are available, but they kill nearly everything else in the soil, such as roots of nearby plants. ■

By Michael MacCaskey

A jungle grows in this San Diego backyard

YOU ALMOST EXPECT to see monkeys swinging in the trees. But Ed Moore didn't plan to create a jungle in his San Diego backyard. As the photograph below shows, he wound up with a lush and botanically diverse garden that flourishes in the subtropical climate of coastal Southern California.

The garden consists primarily of palms (200 species) and cycads (60 species). Begonias, bromeliads, ferns, orchids, tillandsias, and various other tropical plants are used as accents and fillers. What's remarkable is that all these plants are packed into a 62- by 125-foot garden (see the plan below).

Originally, the yard was solid lawn. Then Moore became fascinated with palms. Soon, they shaded the lawn too heavily for it to grow, and he began laying bricks for the pathways that wind between the trees.

As the garden began to take shape, Moore sought design advice from W. F. Sinjen, a plant expert and longtime Ocean Beach resident. Sinjen creates gardens that combine a wide variety of exotic plants to produce junglelike effects.

His influence is evident here: dense planting, but with trees and shrubs pruned so that some light can pass through; and use of all vertical space—fence posts, tree trunks, and lower branches—for bromeliads, epiphytic orchids, tillandsias, and ferns.

Despite the dense vegetation, water use is surprisingly modest. During the dry season, Moore waters the garden with a hose every four days. Maintenance involves mostly periodic grooming. A professional pruner comes every year or so to thin the tallest trees, which reach up to 40 feet. ■

By Michael MacCaskey

SANDRA WILLIAMS

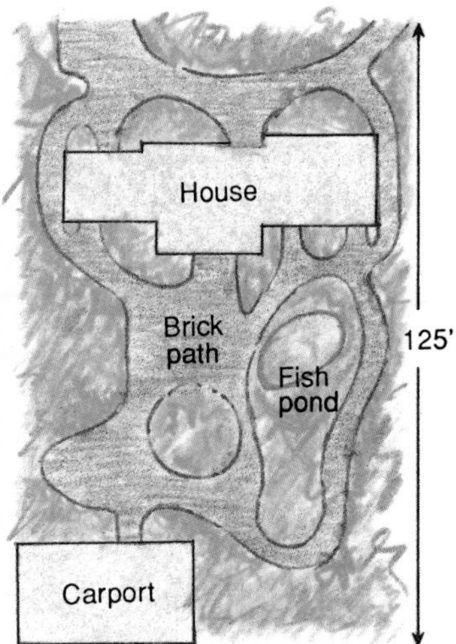

RED FLOWER *bracts belong to Stromanthe sanguinea. The tall fernlike plant above the woman is a cycad, Encephalartos transvenosus; the prickly snakelike plant behind her is Alluaudia procera. The cycads in the left foreground are also Encephalartos. Palms overhead include Rhapis humilis (top left) and Chamaedorea pochutlensis (top right).*

SEPTEMBER

Garden guide....................207
September checklists 212
Miracle of fall planting........216
Northwest wonder plants 222
Carrots for flavor 228
Colorful buckwheats...........229

Sunset's GARDEN GUIDE

K. BRYAN SWEZEY

Under the old oak trees

TAKE THE HUMIDITY OUT OF DOG DAYS AND IT'S STILL HOT—THAT'S THE KIND OF weather gardeners contend with in September. In spite of the warm, dry weather, September is a transition month and the beginning of the fall planting season. It's a great time to change over to a more water-thrifty landscape like this handsome planting of airy grasses and flowering ground covers under oaks—shown above bathed in evening light in Pebble Beach, California. For more on this garden that used to be lawn, see page 211.

Sunset's

GARDEN GUIDE

PETER O. WHITELEY

MINIATURE *species daffodil, yellow hoop petticoat, is 5 to 6 inches tall and naturalizes easily.*

Miniature daffodil for naturalizing

Showy, trumpet daffodils make a wonderful spring display in the garden, but they aren't always dependable for naturalizing in the West's mild-winter climates. Pictured at right is a daffodil that is. Like other species daffodils, it will reappear and increase in numbers every year in mild climates.

Yellow hoop petticoat (*Narcissus bulbocodium conspicuus*) is a miniature daffodil native to Portugal and Spain that reaches only about 5 inches tall. Its unusual 1½-inch-long flaring yellow trumpets are surrounded by narrow petals; they're shaped much like old-fashioned hoop petticoats. The bulbs require very little care other than supplemental water in spring (if rains aren't adequate) when they're growing.

Plants naturalize in two ways. Bulbs increase by divisions. And faded flowers, if left on the plant to dry, form plenty of seed; when a seed pod matures, it breaks open and scatters black seed over the soil. The seeds germinate with fall and winter rains.

One source for yellow hoop petticoat is McClure & Zimmerman, 108 W. Winnebago St., Box 368, Friesland, WI 53935; (414) 326-4220. A dozen bulbs cost $10.40; add $3 for shipping.

RENEE LYNN

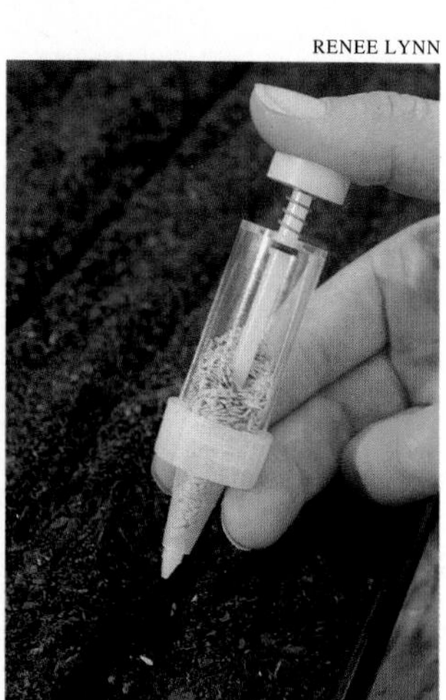

SEED DISPENSER *distributes tiny seeds slowly (these are lettuce) and evenly into flat.*

Tool aids seed planting

The syringe-style seed dispenser pictured at left is designed to plant hard-to-handle small vegetable and flower seeds such as broccoli, lettuce, sweet alyssum, and pansies. It helps you place seeds where you want them, and eliminates the need to thin seedlings later. Use the dispenser for starting seed in flats, or for direct sowing in the garden.

Fill the container with seed, then push the spring-loaded knob to release the seed through the spout. You can adjust the spout opening to accommodate different seed sizes.

The dispenser (called Tiny Tim) is available by mail from Henry Field's Seed & Nursery Co., 415 N. Burnett St., Shenandoah, IA 51602. The cost of $7.79 includes postage and handling.

Potato onions, prolifically

Here's something for gardeners in the low elevations of California and Arizona to try planting this fall: potato onions—mild flavored, old-fashioned relatives of standard single-bulb onions. But unlike them, potato onions multiply. One large bulb (3 to 4 inches in diameter) produces a cluster of 10 to 12 small bulbs. When you plant a small bulb (½ to 2 inches in diameter), you'll end up with a large one. By planting bulbs of different sizes, and saving some of the harvest for planting the following year, you can have a continuous supply of onions for eating and for growing.

Potato onions require loose, fertile, well-drained soil. They are heavy feeders; amend poor soil with decomposed organic matter and a complete fertilizer. Plant bulbs ½ to 1 inch deep; space smaller bulbs 4 to 6 inches apart, large ones 6 to 8 inches apart. Water consistently, and feed early in the growing season.

Bulbs mature in about seven months. Harvest, cure, and store them as you would standard onions.

Potato onions are hard to find. One mail-order source is Southern Exposure Seed Exchange, Box 158, North Garden, VA 22959; (804) 973-4703. A starter package of bulbs (12 ounces of mixed sizes) costs $12.45, including postage and handling. Orders must be received by September 30 in order to be delivered in time for planting in November.

Coming soon—a new botanical garden

Plants from Mediterranean climates around the world will find a home in a new botanical garden. About 150 acres in California's El Chorro Regional County Park, off State Highway 1 between San Luis Obispo and Morro Bay, have been designated for the garden.

Planting began in the fall of 1993, but it will be some time before the garden is open to the public. Still, there are benefits to joining the garden's nonprofit support group now. The group, Friends of SLO Botanical Garden, publishes a quarterly newsletter with updates on the garden's progress, regional home-gardening information, and a calendar of garden events. Members can attend special field trips and presentations on garden-related topics. They also receive discounts at participating local nurseries.

For details, call (805) 546-3501, or write to Box 4957, San Luis Obispo, CA 93403.

Flowering lawns to start now in the Northwest

More meadow than putting green, flowering lawns are made to be cut high, and to offer flowers in spring and summer and various textures year-round. Another bonus: such lawns need minimal mowing and feeding.

The one pictured at right, called Fleur de Lawn, uses dwarf perennial rye grasses selected by region (dwarf tall fescue is added to blends sold east of the Cascades) as the grass part of the mix, with yarrow and strawberry clover mixed in for texture; the last two also stay green during summer when the rye goes dormant.

Large perennial English daisies dot the lawn with white, pink, and red in spring, while pink clover flowers take over in summer. In addition, you might get baby blue eyes and sweet alyssum the first spring, but they tend to drop out of the mix quickly.

Planted now, this blend should be in full bloom by next spring. (Don't sow directly over an existing lawn, and don't mulch or English daisies won't germinate well. Just scatter seed on prepared soil, rake it in, and water.)

Because this lawn uses slow-growing dwarf grasses, you'll have to mow only every three weeks or so in spring, never in summer and winter, and once in fall.

Use your mower's highest setting—4 to 5 inches—so you don't cut off flower heads.

Fleur de Lawn costs about $30 per pound—enough seed to sow 1,000 square feet. To find it, call Pro-Time Lawn Seed at (503) 239-7518.

STEPHEN CRIDLAND

LARGE-FLOWERED *perennial English daisies give flowering lawn a meadow look in spring. Colors are pink, red, and white.*

This hoe has wings

The invention of an Idaho farmer, the Winged Weeder looks like an airplane that's all wing. It's a push hoe: its blade slides under the soil surface and cuts weed seedlings off between root and top.

Such off-with-their-heads hoeing works extremely well when it's done regularly, since tiny weed roots rarely regenerate (big ones do). It also keeps the soil surface loose, inhibiting germination of new weed seeds and reducing evaporation.

Being a push hoe, Winged Weeder isn't made for grubbing out big weeds. It comes as a hand hoe or as a standard hoe you use standing up; blades come in two sizes, 4½ and 8¾ inches. We like the larger version with the broader wing.

PETER CHRISTIANSEN

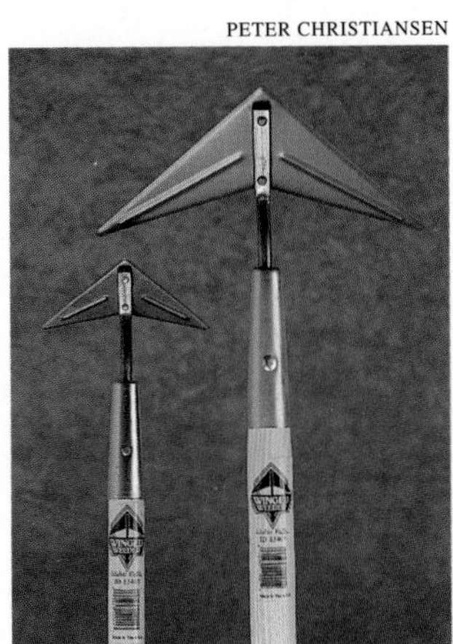

WINGED HOE *has two sizes of blades. The smaller (also used on hand hoe) is for close plantings.*

Mulch, soil, and water

Mulch reduces a garden's water demands, as can the amount of organic matter in the soil itself. But by how much? To find out, visit the soil-and-mulch demonstration project at the Center for Urban Horticulture in Seattle.

Raised beds here are planted in native, amended, and mulched soil. This month, as the demonstration project ends, you can see the results. Signs show what's happening in each test bed.

The project is sponsored by Seattle Water Department, Seattle Solid Waste Utility, and the University of Washington.

The Center for Urban Horticulture is at 3501 N.E. 41st Street, the south end of Union Bay Place N.E. The demonstration beds are about 50 yards behind CUH offices. Visitor parking costs $1.50.

More rainfall-only plants

In the article on page 222, we list 40 excellent drought-tolerant plants for Northwest gardens. The following list includes many good additions.

Trees. Bigleaf maple, Brewer's weeping spruce, California laurel, chestnuts, Chinaberry, Chinese pistache, crape myrtle, Douglas fir, edible fig, English elm, English yew, *Eucalyptus,* European mountain ash, giant sequoia, golden chinquapin, goldenchain tree, goldenrain tree, hackberry, hawthorn, locust, loquat, madrone, Mediterranean fan palm, Modesto ash, osage orange, plane tree, poplar, Port Orford cedar, Serbian spruce, serviceberry, silk tree, silver linden, silver maple, smoke tree, tanbark oak, walnut, Western yew, Wilson holly.

Shrubs. Alpine totara, Apache plume, barberry, big sagebrush, bush anemone, bush germander, butterfly bush, *Ceanothus,* Chinese photinia, cinquefoil, coffeeberry, coyote brush, daphne (*D. cneorum, D. laureola,* and *D. mezereum*), elderberry, escallonia, evergreen huckleberry, flowering quince, forsythia, fountain butterfly bush, hairy manzanita, *Hebe pinguifolia,* Italian buckthorn, *Kerria japonica,* laurustinus, lilac, longleaf mahonia, Oregon grape, Pacific wax myrtle, Portugal laurel, rose of Sharon, salal, Siberian peashrub, silktassel, smooth sumac, sunrose, tree aster, wild mock orange.

Ground covers, vines. Clematis, cotoneaster, cross vine, Hall's honeysuckle, Japanese spurge, kinnikinnick, purple-leaf grape, sageleaf rockrose, spring cinque-

Sunset's

GARDEN GUIDE

DON NORMARK

NODDING ORCHIDS *come in spring and last for weeks. They flower in shade.*

foil, St. Johnswort, wintergreen, wisteria.

Perennials. *Anthemis cupaniana,* bleeding heart, *Calamagrostis stricta* 'Karl Foerster', California fuchsia, California Indian pink, California poppy, cardoon, cast-iron plant, common thrift, coral bells, daylily, dusty miller, *Erythronium,* evening primrose, false lily-of-the-valley, feverfew, foxglove, gaura, herbaceous peony, Jerusalem sage, Johnny jump-up, lady's mantle, liatris, lupine, male fern, mariposa lily, mullein, New Zealand flax, Oregon oxalis, *Osteospermum fruticosum,* penstemon, piggy-back plant, potato vine, *Potentilla villosa,* red-hot poker, *Rhazya orientalis,* ribbon grass, Santa Barbara daisy, *Sisyrinchium striatum,* Solomon's seal, *Vancouveria,* Western columbine, Western sword fern, wild strawberry, winter-blooming bergenia, yucca.

Low ground cover for rock gardens

If you're looking for a low ground cover that blooms over a long period, *Silene vulgaris maritima* (also sold as *S. maritima*) fits the bill.

K. BRYAN SWEZEY

WHITE FLOWERS *fleck Silene vulgaris maritima.*

It grows only 3 to 6 inches tall but spreads 3 feet wide, rooting as it grows. The blue-green foliage is attractive draping over walls or crawling through rock gardens. From spring through autumn, ¾-inch-wide white flowers with green calyxes appear.

Plant silene in an area that has good drainage and gets full sun. It's handsome combined with sunrose (*Helianthemum*) and ground morning glory.

If you can't find silene at a nursery, you can order it by mail from ForestFarm, 990 Tetherow Rd., Williams, OR 97544; (503) 846-7269. Tube-size plants cost $2.95 plus shipping. Or starting in October, ask your nursery to order it for you from Suncrest Nursery, Watsonville, CA (wholesale only).

Hardy orchid for shade

One plant that some gardens should never be without is Chinese ground orchid (*Bletilla striata*), pictured above. A true orchid, it pushes its strap-shaped leaves out of bare ground in spring, and makes cattleya-like, amethyst-purple or white 1- to 2-inch flowers for six weeks in late spring.

This orchid does best in moist, humusy soil in part shade. Though the bulb will take a 15° freeze, you should protect it by planting it about 2 inches deep and mulching. In snowy-winter climates, plant in a container you keep in the garage all winter.

Buy it from nurseries and mail-order bulb suppliers. Plant this month.

Fungus strikes California redwoods

In their native habitats, coast redwoods *(Sequoia sempervirens),* which grow in the Coast Range, and giant sequoias *(Sequoiadendron giganteum),* which are indigenous to the western slope of the Sierra Nevada, are majestic trees. When used in the landscape outside their normal range, they are susceptible to a disease called *Botryosphaeria,* which can eventually kill them.

The disease causes cankers or sunken areas on the undersides of branches, 2 to 3 feet in from the branch ends. The first noticeable sign of infection is dead branch ends in the lower third of the tree canopy. Eventually the disease progresses to the top of the tree and kills it. The fungus usually kills giant sequoias when they're 20 to 40 feet tall, but it can appear even in nursery stock. Coast redwoods are most susceptible when they're drought-stressed (which, surprisingly, often includes trees growing in turf that's only shallow-watered).

On coast redwoods, if you discover the disease in the early stages when only the lower branches are affected, follow these control methods recommended by horticultural consultant Barrie Coate, of

Los Gatos, California. Prune off all branches with cankers and dispose of them. If practical, spray the tree in November and January with fixed copper and heavyweight (dormant) oil to coat all of the woody portions. Apply a 4- to 6-inch layer of organic mulch under the tree canopy. Spray in March with a systemic fungicide. During the dry season, water monthly by slowly applying 10 gallons of water per inch of trunk diameter. Fertilize once between May and September with a controlled-release, high-nitrogen fertilizer applied 8 to 18 inches deep throughout the root zone.

Since the disease is deadly to giant sequoias, avoid planting them outside their native range, except in the Pacific Northwest.

The maximum sunflower

In late summer in Southwest gardens, Maximilian's sunflower (*Helianthus maximiliani*) comes into its glory. Golden daisy blooms—each some 3 inches across—crown this robust, long-lived perennial, brightening otherwise fading gardens. More than 30 closely spaced daisies cover each plant, and each of the daisies is made up of 15 to 30 deep yellow rays, about 1½ inches long.

Besides offering bounteous color, Maximilian's sunflower grows tall enough to make a quick privacy hedge (set plants about 3 feet apart). It looks good against south- and west-facing walls, or use it the way nature does, scattered in grassy meadows. Butterflies and bees visit the flowers for pollen and nectar, and birds like its seeds.

Given occasional water, it grows 6 to 8 feet tall; with more water, it can reach 10 feet. Each plant becomes a clump of woody stems some 3 feet in diameter. Hairy gray-green leaves are typically a foot long and half as wide.

You can grow this dazzler from seeds, plants, or root divisions. Give it full sun and well-drained soil. After frost kills the tops, cut the dead stems back to within 3 inches of the soil.

September's the month to plant. If your nursery doesn't have seeds or plants, small plants ($4 each) are available from A High Country Garden, 2902 Rufina St., Santa Fe, NM 87501; (800) 925-9387.

For a good cook's garden

If you're a cook or a gardener (or both) who likes broccoli, this is the month to get transplants or seeds into the ground. One popular garden variety is 'Packman', which sends out uniform heads with good flavor just 57 days after planting. For a sprouting-type broccoli that you can harvest gradually over time, choose 'Mercedes'. For novelty, try caulibroc, a small-headed greenish cauliflower that tastes better raw than cooked. For strong, rich flavor, plant Chinese broccoli.

Plant in rich soil and a sunny location; allow 1½ to 2 feet between plants.

Check with your nursery for transplants; two sixpacks, plenty for a family, cost less than $4. Or check with seed catalogs such as Park Seed Co., Cokesbury Rd., Greenwood, SC 29647; (800) 845-3369.

Oaks thrive with low-water plants

Faced with dying oaks surrounded by lawn, with voracious deer, and with only filtered sun, designer Michelle Comeau created a handsome, low-water-demand landscape in the Pebble Beach, California, garden pictured on page 207.

The first thing to go was the lawn, which needs supplemental water that's harmful to oaks. In its place, Comeau put plants that were deer resistant and could thrive in the partial sun. For ground covers, she chose 'Wood's Compact' kinnikinnick, *Myoporum parvifolium,* and juniper. Soft, airy grasses and sedges, such as *Carex albula, C. morrowii expallida,* and *Miscanthus sinensis strictus,* punctuate the landscape. For color, Comeau used Australian fuchsia, *Iris douglasiana, Salvia greggii, S. leucantha,* and *Scaevola* 'Mauve Clusters'. Deer nibbled at the plants when they first went into the ground, but once the plants toughened up, the deer left them alone.

During rains, the dry creek bed running through the garden carries runoff from the roof and driveway. The garden is drip-irrigated.

'Texas Gold' columbine

Unlike most columbines, which are typically grown in the Southwest as winter annuals, heat-tolerant 'Texas Gold' stays green through summer. This selection of a Southwestern native (*Aquilegia chrysantha hinckleyana*), which was discovered growing in a shady canyon in the Big Bend area of Texas and introduced by Texas A&M, is accustomed to summer heat that usually dooms hybrid columbines. This is the month to plant it.

'Texas Gold' grows into an 18- to 24-inch-high clump of

attractive, blue-gray, maidenhair fern–shaped leaves. Butter gold flowers are 1½ to 3 inches across with 2½-inch slender spurs. Flowers are good for cutting and, in the garden, attract hummingbirds. Peak bloom lasts about five weeks in spring.

Plant 'Texas Gold' where it gets dappled shade—under deciduous trees such as redbud or Chinese pistache, for example. Space plants about 2 feet apart. Roots tolerate any soil that drains well. Mulch after planting.

Plants are most likely to spread by seed. Leaf miners and spider mites are occasional pests; cut off infested leaves within 2 inches of soil and dispose of them. Plants cost $3 to $6 for gallon size, $1.25 for 4-inch size. ■

By Michael MacCaskey, Jim McCausland, Lynn Ocone, Lauren Bonar Swezey

PETER CHRISTIANSEN

BROCCOLI PLANTS *are edged on both sides with blooming chives—attractive fall-winter garden companions.*

WEST OF THE CASCADES, see items marked with a **W.**

EAST OF THE CASCADES, see items marked with an **E.**

September Checklist

HERE IS WHAT NEEDS DOING

☐ **CLEAN UP THE GREENHOUSE. W, E:** Get ready for winter by replacing broken glazing and loose weather-stripping. Then check vents, and heating and watering systems—you still have time to order replacement parts before frost. Finally, clean out seedbeds and flats.

☐ **DIVIDE IRISES. W:** All the Pacific Coast species and hybrids can be dug, divided (use a sharp knife), and replanted this month for good bloom next spring. Now is also a good time to buy them.

☐ **FERTILIZE LAWNS. W, E:** To support the burst of growth that's about to begin, feed grass at the rate of about 1 pound actual nitrogen per 1,000 square feet of lawn.

☐ **GROOM ROSES. W, E:** Remember that when you cut roses from the fall flush of bloom, you're pruning. Cut stems just above a five-leaflet side branch (instead of a three-leaflet branch), and cut with an eye to the plant's shape. Also let a few roses go to hips (rose fruits) late in the month. On different kinds of roses, the hips vary considerably in size, color, and content. Those on some varieties make good bird food later in the fall.

☐ **MAKE COMPOST. W, E:** Use the summer vegetables and annuals you pull out of the garden to start a new compost pile. At the same time, dig in compost you've made over summer. It restores what nutrients the plants have taken out of the soil.

☐ **MOW LAWNS. W, E:** As cooler weather stimulates fall grass growth, mow often enough that you never have to remove more than a third of the blade's length at once. Mowing every four to seven days should do it.

☐ **MULCH. W, E:** To minimize erosion and frost damage to roots, put a layer of organic mulch (like coarse compost or straw) around shrubs and half-hardy perennials.

☐ **OVERSEED LAWNS. W:** Rough up bare spots with a rake, scratch in grass seed, cover with mulch, and water as soon as the soil surface starts to dry out. A good blend for mild parts of the Northwest contains perennial rye, fine fescue, perhaps bentgrass, and some Kentucky bluegrass as a quick cover that prevents erosion.

☐ **PLANT BULBS. W, E:** Bulbs show up in nurseries right after Labor Day. Shop early to get the best selection, and plant right away so bulbs will have plenty of time to establish roots before spring bloom.

☐ **SHOP FOR BERRY PLANTS. W, E:** Nurseries have plenty of trees, shrubs, and ground covers with beautiful fall berries. Shop for them now so that you'll know exactly what you're getting. This is also a great month to plant.

☐ **WATER. W, E:** When it's cooler, remember that plants still need water. Don't forget those in pots or under eaves.—*J.M.*

IN HIGH ELEVATIONS and intermountain areas of California, and east of the Sierra, see items marked with an **H.**

IN LOW ELEVATIONS of Northern California, see items marked with an **L.**

☐ **CARE FOR CITRUS. L:** To prevent citrus fruit from drying out as they mature, give trees regular deep soakings during warm fall weather. Do not prune trees now; pruning stimulates growth that can be damaged by winter cold.

☐ **FERTILIZE. L:** To get annuals, perennials, and fall-planted vegetables off to a strong start, mix compost into the planting bed or incorporate a complete fertilizer before planting. In two to four weeks (the shorter time if you used compost), follow up with fish emulsion or other fertilizer; for frequency of application after that, follow label directions.

☐ **HARVEST MELONS AND SQUASH. H, L:** As melons start to ripen, check them daily. On cantaloupes and muskmelons, look for thick, corky netting and gold to tan coloring; ripe fruit should slip from stem easily. Crenshaw and Honey Dew melons are ready to pick when skin feels waxy. Winter squash is ready when skin is hard.

☐ **INSPECT FIREWOOD FOR BEETLES. H, L:** Green firewood less than a year old collected from forests may harbor bark beetles that can infest trees in the garden. Signs of insects are holes less than ⅛ inch in diameter and fine sawdust in bark crevices or on the ground beneath stacks of wood. To kill beetles, store wood in direct sun in stacks no larger than 4 feet high by 4 feet wide by 4 feet deep; cover with clear (not opaque) plastic and bury edges. After two to three weeks (unless weather is particularly cool), high temperatures should have killed any beetles that are present.

☐ **PLANT ANNUALS. L:** To get cool-season annuals off to a good start so they bloom this winter and early spring, plant after midmonth. If the weather is hot, shade new seedlings temporarily. Keep the soil moist. Set out calendula, Iceland and shirley poppies, larkspur, ornamental cabbage and kale, primrose, snapdragon, and stock. Near the coast, plant cineraria, nemesia, and schizanthus.

☐ **PLANT PERENNIALS. H, L:** After the weather cools, plant campanula, candytuft, catmint, coreopsis, delphinium, dianthus, diascia, foxglove, gaillardia, geum, penstemon, phlox, salvia, and yarrow. Nurseries have a good selection in sixpacks, 4-inch pots, and gallon cans.

☐ **PLANT VEGETABLES. L:** Set out seedlings of broccoli, cabbage, cauliflower, lettuce, and spinach. Plant seeds of beets, carrots, leeks, onions, peas, radishes, and turnips.

☐ **PREPARE WILDFLOWER BEDS. H, L:** Weeds are the nemesis of wildflower beds. To control them, soak the soil thoroughly to germinate weed seeds, then hoe down or spray them with a contact herbicide such as a nontoxic kind derived from fatty acids (Sharp Shooter). If time permits, repeat the process before sowing wildflowers.

☐ **SHOP FOR BULBS. H, L:** To get the best selection of healthy bulbs, shop soon. Plant anemone, crocus, daffodils, Dutch iris, freesia, homeria, ixia, leucojum, lycoris, oxalis, ranunculus, scilla, sparaxis, tritonia, and watsonia. Buy hyacinths and tulips now, but wait to plant; to bloom well, these two bulbs need chilling in the refrigerator for at least six weeks. Store in a well-ventilated paper bag in the crisper section (away from apples).
—L. B. S.

BUY BULBS. C, L: For best selection, buy anemones, crocus, daffodils, Dutch irises, freesias, hyacinths, ranunculus, scilla, and tulips as soon as they appear in nurseries. Plant freesias now. Plant the others in late October or November, when soil has cooled.

FERTILIZE MANY PLANTS. C: Feed established trees, shrubs, and ground covers now; repeat in a month. Wait about a month after planting to feed recent transplants. **L:** A light application of high-nitrogen fertilizer encourages new growth and helps plants recover from summer's heat. Don't fertilize frost-tender plants like bougainvillea, citrus, hibiscus, Natal plum, or thevetia unless leaves look pale or yellowish.

PLANT BULBS FOR FALL BLOOM. C: Some of the best bulbs for this climate bloom in fall. If you plant soon, most will bloom this year. Choose from large-flowered colchicum (*C. autumnale*), small-flowered *Crocus ochroleucus* and *C. speciosus*, and lycoris. Another possibility is *Amaryllis belladonna*, which blooms in late summer or fall the year after planting.

PLANT FOR WINTER-SPRING COLOR. Cool-season annuals appear in nurseries in mid- to late September. For planting information, variety selection, and design tips, see the article on annuals (page 216).

PLANT (OR SOW) COOL-SEASON VEGETABLES. C: When weather cools, set out seedlings of broccoli, Brussels sprouts, cabbage, cauliflower, celery, chives, kale, and parsley. Sow seeds for beets, chard, chives, collards, kale, kohlrabi, parsnips, peas, radishes, spinach, and turnips. Plant garlic, onions, and shallots. **L:** When temperatures drop below 100°, sow seeds of beets, carrots, celery, chard, endive, green onions, kale, kohlrabi, leaf lettuce, leeks, parsley, parsnips, peas, potatoes, radishes, spinach, turnips. Sow lettuce and cole crops in flats or in containers to transplant in October. **H:** In warm areas like Las Vegas, plant all cool-season crops listed for low desert. In colder areas, plant lettuce and spinach seeds or plants, and radish seeds.

PRECHILL BULBS. C, L: Early shipments of crocus, hyacinths, and tulips will be at most nurseries by midmonth. Buy while supplies are fresh and selections are good, but wait until soil cools down, usually by Thanksgiving, to plant them. Store bulbs in a paper bag in the crisper section of your refrigerator (don't store with ethylene-producing fruit, like apples).

PROTECT AGAINST BRUSHFIRES. In fire-prone areas, cut and remove dead leaves and brush from vegetation close to the house. Clear leaves from gutters. Remove woody vegetation growing against structures.—*L. O.*

September Checklist

HERE IS WHAT NEEDS DOING

☐ **BUY BULBS.** Beginning this month, bulbs arrive in nurseries throughout the Southwest. Shop early for the best selection. Choices include anemones, crocus, daffodils and other narcissus (see page 208), Dutch iris, freesias, hyacinths, ranunculus, scilla, snowdrops, tigridia, and tulips. Store hyacinths and tulips in the refrigerator (not the freezer) for six weeks before planting. Store others in a cool, dry location and plant next month. In the high deserts, plant right away.

☐ **CARE FOR LAWNS.** In low and intermediate deserts, stop feeding Bermuda now in preparation for overseeding. If you don't intend to overseed, feed now with a high-nitrogen fertilizer (½ pound 20-0-0 per 100 square feet) to prolong growth and color into fall. If your lawn is yellow and doesn't respond to nitrogen, apply iron sulfate. In Houston and surrounding counties, tropical sod webworm is a likely September pest of St. Augustine lawns. Douse lawn midmonth with an insecticide that contains *Bacillus thuringiensis*.

☐ **PLANT TREES, SHRUBS, AND GROUND COVERS.** This month begins the best season to start or remodel a garden: plants have time to become established before next summer. Start soon in the high desert; wait until mid-October to plant in the low desert. In fall, put in all landscape plants except frost-tender kinds such as bougainvillea, hibiscus, and lantana.

☐ **SOW CORN AND BEANS.** If you live in the low or intermediate desert and like a Thanksgiving harvest of fresh corn, sow seeds right away. Plant in dense blocks to aid pollination. At the same time, plant a final crop of beans adjacent to the corn and let them climb.

☐ **SOW VEGETABLE GARDENS.** In the low and intermediate deserts, sow seeds of cool-season crops like beets, carrots, chard, endive, garlic, green onions, kale, leeks, lettuce, peas, potatoes, radishes, and spinach. Set out transplants of broccoli, brussels sprouts, cabbage, cauliflower, and lettuce midmonth in the intermediate desert; wait until mid-October in the low desert.

In high-desert gardens, you can still plant transplants of lettuce and spinach, and seeds of radishes.

☐ **START PERENNIALS.** In Phoenix and Tucson, sow carnations, columbine, coreopsis, feverfew, gaillardia, hardy asters, hollyhock, lupine, penstemon, phlox, Shasta daisy, statice, and yarrow. Transplants will be ready in eight weeks.

☐ **WATER CITRUS.** To help reduce fruit split on oranges and tangerines, soak the soil around trees every 10 to 14 days. Lemons should start turning yellow this month. Harvest as needed.—*M. M.*

The miracle of fall planting

START NOW FOR FLOWERS AS SOON AS CHRISTMAS IN MILD CALIFORNIA AND ARIZONA

For sheer quantity of spring-flowering annuals, fall is the best planting season of the year," says Temecula, California, landscape architect and nurseryman Craig Thralls. Though he speaks for Southern California's inland valleys and the Southwest's deserts, where fall really does herald a "spring" of longer duration than elsewhere, most nurserymen

NORMAN A. PLATE

FOR WINTER-SPRING BLOOM, PLANT ON THESE DATES

San Francisco Bay Area:	mid-September through mid-October
Central Valley:	late September through mid-October
Coastal Southern California:	October and November
Inland Southern California:	mid-October through mid-November
Palm Springs and Phoenix:	October through mid-November

RAINBOW MIX *Color comes from fall-planted English daisies (front); 'Imperial Pink' pansies; pink, purple, and white stock; and Iceland poppies, with a few ranunculus bulbs mixed in.*

throughout the low-elevation West agree: cool-season annuals planted in early fall have time to develop better roots before flowering in winter and spring, and—because they start blooming earlier than comparable plants set out in spring (see photo at left)—they bloom over a longer time.

So get out the shovel, prepare your planting beds, and make a shopping list. Now is the time to set the stage in your garden for a grand show of sweet-scented stock, bright yellow pansies, or other dazzling flowers from winter through spring.

APRIL PHOTOGRAPH *contrasts vigorous fall-planted poppies in full bloom with small winter-planted ones; those planted in the fall bloomed earlier and longer.*

NEW PLANTS, NEW COLORS

Among the many cool-season bedding plants that provide winter and spring flower color are some new ones to look for now: pansies in antique shades such as muted rose and soft gold, sweet alyssum in apricot and mixed pastel shades, and two new

HERE ARE 22 FLOWERFUL CHOICES TO PLANT NOW

For a grand show beginning in winter or early spring

Bachelor's button
(Centaurea cyanus)

Upright, from 12 to 30 inches with narrow gray-green leaves and 1- to 1½-inch flowers in blue, pink, red, and white.

How to grow: Prefers light soil. Space transplants adequately to promote branching and minimize powdery mildew. Full sun.

Tips: Good cut flowers. Named varieties give a range of size and form, in single or mixed colors. Tall varieties need staking. Greatest availability is from late fall on.

Calendula
(C. officinalis)

Bushy, upright plants 12 to 30 inches. Abundant blooms like double daisies to 4 inches across in white, cream, orange, yellow, and apricot.

How to grow: Easy by direct seeding or from transplants. Full sun.

Tips: Good cut flower. Petals edible. Powdery mildew is a problem in coastal regions.

Canterbury bells
(Campanula medium)

Upright 2½ to 4 feet tall with long, loose clusters of 2-inch bell-shaped flowers in blue, pink, purple, and white.

How to grow: Set out nursery transplants (from seed, plant takes six months to flower). Full sun, partial shade inland.

Tips: Excellent plant for mixed borders. Long-lasting cut flowers. Usually needs staking.

Chrysanthemum
(C. multicaule, C. paludosum)

Buttery yellow daisies of *C. multicaule* grow 1 to 1¼ inches across on 6-inch stems above mat of green foliage. *C. paludosum* has 1- to 1½-inch flower heads with white rays and yellow centers on 8- to 10-inch stems; dark green leaves are deeply toothed.

How to grow: Give average water, full sun.

Tips: Plants may live a second year. Excellent for edging, containers, hanging baskets.

Dianthus

Annuals, and biennials and perennials often grown as annuals. Fringed flowers are ½ to 1 inch or wider in intense solid colors or in combinations of pink, purple, red, and white on plants 6 to 24 inches tall. Plants bloom from spring or early summer into fall.

How to grow: To ensure spring bloom, start with nursery transplants. Give full sun and light, fast-draining soil. Don't overwater.

Tips: Compact types are excellent for edging. Taller varieties make good cut flowers. Wee Willie sweet William (*D. barbatus*) grows to 6 inches, and Summer Beauty to 12 inches. Common *D. chinensis* hybrids are the Princess series (10 to 12 inches) and the Telstar strain (6 to 8 inches).

English daisy
(Bellis perennis)

Perennials often treated as annuals. Pink, rose, red, or white double flowers 1 to 3 inches across bloom on 4- to 8-inch stems above rosettes of bright green leaves. Blooms from fall into spring, with fewer flowers in coldest months.

How to grow: Give good soil, much moisture, light shade inland, full sun near coast.

Tips: Good edging or bedding plant. Combines well with bulbs.

Flowering cabbage and kale
(Brassica)

Grown for their colorful leaf rosettes. Some turn bright purple or rose with onset of cold weather (best color develops below 40°); others are marked with white or cream. Cabbages are 8 to 12 inches tall with wavy leaves; kales may be compact and fringed or grow to 18 inches and be deeply serrated.

How to grow: Full sun. Control cabbage worm with *Bacillus thuringiensis*.

Tips: Many types available from specialty seed catalogs. More showing up in nurseries. Remove when plants bolt in mid- to late winter.

Forget-me-not
(Myosotis sylvatica, often sold as M. alpestris)

Tiny blue, carmine, or white flowers cover upper portion of 6- to 12-inch stems; leaves are soft, hairy. Bloom begins in late winter, early spring.

How to grow: Easily sown in place. Needs moist soil, partial shade.

Tips: Blues combine nicely with a warmer color such as coral, orange, or yellow. Attractive interplanted with bulbs. Plants self-sow and may become weedy when conditions are right.

Globe candytuft
(Iberis umbellata)

Bushy, free-blooming plants 6 to 15 inches high (depending on variety), with flattened globes of tiny flowers. Lance-shaped leaves to 3½ inches long. Available in pastels (pink, rose, lilac, salmon, white), or intense shades of red and purple.

How to grow: Sow seed now or set out plants in late winter (plants are scarce in fall). Plants are heat sensitive and will stop blooming in hot weather, or if soil dries. Sun, partial shade inland.

Tips: Sow seed where quick color is needed. Good for edging, in rock gardens.

petunias (cool season in desert areas) with colorful centers and white edges. The listings below and on page 220 describe 22 colorful plant groups to choose from. Most are annuals—they complete their life cycles in one season; a few are biennials or perennials treated as annuals. Some old favorites as well as some of the newer varieties are available only through catalogs.

In garden beds, you can orchestrate by flower color—mix and match two or three complementary colors, or two contrasting colors, like red and white, for example. Or plant swaths of the same flowering plant around permanent leafy plants. (For design ideas, see "Tips from the professionals," on page 221).

WHEN TO PLANT

On page 216, we list approximate planting dates for various regions of the low-elevation West. Close to the coast, you can plant earlier or later with good results. Inland, planting before temperatures drop in mid-October is risky.

If you are sowing seed (of plants such as forget-me-nots) directly in garden beds, do it right away. Seed will use the heat of late summer to germinate, and seedlings will come along just as the temperatures begin to cool.

WHAT SIZE TO BUY

Cool-season bloomers are available in a variety of containers. The three commonest containers are sixpack or pony pack (48 plants per flat; about 25 cents per plant); jumbo or color pack (36 plants per flat; 50 cents per plant); and 4-inch or quarts (16 plants per flat; $1.40 per plant). Many horticulturists prefer the old-fashioned straight flats (64 plants; about $15 per flat), believ-

Larkspur
(Consolida ambigua)

Upright branching plants 1 to 5 feet tall (depending on variety), with ferny foliage and dramatic bloom spikes. Delphinium-like 1- to 1½-inch flowers in white, blue, lilac, pink, salmon, and carmine. Peak bloom in spring.

How to grow: Sow seed where plants are to grow or set out transplants. Chill seed for one week before planting. Best in fertile, well-drained soil. Partial shade.

Tips: Large (4- to 5-foot) strains such as Giant Imperial and Regal are good for middle and back of border.

NORMAN A. PLATE

Nemesia
(N. strumosa)

Small (¾-inch) flowers in clusters 3 to 4 inches long and snap-dragon shapes. Colors vary from bright jewel tones to soft pastels, including some bicolors. Plants from 7 to 18 inches.

How to grow: Frost tender away from coastal areas. Cut back after first flush of bloom. Full sun.

Tips: Carnival and Funfair have intense colors. Tapestry combines pastels and deeper colors. 'National Ensign' is a red-and-white bicolor.

Pansy, viola
(Viola)

Pansies and violas (*V. cornuta*) come in many different color variations from plain to blotched. Pansies have large flowers 2 to 4 inches across; violas are about 1½ inches. Johnny-jump-ups (*V. tricolor*) are small (¾-inch), normally purple and yellow bicolors. Plants grow to 8 inches.

How to grow: Pinch leggy plants to encourage new growth. Plants last longer in spring if protected from hottest sun. Full sun or part shade.

Tips: New colors and types introduced annually. Imperial strain Antique shades look like watercolors (plant closer together than normal); 'Pink Shades' opens plum and fades to light pink and white. Princess violas come in single colors and are very floriferous.

Petunia

Plant in fall only in mild desert climates. Funnel-shaped flowers come in many solid and bicolors, singles and doubles. Plants are compact or trailing.

How to grow: Pinch back when young to encourage bushiness. Full sun.

Tips: Many new colors introduced every year. Two new picotee types—Frost and Hulahoop—have colorful centers and white edges.

Annual phlox
(P. drummondii)

Cool-season annual in Southern California and the desert, summer annual elsewhere. Dense clusters of 1-inch-wide flowers form on top of erect, leafy stems 4 to 20 inches tall. Many bright and pastel flower colors, some with contrasting eyes.

How to grow: Plant in rich soil, full sun.

Tips: Newer types (Fantasy Mixed, Promise Pink) are compact, bushy, and covered with blooms.

Poppy
(Papaver)

Iceland poppy (*P. nudicaule*) is a perennial commonly grown as an annual. Three-inch crepe-papery flowers bloom on slender, hairy 1- to 2-foot stems. Slightly fragrant flowers in cream, yellow, orange, and pink. Long bloom season when flowers are picked frequently. Shirley poppy (*P. rhoeas*) is an annual with 2- to 5-foot slender, hairy stems. Flowers are 2 inches or more across with translucent petals in shades of red, pink, white, orange, and bicolors.

How to grow: Set out plants of Iceland poppy. Shirley poppy is best sown in place; you can start with transplants (available starting in late fall). Need good drainage, full sun.

Tips: 'Legion of Honor' Shirley poppy has scarlet flowers with black bases; Mother of Pearl yields smoky pastel shades. All are good cut flowers; sear cut stem ends in flame before placing in water.

Poor man's orchid
(Schizanthus pinnatus)

Also known as butterfly flower. Lilac, pink, purple, rose, salmon, and white orchidlike flowers are produced in profusion on 6- to 15-inch-tall stems. Ferny foliage is bright green.

How to grow: Plants are sensitive to frost and heat (best on coast). If starting from seed, sow about four weeks before planting time (germination is slow). Filtered shade.

Tips: Star Parade grows 6 to 9 inches tall; Angel Wings and Disco grow 12 to 15 inches.

CLAIRE CURRAN

PINK PRIMULA *(P. obconica) infuse tropical-looking Southern California garden with dramatic winter color. Design: Curt Luthy.*

ing that the roots of these small plants are quickest to establish. But these are difficult to find; sixpacks are the modern equivalent.

In mild climates, the smallest plants are probably your smartest choice, especially if you start with well-prepared soil and a good irrigation system. They bloom longer, and they cost less, too. In hot inland areas, start with the jumbo size; they're more resistant to heat and drought, and require water less frequently than small plants. While 4-inch pots bloom more quickly than sixpack plants, their overall bloom cycle is shorter.

Whatever size you choose, look for plants with strong, actively growing roots, and tops not yet in flower. Plants in the bud-and-bloom stage (few flowers, but many buds) provide the longest cycle of bloom; they have roots that are actively growing, so transplant shock is minimal. Keep in mind that all plants are not available in all sizes.

GETTING PLANTS OFF TO A GOOD START

A day or two before planting, prepare soil thoroughly. Over 100 square feet, spread six to twelve 2-cubic-foot sacks of planting mix, commercial

MORE ANNUAL CHOICES

Primrose
(Primula)

English primrose (*P. polyantha*) has strappy leaves and clusters of brightly colored flowers atop 3- to 12-inch stems. *P. obconica* has roundish, hairy leaves and large clusters of 1½- to 2-inch flowers on 10- to 12-inch stalks. Fairy primrose (*P. malacoides*) has lobed leaves and lacy flower whorls on stems 12 to 15 inches tall. Colors include lavender, pink, red, rose, and white.

How to grow: Full sun or part shade in coastal fog belt, part shade inland. In cooler areas, English primrose and *P. obconica* can be kept as perennials.

Tips: New Cantata series of *P. obconica* comes in apricot, blue, carmine, lavender, pink, red, rose, and white. Acaulis types of English primrose (Pageant, Prominent) bloom close to the leaves; Polyanthus types (Pacific Giants) have longer flower stems. Julian types are miniature English primroses.

Snapdragon
(Antirrhinum majus)

Many colors and several forms. Standard one has upper and lower jaws. Newer types include bell-shaped and azalea-shaped (double bell-shaped) flowers. Heights range from 6- to 8-inch dwarfs to 3-foot-tall varieties that are good for cutting.

How to grow: Plants bloom in winter if buds form before night temperatures drop below 50°. To reduce chance of rust, do not water overhead. Full sun.

Tips: Bright Butterflies and Little Darling strains have bell-shaped flowers. Madame Butterfly is an azalea type. Tahiti is a dwarf that blooms in winter when planted in fall (Floral Carpet won't bloom until spring).

Stock
(Matthiola)

Old-fashioned plants with clusters of single or double 1-inch flowers in cream, pink, lavender, purple, red, and white. Flowers form on 1- to 3-foot spikes; tall ones are good for cutting. They have a spicy-sweet fragrance.

How to grow: Plant early so buds form before nights turn chilly; otherwise bloom is late. Full sun.

Tips: Plant column (tall) types for cut flowers; use dwarf types in the front border. Yellow and white Cheerful types produce fully double blooms on 2-foot plants.

Sweet alyssum
(Lobularia maritima)

Trailing, low-growing plants (to 6 inches) have tiny but profuse fragrant flowers in dense clusters. Commonly available in white, pink, or purple.

How to grow: Plant in fall in *Sunset* zones 10 through 24. Easy, blooms from seed in six weeks. Grows in almost any soil. For fresh flowers, shear after four weeks of bloom. Sun or light shade.

Tips: Useful for bulb cover, edging for beds and borders, and in containers. Plant self-sows. New colors include Apricot Shades and Easter Bonnet (mixed pastels). Flowers attract bees.

Sweet pea
(Lathyrus odoratus)

Intensely fragrant flowers on vines 4 inches to 8 feet tall. Dozens of varieties available in shades of blue, pink, purple, salmon, red, white, cream, and bicolors. Magnificent flowers for bouquets.

How to grow: Best when planted from seed. For winter bloom in mildest areas, sow in August or early September (mid- to late September inland). Soak seed for a few hours before planting. Provide trellis or strings for vining types. Full sun.

Tips: Early Multiflora and Early Mammoth have strong flower stems and are early blooming. Old Spice has smaller flowers, but they are very fragrant and somewhat heat resistant. Knee-Hi, a bush type that doesn't require staking, has flowers with long, strong stems.

Toadflax
(Linaria)

Delicate-looking flowers in pastel and bright colors and snapdragon shapes form along upright stems. Narrow leaves are medium green.

How to grow: Easy from seed. Plant in masses; individual plants are wispy. Full sun or light shade.

Tips: *L. maroccana* Fairy Bouquet is 9 to 12 inches tall with ½-inch pastel flowers. Northern Lights has bright, dainty flowers and grows to 24 inches. *L. reticulata* flowers are maroon and gold with yellow throats.

compost, or nitrogen-fortified and composted ground bark. Add to that 2 pounds of a 5-percent nitrogen fertilizer, such as a 5-10-10 (or 1 pound of a 10-percent nitrogen fertilizer). Incorporate the amendment and fertilizer to a depth of 8 to 10 inches, then rake the surface smooth. Water the prepared soil.

Remove plants from containers; if roots have grown into a tight mass, gently ease apart the bottom of the rootball. Space most smaller annuals 8 to 16 inches apart (at this spacing, you'll need about 50 to 100 plants per 100 square feet). Larger plants, such as Canterbury bells and flowering cabbage, need 18 to 24 inches between them (you'll need 25 to 49 plants per 100 square feet).

Plant so the rootball is slightly higher than soil level. Cover it with soil and tamp lightly to firm. Water well.

Keep the newly planted bed moist (not soggy) until roots have taken hold—usually in 10 days to two weeks. Avoid overwatering, which can encourage fungus diseases. A month after planting, begin feeding with liquid fertilizer. ■

By Michael MacCaskey, Lynn Ocone, Lauren Bonar Swezey

NORMAN A. PLATE

CARNIVAL COLORS *of nemesia and yellow ranunculus mix with Princess violas for a brilliant spring show.*

FALL PLANTING: TIPS FROM THE PROFESSIONALS

We asked professional garden makers around the West how they choose and use cool-season flowering plants. Here's what they said.

Dynamite flower combinations

"For a soft watercolor look, I combine pink-leafed flowering kale ('Red Peacock') with gray-green-leafed Giant Imperial stock and pale pink 'Imperial Frosty Rose' pansies. The gray-greens and pinks are complementary; they're gorgeous."

—Cristin Fusano, horticulturist, Roger's Gardens, Corona Del Mar

"One of our favorite combinations is 'Easter Bonnet Mix' alyssum with fairy primroses. The white, pink, violet, and lavender alyssum blends in a most remarkable way with the similarly colored primroses."

—Karen Hedges, superintendent of landscaping, Disneyland

"When designing a bed, I always think in terms of skeleton, tendon, and flesh. The skeleton is dominant in color, texture, or form and makes up 10 to 20 percent of the bed. The tendon (also 10 to 20 percent) connects the skeleton. And the flesh fills in with complementary or contrasting colors.

"I like to mix bulbs or biennials with annuals, so the skeleton might consist of foxglove placed on the points of an unequal-sided triangle. The tendon, connecting these points in weaving lines, could be sweet William. And the flesh or filler might be a wine purple viola such as 'Jersey Gem'. Another handsome combination is hot pink ranunculus as the skeleton, soft salmon Iceland poppies as the tendon, and wine purple violas and pansies as the flesh. For added spirit, you can add what I call sparkle (5 percent) of yellow and pink primroses."

—Peter Lassig, manager, Grounds Services, LDS Church, Salt Lake City

"One of our most popular combinations is forget-me-nots planted with tulips such as 'Angelique'. We set out transplants at the same time we plant bulbs in October."

—Lucy Tolmach, garden superintendent, Filoli Estate, Woodside, California

The most workable flower colors

"Pink is one of the most workable colors in the garden. It forgives and does not assault itself; it's polite and demure with a bit of raciness. On the other hand, orange and yellow are not forgiving and are easy to overdo, but they add a nice surprise. Red is also difficult to work with. Always surround it by green, which is its complementary color."—*P. L.*

"It's best to avoid monochromatic colors; they lack spirit and are more difficult to achieve. It's much safer to do a rainbow effect or use a dominant color that sparkles with complementary or contrasting colors."—*P. L.*

Planting garden beds

"When planting small gardens or beds, 10 square feet or less, it's best to stick to just two or three colors. I combine all light colors, or all deep colors, so the planting doesn't look too busy."—*C. F.*

"At Disneyland, we plant mostly color packs that are in bud and starting to show color. In our experience, these plants have the most vigor and longest blooming cycle. We also use lots of 4-inch and larger plants for instant color and to replace dead or damaged plants."—*K. H.*

"We have the best luck with larkspur if we just toss the seeds over prepared soil, irrigate when necessary, and then don't disturb them. Larkspur doesn't seem to like root disturbance and lacks vigor if we try to sow it in containers and then transplant."—*L. T.*

The most useful fall annuals

"Some of the old-fashioned garden varieties are still the best performers. They may not give you instant color, but their flowers seem to hang on forever, and they're excellent for cutting. I recommend the tall Rocket snapdragons, Giant Imperial stock, and Giant Imperial larkspur."—*C. F.*

"The best cut flowers are Iceland poppies, larkspur, snapdragons, and stock."—*C. F.*

"Iceland poppies and pansies bloom the longest in the garden—if they're planted in fall."—*C. F.*

"To fill space nicely, I choose Johnny-jump-ups because they form fat little mounds of foliage with flowers popping up on top."—*C. F.*

"Primroses are wonderful for winter color. The old-fashioned polyantha types with bigger leaves and long flower stalks are more graceful and interesting. They're also great in containers."—*L. T.*

40 wonder plants for the Northwest

THEY'RE GOOD-LOOKING, EASYGOING, AND, MOST IMPORTANT OF ALL, UNTHIRSTY

hen water was abundant in the Northwest, we could plant anything our climate would allow: big lawns, perennials native to damp meadows, and deciduous plants that thrive on summer rain. Water was never a factor: we were like plutocrats with no sense of our own great wealth.

But times change. As the population grows but water supplies don't, water restrictions that were unheard-of a decade ago are almost annual events now. Dry summers further stress the supplies. Some gardeners see water restrictions as annoy-

DON NORMARK

UNTHIRSTY, YES *Dry-looking, no. This part of Susie Marglin's Bellevue garden, shown in June, was designed by Dan Borroff, Seattle. At left, foxglove towers over Jennifer Marglin. It flowers in May against a background of purple-leafed hazelnut.*

ances, but anybody with a sense of the future knows better: tight water is changing the makeup of Northwest gardens more profoundly than anything that's happened in our lifetimes.

We assembled the plant list that follows after visiting dozens of drought-tolerant gardens; picking the brains of water-conscious designers, horticulturists, and university extension agents; and meeting with Seattle Water Department staffers and advisers. Some of these plants are native to the Northwest; most are not. All have above-average garden character and drought tolerance. All need extra water until roots become well established (in a year or more), but if you plant in autumn, normal rainfall does most of that watering for you.

Appropriate climate zones are noted for all plants on the list. You'll find some real surprises: plants zoned for California only. But the tender plants included in this list give a show good enough to justify them for even a single season. Except where noted, all do best in full sun.

ON PUGET SOUND, *Pat Morgan's garden stays low to preserve the view. Landscape designer: T. M. Holtschlag, Vashon Island.*

Perennials, herbs, grasses, bulbs

These plants are easy to tuck into an established garden. Plant them beneath trees and shrubs, along pathways, or as lawn replacements. They're versatile and inexpensive, and come in seemingly endless variety.

Alstroemeria Zones 5–9, 14–24

The best alstroemerias for rainfall-only gardens are the Ligtu hybrids, which have roots deep enough to take considerable drought. Peruvian lily (*A. aurantiaca*) survives well enough on rainfall only but does better with occasional extra water.

Artemisia All zones

Aromatic silver foliage on knee- to waist-high plants is handsome foil for hot-colored companions. Favorites in the drought-tolerant gardens we scouted were 'Lambrook Silver', 'Powis Castle', 'Silver Brocade', and 'Silver Mound'.

DAVID McDONALD

EXOTIC *alstroemeria flowers in early summer.*

Aster All zones

Rainfall-only gardeners suggested several kinds of these 2-foot-tall daisies, but *A. frikartii* 'Mönch' was the favorite.

Cape mallow (*Anisodontea capensis*) Zones 14–24

Grows into a 3-foot shrublet with mallowlike magenta summer blossoms. Treat it as an annual.

Catmint (*Nepeta faassenii*) All zones

It really does send cats into unfathomable ecstasies, which may explain why they often destroy young plants by rolling on them. Buy gallon-size plants and protect them until they're 18 inches across. Blue or white flowers top gray-green leaves in June.

Corsican hellebore (*Helleborus argutifolius,* usually sold as *H. lividus corsicus*) Zones 4–24

Among the hellebores, this one stands out for its long winter-spring bloom (the chartreuse flowers stop first-time viewers in their tracks), freedom from pests, and excellent performance in shade.

Dead nettle (*Lamium maculatum*) All zones

When planted in soil that's well amended with organic matter, this plant survives on rainfall alone west of the Cascades. The green-edged, gray-white leaves of 'Beacon's Silver' (pink flowers) or 'White Nancy' (white flowers) seem luminous in shade.

DON NORMARK

Epimedium Zones 1–9, 14–17

Heart-shaped leaflets make a beautiful, nearly evergreen ground cover over creeping underground stems. Flowers come in spring; they're mostly yellow or white, though varieties of bishop's hat (*E. grandiflorum*) can produce pink, violet, or red flowers. Full or part shade.

***Erysimum* 'Bowles Mauve'** Zones 4–9, 14–24

Gardeners who grow it like its big flush of mauve spring bloom, and the nonstop dribble of bloom that continues until fall.

Euphorbia Zones 4–24 unless noted

Mostly yellow, white, or chartreuse flowers in spring. Plants grow mainly in the 2- to 4-foot range—about right for planting beside a garden bench. West of the Cascades, start with *E. characias wulfenii, E. martinii,* or *E. rigida. E. myrsinites* (a pretty plant that excels in rockeries) grows anywhere.

Grasses All zones, except as noted

Literally dozens of drought-tolerant grasses to choose from in an amazing number of colors and sizes. After the following ornamental grasses become established, they respond to low water by not growing as tall.

Try 8-inch clumps of blue fescue (*Festuca ovina glauca*); scale up to 2-foot clumps of blue oat grass (*Helictotrichon sempervirens*), or, if you have room, move to giants like eulalia grass (*Miscanthus sinensis*); try the tiger-striped 'Zebrinus' or the silver-plumed 'Silver Feather'. Giant feather grass (*Stipa gigantea*, zones 4–9, 14–24) makes a good intermediate-size choice, with a 6-foot mist of yellow bloom topping a 3-foot clump of grass.

Honey bush (*Melianthus major*) Zones 8–9, 12–24

In his book *Perennial Garden Plants,* British author Graham Stuart Thomas writes that honey bush "has probably the most beautiful large foliage of any plant that can be grown out of doors in these islands." Honey bush sometimes freezes out in the Pacific Northwest, but that's all right; this South African native grows into an imposing, gray-green piece of art in one season.

Iris Zones 4–24, all

Both the Old World and the New contribute fine, low-water irises. The fleur-de-lis (*I. germanica*) produces fragrant, bearded blue flowers on a tough-as-nails plant. *I. pallida,* a likely ancestor of modern bearded irises, also makes fragrant blue flowers; try a variegated form whose gray-green leaves are striped with yellow or cream.

Pacific coast hybrids—there are many, mostly derived from the blue or white *I. douglasiana,* yellow *I. innominata,* and rosy purple *I. tenax*—come in a rainbow of colors, many with colored tracery on the petals. All do well in sun or lightly shaded areas beneath trees. Combine with bleeding heart.

Lavender (*Lavandula*) Zones 4–24

Nurseries and mail-order sources offer at least a half-dozen kinds of English lavender (*L. angustifolia*), from large 'Du Province' to diminutive 'Munstead'. Most lavenders produce blue flowers in late spring, though there is pink as well ('Jean Davis'). Great for borders and bedded out along walkways, where you can breathe its classic fragrance. Lavender grows wild with Spanish sage and rosemary; try it that way in your garden.

Matilija poppy (*Romneya coulteri*) All zones

Maybe one of the finest plants ever to move from California's native flora into Northwest gardens, this shrub-size perennial demonstrates just how showy white flowers can be (especially with tufted yellow centers). Put it at the back of a perennial border, where it can tower over the competition. First bloom comes in May and June, followed by spotty bloom through summer and a late flush in fall. Roots can be invasive.

Rosemary (*Rosmarinus officinalis*) Zones 4–24

Leaves are good for cooking anytime, and tiny blue flowers delight the eye in spring. Many named varieties, from ground cover ('Prostratus') to human size ('Tuscan Blue'). Plants need sandy soil.

Sage (*Salvia*) Zones vary

Garden sage (*S. officinalis*) cooks well, has fragrant blue flower spikes over green, golden, or variegated leaves. Gentian sage (*S. patens*) has larger, lighter blue ('Cambridge Blue') or white ('Alba') flowers on a smaller plant but freezes out in coldest climates. Even more tender, Spanish sage (*S. lavandulifolia*) produces violet blue flowers in reddish purple calyxes (a calyx is to a flower what a socket is to a light bulb); it grows to about 18 inches. Mexican bush sage (*S. leucantha*) grows a little taller, with white flowers in violet calyxes.

Santolina All zones

Most people grow either the gray (*S. chamaecyparissus*) or green (*S. virens*) form, sometimes both together as a 2-foot-tall soft ground cover. Yellow flowers rise above aromatic foliage in late summer.

Sedum, sempervivum Zones vary (sedums); all zones (sempervivums)

Hardy succulents are often thrown together in nurseries, so you may have to pick through lots of plants to find what you want. For the most part, these are extremely tough. (In Dallas, Oregon, Helen and Slim Payne once grew a beautiful mixed succulent garden on a shed roof. They planted by tossing leftover pieces of sedum and sempervivum up there whenever they thought about it.)

Start with *Sedum* 'Autumn Joy' (it flowers pink in fall) for the perennial border, add a small ground cover of *S. spathulifolium* 'Cape Blanco'. Plug in *Sempervivum arachnoideum* and *S. tectorum* wherever there's room (especially among garden rocks).

Thyme (*Thymus*) All zones

For culinary use, grow common thyme (*T. vulgaris,* or its silver form, *T. v.* 'Argenteus'). Like lemon thyme (*T. citriodorus*), it's a foot-tall shrublet. Mother-of-thyme (*T. praecox arcticus*), woolly thyme (*T. pseudolanuginosus*), and caraway-scented

DAVID McDONALD

GRAY *artemisias, 'Bowles Mauve' erysimum, Aster ericoides, Mexican bush sage (top right), and Cape mallow thrive unirrigated.*

thyme (*T. herba-barona*) make good mats between steppingstones; purple flowers cover mother-of-thyme in summer.

Yarrow (*Achillea*) All zones

From foot-tall, pastel-colored bedding plants to bright yellow 5-footers, these bloom long and heavily in summer and early fall. If you start from seed, you'll have to wait two years for flowers.

Shrubs, woody ground cover, vines

While shrubs furnish garden rooms, ground covers carpet them, and vines become their draperies. As you choose any of these, pay special attention to the way leaf colors and textures work with other plants: in most cases, they're more important than flowers because they're all you see for so much of the year.

Broom (*Cytisus, Genista, Spartium*) Zones vary; mostly 2–7, 17

Guilt by association tars this group, Scotch broom (plain *C. scoparius*) being the weedy pest that it is. But if you focus on the right plants, you'll love brooms.

Start with *Genista,* most of which are low and spreading, but not aggressive enough to cause trouble (*G. lydia* and *G. pilosa* 'Vancouver Gold' are especially good choices).

Then move cautiously into the *Cytisus* group: Atlas broom (*C. battandieri,* for zones 5 and 6 only) makes a 12-foot mountain of yellow in summer, *C. beanii* makes a good knee-high cover, and a number of named varieties of man-high Scotch broom (*C. scoparius*) do well (without going wild) as shrub covers in red, orange, pink, purple, and the expected yellow. Spanish broom (*Spartium junceum*), which is invasive in California, stays under control in Northwest gardens, producing fragrant yellow flowers from July to frost on 6- to 10-foot plants.

Camellia Zones 4–9, 14–24

Established camellias thrive well on rainfall alone if you plant them in filtered shade, keep them out of drying winds, and mulch them with a 2-inch layer of organic matter. *C. japonica* in its myriad varieties makes a fine shrub or small tree, while *C. sasanqua* shines as a smaller shrub (most varieties) or classic espalier for winter or early-spring bloom.

Cotoneaster Most grow in all zones, but a few won't make it east of the Cascades

This branch of the rose family includes about 20 kinds of plants that do better in dry soil than in moist. Creeping cotoneaster (*C. adpressus*) has an uncanny ability to mold itself into hollows in rocks. Parney cotoneaster (*C. lacteus*) makes a 7-foot-tall evergreen fountain that's cloaked with red fruit in fall. Rockspray cotoneaster (*C. microphyllus*) excels as a cover for dry banks.

English boxwood (*Buxus sempervirens*) Zones 3–6, 15–17

These are the evergreen hedge plants so common in formal English gardens. Dense green leaves are lush, but the plant holds its own with little extra water. When you shop, pay close attention to the variety: *B. s.* 'Arborescens' grows into a small tree, while *B. s.* 'Suffruticosa' usually stays under 5 feet. All do well clipped or unclipped.

Ramanas rose (*Rosa rugosa*) All zones

You could begin and end your search for drought-tolerant roses with various forms of this thorny customer with big, fragrant flowers, fabulous hips, and fine disease resistance. Its single or double flowers in white, yellow, red, pink, or red-purple grow on a shrub that tops out between 3 and 8 feet. Grow these singly or as a hedge.

MICHAEL THOMPSON

RIPE FRUIT *almost glows against strawberry tree's evergreen leaves.*

Red-flowering currant (*Ribes sanguineum*) Zones 4–9, 14–24

If you wander through European flower gardens in spring, you can't help but notice how well they use this West Coast native that's made good abroad. It bears clusters of small tubular flowers (also available in white and pink) early (mostly in April) and heavily, followed by dusty blue berries in summer. Usually just taller than a human, this upright plant grows best in filtered sunlight.

Rockrose (*Cistus*) Zones 4–9, 12–24

Perhaps a dozen kinds are widely available, mostly with flower colors in the white, pink, or purple range, often with a red or yellow spot at the base of the petals. Blossoms cover these thick, mounding evergreens in spring or summer. Plants range from 5 feet high and wide (*C. hybridus*) to 2 feet high and 6 feet wide (*C. salviifolius*). Because forms vary so much, be sure you know the growth habits of the nursery's rockrose before you buy.

Senecio Zones 5–9, 14–24

A good foil for nearby hot-colored spring flowers, gray *S.* 'Sunshine' (sold as *S. greyi*) looks frosted, as though each of its leaves is edged with rime. Use this 2-foot-tall evergray shrub as a tall filler near bulb beds or beside plants with colored leaves.

Strawberry tree (*Arbutus unedo*) Zones 4–24

This is a fine winter-flowering shrub, whose red to yellow fall berries are delightful as Christmas ornaments. It never gets large (you can use it as a small tree as well), and it attracts early and resident hummingbirds with its winter flowers.

Trumpet vine (*Campsis tagliabuana*) All zones

This deciduous vine combines the best features of its

parents: the common trumpet vine (*C. radicans*) and Chinese trumpet vine (*C. grandiflora*). Give it full sun and a fence or wall to clamber on, and it will reward you with 3-inch, trumpet-shaped salmon red ('Mme. Galen') or pure red ('Crimson Trumpet') flowers in late summer.

Trees

Because trees have relatively extensive, deep root systems, as a group they tend to stand up to summer dry spells better than plants with smaller, shallower root systems. But tree roots can have a darker side: some kinds (willows and large maples, for example) actively seek water, sometimes invading sewers and septic systems.

Black locust (*Robinia pseudoacacia* 'Frisia') All zones

Orange new leaves mature to yellow, making this tree a luminous gold under cloudy skies. Thorns and new wood are red. Black locust grows fast to about 50 feet.

Cedar (*Cedrus*) Zones 2–23 (Atlantic); 2–12, 14–24 (deodar); 2-24 (Lebanon)

In time in all but the very coldest Western climates, all of the cedars become handsome, large skyline trees and do well as stand-alone garden centerpieces. For grace and speed, try deodar cedar (*C. deodara*). If you like trees with rugged character and a canopy that lets more filtered light through, grow the blue-gray Atlas cedar (*C. atlantica*) or the greener cedar of Lebanon (*C. libani*).

Crabapple (*Malus*) Zones 1–21

Crabs are tough, hardy, and beautiful in flower (and often in fruit as well). In the Northwest, buy disease-resistant varieties like 'David', 'Liset', 'Louisa' (a weeper), *M. sargentii, M. zumi* 'Calocarpa', 'Mary Potter', 'Prairiefire', and 'Red Jewel'.

Incense cedar (*Calocedrus decurrens*) Zones 1–12, 14–24

This tree gives its fragrance to freshly sharpened wooden pencils, and gets mistaken for giant sequoia by thousands of Yosemite tourists every year. In the garden, use it in screens, in groves, or (in the long term) as an overstory for rhododendrons and azaleas.

Oaks (*Quercus*) Zones 5–9, 14–24 (canyon); 5–6, 18–23 (cork)

Cork oak (*Q. suber*) is a fine, fascinating garden plant. Its ridged pure cork bark looks something like gray-brown French bread, and the tree's evergreen head can top 40 feet. Canyon live oak (*Q. chrysolepis*) usually grows to about the same size and shape, but with smooth, whitish bark.

'FRISIA' BLACK LOCUST *has yellow leaves, grows 8 feet a year in perfect conditions.*

Pines (*Pinus*) All zones; many choices

Taken together, the pines make up the mother lode of drought-tolerant trees. There are too many excellent choices to name, running from shrub-size to magnificent specimens, short-needled to long, spreading to erect. Most of them are relatively trouble-free (though white pines—the group whose needles come in bunches of five—are susceptible to devastating blister rust). Any good nursery will offer you a host of good choices. Plant only in fast-draining soil.

Redbud (*Cercis*) Zones 1–3, 7–20 (Eastern); 2–24 (Western)

Rare in the Northwest, redbuds deserve more use than they get. In spring, when magenta flower buds hang on these little trees like lights, you'll understand where the redbud name came from.

Eastern redbud (*C. canadensis*) shines east of the mountains. The best of the lot is *C. c.* 'Forest Pansy', whose purple, heart-shaped leaves make the perfect foil for understory plants with light green leaves. Western redbud (*C. occidentalis*) does better on the west side (especially in Oregon), carrying more profuse buds in May, but with smaller leaves.

Staghorn sumac (*Rhus typhina*) Zones 1–10, 14–17

Because this plant is multi-trunked and not very tall, it's often thought of as a shrub. But mature staghorn sumacs have much of the character of good small garden trees: a canopy you can walk beneath, leaves and red fruits that ride on top of the plant, and filtered shade that's just right for understory plants.

Vine maple (*Acer circinatum*) Zones 1–6, 14–17

Anyone who's seen this tree's autumn fire in the forest understory remembers it well. Sinuous multiple trunks give it its name, and many-lobed green leaves make it the lushest of all Northwest deciduous trees. Yet it can do with no extra water in its native range: just grow it as an understory tree (or against the north side of your house). Even in a dry year, it still develops fall color—just earlier than usual.

Make your soil work for you

Much of your success with drought-tolerant plants will depend on soil preparation, but what you do varies according to what you're planting.

Woody plants (trees and shrubs) should be planted in unamended native soil. Dig down 18 to 24 inches, breaking through hardpan when you find it; hole diameter should be about 3 feet. Then set the plant so that its crown (where trunk meets soil) is a couple of inches above ground level. Make a watering well, and cover the ground around the tree with a 2-inch layer of mulch, but don't let it touch the crown.

Perennials usually do best in well-amended soil. Dig a planting bed 12 to 18 inches deep, then till in a 4-inch layer of organic amendment, water, and let the soil settle for a week before planting.

IS THAT EVERYTHING?

Not at all. The Drought Tolerant Study Group of the Northwest Perennial Alliance recently assembled a 2,000-plant list of trees, shrubs, perennials, and ground covers that thrive on little or no extra water west of the Cascades.

Many of the entries are tried-and-true, while others represent educated guesswork by seasoned horticulturists. All plant listings are annotated. For a copy of the list, send $12 plus $3 postage to NPA, Box 45574, University Station, Seattle, WA 98145. For runners-up to the list above, also see page 209. ■

By Jim McCausland

PETER CHRISTIANSEN

HOMEGROWN CARROTS *come in all shapes and sizes—and even in white. From left are 'Caramba', 'Planet', 'Imperial Chantenay', 'Thumbelina', 'A-Plus', 'Little Fingers', 'Belgium White', and 'Short 'n Sweet'.*

Carrots you can count on for flavor

What's the secret to growing them? Choose the right variety and plant seeds now

NORMAN A. PLATE

MASS *of ferny foliage yields plump carrots 60 to 75 days after planting in fall.*

HARVESTING CRUNCHY, sweet carrots from the garden is one of the joys of growing vegetables. Plucked straight from the earth, they're more flavorful than any you can buy in the grocery store.

But flavor differs greatly among varieties, and planting time and maturity also affect flavor. In the mild-winter West, early fall is the best time to plant. Carrots achieve their sweetest taste when the last few weeks of growth occur in cool weather. Also, unless a carrot is bred to be harvested young, it won't develop full flavor until mature.

HOW TO GET THE BEST FLAVOR

Two ingredients determine a carrot's flavor: sugars and terpenoids (volatile compounds that impart the carrot flavor). Some varieties are naturally high in terpenoids, which make the carrots taste bitter or soapy. Because terpenoids develop earlier than sugars, a carrot that is harvested too young might taste bitter.

Commercial carrot varieties have been developed for uniformity of shape, as well as for color, disease resistance, and ease of harvest. But gardeners can select a carrot more for flavor than appearance. How do you choose the sweetest ones to grow?

Select a variety by type (carrots are normally grouped into Chantenay, Danvers, Imperator, Nantes, and Paris Market types; new hybrids blur the definitions). For flavor, it's difficult to beat a Nantes ('Bolero', 'Little Fingers', 'Toudo'), characterized by its blunt ends. It's not a carrot you'll find in the grocery store, because it's difficult to harvest commercially and doesn't store well. Chantenay ('Imperial Chantenay', 'Short 'n Sweet') has broad shoulders and strongly tapered tips. It has good flavor, performs in heavy soil, and stores well.

The sweet, round little Paris Market types ('Planet', 'Thumbelina') do well even in containers or in very heavy, shallow, or rocky soil.

'Belgium White', an heirloom variety, is white, mild tasting, and good for stews.

DON'T LET SEEDS DRY

Prepare the soil deeply with organic matter (not fresh manure, or carrots will develop fine, hairy roots). Soak before planting and scatter seeds thinly on top; cover with ¼ inch of compost (this keeps soil from crusting, so seeds can punch through).

Germination takes 7 to 14 days. To help keep the tiny seeds moist, you can cover the seedbed with wet burlap just until they germinate.

Thin seedlings to 2 inches apart when they have two or three leaves. Allow carrots to mature fully before harvesting; most don't taste good as baby carrots unless they've been bred for this use, such as 'Caramba'. Varieties that store well can stay in the ground and be pulled as needed through midwinter.

WHERE TO BUY SEEDS

For the widest selection of varieties, order by mail. Catalogs are free unless noted.

W. Atlee Burpee & Co., 300 Park Ave., Warminster PA 18991; (800) 888-1447. Sells seven kinds, including 'Short 'n Sweet' and 'Toudo'.

Nichols Garden Nursery, 1190 N. Pacific Highway, Albany, OR 97321; (503) 928-9280. Sells nine varieties, including 'A-Plus', 'Belgium White', and 'Thumbelina'.

Ornamental Edibles, 3622 Weedin Court, San Jose, CA 95132. Catalog $2. Sells five kinds, including 'A-Plus', 'Belgium White', and 'Little Fingers'.

Shepherd's Garden Seeds, 6116 Highway 9, Felton CA 95018; (408) 335-5311. Catalog $1. Sells six kinds, including 'Bolero', 'Caramba', 'Imperial Chantenay', and 'Planet'. ■

By Lauren Bonar Swezey

RUSS A. WIDSTRAND

SULFUR FLOWER'S *yellow-gold blooms fade to tawny red and russet.*

Unthirsty and colorful buckwheats

Plant these California natives soon for bloom next summer

COLORFUL SURPRISES AWAIT you next summer if you plant buckwheats this fall. Most of these unassuming plants start blooming in June and continue until August or later. Most buckwheats are native to California and thrive in *Sunset* climate zones 14 through 24.

The smaller buckwheats are excellent as color accents, in rock gardens, in containers, or in dry borders. Tall growers, like St. Catherine's lace, are best in the background. All are drought tolerant.

Here are the four most colorful kinds to try.

Saffron buckwheat (*Eriogonum crocatum*). Primrose yellow flowers April to August contrast with woolly white leaves. Reaches 1½ feet tall.

St. Catherine's lace (*E. giganteum*). Pale pink clouds of flowers cover plant June to August. Reaches 5 to 8 feet.

Red buckwheat (*E. grande rubescens*). Dusky rose flowers appear in late June and sometimes keep coming until January. Plants can reach 10 to 12 inches high and somewhat wider.

Sulfur flower (*E. umbellatum*). Bright yellow flowers (pictured above) set against green leaves appear June through August. Reaches 1½ feet.

CARE AND FEEDING

Once established, all buckwheats can survive on rainfall alone, but many—especially the colorful kinds shown here—are usually more attractive and flowerful if watered occasionally in summer. Plants in containers need regular supplemental irrigation.

They aren't particular about soil, though it must be well drained.

To keep taller-growing kinds from getting leggy as they grow, start pinching and thinning when they're young.

Gallon-size plants cost about $5. Look for them at nurseries and native plant sales. ■

By Michael MacCaskey

OCTOBER

Garden guide....................231
October checklists..............238
Olive trees are back............243
Flowers by the bunchful 247
Onions that keep on giving...250
Tulips in the mild West........252
Backyard composting 254
Mild-climate peonies...........256
Seeking pink in daffodils 257
A leafy privacy screen.........258
Lush look in a dark entry 259
Vine trellis bolts to fence......259

Sunset's GARDEN GUIDE

CHARLES MANN

Pumpkin patch whimsy

BRIGHT ORANGE PUMPKINS AND FLAMING RED CHILIES GLOW IN THE WARM SUN in this backyard pumpkin patch—sure signs that fall has arrived. In the West's mild, low-elevation climates, this harvest may signal the end of the summer season, but it also ushers in the prime planting time of the year for most bulbs, ground covers, perennials, shrubs, trees, vines, and wildflowers. In cold-winter climates, the gardening season is winding down now and fall cleanup becomes a priority.

Sunset's

GARDEN GUIDE

NORMAN A. PLATE

FALL-PLANTED *ranunculus bloom abundantly in spring in Menlo Park, California. Planted among them are English daisies and purplish blue anemones.*

Spring ranunculus from fall tubers

Although nurseries tempt shoppers with pots of ranunculus in spring, you'll get the best and longest bloom if you plant tubers in October or November (in snowy-winter climates, wait until spring).

During fall and winter, the tubers develop foliage and a healthy root system. Come spring, they burst into full bloom, giving you a brilliant display like the one shown at right.

Tubers are inexpensive (30 to 60 cents each, depending on the quality and supplier), and you can choose the colors you want. In spring, they're often sold in mixed colors.

Set tubers prong side down 2 inches deep (½ to 1 inch in heavy soil) and 6 to 8 inches apart. Water thoroughly, and don't water again, unless it's hot and dry, until sprouts show, in 10 to 14 days. Protect young sprouts from birds with netting.

Help! My ficus has lost its leaves!

You've done the thoughtful gesture for your permanent house plants, having eased them outdoors for the summer, first to the north side of the house, two weeks later to the east side, then into more sun. You've watered and fertilized religiously. Then October rolls around and you move plants back indoors before night temperatures get too brutal. You've earned an A+!

But two days indoors and your beloved *Ficus benjamina* or *F. nitida* begins dropping leaves. In a panic you water, then you withhold water. You fertilize, then you get scared and stick the pot in the bathtub and flush out the fertilizer. The tree keeps dropping leaves until it is leafless! What do you do?

Relax. Ficus are notorious for going into a pout of defoliation with the slightest change in temperature or light level. But they don't stay mad long. Continue to treat the plant with the same respect you've always shown it. Water normally, and hold off on fertilizer. Sweep up the fallen leaves. Keep the plant away from heater vents, and mist the leaves occasionally. You may even want to tell the plant how handsome it is.

Before too long, you'll see new green buds on the ends of the branches, and leaves will begin unfolding. And in no time you'll have a tree full of vigorous new leaves.

Where on Earth!

Want to know where to find a particular plant for sale in California? This handy new 282-page reference, subtitled *A Gardener's Guide to Growers of Specialty Plants in California* and edited by Nancy Conner and Barbara Stevens (agAccess, Davis, Calif., 1993; $12.95), lists 211 retail and wholesale nurseries throughout the state.

For convenience, the book is split into 10 geographical regions, and each entry includes plant specialties, history and description, how to get there, and general information. Also listed are horticultural attractions for each region, 19 mail-order sources in Oregon and Washington, societies and groups, schools, and Master Gardener programs.

The book is a result of nine years of research undertaken on behalf of the San Francisco Landscape Garden Show, held every April. Proceeds from the book and the show benefit San Francisco's Golden Gate Park and other city parks.

Order a copy directly from the publisher for $16.95 postpaid (California residents add 94 cents tax). Write to 603 Fourth St., Davis, CA 95616, or call (800) 235-7171.

A liquidambar without the spiny seed pods

Many homeowners and city officials love to hate liquidambar (sweet gum) trees. The spiny ball-shaped seed pods that drop from the trees in spring can be slippery and hazardous.

But liquidambars have many redeeming qualities. Their bright green leaves change to handsome colors in fall. Established trees need watering only once a month. They're also resistant to oak root fungus.

Now a seedless variety, *L. styraciflua* 'Rotundiloba', is just coming into the nursery trade. Although first identified in the 1930s, it hasn't been available commercially until recently.

Leaves of 'Rotundiloba' are rounded like fig leaves instead of pointed like the common liquidambar's; in fall, they turn burgundy rather than the more typical orange, red, and yellow. This variety also grows fast (to 12 feet the second year), ultimately reaching 45 to 60 feet tall.

In San Martin, California, trees receive no irrigation other than rainfall and are growing slowly, but still look attractive. To avoid surface roots and encourage deep rooting, give established trees periodic deep soakings, particularly if they're planted in lawns.

'Rotundiloba' may be difficult to find, but your nursery can order it wholesale from Monrovia Nursery, Azusa, California. Liquidambar trees in 5-gallon cans cost $35 to $40 retail.

Heavenly flowers for bouquets

Corn cockle (*Agrostemma githago*), also called rose-of-heaven, is tough to beat for its wildflower-like look. Flowers are five-petaled and vaguely trumpet-shaped. On the best variety, 'Milas', they are 3 inches across, lined with deep purplish pink and spotted with deep purple and white in the center. Foot-long stems make the flowers excellent in casual bouquets.

If you live in the low-elevation Southwest, now is the perfect time to sow seeds. They'll germinate in 7 to 10 days, but seedlings are insignificant until early spring, when they shoot upward 3 to 4 feet. Elsewhere in the West, sow seed in spring or early summer.

Plants are too spindly to grow singly; plant them so they'll grow up, through, and around other shrubs, or mass them at the rear of a border.

Give them full sun; they thrive in just about any soil. Pinch off faded flowers to extend overall bloom, but leave a few on the plant to develop seeds for next year's crop. All plant parts are poisonous if eaten.

Order 'Milas' from Thompson & Morgan (address on page 237). A packet costs $2.95.

RUSS A. WIDSTRAND

PURPLE *corn cockle (Agrostemma githago 'Milas') has delicate-looking blooms atop long wiry stems.*

Lupine: easy to grow from seed?

Not as a rule. This handsome wildflower comes from seeds with hard coats that water can't easily penetrate to trigger germination. Here's how to make these tricky seeds sprout.

The evening before planting, cover seeds with boiling water. Then let them soak in the water until morning. Drain off the water and plant the seeds.

If you're planting just a few seeds, simply press them into the soil one at a time. To handle a greater number of seeds efficiently, mix them with about four times their volume of sand or potting soil and scatter; then lightly rake seeds into soil.

In the Southwest, try either arroyo lupine (*Lupinus succulentus*) or desert lupine (*L. sparsiflorus*). As the name suggests, arroyo lupine is greener and more succulent, delphinium-like if given lots of water. The other is, well, sparser—with fewer blooms more widely spaced. Both produce spikes of royal blue flowers.

If you can't find seeds, check with Wild Seed, Box 27751, Tempe, AZ 85285; (602) 345-0669. A packet of either costs $1.25; in greater volumes, desert lupine costs slightly more.

WILLIAM D. ADAMS

FRESHLY DUG *sunchoke tubers are gnarled, like ginger root.*

Sunchoke: harvest or plant it now

Unlike true artichokes, Jerusalem artichokes—also called sunchokes or sunroots (*Helianthus tuberosus*)—develop their crops belowground. Their lumpy, white tubers are crisp—similar to water chestnut or ginger—and taste like jicama. You can grate or chop them into salads or soups. Or you can bake, fry, pickle, purée, or steam them; they'll keep a week or so in the refrigerator wrapped in plastic.

If you already grow sunchokes, you can harvest tubers this month. Use a spading fork to lift all the pieces, or leave a few for next year's crop. Any that remain become new plants in spring.

Even if you don't harvest the roots, the plants are useful as a quick, dense hedge. They grow 6 to 10 feet tall with 8-inch oval leaves, and bear 4-inch golden yellow flowers in summer. The photograph at left shows the plant's flower, leaves, a pile of its tubers.

Sunchoke is easy to grow throughout the West (under the right conditions, it can become weedy). You can plant it any time roots are available—usually fall or early spring. Some nurseries have tubers for sale now. Or order now by mail for delivery in spring. Ronniger's Seed Pota-

toes (Star Route 99, Moyie Springs, ID 83845; catalog $2) offers 'Stampede' (roundish, knobby tubers), 'Fuseau' (smooth, elongated tubers), and 'Red Fuseau' (maroon version of 'Fuseau'). Cost is $3.75 for 1½ pounds of roots.

A leafy screen when you need it

Come autumn, when the sun gets low in the sky and days grow short, you understand the value of deciduous trees, especially in Northwest gardens. If the privacy screen of scarlet-tinged maples pictured at right were evergreens, the garden would be robbed of both sunlight in the dark months and a spectacular show of autumn color. Instead, these trees (*Acer rubrum* 'Armstrong II') provide privacy during the summer, when the owner is outdoors. In autumn, they put on a vivid color performance, then shed their big leaves. Through winter they are handsome sculptures against the gray sky. In spring, they explode in green lace.

NANCY DAVIDSON

LINE OF MAPLES *screens garden from second story of neighboring house from spring to fall.*

These maples are naturally tall, narrow trees. You can plant them close together (the ones pictured are spaced 3 to 6 feet apart). As they grow together, the owner may decide that some are too close, and cut out the weak plants to allow the more vigorous trees to develop. *A. rubrum* is known for fast growth. You can plant these and other trees from nursery cans this month. They'll establish roots through the winter and take off next spring.

The maples written about here do not do well in the mild, low-elevation climates of California and Arizona. But at least three kinds of deciduous plants that grow well in mild climates can serve as a spring-through-fall leafy screen. Here they are; talk to your nurseryman about them: *Lonicera korolkowii, Rosa eglanteria,* and *Salix purpurea* 'Gracilis'.

PUMPKINLIKE *hips dangle from 'Altissimo' rose in fall.*

Pumpkinlike rose hips in time for Halloween

Even after the petals fall, 'Altissimo' climbing rose keeps on giving. The 1-inch-diameter bright orange hips look like miniature pumpkins.

'Altissimo' is a fairly vigorous climber that can reach 10 feet or more. Its 5-inch-wide, brilliant red, single flowers appear throughout the season if deadheaded. For a good show of hips, leave late flowers on to mature.

If planted in a sunny location, 'Altissimo' is easy to grow and resistant to disease. It's also very cold tolerant and will grow in any climate.

Now is a good time to place your order for 'Altissimo', so it arrives in time for bare-root planting this winter. Plants are available from Roses & Wine, 6260 Fernwood Dr., Shingle Springs, CA 95682; (916) 677-9722. Plants cost $11 (plus shipping); they're shipped, ready for planting, in January and February.

A few ferns will take full sun

Northwesterners who've walked along the rockeries on the south slope of Seattle's Queen Anne Hill or, more sadly, over a logging clear-cut, have seen sword ferns (*Polystichum munitum*) growing in full sun, surviving on rainwater alone. In these situations, the fronds are usually stiff and upright, rich apple green in color, and smaller than they are in the shade and moist soil of the forest. But they add handsome texture to mixed plantings.

If you want to try sword ferns in full sun, from now through February is the time to plant them. Have the planting hole waiting, then pull fronds together and tie a piece of twine around them to make digging and handling easier. Take as much rootball as possible and carry the plants with care. Put the ferns in their new home, water well, and remove the twine.

The old fronds may get scorched. If they become too ugly, cut them back; otherwise leave them on until about Valentine's Day, then cut them back.

In March, when the new fronds open, they'll acclimatize to the new sunny location and you'll have healthy, albeit different-looking, foliage from that point on.

Keep these transplanted ferns well watered for their first summer, until their new roots have become established; then they should do well on their own.

Going native with fragrance

When you conjure up images of a scented garden, California native plants may not immediately come to mind. But the state's wild lands do offer many deliciously fragrant garden-worthy plants. We list eight scented perennials and shrubs to try, recommended by Carol Bornstein, director of horticulture at the Santa Barbara Botanic Garden.

Now is prime planting time. Look for these plants at nurseries specializing in natives, or check native plant sales this month.

California sagebrush (*Artemisia californica*). Shrub with finely divided gray-green leaves, aromatic when crushed.

Coyote mint (*Monardella villosa*). Two-foot shrubby perennial with lavender flowers and fragrant foliage.

Matilija poppy (*Romneya coulteri*). Tall perennial with fragrant white flowers to 9 inches wide.

Sage (*Salvia*). Several species, but most pleasing are shrubby Cleveland sage (*S. clevelandii*) and spreading perennial hummingbird sage (*S. spathacea*); both have fragrant foliage and flowers.

Wild buckwheat (*Eriogonum fasciculatum*). Shrub with clusters of white or pinkish flowers; honey-scented.

Wild lilac (*Ceanothus*). Evergreen shrubs with showy, fragrant flower clusters.

Woolly blue curls (*Trichostema lanatum*). Evergreen shrub with dark green, pungently aromatic leaves and profuse purple blooms.

Yerba buena (*Satureja douglasii*). Creeping perennial. Leaves have strong minty scent.

RUSS A. WIDSTRAND

CABBAGE PLANTING *features (from top down) red heading, savoy, green heading, and young red heading types.*

CHAD SLATTERY

'LEMON QUEEN' SANTOLINA, *with a profusion of spring blooms, takes full sun and little water.*

A subtly different santolina

Santolinas are nondemanding and dependable. Most familiar of these shrubby perennials are *S. chamaecyparissus*, with whitish gray leaves and bright yellow flowers, and *S. virens*, with deep green leaves and creamy chartreuse flowers. But one lesser-known santolina—'Lemon Queen' (above)—deserves attention.

It's more compact than its relatives, growing only about 12 to 18 inches wide and 8 to 12 inches tall. The compact habit makes it less prone to open in the middle and flop over. The foliage is gray, and the buttonlike flowers are creamy yellow, lacking tints of orange or green.

Like other santolinas, this one is easy to grow. Plant it in well-drained soil and full sun (or light afternoon shade inland). Once established, 'Lemon Queen' is drought tolerant. Remove spent flowers after peak bloom in late spring or early summer to give lighter bloom later.

Use 'Lemon Queen' as an edging for walks and borders, or in combination with other Mediterranean plants such as lavender and rosemary. It's

attractive massed too, as a ground cover at the edge of an olive grove, for example.

Plants are sold in 4-inch pots for $1 to $2, and in 1-gallon containers for $4 to $5.

Cabbage, an unsung garden hero

"Cabbage is one of the most underrated vegetables in our country," says Wendy Krupnick, horticultural adviser for Shepherd's Garden Seeds. It's a snap to grow, it's ornamental, and it's nutritious. She prefers savoy types (with crinkled leaves, shown below left) for cooking. "They're an absolute delight cooked because they have some bounce. They don't turn mushy." For fresh eating she recommends green 'Grenadier'. "It's sweet tasting, with a crunchy texture." Red cabbage is good fresh or cooked, but it bleeds when cooked.

Start cabbage in flats in dappled shade or under 50 percent shadecloth. Transplant deep enough so the soil comes up to the base of the first true leaves; this keeps plants from toppling. Firm soil over the roots. Immediately after transplanting, cover the bed with a lightweight floating row cover to protect seedlings from insect pests such as aphids, cabbage maggots, and cabbage worms, which can be devastating.

Cabbage prefers rich soil and consistent watering. Fertilize monthly with a complete fertilizer.

In low elevations of California and Arizona, you can plant cabbage from fall to spring but, for best results, try to plant by midmonth and then again in January. In colder climates, plant in mid-

Sunset's

GARDEN GUIDE

summer (for fall harvest).

Seed catalogs offer the best selection of varieties. One mail-order source is Shepherd's Garden Seeds, 6116 Highway 9, Felton, CA 95018; (408) 335-6910 (catalog $1).

JACK NELSON

SHIRLEY POPPIES, *planted in fall at Descanso Gardens, send up brilliant blooms in spring.*

Planting time for Shirley poppies

Also called Flanders field poppies, Shirley poppies (*Papaver rhoeas*) are old-fashioned favorites among connoisseurs of annuals. They bestow a simple elegance with their divided silver-green leaves, slender hairy stems (2 to 5 feet tall), and colorful crepe paper–like flowers (2 inches or more across).

Flanders field poppy generally refers to the scarlet red ancestor of Shirley poppy. Shirley poppies (pictured at right) are commonly pink, white, orange, scarlet, and bicolored. New Mother of Pearl includes unusual smoky pastels in shades of gray, blue, lilac, pink, peach, and white.

Although some nurseries in Southern California offer Shirley poppy seedlings to plant this month, the best way to start the plants—anywhere—is by sowing seed this month. By the time the poppy seedlngs make it to nurseries in color packs or 4-inch pots, they're too overgrown. They'll never catch up to direct-seeded poppies, which are more vigorous and grow taller. You'll also have a greater choice of varieties if you plant by seed.

To plant, choose a spot in full sun, prepare soil, and broadcast seed mixed with fine sand. Thin seedlings to 6 to 8 inches apart. Water regularly.

Plants start blooming in February or March and continue into May or early June. Remove faded flowers to prolong bloom. Toward the end of the season, you may want to leave some seed capsules so that plants self-sow.

WILLIAM. B. DEWEY

SEED-STARTING RACK *has room for newly planted seeds (bottom) and growing seedlings (top).*

A seed-starting rack built like a bookshelf

The handy seed-starting shelf pictured at left, designed by Bryan Rishe for his wife, Peggy, accommodates vegetable seedlings, both newly planted in containers and growing seedlings. Built like a bookshelf with 1-by-10s, the 6½-foot-tall by 5½-foot-wide rack fits neatly into the Rishes' laundry room, where seedlings stay warm. The open back keeps construction simple; a 1-by-6 brace running up the back supports and stabilizes the shelves.

The bottom two shelves are set 9 inches apart so the fluorescent lights can be hung only a few inches above newly planted containers. After seedlings grow a couple of inches tall, they're transferred to three wider-spaced (18 inches apart) upper shelves where fluorescent lights are hung higher to allow room for growth.

Cool-weather care for geraniums

Excessive heat of California's late summer and early fall takes a toll on geraniums (*Pelargonium*). By fall, most look a bit rangy and tired. As the weather cools, it's time to spruce them up and adjust their fall feeding and care. Michael Vassar, former president of the Los Angeles Branch of the International Geranium Society, offers these tips:

- Move plants out from under shadecloth or other summer cover. Adjust them gradually to full light.

•Feed regularly with a complete fertilizer. Once a week, Vassar uses a liquid fertilizer diluted to a third of the recommended strength. He continues this regimen until days are cool and nighttime temperatures drop below 40°.

•Groom and shape plants. Remove faded flowers and dead leaves. To shape and promote branching, cut branches back to just above a node. Always leave at least a third of the branch with some leaves attached.

•Repot, or plant new geraniums. Pot into a slightly larger container—don't jump from a small to a large pot.

Gourmet seedlings now at some nurseries

Gardeners living in and beyond the San Francisco Bay Area (Lafayette, Livermore, Salinas, Santa Cruz, and Carmel) can now buy seedlings of unusual vegetables that are normally sold only in seed catalogs.

For the past five years, a wholesale nursery in Santa Cruz, California, has been supplying retail nurseries in these areas with organically grown gourmet vegetable seedlings. For fall planting, the company offers about 16 varieties of lettuce, such as 'Lollo Rosso' and 'Rouge Grenobloise'; more than a dozen greens, including arugula, escarole, mizuna, and radicchio; unusual broccolis, such as 'Romanesco' and 'Violet Queen'; along with cabbage, kale, herbs, leeks, onions, and peas.

Vegetables are sold in six-packs (price ranges from $2 to $3, depending on the nursery) or 2-inch containers (60 to 90 cents). If your nursery doesn't stock the special seedlings, it can order them for you from Upstarts.

Bright red and green from now into winter

Thirty to 40 years ago, *Skimmia japonica* was so popular that it became a Northwest garden cliché and, as a result of this overexposure, fell from favor with many gardeners. But really, can you beat it? It's been around so long and has performed so well that we must give credit where credit is due. Skimmia flourishes in dry shade, producing a handsome mound of glossy green leaves, fragrant flower clusters in April and May, and masses of bright red berries from now well past Christmas. It's impervious to most diseases and pests, and it is undemanding.

Skimmia does best in rich, quick-draining soil. Female plants produce the fruits, and a male plant is needed for pollination. Broadcast a complete dry fertilizer (12-12-12 is a good choice) around the base of the plant on the same schedule that you fertilize rhododendrons, and you can expect a bumper crop of flowers and fruits.

Plant skimmia this month from 1-gallon cans. You can also take cuttings from existing plants now. They'll root readily in water indoors on an east- or north-facing windowsill through the winter. By April, they'll have a healthy batch of roots and you can set plants directly into beds. Water all new plants well through next summer until they are established.

The plant of many names

The flowers pictured below come from a plant that's as colorful by name as by appearance. Sprays of delicate threadlike foliage topped with blooms the color of sapphires and rubies earned it the most common of its many common names—love-in-a-mist. But this engaging plant is also called fennel flower, devil-in-a-bush, Jack-in-prison, and lady-in-the-bower. Its botanical name—*Nigella damascena*—tells a story: the genus name comes from the Latin *niger* (for the black, irregularly shaped seeds); the species name refers to the city of Damascus, where the plant originated.

In mild-winter regions, scatter the seeds now; in colder regions, sow in spring.

Plants grow 1 to 2½ feet tall. Flowers—typically sky blue, dark blue, white, and rose—develop at branch tips and reach about 1 to 1½ inches across. They last well in bouquets. After flowers fade, papery, horned seed capsules develop; they're decorative in dried arrangements.

Sow seeds on open ground in full sun or part shade. They'll thrive in any soil as long as it's well drained. Seeds germinate easily, but their slender taproots make transplanting difficult.

Varieties include 'Miss Jekyll' (semidouble, cornflower blue blossoms) and Persian Jewels, a strain of mixed colors (blue, pink, white, carmine, mauve, violet). Seeds are widely available in nurseries, or order by mail from Thompson & Morgan, Dept. 149-3, Jackson, NJ 08527; (800) 274-7333. A packet costs $2.25. ■

By Steven R. Lorton, Michael MacCaskey, Lynn Ocone, Lauren Bonar Swezey

WILLIAM D. ADAMS

PERSIAN JEWELS *love-in-a-mist mixes white, red, and blue flowers against feathery foliage.*

Northwest

GARDEN GUIDE

WEST OF THE CASCADES, see items marked with a **W.**

EAST OF THE CASCADES, see items marked with an **E.**

October Checklist

HERE IS WHAT NEEDS DOING

☐ **BREAK UP POTBOUND ROOTS. W, E:** Before planting container-grown perennials or shrubs this month, remove them from containers and check their roots. If roots are growing tightly around the rootballs, massage the roots a bit to loosen them. Or use a sharp knife to make four cuts evenly spaced around the rootball and to cut off some of the twined roots (so there's more room for new roots to spread). The plant will send out new feeder roots at the cut ends.

☐ **CARE FOR HOUSE PLANTS. W, E:** The vacation is over for plants that have been outside for the summer. Hose them off to clean them of dust and insect pests (if you don't, the insects will multiply like gangbusters indoors and spread to other plants). Bring plants in. Clip off yellowed or damaged leaves. Rough up the soil surface a bit if a crust has formed. Water plants well.

☐ **DIVIDE PERENNIALS. W, E:** When perennials like Shasta daisies and daylilies lose their spunk, it is often because clumps are crowded and need dividing. Circle plants with a shovel or spade and pop them out of the ground. Divide gnarled old rootballs, discarding the worst. Put fresh root parts (about the size of a saucer) into a planting hole enriched with compost. Water well. Don't fertilize.

☐ **FLUSH DRIP SYSTEMS. W, E:** Turn drip-irrigation systems on one last time, checking to be certain that each emitter is still irrigating at the proper rate. Clean or replace emitters that are not functioning. Then remove the end caps from systems and flush them with water to blow sediment out of the lines. Finally, drain the lines. Store aboveground systems in a shed or garage for winter. If you have an underground system, disconnect it.

☐ **GROOM LAWNS. W, E:** Mow and edge the lawn. Rake fallen leaves; if you allow them to pile up, they'll become a soggy mass that will smother the lawn below. If you act early, there's still time to seed bald spots and get new grass going before winter halts growth.

☐ **MULCH. W, E:** When you give the garden a complete cleanup at month's end, spread a 3- to 4-inch layer of mulch over beds. Be generous over the roots of tender plants.

☐ **NATURALIZE BULBS. W, E:** To establish beds of bulbs that look as if nature did the work, scatter the bulbs onto spaded soil, rearrange a bit, if necessary, and then plant the bulbs where they landed.

☐ **PLANT BULBS. W, E:** Crocus, daffodils, grape hyacinth, scilla, and tulips can all be set out now. For the best selections, shop early; choose large, firm bulbs. Pot bulbs for winter bloom indoors. Set them close together on a base of potting soil, then cover them with more soil.

☐ **PLANT GROUND COVERS. W, E:** Plant now and you'll see ground covers take off with vigor when spring hits. Choices include ivy, pachysandra, *Rubus calycinoides,* and vinca minor.

☐ **PREPARE PLANTING BEDS. W, E:** After cleaning out spent flower and vegetable beds, enrich the soil with organic matter. You can even turn in leaves and other garden waste that are not fully composted; they'll break down over winter. Leave prepared beds rough. Otherwise, winter's wetness will turn finely worked topsoil into a hard crust. Finish work next spring when the cycles of freezing and thawing have helped break clods apart.

☐ **PROTECT YOUNG TREE TRUNKS. W, E:** In winter, low sunlight can burn tree trunks and cause cracking by repeated freezing and thawing. Trunk wrap is commercially available at garden stores or through mail-order catalogs. One reader wrapped young trunks with old bamboo place mats tied with twine.

☐ **SOW WILDFLOWERS. W, E:** Broadcast seeds now. Nature does it at season's end, and the seeds spend the winter in cold storage in the ground. They'll be up and going earlier next year than spring-sown seeds. Sow seeds on ground you've scratched up with a rake, then cover them with a light layer of organic matter; water well.

☐ **STORE PRODUCE. W, E:** When you harvest members of the squash family for keeping, leave 2 inches of stem on the fruits and store them at 50° to 60°. Apples and pears should be held at about 40°. Beets and carrots can be left in the ground all winter if they have a good covering of mulch. Store onions, shallots, and nuts in mesh bags or in slotted crates. Check all stored produce regularly for signs of rot.

☐ **TRANSPLANT EVERGREENS. W, E:** Dig a hole twice as wide as the rootball. Dig as much of the rootball as possible. Roll the dug plant onto an old blanket or shower curtain, and pull it to its new location.

☐ **WINTERIZE POWER EQUIPMENT. W, E:** At month's end on the east side of the Cascades, next month on the west, get power equipment in shape for winter storage. Drain oil and gas from engines; clean and oil blades and other moving parts to prevent rust. If you are uncertain, look in your instruction booklets for garden equipment.—*S. R. L.* ■

Central

GARDEN GUIDE

IN HIGH ELEVATIONS and intermountain areas of California, and east of the Sierra, see items marked with an **H.**

IN LOW ELEVATIONS of Northern California, see items marked with an **L.**

☐ **COMPOST. H, L:** As you clean up the garden, add disease-free plant debris and leaves to the compost pile. Keep the pile moist but not soggy. To speed decay, add a small amount of nitrogen fertilizer.

☐ **CONTROL SNAILS AND SLUGS. L:** Cool, damp fall weather brings on a full attack. After dark, use a flashlight and search plants in the ground and in containers. Handpick and crush or discard in a closed container. If they're too numerous for handpicking, use a liquid or dry bait.

☐ **FLUSH DRIP SYSTEMS. H:** Before soil freezes, flush drip-irrigation systems to prevent mineral buildup and cracked tubing. Remove end caps from main lines, turn the water on for a few minutes, then shut it off. Make sure all the water has drained out, then replace the end caps. Ooze-type systems will last longer if drained and stored over the winter in a garage or basement.

☐ **NATURALIZE BULBS. L:** To create a mass of plants that looks as if it's spreading naturally, toss handfuls of a single kind of bulb over the planting area, varying their density. Repeat with a second or third kind, if desired. Plant where bulbs fall. Choose bulbs that naturalize easily in your climate, soil, and sun exposure. Try species daffodils, muscari, ornamental alliums, or scilla.

☐ **ORDER GRAPES, FRUIT TREES, BERRIES. H, L:** If you plan to buy special varieties of fruits by mail, get your order in soon, so you're sure to get the types you want and so they arrive in time for dormant-season planting.

☐ **OVERPLANT BULB BEDS. L:** Cool-season annuals planted over bulbs will give a colorful show during the winter before bulbs pop up. Choose colors that complement the bulbs, such as blue violas with yellow daffodils, or white or purple fairy primrose with pink tulips.

☐ **PICK UP FALLEN FRUIT. H, L:** Pick up fruit and leaves that drop to the ground under trees. Compost only pest-free plant debris. If you suspect pests, bag the debris and toss it in the garbage.

☐ **PLANT ANNUALS. L:** Plant soon, so they get established before the weather turns cold. Try calendula, Iceland poppies, pansies, primroses, snapdragons, stock, and violas. In coastal areas, you can also plant calceolaria, cineraria, nemesia, and schizanthus. From seed, plant baby blue eyes, forget-me-nots, sweet alyssum, sweet peas, and spring wildflowers.

To plant from a nursery sixpack, loosen roots by pulling apart the bottom third of the rootball; new roots will grow from broken ends into surrounding soil.

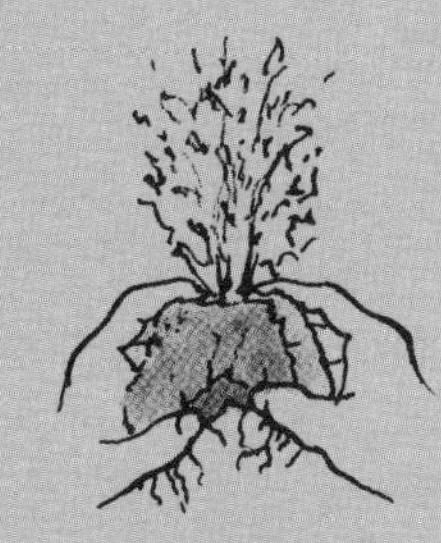

☐ **PLANT BULBS FOR SPRING BLOOM. L:** If you haven't bought bulbs yet, do so as soon as possible. As bulbs hang around in nurseries, they may get soft and start to sprout. **H:** In very cold climates, plant early in the month (warmer high-elevation areas should have been planted by now).

☐ **PLANT SHRUBS. L:** For color with minimal water, try *Anisodontea hypomandarum*, blue hibiscus, ceanothus, feathery cassia, rockrose, and plumbago.

☐ **SET OUT GARLIC. L:** Plant in rich, well-drained soil. Break bulbs into individual cloves a few days before planting and plant the scar end down. Cover regular garlic with 1 to 2 inches of soil, elephant garlic with 4 to 6 inches. Press the soil down firmly and water. Irrigate if the weather is dry.

☐ **SET OUT TREES. L:** Fall is the best time to set out trees. For shade in summer and sun in winter, choose a deciduous tree (ash, Chinese tallow tree, honey locust, liquidambar, oak, redbud). Evergreen trees (acacia, eucalyptus, fruitless olive, tristania) provide shade all year.

☐ **SOW WILDFLOWERS. L:** To get the best show in spring, sow wildflowers now. Choose a weed-free area or weeds will overrun the wildflowers (in mild climates, you still have time to pregerminate weeds: water the soil so they come up, then hoe or spray with a contact herbicide). **H:** Broadcast seed early in the month. In areas where winters are cold but snow cover is minimal, wait until spring to sow seeds.

☐ **TEND LAWNS. L:** Now is the time to plant sod, sow grass seed, or reseed thin spots on bluegrass, fescue, and rye grass lawns. Prepare the soil well first by rotary-tilling it and working in plenty of amendments. Whether using seed or sod, you'll need to water several times a day to get seed to germinate or allow sod roots to knit with the soil. For existing cool-season lawns, fertilize this month.—*L. B. S.* ■

October Checklist

HERE IS WHAT NEEDS DOING

□ C = Coastal and inland zones

□ L = Low desert

□ H = High desert

□ **BUY AND PLANT NATIVES. C, L:** Midmonth marks the beginning of peak planting season for California native plants. Shop at plant sales and nurseries specializing in native and Mediterranean plants. Plant perennials, shrubs, and trees, and sow seeds for annuals. For plants to try, see the item on fragrant native plants (page 235).

□ **CHILL BULBS. C, L:** Place crocus, hyacinths, and tulips in paper bag in refrigerator for at least six weeks before planting. Plant immediately after removing from refrigerator.

□ **DIVIDE PERENNIALS.** If you noticed that blooms on perennials such as asters, bellflowers, callas, daisies, daylilies, helianthus, heliopsis, rudbeckia, and yarrow were smaller this year, and if plants are weak and crowded, it's time to divide. Dig each clump so the rootball comes up intact. Wash or gently shake off excess soil so you can cut off divisions; use a sharp knife. Each division should have some leaves and plenty of roots. Plant immediately.

□ **MANAGE PESTS. C, L:** As temperatures turn cooler, aphids, snails, and whiteflies often multiply. For aphids and whiteflies, hose off plants or spray with insecticidal soap; repeat every three to four days. To guard against snails, put collars or sleeves around vulnerable plants and copper bands or a screen around beds. Handpick at night, using a flashlight.

□ **PLANT BEDDING ANNUALS. C, L:** For winter through spring bloom, plant cool-season annuals now. The sooner you get them into the ground, the faster they get established. Choices include calendula, dianthus, English daisies, Iceland poppies, lobelia, nemesia, pansies, primroses, schizanthus, snapdragons, stock, and violas. Choose small, healthy plants; avoid rootbound ones. To plant, loosen roots by pulling apart the bottom third of the rootball; new roots will grow from broken ends into surrounding soil rather than just circling the existing rootball.

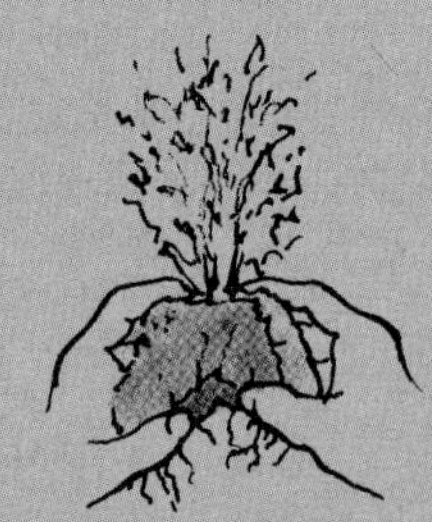

□ **PLANT COOL-SEASON VEGETABLES. C, L:** In Southern California's mildest climates, midmonth begins one of the year's two great vegetable-growing seasons. Set out seedlings of broccoli, cabbage (see item on page 235), cauliflower, and lettuce. Sow seeds of beets, carrots, chard, onions, parsley, peas, radishes, and turnips. **H:** In coldest areas, finish planting by October 1. In warmer zones, plant onions, peas, radishes, and spinach.

□ **PLANT PERENNIALS. C, L:** This is the best time of year to plant perennials. Some undemanding, high-performance ones are coreopsis, daylily, fortnight lily, kangaroo paw, lavender, Mexican evening primrose, rosemary, rudbeckia, *Salvia greggii, S. clevelandii,* santolina (see item on page 235), *Verbena bonariensis, V. peruviana*, and yarrow. **H:** Plant columbine, evergreen candytuft, Shasta daisies, and violets.

□ **PLANT SEEDS FOR ANNUALS. C, L:** Many cool-season annuals planted by direct seeding grow fast and give better results than transplants. Try baby blue eyes, forget-me-nots, globe candytuft, linaria, Shirley poppies (see item on page 236), sweet alyssum, and sweet peas.

□ **PREPARE FOR SANTA ANA WINDS. C, L:** Prevent branch breakage by thinning trees, especially dense and top-heavy ones like California pepper, carob, and jacaranda. Check stakes supporting young trees to be sure they're strong enough. Also check to see that ties are strong and not cutting into the bark. When winds are predicted, mist tender patio plants.

□ **SET BULBS IN GARDEN. C:** In coastal and inland areas, start planting bulbs. Supplies of freesias, daffodils, hyacinths, irises, ranunculus, and tulips are at an annual peak in nurseries. **C, L:** To create an informal mass of plants that looks as if it's spreading naturally, toss out handfuls of a single kind of bulb over the planting area, varying the density. Repeat with a second or third kind, if desired. Plant where bulbs fall. Choose bulbs that naturalize easily in your climate, soil, and sun exposure. Some for mild climates are babiana, homeria, *Ipheion uniflorum, Narcissus tazetta*, sparaxis, and *Tulipa clusiana*. **L:** Before midmonth, plant freesias and irises.

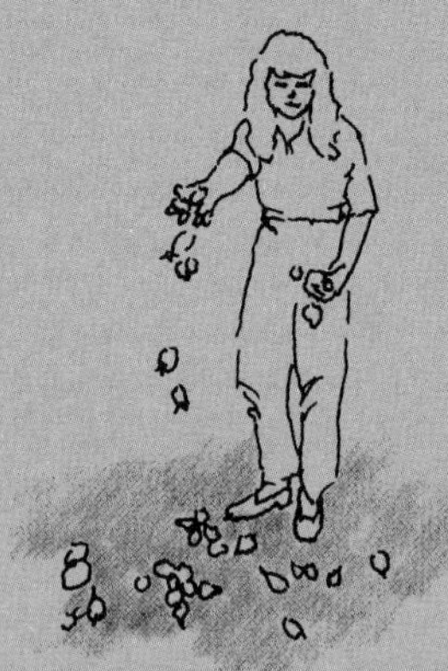

□ **TEND ROSES. C, L:** Most years, you can encourage one more bloom cycle from roses by pruning, feeding, and watering now. When you cut, remove a third of the growth. Given a warm fall, you could have roses blooming again for Christmas.

□ **THIN VEGETABLE SEEDLINGS.** Once seeds germinate and develop true leaves, thin beets, carrots, lettuce, onions, and radishes. Early thinning is especially important to develop well-formed root crops.—*L.O.* ■

DIVIDE PERENNIALS. To restrain the growth of fast-spreading perennials such as Shasta daisies and bee balm, or to reinvigorate stagnating ones such as daylilies, dig up the entire plant. Water first to soften soil, then pry the rootball apart with a fork, or slice into sections with shovel or knife. Partially cut back foliage, and replant.

FEED AND WATER ROSES. In low and intermediate deserts, feed and water now so you can enjoy another flush of bloom. Also cut off spent blooms and remove suckers that rise from below the bud union.

HARVEST VEGETABLES. August-sown bush beans are just beginning to produce. Also keep picking lettuce and radishes.

OVERSEED AND FEED LAWNS. Mow Bermuda lawns closely, overseed with perennial rye grass, and fertilize with ammonium phosphate. When winter lawns are established (about six weeks), use a high-nitrogen fertilizer. Water to supplement rainfall.

PLANT BULBS TO NATURALIZE. Before midmonth in the low and intermediate deserts, plant iris. Anytime during October, plant amaryllis, anemone, calla, crocus, daffodils and other narcissus, harlequin flower, oxalis, ranunculus, and watsonia. Allow tulip bulbs to chill in refrigerator for six weeks before planting. In the high desert, plant daffodils and other narcissus, lilies, and tulips.

PLANT GROUND COVERS. In low and intermediate deserts, consider *Acacia redolens*, Baja and Mexican evening primroses, *Dalea greggii*, dwarf rosemary, gazania, lippia, low-growing junipers, snow-in-summer (*Cerastium tomentosum*), and verbena. In high elevations, plant low-growing junipers.

PLANT PERENNIALS. Throughout most of the Southwest, this is the best month to plant perennials. In sunny areas, sow seeds or set out plants of blanket flower, columbine, coreopsis, candytuft, geranium, and peony.

PLANT SHRUBS AND TREES. Any woody tree or shrub, except cold-tender ones like bougainvillea and hibiscus, can go into the ground now. Dig a hole that's the exact depth of the original rootball and three to five times as wide. Backfill with native soil. Loosen circling roots, and set rootball in hole. Use water to settle soil around rootball as you backfill. Stake trees that need support.

PLANT VEGETABLES. Set out plants or sow seeds of beets, cabbage, carrots, chard, collards, endive, garlic, kale, onion, parsnips, peas, radishes, rutabaga, spinach, and turnips. In low and intermediate deserts, other choices are broccoli, brussels sprouts, cauliflower, and lettuce. Throughout the Southwest, plant roots of asparagus and rhubarb. Lightly mulch around plants; use a row cover to protect from birds and insects.

PLANT WINTER ANNUALS. In low and intermediate deserts, plant these annuals: ageratum, aster, begonia, bells-of-Ireland, calendula, clarkia, cornflower, dianthus, English daisy, forget-me-not, gaillardia, Iceland and Shirley poppies, larkspur, lobelia, nicotiana, painted daisy, pansy, petunia, phlox, primrose, salpiglossis, scabiosa, snapdragon, statice, stock, sweet alyssum, sweet pea, viola.

SET OUT STRAWBERRIES. In the low desert, plant after midmonth for a spring crop. Widely available varieties are 'Sequoia' and 'Tioga'. For high-desert gardens, try 'Ogallala'. Prepare soil with compost and fertilizer, then set plants 6 inches apart in rows 18 inches apart; plant crowns level with soil surface. To retain moisture and protect from frost, place a row cover over the bed.

SOW WILDFLOWER SEEDS. In mountain areas, sow seeds this month for bloom next spring. Scatter seeds of African daisies (*Dimorphotheca*), *Aster bigelovii*, blue flax, coreopsis, Mexican hat, Mexican poppy, and *Penstemon strictus*. Cultivate soil lightly, spread seeds, then mulch with ¼ to ½ inch of ground bark or other organic matter.

TEND VEGETABLE SEEDLINGS. Once seeds germinate and develop the first true leaves, thin young plants of beets, carrots, lettuce, onions, and radishes. Early thinning is especially important to develop well-formed root crops.

WATER. In the low desert, temperatures will likely continue in the 90s for a while longer. Many plants need regular watering, especially those in containers. Water plants deeply and as often as necessary. Check soil moisture with a soil probe or by digging with a shovel.—*M. M.* ■

GRACEFUL CANOPY, STURDY LIMBS

Olive fans out over Mediterranean shrubs and ground covers in this Montecito, California, garden. New Zealand flax provides spiky accents on each side. At right, low-growing 'Little Ollie' olive makes handsome hedge in a Los Angeles garden.

WILLIAM B. DEWEY

RUSS A. WIDSTRAND

Olive trees... back again, and better

PLANT A MATURE ONE, OR BUY A YOUNGER ONE AND WATCH IT GROW

Few trees are as at home in low elevations of California and Arizona as the olive. For many decades after missionaries brought cuttings from Spain to California in 1769 to plant for shade and fruit, this tough, graceful tree became the tree of choice in our arid climates. For one thing, it needs no water—repeat, no water. For another, it grows huge trunks, strong limbs, and clouds of fine-textured foliage—basically, it develops a wonderfully cool and friendly grace. The olive is a gem of a tree.

But in the 1950s and '60s, landscape mistakes temporarily tarnished its reputation. Mature olive trees from groves overrun by suburbia were transplanted seemingly everywhere—over patios, walks, lawns, driveways, and streets. And the falling fruit, which makes a blue-stained

THE AMAZING OLIVE TREE

Grow one of these fruitless varieties, or . . .

45'

30'

15'

'Bonita'

Introduced in 1961. Less popular than the others. Not really fruitless, but has tiny fruit (like privet's).

'Little Ollie'

Introduced in 1987. It's a big, dense shrub, very dark green, excellent as a hedge or screen. Bears almost no fruit.

'Majestic Beauty'

Introduced in 1985. Airy- and fluffy-looking, it's also suitable for a hedge or screen. Bears almost no fruit.

'Skylark Dwarf'

Introduced in 1969. Typically a multiple-trunked, large, compact shrub. Sets a very small crop some years.

'Swan Hill'

From Swan Hill, Victoria, Australia. Introduced to California and Arizona nurseries in 1972. Its leaves are a deep green. Bears no fruit.

'Wilsoni'

Introduced in 1979. It was discovered in a grove of Manzanillo olives. Bears no fruit.

mess, brought disdain.

Now all that has changed. You can buy and plant fruitless trees, or—if you don't want to wait decades for these adolescents to mature fully—50- to 100-year-old orchard trees at the prime of their beauty. To deal with the messy fruit, just plant an olive-swallowing ground cover underneath.

The olive is one of only three good-looking big trees Californians can grow without water; the others are eucalyptus and oak. In outstanding drought tolerance, the three are matched. But the olive has neither the pests of the oak nor (once you plant a ground cover underneath) the mess of the eucalyptus.

YOU'LL LOVE ITS TOUGHNESS

Franciscan fathers planted the 'Mission' olive, which remains California's hardiest. Scores of other varieties came later. The three shown on page 245 along with 'Mission' have become the most grown commercially.

As a xerophyte (a plant adapted to dry air and soil), the olive loved the arid West. The tree's leaves are constructed so that they lose little water through transpiration, and its small, shallow root system quickly brings it what water it can get. California's Central Valley farmers do irrigate olive orchards, which increases fruit production as much as tenfold. But landscape trees need no supplemental water at all as soon as the roots are established, which takes only one to three years (depending on the size of the trees being planted). This is true whether you plant fruiting or fruitless trees.

The fruitless varieties. In landscaping, the olive's fruit is mostly a nuisance. Spattered olives can be an intolerable mess—and how many homeowners have the time, patience, or interest to handpick the olives for curing before they fall? Also, pollen from fruiting olives bothers allergic people so much in some regions—especially Phoenix and Tucson—that a low-pollen variety (the fruitless 'Swan Hill') even makes medical sense.

As a result, since the early 1960s, growers have introduced six varieties of olive that produce no fruit at all, or very little. These are available, in selections varying from minimal to complete, in nurseries. Some so-called fruitless varieties either bear tiny fruits or bear some regular fruits only in some years. Others bear no fruit at all but are alleged (mostly by growers of a competing kind) to bear fruit occasionally.

Even the oldest of the large-tree kinds of fruitless olives have not yet lived long enough to develop the beautiful, massive trunks and branches for which olive trees are famous. You can find that patriarchal look of age only in the fruiting trees, some as old as 100 years.

The fruiting option. In the 1960s, California's commercial olive trees, not just their fruit, became a commodity. As an olive rancher would decide to quit an orchard, he'd find firms to buy his unneeded trees and dig, box, and move them to a landscaping job. By now the market has expanded to the point where it costs homeowners as little as $400 (but most often $1,000 to $1,500, sometimes as much as $3,000) to bring one of those old-timers in.

HOW TO DEAL WITH UNWANTED FRUIT

If you buy a mature olive—or have one already—your options are clear. Either you can pick the fruit every year to preserve or extract oil, or you've got to sweep, rake up, or pick up fallen olives every autumn through early spring.

The easiest solution is to grow a competent olive-swallowing ground cover beneath the tree (see lists at right). The other solution is spraying with a hormone that reduces or eliminates fruit set. Timing is crucial (spraying must be done when the tree is in flower, in midspring), and so is execution (the sprays can cause dieback in nearby plants, or even damage the olive tree if mishandled). Rinse plants beneath and beside the olive afterward. It's best to have a commercial sprayer do the job.

Finally, some homeowners reduce fruit set by spraying open blossoms with a blast of water from the hose. ■

By Joseph F. Williamson

buy a full-grown, fruited type

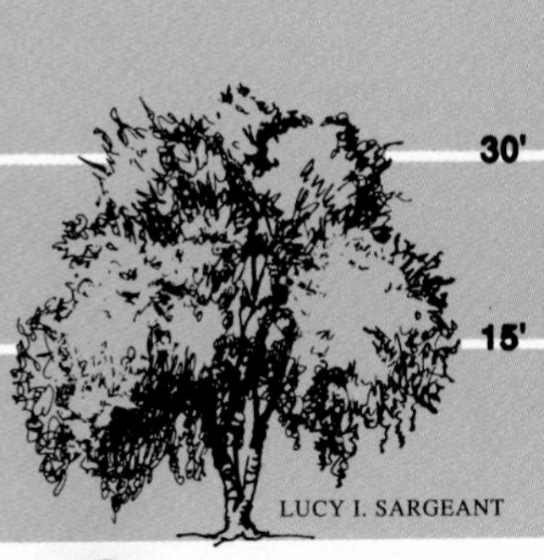

'Ascolana'

Pretty landscape tree. Large fruit (small pit) bruises easily. Makes up only 3.6 percent of commercial acreage.

'Manzanillo'

More spreading growth habit than most. Somewhat apple-shaped fruit. Leading commercial variety (60 percent), so most often sold as a large tree.

'Mission'

Hardier than others. Tall tree with dense vertical growth. Medium-size fruit. Makes up 9 percent of commercial acreage.

'Sevillano'

Second leading commercial variety (26 percent), but losing favor with growers (fruit too large). Oaklike landscaping tree.

Where to buy full-grown fruiting trees

Following are firms that dig, transport, and plant (unless otherwise noted) full-size olive trees from commercial groves to landscaping sites (including home gardens).

Chapo Farms, 1512 W. Elliot Rd., Chandler, Ariz. 85224; (602) 786-3393.

Davis and Son Tree Movers, Box 164, Bangor, Calif. 95914; (916) 679-2591.

Robert Denney and Associates, Inc., Box 2749, Visalia, Calif. 93279; no digging, transporting, or planting.

Ellis Farms, Inc., 1325 Borrego Valley Rd., Borrego Springs, Calif. 92004; (619) 767-5234; no digging, transporting, or planting.

Elmac Industries, 1170 N. Maston St., Porterville, Calif. 93257; (209) 781-7542.

Land-scape Innovations, Box 4349, Napa, Calif. 94558; (707) 252-4627.

Mel's Tree Service, 1523 Timberlake Circle, Lodi, Calif. 95242; (209) 368-4767.

Morales Olive Trees, 24631 Seth Circle, Dana Point, Calif. 92629; (714) 545-8011.

Nor Cal Trees, 22000 Silver Spur Rd., Palo Cedro, Calif. 96073; (916) 244-6278.

The Olive Branch, Box 2458, Santa Barbara, Calif. 93120; (805) 962-6272.

Jerry Rhodes, 2133 S. Jacob St., Visalia, Calif. 93277; (209) 732-9890.

Roadrunner Tree Farm, Box 1900, Borrego Springs, Calif. 92004; (619) 767-3310.

Gil Sariana & Sons Olive Trees, 217 Curtis Way, Anaheim, Calif. 92806; (714) 535-8241.

Swan Hill Nurseries, 6244 E. Berneil Dr., Paradise Valley, Ariz. 85253; (602) 228-7352; bags and ships only.

Tree Movers, 2190 Crittenden Lane, Mountain View, Calif. 94043; (800) 498-7337.

Trees of California, Box 13189, Coyote, Calif. 95013; (408) 264-3663.

Trees to Go, 3060 El Centro Rd., Sacramento, Calif. 95833; (916) 920-8733.

What to plant under them to limit the mess

Out of more than 140 ground covers on the market, these 26 are said by landscape architects and nurserymen to work best at swallowing olives. Each plant is thick yet permeable, lacks heavy stems olives might bounce off, and can handle root competition, sun, and shade. All are handsome companions to olive trees.

Drought tolerant

Acacia redolens • *Arctostaphylos manzanita* • *Ceanothus gloriosus, C. griseus horizontalis* • *Cistus*, low-growing • *Cotoneaster*, low-growing • *Hypericum calycinum* • Lantana, lavender-flowered • *Myoporum* • *Polygonum capitatum* • Rosemary (*Rosmarinus officinalis*) • *Sollya heterophylla*

Needs watering

Aptenia 'Red Apple' • Asparagus • *Cerastium tomentosum* • *Ceratostigma plumbaginoides* • *Duchesnea indica* • Ivy (*Hedera helix*) • Japanese honeysuckle (*Lonicera japonica*) • Oregon grape (*Mahonia aquifolium*) • *Pelargonium tomentosum* • *Ribes viburnifolium* • *Rubus calycinoides* • *Sarcococca hookerana humilis* • Star jasmine (*Trachelospermum jasminoides*) • *Vinca major*

LARKSPUR, *in cotton candy colors, spreads rows of pink and blue flowers across Don Thompson's sunny field in spring. Don harvests bunches of blooms regularly for bouquets.*

SAM KWONG

Flowers by the bunchful

IN WALLA WALLA, TWO GROWERS HARVEST FLOWERS AND FOLIAGE FOR BOUQUETS

Grow flowers for a living and you'll quickly learn which plants bloom prolifically, which ones cause the least amount of trouble, and which ones yield cut flowers over a long period and add color to garden borders.

Cyndi and Don Thompson grow flowers in and around their Walla Walla garden to use fresh in their wedding flower business, to sell wholesale, and to dry for bouquets. What do they grow? Mostly common favorites. As Don puts it, "The old favorites got that way because they work hard and are trustworthy."

Here are plants the Thompsons grow for surefire success, with details on how they grow them. The Thompsons' lists on page 249 show cold-winter gardeners what can be planted now and what should wait until

PLANTED CLOSELY *in clumps and sweeps, perennials and annuals color garden beds. Roses and dahlias enhance this border.*

spring. In mild climates, plant what you want now.

CHOICE FLOWERS FOR CUTTING

For old-fashioned bouquets, prolific perennials fill beds around the cottage. Annuals such as snapdragons and sweet peas (for spring bloom) and salvias and zinnias (for summer bloom) are mixed among them. The Thompsons crowd the plants—often in sweeps—and choose ones that don't require frequent dividing or much staking.

Tall growers like delphinium, hollyhock, monarda, and *Nicotiana sylvestris* grow at the back of borders and in the center of island beds. Asters, 'Victoria' blue salvia, *Nicotiana alata,* snapdragons (the Madame Butterfly strain is a favorite), 'Coronation Gold' yarrow, and *Centranthus ruber* 'Albus' grow in the middle of the beds. Low growers like 'Moonbeam' coreopsis and 'Lemon Gem' signet marigolds ruffle along at the edges.

For punch, the Thompsons plant big annual sunflowers or *Helianthus multiflorus,* or they build a tepee from cut saplings and let scarlet runner beans, blue morning glories, and sweet peas scramble over it.

The biggest producer is larkspur (*Consolida am-*

SAM KWONG

BRIGHT SUNFLOWER, *a volunteer in the Thompsons' garden (probably sown by a passing bird), was allowed to grow and produce seed for subsequent crops.*

bigua). The Thompsons sow seeds of this annual delphinium in October in a field next to the garden, and harvest the blossom spikes in June and July.

They also grow roses to cut fresh and to dry. Old hybrid teas like 'Medallion', 'Peace', and 'Pristine', and grandifloras like 'Aquarius' fill the garden. Old-fashioned shrub roses, English roses, and 'Simplicity' (a good hedge rose) are other favorites.

When frost hits in late October, the Thompsons cut back plants, give the garden a thorough cleanup, and cover beds with a 2-inch layer of rotted cow manure. ■

By Steven R. Lorton

The Thompsons' favorite flowers for bouquets

Plant these in fall

Crambe cordifolia
Larkspur
Monarda
David Austin English roses:
'Abraham Darby', 'Bibi Maizoon', 'Graham Thomas', 'Mary Rose', 'Othello', 'Perdita'
Scabiosa
Verbena bonariensis
Yarrow (*Achillea filipendulina* 'Coronation Gold')

Plant these in spring

Ageratum 'Blue Horizon'
Asters:
A. 'Operetta', Pastel Mix, 'Tiger Paws', 'Super Princess Symphonie'
Mexican tulip poppy
(*Hunnemannia fumariifolia* 'Sunlite')
Salvias:
S. farinacea 'Victoria', *S. coccinea* 'Cherry Blossom'
Snapdragon (Madame Butterfly)
Sunflowers:
'Orange sun', 'Valentine'
Stock ('Legacy')
Sweet peas
Zinnia

Favorite foliage for bouquet fillers and fragrance

Plant these in spring

Bronze fennel
Scented geraniums:
'Apricot', 'Clorinda', 'Copthorne', 'French Lace', 'Mabel Grey'
Mint

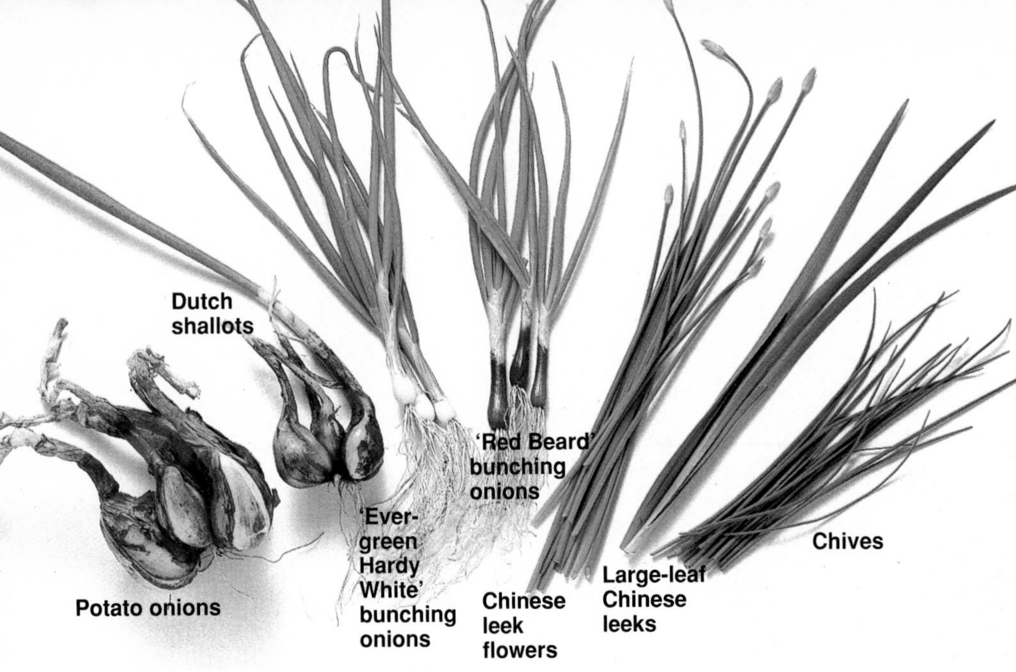

Onions that keep on giving

Plant them now and you can harvest them for years to come

PETER CHRISTIANSEN

TOPSET ONIONS *produce small, edible bulblets on the ends of leaves. Tender young leaves and underground bulbs (shown at right) are also edible.*

POTATO ONIONS, Egyptian onions, and Chinese leek flowers are seldom featured prominently on supermarkets' produce counters. In fact, there's a good chance you won't find them in most home gardens either.

These cousins of the ordinary bulbing onion are part of a diverse group in the *Allium* family that are all perennial onions. Once you plant them, they'll provide many crops.

If planted in October in the mild-winter West, they grow and develop through the cool season, with harvest the following spring.

GROW ONIONS FOR BULBS OR LEAVES

Among perennial onions, you'll find a wide selection.

Multipliers. The closest relatives of common single-bulb onions are multipliers, which include potato onions and shallots.

Multipliers grow by dividing. If you plant a larger (about 2- to 3-inch-diameter) potato onion, it will divide into a cluster of bulbs of mixed sizes. Each smaller onion (about 1 inch in diameter) usually grows into one large bulb. Shallots always divide, and they're often smaller than potato onions.

Multipliers can be left in the ground, where they will continue to multiply. But most gardeners lift the bulbs at harvesttime, store some for eating, and replant the rest in fall.

Both potato onions and shallots are good keepers, flavorful, and fairly mild. But they're best for cooking rather than for eating fresh.

Topset onions. This type, called Egyptian onion (it's not really from Egypt), produces many leafy green stalks; small bulblets form on their tops. If bulblets are not harvested, the leaves bend and the bulblets fall to the ground and take root.

When left in the ground, Egyptian onion plants increase in size. To expand the size of your planting, harvest the bulblets and plant them individually in fall (if bulblets are very small, don't separate them before planting).

Several parts of this onion are edible. Mild, tender young leaves (with no bulblets) can be used like green onions. The bulblets make tasty pickles (see recipe on facing page). The bulbs normally are left in the ground, but some can be harvested. Since their flavor is very strong, they're best cooked.

Bunching onions. These onions may be called Japanese bunching onions, Welsh onions, or sometimes scallions (although scallions can refer to any onion at the green onion stage of growth).

Although these onions are often grown as annuals, you can leave some plants in the ground to allow offshoots to develop and continue to divide. Harvest older ones carefully by gently pulling them up, so the young ones remain in the soil to grow.

Bunching onions are mild and can be used fresh or in cooking just like any green onions.

Chives. Common chives have leafy growth 12 to 24 inches tall, lavender-pink flowers in spring, and a mild green onion flavor. To harvest them, snip leaves as needed.

Chinese leeks (also called Oriental garlic chives) form foot-tall plants; the foliage has a distinctive mild garlic flavor. Common Chinese leek plants have fairly narrow leaves (there's also a broad-leafed type) and produce white flowers in late summer. Another type—Chinese leek flower—is grown especially for its flowers, which appear starting in spring. The flowers are harvested in bud stage when stalks are about a foot tall and stems are pliable.

PROVIDE RICH SOIL

Till the soil and turn in plenty of organic material. Since onions have shallow roots, they don't compete well with weeds. Lightly hoe or hand-weed regularly; deep hoeing can damage roots. Keep the soil moist (Chinese leeks prefer to be on the dry side) and fertilize every two weeks with fish emulsion.

Planting and harvesting techniques vary by type.

Multipliers. Cover bulbs with 1 inch of soil. In cold-winter climates, cover soil with about 2 inches of mulch in fall; remove in February. Stop fertilizing one month before harvest (late April or early May in mild climates); cut off water a week before harvest. Harvest when necks are dry and most of the leaves are turning brown.

Cure bulbs for one to two months in a protected spot out of sunlight; handle gently to avoid bruising them. When bulbs have cured, clip off tops, leaving about 1 inch of neck. Store in a dry place.

Topset. Cover bulbs with 1 to 1½ inches of soil. Harvest tender green leaves when plants grow large enough to snip some off. Cut off bulblets when they're ½ to ¾ inch in diameter. Harvest underground bulbs in late spring.

Bunching. Scatter seeds about 1 inch apart. Cover with ¼ inch of soil; thin to 2 to 3 inches apart. Harvest as needed.

Chives and Chinese leeks. Sow seeds about 2 inches apart and ¼ inch deep; thin to 4 to 6 inches apart. Harvest individual leaves as needed or cut back the entire plant.

WHERE TO BUY ONIONS

The more unusual perennial onions must be ordered by mail. Here are four sources.

Nichols Garden Nursery, 1190 N. Pacific Highway, Albany, OR 97321; (503) 928-9280 (free catalog). Chives, Oriental garlic chives, and onions (bunching, Egyptian).

Seeds Blüm, Idaho City Stage, Boise, ID 83706 (catalog $3). Welsh onions and potato onions.

Southern Exposure Seed Exchange, Box 158, North Garden, VA 22959; (804) 973-4703 (catalog $3). Shallots, and bunching, Egyptian, and potato onions (call for fall availability).

Sunrise Enterprises, Box 330058, West Hartford, CT 06133; (203) 666-8071 (catalog $2). Bunching onions, and broad-leafed, common, and Chinese leek flowers. ■

By Lauren Bonar Swezey

COOKING WITH ONION BULBS, LEAVES, BUDS, AND STALKS

PETER CHRISTIANSEN

TENDER STALKS *of Chinese leek flower accompany ginger- and sherry-flavored chicken with rice.*

Chive Mayonnaise

Serve as a dip for vegetables or as a sandwich spread.

- 1 cup thinly sliced chives, Chinese leeks, or Chinese leek flower leaves
- ½ cup unflavored nonfat yogurt
- ½ cup reduced-calorie or regular mayonnaise
- Salt

In a blender or food processor, combine the chives, yogurt, and mayonnaise; whirl until smoothly blended. Add salt to taste. Serve, or cover and chill up to 1 day. Makes 1¼ cups.

Per tablespoon: 20 cal. (72 percent from fat); 0.4 g protein; 1.6 g fat (0.4 g sat.); 0.9 g carbo.; 37 mg sodium; 2 mg chol.

Pickled Egyptian Onions

- 1 cup Egyptian onion bulblets (about ½ in. wide)
- ⅔ cup seasoned rice vinegar (or ½ cup rice vinegar plus 3 tablespoons sugar, and salt to taste)

Separate bulblets, trim ends, peel, rinse, and drain. In a 1- to 2-quart pan, combine bulblets and vinegar. Bring to a boil over high heat; boil, uncovered, for 1 minute. Pour into a wide-mouthed jar; cover. Cool, and chill at least 1 day or up to 1 month. Makes 1 cup.

Per ¼ cup: 49 cal. (0 percent from fat); 0.4 g protein; 0 g fat; 12 g carbo.; 800 mg sodium; 0 mg chol.

Gingered Chicken with Leek Flowers

When using the Chinese leek flowers, pick young tender stalks with tightly closed buds. As the flowers open and plant matures, the stalks become woody and tough.

To determine where the tender part begins, gently bend stalk, working up from the tough end; the stalk will snap where tender, much like asparagus.

- 1 tablespoon butter or margarine
- 2 skinned and boned chicken breast halves (about 6 oz. each)
- ⅓ cup dry sherry
- ⅓ cup regular-strength chicken broth
- 1 teaspoon finely shredded fresh ginger
- 4 to 6 ounces tightly closed Chinese leek flowers with stalks, or 6 bunching (or green) onions
- 1 teaspoon cornstarch mixed with 1 tablespoon water

In a 10- to 12-inch frying pan, melt butter over medium-high heat. Add chicken; cook, turning to brown on all sides, 2 to 3 minutes total. Add sherry, broth, and ginger. Reduce heat to low, cover tightly, and simmer 3 minutes.

Meanwhile, snap off tough ends from leek flower stalks (see preceding; or trim ends and tops of bunching or green onions); rinse. Add leek flower stalks (or onions) to chicken; simmer, covered, until breast halves are no longer pink in thickest part (cut to test) and leeks are tender when pierced, 4 to 6 minutes. With a slotted spoon, transfer chicken and leek flowers to a warm platter; keep warm.

Measure pan juices. If needed, add water to make ½ cup; stir in cornstarch mixture. Return mixture to pan and stir over high heat until boiling. Pour sauce over chicken and leeks. Makes 2 servings.

Per serving: 346 cal. (22 percent from fat); 41 g protein; 8.3 g fat (4.2 g sat.); 15 g carbo.; 193 mg sodium; 114 mg chol.

By Linda Lau Anusasananan

PURE PINK *blends into white of 'Dreamland', left. White and pink fairy primroses and blue pansies provide accent. All tulip photos were taken in the Fallbrook, California, garden of Charles Cozzens.*

ABOUT TO UNFURL, *'Apricot Beauty' has mostly pink flowers that show richer tones in veins and at edges.*

And what about tulips in Southern California?

Chill bulbs in the fridge for best blooms

NOTHING IS MORE demoralizing than investing the money, time, and energy to plant a bed of tulips only to get so-so flowers. But once you know a few secrets, you can succeed with tulips. If you garden in the mild-winter West—coastal California, low elevations of southern Arizona, Houston, and South Texas—follow these steps:

Plant tulips that are proven in warm climates. Use the ones listed at right.

Refrigerate bulbs at least six weeks before planting. Place bulbs in paper bags (not sealed plastic) and chill them in the refrigerator, away from ripening fruits (especially apples), until planting day.

Plant between Christmas and mid-January. A heat wave between Thanksgiving and Christmas is a given in Southern Calfifornia. And if leaves or buds dry out early on, blooms will be diminished or even nonexistent.

Treat tulips (except some species) as annuals. After they bloom, pull the bulbs and discard them.

BEST-BET TULIPS FOR THE MILD WEST

Only by trying different tulips in your own garden will you learn which ones perform best. Start with those recommended here.

Classic tulips

Orange: 'Avignon', 'Orange Grove'
Pink: 'Apricot Beauty', 'Carmel', 'Hermosa', 'Menton', 'Pink Impression', 'Rosy Wings'
Purple: 'Blue Jay', 'Purple Star'
Red: 'Apeldoorn', 'California Giant', 'Oxford', 'Red Bluff', 'Redwood'
Red-white: 'Fiesta', 'Lucky Strike', 'Saratoga'
Red-yellow: 'Apeldoorn's Elite', 'Gudoshnik', 'Mojave', 'Newport', 'Silverstream' (variegated leaves), 'Sunrise'
White: 'High Sierra', 'Maureen', 'Sigrid Undset'
White-pink, lavender: 'Cocktail', 'Dreamland', 'Marina', 'New Design', 'Shirley'
Yellow: 'Asta Nielsen', 'Forty Niner', 'Golden Apeldoorn', 'Golden Giant', 'Golden Oxford', 'Lemon Grove', 'Mrs. J. T. Scheepers'

Tallest tulips

Like most of those listed at left, these are also Single Late tulips, but their height is enormous. At Descanso Gardens in Southern California, 8-inch-tall flowers sit atop 24-inch stems. Two named kinds are 'Blushing Beauty' (pink with white edges), and 'Hocus Pocus' (yellow tipped with pink).

Lily-flowered tulips

Ones particularly recommended for Southern California include 'Ballade' (reddish magenta with white edges), 'Marilyn' (white striped with red), and 'Queen of Sheba' (dark red edged with gold). Houston gardeners endorse 'Queen of Sheba', as well as 'Mariette' (pink) and 'West Point' (yellow).

Fancy and novelty tulips

'Angelique' (Double Late, pale pink with lighter margins); 'Burgundy Lace' (Fringed, red); 'Estella Rijnveld' (Parrot, red and white); 'Georgette' (Multiflowered, yellow edged in red); and 'Toronto' (Multiflowered, pink).

KINDS OF TULIPS

All tulips are classified into three main groups and many subgroups. The main groups relate to flowering time: early, midseason, and late. In the mild-winter West, *early* means the end of March, *midseason* is April, and *late* is late April into May. Two to three weeks separate the peak bloom seasons of each group.

Here are brief descriptions of the most important kinds of tulips for warm climates.

Early. Single or Double Early are short-stemmed in warm climates—about 14 inches (single) and 10 inches (double). Double Early tulips have double or many-petaled flowers. Few of these early bloomers do well in warm climates, but two important—and taller—exceptions are 'Angélique' and 'Apricot Beauty'.

Midseason. These include Darwin Hybrids and Triumph. Both are tall and large-flowered. Again, few are good warm-climate performers, but for some surprises, consider the Darwin Hybrids 'Apeldoorn' and 'Gudoshnik', and the Triumph 'Blue Jay'.

In South Texas, the short and stocky Darwin Hybrids are preferred for their superior tolerance to wind and rain. Taller late-season tulips grow well but too often fail to survive spring weather.

Late. This group of tulips is usually tallest and most reliable in warm climates. These tulips include primarily the Single Late (now including Darwin and Cottage) and Lily-flowered types as well as specialties such as Fringed and Parrot.

Lily-flowered tulips are noted for their pointed and reflexed petals. Many perform well in warm areas.

The best species tulips for warm climates are *Tulipa clusiana* and *T. saxatilis.* Neither requires chilling.

Fancy and novelty tulips include Fringed (tiny featherings on petal margins), Viridiflora (the green of the stem extends up center of petals), Rembrandt (Darwin tulips with unusual color combinations), Parrot (flower petals have deeply fringed margins), Double Late (many petals, shorter plants), and Multiflowered (more than one flower per stem).

MORNING LIGHT *captures rosy pink and soft yellows of 'New Design', a variety also noted for its white-variegated leaves. Blue flowers are nemesia and pansy.*

RUSS A. WIDSTRAND

BUYING AND PLANTING

Your odds for success increase if you buy tulips from a well-stocked garden center. It's more likely that most of the bulbs displayed have been preselected for your area and will be accurately named by variety. Choose bulbs that are 12 to 14 centimeters in circumference, or 1½ inches in diameter. Expect to pay 40 to 60 cents per bulb, depending upon variety.

Buy tulips from September through December, or place catalog orders as early as July for fall delivery.

Tulips grow best in rich, well-drained soil. Before planting, mix in a low-nitrogen granular fertilizer. Use ½ to 1 pound of 10-10-10 per 100 square feet.

Set bulbs in the ground at equal depths under 4 to 6 inches of soil. (If planting in pots, set bulbs so tips project slightly above the soil surface.) Water once after planting, sparingly until leaves emerge, then generously. If aphids appear, spray with insecticidal soap. ■

By Michael MacCaskey

Turn your garden trimmings into soil conditioner

Backyard recycling is simple with the right composter

NORMAN A. PLATE

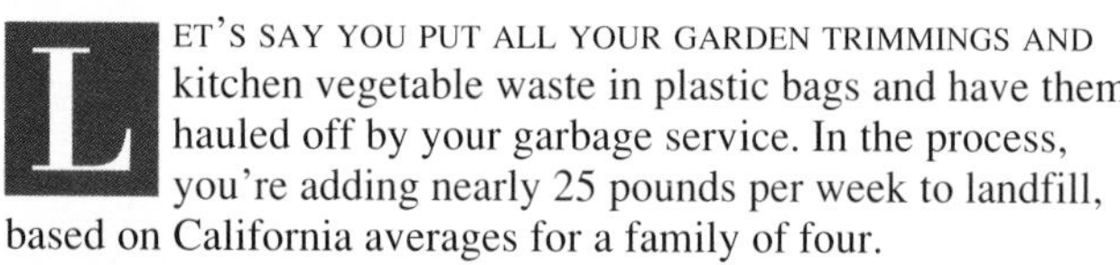

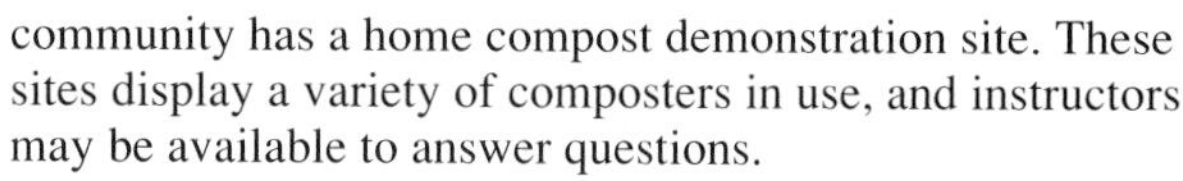

LET'S SAY YOU PUT ALL YOUR GARDEN TRIMMINGS AND kitchen vegetable waste in plastic bags and have them hauled off by your garbage service. In the process, you're adding nearly 25 pounds per week to landfill, based on California averages for a family of four.

Then you go out and buy plastic bags of soil conditioner to haul back to your garden. Now you and your garbage have just made what amounts to a costly round trip.

That's why backyard composting makes so much sense. And the payoff for your garden is a ready supply of soil conditioner that will improve soil texture, enhance nutrients, and increase water retention.

SHOPPING FOR COMPOSTERS

Essentially, you can make compost in a fancy bin or simply dump your garden waste in a pile. The manufactured models illustrated here get you started with a tidy container and a choice of composting methods. In addition to price, you'll want to consider convenience: the quicker you want results, the more maintenance (balancing different raw materials, turning, and moistening) you need to do.

Although composters are designed for utility, not aesthetics, these models can be tucked out of sight. If you think of them as just another type of recycling bin, they easily earn the space they occupy.

All types of composters are available by mail order, and most through garden supply and seed catalogs. Many are advertised in garden magazines. Increasingly, nurseries, garden centers, and even discount warehouses sell composters. The American Horticultural Society offers several types by mail; for a free brochure on its composters, as well as a source list for additional composters and composting supplies, call (800) 777-7931.

The California Integrated Waste Management Board's recycling hotline offers a free home-composting bin list that describes types of composters and gives their prices and manufacturers or distributors; call (800) 553-2962.

If you want to check out composters before buying, call your city or county recycling program to find out whether your community has a home compost demonstration site. These sites display a variety of composters in use, and instructors may be available to answer questions.

ESSENTIALS OF GOOD COMPOSTING

Composting enhances the natural process of decomposition in which microorganisms in the soil break down organic debris. By providing the optimum conditions for the organisms to thrive—a balance of raw materials, air, and water—you can help speed decomposition.

A composter's design influences the ease of composting and tidiness of the process, but it doesn't compensate for technique. Here are the fundamentals for getting the fastest results in any composter in which you turn the contents:

• Combine equal parts by volume of dried, brown, carbon-rich material, such as old leaves or straw, with fresh, green material high in nitrogen, such as fresh-cut grass and kitchen waste (excluding animal products).

• Ideally, a pile should have a volume of 27 cubic feet (1 cubic yard).

• Chop or shred organic materials into pieces ¾ inch or smaller.

• Keep the pile as moist as a wrung-out sponge. Wet the pile as you build it, and then again as you turn it.

• Turn the pile regularly—about once a week. The heat in a well-built pile will peak between 120° and 160°. When the temperature begins to decrease, turn the pile.

HOW THE MODELS STACK UP

At right, we compare the four basic types of composters. The first two types are the fastest but most work-intensive; the other two are slower but more carefree. For help evaluating the pros and cons of each type, we consulted Sherl Hopkins of the University of California Cooperative Extension Service. As demonstration projects coordinator, he manages the home composting program for Los Angeles County and teaches backyard composting.

By Lynn Ocone

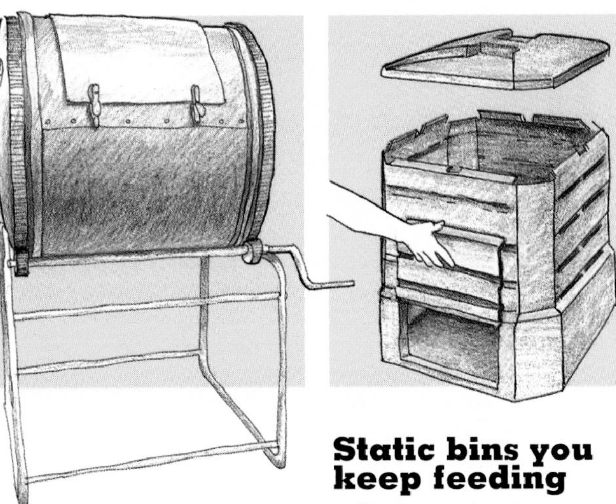

LUCY I. SARGEANT

Bins for hot, tossed compost

These movable containers—usually designed as bottomless boxes or cylinders—easily lift off so you can turn the contents with a pitchfork. Holes or slats allow air circulation. It's best to fill the bins completely with balanced materials and let decomposition finish without adding materials during the process. If turned regularly, the contents heat to 120º or more. You may have finished compost in as little as 14 days, but it usually takes four to six weeks.

Pros: Materials compost quickly, with no odors. The heat destroys most plant diseases and weed seeds.

A simple cylinder costs only about $30. The unit above, about $100, has three bottomless snap-together tiers that ease turning; add-on tiers are available.

Cons: This method is labor-intensive. Waste materials need to be stockpiled until there are enough to fill the container.

Shopping tips: In order for the pile to hold its heat, choose a unit with at least a 12-cubic-foot capacity. Aeration holes should be small to keep rodents out and moisture in. A lid also helps retain moisture and deter rodents. If possible, test the unit for ease in assembling and disassembling for removing compost. Hopkins gives the stackable composter top rating; it's commonly sold as Bio-Stack.

Tumblers that do the turning

With tumblers, you turn the container to toss the compost; otherwise, the principles are the same as for piles you turn with a pitchfork. The tumbler above is one of several models with a crank handle. You turn others by pushing them on an axle or on the ground.

Pros: Like bins whose contents you turn, these are among the fastest composters. Most are fully enclosed with small aeration vents, which keep moisture in and animals out. They are attractive and neat. It's convenient to empty a unit that sits high above the ground, since you can push a wheelbarrow beneath it.

Cons: Units with cranks are expensive; the one above costs about $400. Those with moving parts may be difficult to assemble. It's hard to load tumblers that sit high above ground (although easier to empty them). Large tumblers are heavy when full, and some are hard to turn.

Shopping tips: Choose units with at least a 12-cubic-foot capacity. If possible, test large units for ease of turning; a full load will make turning harder. Aeration holes should be small so compost doesn't fall out. For its overall design and capacity, Hopkins prefers the 18-bushel (22-cubic-foot) tumbler made by Kemp Company, even though its size makes a full load that much harder to turn.

Static bins you keep feeding

In these units, the contents sit without being turned, although occasional aerating with a pitchfork is required. You need to properly balance materials, but volume is not critical: as the waste decomposes, you add more to the top. Finished compost starts to appear at the bottom of the pile in about three months, and is supplied continuously (in small amounts) as long as you keep adding to the pile. Containers have a door at the bottom for removing compost.

Pros: The containers and the process are neat. Most units hold moisture and deter critters well. No turning is required, and you can add organic waste as it accumulates.

Cons: The process is slow, and it delivers small amounts of compost. Plant diseases and weed seeds may survive since the pile does not become very hot.

Shopping tips: Choose a unit low enough and with a top opening large enough so you can easily load it. The bottom door should open easily and be large enough to shovel out finished compost. Hopkins prefers conical units (about $100) for best air circulation and moisture retention.

Anaerobic composters

Anaerobic bacteria, which thrive without exposure to air, do the composting in these fully enclosed systems—no turning or aerating is necessary. In the model shown above, the open bottom is buried underground. Some models have a buried waste chamber.

With either type, you simply fill the container with organic material and close the lid. You can add more material at any time. (Some manufacturers suggest adding small amounts of lime, bonemeal, and soil.) To remove compost, you must shovel out the unit. Finished compost takes six months or more, including drying time.

Pros: Little care or attention is required.

Cons: In Hopkins's experiments, the process created insect and odor problems. The decomposed waste was slimy and hard to retrieve. It required drying before use. Although the unit may be useful for waste disposal, Hopkins does not recommend it for home gardeners desiring high-quality compost. ■

Grow peonies in mild climates?

It's possible ... if you choose the right varieties

MARDE ROSS KNOWS about growing peonies in mild climates. In spite of myths that these tuberous-rooted perennials demand lots of winter chill to produce lush foliage and large blossoms, she has grown them successfully for 15 years in Palo Alto, California, where winter temperatures seldom drop below 30°. In spring, pots of these beauties grace her patio (two are pictured below). The key to her success? Choosing the right varieties.

When Ross's plants are in full bloom, it's easy to understand why avid mild-climate gardeners buck the odds to grow peonies. The 5- or 6-inch, often fragrant, single or double flowers are thoroughly enchanting when they appear in spring. Also, they come in a range of colors—from white, cream, and salmon to pink and red—that combine well with many plants. And the deeply cut, glossy green leaves look handsome for months, especially when planted amid other perennials and shrubs.

VARIETIES FOR MILD CLIMATES

The most successful varieties for mild climates, according to Ross, are early blooming double-flowered peonies and any single-flowered and Japanese types (the early, mid-, and late season ones all do fine). Double varieties that bloom mid- to late season are poor candidates for mild climates: they may produce flower buds, but warm weather usually keeps them from opening properly.

And don't expect any peonies to reach their normal, cold-climate heights of up to 3 feet. In Ross's garden, the foliage grows to about 2 feet tall, with the flowers rising above the leaves.

Some of her successes include 'Charlie's White', 'Coral Charm', 'Doreen', 'Fairy's Petticoat', 'Krinkled White', 'Mons. Jules Elie', 'Mrs. F. D. Roosevelt', 'Richard Carvel', and 'Toro-No-Maki'.

WHILE IN BLOOM *container-grown 'Mrs. F. D. Roosevelt', below, makes an attractive patio plant in Marde Ross's garden. Afterward, the container is moved out of sight. At right, 'Krinkled White' has the typical form of single peonies.*

NORMAN A. PLATE

PLANT IN AMENDED SOIL

Select a site in full sun (late afternoon shade is okay), with good air circulation and good drainage; in windy areas, choose a sheltered location. Prepare the soil well by mixing in organic matter to a depth of 18 inches (never use manure). Refill the hole almost to the top and tamp down well.

Peonies are sold bare-root in fall. Plant the root no more than 1½ inches deep (½ inch deep in Southern California); do not follow the usual 2-inch recommendation for cold-winter areas. Space roots 3 to 4 feet apart. Keep soil moist; don't fertilize the first year. Apply moderate amounts of fertilizer thereafter.

Flowers appear in April. The first year you'll probably get one or two blooms. By the third year, you should get a good show. You'll probably find ants crawling on the buds of peonies, but don't try to control them; longtime peony growers say they help the flower buds open. Cut off flowers after they fade. Plants die back in fall.

WHERE TO BUY PEONIES

The price of roots starts at $14 to $16 and can go as high as $55 for rare varieties.

A & D Peony And Perennial Farm, 6808 180th S. E., Snohomish, WA 98290; (206) 668-9690. Catalog $1.50 (deducted from first order).

Caprice Farm Nursery, 15425 S. W. Pleasant Hill Rd., Sherwood, OR 97140; (503) 625-7241. Catalog $2.

Marde Ross & Campony, Box 1517, Palo Alto, CA 94302; (415) 328-5109. Free catalog.

Klehm Nursery, Route 4, Box 197 Penny Rd., South Barrington, IL 60010; (800) 553-3715. Catalog $4. ■

By Lauren Bonar Swezey

Seeking the pink in daffodils

There isn't a true pink yet, but hybridizers are getting closer

THUMBING THROUGH bulb catalogs, you can easily be seduced by the gorgeous flowers that stare back at you from the colorful photographs. Unusual varieties like "pink" daffodils are particularly hard to resist. But gardeners should be aware that what you see is not always what you get.

The first pink daffodil, 'Mrs. R. O. Backhouse', was introduced more than 40 years ago. Like the first so-called black tulips or yellow petunias, it doesn't really live up to its billing; its trumpet is actually more apricot and yellow than pink. Nevertheless, increased demand has inspired bulb hybridizers to introduce many new pink varieties over the past five years, and some of them are getting closer to their goal. Still, don't expect to find a true pink yet.

PUTTING THE PINKS TO THE TEST

Enticed by the catalog pictures, we planted 17 varieties of daffodils last fall in *Sunset*'s experimental garden in Menlo Park, California. We included any that had the word *pink* in its name or was described or shown in at least one catalog as pink (one catalog might describe a daffodil as pink while another one says it's apricot). The results, shown here, speak for themselves.

Although all the plants produced very attractive flowers, we didn't find any truly pink ones. The closest was 'Pink Wonder' with its soft coral trumpet. Others ranged from yellowish ('Palmares') to coral or orange and yellow ('Petit Four', 'Pink Charm', 'Romance') to apricot ('Rose Caprice'). In our test, apricot daffodils often faded to coral, coral faded to pale yellow.

Some growers suggest that pink daffodils may grow pinker in cool, moist springs like those in Holland. Soil acidity may also affect color. But our survey of professional growers and gardeners around the West suggests that you can expect the results you see here in other Western climates.

To get the most intense color with minimal fading, plant daffodils in filtered or partial shade, especially in hot inland climates.

WHERE TO GET PINK DAFFODILS

Nurseries carry some pink daffodils, but mail-order suppliers such as those listed here generally carry a wider selection. Catalogs are free.

Dutch Gardens, Box 200, Adelphia, NJ 07710; (908) 780-2713. Sells 'Palmares', 'Petit Four', 'Pink Pride', 'Romance', and 'Salome'.

K. Van Bourgondien & Sons, Inc., 245 Farmingdale Rd., Box 1000, Babylon, NY 11702; (800) 552-9996. Sells 'Accent', 'Filly', 'Foundling', 'Mrs. R. O. Backhouse', 'Palmares', 'Passionale', 'Petit Four', 'Pink Charm', 'Romance', 'Rose Caprice', 'Roseworthy', 'Salome', and 'Solo' (total order must be at least $50).

Netherland Bulb Co., Inc., 13 McFadden Rd., Easton, PA 18042; (800) 788-8547. Sells 'Pink Wonder'.

Park Seed Co., Cokesbury Rd., Greenwood, SC 29647; (800) 845-3369. Sells 'Accent', 'Palmares', 'Replete', and 'Rosy Cloud'. ■

By Lauren Bonar Swezey

BUTTERFLY-TYPE *daffodil 'Palmares' appeared much pinker in catalog than in Sunset's test garden.*

LINEUP *of so-called pink daffodils shows range of colors, from coral to orange-red.*

NORMAN A. PLATE

MICHAEL THOMPSON

A TANGLE OF SHRUBS, *including variegated redtwig dogwood in the foreground, masks the front of the house.*

A leafy privacy screen

In October this Portland border is at its fiery best

A 60-FOOT-LONG THICKET OF shrubs and grasses replaced a lawn to create seasonal interest in this garden and to screen the house from the street. "It took courage to tear up lawn in this neighborhood, put in little plants, and then look at them all winter," says John Nausieda, the garden's designer. "But it paid off."

For quick cover and continuity in plant form and foliage texture, he spotted big grasses, mostly various forms of *Miscanthus sinensis,* throughout the border.

Then Nausieda set out plants for seasonal interest: the variegated form of redtwig dogwood (*Cornus stolonifera* 'Elegantissima'), which in summer is covered with green leaves edged with silver, and in winter drops them to reveal bright red winter twigs; witch hazel (*Hamamelis intermedia*), which produces fragrant yellow flowers in February, a thick screen of leaves in summer, and brilliant color in autumn; and Alaska blue willow (*Salix purpurea*), which sprouts up in great feathery wands. Assorted conifers, shrubs, and Japanese maples add more color and texture.

Finally, Nausieda added accents to the garden: heavenly bamboo (*Nandina domestica*), for lacy foliage and red new growth; New Zealand flax (*Phormium tenax*), for bold spots of blood red and for soaring form that will stand up to most Portland winters; and barberry (*Berberis thunbergii* 'Rose Glow'), for a similarly powerful color punch in a different shape. Beautyberry (*Callicarpa bodinieri giraldii*) bejewels the border with clusters of violet fruits in winter, and *Viburnum bodnantense* 'Pink Dawn' adds clusters of fragrant flowers from November through February.

All plants are pruned and groomed as needed. In late February and early March, the rustling dry blades and blossoms of miscanthus (left standing in the fall for winter interest) are cut down to ground level. In November, after all leaves have dropped, the garden is given a complete cleanup.

As the plants grow, they'll be thinned and pruned to become a managed tangle of foliage and branches that will shelter an active community of urban wildlife. ■

By Steven R. Lorton

NEW ZEALAND FLAX *and Japanese blood grass flaunt fall hues.*

FLAMING FOLIAGE *of Cotinus obovata burns bright in border.*

CHAD SLATTERY

PLANTS, *aided by artificial light, transform bleak corridor into lush garden.*

Lush look in a dark, dark entry

The right plants and artificial lighting make the difference

SANDWICHED BETWEEN TWO buildings, the once-dim entranceway of this Santa Monica, California, condominium called out for greenery. Natural light was not sufficient for plants to flourish, so designer Stephanie Wilson-Blanc added artificial light and chose plants that require little light.

Overhead metal-halide HID (high-intensity discharge) lights supplement natural light to provide adequate intensity and spectrum of light for photosynthesis, and even flowering in some plants. Lights stay on 12 hours a day.

Decorative lamps with 10-watt bulbs are tucked among the plants. Alone, these low-intensity incandescent bulbs will not support plant growth, but collectively the light and heat may give a boost.

Most plants are in three large, permanent containers. Small-leafed ivy, hoya, wandering Jew, and miniature bamboo provide a backdrop for bright accents. Showy foliage plants such as breynia, caladium, and leopard plant add year-round color.

Small pots of flowering plants, including orchids, are rotated in to give additional seasonal color.

Foliage plants usually require less light than flowering plants. Even with supplemental light, relatively few permanent plants flower here. Successes include rhizomatous begonias, single-flowered impatiens, and, surprisingly, *Camellia sasanqua* 'Tanya'. Pansies from sixpacks provide color for several weeks but won't rebloom.

The plants require slightly moist soil, and infrequent feeding with diluted house plant fertilizer. Self-watering pots, for individual plants, reduce the frequency of watering. ■

By Lynn Ocone

Vine trellis just bolts to the fence

Built of scrap wood, painted to match lavender flowers

WOODEN FENCES AGE to a nondescript silver gray. To enliven a long backyard fence, landscape architect Scott Smith, of Mill Valley, California, designed a series of multilayered trellises and painted them to match flowers in the bordering beds.

The trellises were built of scrap wood that was ripped to size. Each of the units measures 9 feet long by 5 feet tall and has four layers: horizontal 2-by-4s against the fence at top and bottom; vertical ½-by-1½s; and pairs of horizontal 1-by-1½s that sandwich the vertical pieces. A curved 1-by-8 top and a 1-by-4 bottom mask the 2-by-4 spacers.

Before adding the top 1-by-8s, Smith painted the trellises and mounted them to the fence with carriage bolts through the top 2-by-4s. The 1-by-8s mask the bolt ends.

Eventually, climbing hydrangeas (*H. anomala*) will cover the trellises. ■

By Peter O. Whiteley

PETER O. WHITELEY

TRELLIS FOR VINE *is painted to match flowers in the bed.*

NOVEMBER

Garden guide....................261
November checklists...........268
Robust, rugged rosemary.....272
Choosing the right gloves 275
From seed to bread.............276
Plants for winter sparkle 281
Landscaping under oaks......283
Natural look, artificial rock..284

Sunset's

GARDEN GUIDE

MICHAEL LANDIS

Maples aflame in Napa

GLOWING FALL FOLIAGE SETS THE TONE FOR NOVEMBER AS TREES SUCH AS maple (above), ginkgo, and liquidambar turn shades of gold and orange. It's time to rake leaves and clean up the garden, while children frolic beneath colorful canopies. With luck, this month may bring the first winter rains and the hope of a wet winter. If rains don't come, newly planted flowers, vegetables, and permanent plants will need regular irrigations. By the end of the month, put aside chores and celebrate the holidays.

Easy-care combo for coastal gardens

The pretty, spring-flowering shrub-perennial combination pictured at right can come from fall planting in California's coastal and coastal-influenced areas. The three colorful performers are New Zealand tea tree (*Leptospermum scoparium* 'Ruby Glow'), blue-flowered *Ceanothus* 'Concha', and statice (*Limonium perezii*).

At maturity, the tea tree stands upright, 6 to 10 feet high; its profuse double flowers are blood red. The ceanothus will eventually mound 5 to 7 feet high and spread 6 to 10 feet wide; the cobalt blue flowers bloom in tight, round clusters. Statice grows 12 to 18 inches high with 2- to 3-foot flower stalks; bloom continues from spring through summer.

All three are available at nurseries this month. The plants need little water or attention once established. Tea tree and statice need occasional supplemental water during the dry season; ceanothus requires none but will tolerate it if planted in well-drained soil.

RUSS A. WIDSTRAND

COLORFUL COMPANIONS *are (from top to bottom) 'Ruby Glow' New Zealand tea tree, Ceanothus 'Concha', and statice.*

NORMAN A. PLATE

TERRA-COTTA PLANT TAGS *make attractive markers for herbs and perennials.*

Give a gift of terra-cotta garden markers

Here's a gift that's sure to please gardening friends—handmade terra-cotta plant markers (shown at left). Each simple but elegant tag is impressed with a plant name, then washed with a verdigris patina; each comes with a 10-inch copper stake to hang on. Unlike plastic markers you write on, the engraved names on these markers will never fade or smear.

You can choose from 214 round plant labels for perennials and herbs (including 16 thymes and 12 mints). The small Oregon company that makes them also makes special heart-shaped or oval message markers such as "Best wishes" and "Le Jardin."

These tags are available from Vicki Antelope Bear, Box 926, Rogue River, OR 97537. Round and heart-shaped markers cost $2.50 each, oval markers $3.50; shipping is extra. Discounts are given for quantity orders. You can also buy an herb garden collection containing seven markers for $17.95. For a free brochure, send a self-addressed, stamped business-size envelope.

Powdery mildew-resistant roses

In coastal climates, powdery mildew is the commonest and most serious foliar disease of roses. Patches of powdery white fungus form on leaves and buds, distorting them and killing the leaves. Trying to combat or prevent powdery mildew by using chemicals can become a great inconvenience. A much easier and wiser plan is to select and plant varieties that naturally resist the disease.

Contra Costa County rose breeder and cooperative extension Master Gardener John Ohlson recommends the following varieties:

'Cherish' (orange-pink floribunda), 'Double Delight' (red blend hybrid tea), 'Gold Medal' (medium yellow grandiflora), 'Honor' (white hybrid tea), 'Iceberg' (white floribunda), 'Olympiad' (red hybrid tea), 'Pink Parfait' (pink blend grandiflora), 'Pristine' (white hybrid tea), 'Queen Elizabeth' (medium pink grandiflora), 'Shreveport' (orange grandiflora), 'Silver Jubilee' (pink blend hybrid tea), 'Spartan' (orange-red floribunda), and 'Sunsprite' (deep yellow floribunda).

Miniature amaryllis in bloom for the holidays

Those tall, large-flowered amaryllis (*Hippeastrum*) you see around the holidays are dramatic plants, but they can sometimes look gawky and out of scale with their surroundings. For a fuller, more compact plant, try miniature amaryllis (*H. gracilis*), shown on the facing page.

It's only a bit shorter (15 to 20 inches tall instead of up to 25 inches for the standard amaryllis), but each bulb produces two or three flower stems, giving the plant a fuller appearance. The flowers are smaller, but there are more of them. Each stem is topped with about four 4- to 5-inch-wide slightly ruffled blooms.

The miniatures come in a variety of colors, including pink, white, yellow, and red. 'Scarlet Baby' makes an especially festive display for the holidays.

Amaryllis are easy to force into bloom. Plant three bulbs in an 8-inch-wide pot. Fill pot with a container mix so that each bulb's upper half protrudes. Initially, keep the pots in any area that's protected from frost. Water after planting and again when the soil is almost dry. After shoots appear, in about six weeks, place pots in bright light; water when the top inch of the soil is dry to the touch.

Miniature amaryllis are available from Amaryllis, Inc., Box 318, Baton Rouge, LA 70821; (504) 924-5560 (catalog $1). Most miniatures cost $9 plus shipping.

Save seeds in powdered milk

Leftover seeds from this past planting season can be saved for next year if you provide the proper storage conditions. Low humidity and low temperature are keys.

To keep seeds dry, some gardeners store them with little pouches of silica gel. But James Harrington, professor emeritus of vegetable crops at UC Davis, makes moisture-sucking pouches from a product that's inexpensive and much more widely available—powdered milk.

Before storing seeds, make sure they're dry. If they have been lying around in moist areas, spread them in a single layer on paper for a week or so first.

Buy fresh powdered milk in sealed packages (cans or cartons that have been open for a while may have absorbed moisture already). To make the pouch, place 2 tablespoons of milk on top of a stack of four facial tissues. Roll up the tissues and fold over the ends so the milk won't spill out; tape the ends closed.

Place the milk pouch and seeds in a glass canning jar or other container with a tight seal. Tighten the lid and place the jar in the refrigerator—never the freezer (this will kill the seeds).

Seeds can be stored like this for several years, but the powdered milk should be replaced annually. Since stored seeds are drier than freshly packaged seeds, they may take longer to germinate because they have to absorb more water.

The tastiest garlics

If you love flavorful garlic, here's one to try growing. 'Special Idaho', named after the area where it was recently introduced, is a hard-necked rocambole type that produces extra-large cloves.

Each clove is two to three times larger than a standard clove and about two-thirds the size of elephant garlic. Unlike mild-flavored elephant garlic, the cloves are intense and flavorful. Cooks will like it, too, because the skins are easy to peel.

Like all rocamboles, this garlic sends up a flower stalk in spring that curls as it grows but straightens out before harvesttime. Flower heads form little bulblets that can be replanted, but the heads that grow from these bulblets will be smaller.

'Special Idaho' is available from Seeds Blüm, Idaho City Stage, Boise, ID 83706. Bulblets cost $2.95 per packet plus $1.50 postage.

Hummingbirds still need a nectar source

In fall, some backyard birders take down hummingbird feeders and store them for winter, mistakenly believing that an artificial food source prevents the natural southward migration of these tiny birds. But according to Rick Held of the Wild Bird Center in San Carlos, California, that isn't true.

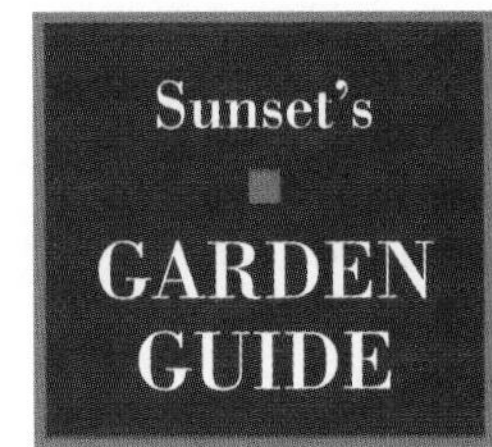

First of all, not all hummingbirds migrate in winter. Anna's, for example, are more likely to hang around their coastal range. As for those that normally migrate in search of winter nectar sources, there's no evidence that an artificial food supply can keep them from making their journey. In fact, having access to a large nectar supply allows them to stock up before a long migration.

So keep cleaning and filling those hummingbird feeders regularly.

PETER CHRISTIANSEN

MINIATURE AMARYLLIS *'Scarlet Baby' produces clusters of 4- to 5-inch-wide flowers on 15- to 20-inch-tall stalks.*

Dig your own pansies in Encinitas

November is the ideal pansy planting time in the low elevations of Southern California. And because pansies are in bloom in nurseries this month, it's easy to choose plants for the flower color you prefer.

At Weidners' Gardens in Encinitas (see photo below)—in a pansy field that displays about 20,000 plants representing more than 30 cultivated varieties—you can even dig your own. Among the new types are the Imperial strain Antique Shades, in warm pastels, and the Masterpiece series, with ruffled blooms.

Weidners' pansy field is open for digging from November 1 through December 22. The plants are started from seed at the nursery and later transplanted to the field. At their prime in the field, plants are about 12 inches in diameter. Since the roots have grown unchecked by containers, the large flowering plants transplant well.

Plants cost $1.10 each (or 13 for the price of 12); 50 or more plants cost 60 cents each. The nursery supplies boxes and a digging fork. It will even lend you scissors to cut free pansy bouquets.

This month, the nursery is open 9:30 to 4:30 every day except Thanksgiving. For information and directions, call (619) 436-2194.

STEPHEN SIMPSON

ROWS OF COLORFULLY BLOOMING PANSIES *fill planting beds at Weidners' Gardens this month. You can dig your own to plant at home for winter to spring bloom.*

Insects, good and bad, of the L.A. Basin

Los Angeles residents—and gardeners in particular—are fortunate to have available a complete and authoritative reference book: *Insects of the Los Angeles Basin,* by Charles L. Hogue (Natural History Museum of Los Angeles County, Los Angeles, 1993; $27.95 paperback, $42 hardbound).

The 448-page book includes descriptions of 430 insects and 70 spiders, ticks, and mites that are common to the region. Its chief value is to aid identification (many insects are beneficial, and less than 1 percent are harmful).

Readers familiar with the 1974 version of the book will appreciate the new one's 370 high-quality color photographs, many of them made by Hogue himself, and the 130 black-and-white photographs and line drawings made by the museum's illustrator, Tina Ross.

Insects of the Los Angeles Basin is available at all museum stores: Exposition Park, 900 Exposition Boulevard; Page Museum, 5801 Wilshire Boulevard; and Burbank Museum, 555 N. Third Street.

How to force bulbs to bloom in water

Hyacinths, crocus, and several varieties of *Narcissus tazetta* are ideal for growing indoors in water because the bulbs store all the food needed for growth. Garden centers and florists offer glass vases designed to hold single hyacinth and crocus bulbs. The narcissus, including paper whites, Chinese sacred lilies, and 'Soleil d'Or', grow well set in bowls filled with gravel and water, or in vases with just water.

For hyacinth and crocus, fill the vases with water so that it just barely touches the bases of the bulbs. Place the vases in a cool, dark place, and check the water level regularly.

When the first roots develop, keep the water level just below the bases of the bulbs. Store in darkness until roots are well developed and top growth shows.

When flower buds on crocus are a couple of inches tall move the vases to a bright location. Hyacinths should be moved to light when the buds are about 4 inches tall. Bulbs bloom in three and a half to four months.

Place narcissus in a shallow bowl filled with gravel; mound gravel around the sides of the bulbs. Fill the bowl with water so it barely touches the bulbs, and place it in a dark location.

Once the roots start to grow, keep the water below the bulbs. When top growth begins, move the container to light. The bulbs bloom in about six weeks.

Change water in containers regularly. Run a gentle stream

of water through the container to flush out the old water, or, with vases, hold the bulbs in place and spill out the old water. As an alternative, use activated charcoal in the water to prevent algae growth.

WILLIAM D. ADAMS

BRIGHT SCARLET *'Champion' radishes mature less than a month after sowing. Grow them in moist, rich soil, and interplant them among other vegetables to save space.*

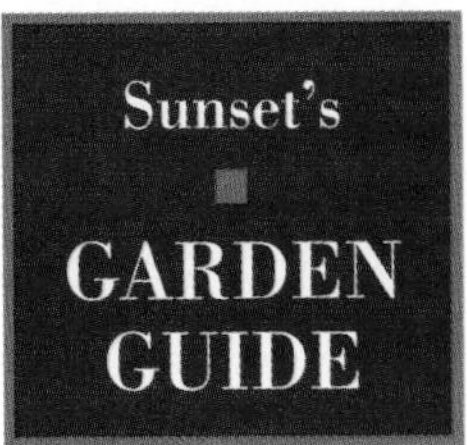

If only Alice's Restaurant sold plants

You can get anything you want for the garden if you know where to look. Three Northwest sources can help greatly. For native plants, consult *Hortus Northwest* (Vol. 4), by Dale Shank (Hortus Northwest, Box 955, Canby, OR 97013, 1993; $9). It lists sources for about 900 species of trees, shrubs, annuals, and perennials native to the Northwest.

Codes tell whether plant sources are retail, wholesale, or mail order, and whether they offer seeds or plants. To order *Hortus Northwest*, send $9 to the publisher (address above); the price includes shipping and handling.

For ornamentals in general, you can subscribe to *PlantSource Journal*, a magazine published six times a year. Designed for plant professionals, it's like a master catalog for about 80 wholesale nurseries, listing their changing nursery stocks both in print and in a database on computer disk (DOS presently available; Windows and Mac versions due by winter). It covers woody plants, perennials, and annuals. To subscribe, send $68 to *PlantSource Journal*, 606 110th Ave. N.E., Suite 301, Bellevue, WA 98004.

For everything else, pick up the fourth (1993) edition of *The Northwest Gardeners' Resource Directory*, by Stephanie Feeney (Whatcom In Bloom Garden Society, Bellingham, Wash., 1993; $10). This lists everything from lectures to public gardens, nurseries to books and tools. The book's regional focus is on northern Washington west of the Cascades, but it has much broader application. Order from Stephanie Feeney, 59 Strawberry Point, Bellingham, WA 98226; a $12 check, payable to Whatcom In Bloom Garden Society, will cover shipping and handling.

Putting weeds on hold

If your low-elevation mild-winter garden gets overrun by weeds every winter, and if you are not adverse to using chemicals, now—before weeds sprout and grow—is the time to take preventive measures. The most effective method is to apply a preemergence herbicide.

Preemergence herbicides work by inhibiting germination of seeds or growth of very young seedlings.

Treat only weed-free soil. If weeds are already growing, pull or hoe them before treatment.

To prevent grassy weeds from germinating, use the preemergence oryzalin (sold as Surflan). It's normally available as a liquid; apply it with a hose-end sprayer. One pint (about $22) treats 5,000 square feet.

Water thoroughly the day before application and immediately afterward. Also wash off any trees and shrubs that may have been inadvertently sprayed.

If your weeds include both grasses and broad-leafed plants such as mustard and sow thistle, use Snapshot 80DF. A combination of Gallery (isoxaben) and Surflan, it prevents growth of both types of seeds. Apply it in the same way as Surflan, following all label directions. Enough Snapshot 80DF to treat 5,000 square feet costs about $35.

Quick as a radish

Few cool-season vegetables are as quick, easy, and fun to grow as radishes. And if you grow them when weather is cool, they taste sweeter and less pungent.

Radishes now come in a variety of colors and shapes, including spherical 'Champion' (pictured at left), 'Easter Egg II' (red, white, purple, and rose; egg-shaped), 'Flamboyant' (red; 3 inches long, cylindrical), and 'Purple Plum' (bright purple skin, white flesh; oblong).

Sow seeds about ½ inch deep in rows 8 inches apart in well-amended soil. Seedlings appear in three to seven days; thin until plants are 1 to 2 inches apart.

Most varieties are ready to harvest in three weeks, though a few take slightly longer. Mix seeds of several varieties so that every radish you harvest is a surprise, or interplant with carrots and harvest before the carrots need the space.

The four varieties listed are available by mail from the following sources. *'Champion':* DeGiorgi Seed Company, 6011 N St., Omaha, NE 68117; (402) 731-3901 (catalog $2). *'Easter Egg II':* Park Seed Co., Cokesbury Rd., Greenwood, SC 29647; (800) 845-3369 (catalog free); and Shepherd's Garden Seeds, 6116 Highway 9, Felton, CA 95018; (408) 335-5311 (catalog $1). *'Flamboyant'* and *'Purple Plum':* Shepherd's Garden Seeds (address above).

Colorful kalanchoe for Thanksgiving

Gift plants, like the vibrant kalanchoe pictured at right, displayed at Roger's Gardens in Corona del Mar, show up in abundance in nurseries this month—in time for Thanksgiving and Christmas entertaining. If you're looking for a plant that gives indoor color for a very long time in autumn and winter, then give kalanchoe (*K. blossfeldiana*) a try.

Its small, bright flower clusters bloom indoors for up to three months. The trick for long bloom is to buy the plant in bud stage with just a bit of color showing. If you buy it in full bloom, the flowers last just a month or so.

Kalanchoe comes in an ever-expanding array of colors—among them a good selection of autumn yellows and oranges. Other popular colors are red and pink. Newer colors include purple 'Timor' and white 'Snow Cap' and 'Mount Robson'. The supply of whites is still limited, but it's increasing.

Give kalanchoe bright indirect light. Direct sun turns the leaves red and diminishes the size of new growth. Let the soil dry out between waterings; too much water turns the leaves yellow. From March through October, fertilize with a house plant food according to package directions. Kalanchoe has two natural bloom periods, one in March and the other in September. Cut spent blooms to prolong flowering.

Although kalanchoe is generally grown indoors, in *Sunset* climate zones 17 and 21 through 24 many of its varieties grow successfully outdoors, most commonly as color accents in containers.

RUSS A. WIDSTRAND

DECORATIVE BASKET *holds three small pots of kalanchoe; they're covered with blooms in autumn colors.*

Putting worms to work

Without much to do besides eat and reproduce, worms can quickly reduce kitchen waste to compost.

In Kathy Elshire's Lake Oswego, Oregon, garden, a pound of them eat about 3½ pounds of fruit and vegetable scraps per week, churning out two 5-gallon buckets of worm castings every four months or so. The fine castings make an excellent amendment for potting soil and seedbeds.

The worms do their work in a rough wooden box that's 2 feet by 4 feet and 16 inches tall. Pencil-size holes were drilled in the bottom for drainage and ventilation, and a cover keeps rain out. (Elshire avoided using pressure-treated wood, which kills the worms.)

The bin rests in a shady spot that's protected from the year's hottest and coldest temperatures.

You can start a worm bin by building a box like the one described above. When the box is ready, put a 12-inch-deep layer of bedding in the bottom; make it from shredded newspaper and straw. It should have about the same dampness as a squeezed-out sponge.

Begin with worms you get out of your own compost pile, from a feed store, or by mail.

Why won't my rhodohypoxis rebloom?

During the past few years, *Rhodohypoxis baurii* has managed to float out of horticultural obscurity and into the mainstream. Most gardeners are attracted by the long season of spring and summer bloom—but it's bloom that many never see again. There's a trick to getting this temperamental plant to rebloom: This month, let your plants dry off completely. Don't water again until May 1.

This process ultimately ensures that sometime in spring (after you start watering and feeding again), plants will be covered by inch-wide white, pink, or rose-colored flowers. If you've never grown rhodohypoxis, you can buy corms this month, plant in a shallow container, and water once to settle bulbs into the soil. Then leave them in a dark, cool, frost-free place until spring, and you'll have what is sure to become one of your favorite pot plants.

Making more forsythias

Forsythias naturally layer themselves—that is, their lowest horizontal branches often take root and become viable plants on their own.

If you (or a generous gardening friend) have a forsythia and you want more, look under the plant after leaves have fallen and see whether any branches have layered. If they have, cut the branches between the main trunk and the rooting places. Dig up the new plants and move them right away to wherever you want new forsythias, and they may flower in late winter, if they're mature.

If you come up empty-handed in your search for layered plants, scrape a dime-size piece of bark off the bottom of a low branch 18 inches from the trunk, and hold the branch to the ground with a tent stake. By this time next year, it will be rooted.

Blessing or curse? Jujube

Jujube (*Ziziphus jujuba*) is "one of the best small trees for Phoenix," says Jim Baker of Baker Nursery. It's attractive and obliging, and yields tasty fruits. But you've got to plant it in the right spot, or you may curse the day you bought it.

Near a path, entry, or walkway, its thorny branches can scratch passersby, and its fruit can drop and mess the paving. Plant it where the fruit drop isn't a problem—such as in a wide bed near a back fence or wall; give it full sun and any type of soil except wet clay. Plant right away (or bare-root in January).

Unpruned, the tree reaches 20 to 30 feet high, but with pruning it can be kept smaller. Branches are spiny and gnarled. Leaves are a shiny kelly green, and 1 to 2 inches long; they look fresh even on the hottest days. Flowers, in spring, are yellowish and barely noticeable. In Phoenix, fruits begin ripening in July and last through August.

Jujube trees tolerate heat and drought as well as salty, alkaline soil. Best growth occurs in moist, well-drained soil (the trees thrive in lawns). Prune in winter to shape.

For best fruit, plant grafted trees; seedling trees produce ½-inch-diameter, tasteless fruits. Two named varieties are available: 'Lang' has fruits 1½ to 2 inches long, and 'Li' has spherical 2-inch fruits. Both have superior flavor and an occasional seed; once dried, they keep indefinitely. Trees in 5-gallon containers cost about $20.

A "looks-like-the-desert" garden

Natural-looking mounds covered with drought-tolerant plants mimic the wild desert in Ann and Bill Marchiony's garden in Phoenix. But before the garden (pictured at right) was planted, the lot was as flat as a billiard table. To add contour to the lot, the Marchionys brought in topsoil and shaped it into mounds.

Then, with the help of Peter Curé of Arterra Design, the Marchionys chose 17 trees and 150 shrubs, vines, and ground covers for the 70- by 100-foot lot. Each is native to the desert. Trees, mostly 15-gallon size to start, include Chilean mesquite, Sonoran palo verde, sweet acacia, and Texas ebony. Gallon-size shrubs include penstemon, salvia, and verbena.

Plants were delivered in stages over several days. "It took me about a week to get them all in," Bill Marchiony says. After planting and completing the installation of a drip-irrigation system, he applied a 3-inch layer of ¾-inch decomposed granite.

The fruit that acts like a grape, tastes like a kiwi

Grown over an arbor or trellis like grapes, hardy kiwis also produce sweet, green to reddish purple fruits you can eat off the vine without peeling. These are small fruits—not the big fuzzy kinds you buy at the store. The vines they grow on make perfect covers for a patio or arbor.

Following are some good choices. We've classed them as edible or ornamental, based on each plant's strongest garden value. Female plants of both groups produce edible fruits, though silver vine fruit is of poor quality.

Edible. *Actinidia arguta* 'Issai' is self-fruitful, grows to about 15 feet, and starts producing after only two years (it takes four years for most other *A. arguta* varieties). *A. a.* 'Ananasnaja' has pineapple overtones to its fruity flavor, and needs a pollinator. *A. melanandra* tastes great when it's vine ripened, terrible when it's overripe.

Ornamental. Male plants of *A. kolomikta* have beautifully variegated leaves in spring, a tricolored look in summer, and red leaves in fall; color holds best in bright, indirect light. Silver vine (*A. polygama*) has silvery, fuzzy, heart-shaped leaves on a vigorous, tree-climbing vine.

To learn more about kiwis of all kinds, order *Kiwifruit Enthusiasts Journal Vol. 6,* an occasionally published compendium. For a copy, send $17.20 to Friends of the Trees, Box 1064, Tonasket, WA 98855. ■

By Michael MacCaskey, Jim McCausland, Lynn Ocone, Lauren Bonar Swezey

RICHARD MAACK

FLECKED WITH BLOOM *around a sprawling mesquite tree, this Phoenix garden was planted during the fall, just 18 months before the photo was taken. See item at left.*

Northwest

GARDEN GUIDE

WEST OF THE CASCADES, see items marked with a **W.**

EAST OF THE CASCADES, see items marked with an **E.**

November Checklist

HERE IS WHAT NEEDS DOING

☐ **CARE FOR HOUSE PLANTS. W, E:** If you haven't brought in all your house plants yet, do it now, before the first frost burns them. Before you make the transfer to a well-lit spot indoors, make sure you don't bring slugs and insects in as well; some gardeners rinse leaves off in a lukewarm shower first.

☐ **CUT BACK CHRYSANTHEMUMS. W, E:** When the last flowers fade, cut plants back to within 6 inches of the ground. They'll send out new shoots again in spring.

☐ **DIVIDE OR MULCH DAHLIAS. W, E:** West of the Cascades, you may be able to get away with mulching dahlias with 4 inches of straw or leaves. In a normal winter, they'll make it through, but, if things stay well below freezing for more than a few days, you'll likely lose all or some of them. If you don't like to gamble, haven't divided your dahlias in at least three years, or if you live east of the Cascades, dig and divide your dahlias now. Store them in peat moss–filled bags or boxes in a cool, dark, dry, frost-free place for the winter.

☐ **DIVIDE LILIES. W:** On a dry day, carefully dig up lily bulbs with a spading fork and tease them apart. Weed and amend the soil, and replant. The smallest bulbs you replant now won't rebloom for a couple of years, but eventually they'll size up and flower well.

☐ **DIVIDE RHUBARB. W:** Lift and divide rhizomes now, replanting them at least 36 inches apart in well-amended soil that drains well.

☐ **GROOM LAWNS. W, E:** Wet weather makes grass hard to mow, so take advantage of any dry day to get the lawn in shape for winter. You may not have another chance to mow (and you may not need to) until December or January. Keep leaves raked as well, since they can smother and kill the grass beneath them.

☐ **GROOM PERENNIAL BORDERS. W, E:** Most perennials can be cut back for the winter, but you may want to leave some grasses and dried flower heads for winter interest. Pull winter weeds while they're small, and mulch half-hardy perennials to carry them through hard freezes.

☐ **LIME LAWNS AND FLOWER BEDS. W, E:** Apply lime to lawns and flower beds now, since it can take months to wash down around roots and make a difference to plant growth. To speed the process in annual beds and next year's flower beds, dig in lime with a spading fork. Use dolomitic lime if you need to add magnesium to your soil as well as calcium.

☐ **MAKE COMPOST. W, E:** Everything from fall leaves to weeds and grass clippings can go into the fall compost pile. If you have lots of tough waste (like corn stalks), consider renting a grinder for a half-day to reduce it to a mass that will compost quickly over winter. To start a simple compost pile, layer greens (grass and weeds) with browns (straw, dried leaves) as shown below.

☐ **MULCH TREE AND SHRUB BEDS.** Use the coarse leftovers from sifted compost to make an organic mulch that keeps roots from freezing and minimizes weed growth.

☐ **PLANT BERRIES. W:** Plant small fruits (blackberries, blueberries, grapes, raspberries, strawberries) as soon as you can get them. They'll have all winter to send out roots, and some kinds will give you fruit next year.

☐ **PLANT BULBS. W, E:** As early in the month as possible, plant spring-flowering bulbs in well-amended soil. You can buy bulbs clear through December, but earlier planting is better: roots have a chance to become established before spring bloom comes on.

☐ **PLANT CAMELLIAS. W:** The earliest kinds, mostly sasanquas, will be in flower this month. They work well espaliered under a house eave, where blooms have protection against rain and rot.

☐ **PLANT PEONIES. W:** Herbaceous and tree peonies can go into rich, well-amended soil now for spectacular bloom next spring and summer.

☐ **PRUNE SHRUBS AND TREES. W, E:** Pick a comfortable, dry day that's above freezing. First remove dead, diseased, and injured wood, then closely parallel and crossing branches. That done, step back and size up the plant, then go back and prune for shape.

☐ **SOW HARDY ANNUALS. W, E:** If you plan to sow wildflower mixes in your garden for color or to attract butterflies, do it now. Also sow other hardy annuals like candytuft, clarkia, larkspur, and linaria. They'll germinate and flower earlier than the same seeds sown in spring.—*J. M.* ■

Central

GARDEN GUIDE

IN HIGH ELEVATIONS and intermountain areas of California, and east of the Sierra, see items marked with an **H.**

IN LOW ELEVATIONS of Northern California, see items marked with an **L.**

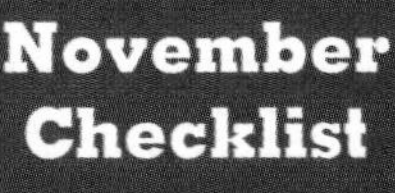

☐ **CHOOSE TREES FOR FALL COLOR. L:** Now—while leaves are still on the trees—is the time to shop for such trees as Chinese pistache, Chinese tallow tree, crape myrtle, ginkgo, liquidambar, maple, persimmon, Raywood ash, redbud, and sour gum.

☐ **CLEAN UP DEBRIS. H, L:** Pull up spent annuals and vegetables that have stopped producing. Rake up leaves. Add debris to the compost pile (except weeds that have gone to seed, and diseased plants).

☐ **COMPOST. H, L:** Start a simple compost pile by layering greens (grass and weeds) with browns (straw, dried leaves) as shown below. Or build a simple wire one: bend a 4-foot-high piece of 12- to 14-gauge wire fencing into a cylinder about 4 feet across and hook the cut edges together. To fill, alternate 1- to 1½-foot layers of garden debris with 2- to 3-inch layers of soil. Sprinkle nitrogen fertilizer every 1½ feet. Keep the pile evenly moist, and aerate it by turning it every two weeks or so.

☐ **CUT BACK CHRYSANTHEMUMS. L:** As soon as flowers die, cut back plants to within 6 inches of the ground.

☐ **DIVIDE DAHLIA TUBERS. H, L:** Withhold water to allow plants to go dormant. Then dig them carefully with a spading fork; trim away brown foliage and most of the stems, and brush off soil. Allow to dry for a few hours before storing or dividing. To divide clumps, use a sharp knife to cut each clump into sections; include an inch of stem and an eye with each division. Discard soft or diseased tubers. Store in peat moss, vermiculite, or sand.

☐ **DIVIDE PERENNIALS. L:** Lift and separate overgrown clumps, add organic matter to the soil, then divide and replant. To divide acanthus, agapanthus, and fortnight lily, you may need to force them apart with a spading fork.

☐ **FERTILIZE COOL-SEASON CROPS. L:** If you didn't mix a controlled-release fertilizer into the soil at planting time, feed annuals and vegetables with an organic fertilizer such as fish emulsion, or apply a commercial pruct in either liquid or dry form.

☐ **FERTILIZE LAWNS. L:** If you haven't already done so this fall, or if your fertilizer requires a second application (check label), feed lawns now with a granular lawn food. Use one that's designed to release nutrients over a long period.

☐ **FIGHT EROSION. L:** On slopes, make sure there's enough plant material to keep the hillside from eroding if rains are heavy this winter. If the slope is bare or is covered with young plants whose roots haven't knitted the soil together yet, sow seeds of wildflowers and a perennial grass, such as blue wild rye *(Elymus glaucus).*

☐ **PLANT ANNUALS. L:** For instant color, you can still buy 4-inch plants. Gently loosen the roots before planting them in the ground or a container.

☐ **PLANT FOR PERMANENCE. L:** In mild climates, November is still a good time to set out cold-hardy ground covers, shrubs, trees, and vines. Wait until spring to plant tender plants such as bougainvillea, mandevilla, and princess flower.

☐ **PLANT PERENNIALS. L:** Nurseries have a wide assortment. Choices include campanula, columbine, coral bells, coreopsis, delphinium, gaillardia, penstemon, phlox, salvia, and species geraniums.

☐ **PLANT SPRING BULBS, CORMS, TUBERS. L:** Buy only firm bulbs that are not sprouting. Chill crocus, hyacinths, and tulips in the refrigerator for four to six weeks before planting. Place in paper bags and keep away from apples, which produce ethylene gas that can cause bulbs to sprout.

☐ **PROTECT TREES. H:** Cover trunks of young trees with tree wrap to protect them from frost cracks and sunscald. Begin near the soil line and work partway up the major branches.

☐ **PULL MULCH BACK FROM CITRUS. L:** To help protect citrus from frost damage, pull mulch back from below the tree canopy. This allows the ground to absorb heat during the day and release it at night.

☐ **SOW WILDFLOWERS. L:** For colorful spring bloom, choose a mix that's suited to your climate (available in many seed catalogs), or buy individual kinds and develop your own color combinations. You can also buy mixes for specific purposes, such as wildflowers that attract butterflies.

☐ **STAKE TREES. H, L:** Trunks with leaning tops or those planted in very windy areas need support. To determine how high to place ties, move your hand up the trunk until the treetop straightens (if it's not bent, place tie about two-thirds of the way up the trunk). Tie tree to stakes with commercial ties or with wire or rope covered by hose or tubing. Make sure ties are not digging into the trunk; loosen if necessary. Remove when the tree can support itself.

☐ **WATER. L:** If rains are infrequent or absent, water newly planted lawns, landscape plants, and vegetables often enough to keep the soil moist.—*L.B.S.* ■

November Checklist

HERE IS WHAT NEEDS DOING

☐ **BUY AND PLANT BULBS. C, L:** While supplies last, buy anemones, daffodils, freesias, and ranunculus. Also look for allium, Asiatic lilies, bearded iris, Dutch iris, grape hyacinth, ixia, sparaxis, and watsonia. **H:** Hurry to plant the last of the spring-blooming bulbs.

☐ **CHILL BULBS. C, L:** Before supplies are depleted, buy crocus, Dutch hyacinth, and tulips, but keep bulbs in the refrigerator crisper for four to six weeks. Plant after Thanksgiving at the earliest; plant bulbs immediately after removing from refrigerator.

☐ **CONTROL SNAILS, SLUGS.** Handpick snails in the early evening or morning. Or use barriers (row covers, copper stripping), baits, or traps. A jar or can set on its side near a vulnerable plant and held in place with a stick or stone makes a good trap; put a tablespoon of bait inside. Carefully check seedlings and tender-leafed plants; these are snail favorites.

☐ **CONTROL WEEDS.** Fall rains encourage weed seeds to germinate. Control sprouts with a garden hoe, and mulch heavily around annuals, shrubs, and trees.

☐ **CUT BACK ASPARAGUS.** As soon as tops brown, cut stalks to the ground. Renew mulch.

☐ **DIG AND DIVIDE DAHLIAS.** If you haven't done so already, dig dahlia tubers. Trim remaining foliage and stems, and brush off soil. Use a sharp knife to divide tuberous roots. Each division should have an inch of stem and one or more buds at the base. Discard soft or diseased sections. Store healthy tubers in a cool spot until spring planting time.

☐ **DIG TUBEROUS BEGONIAS.** Trim dried leaves and stalks, brush off soil, and store tubers in a cool, dry place until spring.

☐ **MAINTAIN GARDEN TOOLS.** Late-fall days are great for getting tools in shape. Sand wooden handles, then paint or oil them. You can also use fine sandpaper or steel wool to clean and smooth the steel parts of cultivators, hoes, shovels, or other tools. Then go over them with a well-oiled rag to ward off rust.

☐ **MANAGE CABBAGE WORM.** The white butterflies flitting above broccoli, cabbage, and cauliflower have larvae that eat these vegetables' leaves. To prevent infestation, cover seedlings with a floating row cover immediately after planting. If uncovered plants are bothered, spray with *Bacillus thuringiensis*, which kills larvae only.

☐ **PLANT BULB COVER. C, L:** Scatter seeds of blue forget-me-not (*Myosotis sylvatica*) in beds of yellow daffodils, or seeds of white sweet alyssum in beds of mixed bulbs.

☐ **PLANT FOR WINTER, EARLY-SPRING COLOR. C, L:** You have just enough time to set out transplants. Choices for sun include bells-of-Ireland, calendula, clarkia, cornflower, foxglove, larkspur, lobelia, painted daisy, pansy (coast), petunia, phlox, snapdragon, stock, sweet alyssum, and sweet pea. For afternoon shade, try dianthus, English daisy, lobelia, pansy (inland), primrose, sweet alyssum, and viola.

☐ **PLANT NATIVES. C, L:** Plant shrubs such as manzanita, toyon, and wild lilac, and perennials such as California fuchsia and coral bells. Sales put on this month by botanical gardens and native plant societies are good sources.

☐ **PLANT PERENNIALS. C, L:** Spring-flowering perennials planted now will become established in warm soil and fall rain. Look for seedlings of carnation, columbine, delphinium, gaillardia, gloriosa daisy, penstemon, and yarrow.

☐ **PLANT VEGETABLES. C, L:** There's still time to plant seeds of beets, carrots, kohlrabi, lettuce, mustard, peas, radishes, rutabaga, spinach, Swiss chard, and turnips. Plant seedlings of broccoli, cabbage, cauliflower, celery, collards, endive, kale, leeks, lettuce, and parsley.

☐ **PUT IN GARLIC, ONIONS. C, L:** Separate cloves from garlic bulbs; plant largest ones, base down, 1 to 2 inches deep and 3 inches apart. Harvest when the leaves are half brown. Start onions from seeds or sets (tiny onions). Use sets larger than a dime for green onions, smaller than a dime for bulbs.

☐ **REDUCE CITRUS WATERING. C, L:** Reduce the frequency but not the duration of irrigation for citrus and subtropical plants. Too much water stimulates new, frost-tender growth. In some areas, rain will supplement regular watering.

☐ **SOW WILDFLOWER SEEDS. C, L:** Broadcast seeds by hand over weed-free soil. Rake the area lightly to cover seeds with soil. Wait for rain, or water them yourself. Once watered, the soil should be kept consistently moist until seeds germinate.

☐ **STAKE TREES.** Trees grow better unstaked, but rubbery trunks may need some support. If an unstaked tree is leaning, place ties just above the point where the trunk starts to bend. Tie tree to stake or stakes using wire covered by hose or tubing. Check ties periodically to make sure they're not girdling the tree. When the tree can support itself, remove ties and stakes.

☐ **SURVEY SASANQUAS. C:** Early-flowering sasanqua camellias begin blooming this month. Visit nurseries and gardens to see flower colors and the range of upright and sprawling types available. If space is limited, plant in containers or espalier against a fence.—*L. O.* ■

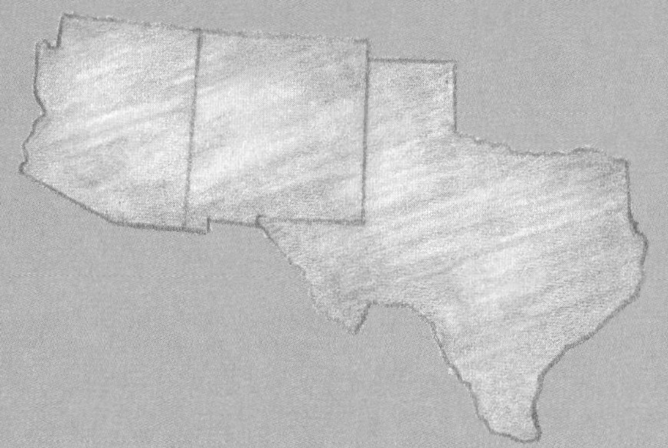

November Checklist

HERE IS WHAT NEEDS DOING

☐ **DRAIN DRIP SYSTEMS.** If below-freezing temperatures are common where you live, drain water out of drip systems to prevent breakage caused by ice. If you use an underground drip (or spray) system, install a weeper valve to automatically drain the system after each use.

☐ **OVERSEED BERMUDA.** To keep your winter lawn green, overseed with annual or perennial rye grass. Annual rye is cheaper but needs more frequent mowing, stains clothes, and is coarser-textured. Sow 10 to 20 pounds of either rye over 1,000 square feet of scalped (mowed very low) Bermuda; keep the seedbed moist until seedlings are ½ inch high. A month later, feed with a nitrate-containing fertilizer such as ammonium nitrate.

☐ **PICK SPLIT CITRUS.** Mild November weather spurs most citrus into growth. Sometimes this causes existing fruit to split, especially if your trees were kept on the dry side through summer. Pick right away, because split fruit attracts insects and fungus.

☐ **PLANT BULBS.** This is the best month of the year to plant most spring-flowering bulbs. Even if you can't plant right away, shop now while selection is good. After purchase, chill bulbs of crocus, hyacinth, and tulips for six weeks before planting. In the mountains (Prescott and Santa Fe), hurry to complete planting.

☐ **PLANT FOR COLOR.** It's not too late to plant many annuals. For sunny locations, plant ageratum, aster, bells-of-Ireland, calendula, candytuft, clarkia, cornflower, foxglove, larkspur, lobelia, painted daisy, petunia, phlox, snapdragon, stock, sweet alyssum, and sweet pea. In shady areas, try dianthus, English daisy, pansy, primrose, and viola.

☐ **PLANT TREES AND SHRUBS.** Right now is a perfect time to put in hardy trees and shrubs. Consider acacia, cassia, *Cordia boissieri*, desert spoon, fairy duster, mesquite, oleander, palo verde, *Salvia greggii*, and Texas ranger. All will tolerate summer heat, but winter hardiness of plants varies; check with your nursery or the *Sunset Western Garden Book*.

☐ **PLANT VEGETABLES.** In low and intermediate deserts, there's still time to plant asparagus, beets, broccoli, brussels sprouts, cabbage, carrots, cauliflower, celery, endive, garlic, kale, kohlrabi, leeks, lettuce, mustard, parsley, peas, radishes, spinach, Swiss chard, and turnips. Nursery-grown transplants of long-season vegetables such as cabbage, celery, parsley, spinach, and Swiss chard are usually more successful than seeds.

☐ **PRUNE AND FEED ROSES.** For best fall flowering and to shape plants, remove spent flowers and dead, crossing, or weak stems and twigs. Then feed with a fertilizer formulated especially for roses, or any complete fertilizer. As a guide, apply about 4 ounces of a 10-10-10 fertilizer per bush. On roses in containers, decrease quantity but apply more often; check directions on product label.

☐ **REDUCE CITRUS WATERING.** Cut back on irrigations to one deep soaking every three to four weeks in clay soils, one a week in sandy soils. If you use a hose, build a basin 2 feet beyond the tree's drip line, then run the water slowly into it. Fill the basin several times to wet the root zone thoroughly. If you use a drip system, allow enough time for water to soak soil thoroughly. Time varies with the number of emitters and their gallon-per-hour rating; a large tree could take 12 hours or longer to water properly.

☐ **SOW WILDFLOWERS.** In low and intermediate deserts, sow seeds of blackfoot daisy (*Melampodium leucanthum*), desert bluebells (*Phacelia campanularia*), desert globe mallow (*Sphaeralcea ambigua*), fire-wheel (*Gaillardia pulchella*), Mexican hat (*Ratibida columnifera*), Mexican tulip poppy (*Hunnemannia fumariifolia*), and owl's clover (*Orthocarpus purpurascens*). If rains are infrequent, keep seeds moist until plants reach about 2 inches tall.

☐ **STAKE YOUNG TREES.** Determine direction of prevailing wind; place stakes at right angles to wind. Drive two stakes into soil outside of rootball, not through it. Use rope, hose, or plastic nursery tape to connect stakes and tree. Determine tie height by sliding your hand up the trunk until treetop straightens.

☐ **START COMPOST.** As summer flowers and produce die back, pull and use the plants to make compost. Don't add Bermuda clippings, weeds, or diseased plants to the pile. To speed breakdown, chop or shred garden debris before adding it to the pile.

☐ **TRAP AND BAIT SLUGS AND SNAILS.** Try to keep them in check by handpicking them at night or early in the morning. Or set out barriers, traps, and baits.

☐ **WATCH FOR PESTS.** Aphids often reappear in fall's cooler weather. Wash plants with spray from the hose, or spray with insecticidal soap. Protect seedlings with cardboard collars.

☐ **WRAP TREE TRUNKS.** To protect young trees from winter frost damage, cover trunks with cardboard or burlap. Leave the protective covering in place until danger of frost is past.—*M. M.* ■

Robust and rugged rosemary

IT'S OUTSTANDING FOR FRAGRANCE, FLAVOR, AND GARDEN ARTISTRY

One of the most versatile of all herbs, rosemary can be used in a variety of ways in both garden and kitchen. Gardeners cherish it for its many landscape uses—from tall, narrow screens to picturesque spreading groundcovers to little potted trees that bring their pungent fragrance onto patios or decks. Cooks use it to flavor barbecued meats, vinegars, and sauces.

PETER CHRISTIANSEN

But rosemary's greatest attribute is its toughness. This rugged perennial, native to the Mediterranean region, tolerates a wide range of growing conditions; it endures both hot sun and cool ocean spray and survives temperatures down to around 15°. Rosemary also tolerates drought, but

RUSS A. WIDSTRAND

FRAGRANT SLOPE

At home in Mediterranean climates, rosemary grows with gusto in Norma Jean and Bill Lathrop's garden in Glendora, California. 'Prostratus' cascades down the hill as 'Collingwood Ingram' reaches skyward. Blooming wisteria caps the slope. In pot shown on opposite page, pruned rosemary makes patio topiary.

FLOWERS *grow ¼ inch across or larger in small clusters.*

CHAD SLATTERY

ERECT 'BLUE SPIRE' *in Montecito patio garden grows in small pocket about 1-foot deep. Santa Barbara daisy blooms at its base. Design: Dennis Shaw.*

it welcomes some supplemental water.

Most types of rosemary (*Rosemarinus officinalis*) fall into one of two categories: upright or prostrate. Some have straight branches, others arch or undulate. Among the uprights, you'll find some with basal growth forming an attractive "skirt." Types with branches touching the ground root as they spread.

Leaf color varies. The needlelike leaves are usually green on top and grayish white beneath; the shade of green changes slightly through the year. One rosemary has green-and-gold variegated foliage, but horticulturists tend to agree it looks more diseased than attractive.

Flowers come mostly in shades of blue, but novel pink and white varieties exist as well. All fade as they age. Peak bloom is in late winter or early spring, with flowers intermittently through the year. Flowers attract bees.

MAINTENANCE IS MINIMAL

Rosemary's primary requirements are sun and well-drained soil; given these, it is practically trouble-free.

Plants grow at a moderate pace and can live for decades; the ones on page 273 are about 15 years old. Too much fertilizer and water result in rank, shorter-lived plants.

Shape young rosemary plants by tip-pruning. On older plants, cut back branches; when spring bloom is over, make cuts in green wood only.

HARVEST TIPS

You can harvest leaves for cooking anytime, although some growers say leaves are most flavorful just before the plant flowers. Consider planting rosemary near the barbecue so you can toss plant sprigs over the coals to flavor food as it cooks. Or use rosemary branches dipped in sauce to baste grilled food.

Carole Saville, food and garden writer and garden designer, makes rosemary-flavored vinegar. Since blossoms impart a more subtle rosemary flavor than whole sprigs do, she steeps a 2-inch layer of fresh blossoms in a 12-inch-deep bottle of white wine vinegar; once the vinegar assumes a subtle flavor, she strains the infusion. ■

By Lynn Ocone

Rosemary: 10 good choices

Rosemary variety names and plant characteristics are often confused. Descriptions below are based on the collective experience of four California nurseries that specialize in Mediterranean plants; all agree on these plant names.

*An asterisk indicates varieties most favored by these experts for appearance and performance.

Prostrate kinds for low ground covers

These eventually spread 4 to 8 feet or more.

***'Corsican Prostrate'.** Billowing, with arching branches to 2 feet high; dark blue flowers. Prominent undersides of leaves give plant a silver-blue cast.

'Huntington Carpet'. Billowing, with arching branches 1½ to 2½ feet high; light to medium blue flowers; dull, light green leaves. Not as showy as 'Corsican Prostrate' or 'Ken Taylor'. Slower, more compact than 'Prostratus'.

'Prostratus'. Ground-hugging to 2½ feet high; cascading; light to medium blue flowers; dull green leaves. (Plants sold as 'Prostratus' vary widely. Plants currently sold as 'Lockwood de Forest' may be 'Prostratus'.)

Semiupright kinds for ground covers

***'Collingwood Ingram'** (also called 'Benenden Blue' and 'Ingramii'). Vertical stems to 5 feet with basal branches sprawling outward and arching upward; spreads to 6 feet or more; showy in bloom, with rich medium to dark blue flowers.

***'Ken Taylor'.** Similar to 'Collingwood Ingram', with vertical stems to 3 feet and looser habit; showy in bloom, with bright lavender-blue flowers; dark green leaves.

Upright kinds for hedges

'Albus'. Bushy to 3 feet tall and wide; white flowers.

'Blue Spire'. Very erect; 4 to 6 feet tall, equal width; no basal growth; medium to dark blue flowers.

'Majorca Pink'. Vase-shaped; 3 to 5 feet tall and to 6 feet wide; lavender-pink flowers; short, dull green leaves; opens in center as it grows; grown for unusual flower color.

'Miss Jessop's Upright'. Five to 8 feet tall, spreading 4 feet; multistemmed; branches arch and dip when 2 to 3 feet long; medium to medium-dark blue flowers; rich olive leaves are longer and wider than on others; not a dense grower.

***'Tuscan Blue'.** Erect to 6 feet or more with basal branching; 4 to 5 feet wide; radiant dark blue flowers are larger than others; dusty olive leaves on stems.

PETER CHRISTIANSEN

LEATHER, *cotton, and waterproof vinyl gloves each offer different kinds of protection from thorns, blisters, chemicals, and dirt. Leather gloves are cut in two patterns: gunn (left) and clute (next to it).*

Matching gloves to garden chores

Choices range from heavy-duty leather to lightweight cotton

EVERY GARDENER'S supply closet should include a pair of good gloves. Beyond providing protection against blisters, dirt, and scratches, gloves—in any kind of fabric or leather—significantly reduce the risk of nerve damage to your hands and wrists from vibrating power tools, like rotary tillers and chain saws.

INDUSTRIAL-STRENGTH GLOVES

Leather gloves offer the best protection for most garden jobs, but there are huge differences among skins (explanations follow). Also, most kinds of leather are split when they're tanned. The bottom (flesh) side of the skin, called split leather or suede, is stronger. The top (hair) side, called grain leather, is smooth.

Cowhide. Inexpensive and tough, cowhide is used in most all-purpose leather gloves. If you never plan to use these for handling thorny or stickery plants, get the kind with cotton backs—they're cooler in summer. For winter use, buy the insulated kind.

Deerskin. Usually tanned yellow-orange, deerskin is extremely soft, and, while it's difficult to puncture, it's not particularly abrasion or tear resistant. It offers good protection when you're working with tools and regains suppleness well after it's wet.

Elkskin. Also fairly soft, elk is thicker and tougher than deer but not as tough as cowhide. Elk gloves are expensive (around $25 a pair) and effective for most jobs. They won't hold up well for work like rock handling.

Goatskin. Though it makes the toughest gloves, goat is very soft; it's probably the best glove leather you can buy for gardening. Goat leather is almost never split: gloves are made from intact, tanned skin.

Pigskin. Tough and often brushed (sueded) for softness, pigskin retains much of its supppleness after going through repeated wet-dry cycles, and breathes well. It tears fairly easily, and thorns can poke through the skin's hair follicles.

Sheepskin. It's rarely used for gloves, deerskin being the more common, feel-alike alternative. But sheepskin is infused with lanolin that leaves the skin on your hands softer than before you started.

To preserve their natural lanolin, these gloves are undyed. To keep them white, use only for pruning (not weeding or rock handling).

Sheepskin gloves are difficult to find, but you can order from Little's Good Gloves, Box 808, Johnstown, NY 12095.

LIGHTER GLOVES FOR LIGHTER TASKS

Cotton. These gloves remain one of the world's great deals. For less than $5, these do a great job of protecting your hands against blisters and dirt. They're also cool and absorbent—great for wiping the sweat from your brow. Buy the kind with nylon dots on the palms for extra grip and wear resistance.

Synthetic. Vinyl or latex gloves provide essential skin protection for handling garden chemicals. (We also know a physician who slips on surgical gloves for working with potted plants; they keep his hands clean.)

I SEE A PATTERN HERE

Gloves are sewn to either of two patterns (though each has variations).

The clute pattern has seams between the fingers. The gunn pattern has a seam along the base of the middle and ring fingers on the palm side of each hand. (Both are pictured above.) Try on each and make a fist. We find that seams bunch up between and beneath the fingers of clute-sewn gloves. Prices are comparable. ■

By Jim McCausland

ROSALIND CREASY

1. ■ Grain is planted in November in Rosalind Creasy's Los Altos, California, garden. After broadcasting seeds, Sandra rakes them into the soil (left). Come spring, grain develops heads, although it is still green (below).

2. ■ Jill's favorite part of the early-July harvest is cutting off the "heavy gold tops." She uses scissors to snip off the heads while Sandra, C. J., and Creasy help out. Later, leftover stalks will be cut down with grass clippers.

From seed to bread

Kids gain hands-on experience with the staff of life

By Lauren Bonar Swezey with Linda Lau Anusasananan

Ask a kid where bread comes from, and "the grocery store" is the probable answer. Unlike children of earlier generations, whose parents most likely lived on a farm, grew much of their food for the table, and baked bread every week from grain they had raised in the fields, children today don't usually make a connection between what they eat and where it came from. But landscape designer and author Rosalind Creasy is changing the way some kids think of bread.

"I started growing grain as an experiment to see if fresh grain really would make a difference in the flavor of homemade bread," Creasy explains. "As a gardener and cook, I'm always looking for the most flavorful ingredients.

"The growing and harvesting turned out to be so much fun, I got the neighborhood kids involved. It's amazing to watch the light bulb go off in their heads—they suddenly understand the connection between the earth and the food they eat."

Creasy has been holding her neighborhood harvest party for eight years now. The ritual actually begins in fall, when the children help sow the seeds, watch the grain grow through the winter and spring, and then check its progress as it slowly turns brown. By early July, it's ready to harvest.

First grader C. J. Lion com-

3. ■ C. J. carts the wheat heads to the driveway, where a sheet is laid out for the "tennis-shoe twist" (right). Creasy makes sure that the bottoms of everyone's shoes are clean before they start.

pared his harvesting experiences to those of the Little Red Hen in the classic children's book. None of the animals would help her harvest the wheat, but they all wanted to eat the bread. C. J. told his mom, "No wonder the Little Red Hen didn't want to share. It's a lot of work to harvest."

Nine-year-old Sandra Chang says she'd never thought about where bread comes from. "Now I know you have to grow the wheat, harvest the heads, and grind the berries to get flour."

Eleven-year-old Jill Main says she likes the harvest togetherness—and doing things the old-fashioned way. But at

PETER CHRISTIANSEN

4. ■ Sandra uses a modern invention to separate the wheat from the chaff—a vacuum cleaner with hose positioned on the outlet (so air blows out).

PETER CHRISTIANSEN

first she wasn't sure about eating the bread. "I like whole-wheat bread from the store, but I thought home-grown wheat bread would taste gross. I was surprised. It tastes really good!"

"You don't need 2½ acres and a McCormick reaper to grow wheat"

"The great thing about wheat," says Creasy, "is that it's one of the easiest crops to grow. Since it's planted in fall, winter rains do most of the watering for you when it's a moist year."

Creasy found that a patch of soil of about 100 square feet (hers is 4 feet by 24 feet) provides flour for about 20 loaves. "The learning process is much more important than how much wheat you harvest and store," she explains.

To get the best production, soil should be well drained and thoroughly tilled, with plenty of compost mixed in. Before planting, Creasy tills in blood meal and bonemeal (about 1 pound each per 100 square feet).

She grows hard red spring wheat, but she's also had success with winter wheat from a natural-food store. If you buy wheat seeds—also called wheat berries—at a natural-food store, check to make sure they'll grow before you plant them by putting some in a damp paper towel. Keep the towel moist until they sprout.

The best time to plant is two to three weeks before winter rains set in—in most of the West, that means planting in October or November for a June or July harvest. In cold climates, gardeners must wait to plant spring wheat until the soil can be worked in March or April (expect an August or September harvest).

To plant, scatter seeds over the prepared soil (about 6 handfuls, or ¼ pound, per 100 square feet), then rake seeds in so they are buried to about three times their diameter. This allows plants to get a strong foothold and helps prevent them from lodging—falling over—later.

After planting, soak the soil thoroughly; water to keep moist (every week or two if rains don't come). If cats are a nuisance, stretch bird netting tautly over stakes about 4 to 5 inches off the ground.

As the wheat sprouts, weeds can be a big problem. Creasy advises weeding regularly, so weeds don't compete with the young wheat shoots.

When the wheat is about

knee-high, Creasy ties it up to keep it from lodging in the wind and rain. She places heavy wooden stakes at the corners, then encircles the area at knee height with heavy twine. If the twine needs more support, place more stakes between the corner stakes.

Once winter rains end, continue watering (about once a week) until the wheat starts turning brown. Creasy says the experienced young wheat harvesters often stop by to check the progression. They've learned that when the wheat turns brown and a tooth can no longer dent the berries, the wheat is ready to harvest.

5. ■ The children pour wheat berries collected in the bottom of the red tub into a grain-grinding mill attached to an electric mixer. The result is fine whole-wheat flour. (A blender also works well.)

In mild climates, you can normally start harvesting in early June, but Creasy lets her crop stand awhile to harvest at her traditional Fourth of July party. To harvest, follow her step-by-step process pictured on these pages.

Where to get seeds

Buy wheat berries at natural-food and farm supply stores. Or order by mail from Bountiful Gardens, 18001 Shafer Ranch Rd., Willits, CA 95490; (707) 459-6410 (catalog free).

Grow- Your-Own Whole-wheat Bread

Enjoy the aroma of bread made with freshly ground flour. Use home-grown hard spring or winter wheat or buy it at a natural-food store.

- 1 package active dry yeast
- 2¾ cups warm water (110° to 115°)
- ½ cup firmly packed dark brown sugar
- ¼ cup (⅛ lb.) butter or margarine, at room temperature
- 2 teaspoons salt
- 4 cups bread flour
- About 3½ cups freshly ground whole-wheat flour (directions follow)

In a large bowl, soften yeast in ¼ cup of the water, about 5 minutes. Blend in remaining 2½ cups water, sugar, butter, and salt. Stir in all the bread flour until moistened. Beat with an electric mixer or a heavy spoon until dough is stretchy, 10 to 15 minutes. Add 3½ cups whole-wheat flour.

If using a dough hook, beat on low speed until flour is moistened. Then beat at high speed until dough pulls cleanly from sides of bowl, 5 to 7 minutes. If dough still sticks, add whole-wheat flour 1 tablespoon at a time until it pulls free.

If mixing by hand, with a heavy spoon stir flour into dough until moist. Scrape dough onto a lightly floured board. Knead until smooth and elastic, adding as little flour as possible to prevent sticking, about 15 minutes. Place dough in a large bowl.

Cover dough with plastic wrap; place in a warm, draft-free place. Let dough rise until almost doubled, 1 to 1½ hours.

Knead with dough hook or on a lightly floured board to expel air bubbles. On a floured board, divide dough in half and shape each portion into a loaf. Place each loaf in a greased 4- by 8-inch loaf pan. Cover lightly with plastic wrap and place in a warm, draft-free place. Let rise until almost doubled, about 45 minutes.

Uncover and bake in a 375° oven until richly browned, 40 to 50 minutes. Turn loaves onto a wire rack to cool. Makes 2 loaves (each about 1¾ lb.).

Per ounce: 76 cal. (14 percent from fat); 2.2 g protein; 1.2 g fat (0.6 g sat.); 14 g carbo.; 89 mg sodium; 2.3 mg chol.

Freshly ground whole-wheat flour. Sort through 3 cups (about 1⅓ lb.) **hard spring** or winter **wheat;** remove any grit or dirt (some chaff is all right). Grind wheat in a grain grinder or whirl 1-cup portions in a blender until finely ground. Makes about 4 cups flour. If flour isn't used at once, store airtight in freezer. ■

6. ■ The best part of the harvest party is biting into nutty-tasting, fresh whole-wheat bread.

A PUFF OF SUNSHINE
On a gray January day, Chinese witch hazel blooms brightly (and fragrantly) in a rain-soaked garden.

BILL ROSS

Winter sparklers

THESE PLANTS BLAST THE BLAHS FROM YOUR GARDEN WITH FRAGRANCE, WITH COLOR

It takes a brave shrub to bloom in the gray chill of winter in Northwest gardens. But courageous plants do pop up, set buds, and even bloom in winter—providing sparkle in gardens suffering from the midwinter blahs. All you have to do is choose the right plants and set them out this month. These permanent investments will grace your garden for years to come.

Nature takes care of winter bloomers, equipping them with the rich colors (often vivid yellow) or strong fragrances that they need to attract pollinators. And that makes them attention grabbers, especially since many of them bloom on winter-naked branches. Positioned outside a window, along a walk, or by an entry, they invite regular glimpses or sniffs.

Unless nipped by an especially hard cold snap, their flowers stay perky for a month or more—they're essentially in cold storage.

Below, we list 13 of the top winter bloomers. Look for them in nurseries now, and plant them soon so late-fall and winter rains can get them off to a good start.

Give all these plants rich, fast-draining soil. Some, like *Arbutus unedo* and the witch hazels, take full sun. Others, like wintersweet (*Chimonanthus praecox*) and *Viburnum bodnantense,* need at least strong morning light but will take some shade. And *Sarcococca hookerana humilis* will flourish in deep shade.

Once established, none of these plants are fussy. Give them normal summer water (if our water supplies allow). Feed them with a complete fertilizer as often as four times a year, spacing applications evenly between Valentine's Day and the Fourth of July. Prune errant branches (the perfect time is when they're blooming, to take indoors). Otherwise, let them grow and enjoy them. ■

By Steven R. Lorton

BILL ROSS

LOOSE CLUSTER *of delicate, bell-shaped blooms dangles from woody branches of Viburnum bodnantense, sweetening the air with fragrance.*

BOLD, PRICKLY FOLIAGE *of Mahonia 'Arthur Menzies' sets off big yellow blooms for a month-long show.*

Here are 13 winter sparklers

Camellia sasanqua. Many varieties with small flowers, usually single or semidouble, in a range of colors from white ('Apple Blossom') through pink and rose, and on to deep red ('Yuletide'). Excellent for espaliers.

Cornelian cherry (*Cornus mas*). Small deciduous tree (to 20 feet). Brilliant yellow blooms appear on a delicate network of bare branches. Hardy on both sides of the Cascades (but blooms later east of the mountains).

Chinese witch hazel (*Hamamelis mollis*). Deciduous tree to 30 feet tall. Brilliant yellow blooms with a strong, spicy scent appear on naked branches.

Flowering cherry (*Prunus subhirtella* 'Autumnalis'). A classic tree for Northwest parking strips. It begins showing blooms in late autumn, holding pink buds all through winter. With each warm spell, a few flowers emerge.

Hamamelis intermedia. Deciduous shrub, like Chinese witch hazel but smaller, can be trained as a small garden tree to 15 feet. Numerous varieties have colorful flowers and autumn foliage; among them are 'Copper Beauty', 'Diane', 'Magic Fire', and 'Ruby Glow'.

Lonicera standishii. A rare honeysuckle, well worth the search. Check arboretum and plant society sales, or take a cutting from a friend. Cream-colored flowers have a sweet fragrance and appear on the leafless shrub. Flowers of *L. fragrantissima* are similar but more intensely fragrant. Both work well for informal espaliers.

***Mahonia* 'Arthur Menzies'.** Brilliant yellow blooms atop stems filled with holly-like evergreen leaves. Often begins flowering before Christmas.

Leatherleaf mahonia (*M. bealei*). Much like mahonia listed above, but easier to find and with broader leaves. Plant blooms with a big upright cluster of torch-like flower spikes.

Sarcococca hookerana humilis. Shrubby, low-growing evergreen (to 1½ feet). Many tiny cream-colored flowers hide among small waxy green leaves. Powerful fragrance (some gardeners love it; others consider it too strong). Black fruits follow the flowers.

S. ruscifolia. Larger, coarser plant than *S. h. humilis* (to 3 to 4 feet tall; tends to flower a bit later). Fruits are red.

Strawberry tree (*Arbutus unedo*). Small evergreen tree (to 8, maybe 20 feet). Clusters of sparkling white flowers becoming brilliant red gum ball–size fruits later. Though flowers have little fragrance, they're handsome on the plant and in arrangements.

Viburnum bodnantense. Deciduous shrub (to 10 feet) with an open growth habit. Richly fragrant pink bloom clusters hang from bare branches. An all-time favorite for Northwest gardeners.

Wintersweet (*Chimonanthus praecox*). Rangy, deciduous shrub (to 15 feet and half as wide) with pale yellow flowers. Wonderful fragrance fills the cold air around a doorway or along a walkway.

by with watering once every two weeks.

PLANTING GUIDELINES

To choose plants, consider watering and light requirements, soil type, and slope.

Also aim to keep 80 percent of the oak's root area dry in the summer.

An exception to the limited-water rules and guidelines: If you grow an oak from an acorn, or plant it as a small seedling, you can give it full garden watering all its life. ■

By Emely Lincowski

NORMAN A. PLATE

SCATTERED *as though planted by nature, perennials and shrubs add color and help retain soil on slope around valley and coast live oaks in this Santa Rosa, California, garden. Pink-flowered Spiraea 'Trinity Rose' grows in foreground.*

Under oaks and with oaks

Here are plants that do well and minimize oak troubles

MATURE OAKS IN THE garden are a mixed blessing: they lend a woodsy ambience few other trees can equal, but landscaping under them can jeopardize the trees' health from too much watering. Pictured here are two approaches to planting near oaks with minimum risk. If you act now, winter rains can help establish plants.

The retreat pictured above was designed by Kent Calkins of Creative Landscape Consultants. Surrounding the deck for shady color and foliage are daylilies, Serbian bellflower, Western spiraea, mahonia, evergreen currant, and giant chain ferns.

Calkins also planted some thirsty plants (rhododendrons and Japanese maple) as accents. Used correctly—8 feet or more apart, at least 10 feet from the trunk, and on slopes that allow water to drain away—they give oaks a small amount of summer water, a benefit in dry years. Drip irrigation is used for the thirsty plants.

In the garden pictured at the bottom of the page, native oaks with branches pruned up provide a sunnier setting to grow a variety of colorful plants. These bloom from spring into summer and get

SUN-LOVING, *unthirsty perennials—dwarf hollyhock, Peruvian verbena, twinspur, and rose-colored yarrow—surround coast live oak.*

Plants under oaks

These plants require little summer water.

Blooming perennials

Common yarrow (*Achillea millefolium*), Dalmatian bellflower (*Campanula portenschlagiana*), dwarf hollyhock (*Sidalcea candida*), gaura (*G. lindheimeri*), ground morning glory (*Convolvulus mauritanicus*), Mexican lobelia (*L. laxiflora*), Peruvian verbena (*V. peruviana*), Serbian bellflower (*C. poscharskyana*), twinspur (*Diascia*), Western columbine (*Aquilegia formosa*), yerba buena (*Satureja douglasii*).

Ferns and grasses

Autumn fern (*Dryopteris erythrosora*), blue fescue (*Festuca ovina glauca*), giant chain fern (*Woodwardia fimbriata*), lily turf (*Liriope* and *Ophiopogon*).

Shrubs

Australian bluebell creeper (*Sollya heterophylla*), bush anemone (*Carpenteria californica*), Darwin barberry (*Berberis darwinii*), flowering currant (*Ribes*), heavenly bamboo (*Nandina domestica*), island bush-snapdragon (*Galvezia speciosa*), Oregon grape (*Mahonia*), salal (*Gaultheria shallon*), spice bush (*Calycanthus occidentalis*), sticky monkeyflower (*Mimulus aurantiacus*).

The natural look...with artificial rock

Boulders, steps, waterfalls—all built of artificial materials

ROCKS AND BOULDERS can lend a rugged texture to a residential landscape. Since few suburban building sites are rock strewn, it's common for landscapers to haul in truckloads of small boulders and river rocks. However, big boulders can be hard to find and difficult to transport and install.

These hillside gardens are not quite what they appear to be: most of the "rocks" are artificial. In each garden, the owners wanted the natural look of stone, but the site conditions or the scope of the landscape design made it impractical to install the real thing. So the owners turned to a technology that produces artificial rocks shaped, textured, and colored to resemble their natural counterparts.

ROCK-MAKING TECHNOLOGY

Originally, artificial rocks formed with concrete were often used to create animal habitats in zoos or to build large retaining walls along roads. Manufacturers have since adapted the technology

STACKED FLAGSTONES *were built on site to create outcrop with waterfall; stones in foreground are real. Design: Bob Morris and Associates of Hemet, California.*

NORMAN A. PLATE

COUNTERFEIT ROCKS *can be formed over metal lath–covered frame or cast in concrete from textured latex molds.*

PETER CHRISTIANSEN

for residential landscaping. Today, skillful technicians can match the form, texture, and color of any true rock.

Concrete rocks are not a solid mass—most are hollow shapes that can be built in several ways. One style starts with a boulder-shaped frame of reinforcing bar. A layer of wire mesh or expanded metal lath is secured to the frame, and then several layers of concrete are applied to the shell. The result is a hollow igloo that can be as small as a breadbox or tall enough for an adult to stand in.

To re-create the cracks and fissures of natural rock, the still-wet concrete may be carved with tools or embossed with crinkled aluminum foil, clear plastic wrap, or custom latex molds cast from actual rock formations.

PETER O. WHITELEY

CASCADING STEPS *and retaining wall were formed on hillside. Design: Ron Taylor of Natural Design, Santa Clara, California.*

WATERFALL *tumbles into spa on hillside terraced by retaining walls with precast rock veneer. Design: Lehmann Landscaping Co. and Ransohoff, Blanchfield, Jones.*

Another popular rock-forming technique even more accurately re-creates the subtle forms and textures of nature. The process starts with latex molds that are cast on real rocks. The molds are then sprayed with a mixture of concrete and strands of fiberglass or polypropylene. When the mixture dries, the forms are removed, and the builder has a thin but sturdy panel with a rock-textured veneer. The molds produce identical panels, which can be joined together horizontally or vertically so you don't notice the repeated shape. (Other manufacturers make lightweight rocks by spraying fiberglass onto latex forms.)

At this point, the artificial rocks still wear the drab gray of concrete. True rock is often a pastiche of colors and may also be flecked with lichen and specks of soil. To imitate this look, installers color the concrete with layers of diluted acrylic stains that are brushed, sprayed, or splattered on.

Manufactured rocks offer some other landscaping features: they can be formed with pockets for plants, lights, or ponds, and can hide pumps and electrical or water lines and mask retaining walls.

Because of labor and materials, the cost of installing artificial rock is usually slightly higher than bringing in real boulders. Installers often estimate the cost based on the square footage of the finished surface area and the complexity of site preparation work. Cost can range from $10 to $30 per square foot, depending on the site. ■

By Peter O. Whiteley

DECEMBER

Garden guide....................287
December checklists...........292
The Western wreath...........296
Camellias for Christmas......304
Lights for winter flowers......307
Berries to deck the garden...309
Quick holiday centerpieces..311
L.A.'s flower market...........312
Tools for a plant collector....313

Sunset's

GARDEN GUIDE

CHARLES MANN

High-country winter

DUSTED WITH SNOW, SPIKED LEAVES OF SOAPTREE YUCCA (Y. ELATA) FAN OUT from a sturdy trunk against a backdrop of adobe walls (and Sandia Peak) in Albuquerque. In winter, this tough yucca—a Southwest native—takes on a sculptural beauty all its own, especially when surrounded with snow. Despite the cool temperatures, high-desert gardeners should remember that the air is dry, so new plants need regular watering to survive. In the West's low elevations, gardeners can still plant for winter and spring color.

Living rosemary trees—for gifts or decorations

Rosemary trained as a Christmas tree makes an enduring holiday gift. This month, some Western nurseries will be selling trees like the one pictured at right—several years old and usually in 2- or 5-gallon containers. The growers have done the training for you. Some trees are staked and have arching branches, while others are rigid and upright. The variety of rosemary that's used varies from grower to grower and will determine the plant's form.

To maintain the established shape, you just snip young branches as they grow (cuttings are excellent for flavoring sauces and barbecued foods). You can decorate the tree with small, lightweight ornaments, but do so carefully to avoid breaking branches.

Adventurous gardeners with time and patience can train rosemary from small plants. Start with a young plant that is full, especially at the base, and has a somewhat pyramidal shape; it should look good from all angles. For an unstaked, upright tree, choose a plant with a strong, straight central stem. Prune as needed, three or four times a year, except in late summer or early fall, when pruning will diminish bloom.

All tree-shaped rosemaries look best in containers. Keep them outdoors in a sunny location, except for a brief stint in the house for holiday decoration. Give them well-drained soil; keep it on the dry side, since plants can't tolerate soggy soil. This Mediterranean plant adapts well to the low-elevation West's mild climate and can thrive for years.

RUSS A. WIDSTRAND

TABLETOP CHRISTMAS TREE *is prostrate rosemary that has been staked and clipped into a cone shape.*

Additives your compost can live without

If your compost pile is slow to decompose, you may be tempted to try a compost activator—a powder promoted and sold to speed up the decomposition of leaves and other materials. Before you buy it, though, consider the advice of University of California Cooperative Extension staff.

"Gardeners would be better off saving their money," says Dennis Pittenger of the Department of Botany and Plant Sciences at UC Riverside. "The microorganisms introduced by activators are already present in the plants and soil introduced to the compost. The claim that compost activators get your pile cooking fast won't overcome improper management of the pile."

"Adding an activator is like adding a grain of yeast to bread that is already leavened," adds Jim Downer, farm adviser for Ventura and Santa Barbara counties.

Both agree that the key to a fast-acting pile is the proper balance of raw materials, moisture, and aeration. The pile should include equal parts by volume of dried, brown carbon-rich materials (dried leaves, straw) and fresh, green material high in nitrogen (fresh lawn clippings). Ingredients should be chopped or shredded into small pieces, about ¾ inch or less. The ideal volume for the pile is 1 cubic yard (3 feet by 3 feet by 3 feet). Wet the pile as you build it, and rewet it each time you turn it; keep it moist, not soggy. To ensure aeration and thoroughly process the raw materials, turn the compost weekly.

California plants to know and grow

Botanically speaking, California is perhaps the richest state in the nation: more kinds of plants grow wild here than anywhere else in the country. Now, after 10 years in the works, 200 authors, and the cooperation and assistance of nearly 2,000 friends and supporters, a book is available that describes nearly 8,000 kinds of native and naturalized plants that grow wild in the Golden State. *The Jepson Manual: Higher Plants of California,* edited by James C. Hickman (University of California Press, Berkeley and Los Angeles, 1993; $65), is a massive work (1,400 pages) that's intended to be useful to botanists, native plant enthusiasts, and home gardeners alike.

The heart of this comprehensive reference is a plant encyclopedia. Descriptions include information about horticultural value, rarity, weediness, and plant toxicity. Line drawings are lavishly used.

Native plants deemed worthy of garden use are indicated by a small flower symbol following the plant description. This symbol followed by the word TRY indicates that a plant is attractive and worth a try in home gardens but hasn't proved itself there yet.

To save space, abbreviations are used for cultural information; for example, DRN means needs excellent drainage, and DRY indicates that the plant dislikes summer water. Regions where plants are likely to succeed are keyed to climate zones in the *Sunset Western Garden Book,* with the most favorable zones listed in boldface type.

Beginners will find the glossary and the pronunciation guide to botanical names especially useful. *The Jepson Manual* is available at bookstores.

Hanging a Christmas cactus

Long-lived, easy to grow, prolific bloomer: it's little wonder that Christmas cactus (*Schlumbergera bridgesii*) is such a dearly loved house plant. As shown at right, it grows happily in a hanging pot in Marietta and Ernie O'Byrne's house in Eugene, Oregon. Hanging baskets are perfect for these sprawling plants. If you hang them near a window (in summer, this one enjoys the dappled shade of bigleaf maples outside), they're often exposed to more light than they'd get sitting on a table. And the branches can droop, allowing the vivid flowers to dangle at eye level.

To keep this plant looking its best, the O'Byrnes treat it well. They water it regularly. To keep a bumper crop of flowers coming, they feed it with a complete liquid fertilizer (such as 10-10-10) monthly, except when the plant is in bloom. They pick off faded flowers, and snip off branch segments that grow too far or too fast.

The plant is growing in a rich indoor potting mix, and gets repotted to a larger container when needed (every three to four years).

Christmas cactus are available in nurseries (and even some grocery stores) this month.

MICHAEL THOMPSON

MORE THAN *two decades old, this Christmas cactus thrives in a hanging basket in a west-facing window. Its weekly drink gets poured into an oversize plastic saucer beneath.*

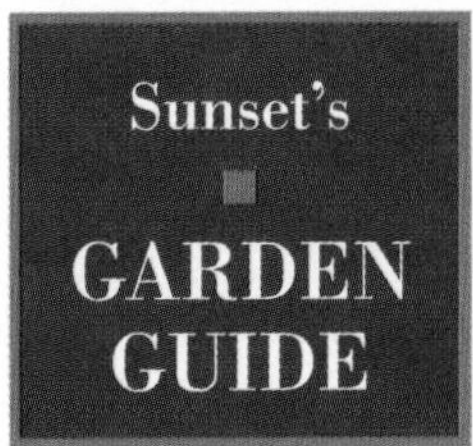

Don't trash the Christmas tree

Drive down any street in suburbia after the holidays and you'll likely see plenty of Christmas trees, stripped of their trimmings and languishing on the curb beside the garbage cans.

But cut trees can have a useful life in the garden long after their moment of glory indoors. In cold-winter climates, cut off the needle-clad branches and place them over tender plants to protect them from winter cold snaps. Saw the thick part of the trunk into firewood, or find out if your disposal service has a tree recycling program. If it doesn't, ask who does. If you can't find one, rent a chipper with your neighbors and grind all your trees on the same day. Use the grindings immediately for mulch, or let the pile rot for later use as soil amendment.

Dudleyas for shape, color, texture

Dudleyas are striking plants with rosette-forming succulent leaves. In the wild, these natives to western North America often grow on steep, rocky slopes. In the garden, they're especially handsome in containers and rock gardens, or growing out of pockets in garden walls.

Several gardenworthy dudleyas are available. Elegant (though somewhat temperamental) *D. arizonica* grows in clusters of 8- to 12-inch rosettes; the attractive powdery-coated leaves look as though brushed with chalk. *D. brittonii* has broad 1½-foot-wide rosettes of green to gray leaves that gradually lengthen into short, thick trunks up to 2 feet high. *D. pulverulenta,* with broad, chalky white leaves, forms a single large rosette a foot or more across; its coral red flowers bloom on long flower stems. *D. virens* has green strap-shaped leaves.

All dudleyas require rich, well-drained soil, and most prefer light shade, especially inland. Dudleyas are very drought resistant, although they look best with occasional water in summer. When you plant them, tilt them slightly to allow water to run off their centers. Also avoid overhead irrigation: it's bad for the plants and removes the chalk from some species.

For the best selection, check botanic gardens or nurseries that specialize in native plants (it's illegal to harvest dudleya from public land). Santa Barbara Botanic Garden has a new display featuring 38 species of dudleya; plants are labeled for identification. The garden's nursery also sells dudleyas; a 1-gallon container costs $6 to $8. For botanic garden information and nursery hours, call (805) 682-4726.

CHAD SLATTERY

DUDLEYA ARIZONICA *thrives in a container in light shade.*

Quick winter crop: mustard

A fast and gratifying crop that mild-winter gardeners can sow now is broad-leafed Oriental mustard (*Brassica juncea rugosa*). It thrives in the cool of such winters; its large, attractive, deeply colored leaves are good to eat sautéed or chopped in stir-fry.

You can sow seeds indoors and transplant seedlings in garden beds now, but it's easier to sow seeds directly where you want plants to grow. Optimum growth occurs at temperatures between 60° and 65°, but plants are quite frost-hardy. Later in spring, as days become warmer and longer, plants bolt and produce seed stalks.

Sow seeds ½ inch deep in rows 15 to 24 inches apart. Thin seedlings to about 4 inches apart. Maintain soil moisture and watch for aphids and cabbage worms (use insecticidal soap on aphids, *Bacillus thuringiensis* on cabbage worms).

You can begin to harvest leaves in only six weeks, or once they reach 6 to 8 inches long. Pull out the entire plant at once or harvest only the young, lower leaves continuously through the season.

If you sow seeds right away, you can harvest 'Osaka Purple-leaved' by mid-January; allow 45 days, but weather will speed up or slow down growth. It grows to a foot or taller with white leaf stalks, which are also good to eat. Large leaves are some 2 feet long. 'Red Giant' looks similar to it but has a milder flavor.

Seeds of these and other mustards are available from The Cook's Garden, Box 535, Londonderry, VT 05148, (802) 824-3400 (catalog $1); Nichols Garden Nursery, 1190 N. Pacific Hwy., Albany, OR 97321, (503) 928-9280 (catalog free); and The Redwood City Seed Co., Box 361, Redwood City, CA 94064 (catalog $1).

WILLIAM D. ADAMS

YOUNG LEAVES *of 'Osaka Purple-leaved' mustard are tinged purple-red.*

MICHAEL THOMPSON

GLISTENING LEAVES *and bright berries cover Stranvaesia davidiana, which grows best west of the Cascades.*

Why don't we see more of it?

When it comes to handsome evergreen shrubs with red berries, few plants can match *Stranvaesia davidiana.* In time, this plant (pictured above right) forms a massive mound that can grow as tall as 6 feet and spread 20 feet. Leaves are a waxy, rich green; when cold weather hits, they can turn purplish bronze. White flower clusters appear in June. Bright red fruits, a bit bigger than holly berries, follow.

Stranvaesia grows well in the rich acid soils of the Northwest and Northern California. It likes full sun but will flourish in shade. For maximum flower and fruit crops and shiniest foliage, water it during driest weather and fertilize it just as you would rhododendrons. Give stranvaesia room to spread out, and go light on pruning. Now is a perfect time to groom the plant; cut branches will do well indoors in arrangements.

This plant is difficult to find in nurseries. Either ask your nursery to hunt one down or shop at plant sales of arboretums and horticultural clubs and societies. One Northwest source is Hart's Nursery in Mount Vernon, Washington.

Come cut your tree at my house

Take a stroll around Grethe and Soren Vestergaard's garden near Beaverton, Oregon, and you'll see lots of beautiful noble firs growing there, all 8 feet tall or less. The Vestergaards like the handsome symmetrical shape of these trees—but they like them garden scale.

So each year they tag the trees that are getting too tall. Shortly after Thanksgiving, they cut one tree for their living room, then invite friends over for dinner and to cut more trees for their own homes. Away go the happy guests with their trees tied to the tops of their cars.

As soon as possible, the Vestergaards plant new seedlings from 1-gallon cans; each one goes next to the stump of a harvested tree (or fills in another bare spot in the garden). The Vestergaards normally plant 30 new trees each year in their 2½-acre garden, so the tradition is an easy one to perpetuate.

Holiday events in Eastern Washington

If you're not quite certain where the Yakima Area Arboretum is, you can't miss it at Christmastime. Its western boundary is the freeway (Interstate 82). And in early December, local Kiwanians will turn on 10,000 lights that decorate a 65-foot spruce near the highway. The lights will blaze through New Year's. This month is an excellent time to view all the deciduous trees showing off their handsome forms in their seasonal naked-

ness, perhaps with a dusting of snow.

In mid-December, Friends of the Arboretum and the cosponsoring Cascadians celebrate too, with a Luminaria—a mile-long walk through the wintry landscape by candlelight. Candles will burn along pathways from 5 P.M. until 8 the following morning. After the walk, warm up with hot cider in Jewett Interpretive Center, festive with banks of poinsettias. The Tree House is a great stop for Christmas garden gifts—quality tools, garden art, and books.

If you wish to join Friends of the Arboretum or offer a membership as a gift, cost is $25 for individuals, $50 for families, $10 for students and seniors. To reach the arboretum, take exit 34 off I-82. Go east on Nob Hill Boulevard; the arboretum is the second turn to the left.

Red berries for the holidays

For attractive holiday berries that last well into the new year, it's tough to beat evergreen cotoneasters. Although these rugged, small-leafed plants are most often thought of as practical, low-maintenance shrubs or ground covers, some varieties grow taller with a more upright habit. These can be easily trained into stately trees with arching branches.

Tiny white or pinkish spring blooms are followed in fall or winter by abundant orange or red berries—loved by birds as well as holiday wreath makers.

Among the tallest varieties readily available, *C. parneyi* has willowy branches that stretch to 8 feet. Stouter *C. glaucophyllus,* with orange berries, may reach 6 feet. Two cotoneasters suitable for containers on a patio are *C. dammeri* 'Coral Beauty', with coral berries and prostrate branches that spread to several feet, and *C. congestus* 'Likiang', which grows up to 3 feet tall with red berries and weeping branches.

All cotoneasters produce better crops of berries if you plant them in poor soil—such as on dry slopes—rather than in moist garden soil. They prefer sunny locations. They're sold in gallon containers and as patio trees and espaliers.

Read about cotoneasters' Northwest Christmas performance on page 309.

The woodsy primrose

By now most nurseries in the low elevations of California and Arizona are offering primrose plants—to be set out for display in late winter and early spring. English primroses and fairy primroses are probably the most shown. But consider a third kind, *Primula obconica*: it blooms longer than the others, it's more heat tolerant, and its flowers come in Easter egg hues.

A bedding plant in mild-winter areas, this one has a woodsy look. Apple green leaves are large and roundish with minute, soft hairs (which irritate the skin of some people; when planting, wear a long-sleeved shirt and gloves). They combine attractively in lightly shaded garden beds with baby's tears or blue star creeper. (In cold-winter areas, grow this primrose in pots in a protected spot.)

Flowers are $1\frac{1}{2}$ to 2 inches across in clusters atop foot-tall stems. Standard colors include white, pink, lavender, and reddish purple. New colors to look for include (separate or mixed) apricot, blue, carmine, lavender, and red.

Blooming plants are available now in nurseries; a 4-inch container costs about $2. Plant in moist, rich soil. Snails and slugs love all primroses; set out traps or bait. ■

By Kimberly Chrisman, Nancy Davidson, Richard Dunmire, Steven R. Lorton, Michael MacCaskey, Lynn Ocone

SAXON HOLT

PRIMULA OBCONICA *in one of its many flower colors. It is characteristic for mature leaves to be roundish with overlapping lobes, as you see at lower left.*

WEST OF THE CASCADES,
see items marked with a **W.**

EAST OF THE CASCADES,
see items marked with an **E.**

December Checklist

HERE IS WHAT NEEDS DOING

☐ **ADD TO COMPOST. W, E:** If you have any time left this month to garden, now is a good time to prune and clean up wind-downed debris. Add it to the compost pile along with spent Christmas greens.

☐ **CHECK STORED BULBS. W, E:** Throw out any bulbs (except dahlias) that show signs of rot. Cut rotten spots out of dahlias, then dust the opening with sulfur and store bulbs separately. If you sprinkle water on shriveling bulbs, corms, or tubers, they'll usually plump up again.

☐ **GROUND-LAYER EVERGREENS. W:** You can increase evergreen shrubs by ground layering. Scrape away a fingernail-size bit of bark on a small lower limb, treat it with rooting hormone, and stake it to the ground (or put a stone atop it to keep it in contact with the soil). By the end of next summer, the branch should have a self-sustaining clump of roots, and you can sever and transplant it.

☐ **MAINTAIN HOLIDAY PLANTS. W, E:** Give them good light, keep them away from drafts and heater vents, and don't let them dry out. Remove any decorative foil from the pot, or perforate its bottom and set the pot in a saucer.

☐ **PREPARE CACTUS FOR BLOOM. W, E:** To stimulate spring-flowering indoor cactus plants into setting buds for spring flowers, keep them cool and on the dry side from mid-December to February. In February, begin feeding with quarter-strength liquid fertilizer every second watering.

☐ **PROPAGATE HARDWOODS. W:** Aucuba, barberry, forsythia, holly, honeysuckle, hydrangea, rose, rose of Sharon, spiraea, and weigela can be propagated from cuttings now. Take pencil-size tip cuttings, dip cut ends in rooting hormone, and plant in a potting mix (you may want to mix equal parts potting mix and sand). Keep the rooting medium constantly moist. A pot of cuttings with instructions on how to care for and later transplant them is a thoughtful and interesting Christmas gift.

☐ **PRUNE FOR HOLIDAY DECORATIONS. W, E:** Follow pruning rules when you cut boughs from conifers and other evergreens for wreaths and swags. Remove diseased or injured branches first, then cut those that cross or are closely parallel. Make cuts so you don't leave stubs, and angle your cuts so that they aren't visible from eye level.

☐ **ROTATE INDOOR PLANTS. W, E:** For even growth, give indoor plants a quarter turn every week. A chalk mark on the pot helps you keep track.

☐ **SAND ICY WALKWAYS AND PATIOS. W, E:** Unlike salt, sand isn't harmful to plants, so use as much as you need. You can hose it off, right into adjacent beds, when weather warms. Don't use sand on decks; it scars the wood.

☐ **SHOP FOR CAMELLIAS. W:** Nurseries have a good selection of winter-flowering plants now. They make spectacular Christmas gifts. Or you might want to buy one to set in a highly visible place outdoors for the holidays. You can put it in the ground in January or February.

☐ **WATER. W, E:** When temperatures are above freezing, water spots in the garden that look dry—especially pots and plantings under eaves that are sheltered from rain. In a hard freeze, plants that have been well watered stand a better chance of surviving.
—S. R. L.

IN HIGH ELEVATIONS and intermountain areas of California, and east of the Sierra, see items marked with an **H.**

IN LOW ELEVATIONS of Northern California, see items marked with an **L.**

December Checklist

HERE IS WHAT NEEDS DOING

☐ **APPLY DORMANT SPRAY. L:** To smother overwintering insects such as aphids, mites, and scale, apply horticultural oil to roses and deciduous flowering and fruit trees after leaves have fallen. Rake out and dispose of leaves. For complete coverage, spray branches, crotches, trunks, and ground out to the drip lines.

☐ **BUY GIFT PLANTS. H, L:** Nurseries should be well stocked this month with plenty of flowering plants for gifts and decorations. Choices include amaryllis, azaleas, Christmas cactus, cyclamen, paper white narcissus, and orchids. Besides traditional red poinsettias, look for miniature poinsettias and kinds with pastel blooms, such as 'Marble', 'Lemon Drop', and 'Pink Peppermint'.

☐ **CLEAN UP. H, L:** Remove dead foliage and stems from dormant perennials such as *Salvia patens* and *S. uliginosa*. Cut back chrysanthemums to about 6 inches. Chop the prunings into tiny pieces using loppers or a shredder; most of it can be composted.

☐ **KEEP CHRISTMAS TREES FRESH. H, L:** The best way to prolong the freshness of a cut tree is to trim an inch or so off the bottom of the trunk when you get home, place the tree in a stand that holds water, and keep the reservoir full (check daily the first week). The day before moving it indoors, wash off foliage with the hose. Living trees should be kept indoors two weeks at the most. Keep all trees away from heaters and avoid hot-burning tree lights.

☐ **PLANT BERRIES AND VEGETABLES. L:** Late in the month, bare-root plants start arriving in nurseries. Choices include artichokes, grapes, fruit trees, raspberries, strawberries, and roses. Among the fruit trees are tasty 'Fuji' and 'Braeburn' apple. Buy and plant early while roots are still fresh. If soil is too wet, heel in or plant in containers; roots must stay moist.

☐ **PROTECT AGAINST FROST. H, L:** Killing frosts often hit this month. Watch out for still, starry nights, and be prepared to protect tender plants with sheets, tarps, big cardboard boxes, or plastic (held up with poles, not draped over leaves). Plants must be adequately watered to survive a freeze; drought-stressed plants are more susceptible to damage.

☐ **PRUNE FOR HOLIDAY GREENS. H, L:** Long-lasting choices include evergreen magnolia, juniper, pine, and redwood. Deodar cedar, spruce, and Western hemlock drop needles sooner.

☐ **SPRAY FOR PEACH DISEASES. L:** To control peach blight and peach leaf curl, spray trees with fixed copper (in wettable powder form) or lime sulfur. Repeat spray in January or early February.

☐ **TEND GIFT PLANTS. H, L:** Place plants in a cool spot with bright, indirect light away from drafts and furnace vents. Don't let them sit in water; remove any decorative foil from the pots, or perforate the bottoms and set the pots in a saucer. Feed every two weeks with high-nitrogen fertilizer.—*K. C.*

December Checklist

HERE IS WHAT NEEDS DOING

☐ **CARE FOR LIVING CHRISTMAS TREES.** Even if you buy a living tree early in the month, when nurseries have good supplies, keep it outdoors until shortly before the holidays. Water regularly; don't let the rootball dry out. Indoors, place the tree away from heating vents and fireplaces. Move it outside again after no more than two weeks indoors.

☐ **CHOOSE CAMELLIAS. C:** Early in the month is the best time to choose plants for the flower color you want. You'll find the last of autumn-blooming sasanquas and the early japonicas in bloom now.

☐ **CLEAN UP.** Remove dead foliage and stems from dormant perennials. Rake up fallen leaves. Chop debris into small pieces and add to the compost pile.

☐ **NURTURE GIFT PLANTS.** Remove wrapping paper or foil so water won't collect at the bottom of the pot. Put plants indoors where they'll get natural light but no direct sun. Keep them away from heating vents and warm spots like the top of the television. Once blooms on azaleas, cyclamen, and kalanchoe fade, put plants outside if they are hardy in your zone.

☐ **PLANT ANNUALS AND PERENNIALS. C, L:** If soil isn't soggy, plant calendula, candytuft, cyclamen, dianthus, Iceland poppy, pansy, primroses, snapdragons, and viola. In frost-free areas, try bedding begonias and cineraria.

☐ **PLANT BULBS. C, L:** Put in anemone, Asiatic lily, daffodil, gladiolus, and ranunculus bulbs as soon as you get them home. Also plant prechilled tulip bulbs. **H:** If the ground is still workable, plant any leftover bulbs; they may bloom late.

☐ **PLANT NATIVES. C, L:** Unless soil is soggy, early this month is still a good time to plant California natives. If rains are light, water regularly to get plants established.

☐ **PRUNE.** Cut branches of holly, juniper, nandina, pine, pittosporum, podocarpus, pyracantha, and toyon for holiday decorations. Prune plants to shape at the same time. Cut to side branches or buds, trim overlong branches, and thin out dense centers.

☐ **RECYCLE CHRISTMAS TREES.** Many cities now sponsor programs that convert Christmas trees into compost. Usually, you drop the tree off at a specific site, where city crews handle chipping and composting; some cities return it as mulch. Some cities may also offer curbside pickup; check with your disposal service.

☐ **SHOP FOR BARE-ROOT PLANTS. C, L:** Nurseries sell bare-root cane berries, fruit trees, grapes, roses, and perennial vegetables such as asparagus, horseradish, and rhubarb.

☐ **SPRAY DORMANT PLANTS.** As soon as leaves fall, spray roses and deciduous flowering and fruit trees with dormant oil to smother overwintering insect pests such as scale, mites, and aphids. For diseases such as brown rot, peach leaf curl, and shot hole, mix lime sulfur or fixed copper into the oil. Spray branches, crotches, trunks, and ground beneath the trees' drip lines.—*L. O.*

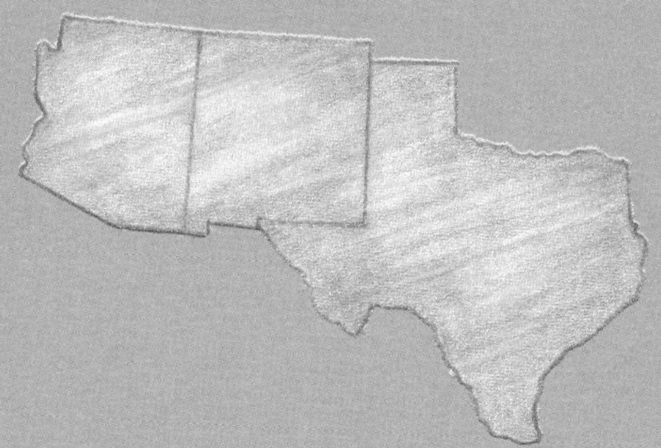

December Checklist

HERE IS WHAT NEEDS DOING

☐ **APPLY DORMANT SPRAY.** As soon as leaves fall, spray roses and deciduous flowering and fruit trees with dormant oil to smother overwintering insect eggs, and pests such as scale, mites, and aphids. Spray enough to drench both the plant and the soil around it out to the drip line.

☐ **CARE FOR LIVING CHRISTMAS TREES.** Place tree in a bright, cool location away from heater vents. Water to keep soil moist. Move tree outdoors as soon as possible, preferably after a week. High-desert tip: If you're going to plant the tree after Christmas, dig the hole now before soil freezes. Cover backfill with a plastic tarp.

☐ **FERTILIZE DECIDUOUS FRUIT TREES.** They benefit most from fertilizer applied this month. Four-year-old trees need about 9 pounds of a 10-10-10 fertilizer in winter, 3 pounds after harvest.

☐ **MULCH.** In high-desert regions, cover perennials with a thick layer of coarse mulch. The mulch will keep soil from alternately freezing and thawing and prevent frost heaving.

☐ **PLANT ANNUALS.** Still available in nursery cell-packs are calendula, candytuft, clarkia, cornflower, dianthus, Iceland poppy, larkspur, pansies, petunia, primroses, snapdragon, stock, sweet alyssum, sweet pea, and violas.

☐ **PLANT BARE-ROOT.** Bare-root cane berries, fruit trees, and ornamental plants show up in nurseries this month—and cost less than when sold in containers. Prepare planting holes before shopping. To get the best selection and healthiest plants, buy them as soon as possible. Look for plump, unbruised trunks and branches, and full—not shriveled—root systems. Don't buy plants that have started sending out leaves. Plant immediately once you get home.

☐ **PLANT BULBS AND CHILLED TULIPS.** Many nurseries still have some daffodils, hyacinths, and narcissus, and there's time to plant them. It's too late to plant unchilled tulips because they need six to eight weeks in the refrigerator before planting. But if you have already chilled some of these, plant now.

☐ **SHOP FOR ROSES.** Bare-root plants are available at nurseries (or by mail) this month. Plant soon after getting them home. Soak the entire plant in a bucket of water while you dig the hole. Then set bud union (swollen section on lower stem) just at or slightly above soil surface.

☐ **SOW SEEDS OF PEPPERS, TOMATOES.** In the low desert and in warmer areas of the intermediate desert, get a jump on the season by starting pepper and tomato seeds indoors in small containers; set in a warm spot by a bright window or under fluorescent lights. Seedlings will be ready to plant outdoors by late February or early March.

☐ **WATER.** In the high desert, early December is usually very dry. Plants set out last season are likely to need a good soaking every other week or so. Also, established plants such as dwarf Alberta spruce, holly, and mahonia benefit from antidesiccant spray to prevent winter leaf burn.—*M. M.*

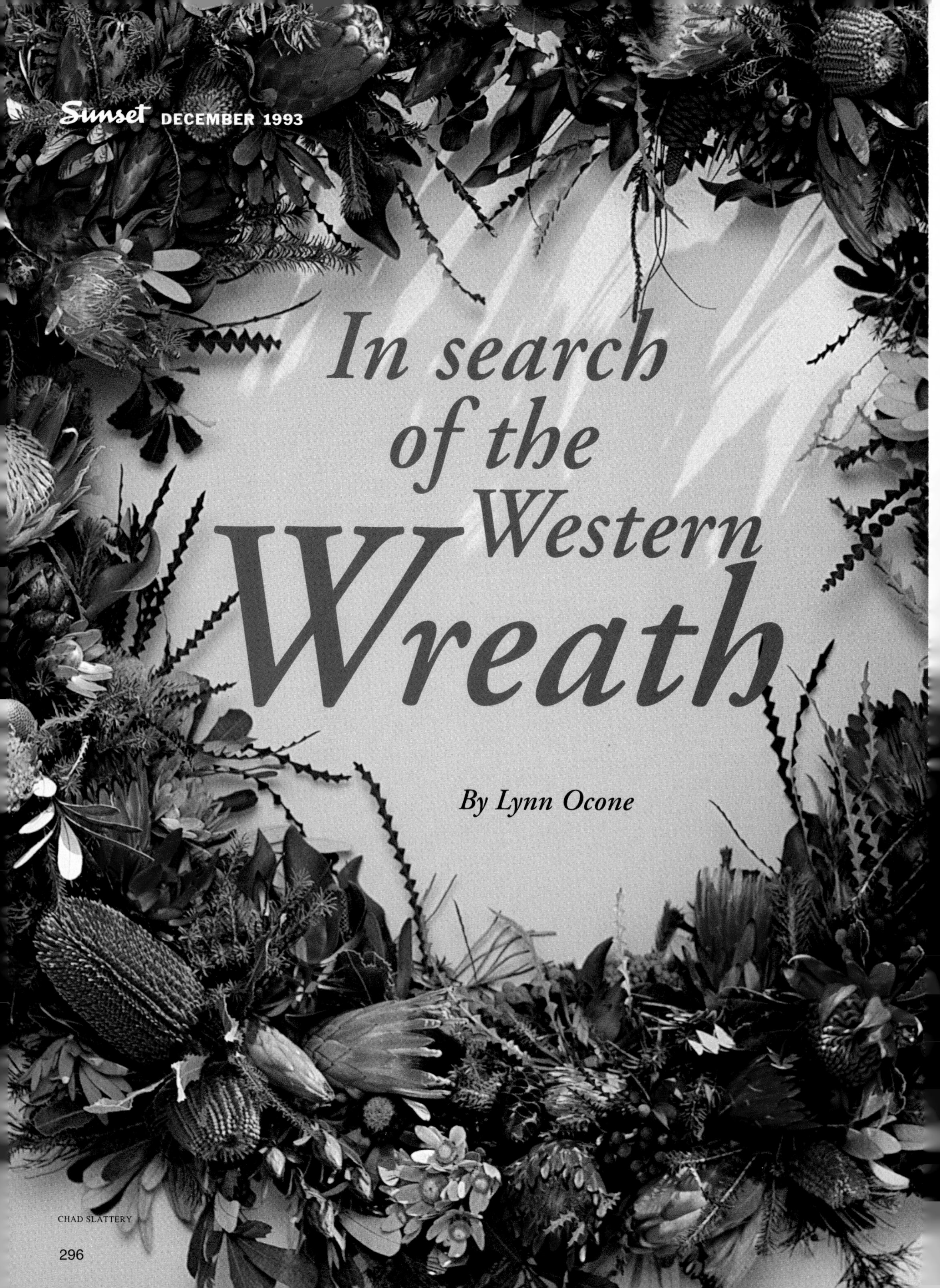

In search of the Western Wreath

By Lynn Ocone

CHAD SLATTERY

Northwest woods

Loosely woven grapevines form wreath base. Evergreens, cones, moss, and sword ferns provide regional accents.

DON NORMARK

"Deck the halls with boughs of holly": Regardless of your cultural or religious upbringing, there's no denying the universal appeal of this midwinter sentiment, best exemplified by the wreath. For many, wreaths symbolize the instinctive urge to feather our nests, to freshen up the old cave with a bit of scented green.

In the West, green is only one of the colors available to the amateur or professional wreath maker. In addition to ubiquitous holly, Western wreaths can be trimmed with clusters of pink proteas, strings of tawny pine cones, garlands of dried red chilies, and bouquets of fragrant purple lavender. Some of these plants are native, others are imports, but all grow well in the West. As a result, the colors, textures, and smells of Western wreaths don't just evoke a particular region—be it Washington's damp forests or California's sun-drenched coast—they also conjure the abundance of the West.

Exotic California

Proteas (and relatives) emblazon a 44-inch base of woven honeysuckle. The flowers hold their color for weeks and dry beautifully in place.

Tips from the pros

Perhaps the most important thing about wreaths, though, is that just about anyone can make one—which is not to say that all wreaths are created equal. That's why we asked several artists to give us something to aspire to. A

Apples and oaks

Native coast live oak conceals a 12-inch wire frame in a wreath by Françoise Kirkman. Kumquats add color. (Instructions for a similar wreath begin on page 302.)

NORMAN A. PLATE

few of them constructed large and complex circles of exotic materials; others were satisfied by smaller rings made of clippings from their gardens. All had a ball doing it, and agreed to share their tips and ideas.

Landscape horticulturist Roger Boddaert created the exuberant exotic California wreath on page 297 out of flowers, foliage, and seed pods exclusive to the protea family (there are 47 kinds). All of the plants used were taken from gardens and farms in San Diego County; many were grown at Boddaert's own backyard protea farm in Fallbrook. Although some people associate these bizarre flowers with the tropics, Boddaert's neighbors are more familiar with the plant, thanks to the protea farms that dot the slopes of the county's steep, dry hills. For Boddaert, wreaths are "an appendage of nature," and wreath making is a way of sharing with others the beauty he experiences daily in his landscaping profession.

Working out of her home in Issaquah, Washington, floral designer Sylvia Breece Willard created the traditional-looking Northwest woods wreath on page 297. This technical tour-de-force measures 6 feet across

Southwest sizzler

Chili peppers rule on this Sante Fe wreath, which also features gourds, ornamental corn, and pine cones.

DON NORMARK

Desert harvest

Bright color from cockscomb, safflower, California pepper berries, pequin chilies, and pomegranates combines with eucalyptus leaves and raffia.

Soft and fragrant

Lavender and lamb's ears give color and scent to this unusual wreath by self-proclaimed "wildcrafter" Sandy Worth.

STEVEN R. LORTON

Yakima hawktail

Native American Leo Adams made his wreath out of dried weeds and folded paper (to symbolize feathers).

CHARLES MANN

Stocking supplement

Some folks decorate their wreaths as if they were mini–Christmas trees.

Mild-climate medley

Eucalyptus leaves dominate this citrus-studded wreath. Exposed honeysuckle base adds a spiky texture.

CHAD SLATTERY

STEPHEN CRIDLAND

Status symbol

What becomes a legend most? Why, a wreath tied to the front of your Benz, of course!

Western wreaths are made of more than just pine boughs (although they're okay, too)

PETER CHRISTIANSEN

and is constructed of mixed evergreens wired to a loosely woven grapevine base. Sword ferns, moss, and pine cones were incorporated as accents. "I chose natural materials," she says, "so when you look at the wreath you feel the forest."

Phoenix interior designer Luis Corona also stuck to fresh material. He created his elaborate 40-inch desert harvest wreath on page 299 from desert-grown plants, including the pink fan-shaped cockscomb cultivated in his garden. Corona sells custom-made wreaths year-round at his interior design store, Casa del Encanto. "Most of

the plants I use originally came from somewhere else, since native plants are mostly cactus," says Corona. "But," he adds, "with a little water and fertilzer, almost anything grows here."

The sweet-scented mild-climate medley wreath of citrus and eucalyptus on page 299 practically shouts "Southern California." Once exotic imports, these stalwart trees are now integral to the region's landscape. That suits designer Walter Hubert, of Silver Birches florist shop in Pasadena, just fine. His familiarity with citrus and eucalyptus (he's worked with the plants his whole professional life) helps him approach wreath making from an artistic rather than a botanic point of view, choosing plant combinations as an artist would colors on a palette.

The basics

All wreaths start with a base, sometimes entirely concealed by decorative materials, sometimes showing through to add color and texture, as in the Northwest woods and mild-climate medley wreaths. You can make your own base by weaving or tying together the branches of any thin, supple plant, or you can buy a ready-made base of plant material, wire, or plastic foam. Florists and craft supply stores offer good selections. Some Western plants commonly used for bases include grapevine, honeysuckle, and willow.

The fresh greenery, fruits, cones, seeds, and berries in the assortment on pages 300 and 301 were collected from landscapes around the West, and are just a sampling of materials that work well in wreaths. You'd probably be surprised by what you can find in your own backyard, but if it's short on variety, you might want to consider a trip to the grocery store for a few can't-miss accents—among them, dried ornamental corn, lady apples, and kumquats. While it is tempting to gather plants from the wild, it is not always legal, so be sure to check local regulations before collecting on public land.

RENEE LYNN

Craftsman at Wente Brothers Winery in Livermore, California, weaves fresh-cut vines from dormant grapes.

Finally, be sure to experiment with your favorite materials to learn how they dry before gathering large quantities to make your wreath. Some plants shrink and others may turn brittle. Proteas are examples of plants that dry beautifully, better, perhaps, than you'd think at first glance. As a rule of thumb, wreaths made out of freshly cut pine branches can last six to eight weeks if hung outdoors in cool weather.

Making your own

Designer Françoise Kirkman created the 13-inch willow-base wreath (at right above) and the 12-inch wire-frame wreath (at right below) using materials mostly from her Northern California garden. You can substitute plants common to your neighborhood.

In addition to a base and plenty of plant material, you'll need a spool of florist's wire, scissors or wire cutters, floral picks with attached wire to hold stems of fresh fruit (see top right photo on facing page), and a decorative bow. For more detailed instructions, follow the construction steps at right. ■

Willow base adds character to kumquat wreath

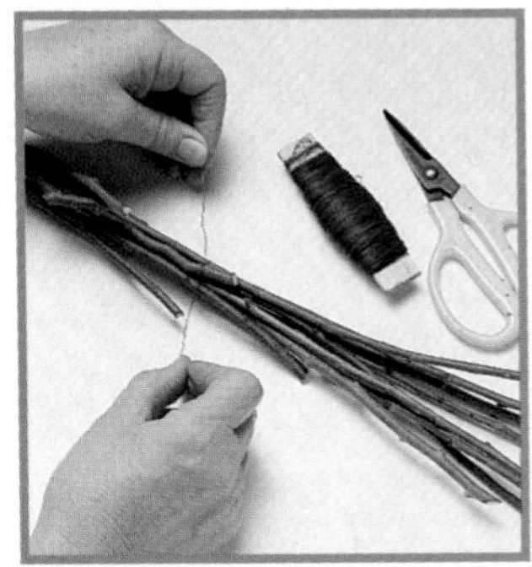

Stagger 15- to 20-inch-long branches of willow (¼-inch diameter or smaller) to form a 55-inch-long "rope" about 2 inches in diameter. Bind with wire.

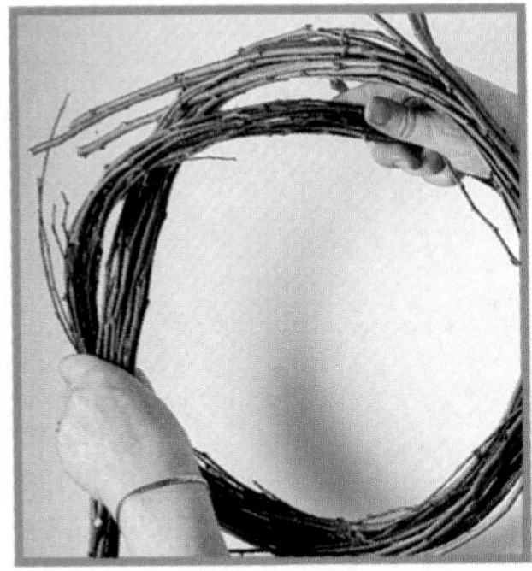

Carefully bend and weave together the ends of your willow rope to form a circular base about 13 inches across. Tie the ends together with florist's wire.

Oak clippings and branches hide wire frame

Attach oak cuttings to frame with florist's wire. Leave wire on the spool to make wrapping of other cuttings easier.

Lay foliage of second cutting over stem of first and wrap with wire. Work in one direction until the frame is covered.

Wrap wire around base at several points to secure loose ends (left). Insert branches of Myers asparagus or other decorative foliage into openings between strands.

Attach kumquats to floral picks by wrapping wire around the fruit's stem. Leave foliage on some. Insert pointed ends into wreath base, then attach bow with florist's wire.

Use raffia or wire to attach a moss-covered branch to the back of the frame. Extend end of the branch beyond the foliage.

Add holly, oak galls, and, if you like, fruit. You can insert them into oak cuttings, or attach with floral picks (as shown above).

California kumquat

In just a few hours and using only three plants, you can make this striking wreath. It will stay green indoors for about two weeks.

PETER CHRISTIANSEN

Camellia blooms for Christmas

BRING WINTER COLOR TO YOUR GARDEN BY SETTING OUT PLANTS THIS MONTH

Luscious blooms unfurl on many camellias this month in the mild-winter West, just in time for the holidays. Their delicate rounded and often frilled petals range from pale shell pink, rich rose, and vibrant white splashed with scarlet to fiery orange-red surrounding starbursts of yellow stamens. They stand out as visual poetry against glossy, dark green foliage, especially when flecked with raindrops.

Native to mild-winter areas of Asia, camellias thrive outdoors along the Pacific Coast. Despite their tender, hothouse looks, these plants are rugged; once established,

ROBIN HIGGIN

'Alba Plena'

'Rainbow'

'Nuccio's Carousel'

'Chandleri Elegans'

'Magnoliaeflora'

'Debutante'

DECEMBER FLOWERS
Arrangement of camellia flowers in confetti colors and various shapes shows some of the many kinds that bloom in December. At left, young plant in container dresses up front entry for the holidays.

'Freedom Bell'
'Shibori Egao'
'Shishi Gashira'
'Nuccio's gem'
'Daikagura'
'Coral Delight'
'Wildfire'
'Egao'
'Yuletide'
'Adolphe Audusson Variegated'

most camellias thrive on surprisingly little water.

Of the many kinds that grow in the West and bloom between September and March, the ones that bloom mostly in December are *C. japonica* (which typically grow into 6- to 10-foot shrubs or small trees) and *C. sasanqua* (versatile, smaller-leafed shrubs that vary in habit from bushy and upright to floppy and vinelike). The chart at right lists 16 varieties that bloom most reliably in December, according to nurserymen and home growers we interviewed. The taller ones make handsome hedges; smaller ones (mostly sasanquas) can be trained as espaliers or grown in pots.

This month, while camellias are in bloom, is the best time to shop for them. The plants make elegant gifts for gardening friends or for your own garden.

STARTING CAMELLIAS RIGHT

Plant camellias in a spot that's sheltered from hottest sun and drying winds (although some kinds, noted on the chart, are more sun tolerant than others). Young plants grow and flower better in part shade. Tall plants in old gardens survive (but don't thrive) in full sun; their broad canopies shade their roots.

Provide well-drained soil that is rich in organic matter. Never plant camellias so the trunk base is below the soil line, and never permit soil to wash over and cover the base. Keep roots cool with a 1- to 2-inch-thick mulch (apply it away from the trunk).

If your water is high in salts, give plants a deep soaking at least twice in summer to wash accumulated salts past the root zone.

In spring and fall, apply a commercial camellia fertilizer according to package directions, and prune just after flowering only to control size and shape. ■

By Michael MacCaskey

December-blooming camellias:

Here are 16 favorites

WILLIAM B. DEWEY

IN LIGHTLY SHADED GARDEN, *bright flowers show off handsomely against lustrous deep green leaves of 'Chandleri Elegans'. Arching branches give this graceful shrub a loose, informal look.*

White

'Alba Plena' (*C. japonica*). Double 2½-inch blooms on 8- to 10-foot plants.

'Nuccio's Gem' (*C. japonica*). White, beautifully petaled 3- to 4-inch double blooms of outstanding beauty and quality. A full, upright, and vigorous grower to 6 to 8 feet tall.

Pink and coral pink

'Chandleri Elegans' (*C. japonica*). Rose pink, anemone-like 3½-inch semidouble blooms splashed with white. Grows to 8 feet.

'Coral Delight' (*C. saluenensis* and *C. japonica* hybrid). Deep coral pink 3-inch semidouble blooms sometimes mottled with white; small, dark green leaves. Upright, bushy plant grows slowly to 6 to 7 feet.

'Debutante' (*C. japonica*). Light pink 3-inch peony-like blooms. One of the best all-round camellias. Grows 10 to 12 feet tall.

'Egao' (*C. sasanqua*). Deep pink 2½-inch semidouble blooms. Grows 6 to 8 feet tall. Sun-hardy.

'Magnoliaeflora' (*C. japonica*). Blush pink 3-inch semidouble blooms. Grows 6 to 10 feet tall.

'Nuccio's Carousel' (*C. japonica*). Soft pink 3-inch semidouble blooms with darker pink edges. Grows 6 to 8 feet tall.

'Rainbow' (*C. sasanqua*). White 2½-inch single blooms with red border on each petal. Grows 6 to 8 feet tall. Sun-hardy.

'Shibori Egao' (*C. sasanqua*). Deep pink, shatter-resistant 3-inch semidouble blooms variegated with white. Grows 6 to 8 feet tall. Sun-hardy.

Red or orange-red

'Adolphe Audusson Variegated' (*C. japonica*). Dark red 3½-inch semidouble blooms mottled with white. Grows 8 to 10 feet tall.

'Daikagura' (*C. japonica*). Bright rose red, peony-like 3- to 4-inch double blooms splotched with white. Grows 8 to 9 feet tall.

'Freedom Bell' (*C. saluenensis* and *C. japonica* hybrid). Bright red, bell-shaped 2½-inch semidouble blooms. Grows 6 to 8 feet tall.

'Shishi Gashira' (*C. hiemalis*, usually sold as *C. sasanqua*). Bright rose red 2½-inch double blooms. Reaches 2½ to 5 feet tall; good as espalier or vine. Sun-hardy.

'Wildfire' (*C. japonica*). Fiery orange-red 3½-inch semidouble blooms with yellow stamens. Grows 6 to 8 feet tall.

'Yuletide' (*C. sasanqua*). Brilliant orange-red 2-inch single blooms with bright yellow stamens. Compact, upright grower to 6 to 8 feet tall. Sun-hardy.

PETER CHRISTIANSEN

SUSPENDED ABOVE *a collection of orchids and hibiscus, halide light is bright enough to keep plants flowering for months.*

Plant lights for winter flowers

Here are options for plants of all sizes

FLOWERING INDOOR plants are most welcome in winter, when there's little in bloom outside. But to flower, house plants need plenty of light—a commodity that's in short supply during the dark days of winter.

That's where plant lights come in. Using low-intensity lights for small plants, or stronger, more expensive lights for larger ones, you can induce heavy winter flowering in everything from orchids to African violets.

KEEPING IT SIMPLE

Both fluorescent and incandescent lights are easy to find, and come in versions engineered for plants.

Fluorescents do the best overall job because they produce abundant light and little heat. The full-spectrum kind works best for flowering plants. For good results, use four 48-inch, 40-watt tubes in a fixture with a built-in reflector to increase the light that reaches plants. Put the fixture about a foot above the plants, and keep it on 16 hours per day. Because large fluorescent fixtures tend to block views of the plants underneath them, they're best used in elevated plant displays.

Incandescents can help with slightly taller plants, since they come in higher-intensity versions that bathe more of the plant in light. Use 150-watt bulbs, preferably shining on the plant at a 45° angle. Incandescents don't put out many lumens per watt: even powerful ones are only effective up to about 2 feet from the plant. Concentrating heat as well as light, they'll burn plants if they're placed too close.

BRINGING IN THE HEAVY ARTILLERY

To get bright light without the massiveness of fluorescent fixtures or the heat of incandescents, you'll need to turn to one of the high-tech options. In earlier days, high-intensity-discharge lights—halide, mercury vapor, and sodium—had to be purchased in pieces (separate fixtures, ballasts, and wires), then assembled by an electrician. Now such lights come complete and ready to plug in. They're installed either above a plant or angled at it from the best viewing side, since plants tend to face the light.

Halide light approaches the color of daylight and is the best all-around light source for plants: they look good under it and flower well. A 175-watt halide light suspended from the ceiling can induce flowering in desktop plants.

Bulbs alone cost $40 (175 watts) to $80 (1,000 watts), and they must be mounted in ballasted fixtures. With the most powerful lights, the heavy ballast sits on the floor, and the light hangs above the plants. Add in the cost of the fixtures, and the total runs from $165 to $300.

Mercandescent lights are mercury vapor lights that use an incandescent filament instead of a ballast. They also have phosphors added to the light to broaden the color spectrum for good plant flowering.

Available in 160- and 300-watt versions (about $70 and $100, respectively), they can be screwed into inexpensive conventional ceramic sockets (but check socket ratings: most are rated for 250 watts or less). Mercandescents put out more light per watt than incandescents, but not as much as halide or sodium lights.

Sodium lights are longer-lived than halide, and about 15 to 20 percent more expensive. They're extremely efficient, giving more light for the energy used than other lights mentioned here. However, their yellow light is unflattering to most plants; use them to supplement natural light, not as a primary light source.

SOURCES

Incandescent and fluorescent plant lights are sold at hardware stores and garden centers.

For prewired sodium and halide lights, try Hydrofarm, 3135 Kerner Blvd., San Rafael, CA 94901. You can get a copy of the company's free mail-order catalog by calling (800) 634-9999.

To order mercandescent lights that fit into standard sockets, call Public Service Lamp Company at (800) 221-4392. ■

By Jim McCausland

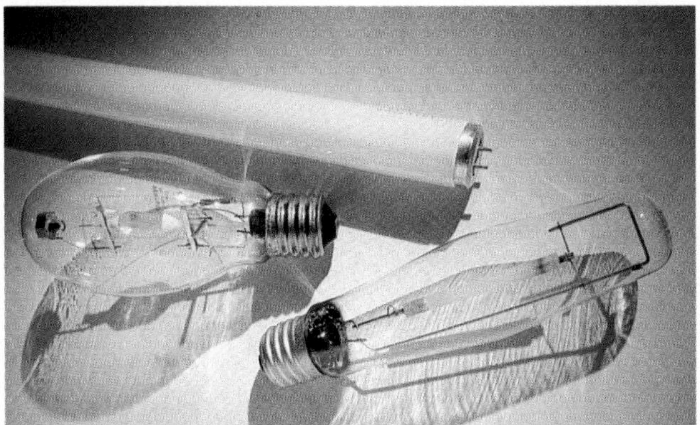

THREE LIGHTING CHOICES *(from top): Fluorescent tube, high-intensity halide bulb, and sodium bulb.*

Deck the garden with berries

COTONEASTER BRIGHTENS NORTHWEST WINTERS WITH ITS NATURAL ORNAMENTS

DON NORMARK

ALL ATWINKLE
Trained up a wall, Cotoneaster horizontalis (leafless after a cold snap) sparkles with red berries and white lights at Peggy Moe's Seattle house. Ceramic pot (inset) contains a 1-gallon can of perky C. buxifolius, brought indoors for the holidays; excelsior camouflages can.

Come December, cotoneasters are as merry as a shop full of elves: bright berries ornament these shrubs profusely just in time for the holidays. Although these plants are versatile performers any time of year—with varieties you can train as small, gracefully arching trees, as lacy espaliers against a wall, or as sprays of foliage beside an entry—they're downright show-offs in December.

This month, a number of cotoneasters will be in fruit and avail-

NORMAN A. PLATE

FRUIT-LADEN, *Cotoneaster lacteus has long, graceful branches that look best arching freely, rather than clipped. Shown here as a shrub, it can also be trained as a tree.*

able in nurseries in 1-gallon cans. Pop one into a decorative container to use temporarily indoors. If the soil is still workable, you can even plant them outdoors, where they'll shine for many winters to come.

Plant a tall-growing variety for a fountain of winter berries (birds will love you: the big species provide excellent cover for them, and the fruit provides good forage). No matter where you put plants, keep them well watered the first year in the garden to prolong the winter berry show.

For a gardener who has everything, give him or her a cotoneaster. Hardly a garden in the Northwest doesn't have room for one more. It's a plant for a Good Samaritan to give if ever there was one—easy to grow, no pruning needed, no problems.

CHOICE PLANTS FOR MANY GARDEN USES

Of the more than 50 species of cotoneaster in cultivation, several provide a crop of red or orange berries for the holidays and stand out as top performers for winter gardens. These bear clusters of tiny white flowers in spring.

Nothing spills over a retaining wall better than *C. dammeri* (you'll see it used extensively atop the walls of Seattle's Freeway Park). This plant has masses of leathery, dark green fingernail-size leaves, with fruits all along cascading boughs that can dangle 10 feet.

For stiff, horizontal branches that jut handsomely out of a rockery, use *C. horizontalis*. In all but the mildest Northwest winters, this plant—which spreads to 15 feet—defoliates, leaving its abundant crop of berries as pictured on pages 308 and 309. Landscape designer Doug Bailey touts the virtues of a variegated form, *C. horizontalis* 'Variegatus', with dainty leaves edged in white. "It's dynamite! Great, glistening foliage, decorative berry crop, interesting black branch pattern against the snow, spectacular outlined with rime . . . it's worthy of a place next to the front door."

For a big, generously berried burst of loose branches that can grow to 7 feet or more, plant *C. lacteus*. It makes an excellent informal hedge. A single plant can fill the corner of a city garden, or tough it out under a limbed-up Douglas fir or native cedar, softening a big expanse of naked trunk. Growing to a height of about 6 feet, *C.* 'Hybridus Pendulus' has a similarly upright form, but the main branches are erectly vertical with curving, weeping side branches.

If you want a showy plant in a container, look for *C. buxifolius,* not as commonly available as *C. lacteus*. This sturdy little plant arches up 2 feet and can stretch out twice that distance. Its rigid branches carry masses of tiny leaves that are a dull blue green on top and silvery and fuzzy underneath. It makes a great indoor plant for the holidays, but be especially certain not to let it dry out, and keep it away from heater vents. You may want to move it outdoors at night, or onto a covered porch where it will be protected from the shock of a hard freeze but still get a refreshing chill.

DON NORMARK

PLANTS ARE CAREFREE, EASYGOING

Cotoneasters are drought tolerant, performing happily through our driest summers without help from the hose. They're unfussy about soil, though they do best in the rich acid soil of Western Oregon and Washington—showing more vitality there than in the alkaline soils of most of the West.

Although the big fountaining varieties can be espaliered with some success, cotoneasters don't take well to heavy pruning and are not plants for clipped hedges or topiaries. But you can clip off errant switches when they shoot out and snip branches for bouquets or holiday wreaths.

Plants are generally robust. If we have a cold spell, leaves can take on a deep bronzy cast, or some of the leaves and some of the fruits may drop. In one of our occasional streaks of near 0° weather, plants will defoliate altogether and, in some cases, die back to the ground. If this happens, cut back dead growth when warmer weather returns in spring, and the plants will leaf out again. ■

By Steven R. Lorton

ONE PLANT *of Cotoneaster horizontalis, trained and clipped regularly, edges these front steps in Seattle.*

RED CHILI PEPPERS *spice up this festive arrangement, designed by Kim Haworth, of camellia, holly, and redwood foliage.*

Winter greens, winter wonders

Here's how one Sunset gardener puts together holiday centerpieces quickly

You're getting the house ready for a holiday party, and you need a centerpiece quickly. But you have no flowers and no time to run to the florist or nursery. What do you do? If you live in a mild-winter area, grab the clippers and step outside: there's probably a wealth of greenery to choose from.

Each year at *Sunset,* gardener Kim Haworth does just that. She put together the arrangement pictured above in about 20 minutes to decorate the lobby at *Sunset*'s headquarters. Her tools: a plastic-lined basket, a block of florist's foam, florist's wire (all available at craft stores), and garden prunings.

After she harvests and washes prunings of such plants as *Aspidistra elatior,* camellia, holly, juniper, mullein, and redwood, she cuts the stems at an angle and secures them firmly—at least an inch deep—in moistened florist's foam set in the basket. She works from the outside in, placing the tallest pieces in the center.

For variety, she then adds snippets of silvery plants such as gray dusty miller. "The lighter foliage makes a nice contrast, especially in the winter, when it gets dark indoors," she says.

Berries (holly, nandina, or toyon), small ornaments, or candles complete many of her arrangements; Haworth especially likes nandina because its berries last longer than the others'. For bright accents in the arrangement above, she used red chili peppers. She threaded florist's wire through the base of each pepper, then doubled the wire back a few inches, twisted it, and poked it into the florist's foam.

The arrangements are kept fresh-looking by keeping the foam moist. ■

By Kimberly Chrisman

NORMAN A. PLATE

TO CREATE *a base of greenery, poke foliage stems into the sides of a block of florist's foam.*

Two-stop shopping at L.A.'s flower market

This downtown district offers everything you need for holiday decorating . . . wreaths, flowers, and Christmas trees

CHAD SLATTERY

FRESH CONIFER WREATHS *scent the air at Mellano & Company, and tempt holiday shoppers to stop and sniff.*

WALL STREET IN NEW York may mean stocks and bonds, but Wall Street in Los Angeles means flowers and greens, especially at Christmas. For many Angelenos, it's a tradition: pack up the kids and head downtown to the floral district for wreaths, mistletoe, and other holiday greenery. Then head over to Alameda Street to pick out a tree, or bid on one at a tree auction.

The Los Angeles Flower Market (754 Wall Street) and adjacent wholesale florists constitute the largest floral district in the country. At holiday time, it's one of the city's most festive areas—colorful and fragrant. Whether you're looking for juniper branches, garlands, swags, centerpieces, or holly, the floral district has the freshest and least expensive selection around, with prices just above wholesale. Some wholesalers offer floral services, and will even customize wreaths with such decorations as angels or little apples.

Interspersed with the florists are floral supply houses, so if you'd rather do your own decorating you can buy miniature sleighs (or Cadillacs) to put your greenery or flowers in.

The best time to shop is early. The market and most wholesalers open at 6 A.M. and generally close by early afternoon. Some offer extended holiday hours, but for the best selection, go between 6 and 11. (A thermos of coffee isn't a bad idea.)

Some wholesalers with large selections of greens and plants include Buford W. Hall Wholesale Florists, 750 Wall Street, (213) 623-2882; California Flower Distributors, 778 Wall, 623-2514; Mellano & Company (inside the market), 754 Wall, 622-0796; and Valle Wholesale Flowers, 754 Wall, 688-8810.

Jim Hall of Buford W. Hall offers these tips: "Park in a pay lot to avoid a ticket. And call ahead if you're unsure of holiday hours."

DON'T FORGET THE CHRISTMAS TREE

If you're going to shop for a Christmas tree, too, head up Eighth Street and east to Alameda. Huge Christmas tree lots line the east side of the street. Every type and size of tree imaginable, from a tiny "top" on a redwood base to an enormous noble fir, is stocked here beside the Alameda railyard. This month almost a million trees will pass through these lots, which have sprung up every Christmas since 1931.

True bargain hunters will want to attend the Holiday Tree Farms Christmas Tree Auctions, held from boxcars at Alameda and Eighth. Trees sell for an average of $8 below retail. Holiday Tree Farms of Oregon ships in the Douglas firs, which are bid on one by one. This year, the auctions run from December 3 through 19; hours are 5 to 10 P.M. weekdays, 10 to 10 weekends. ■

By Janis Hashe

Tool kit for a plant collector

Avid gardeners find plant collecting an incurable obsession that can strike at any time or place. But it takes the right tools to dig seedlings, harvest seeds, or take cuttings, and then transport them safely home. You can make life easier for the plant nut in your life by giving him or her this easy-to-assemble traveling kit. Here are the components, A through N (clockwise from top):

A. ***One yard of heavy denim or canvas*** (45 or 60 inches wide). Folded package-style and secured with twine, it contains other components for the kit and can fit conveniently in the trunk of a car. Open, it's a drop cloth to protect a car seat or trunk from spilled soil. Hem the raw edges if you like.

B. ***Two clear tennis ball cans.*** One stores plastic bags; the other stores items H, I, and J. Empty, these are good containers for transplants. Put a bit of soil in the bottom of one of the containers and dig up the plant with as much soil around the root as possible. Slip the plant into the can, water well, and pop on the lid for travel. When you get home, remove the plant and set it out in the garden.

C. ***Green twine and wired twist tape*** to secure floppy branches or shoots to a stake. Natural twine ties up the kit.

D. ***Plastic bags.*** Include three sizes. Use small zip-lock bags for seed collecting (to keep seeds contained and dry) and for small cuttings that you've wrapped in wet paper towels. Medium-size bags (used for bringing produce home from the grocery) work for collecting small plants like clumps of violets. Use large plastic bags for large plants, or slip a 1- to 5-gallon plant from a nursery into one to keep the moisture in the container from leaking onto the car, camper, or motel room floor.

E. ***Paper towels*** to clean up spills and hold water for wrapping up roots and ends of cuttings. Stack up a good supply, fold them into quarters, and store them in one of the zip-lock bags.

F. ***Trowel*** for digging plants.

G. ***Pruners*** for cutting.

H. ***Plastic plant labels and a waterproof marking pen*** for making on-the-spot plant tags.

I. ***Rooting hormone.*** This powder helps ensure the success of cuttings. Store it in a plastic film canister.

J. ***Rubber bands*** to secure the tops of plastic bags.

K. ***Water-filled plastic bottle.***

L. ***Stakes.***

M. ***Cultivating fork and narrow trowel*** (optional). Fork is for gently lifting shallow-rooted plants. The narrow trowel allows you to dig up seedlings from tight places.

N. ***A can of sterile potting soil*** for rooting as many as four small cuttings that you won't disturb until roots are established and you're ready to transplant. Wash a 6- to10-ounce metal can with one end removed. With a hammer and nail, punch four small drain holes in the bottom. Fill the can with sterile mix. Pop pet food can lids (available at grocery stores) on the top and bottom to contain the soil. When you make cuttings, wet the soil thoroughly and press it down firmly (allowing excess water to drain out of the holes). Put the snap-on lid back on the bottom to contain drips. Push in a stake to tie up a limp vine. Push in three or four stakes to make a frame for a mini-greenhouse (slip a plastic bag over it and secure with a rubber band). ■

By Steven R. Lorton

PETER CHRISTIANSEN

DROP CLOTH, *folded into an easy-to-carry package, contains all the tools needed to collect and bring home plants, cuttings, and seeds.*

Article Titles Index

And what about tulips in Southern California, 252–253

Basic or fanciful baths for birds, 192–195
Bulbs to plant in winter, 43

Camellia blooms for Christmas, 304–306
Carrots you can count on for flavor, 228
Checklists. *See* Garden checklists
Citrus breakthroughs, 20–22
Colorado country gardens, 144–149
Creative containers, 176–177
Crinkly, colorful crispheads, 200–201

Daisy standouts from seed, 98
Dazzle of dahlias...from a pack of seeds, 23
Deck the garden with berries, 308–310
Dinosaur food? Not exactly, 202

Easy, enchanting everlastings, 136–139
Elegant and easy...orchids to grow indoors, 18–19

First house, first garden, 164–166
Flowers by the bunchful, 246–249
Forty wonder plants for the Northwest, 222–227
From seed to bread, 276–279

Garden checklists, Central region
- April, 81
- August, 185
- December, 293
- February, 31
- January, 11
- July, 161
- June, 133
- March, 53
- May, 111
- November, 269
- October, 239
- September, 213

Garden checklists, Northwest region
- April, 80
- August, 184
- December, 292
- February, 30
- January, 10
- July, 160
- June, 132
- March, 52
- May, 110
- November, 268
- October, 238
- September, 212

Garden checklists, Southern California
- April, 82
- August, 186
- December, 294
- February, 32
- January, 12
- July, 162

Garden checklists, Southern California *(cont'd)*
- June, 134
- March, 54
- May, 112
- November, 270
- October, 240
- September, 214

Garden checklists, Southwest region
- April, 83
- August, 187
- December, 295
- February, 33
- January, 13
- July, 163
- June, 135
- March, 55
- May, 113
- November, 271
- October, 241
- September, 215

Garden Guide
- April, 73–79
- August, 179–183
- December, 287–291
- February, 25–29
- January, 7–9
- July, 155–159
- June, 125–131
- March, 46–51
- May, 103–109
- November, 261–267
- October, 231–237
- September, 207–211

Garden of the future in Riverside, 70
Graceful grasses, 34–37
Grow peonies in mild climates, 256

Hang up some quick color, 42

Impatiens: the easy garden show-off, 91
In search of the Western wreath, 296–303
It's a cloister garden, 203

Jungle grows in this San Diego backyard, 205

Keep your roses blooming...by cutting them properly, 99

Leafy privacy screen, 258
Lessons for lofty landscapes, 191
Like a slice of the wild North woods, 196–198
Look is "controlled wildness," 40
Lush look in a dark, dark entry, 259

Matching gloves to garden chores, 275
Miracle of fall planting, 216–221
Mountain retreat or coastal dell, 199

Natural look...with artificial rock, 284–285
New ardor for Arbor Day, 101
No space, no time? Yes, you can grow vegetables, 84–90

Oasis for wildlife—and people, 188–190
Olive trees...back again, and better, 242–245
Onions that keep on giving, 250–251

Perennials come back—stronger than ever, 114–120
Plant lights for winter flowers, 307
Plants that invite beneficial insects into your garden, 71
Pretty small gardens, 170–175
Pruning a hybrid tea rose, 41

Quick and easy compost, 152

Real geraniums: versatile and hardy, 66
Right hoe for the right job, 69
Robust and rugged rosemary, 272–274
Rock garden to end all rock gardens, 96–97
Roses high and mighty, 14–17

Saguaros on the sofa, 92–95
Seeking the pink in daffodils, 257
Sharing the harvest, 64–65
Showy sunroses add zest to spring gardens, 100
Southwest beans, 56–58
Start seeds from scratch, 62–63
Summer pruning for more apples and pears, 153
Sweet? Sweeter? Sweetest? What's best, 122–123
Switching to drip, 167–169

Tapestry of herbs for a Northwest border, 59
Thirty minutes or less, 140–143
Tool kit for a plant collector, 313
Top tomato, 38–39
Turn your garden trimmings into soil conditioner, 254–255
Two-stop shopping at L.A.'s flower market, 312

Under oaks and with oaks, 283
Unthirsty and colorful buckwheats, 229

Vine trellis just bolts to the fence, 259

West's spreading compost movement, 60–61
What about a rabbit in your garden, 150–151
What about "natural" fertilizers, 121
When leaves turn a sickly yellow, 67
When plants die mysteriously...suspect nematodes, 204
Wildflower time in Golden Gate Park, 68
Winter greens, winter wonders, 311
Winter sparklers, 280–282

General Subject Index

Acer circinatum, 227
Acer rubrum 'Armstrong II', 234
Achillea, 71, 73, 116, 139, 182, 226, 249
Achillea ptarmica 'The Pearl', 182
Acidanthera, 43
Acroclinium, 27, 139
Agave vilmoriana, 183
Ageratum 'Blue Horizon', 249
Agrostemma, 71, 233
Agrostis nebulosa, 139
Alcea rosea, 107
Alchemilla, 116
Algae, removing from ponds, 158
All-America selections for 1993, 8
Allium, 139
Alstroemeria, 224
Amaranth, 130
Amaranthus, 130
Amaryllis, miniature, 262
Ammi majus, 71
Ammobium alatum, 27, 139
Anemone hybrida, 116, 180
Anemone vitifolia 'Robustissima', 127
Anisodontea capensis, 224
Annual phlox, 219
Annuals
  attractive to beneficial insects, 71
  best time to plant, 29
  at Clear Water Farm in Colorado, 148–149
  for fall planting, 216–221
  for hanging baskets, 42
  heat-tolerant, 183
  nursery packs and flats, 27
  from seed, 42, 62–63
Antirrhinum majus, 220, 249
Apples, summer pruning, 153
April, 72–101
  checklists, 80–83
  garden guide, 73–79
Aquilegia chrysantha hinckleyana 'Texas Gold', 211
Arbutus unedo, 226, 282
Armeria, 116
Arrhenatherum elatius bulbosum 'Variegatum', 36
Artemisia, 116, 224, 235
Artichoke, 139
Arugula, 129
Asparagus, 49
Aster, 116, 180, 224, 249
Astilbe, 117
August, 178–205
  checklists, 184–187
  garden guide, 179–183
Avocado mites, 130
Azadirachta indica (neem), 131

Baby blue eyes, 71
Baby's breath, 139
Bachelor's button, 218
Beans
  harvesting times, 130
  pole versus bush, 109
  Southwest natives, 56–58
  trellis for, 104
Begonia, 43
Bellflower, 117
Bellis perennis, 218
Beneficial insects, plants attractive to, 71
Bergenia, 28, 117
Birches in Central Valley backyard garden, 199
Birdbaths, 192–195
Bishop's weed, 71
Black-eyed Susan, 106, 181
Black locust, 227
Blanket flower, 118
Bleeding heart, 118
Bletilla striata, 210
Blue fescue, 36
Blue-flowered plants, two new or rediscovered choices, 49, 107
Blue oat grass, 36, 127
Bonsai planters, 51
Botryosphaeria, 210
Brachycome multifida, 117
Brassica, 218
Bread baked from home-grown wheat, 279
Briza, 36, 139
Broccoli, 49, 211
Broom, 226
Brunnera macrophylla, 117
Buckwheat, 71, 229, 235
Buddleia davidii, 47
Bulbous oat grass, 36
Bulbs
  drought-tolerant, for Northwest, 224–225
  forcing in water, 264
  for winter planting, 43
Butterfly bush, 47
Buxus sempervirens, 226

Cabbage, 235
  flowering, 218
Cacti
  animal damage to, in desert gardens, 109
  in Rancho Mirage garden, 92–95
Calamagrostis acutiflora 'Stricta', 36
Calendula, 218
California sagebrush, 235
Calla, 43
  in containers, 48
Callirhoë involucrata, 130
Calocedrus decurrens, 227
Camellia, 226, 282
  December-blooming, 304–306
Camellia sasanqua, 282
Campanula, 117, 218
Campsis tagliabuana, 226
Candytuft, 119, 218
Canterbury bells, 218
Cape mallow, 224
Carex, 36
Carrots, 228
Carthamus tinctorius, 27, 139
Catananche caerulea, 139
Catmint, 119, 224
Cattleya, 18–19
Ceanothus, 235, 262
Cedar, 227
Cedrus, 227
Celosia, 139
Centaurea cyanus, 218
Centerpieces for the holidays, 311

NORMAN A. PLATE

Tuberose (see page 43)

Central region
Central Valley backyard oasis, 199
Colorado country gardens, 144–149
fall planting in (annuals), 216–221
garden checklists for. *See* Garden checklists in the Article Titles Index
growers of specialty plants in (reference book), 232
Lake Tahoe demonstration garden, 191
peonies for, 256
source for unusual vegetable varieties in, 237
Cercis, 227
Chard, 129
Cherries, new sweet varieties, 8
Chimonanthus praecox, 282
Chinese ground orchid, 210
Chinese lantern, 139
Chinese leeks, 250, 251
Chinese witch hazel, 282
Chive mayonnaise, 251
Chives, 250, 251
Chlorosis, 67
Choisya ternata, 47
Christmas cactus, 289
Christmas trees, recycling, 289
Chrysanthemum, 71, 98, 117, 126, 139, 180, 218
Cistus, 226
Citrosa, 105
Citrus
flower drop from trees, 104
new varieties, 20–22, 47
Cladanthus arabicus, 98
Clay pots. *See also* Containers
how to keep moist, 182
painting (quick garden project), 140
rejuvenating appearance, 105
Cleveland sage, 78
Cloister garden, 203
Cloud grass, 139
Cockscomb, 139
Colorado country gardens, 144–149
Columbine, 'Texas Gold', 211
Common fennel, 71
Composters, 254–255
Composting, 60–61, 79, 254–255
compost activators, 288
quick and easy, 152
worms as compost-makers, 266
Consolida ambigua, 139, 219
Containers, 176–177. *See also* Clay pots
for bonsai, 51
callas in, 48
"feet" for, 180
hanging baskets of annuals, 42
herbs in, 143
large pots for spring display, 77
Mediterranean plants in, 126
recycling plastic pots, 49
succulents in, 104, 183
watering container plants, 76
Coral bells, 119
Coreopsis, 71, 76, 98, 117
Coreopsis verticillata 'Moonbeam', 76
Coriander, 71
Coriandrum satirum, 71
Corn
extra-sweet varieties, 122–123
testing ripeness, 126
Corn cockle, 71, 233
Cornelian cherry, 282
Cornus, 157, 282
Corsican hellebore, 224
Cortaderia selloana 'Gold Band' or 'Sun Stripe', 36
Corylopsis, 49
Cosmos, 71
Cotoneaster, 77, 226, 291, 308–310
Coyote mint, 235
Crabapple, 227
disease resistance, 9
Crambe cordifolia, 249
Cranesbill, 66, 118
Craspedia globosa, 27, 139
Creeping zinnia, 98
Crocosmia, 43
Crown pink, 71
Cupid's dart, 139
Curly-top sedge, 36
Cut flowers
and foliage, garden choices for (Walla Walla garden), 246–249
keeping fresh, 9
roses as, how to cut, 99
Cycads, in San Diego jungle-style garden, 205

Gladiolus, dahlias, and lilies (see page 43)

Cynara, 139
Cytisus, 226

Daffodils
for naturalizing, 208
pink varieties, 257
Dahlberg daisy, 98
Dahlia, 43
from seed, 23
staking, 28
Daisies from seed for summer color, 98
Dalea greggii, 78
Daphne odora, 47
Daylily, 119
Dead nettle, 119, 224
De-Bug, 159
December, 286–313
checklists, 292–295
garden guide, 287–291
Deer grass, 36
Deer-resistant garden, 76
Delosperma nubigenum, 183
Delphinium, 117
Desert four o'clock, 127
Desert plumbago, 105
Dianthus, 118, 218
Diascia, 118
Dicentra, 118
Dierama pulcherrimum, 118
Digitalis mertonensis, 108
Diseases
fungal, of redwoods *(Botryosphaeria),* 210
iron chlorosis, 67
powdery mildew
roses and yuccas as indicators for, 107
roses resistant to, 262
root rot, 46
rust fungus, 76
Dogwoods, disease-resistant, 157
Drip irrigation, 167–169
book about, 9
Drought-tolerant plants. *See also* Heat-tolerant plants; Watering
buckwheat, 229
for California hillside garden, 188–190
for desert courtyard, 50
for desert-style garden in Phoenix, 267
guides to, 29, 156, 159
in Healdsburg garden, 76
for herb borders, 59
in Lake Tahoe demonstration garden, 191
for Northwest gardens, 209–210, 222–227
with oaks in Pebble Beach garden, 211
olive trees, 243–245
soil preparation for, 227
Drumstick flower, 27, 139
Dudleya, 289
Dyssodia tenuiloba, 98

Eccremocarpus scaber, 8
Echinacea purpurea, 98
Echinops, 139
Elaeagnus philippinensis, 159
Elymus condensatus 'Canyon Prince', 36
Emu bush, 78, 79
English boxwood, 226
English daisy, 218
Epimedium, 225
Eremophila, 78, 79
Erigeron 'Blue Beauty', 98
Erigeron karvinskianus, 118
Eriogonum, 71, 229, 235
Eryngium, 139
Erysimum linifolium 'Bowles Mauve', 118, 225
Eulalia grass, 36
Euphorbia, 78, 118, 225
Evening primrose, 119
Evergreen candytuft, 119
Evergreen maiden grass, 36
Everlasting flowers, 27, 136–139

Fairy wand, 118
Fall planting, annuals for, 216–221
False spiraea, 117
Feather reed grass, 36
February, 24–43
checklists, 30–33
garden guide, 25–29
Feijoa sellowiana, 78
Ferns for full sun, 234
Fertilizers
"natural," 121
for Northwest lawns, 49
planting after use (avoiding root burn), 74
strong, how to use, 28
Festuca amethystina, 36
Feverfew, 71, 98, 139
Ficus, causes of leaf-drop in, 232
Flagstone garden table, easy-to-make, 141
Flanders Field poppy, 236
Fleabane, 98
Flour, freshly-ground whole-wheat, 279
Flowering cabbage and kale, 218
Flowering cherry, 282
Flower market in Los Angeles, 312
Foeniculum vulgare, 71
Foliage centerpieces for the holidays, 311
Food preservation, 181
Forest-style Northwest garden, 196–198
Forget-me-not, 218
Forsythia, 266
Foxglove, 108
Fox red curly sedge, 36
Fruit. *See also* specific fruits
growing in Northwest, books about, 8
Fuchsia, 74, 155
Fungal disease of redwoods *(Botryosphaeria),* 210

Gaillardia grandiflora, 118
Garden books and references. *See* Reference books and guides

Garden ideas
backyard oasis in Central Valley, 199
cloister garden, 203
Colorado country gardens, 144–149
cut-flower garden in Walla Walla, 246–249
deciduous privacy screen, 258
drought-tolerant plants for Northwest, 209–210, 222–227
entryway ideas, 259
first garden (starting from scratch), 164–166
"forest" in a Northwest backyard, 196–198
hillside oasis in Southern California, 188–190
indoors and outdoors working together (Rancho Mirage garden), 92–95
"jungle" in San Diego, 205
for mountain dwellers (Lake Tahoe demonstration garden), 191
plant collectors' kits, 313
plant labels and markers, 182, 262
plant shelves, 142
plant stands, 141, 143
rock garden in Washington, 96–97
shade gardens (book about), 157
small-space gardens in Southern California, 170–175
starter garden, 164–166
vegetable garden for charity, 64–65
vegetable gardens for small spaces, 84–90
water-conserving gardens, guides for, 29, 156, 159
winter-blooming plants for Northwest, 280–282
Gardens, public
in California, 68, 70, 180, 191, 208
in Northwest, 290
Garlic, 263
Gaura, 118
Gazania, 78
Genista, 226
Geranium, 66, 75, 118
Geranium *(Pelargonium)*, cool-weather care for, 236
Germander, 120
German statice, 139
Giant blue wild rye, 36
Giant feather grass, 36
Giant palm borer, 50
Gingered chicken with leek flowers, 251
Gladiolus, 43
why flowers fail to open (gladiolus thrips), 126
Gladiolus callianthus, 43
Globe amaranth, 139
Globe candytuft, 218
Globe thistle, 139
Gloriosa daisy, 98, 106, 181
Glory vine, 8
Gloves, garden, 275

NORMAN A. PLATE
Seedlings and peat pots (see page 63)

Golden crownbeard, 78
Goldenrod, 127, 139
Gold locust, 26
Gomphrena globosa, 139
Goniolimon tartaricum, 139
Grapefruit and grapefruit hybrids, new varieties, 22
Grasses, ornamental, 34–37
cutting back, 47
drought-tolerant, for Northwest gardens, 225
encyclopedia of, 75
Grasshoppers, 159
Green fruit beetle, 48
Ground covers
drought-tolerant, for Northwest, 209, 226
for rock gardens, 210
shearing, 79
for summer bloom, 156
Gunnera, 202
Gypsophila, 139

***H**amamelis,* 282
Hanging baskets, annuals for, 42
Hare's tail grass, 139
Heat-tolerant plants, 183. *See also* Drought-tolerant plants
Helianthemum, 100
Helianthus maximiliani, 211
Helianthus tuberosus, 233
Helichrysum, 27, 139
Helictotrichon sempervirens, 36, 127
Heliopsis helianthoides scabra 'Incomparabilis', 127
Helipterum, 27, 139
Hellebore, 118, 224
Helleborus, 118, 224
Hemerocallis, 119
Herb border for Seattle garden, 59
Herb pot, 143
Heuchera, 119
Hippeastrum, 262
Hoes, 69
for weeding (Winged Weeder), 209
Hollyhock, 107
Homalomena 'Emerald Gem', 9
Honey bush, 225
Honeysuckle, winter-blooming, 282
Hosta, 119
House plants
new selection *(Homalomena* 'Emerald Gem'), 9
plant lights for, 307
Houttuynia cordata 'Variegata', 119
Hummingbirds
feeders, cleaning, 26
plants attractive to, 8, 108
winter care, 263
Hunnemannia fumariifolia 'Sunlite', 249

***I**beris,* 119, 218
Immortelle, 27, 139
Impatiens, 91
Incense cedar, 227
Insects
avocado mites, 130
beneficial, plants attractive to, 71
giant palm borer, 50
gladiolus thrips, 126
grasshoppers, 159
green fruit beetle, 48
of the Los Angeles Basin, reference book about, 264
mosquitoes, 105, 183
nematodes, 204
ticks, 183
Iris, 78, 225
failure to bloom, 27
Iron chlorosis, 67
Ivy, training in decorative pattern, 128

January, 6–23
checklists, 10–13
garden guide, 7–9
Japanese anemone, 116, 180
Jasmine, 47
Jasminum, 47
Jerusalem sage, 119
Jujube, 266
July, 154–177
checklists, 160–163
garden guide, 155–159
June, 124–153
checklists, 132–135
garden guide, 125–131
Jungle-style garden in San Diego, 205
Justicia spicigera, 108

Kalanchoe, 266
Kiwi fruit, 267

Labels for garden plants, 182, 262
Lady's mantle, 116
Lagurus ovatus, 139
Lamb's ears, 120, 139
Lamium maculatum, 119, 224
Larix occidentalis, 182
Larkspur, 139, 219, 249
Lathyrus odoratus, 220, 249
Laurels, when to shear in Northwest, 182
Lavandula, 119, 225
Lavender, 119, 225
Lawns
feeding, in Northwest, 49
flowering, for Northwest, 209
lightweight sod for, 74
rust fungus, 76
Lawrencellia rosea, 27
Layia platyglossa, 71
Leatherleaf mahonia, 282
Lemons, new varieties, 22
Leonotis leonurus, 119
Leptospermum scoparium 'Ruby Glow', 262
Lettuce
crisphead, 200–201
seed, easy-to-handle, 26
Liatris, 43
Lily, 43
Limonium, 127, 139, 262
Linaria, 220
Lingaro, 159
Lion's tail, 119
Liquidambar, 232
Lobularia maritima, 71, 220
Locust, 26, 227
Lonicera standishii, 282
Love-in-a-mist, 139, 237
Lunaria annua, 139
Lupine from seed, 233
Lychnis coronaria, 71

Mahonia, 48, 282
Malus, 227
disease resistance, 9
Mandarins, new varieties, 22
March, 44–71
checklists, 52–55
garden guide, 45–51
Marguerite, 125, 126
Marigold, 'French Vanilla', 74
Markers for garden plants, 182, 262
Matilija poppy, 120, 225, 235
Matthiola, 220, 249
Maximilian's sunflower, 211
May, 102–123
checklists, 110–113
garden guide, 103–109
Mediterranean plants
in California hillside garden, 188–190
in pots, 126
public garden featuring, 208
Melianthus major, 225
Mexican honeysuckle, 108
Mexican orange, 47
Mexican sunflower, 98
Mexican tulip poppy, 249
Mirabilis multiflora, 127
Miscanthus, 36
Monarch of the Veldt, 98
Monarda, 249
Monardella villosa, 235
Money plant, 139
Montbretia, 43
Mosquitoes
repellent you can grow, 105
and ticks, protecting against, 183
Mother-of-thyme, 120, 127
Mountain gardens
good perennials for, 127
Lake Tahoe demonstration garden, 191
Muhlenbergia rigens, 36

Mulching, 209
with newspaper, 26
Music to garden by, 51
Mustard, 290
Myosotis sylvatica, 218

N*arcissus bulbocodium conspicuus,* 208
Native plants
California
fragrant, 235
nurseries selling, 181
reference book to, 288
golden crownbeard, 78
in Golden Gate Park, 68
in Lake Tahoe demonstration garden, 191
in Northwest forest-style garden, 196–198
Northwest, sources for, 265
wildflowers, new source book for, 107
wine-cups, 130
Naturalizing, daffodils for, 208
Neem, 131
Nematodes, 204
Nemesia, 219
Nemophila menziesii, 71
Nepeta faassenii, 119, 224
New Zealand tea tree, 262
Nicotiana, 129
Nierembergia 'Mont Blanc', 8
Nigella damascena, 139, 237
Northwest region
cloister garden, 203
deciduous privacy screen, 258
drought-tolerant plants for, 209–210, 222–227
feeding lawns in, 49
ferns for full sun, 234
flowering lawn for, 209
forest-style garden, 196–198
fruit-growing in, books about, 8
garden checklists for. *See* Garden checklists in the Article Titles Index
garden for cut flowers and foliage, 247–249
herb border in Seattle, 59
landscape plants for, booklet about, 77

NORMAN A. PLATE

'Golden Rosette' coreopsis (see page 98)

Northwest region *(cont'd)*
laurels in, when to shear, 182
maples as privacy screens, 234
music for gardening, 51
plant-purchasing guides for, 265
rhododendrons in, when to transplant, 129
rock garden in Washington, 96–97
shade tree for, 182
skimmia in, 237
winter-blooming plants for, 280–282
Nosema locustae, 159
November, 260–285
checklists, 268–271
garden guide, 261–267
Nurseries in California, directory of, 232

Oaks
companion plants for, 211, 283
drought-tolerant, for Northwest gardens, 227
October, 230–259
checklists, 238–241
garden guide, 231–237
Octopus agave, 183
Oenothera, 119
Olive trees in the garden, 242–245
Onions, 139, 250–251
potato, 208, 250, 251
recipes using, 251
Orange-colored sedge, 36
Oranges, new varieties, 22
Orchids
to grow indoors, 18–19
for shade, 210
Oregano, 158
Oriental fountain grass, 36
Origanum hybridum, 158
Osmanthus fragrans, 47
Oxypetalum caeruleum 'Blue Cheer', 49

Palms
collection of, in Costa Mesa, 128
pruning, 127
in San Diego jungle-style garden, 205
Palm Springs daisy, 98
Panicum virgatum 'Haense Herms', 36
Pansy, 7, 219, 264
Papaver, 139, 219, 236
Papaver rhoeas, 236
Paper daisy, 27
Paphiopedilum, 18–19
Peach for Southern California, 158
Pears, summer pruning, 153
Pennisetum, 36
Penstemon, 119, 127, 131
Pentas lanceolata, 127
Peonies for mild climates, 256
Perennials
attractive to beneficial insects, 71

Perennials *(cont'd)*
best choices for today, 114–120
drought-tolerant, for Northwest, 210, 224–225
heat-tolerant, 183
for late summer and fall bloom, 180
low-growing, for borders, two good choices, 76
meadow of, in Colorado, 146–147
for mountain climates, 127
to plant under oaks, 283
Perovskia, 119
Pesticides
De-Bug, 159
neem, 131
Nosema locustae, 159
sabadilla, 75
Petunia, 219
fragrant, 46
for six-month-long bloom, 128
Phalaenopsis, 18–19
Phlomis fruticosa, 119
Phlox, 120
annual, 219
Physalis alkekengi, 139
Pickled Egyptian onions, 251
Pineapple guava, 78
Pineleaf penstemon, 127, 131
Pines, drought-tolerant, for Northwest gardens, 227
Pink, 118, 218
Pink pokers, 139
Pinus, 227
Plains yucca, 50
Plantain lily, 119
Plant collectors' kits, 313
Plant lights, 307
Plant shelves, 142
Plant stands, 141, 143
Plastic pots, recycling, 49
Plumbago scandens, 105
Polianthes tuberosa, 43
Polystichum munitum, 234
Ponds
removing algae from, 158
tips for increasing garden impact, 77
Pony packs, 27
Poor man's orchid, 219
Poppy, 139, 219, 236
Portulaca, 159
Potato onions, 208, 250, 251
Powdery mildew
roses and yuccas as indicators for, 107
roses resistant to, 262
Primrose, 220, 291
Primula, 220, 291
Privacy screens, deciduous, 234
Prunella vulgaris, 156
Pruning and shearing
apples and pears, in summer, 153
ground covers, 79
laurel hedges, 182
palms, 127
roses, 40, 41
Prunus subhirtella 'Autumnalis', 282
Psylliostachys suworowii, 139
Pumpkin, 'Baby Bear', 8
Purple coneflower, 98
Purple-leafed fountain grass, 36

Purple sage, 29
Purslane, 159

Quaking grass, 36, 139
Quercus, 211, 227, 283

Rabbits
  as pets, 150–151
  plants resistant to, 78
Radishes, 265
Ramanas rose, 226
Ranunculus, when to plant, 232
Red buckwheat, 229
Redbud, 227
Red-flowering currant, 226
Red switch grass, 36
Redwoods, fungal disease of *(Botryosphaeria),* 210
Reference books and guides mentioned in this volume
  Complete Shade Gardener, 157
  Drip Irrigation for Every Landscape and All Climates, 9
  Encyclopedia of Ornamental Grasses, 75
  Gardener's Guide to Growers of Specialty Plants in California, 232
  Growing Grapes in Your Home Garden, 8
  Growing Small Fruits for the Home Garden, 8
  Hortus Northwest, 265
  Insects of the Los Angeles Basin, 264
  Jepson Manual: Higher Plants of California, 288
  Landscape Plants for the Inland Northwest, 77
  Landscape Plants for Western Regions, 159
  Low-Water Flower Gardener, 29
  Low-Water-Use Plants for California and the Southwest, 156
  National Wildflower Research Center's Wildflower Handbook, 107
  Northwest Gardeners' Resource Directory, 265
  PlantSource Journal, 265
  Tree Fruit Varieties for Western Washington, 8
Rhododendron, when to transplant in Northwest, 129
Rhodohypoxis baurii, 266
Rhus typhina, 227
Ribes sanguineum, 226
Robinia pseudoacacia 'Frisia', 26, 227
Rock, artificial, garden uses for, 284–285
Rock gardens
  ground cover for, 210
  extensive, in Washington, 96–97
Rockrose, 226
Romneya coulteri, 120, 225, 235
Root rot, 46
Rosa. See Roses
Rosa rugosa, 226
Rosemary, 78, 225, 272–274, 288
Roses
  climbing types, 14–17
    'Altissimo' (for rose hips), 234
    source for 'Cl. Iceberg', 108
  for cut flowers, 249
    how best to cut, 99
  as indicators for powdery mildew, 107
  pruning and tying for "wild" look, 40
  pruning hybrid teas, 41
  resistant to powdery mildew, 262
  tree types with weeping form, 8
Rosmarinus, 78, 225, 272–274, 288
Rudbeckia hirta, 98, 106, 181
Rue, 71
Russian sage, 119
Rust fungus, 76
Ruta graveolens, 71

Sabadilla, 75
Safflower, 27, 139
Saffron buckwheat, 229
Sage, 29, 78, 120, 225, 235, 249
St. Catherine's lace, 229
Salt-tolerant plants (for seaside), 106
Salvia, 29, 78, 120, 225, 235, 249
Santa Barbara daisy, 118
Santolina, 225, 235
Sanvitalia procumbens 'Mandarin Orange', 98
Sarcococca, 282
Satureja douglasii, 235
Scabiosa, 76, 139, 249
Schizanthus pinnatus, 219
Schlumbergera bridgesii, 289
Sea holly, 139
Sea lavender, 127
Sea pink, 116
Sedges, 36
Sedum, 120, 180, 183, 225
Seed
  annuals from, 62–63
    for hanging baskets, 42
  dahlias from, 23
  daisies from, 98
  lupine from, 233
  seed-planting tool, 208
  seed-starting rack, 236
  storage methods, 263
Sempervivum, 225
Senecio, 226
September, 206–229
  checklists, 212–215
  garden guide, 207–211
Shade gardening, book about, 157
Shearing. *See* Pruning and shearing
Shelves for plants, easy-to-make, 142
Shirley poppy, 236
Shrubs
  drought-tolerant, for Northwest, 209, 226–227
  fragrant, 47

Monarch of the Veldt 'Zulu Prince' (see page 98)

Shrubs *(cont'd)*
  to plant under oaks, 283
  preventing snow damage to, 9
Silene, 210
Skimmia japonica, 237
Skunks, protecting against, 108
Snapdragon, 220, 249
Soaker hoses, 157
Solidago, 127, 139
Sophora secundiflora, 78
Southern California
  fall planting in (annuals), 216–221
  flower market in Los Angeles, 312
  garden checklists for. *See* Garden checklists in the Article Titles Index
  growers of specialty plants in (reference book), 232
  hillside garden, 188–190
  insects of the Los Angeles Basin (reference book), 264
  "jungle" in San Diego backyard, 205
  peach variety for, 158
  peonies for, 256
  purple sage for, 29
  small gardens in, 170–175
  tulips for, 252–253
Southwest region
  beans native to, 56–58
  desert courtyard ideas, 50
  desert plumbago in, 105
  desert-style garden in Phoenix, 267
  fall planting in (annuals), 216–221
  garden checklists for. *See* Garden checklists in the Article Titles Index
  purple sage for, 29
Spartium, 226
Specialty plants in California, guide to growers, 232
Speedwell, 120
Spruces, sheared and trained as garden arch, 28
Stachys byzantina, 120, 139
Staghorn sumac, 227
Stands for plants, easy-to-make, 141, 143
Star clusters, 127
Starflower, 139
Statice, 139, 262
Stipa gigantea, 36
Stock, 220, 249
Stranvaesia davidiana, 290
Strawberries, lack of sweetness in, 46
Strawberry foxglove, 108
Strawberry tree, 226, 282
Strawflower, 27, 139
Succulents. *See also* specific succulents
  in containers, 104, 183
Sulfur flower, 229
Sunchokes, 233
Sunflower, 104, 211, 249
Sun protection for plants, 109
Sunrose, 100
Swan River daisy, 117
Swan River everlasting, 139
Sweet alyssum, 71, 220
Sweet gum, 232
Sweet olive, 47
Sweet pea, 220, 249
Sword fern, 234

Tanacetum vulgare, 71
Tangelolo, 22
Tansy, 71
Teucrium, 120
Texas mountain laurel, 78
Thrift, 116
Thyme, 225
Thymus, 120, 127, 225
Thymus praecox, 120, 127
Ticks and mosquitoes, protecting against, 183
Tidytips, 71
Tigridia, 43
Tithonia rotundifolia 'Goldfinger', 98
Toadflax, 220
Tomatoes
  'Early Girl', as all-time *Sunset* favorite, 38–39
  for hot areas ('Heatwave'), 26, 78
  'Husky Gold', 8, 78
Trailing indigo bush, 78
Tree basins, 156
Trees. *See also* specific trees
  "adopting" for Arbor Day, 101
  drought-tolerant, for Northwest, 209, 227
  historic, available for sale, 51
  preventing snow damage to, 9
  watering in summer, 156
Trellises
  for beans, 104
  for vines, 259
Trichostema lanatum, 235
Trumpet vine, 226
Tuberose, 43

Tuberous begonia, 43
Tulips, growing in Southern California, 252–253
Twinspur, 118

Variegated Japanese sedge, 36
Vegetables. *See also* specific vegetables
  garden for charity in Santa Rosa, 64–65
  gardens for small spaces, 84–90
  unusual varieties, source for seedlings of, 237
Venidium fastuosum 'Zulu Prince', 98
Verbena, 8, 120, 249
Verbena 'Imagination', 8
Verbesina encelioides, 78
Veronica, 107, 120
Veronica 'Sunny Border Blue', 107
Viburnum bodnantense, 282
Vine maple, 227

Watering. *See also* Drought-tolerant plants
  container gardens, 76
  drip irrigation, 9, 167–169
  low-water-use gardens, 50, 70, 76, 188–190, 211
    guides for, 29, 156, 159
  soaker hoses, 157
  tree basins, 156
  water meters, 156
Watermelon, Moon and Stars types, 46
Water meters, 156
Weeds, winter control of, 265
Western larch, 182
Wheat, growing for bread, 276–279
Wild buckwheat, 235
Wildflowers. *See also* Native plants
  in Golden Gate Park, 68
  new source book for, 107
Wild lilac, 235
Wind-tolerant plants (for seaside), 106
Wine-cups, 130
Winged everlasting, 27, 139
Winter daphne, 47
Winter hazel, 49
Wintersweet, 282
Wisteria, 106
Woolly blue curls, 235
Worms as compost-makers, 266
Wreaths for the holidays, 296–303

Xeranthemum annuum, 27, 139

Yarrow, 71, 73, 116, 139, 182, 226, 249
Yellow hoop petticoat, 208
Yellow leaves (from iron chlorosis), 67
Yellow pampas grass, 36
Yerba buena, 235
Yucca elata, 287
Yucca glauca, 50
Yuccas as indicators for powdery mildew, 107

Zantedeschia, 43
  in containers, 48
Zinnia, 249
Ziziphus jujuba, 266
Zucchini, 76